From Neighborhoods to Nations

From Neighborhoods to Nations

The Economics of Social Interactions

Yannis M. Ioannides

PRINCETON UNIVERSITY PRESS
PRINCETON AND OXFORD

Published by Princeton University Press, 41 William Street, Princeton,
New Jersey 08540
In the United Kingdom: Princeton University Press, 6 Oxford Street, Woodstock,
Oxfordshire OX20 1TW
press.princeton.edu

Jacket illustration: *Chance Construction 2*, 2008, 59″ × 59″ m/m on sintra.

Library of Congress Cataloging-in-Publication Data

Ioannides, Yannis Menelaos.
From neighborhoods to nations : the economics of social interactions / Yannis M. Ioannides.
p. cm.
Includes bibliographical references and index.
ISBN 978-0-691-12685-2 (hardcover : alk. paper) 1. Social interaction—Economic aspects.
2. Economics—Sociological aspects. I. Title.
HM548.I63 2012
306.3—dc23

2012002809

British Library Cataloging-in-Publication Data is available
This book has been composed in Verdigris MVB Pro Text
Printed on acid-free paper. ∞
Typeset by S R Nova Pvt Ltd, Bangalore, India
Printed in the United States of America
10 9 8 7 6 5 4 3 2 1

TO ANNA

CONTENTS

Preface xi

Chapter 1 Introduction 1
1.1 From Urban Externalities to Urban Interactions 2
1.2 Economies of Cities and New Economic Geography 6
1.3 Urban Structure and Growth 8
1.4 Urban Interactions, Politics, and Urban Design 9
1.5 Moving Forward 9

Chapter 2 Social Interactions: Theory and Empirics 11
2.1 Introduction 11
2.2 A Simple Linear Model 14
2.3 Endogenous Social Structure 22
2.4 Nonlinear Models 30
2.5 Why Experimental Data Can Help 38
2.6 Endogenous Social Structure Revisited: Dynamics 44
2.7 Econometrics of Social Interactions in Social Networks 53
2.8 Spatial Econometrics Models as Social Interactions Models 61
2.9 Social Learning in Urban Settings 64
2.10 Conclusions 66
2.11 Highlights of the Literature and Further Study 67
2.12 Appendix: Basic Facts of Graph and Network Theory for Social Network Modeling 68
2.13 Appendix: Survey of Micro Data Sources with Rich Contextual Information 71

Chapter 3 Location Decisions of Individuals and Social Interactions 79
3.1 Introduction 79
3.2 Aspatial Models of Location with Social Interactions 82
3.3 An Exact Solution for Hedonic Prices in a Model of Sorting 88
3.4 A Discrete Location Problem with Endogenous and Contextual Effects 95
3.5 Endogenous Neighborhood Choice and Contextual Effects in Housing Decisions 97
3.6 Spatial Clustering and Demographic Characteristics: Schelling's Models 115
3.7 Hierarchical Models of Community Choice with Social Interactions 126

3.8 Conclusion 134
3.9 Appendices 135

Chapter 4 Location Decisions of Firms and Social Interactions 148
4.1 Introduction 148
4.2 Models of Location of Firms 150
4.3 Location of Firms under Uncertainty 153
4.4 Testing for Agglomeration 158
4.5 Other Approaches to Studying Agglomeration Economies 169
4.6 Empirical Evidence on Urbanization (Jacobs) Externalities: A Look from the Total Factor Productivity of Firms 180
4.7 The Role of Inputs and Geography in Location Decisions of Firms 183
4.8 Economic Geography Models for Firms' Location Decisions 188
4.9 Risk Pooling by Firms in the Urban Economy 192
4.10 Conclusion 198

Chapter 5 Social Interactions and Urban Spatial Equilibrium 200
5.1 Introduction 200
5.2 Urban Spatial Equilibrium with Social Interactions 206
5.3 Location Decisions of Firms in Urban Space 212
5.4 Monocentric versus Polycentric Models of the Urban Economy 217
5.5 The Lucas–Rossi-Hansberg Models of Urban Spatial Structure with Productive Externalities 219
5.6 Neighborhood Effects and the Geometry of the Canonical Urban Model 226
5.7 Transmission of Job-Related Information and Urban Equilibrium 234
5.8 Choice of Job Matching and Spatial Structure 240
5.9 Conclusions 246

Chapter 6 Social Interactions and Human Capital Spillovers 248
6.1 Introduction 248
6.2 Spatial Equilibrium 251
6.3 Spatial Interactions and Spatial Economic Activity 253
6.4 The Urban Wage Premium and Spatial Equilibrium 259
6.5 Social Interactions and Human Capital Accumulation 268
6.6 Social Interactions in Synthetic Neighborhoods 284
6.7 Conclusions 286
6.8 Guide to the Literature: Chapters 3–6 287

Chapter 7 Specialization, Intercity Trade, and Urban Structure 292
7.1 Introduction 292
7.2 Empirical Evidence on Urban Specialization and Diversification 294

7.3 Simple Economics of Urban Specialization 297
7.4 Specialization, Diversification, and Intercity Trade 306
7.5 Equilibrium Urban Structure with Intercity Trade 318
7.6 Richer Urban Structures 323
7.7 The Role of Geography 326
7.8 Labor Market Frictions in a System of Cities 330
7.9 Modeling Lessons from the Empirics of Urban Specialization and Diversification 344
7.10 Summary and Conclusions 346

Chapter 8 Empirics of the Urban Structure and Its Evolution 349
8.1 Introduction 349
8.2 Zipf's Law for Cities 350
8.3 The Duranton Model of Endogenous City Formation 364
8.4 The Hierarchy Principle 368
8.5 Cities versus Metropolitan Areas versus Urban Places versus Densities versus Clusters 371
8.6 Evolving Urban Structures with General Intradistribution Dependence 379
8.7 Geography and Spatial Clustering 390
8.8 Studies of Urban Structure Based on "Quasi-Natural Experiments" 393
8.9 Global Aspects of City Size Distribution and Its Evolution 395
8.10 Conclusion 396

Chapter 9 Intercity Trade and Long-Run Urban Growth 398
9.1 Introduction 398
9.2 Growth of Isolated Cities 401
9.3 A Ventura-Type Model of Intercity Trade and Economic Growth 409
9.4 Growth in an Economy of Autarkic Cities 412
9.5 Economic Integration, Urban Specialization, and Growth 420
9.6 The Rossi-Hansberg–Wright Model of Urban Structure and Its Evolution 429
9.7 Empirical Aspects of Urban Structure and Long-Run Urban Growth 434
9.8 Sequential Urban Growth and Decay 440
9.9 "Space: The Final Frontier?" 444
9.10 Why Does a City Grow? 447
9.11 Guide to the Literature for Chapters 7–9 448

Chapter 10 Urban Magic: Concluding Remarks 451
10.1 Networks, Urban Infrastructure, and Social Interactions 452
10.2 Graphs and the City 454

Notes 457
Bibliography 483
Index 517

PREFACE

Individuals share information; we self-select into social groups; most of us live and work in close proximity in cities and in firms, both important features of modern economic life. Economists, influenced by other social scientists and recognizing that disciplinary boundaries are sometimes arbitrary, have developed new theoretical models and empirical tools for understanding the social interactions that underlie interpersonal and community life.

This book offers a synthesis of research on the economics of social interactions, a body of knowledge made up of strands from several areas of economics. My goal is to provide a set of tools that can be used to structure empirical investigations and to interpret empirical findings in ways that make recent research in economics accessible as a tool to scholars in other social science disciplines. In other words, the book is designed to enrich our set of metaphors for understanding and modeling the fabric of communities, their neighborhoods, and their consequences for studying larger regional and national economies. Identifying and measuring the importance of social interactions is a challenging task because of the inherent difficulty in separating personal, social, and cultural forces from purely economic ones. Social interactions have important impacts on phenomena ranging from the diffusion of norms to how students learn from one another, and from causes of urban decay to explanations for economic growth.

The concept of social interactions has already shown its value in exploring many facets of interdependence between actors in the modern economy. In economics, social interactions are defined as direct agent-to-agent interactions that are not mediated by price. My overarching theme in this book is proximity in all of its dimensions and its impact on interactions among individuals and firms in society and in the economy. Chapter 1 introduces highlights of the significance of social interactions. Chapter 2 sets out the basics of the analytical language that I then use throughout the book to describe social interactions. The subsequent chapters use that analytical language. Chapter 3 examines location decisions of individuals and emphasizes the study of neighborhood effects in housing markets and their interaction with the role of prices in rationing admission to communities and neighborhoods in market economies. Chapter 4 looks at the impact of interactions on firms' location decisions, focusing on the effects of proximity to other firms, the size of the total urban economy, the availability of a suitable labor force, and risk pooling. Chapter 5 builds on the foundations laid down in earlier chapters when economic agents interact in physical space. It examines how the interactions of individuals and firms in their vicinity and in broader communities help us understand the spatial structure of cities as self-organization by agents. Chapter 6 documents spatial patterns in productivity, wages, and incomes and addresses the origin of the idea that spatial concentration causes higher productivity. The chapter starts with aggregative spatial measures, such as economic activity at the level of states, regions, and counties, and moves to the smaller scale of cities and their neighborhoods. In chapters 7–9 the city is ultimately the unit of analysis. Those chapters address urban structure, industrial specialization and diversification, and urban growth in the context of national economic growth. Each chapter provides its own microfoundations and moves progressively from static settings to dynamic economies in steady states, such as the model of labor market turnover in chapter 7 and the empirics of urban evolution in chapter 8. Chapter 9 explores models of long-run growth with factor accumulation and endogenous technological change.

Finally, chapter 10 speculates about the prospect of a deeper understanding of social interactions in urban settings, introducing broader sets of tools for describing the entire social fabric. I cogitate about ways the interplay of actors in the physical, economic, and social space allows interactions to make the global local. It ends by comparing individuals and their social interactions to an archipelago. Components of the urban economy and social structure interact in numerous ways, sometimes reaching far and other times concentrating locally as they react to economic and social forces. The models can allow an economy to self-organize in the face of vicissitudes within an ever-changing environment, as adverse shocks alternate with payoffs from increasing returns.

My goal is to emphasize that our knowledge of social interactions rests on data, on the empirical findings that derive from them, and on the applied economics that made those findings possible. It also reflects my view that the only way to do justice to the empirical findings is to present their theoretical underpinnings. Each chapter interweaves original material with syntheses of the existing literature, going back and forth between theory and empirics.

The book comes at a time when a torrent of new research has become available. Among several particularly elegant new books, those by Glaeser (2008), Jackson (2008), and Zenou (2009a) stand out. My goal is to provide a synthesis for economist and noneconomist readers that organizes the interacting areas of this very active research topic. Of course, I hope that others will build on my synthesis.

I am truly grateful to a great number of friends, some of whom also happen to be colleagues and research collaborators (from whom I have learned enormously, and especially from Vernon Henderson and Christopher Pissarides), who have shown great selflessness and immeasurable patience in reacting to my work over many years. Many offered suggestions and corrections during presentations of parts of the research that led to this book. Some generously offered thoughtful suggestions on earlier related work and on drafts of parts of the book. They include Tom Bender, Marcus Berliant, Larry Blume, John Boulton, Yann Bramoullé, Drusilla Brown, the late Toni Calvó-Armengol, David Cuberes, Linda Harris Dobkins, Gilles Duranton, Steven N. Durlauf, Dennis Epple, Yannis Evrigenis, Xavier Gabaix, Dominique Goux, Bryan

Graham, Hans Haller, Bob Helsley, Vernon Henderson, Wen-Tai Hsu, Panle Jia Barwick, Matt Kahn, Tomoo Kikuchi, Alan P. Kirman, Anne Laferrère, the late Linda Datcher Loury, Stelios Michalopoulos, Tomoya Mori, Henry G. Overman, Theodore Palivos, Christopher A. Pissarides, Diego Puga, Danny Quah, Esteban Rossi-Hansberg, Kjell Salvanes, Kurt Schmidheiny (and his and Giacomo Ponzetto's students at Pompeu Fabra), Tracey N. Seslen, Spyros Skouras, Adriaan Soetevent, Michael Sobel, Enrico Spolaore, Takatoshi Tabuchi, Chih Ming Tan, Heiwai Tang, Giorgio Topa, David Warsh, Bruce Weinberg, Jeff Zabel, Marios Zachariades, Giulio Zanella, Yves Zenou and Junfu Zhang. I benefited from a wonderful research environment provided by my colleagues at Tufts and by the MacArthur Research Network on Social Interactions and Economic Disparities, directed by Kenneth J. Arrow and Steven N. Durlauf during 1998–2005. The interactions in the network helped me decisively in clarifying my ideas. I acknowledge with gratitude resources from the MacArthur Foundation, the Max and Herta Neubauer Chair in Economics at Tufts, and the National Science Foundation under grants SBR-9618639 and ACI-9873339. I benefited greatly from the regular compilations of working papers produced as "New Economics Papers: Urban and Real Estate Economics," part of Research Papers in Economics (RePEC), edited by Stephen Ross, and *Economics of Networks eJournal*, part of the Social Science Reasearch Network (SSRN), edited by Nicholas Economides. I thank Thad Beal whose *Chance Construction 2* is so brilliantly evocative of how human networks overlay urban geography.

I wish to especially acknowledge my intellectual gratitude to Alan Kirman for encouraging me early on, and to Steven Durlauf, whose own research in related areas and whose comments and friendship over more than 15 years have had an extraordinary influence on much of my work reflected in this book. My friends Costas Azariadis, Dimitri P. Bertsekas, and Christopher A. Pissarides taught me the importance of setting high standards for oneself. I am grateful to the anonymous reviewers at Princeton University Press whose comments improved the manuscript enormously. Peter Dougherty, Tim Sullivan, and Seth Ditchik at the Press have been enthusiastic, very encouraging, and extraordinarily patient, and so has Janie Chan. Very special thanks go to Carol Dean for superb copyediting, and to Natalie Baan for meticulous care of the manuscript. Finally, Anna Hardman and Kimon Ioannides in different ways have been wonderfully helpful to me throughout this undertaking: Anna, with her tireless advice and editorial help, and Kimon, whose steadfast advice that writing a book is a different and worthy kind of challenge, kept me going.

September 25, 2011

From Neighborhoods to Nations

CHAPTER 1
Introduction

PHILOSOPHY MASTER: [E]verything that is not prose is verse, and everything that is not verse is prose.
MONSIEUR JOURDAIN: And when one speaks, what is that then?
PM: Prose.
MJ: What! When I say, "Nicole, bring me my slippers, and give me my nightcap," that's prose?
PM: Yes, Sir.
MJ: By my faith! For more than forty years I have been speaking prose without knowing anything about it, and I am much obliged to you for having taught me that.

—Moliére, *Le Bourgeois Gentilhomme*, 1670, act two. scene 4

We engage in social interactions "without knowing anything about it" throughout our lives; these interactions teach us new skills and influence our choices. Examples are easy to find: recycling and composting practices; sending a child to a charter school; ideas for software innovations that come from a chance encounter in a Silicon Valley, California, or Austin, Texas, bar; learning from classmates—about schoolwork or about getting pregnant or how to avoid it; gaining weight; attending a church, synagogue, or mosque; joining a gym or a country club; supporting a sports team; getting involved in a civic association or spending time working for a nonprofit; keeping up with college friends in person or on Facebook; enforcing, or failing to enforce, building code and zoning regulations; dying one's hair to hide the gray. These are just a few examples.

Economic models of cities increasingly focus on the microfoundations of the multitude of interactions underlying innovation and creativity as well as on the pollution and congestion associated with cities as places where social interactions are most dense. Empirical work using data made more accessible by modern technologies of interpersonal communication has followed suit and is expanding the set of metaphors we can use to understand cities and urbanization. While social interactions are most dense in cities, this is not the only place where they are found.

Scholars in recent years have begun to explore the ways these social interactions influence our behavior and their broader implications for policy, asking questions like: How does access to mobile telephones in Africa influence farmers' productivity and the farming techniques they use; does that in turn influence the size and growth of settlements? What is the reach and influence of places where urban buzz occurs? Is obesity—or depression or acne—contagious? How do racial and ethnic prejudices start and evolve, and can we deter them? Can interactions between neighbors help revitalize a decaying urban neighborhood, and why do they cause urban decline in one neighborhood and not in another? Did Edinburgh's streets and urban form contribute to the interactions that led to the Scottish Enlightenment in the eighteenth century?

Some of our actions change prices. When families move to a community with good schools, property values rise, and that in turn is relevant for people who do not have school-age children. In other words, prices record the value of social interactions and can signal their quality. Economists' questions about interactions started from but have moved well beyond direct influences on prices and markets.

In all the examples above social interactions are present, making individuals' actions interdependent and in turn affecting their lives. Sometimes spatial proximity implies interaction, as in keeping up with the Joneses. Other times the links are professional, social, or familial, and agents interact at long distances from each other. Widespread adoption of information and communication technologies means that personal and social interaction tempt some to claim "the death of distance." Travel (still costly albeit cheaper than in the past) is also growing, allowing the physical proximity we sometimes need to clinch deals or collect ideas, to share unique events, or just to spend time together. International migrants now use email and the Web, and make telephone calls using Skype—but that communication is a complement and not a substitute for visits home and from family members. Academics work on joint papers on the Web, but conferences become even more important as an opportunity for face-to-face contact that consolidates the trust needed for long-distance collaboration.

The United Nations has already defined more than half the world's population as being *urban*, with rapid further growth forecast in urban populations. Face-to-face interpersonal interactions remain indispensable, and research on social interactions has strengthened the argument that the close proximity of economic, social, and cultural forces (and the density of social interactions) in cities is one, perhaps the most, important reason for cities' continued growth and economic relevance.

1.1 FROM URBAN EXTERNALITIES TO URBAN INTERACTIONS

Economists typically emphasize the role of markets. Thus, urban economists focus on housing and labor markets and on the economic activities of households, firms, and public institutions that define modern economies. A common concern of economists is what to do if markets are not "functioning well." A common cause of dysfunctionality in urban markets is widespread *externalities*—direct agent-to-agent interactions that are *not* mediated through the markets. Externalities are pervasive and naturally generated in urban settings with their high density of population and economic activity. Market outcomes in such cases are typically socially inefficient. It is possible to rearrange things and make some individuals better off without hurting others. An earlier urban economics and policy literature used the pervasiveness of allegedly *negative* externalities to justify the massive interventions in cities in the 1960s and 1970s that came to be known as *urban renewal* in the Western world and *slum clearance* in developing countries.[1]

Some of these projects rejuvenated urban downtown areas; many others were disastrous. The character of the urban neighborhoods and urban life and lives destroyed has since been mourned as a lost positive force in those cities' economic and social spheres. Economists and other social scientists now see many kinds of urban externalities instead as instances of *social interactions*. This broader term refers to preferences or tastes that individuals have for the types of other individuals near whom they live and for those individuals' actions. Interactions may be undesirable, but they cannot be ignored. Urban amenities are not only attractive scenery, parks, and natural settings but also the characteristics, habits, and activities of individuals' neighbors. The examples at the beginning of the chapter all involve such direct agent-to-agent interactions. Urban places acquire a "life" of their own as magnets for formal and informal activities. Some of these activities are so persistent that they confer some specialization on their particular locales, contributing to the vibrancy and variety of life in large cities. Some come to be seen by outsiders as characterizing the larger city. Such places attract professionals, tourists, and locals in varying proportions. Well-known locales in this sense include Soho and the City in London; the Left Bank and the Marais in Paris; Wall Street, Greenwich Village, the Garment District, and Brooklyn Heights in New York; Harvard Square in Cambridge, Massachusetts; Hollywood in Los Angeles; Ginza in Tokyo; the Grand Bazaar and Istiklal Caddesi in Istanbul; and Darb Al-Ahmar (the historic city) and Tahrir Square in Cairo.

Why do some urban activities produce great things? Peter Dougherty (2002, 19) urges economists to talk about cities not in the same way that psychologists talk about sex, that is, without taking "the fun out of it." How can the tools of economics help explain the role of cities in bringing "the vast variety of human creative resources together in an ongoing spontaneous and combustible mix"? (Dougherty 2002, 18). Can rigorous theory support Florida's (2002) claim that imaginatively selected measurable variables (such as the percentage of gays or of people with bohemian lifestyles) can explain a big part of a city's attractiveness. Can economists marry "thought to feeling" so as to help in "reaffirming the exciting connections that unite the historic wisdom of Adam Smith with city life"? (Dougherty 2002, 19).

An answer needs to combine economic variables, such as prices, with noneconomic ones. Education and health are critical in individuals' social personas and yet are components of human capital, an economic concept par excellence. The distinction between economic and noneconomic variables has become increasingly blurred, but in the analysis explored here the strength of economics is the rigor and discipline afforded by its theoretical and empirical tools.

The contemporary theory of social interactions is an important example of how these tools provide a powerful framework. Becker (1974) was one of the earliest economists to talk explicitly of social interactions; subsequently they were used extensively in empirical work. Loury (1982) pioneered using variables to measure the impact of community and family background on educational achievement. Yet, it was the Manski (1993, 2000) model that provided the canon for empirical modeling of social interactions. Manski's approach provides a typology of social influences within individuals' social milieus and raises key identification issues.

The Manski model distinguishes influences that emanate from: one, the *decisions* of members of one's reference group (*endogenous* social effects), such as keeping up with the Joneses; two, the effects on an individual of *characteristics* of members of one's reference group(s) (*exogenous* or *contextual* effects), as when individuals value living close to others with similar ethnic backgrounds, or with other characteristics they view as conducive to practices they themselves value; and three, individuals acting similarly because they have similar observable or unobservable characteristics, or face similar institutional environments (*correlated* effects). This book adds the role that prices play in conveying "social" effects to the categories proposed in Manski's paper. It is precisely because individuals take the price of a good as given and beyond their control, making their decisions accordingly, that equilibrium prices ultimately reflect the characteristics of all market participants.

The fact that the actions of individuals in social contact with one another are interdependent is an important notion, and the concept of social interactions can be a powerful tool, as the following examples demonstrate. In seeking to explain one individual's actions, we can no longer use just the actions (or choices) of neighbors as explanatory variables in a regression. Such magnitudes are not independent of the error. Instead, more elaborate econometric approaches are called for. Nonetheless, even when individuals choose their neighbors and thus their neighborhood effects, results by Brock and Durlauf (2001b) establish that it is possible to actually identify different social effects separately. To do that we need to correct appropriately for the selection bias associated with individuals' having chosen their neighbors. Sometimes interactions are group-based, in which case individuals value aggregates describing entire communities and aggregates of the actions of the members of those communities. At other times, interactions are one-to-one. In the second case social network models can provide a critical focus on the microstructure of interactions. Heterogeneity in interactions across individual pairs is an important focus of the econometric analysis.

1.1.1 Location Decisions of Individuals

In deciding whether or not to locate in a particular city or neighborhood, each individual weighs numerous factors from their own perspective. These factors can be classified neatly as market variables, endogenous social effects, and contextual variables. When individuals decide where to locate, pursuing equilibrium strategies, their own individual characteristics contribute to defining the equilibrium values of prices and the distribution of characteristics by location. In the process individuals sort themselves into neighborhoods. Some of the sorting is sorting on observables. As Rosen (2002) underscores, it is important to assess such sorting in order to, inter alia, understand the social valuation of neighborhood amenities when individuals are heterogeneous. For example, if some people value neighborhood safety more than others, then those who value it less will sort to less safe neighborhoods. Estimates of the average value to society of neighborhood safety based on those who sort to more safe neighborhoods will be biased upward, while estimates based on those who locate in less safe neighborhoods will be biased downward. Most realistic settings with social interactions involve sorting on unobservables as well as observables. Social interactions models help us understand individuals' location decisions, as well as membership decisions more generally.

The inherent difficulty in determining what drives the growth of cities is an example of the problem of correcting for sorting on unobservables. We want to know whether the factors that drive location decisions are due to the direct attraction of being near many others (agglomerative forces) or to underlying (unobserved) factors that those who make the location decision have in common. Economic geography provides examples where we can distinguish between the attraction of natural features of the landscape, *first nature*, and spatial features of the economic system, which include but are not limited to the effects of the landscape, *second nature*. I discuss the relative importance of first nature versus second nature and how it motivates empirical research at length in several chapters.

1.1.2 Location Decisions of Firms

Decisions made by firms, like those made by individuals, are influenced by factors resembling social interactions; this book exploits this similarity methodologically and links decisions of firms, in particular, with the theoretical underpinnings of new economic geography (NEG) (Fujita, Krugman, and Venables 1999). The case of firms introduces a new angle—spatially dispersed social interactions. The idea that firms interact in the context of the urban economy is an old concept, but to fully understand the benefits firms derive from being near other firms we need to articulate the origin of those benefits. In particular, economists since Marshall (1920) have asked whether proximity to other firms in the same industry generates an effect that is different from proximity to firms in other industries or from other factors such as proximity to a larger city or to a particularly suitable labor force. Moreover, numerous firms may be attracted by the same advantageous local factor, such as attributes of the local labor force. Similarly, workers may be attracted to a location by a factor in common with firms such as good weather and/or other physical amenities in addition to the job opportunities at that location. In such cases it may appear that a single common factor operates as a force of attraction for both individuals and firms.

Yet to understand what is really happening we must distinguish among the multiple types of attractions that are in fact involved. Distinguishing the attraction of other firms, for example, from the attraction of labor force characteristics or of first nature attributes of a place, such as the weather, can be critical for public policy choices that set out to encourage local economic development. If firms are attracted by the presence of a skilled labor force and those workers in turn are attracted to Silicon Valley by the weather, then investments that attempt to reproduce other aspects of that region in a midwestern city are likely to fail.

1.2 ECONOMIES OF CITIES AND NEW ECONOMIC GEOGRAPHY

Since individuals and firms benefit by locating in close spatial proximity to one another, it is fruitful to apply the analysis of social interactions in examining the economies of cities. The social interactions approach to the study of economies made up of cities is contributing much improved microfoundations that allow us to understand and predict how individual economic agents benefit from the size of the city where they live and work. Urban concentrations generate costs as well as benefits. The most obvious costs are those due to pollution and congestion. Two natural questions follow: How large should cities be? Will cities in free market economies attain their optimum sizes? The system-of-cities literature has dealt elegantly with these questions (Henderson 1974, 1977a, 1988a).

Questions about city size have attracted attention for a long time, at least since Plato and Aristotle (Papageorgiou and Pines 2000, 520). In *The Laws*, Plato (ca. 350 BC) sets the optimal city size precisely at $7! = 5{,}040$ (male) citizens.[2] This number does not include optimal support personnel (women, children, slaves, and alien residents) whom we would include in the population and who would make the size of Plato's city considerably larger. According to Aristotle's (ca. 340 BC) *Politics*, optimal city size should be constrained from below by *self-sufficiency*: "a city only comes into being when the community is large enough to be self-sufficing. If then self-sufficiency is to be desired, the lesser degree of unity is more desirable than the greater." And it should be constrained from above by *efficiency*. Too small a city cannot satisfy all the needs of its citizens; if it is too large, it becomes unwieldy. Thus, "You cannot make a city of ten men, and if there are a hundred thousand it is a city no longer. But the proper number is presumably not a single number, but anything that falls between certain fixed point" (Aristotle, *Nicomachean Ethics*, Book IX, 10, ca. 330 BC). Chapters 7 and 9 offer more modern perspectives on this issue.

Using the tools of new economic geography and casting them in a system-of-cities model, Au and Henderson (2006) take a modern stand and show that Chinese cities are too small.

The system-of-cities approach I cited above adopts a market-based approach to optimal city size. Different industries located in a city all benefit from external economies. People need to commute to their places of work. That creates congestion costs (time wasted in traffic, noise, and air pollution). Each individual contributes more to total congestion than he or she experiences, thus generating a social cost of congestion. When cities specialize in producing a single product or a group of related products, congestion costs are lower: the software industry is not saddled with the social costs generated by the metal-processing industry, as it would be if both industries were to locate in the same city. It follows that cities should specialize once their survival is ensured. It is hard nowadays to think of cities without industries or marketable services. It is thus interesting to contrast with Plato's proscription (accompanied by severe penalties) against the citizens' being retail traders or merchants!

In most modern economies governments cannot directly regulate what different cities produce or who lives where. A variety of city types emerge including both industrially diversified and specialized cities. Local and national governments defer to political realities generating favorable treatment for particular cities and their hinterlands, especially via subsidized transportation and other infrastructure. It is thus important to be able to assess how such policies impact the urbanization process and the nature of outcomes in large economies.

Just as local increasing returns to scale are a driving force of the urban economy, similar forces underpin endogenous growth theory, that is, growth driven by endogenous technological change (Lucas 1988; Romer 1990). This research has built on increasing returns-to-scale technologies from plausible assumptions without ending up with an extreme and counterfactual market structure, such as an economywide monopoly. Spatial economics has dealt with a similar challenge so as to navigate carefully between a high concentration of activity in some locations and a low concentration in the rest of space. In hailing the value of proximity, Lucas (1988) credits Jane Jacobs (1969), whose writings had been treated as anathema by the earlier generation of economists.[3] The use of increasing returns in these literatures is conceptually related to Adam Smith's (1776) famous analysis of the division of labor and its being limited by the extent of the market. Urban economics also owes a lot to Alfred Marshall's (1920) trilogy, now part of the canon. Local increasing returns could arise because of knowledge spillovers, linkages between input suppliers and final producers, and thick local labor market interactions.

1.2.1 New Economic Geography

Paul Krugman's research and its early popularization in his *Geography and Trade* (Krugman 1991b), eloquently outlined in his Nobel lecture

(Krugman 2008), contributed to the momentum of new economic geography. The approach seeks to integrate urban and regional economics, both in a national as well as an international context, and takes the form of economists' directing their traditional tools to questions with space as a key dimension.

The emergence of regional disparities within an economy, especially when different regions share the same institutional framework (Kaldor 1970), is emphasized as a key puzzle, as are the origins of international inequalities. Recent interest by economists in European economic integration and in globalization has renewed interest in the study of regional, as opposed to national, phenomena. In the context of European integration, more generally, it is often argued that the abolition of economic borders will shift the playing field of economic interactions to regional entities. New economic geography addresses concerns such as, for example, whether improvements in transportation links intended to break the isolation of lagging regions may have the opposite effect, strengthening the forces of agglomeration in leading regions and thus further exacerbating regional inequalities.

1.3 URBAN STRUCTURE AND GROWTH

Urban agglomeration is a social invention determined by the interplay between the value of concentration relative to the cost of congestion. If the former dominates, spatially uniform steady states cannot sustain themselves. Agglomerations were originally limited by the need for genetically related individuals to live close to one another and to avoid encounters and unnecessary conflicts with strangers, a situation that reduced the attractiveness of large agglomerations (Seabright 2004). Social interactions within cities give rise to innovative ideas. The advantages of interactions themselves, as well as their fueling of technological progress and especially the advent of improvements in public health (Cairns 1997), however, came to outweigh the disadvantages of close proximity. Increasing interactions accommodate an ever finer division of labor that in turn mitigates hostility among unrelated individuals [cf. (Seabright 2004)].

An economy's urban system is not a static entity. Populations grow, in part, for reasons that are endogenous to the economies that host them. A growing population will be accommodated in growing cities as well as in newly created urban settlements of all kinds. Technological change and infrastructural development can make existing cities function better and accommodate increased populations and diverse industries. Casual observation suggests that there is considerable arbitrariness in the location of cities. Why should Santa Fe, New Mexico, be where it is? For visitors and residents today, its charm is directly due to its location in the mountains of New Mexico. But is that why the city developed there? Natural features of the geographic landscape, such as access to waterways and natural harbors, are important. Proximity to natural or historically given hubs and being in a place where transshipment occurs (boat to rail; air to truck) allow a city to function as a cusp in total transport costs. Once established, a new city itself serves as a cusp for further development of the urban system. Even if the original "cause" is no longer present, a city rarely disappears.

Even within a mature urban system, existing cities may renew their prominence by reinventing themselves. Cities can also become obsolete, often because they are perceived as unattractive places to live, and when their industries relocate to more attractive sites nationally and internationally. Urban structure adapts through the birth, growth, and death of cities. Urban reinvention may not always prevent urban decay. Urban growth under certain conditions provides a margin that eliminates local increasing returns to yield constant returns to scale at the level of the national economy. This outcome helps reconcile the exploitation of increasing returns in an economy with non-explosive national economic growth (Rossi-Hansberg and Wright 2007). In this context, it is interesting to ask whether urban growth imposes restrictions on national economic growth.

1.4 URBAN INTERACTIONS, POLITICS, AND URBAN DESIGN

The interplay between the spatial and social configurations of cities is important in much of the book. The serendipity of interactions among urban dwellers is a big part of urban living. That public opinion formation is influenced by the topology of social interactions within existing social milieus is long-standing. For example, consider the observation by Doxiadis (1970, 398): "Pericles in ancient Athens could get a reasonable sample of public opinion by meeting 100 to 150 people while walking from his home to the Assembly." Ober (2008) interprets the famous political reforms in classical Athens instigated by Cleisthenes by means of modern social network theory. He studies how the administrative rearrangements of the Cleisthenes reform, whereby urban, "suburban," and rural communities were grouped together, allowed for artful mixing of opinions as representatives from distant communities sampled public opinion on their way to the agora in the central city. Nowadays, it is the media and social networking that help form public opinion, in addition to locally hosted interactions facilitated by civic associations and local governmental institutions, especially in Anglo-Saxon countries.

1.5 MOVING FORWARD

Many though *not all* of the questions rhetorically posed at the beginning of this chapter are dealt with formally in the book. Social interactions are the overarching theme that allows me to structure the book and helps embed it within the economics literature. While urban economics lends basic components to social interactions as an organizing principle, it is not the only branch of economics in which the social interactions approach is leading to significant advances. Labor economics, the economics of health, and the economics of education have benefited enormously from this perspective. So too have spatial economics and the economics of international trade. For example, individuals and firms benefit from being in a larger city because its economy can accommodate a greater variety of goods and services. They in turn allow for more attractive lifestyles, greater ability to innovate, and improved ways to mitigate risk. The role of city size serves as an important analytical link between the microbased chapters of the book and the more aggregative ones. Understanding international trade through the lens of an economy's urban structure is a promising area of research, and so is understanding the forces of urban business cycles, a new area of research, where several chapters of the book propose promising new inroads. Yet above all, the book aims at integrating empirical findings, mainly by economists, and thus helps establish social interactions as a central tool of modern economics.

CHAPTER 2
Social Interactions

Theory and Empirics

2.1 INTRODUCTION

This chapter addresses the role of the social context in individual decisions. Many important markets continue to coexist with nonmarket arrangements. Social interactions, that is, nonmarket interactions, are ubiquitous, and social institutions do matter to an extent not fully appreciated by economics (Arrow 2009). Understanding the social consequences of economic decisions requires that we acknowledge their social context. With economics increasingly venturing into the traditional realms of other social sciences, recognizing the importance of social interactions can be particularly helpful in understanding a diverse set of phenomena, from obesity and cigarette smoking to economic inequality.

In the canonical case of individual decision making when goods and services are procured from markets, individuals are assumed to choose quantities of goods and services to maximize utility subject to a budget constraint. The basic model has been extended to allow for *externalities*, that is, direct effects from an individual to another that do not involve market transactions. In the presence of externalities, market prices may not reflect the full social value of the respective goods and services. For example, my neighbor's playing loud music bothers me, and there is no direct market-mediated way for my unhappiness to be transmitted to him and hence to affect his behavior. This might prompt me to leave the area and perhaps to move near people whom I think are less likely to engage in behaviors that I find unpleasant or perhaps who are like me. When I rent a particular apartment in a multiunit complex or buy a home in a suburban subdivision, I can expect that my daily life will be affected by the behavior of my neighbors as they, too, go about their daily lives. Such effects are "bundled" with my choice of residence. My own actions will in turn affect the welfare and perhaps actions of my neighbors who are sensitive to them.

The part of the marginal value of a good that is due to its being appreciated by those consuming it is equal to the marginal cost to them of acquiring it. In competitive markets, it is also equal to the cost of producing an additional unit. Yet, an additional unit of the good may have adverse effects on some individuals and beneficial effects on others. Individuals' preferences differ. Externalities can also be beneficial. My neighbor's male winterberry plants help my female winterberry plants produce lovely berries profusely, and such neighborly habits improve the productivity of the apiary further down the street.

Even though the case of music playing bothering me does connote physical proximity, this need not be so for all externalities. There are examples of consumption practices by people far away raising objections on deeply felt ethical or religious grounds. Some people object to the hunting and consumption by others of meats of certain species even though these acts occur far away. This is the case of Japanese consumption of whale meat raising objections in some quarters in the United States. This example may be an instance of someone else's consumption affecting my enjoyment, as a matter of principle or because I like to have the option of going on whale-watching trips.

It is arguably less well understood that externalities from some aspects of consumption (broadly construed) are critical for defining social structure and cohesiveness. These range from patriotic activities such as raising flags, displaying national symbols, and celebrating national holidays, to participating in music, sports, and other performances and cultural events. Such activities suggest sharing of values and personal tastes. It would be natural to suppose that people tend to cluster near others with similar values and tastes.

For example, the availability of a variety of different ethnic foods in supermarkets and restaurants is attractive for some but off-putting for others. Therefore, one would think that to the extent possible individuals who are free to choose where to locate will seek to be near others with like tastes and values and far from others with different ones. This may be due to several reasons: either pure preference for the values of others or anticipation that being near others with similar preferences will make it more likely that desirable goods will be readily available. These effects may coexist with externalities. For example, I might want to live near others who take good care of their yards and gardens or decorate their balconies and windows with beautiful flowering plants and keep up with maintaining their houses. I value living near others who are highly educated or artistically inclined because I enjoy engaging in intellectual or artistic casual conversations with my neighbors. Firms seeking to locate near other firms is a similar phenomenon.

I have implied so far that interpersonal effects are passive. They can also be deliberate. Individuals derive satisfaction from displaying their consumption activities conspicuously, perhaps regardless of whether or not others are positively influenced. This is an important phenomenon sometimes referred to as *Veblen effects* in consumption (Leibenstein 1950).

This book is about *social interactions*. As we shall see, distinguishing between different types of effects is important for drawing reliable conclusions from observing individual behavior and for designing policy. It is important to have a theory to guide us in interpreting the evidence from a variety of settings where individuals may seek deliberately to mix or to segregate. It is also important to be able to design different types of policy interventions.

The canonical formulation that I develop in this chapter can accommodate, in particular, phenomena that have been emphasized recently by such a diverse set of scholars as Christakis and Fowler (2009) and Wilson (2009). Specifically, Wilson (2009, 5) distinguishes two types of *structural forces*, social acts and social processes, and two types of *cultural forces*, national views and beliefs on race, and cultural traits, that is, shared outlooks, modes of behavior, traditions, belief systems, world views, values, skills, preferences, styles of self-presentation, etiquette, and linguistic patterns. These are seen, Wilson (2009, 15) adds, "[as they] emerge from patterns of group interaction in settings created by discrimination and segregation and that reflect collective experiences within those settings." Prevailing outcomes associated with the phenomena that Wilson emphasizes as having race as a key salient factor can be modeled as group equilibrium outcomes for analytical convenience. However, they can reflect the full range of concerns described by Wilson. Social acts that Wilson defines as the behavior of individuals within society, including stereotyping, stigmatization, discrimination, and others, may be modeled as contextual effects or endogenous social effects, as when individuals conform to the behavior of others.

As another example, consider one of the phenomena discussed by Christakis and Fowler where it is vitally important to distinguish the spread of behavior from the spread of norms. Reaction to particular behaviors by others in individuals' social milieus and adherence to norms are both instances of endogenous social interactions. In the case of obesity, as Christakis and Fowler (2009, 105–112) argue (and I discuss in further detail in section 2.7.2.3 below), it may be possible to distinguish between the spread of behavior and the spread of norms as the main force driving its social incidence provided that additional information on physical versus social proximity (and its direction) is utilized.

I proceed next by introducing a sequence of models that highlight applications in different empirical social interactions settings. I start with a simple static model, which I use to demonstrate the basic concepts of the social interactions approach, and then apply it to the case of coexistence, in a market context, of individual actions that are private with actions that have social consequences, and to endogenous networking. Social networks are jointly determined with individual actions. A special case of this model where the endogenous social structure is probabilistic allows me to link social interactions theory with social networks theory (including, in particular, random graph theory). I follow up with a dynamic model where the social structure accommodates a variety of social interaction motives. It is solved as a dynamic system of evolving individual actions. The solution links social interactions theory with spatial econometrics. I conclude with an appendix that surveys available data sets that lend themselves particularly well to social interactions studies.

2.2 A SIMPLE LINEAR MODEL

The empirical economics literature on social interactions addresses the significance of the social context in economic decisions. Decisions of individuals who share a social milieu are likely to be interdependent. Recognizing and identifying the origin and nature of such interdependence in a variety of conventional and unconventional settings and measuring empirically the role of social interactions pose complex econometric questions.

The actions of different individuals in a group are interdependent if they reflect the actions, or expectations of the actions, of all others in the group. This is known as an *endogenous* social effect (or interaction). This is the case when individuals care not only about the kinds of cars they themselves drive or the education they acquire but also about the kinds of cars or the education obtained by their friends. Therefore, their own *decisions* and those of others in the same social milieu are simultaneously determined. Individuals may also care about personal characteristics of others, that is, whether they are young or old, black or white, rich or poor, trendy or conventional, and so on, and about other attributes of the social milieu that may not be properly characterized as deliberate decisions of others. Such effects are known as *exogenous* social or *contextual* effects. I address below the particular difficulties that these different effects pose for estimation. In addition, individuals in the same or similar social settings tend to act similarly because they share common observable and/or unobservable factors or face similar institutional environments. Such interaction patterns are known as *correlated* effects. This terminology is due to Manski (1993), who emphasizes the difficulty of identifying econometrically endogenous effects separately from contextual effects in linear-in-means models, and social effects, endogenous or exogenous (contextual), from correlated effects.

Theorizing in this area lies at the interface of economics, sociology, and psychology and is often imprecise. Terms like "social interactions," "neighborhood effects," "social capital," "network effects," and "peer effects" are often used as synonyms although they may have different connotations. Empirical distinctions among endogenous, contextual, and correlated effects are critical for policy analysis because of the "social multiplier," as I explain in more detail further below.

Joint dependence among individuals' decisions *and* characteristics within a spatial or social milieu is complicated further by the fact that in many circumstances individuals in effect "choose their own context." That is, in choosing their friends and/or their neighborhoods, individuals also choose their neighborhood effects. Such choices involve information that is in part unobservable to the analyst and therefore require making inferences among the possible factors that contribute to decisions (Brock and Durlauf 2001b; Moffitt 2001).

Let individual i's action y_i be a linear function[1] of a vector of observable individual characteristics, $\mathbf{x}_i$, of a vector of contextual effects, $\mathbf{z}_{\nu(i)}$, which describe i's neighborhood (or social milieu) $\nu(i)$, and of the expected action $\frac{1}{|\nu(i)|}\sum_{j\in\nu(i)}\mathcal{E}[y_j|\Psi_i]$ among the members of i's neighborhood $\nu(i)$, the endogenous social effect, conditional on information known to i, Ψ_i. That is,

$$y_i = \alpha_0 + \alpha\mathbf{x}_i + \theta\mathbf{z}_{\nu(i)} + \beta\frac{1}{|\nu(i)|}\sum_{j\in\nu(i)}\mathcal{E}[y_j|\Psi_i] + \epsilon_i, \quad i = 1, \ldots, I, \tag{2.1}$$

where parameters α and θ are row vectors, α_0 and β are scalar, and the stochastic shock ϵ_i is independent and identically distributed across observations.

I note that the endogenous social effect is defined with respect to the expectation of the average action within group $\nu(i)$. Abstracting at the moment from the issue that individual i may have deliberately chosen her group (or neighborhood), $\nu(i)$, and stating that conditional on individual characteristics, contextual effects, and the event that i is a member of neighborhood $\nu(i)$, the expectation of ϵ_i is zero, allows me to focus on the estimation of such models. I assume *social equilibrium* within the group and that individuals hold *rational expectations* over $\mathcal{E}[y_j|\Psi_i]$. That is, individuals' expectations are confirmed; they are equal to what the model predicts. So, taking the expectations of both sides of (2.1) and setting the expectation of y_i equal to $\frac{1}{|\nu(i)|}\sum_{j\in\nu(i)}\mathcal{E}[y_j|\Psi_i]$ allows me to solve for this expectation, an endogenous variable. Substituting back into (2.1) yields a *reduced form*, an expression for individual i's outcome in terms of all observables $(\mathbf{x}_i, \mathbf{x}_{\nu(i)}, \mathbf{z}_{\nu(i)})$:

$$y_i = \frac{\alpha_0}{1-\beta} + \alpha\mathbf{x}_i + \frac{\beta}{1-\beta}\alpha\mathbf{x}_{\nu(i)} + \frac{\theta}{1-\beta}\mathbf{z}_{\nu(i)} + \epsilon_i. \tag{2.2}$$

Suppose that y_i is i's educational attainment. One's socioeconomic characteristics, $\mathbf{x}_i$, typically do affect educational attainment. The socioeconomic characteristics of adult neighbors, including measures of economic success, are often used as contextual effects and are included in $\mathbf{z}_{\nu(i)}$. They could stand for *role model effects*. In contrast, the effect of educational attainment by one's peers in schools and neighborhoods, an endogenous social effect, is an example of a *peer group effect*. Note that these effects are associated with distinct populations and can be fully articulated in a dynamic model. See chapter 6, section 6.5.4.1, below.

Comparison of model (2.1) and its reduced form (2.2) shows clearly that endogenous social effects generate feedbacks that magnify the effects of neighborhood characteristics. That is, from (2.1), the effect of $\mathbf{z}_{\nu(i)}$ on y_i is $\frac{\theta}{1-\beta}$ and thus magnified, if $0 < \beta < 1$, relative to θ. Consider the effect on the academic performance of a particular medical student caused by the presence of women in the classroom, measured as a percentage. This problem is addressed by Arcidiacono and Nicholson (2005).[2] According to (2.1), the partial effect is given by θ. However, this ignores the fact that there is such an effect on all the other students conditional on their characteristics. Therefore, the effect magnified by feedback adds up to $\theta + \beta\theta + \beta\theta^2 + \cdots = \frac{\theta}{1-\beta}$, exactly as shown in equation (2.2).

Following the pioneering work of Datcher Loury (1982), a great variety of individual outcomes have been studied in the context of different notions of neighborhoods. This chapter seeks to show how to interpret findings of significant coefficients for contextual effects. The model in equation (2.1) is the bare minimum of interactions needed in order to express essential complexities of social interdependence. In practice, empirical researchers deal with models considerably more complex than (2.1). For example, it is possible that the marginal effect of a neighbor's actions may depend on neighborhood characteristics. This can be expressed by an additional term $\mathbf{z}_{n(i)} \frac{1}{|\nu(i)|} \sum_{j \in \nu(i)} \mathcal{E}[y_j | \Psi_i]$ in (2.1). See sections 2.3 and 2.6 below. Linearity obscures the richness that comes with nonlinear social interactions models like multiplicity of equilibria; see section 2.4 below.

2.2.1 Econometric Identification and Manski's Reflection Problem

Including as contextual effects only neighborhood averages of individual effects, $\mathbf{z}_{\nu(i)} \equiv \mathbf{x}_{\nu(i)}$, is a common practice but may cause failure of identification of endogenous separately from exogenous interactions. That is, we may not be able to estimate separately coefficients β and θ by means of a linear model like (2.1). Manski (1993) terms this the *reflection* problem: it arises because the direct effect of the social context variables $\mathbf{z}_{\nu(i)}$ shows up together with the indirect effect as reflected through the endogenous effect represented by $\frac{1}{|\nu(i)|} \sum_{j \in \nu(i)} \mathcal{E}[y_j | \Psi_i]$. By imposing in equation (2.1) that $\mathbf{z}_{\nu(i)} \equiv \mathbf{x}_{\nu(i)}$, that is, contextual effects coincide with neighborhood averages of individual characteristics, (2.2) becomes

$$y_i = \frac{\alpha_0}{1-\beta} + \boldsymbol{\alpha}\mathbf{x}_i + \frac{\beta\alpha + \theta}{1-\beta}\mathbf{x}_{\nu(i)} + \epsilon_i .$$

The coefficient of $\mathbf{x}_{\nu(i)}$ is now the combined effect $\frac{\beta\alpha+\theta}{1-\beta}$. A statistically significant estimate of this coefficient in a reduced-form regression of individual outcomes on individual characteristics and neighborhood averages of individual characteristics $(\mathbf{x}_i, \mathbf{x}_{\nu(i)})$ allows a researcher to infer that at least one type of social interaction is present: β is nonzero and there is an endogenous effect, or θ is nonzero and there is a contextual effect, or both. Therefore, partial identification is possible for some type of social effect. This instance of failure of identification is a direct consequence of the linearity of the endogenous social effect in the behavioral model and of the unobservability of the expectation[3] $\frac{1}{|\nu(i)|} \sum_{j \in \nu(i)} \mathcal{E}[y_j | \Psi_i]$ in (2.1).

If the underlying economic model suggests that some neighborhood averages of individual covariates should be excluded from $\mathbf{z}_{\nu(i)}$, then the econometric model is identified. More precisely, for the identification of (2.1), the vector $\mathbf{x}_{\nu(i)}$ must be linearly independent of $(1, \mathbf{x}_i, \mathbf{z}_{\nu(i)})$. It is thus necessary that there be at least one element of $\mathbf{x}_{\nu(i)}$ whose group-level average is not a causal effect and therefore not included in $\mathbf{z}_{\nu(i)}$.

When individuals belong to different groups, there could well be group-level heterogeneity that might not necessarily arise from group-level social interactions. Graham (2008a) proposes a method that separately identifies the social interactions component of any excess variance from that due to group-level heterogeneity and/or sorting. To see this in simple terms, suppose groups come in singletons or in pairs. Let the outcome for singletons be $y_i = \epsilon_i$. The outcome for individual i in a pair $\{i, -i\}$ is $y_i = \beta y_{-i} + \epsilon_i$. The shock ϵ_i has 0 mean and variance σ_ϵ^2, which is assumed to be independent of group size. The outcome for one of the individuals in a pair may be solved for in terms of both shocks: $y_i = \frac{1}{1-\beta^2}(\epsilon_i + \beta\epsilon_{-i})$; its variance is $\frac{1+\beta^2}{(1-\beta^2)^2}\sigma_\epsilon^2$. The ratio of the variance of individuals in pairs to those who are singletons, $\frac{1+\beta^2}{(1-\beta^2)^2}$, identifies β.

Graham (2008a) reports an application, based on data from Project STAR, where kindergarten students and teachers were randomly assigned to large and small classrooms. The performance of talented students is typically offset by that of below-average students, resulting in little variation in mean student ability in large classrooms. In small classrooms, however, groups composed of mostly above- or below-average students are more frequently observed, generating greater variation in mean ability. As a result, the variance of peer quality is greater across the set of small than across the set of large classrooms, while the random assignment of teachers ensures that the distribution of their characteristics is similar across the two types of classrooms. Graham decomposes the unconditional between-group variance of outcomes into the sum of three terms. The first term equals the variance of any group-level heterogeneity. In Graham's application, that could be due to teacher quality. The second term equals the between-group variance of any individual-level heterogeneity. In Graham's application, that is the variance of average student ability across classrooms. It is the third term that reflects the strength of any social interactions. When social interactions are present, between-group variation in outcomes should mirror between-group variation in "peer quality." The third term therefore depends on the variance of peer quality across groups. When group sizes differ, as they do in the Project STAR–based data that Graham uses, it is possible to identify the endogenous social effect. Graham (2008b) reports evidence of social interactions; that is, differences in peer group quality were an important source of individual-level variation in academic achievement for Project STAR kindergarten students. Lee (2007) examines in detail the econometric properties of models where group sizes differ exogenously.

2.2.1.1 *The Social Multiplier*

The fact that social interactions, exogenous and endogenous, help amplify differences in average neighborhood behavior across neighborhoods can itself serve as a basis for identification. Glaeser, Sacerdote, and Scheinkman (2003) use patterns in the data to estimate a *social multiplier*.[4] For an incremental change in a particular fundamental determinant of an outcome, the *social multiplier* is defined as the equilibrium effect in the social group to the direct effect on each individual. In addition to the direct effect on an individual, this includes the sum total of the indirect effects through the feedback from the effects on others in the social group.

To see this clearly, consider the group-level counterpart of equation (2.1) with $\theta = 0$, that is,

$$y_{\nu(i)} = \alpha_0' + \mathbf{x}_{\nu(i)}\alpha' + \bar{\epsilon}_{\nu(i)},$$

where the group-level stochastic shock $\bar{\epsilon}_{\nu(i)}$ is suitably defined. For simplicity let $\mathbf{x}$ be a scalar. Put crudely, an estimate of the multiplier could be seen as the ratio of the group-level coefficient to the individual-level coefficient, the coefficient of x_i in equation (2.1): $\frac{\alpha'}{\alpha}$. The group-level regression may be seen as being obtained by summing up the reduced forms according to equation (2.2) over all members of each group. As a result, the coefficient of $x_{\nu(i)}$ in the reduced form is given by $\alpha' = \alpha + \frac{\beta}{1-\beta}\alpha = \frac{\alpha}{1-\beta}$. The multiplier is

$$\text{multiplier}_x = \frac{\alpha'}{\alpha} = \frac{1}{1-\beta}. \tag{2.3}$$

A more precise estimate of the multiplier requires that one account for sorting. Blume, Brock, Durlauf, and Ioannides (2011, 885) show that the ratio of the coefficient associated with $\mathbf{x}_{\nu(i)}$ in a group-level regression of neighborhood outcomes on neighborhood attributes ($y_{\nu(i)}$ on $\mathbf{x}_{\nu(i)}$) to the individual-level coefficient associated with $\mathbf{x}_i$ when regressing y_i on $\mathbf{x}_i$ is equal to $1/1-\beta+\sigma_s\beta$, where $\sigma_s = \text{Cov}(\mathbf{x}_i, \mathbf{x}_{\nu(i)})/\text{Var}(\mathbf{x}_i)$ corrects for the portion of the variation in individual attributes due to the group-level variation. With random sorting, $\sigma_s = 0$, we are back at (2.3). Therefore, one can obtain an estimate of β from the ratio of group-level to individual-level regression coefficients and an estimate of σ_s. If sorting is perfect, on the other hand, that is, groups are perfectly segregated, $\sigma_s = 1$ and the multiplier is equal to 1 and thus smaller.

It follows that an estimated social multiplier greater than 1 implies magnification of the direct effect and thus endogenous social interactions, $0 < \beta < 1$. This estimate is positive if the underlying social equilibrium is stable, a condition that Glaeser, Sacerdote, and Scheinkman (2003) term *moderate social influence*. As Burke (2008) emphasizes, while much of the literature on the social multiplier so far rests on linear models in static settings, the concept may be extended to dynamic settings (Binder and Pesaran 2001), to nonlinear settings (Brock and Durlauf 2001a), to settings with complete versus incomplete information (Bisin, Horst, and Özgür 2004), and to economies with more complex interaction topologies (Ioannides 2006). So far, my emphasis is on measuring the strength of social interactions but not necessarily their topology or the dependence of the feedback on incomplete access to information by different agents. Bisin, Horst, and Özgür (2004) show that incomplete information has the effect of dampening the aggregate effects of the agents' preferences for conformity, thus reducing the social multiplier relative to complete information.

The above discussion shows that in measuring the social multiplier one must deal, in practice, with dependence across decisions of individuals belonging to the same group. This occurs with nonrandom sorting in terms of observables and of unobservables. If educated people prefer to have other educated people as neighbors, the effect of one person's education (in an individual-level regression) will overstate the true impact of education because it includes spillovers. So, with sorting on observables and positive social interactions, the individual-level coefficient will overstate the true individual-level relationship and the estimated social multiplier will tend to underestimate the true level of social interactions. On the other hand, correlation between aggregate observables and aggregate unobservables will cause the measured social multiplier to overstate the true level of social interactions.

The social multiplier approach is particularly useful in delivering a range of estimates for the endogenous social effect especially when individual data are hard to obtain, as in the case of crime data. Glaeser, Sacerdote, and Scheinkman (1996) motivate their study of crime and social interactions by the extraordinary variation in the incidence of crime across U.S. metropolitan areas over and above apparent differences in fundamentals. If social interactions in criminal behavior are present, variations in observed outcomes are larger than what would be expected from variations in underlying fundamentals, precisely because of the social multiplier. Their results show that the estimated interactions coefficient is highest for petty crimes and declines for more serious crimes to become negligible for the most serious ones. Across cities, the implied extent of interactions is roughly constant.

Glaeser, Sacerdote, and Scheinkman (2003) report results using a multiplier-based model with three different alternative outcomes. One is fraternity/sorority participation by students at Dartmouth College. This setting exploits the advantage that students are randomly assigned to residences at Dartmouth College; in other words, there is no sorting. So, aggregating at the room, floor, and dormitory levels allows these researchers to apply the multiplier technique in the presence of random group assignments. The coefficient of having drunk beer in high school as an explanatory variable in regressions with fraternity/sorority participation as a dependent variable rises with the level of aggregation due to reduced sorting, exactly as the model predicts. This allows them to predict the endogenous social interaction effect of beer drinking associated with large multipliers. A second outcome they study is crime, for which individual data are not reliable. These researchers regress actual crime rates against predicted crime rates, which are formed by multiplying percentages of U.S. individuals in each of eight age categories by the estimated crime rate of persons in that category. They perform such regressions at the level of U.S. county and U.S. state cross-sectionally, and for the entire United States over time. Their results imply large social multipliers that increase with the level of aggregation, specifically from 1.72 at the county level to 2.8 at the state level to 8.16 at the national level. The basic theory would predict that these estimates are consistent with large endogenous social interaction coefficients. Working with data on wages and human capital variables, these authors again find further evidence of large social multipliers. The authors are aware of the fact that their results should be accepted cautiously because they do not control for sorting on unobservables, which may increase with the level of aggregation.

2.2.2 Identification of Social Interactions with Self-Selection to Groups and Sorting

The presence of nonrandom sorting in terms of unobservables is a major challenge for the econometric identification of social interactions models. The deliberate choice of a neighborhood, $\nu(i)$, by individual i suggests that the unobserved elements in the actions of individuals who have chosen the same neighborhood (or social group, more generally) are not independent of one another. The random shock on the right-hand side of (2.1) may not be independent of the other regressors. Conditional on their characteristics, different individuals might still be influenced by unobservable factors in common, rendering $\mathcal{E}[\epsilon_i | \mathbf{x}_i, \mathbf{z}_{\nu(i)}; \Psi_i; i \in \nu(i)] \neq 0$ and thus lowering the quality of regression coefficients estimated using equation (2.1).

I formalize this notion by supposing that evaluation of the attractiveness of a neighborhood ν may be expressed in terms of an unobservable "latent" quality variable $\mathcal{Q}^*_{i,\nu}$.[5] That is, individual i evaluates neighborhood ν by means of observable attributes $W_{i,\nu}$ that enter with weights ζ, and an unobservable component $\vartheta_{i,\nu}$:

$$\mathcal{Q}^*_{i,\nu} = \zeta W_{i,\nu} + \vartheta_{i,\nu}, \quad i = 1, \ldots, I. \tag{2.4}$$

Random shocks ϵ_i in (2.1) and $\vartheta_{i,\nu}$ in (2.4) are assumed to have zero means, conditional on (are orthogonal to) regressors $(\mathbf{x}_i, \mathbf{z}_{n(i)}, W_{i,\nu})$, across the population. If individual i chooses the neighborhood that affords her the highest possible evaluation, $\mathcal{Q}^*_{i,\nu} \geq \mathcal{Q}^*_{i,\nu'}$, $\nu' \neq \nu$, then conditions on the $\vartheta_{i,\nu}$'s are implied that make the respective errors in (2.1), conditional on choosing neighborhood $\nu(i)$, no longer have zero means. Once parametric assumptions are made about the joint distribution of $(\epsilon_i, \vartheta_{i,\nu})$, an expression for $\mathcal{E}[\epsilon_i | \mathbf{x}_i, \mathbf{z}_{\nu(i)}; \Psi_i; i \in \nu(i)]$ may be obtained (Heckman 1979) and written as proportional to a function $\delta(\zeta; W_{i,\nu(i)}, W_{i,-\nu(i)})$. This so-called Heckman correction term[6] allows me to rewrite (2.1) as

$$y_i = \alpha_0 + \mathbf{x}_i\alpha + \mathbf{z}_{\nu(i)}\theta + \beta \frac{1}{|\nu(i)|} \sum_{j \in \nu(i)} \mathcal{E}[y_j | \Psi_i] + \kappa\delta(\zeta; W_{i,\nu(i)}, W_{i,-\nu(i)}) + \xi_i, \tag{2.5}$$

where $W_{i,-\nu(i)}$ denotes the observable attributes of all neighborhoods other than $\nu(i)$ and $\mathcal{E}[\xi_i] = 0$.

Combining information on the discrete choice of neighborhood problem (2.4) with information on the continuous decision allows us to estimate such models.[7] The additional regressor $\delta(\hat{\zeta}; W_{i,\nu(i)}, W_{i,-\nu(i)})$, where $\hat{\zeta}$ is obtained from the estimation of (2.4), in (2.5), even if it also included $\mathbf{z}_{\nu(i)}$, is generally nonlinear in it and therefore linearly independent of $(1, \mathbf{x}_i, \mathbf{z}_{\nu(i)})$. If it is possible to estimate the neighborhood selection rule (2.4), then correction for selection bias via the mean estimated bias, the Heckman correction term, introduces an additional regressor, $\delta(\hat{\zeta}; W_{i,\nu(i)}, W_{i,-\nu(i)})$, on the right-hand side of (2.5) relative to (2.1) whose neighborhood average is not on the right-hand side of equation (2.1), in other words, is not a causal effect. Econometrically speaking, this approach supplies instruments that enable identification of the model.

Additional details on this approach are given in chapter 3, section 3.5, 3.9.2.1 and 3.9.2.2. The approach is helpful in empirical analyses of community choice with U.S. data. Local public financing of education in the United States creates a link between sorting into residential communities and educational outcomes. See discussion of papers by Epple et al. in chapter 3, section 3.7 below.

In multiethnic countries like the United States there is interest in assessing the impact of public school integration on the performance of students. The Boston Metropolitan Council for Educational Opportunities (METCO) program is a long-standing voluntary public school desegregation program. The program assists mainly black inner-city kids from Boston public schools in enrolling in, and commuting to, mainly white (and more prosperous) suburban Boston communities that accommodate them in their own public schools. Angrist and Lang (2004) evaluate the program and show that the receiving school districts, which have a higher mean academic performance than the sending ones, do experience a mean decrease in performance because of the program. However, they also show that the effects are merely "compositional," and there is little evidence of statistically significant effects of METCO students on their non-METCO classmates. Their analysis with microdata from one receiving district (Brookline, Massachusetts) generally confirms this finding but also produces some evidence of negative effects on *minority* students in the receiving district.

METCO is noteworthy as a social experiment, having been initiated in 1966 by civil rights activists seeking to bring about de facto desegregation of schools. It is a voluntary program for both sides, making self-selection a problem for its evaluation. There is self-selection at the individual level and at the receiving school district level. If individual data were available, this could be accounted for by a bivariate version of equation (2.4); that is, the community must be agreeable to METCO and the individual chooses to participate, which then leads to the appropriate selection correction on the right-hand side of (2.5). There are numerous factors specific to how welcome the program is in each receiving school district, which is administered academically and fiscally by its respective hosting community. Therefore, the Angrist–Lang results must be viewed with caution and do depend on the absence of self-selection.

2.3 ENDOGENOUS SOCIAL STRUCTURE

Implicit in formulating the model of individuals' actions subject to social interactions and in elaborating the group choice problem is that each individual is affected by group averages of contextual effects and of decisions. It is easy to contemplate that individuals may deliberately seek social interactions that are not necessarily uniform across their social contacts. Here I follow Cabrales, Calvó-Armengol, and Zenou (2011) and introduce a simple model of individuals engaging in networking (socialization, in their terminology) efforts that determine the probabilities of contacting others simultaneously with deciding on their own actions. (See chapter 2, section 2.12, for more technical details on graph and network theory for social network modeling.)

Individual i chooses action y_i and socialization effort γ_i, taking as given actions and socialization efforts by all other individuals, $i, j \in \mathcal{I}$, so as to maximize

$$U_{i,\tau(i)}(\mathbf{g}, \mathbf{y}) \equiv \alpha_i y_i + \beta \sum_{j=1, j\neq i}^{I} g_{ij}(\mathbf{g}) y_i y_j - a\frac{1}{2}y_i^2 - \frac{1}{2}\gamma_i^2, \quad (2.6)$$

where $\tau(i)$ denotes the individual type[8] individual i belongs to, $\mathbf{g} = (\gamma_1, \ldots, \gamma_i, \ldots, \gamma_I)$ denotes the full vector of socialization efforts, and $\mathbf{y} = (y_1, \ldots, y_i, \ldots, y_I)$, that of actions. The weights of social interaction g_{ij} are defined in terms of socialization efforts as follows:

$$g_{ij}(\mathbf{g}) = \frac{1}{\sum_{j=1}^{I} \gamma_j} \gamma_i \gamma_j, \quad \text{if } \forall \gamma_i \neq 0; \quad g_{ij}(\mathbf{g}) = 0, \quad \text{otherwise.}$$

The interactive term in definition (2.6) is general enough to accommodate many other possibilities, such as conformism, as we will see in further detail later in this chapter.

The necessary conditions for individuals' choices may be manipulated so as to express optimal individual actions and socialization efforts in terms of a pair of baseline values for socialization effort and action, denoted by (γ^*, y^*). These baseline cases are the roots of the system

$$\gamma^* = \beta_{\text{adj}} y^{*2}, \quad y^*[a - \beta_{\text{adj}}\gamma^*] = 1, \quad (2.7)$$

where $\beta_{\text{adj}} \equiv \beta \frac{\sum_i \alpha_i^2}{\sum_i \alpha_i}$. I note that β_{adj} in equation (2.7) adjusts β, a component of the coefficient of the endogenous social effect, to account for heterogeneity in the α's, the constant terms of individuals' marginal utilities. Optimal individual actions and socialization efforts are expressed in turn in terms of the baseline values as follows:

$$y_i = \alpha_i y^*, \quad \gamma_i = \alpha_i \gamma^*. \quad (2.8)$$

Comparison of this solution with the case of autarky, where all γ's are zero, is revealing. If individuals exert no socialization effort, they are isolated, and their actions are given by $y_{\text{aut},i} = \frac{\alpha_i}{a}$. If individuals do exert their optimal efforts, their actions from (2.7) and (2.8) may be written as

$$y_{\text{aut},i} = \frac{\alpha_i}{a}, \quad y_i^* = y_{\text{aut},i} \frac{1}{1 - \beta_{\text{adj}} \frac{\gamma^*}{a}}.$$

That is, each individual's optimal action is uniformly scaled up from their action under autarky by a uniform factor across all individuals. Cabrales et al. refer to this factor,

$$\left(1 - \beta_{\text{adj}} \frac{\gamma^*}{a}\right)^{-1}, \tag{2.9}$$

as the *synergistic* multiplier. The multiplier increases with β_{adj} and thus increases with heterogeneity in the α's across individuals. It decreases with the coefficient of y_i in the marginal disutility of individual action a, but both total effects also depend on γ^*, which is determined by (2.7).

The baseline values for socialization effort and actions (γ^*, y^*) may actually be obtained in closed form. That is, substituting for γ^* from the first into the second equation in (2.7) yields a *cubic* equation in y^* (see also section 2.6.5 below). It is a standard property of cubic equations that they admit three real solutions, of which two are positive, provided that $0 < \beta_{\text{adj}} < 2(\frac{a}{3})^{3/2}$.[9] This condition restricts the heterogeneity in the α_i's relative to the endogenous social effect coefficient β. The positive values characterize feasible Nash equilibria for the problem. The model admits two sets of solutions for (γ^*, y^*), one associated with high and the other with low baseline values. It is possible to prove that the high value is stable and the low value is unstable. Section 2.3.3 below uses this model to analyze probabilistic social structures.

2.3.1 Social Interactions Topology

The social structure introduced above is inherently symmetric. This need not be the case. Next I follow the literature and define the social setting by means of a social interactions *structure* (or *topology*; the two terms are used interchangeably in the literature and here). The associated adjacency matrix (or sociomatrix, a standard tool) $\mathbf{\Gamma}$ (Wasserman and Faust 1994) of the graph $\mathcal{G}$ of connections among individuals, indexed by $i = 1, \ldots, I$, is defined as follows:

$$\Gamma_{ij} = \begin{cases} 1, & \text{if } i \text{ and } j \text{ are } \textit{direct} \text{ neighbors in } \mathcal{G}; \\ 0, & \text{otherwise.} \end{cases} \tag{2.10}$$

If for any two individuals i and j, $i,j \in \mathcal{I}$, action by i affects the utility of j *and* action by j affects the utility of i, then we say that social interactions are *undirected*. The adjacency matrix $\mathbf{\Gamma}$ is symmetric in that case. If interactions are directed, that is, influence by i on j does not imply influence by j on i, the respective adjacency matrix is not symmetric.

An individual i's *neighborhood* is the set of other agents she is directly connected with in the sense of the adjacency matrix, $\nu(i) = \{j \in \mathcal{I} : \Gamma_{ij} = 1\}$. Let $\mathbf{\Gamma}_i$

denote row i of $\mathbf{\Gamma}$. Then nonzero elements of $\mathbf{\Gamma}_i$ correspond to individual i's neighbors. It is also straightforward to allow for interactions of varying intensities. For example, some of the people I am connected with can have greater influence on me than others. This is accomplished by a *weighted* adjacency matrix, with entries being positive numbers of varying magnitudes. I make further use of this concept in section 2.6.5 below where I discuss endogenous networking. Section 2.12 provides additional details.

2.3.2 Centrality in Social Structures and Consumption Decisions

Suppose that individual actions denote quantities of different goods consumed and that only some goods are *socially sensitive (social* for short) in the sense that their consumption generates influences on others via social interactions, and the remaining ones are *private*. Next I demonstrate the significance of the social structure in a static setting, where all goods are traded (Arrow and Dasgupta 2009; Ghiglino and Goyal 2010).

I follow Ghiglino and Goyal (2010) and assume a Cobb–Douglas utility function of the quantity of a private good y_i and of the socially sensitive good $y_{s,i}$, adjusted to reflect *social interaction*. This adjustment is the excess of an individual's consumption of the social good over its average consumption by i's neighbors multiplied by the *number* of i's neighbors. Specifically, let individual i's utility function be

$$U(y_i, y_{s,i}; \mathbf{y}_s) \equiv y_i^{\alpha} \left(y_{s,i} + \beta|\nu(i)| \left[y_{s,i} - \frac{1}{|\nu(i)|} \sum_{j\in\nu(i)} y_{s,j} \right] \right)^{1-\alpha}, \quad 0 < \alpha < 1, \tag{2.11}$$

where $\mathbf{y}_s$ denotes the I-vector of consumptions of the social good by all agents. Individual i chooses $(y_i, y_{s,i})$ so as to maximize utility function (2.11), subject to budget constraint $y_i + py_{s,i} = \bar{y}_i + p\bar{y}_{s,i}$, where $(\bar{y}_i, \bar{y}_{s,i})$ are i's endowments and p is the price of the social good in terms of the private good. Let $\bar{\mathbf{y}}_s = (\ldots, \bar{y}_i + p\bar{y}_{s,i}, \ldots)$ denote the I-vector of individuals' wealths.

Solving the resulting system of demands yields the following solution for the aggregate demand for the social good:

$$\mathbf{y}_s = \frac{1-\alpha}{p}[\mathbf{I} - \beta\alpha\tilde{\mathbf{\Gamma}}]^{-1}\bar{\mathbf{y}}_s, \tag{2.12}$$

where $\mathbf{I}$ is the $I \times I$ identity matrix, $\tilde{\mathbf{\Gamma}}$ denotes the adjacency matrix normalized so that the sums of the elements of each row are equal, $\frac{|\nu(i)|}{1+\beta|\nu(i)|}$. Given price p, the solution for the aggregate demand for the social good is well defined provided that $[\mathbf{I} - \beta\alpha\tilde{\mathbf{\Gamma}}]^{-1}$ exists. If $\beta\alpha$ is smaller than the magnitude of the largest eigenvalue of the normalized adjacency matrix $\tilde{\mathbf{\Gamma}}$, then the inverse matrix exists. This condition is satisfied because of the Perron–Frobenius theorem, which ensures that all eigenvalues of $\tilde{\mathbf{\Gamma}}$ are less than the maximum sum across all of its rows [see (Ghiglino and Goyal 2010, 9) and section 2.12 on graph and network theory].

What can one say about the impact of agents' social positions on agents' outcomes in general equilibrium? Here the concept of centrality for each individual within the social structure, proposed by Bonacich (1987) and recently used in economics by Ballester, Calvó-Armengol, and Zenou (2006), becomes handy. This concept teases out of the spectral properties of the normalized adjacency matrix the social importance of each individual measured in terms of their social connectedness. That is, the centrality vector for the social structure represented by $\mathbf{\Gamma}$ is defined as

$$\mathbf{B} = [\mathbf{I} - \beta\alpha\tilde{\mathbf{\Gamma}}]^{-1}\iota,$$

where ι denotes an I-vector of 1s. Since the matrix $[\mathbf{I} - \beta\alpha\tilde{\mathbf{\Gamma}}]$ is invertible, its inverse may be written out in terms of its power expansion, so that the above vector of centralities may be written as

$$\mathbf{B} = \sum_{l=0}^{\infty}(\beta\alpha\tilde{\mathbf{\Gamma}})^l\iota. \tag{2.13}$$

By a standard interpretation of the powers of $\tilde{\mathbf{\Gamma}}$ [see section 2.12 below and (Wasserman and Faust 1994)], element (i, j) of $\tilde{\mathbf{\Gamma}}^l$ gives the number of paths of length l within the social structure that start from an individual j and end at an individual i, weighted by the powers of $\alpha\beta$ that account for attenuation of the effect. Therefore, the centrality of each individual in the social structure reflects the sum of the lengths of paths along the interaction structure of all different possible lengths, weighted by the endogenous social interaction coefficient, β, times the elasticity of the private good in the utility function, α.

The solution for equilibrium allocations and price for the simple case of equal endowments is

$$y^*_{s,i} = \frac{B_i}{\bar{B}}\bar{y}_{s,i}, \quad p^* = \frac{\bar{y}_i}{\bar{y}_{s,i}}\left[\frac{1}{1-\alpha}\frac{1}{\bar{B}} - 1\right]^{-1},$$

where B_i denotes the i-component of $\mathbf{B}$ and $\bar{B}$ denotes average centrality defined as $\bar{B} = \frac{1}{I}\sum_i B_i$. Furthermore, the equilibrium price depends on average centrality in the social network and equilibrium allocations on each individual's relative centrality. Ghiglino and Goyal show that as new links are added to the social network individuals' centralities rise, which in turn pushes up the price of the socially sensitive good. Newly linked agents demand more of the socially sensitive good and less of the other (private) good. It is possible to compute the *critical link*, that is, the new link that maximizes the price increase. Roughly speaking, when social interaction effects are weak, the critical link is the one that connects the two least linked agents.

When individuals differ in terms of endowments, inequality in network centrality and in wealth inequality reinforce each other. Thus, redistributing wealth from less to more central agents raises the price of the socially sensitive good and affects outcomes for all agents. Ghiglino and Goyal show that as a society moves from segregation to integration, poor individuals lose while rich individuals gain. This finding prompts interesting questions about the welfare effects of integration versus segregation, in that it suggests that richly endowed agents will desire links with their poor cohorts, while the opposite pressures will work on the poor. In a world where link formation requires consent on the part of both types of agents, this suggests that stable communities should consist of agents with similar endowments. In other words, societies would be segregated by wealth. Of course, these specific conclusions depend critically on the properties of the preferences assumed in (2.11) above.

Interestingly, when both goods are socially sensitive, Ghiglino and Goyal show that there exists an equilibrium that is identical with respect to prices and allocations to an equilibrium in the economy with no social interactions. This point in fact first made by Arrow and Dasgupta (2009), who show (in a dynamic model of work, leisure, and savings) that when consumption is socially sensitive and individuals derive utility from average consumption, but leisure is not, individuals consume more and work harder in a market economy than they would at the social optimum. If, on the other hand, consumption and leisure are equally socially sensitive, then equilibrium is not distorted by social interactions.

2.3.3 Probabilistic Social Structures

With a large number of agents, one may interpret the interaction weights derived in section 2.3 above as defining interaction probabilities $g_{ij}(\mathbf{g})$, provided, of course, that they do not exceed 1. Under symmetry, that is, when all individuals are of the same type, the weight individual i attaches to interaction with individual j becomes equal to $g_{ij}(\mathbf{g}) = \frac{I(\gamma^*)^2}{I\gamma^*} = \frac{\gamma^*}{I}$. This is less than 1 when the number of individuals I is sufficiently large. In other words, individual i weights the term $\beta y_i y_j$ in her utility function (2.6) according to probability $\frac{\gamma^*}{I}$. It follows that, under symmetry, the expected number of connections each individual has with others is equal to $I\frac{\gamma^*}{I} = \gamma^*$ and is thus independent of the number of individuals.

A social structure where any two individuals are connected with probability equal to $\frac{\gamma^*}{I}$ may be analyzed as an Erdös–Renyi random graph. Specifically, graphs where each possible edge is present *independently* of any other edge and occurs with probability $\frac{\gamma^*}{I}$ have been studied extensively since the pioneering work by Erdös and Renyi (1959, 1960). In such a graph, the probability that an agent has exactly k connections with other agents is given by

$$p_k = \binom{I-1}{k}\left(\frac{\gamma^*}{I}\right)^k\left(1-\frac{\gamma^*}{I}\right)^{I-1-k}. \tag{2.14}$$

Here the random quantity is the entire graph, and the probability given by (2.14) pertains to a typical node. In the limit, when the number of agents is much greater than the average number of connections each agent has, $I \gg (I-1)\frac{\gamma^*}{I} \approx \gamma^*$, then the binomial probability function is approximated by the Poisson distribution for large I:

$$p_k = \binom{I-1}{k}\left[\frac{\gamma^*}{I-1-\gamma^*}\right]^k\left[1-\frac{\gamma^*}{I-1}\right]^{I-1} = \frac{(\gamma^*)^k e^{-\gamma^*}}{k!}. \qquad (2.15)$$

In other words, the degree distribution for the Erdös–Renyi random graph is Poisson.[10]

A particularly interesting feature of random graphs as probabilistic structures is their *threshold* properties. That is, as the value of γ^* varies, the topological properties of the associated random graphs change dramatically when γ^* passes the value 1, this being a threshold value in this case. For values of the socialization effort less than 1, the groups of individuals who are interconnected are small; above that value, a fraction of the entire society belongs to a single, *giant* component. This value is associated with a stark qualitative change in the topology of the graph, a *phase transition*. See (Ioannides 2004b; Kirman 1983) for more details.

There is no reason why the number of connections created by the uncoordinated action of individuals, or the probability of each connection, should satisfy the condition for a phase transition. Diverse sets of outcomes are possible. A simple condition for phase transition is straightforward to express within the Cabrales et al. model. From the discussion in section 2.3 we have that, given β_{adj}, higher values of a widen the gap between the baseline values for the two equilibria. On the other hand, given a, greater heterogeneity in the α's brings the two baseline values closer together. For the larger of the two positive roots to be greater than 1, it must also be the case that $a > \beta^2_{\text{adj}} + 1$. In other words, the marginal disutility of effort parameter, a, must be sufficiently large, relative to the heterogeneity among individuals, in order for a proportion of the entire economy to be interconnected. Thus, the topological properties of the resulting endogenous social structure are linked to underlying behavioral parameters. Thanks to Cabrales et al., the conditions under which phase transition occurs in random graphs are given precise behavioral underpinnings [see also (Ioannides 1990)].

The fact that the degree distribution for the Erdös–Renyi random graph in (2.15) is Poisson has been a limitation for numerous applications for which random graphs would have been natural modeling tools. Specifically, the degree distributions for many real-life networks have demonstrably fatter tails than those of the Poisson and are better described by means of power laws.[11] As a number of authors, but in particular Dorogovtsev and Mendes (2003, 80–81), document in detail, different social (but also biological, physical, and engineering) networks differ considerably in terms of their degree distributions and their clustering properties. Also, connections among agents are typically dependent. This failure motivated additional research that led to a revival of random graph theory, which I review immediately below. I discuss econometric approaches and empirical aspects of networks further in section 2.7 below.

2.3.3.1 The Revival of Random Graph Theory

Mark Newman and a number of collaborators use results from the combinatorics literature (Molloy and Reed 1995) and recast random graph theory leading to arbitrary degree distributions. Newman, Strogatz and Watts (2001) discuss data on degree distributions from some actual real-life social networks and note important differences among different types of networks, ranging from networks of scientific collaborators to networks of movie actors who have costarred and of directors of Fortune 1000 companies. The latter has a peak and is much less skewed; the former resemble power laws with exponential cutoffs. The authors attribute these differences to the fact that connections due to memberships on company boards require maintenance, while ties gained by coauthorships remain present indefinitely. Optimizing over connections reflects different objectives and may imply sharply different distributions of social connections from those of other, passive, relationships.

Newman, Strogatz, and Watts (2001) take off from the work of Molloy and Reed (1995) and apply the basic mathematics of random graph theory with arbitrary degree distributions also to cases of directed graphs and of bipartite graphs. Newman (2010) highlights the importance of *connection bias*. That is, even when the numbers of individuals' acquaintances vary randomly across the population and are probabilistically independent, the set of an individual's acquaintances is not a random sample of the population. Given a randomly chosen acquaintance from among an individual's acquaintances, that individual's total number of acquaintances, $\tilde{p}_k$, will be distributed in proportion to kp_k. That is, an individual's sampling others on that basis is subject to a bias because there exist k times as many links for an individual of degree p_k than for an individual with only a single link, where p_k is the degree distribution. Since the degree distribution for any given neighbor is proportional to the number of acquaintances the other person already has, $\tilde{p}_k$ is given by

$$\tilde{p}_k = \frac{kp_k}{\mathcal{E}[k]}. \tag{2.16}$$

I will refer to $\tilde{p}_k$ as the induced distribution of neighbors' degrees. Exploring this notion in the context of these new analytical tools turns out to be particularly fruitful in understanding the number of acquaintances of one's acquaintances of one's acquaintances, and so on, that is, of one's neighbors' neighbors in the acquaintance network. This bias is conceptually similar to the length-biased sampling associated with sampling employment or unemployment spells by means of data collected from employed or, respectively, unemployed individuals. This also suggests that it is important to know how data on social networks are actually collected.

In a number of papers, Newman and coauthors have emphasized properties that are particularly prevalent in social networks. These include high degrees of clustering—the friends of my friends are often my own friends, too—and positive correlations between the degrees of adjacent vertices (assortative mixing)—gregarious individuals tend to know one another. High clustering has been attributed to community structure in networks. Newman and Park (2003) demonstrate that community structure can also account for assortative mixing. Newman (2002) examines patterns in mixing by degree in different types of networks. He notes that whereas social networks are assortatively mixed, technological and biological networks tend to be disassortative. This is perhaps due to the fact that deliberately designed engineering systems reflect concerns for reliability that require redundance, whereas individuals' choices of the number of connections may be less sensitive to such concerns.

Social interactions in networks have proven hard to deal with theoretically by means of economic models, even with exogenous networks. This is in part so because, in network settings, small numbers of individuals are involved, which in turn necessitates game-theoretic treatments. However, even the simplest examples of games on networks have multiple equilibria that possess very different properties. Galeotti, Goyal, Jackson, Vega-Redondo, and Yariv (2010) offer a major advance. These authors assume that, whereas individuals know their own number of connections with others (their own network degree), they are uncertain about the degrees of others in the network. It turns out that the introduction of imperfect information about the network in games played on networks eliminates the multiplicity of equilibria because the limited information makes agents unable to condition their behavior on fine details of the network. These authors do show that when actions are strategic substitutes (complements), they are nonincreasing (nondecreasing) in players' degrees. When (symmetric) equilibrium actions are monotone and externalities across players are positive, well-connected players have higher outcomes irrespective of whether actions are substitutes or complements. A number of other important aspects of networks, such as clustering, centrality, proximity, and others [see (Jackson 2008, 54–73, chap. 3)] have yet to be incorporated into theoretical models of comparable rigor. The Galeotti et al. (2010) study is also significant because the prominent role played by individuals' network degrees can facilitate empirical investigations with data, like Add Health, where they are directly observable. See section 2.13.5.2.

2.3.4 Spatial Positioning and Social Structure

So far, I have modeled social structure in terms of individuals' forming connections with others. Further, below I analyze how social structure emerges from individuals' self-selections into social groups and neighborhoods. Another dimension involves social structures that emerge from the salience of spatial positioning when individuals differ. Specifically, consider two types of individuals, black and white, who choose locations on a lattice and have preferences concerning how many of their neighbors have the same skin color as themselves. We owe this view to research by Thomas Schelling (1978), which is discussed in further detail below in chapter 3, section 3.6. In particular, there I follow Zhang (2004) and consider location decisions on a lattice, where each node has a fixed number of neighbors, from the vantage point of the set of edges that connect different individuals at equilibrium. For the particular parsimonious specification of preferences that Zhang adopts, which does express that whites have some (but not necessarily a large) preference in favor of being near other whites but blacks are indifferent to the skin color of their neighbors, it turns out that social welfare is maximized when the *number* of edges connecting whites is *maximized.* As I discuss in more detail in section 3.6, this implies segregation of whites from blacks. In terms of the basic terminology of the present chapter, individuals' choices express endogenous social effects. As in the discussion of self-selection and sorting, in section 2.2.2 above and in greater detail in chapter 3, section 3.6, bringing into the choice process additional attributes leads to a much richer view of spatial positioning and social structure.

2.4 NONLINEAR MODELS

I turn next to models of discrete decisions with a given social structure. A path-breaking model of discrete binary choice with social interactions is due to Brock and Durlauf (2001a) and is extended to multinomial choices by them (Brock and Durlauf 2002, 2006) and by Durlauf and Ioannides (2010). Each individual seeks to maximize utility from her own actions while being influenced by the actions of others with whom she is connected socially. Following my earlier work (Ioannides 2006), in this section I make use of notation introduced in section 2.3.1 and adapt the original Brock–Durlauf model of interactive discrete choice to arbitrary but given interaction topology, described by a weighted adjacency matrix $\mathbf{\Gamma}$.

2.4.1 The Brock–Durlauf Interactive Discrete Choice Model

Let agent i choose action ω_i, $\omega_i \in S = \{-1, 1\}$ so as to maximize her utility, which depends on the actions of her neighbors: $U_i = U(\omega_i; \tilde{\omega}_{\nu(i)})$, where $\tilde{\omega}_{\nu(i)}$ denotes the vector of dimension $|\nu(i)|$ containing as elements the decisions made by each of agent i's neighbors, $j \in \nu(i)$. The I-vector of all agents' decisions, $\tilde{\omega} = (\omega_1, \ldots, \omega_I)$, is also known as a *configuration*, and $\tilde{\omega}_{\nu(i)}$ is known as agent i's *environment*. I assume that agent i's utility function U_i is additively separable in: a private utility component, which without loss of generality (because of the binary nature of the decision) may be written as $h\omega_i$, $h > 0$; a social interactions component, which is written in terms of quadratic interactions between her own decision and of the expectations of the decisions of her neighbors, $\omega_i \mathcal{E}_i\{\frac{1}{|\nu(i)|}\sum_{j \in \nu(i)} J_{ij}\omega_j\}$; and a random utility component, $\epsilon(\omega_i)$, which is observable only by the individual i. That is, U_i may be written as

$$U_i(\omega_i; \mathcal{E}_i\{\tilde{\omega}_{\nu(i)}\}) \equiv h\omega_i + \omega_i \mathcal{E}_i \left\{ \frac{1}{|\nu(i)|} \sum_{j\in\nu(i)} \Gamma_{ij}\omega_j \right\} + \epsilon(\omega_i). \tag{2.17}$$

The interaction coefficients may be positive (individuals are conformist) or negative (individuals are nonconformist). I define $\mathbf{\Gamma}$ as an $I \times I$ adjacency matrix with element Γ_{ij}. Also, let $\epsilon_i(\omega_i)$ denote independent and identically type I extreme-value distributed random variables across all alternatives and agents $i \in \mathcal{I}$. Following Brock and Durlauf (2001a),[12] individual i chooses $\omega_i = 1$ with probability[13]

$$\text{Prob}[\omega_i = 1] = \text{Prob}\left[2h + 2\mathcal{E}_i \left\{ \frac{1}{|\nu(i)|} \sum_{j\in\nu(i)} \Gamma_{ij}\omega_j \right\} \geq -(\epsilon_i(1) - \epsilon_i(-1)) \right]. \tag{2.18}$$

In view of the above assumptions, this probability may be written in terms of the logistic cumulative distribution function:

$$\text{Prob}[\omega_i = 1] = \frac{\exp\left[\varpi\left(2h + 2\mathcal{E}_i\left\{\frac{1}{|\nu(i)|}\sum_{j\in\nu(i)}\Gamma_{ij}\omega_j\right\}\right)\right]}{1+\exp\left[\varpi\left(2h + 2\mathcal{E}_i\left\{\frac{1}{|\nu(i)|}\sum_{j\in\nu(i)}\Gamma_{ij}\omega_j\right\}\right)\right]}, \tag{2.19}$$

where $\varpi > 0$ is a dispersion parameter, the degree of precision in the random component of private utility, $\epsilon(\omega_i)$ in (2.17). If $\varpi = 0$, then (2.19) implies purely random choice and the two outcomes are equally likely; if $\varpi \to \infty$, then it implies purely deterministic choice. The assumption of extreme-value distribution for the ϵ's is not only convenient for writing (2.19) but also links with the machinery of the Gibbs distributions theory (Blume 1997; Brock and Durlauf 2001a). It is not necessary either, as the asymptotic theory of extreme-value distributions suggests. More details on extreme-value distributions are given in chapter 3, section 3.9.1.

To characterize social outcomes, I assume that all agents are identical in terms of preferences but that each agent holds expectations of other agents' decisions that are *contingent* on those agents' *positions* in the social structure. At the social equilibrium, expectations are confirmed:

$$\mathcal{E}_i(\omega_j) = m_j, \quad \forall i, j \in \mathcal{I}. \tag{2.20}$$

By writing $\mathbf{m}$ for the vector of expectations of decisions, where $m_i = 1 \times \text{Prob}(\omega_i = 1) + (-1) \times \text{Prob}(\omega_i = -1)$, and using the hyperbolic tangent function, $\tanh(x) \equiv \frac{\exp(x)-\exp(-x)}{\exp(x)+\exp(-x)}$, $-\infty < x < \infty$, we have:

$$m_i = \tanh\left[\varpi h + \varpi \frac{1}{\nu(i)} \Gamma_i \mathbf{m}\right] \quad i = 1, \ldots, I, \tag{2.21}$$

where $\mathbf{\Gamma}_i$ denotes the ith row of the adjacency matrix. Ioannides (2006) proves that under the assumption of location-contingent expectations (2.20), the system of social interactions with an arbitrary topology admits an equilibrium that satisfies (2.21).

In the mean field theory case, which is equivalent to global interactions (Brock and Durlauf 2001a), each individual's subjective expectations of other agents' decisions are equal, $\mathcal{E}_i(\omega_j) = m, \forall i, j \in \mathcal{I}$, and the Nash equilibria satisfying (2.21) now satisfy

$$m = \tanh[\varpi h + \varpi \beta m], \tag{2.22}$$

where β denotes the now uniform social interactions coefficient, $\beta = \frac{\gamma(I-1)}{I-1}$.

An important implication of these results follows. Consider that all agents have the same number of neighbors, $d = |\nu(i)|$; that is, the graph is *regular*, and the interaction coefficients are equal, $\Gamma_{ij} = \beta$. Then a question arises whether or not equilibria exist with agents' behaviors being differentiated by their locations on the graph. We call such equilibria *anisotropic* in order to distinguish them from the *isotropic* case, where individuals are not distinguished in this fashion (Ioannides 2006).

For an isotropic equilibrium in the regular graph case, $\frac{1}{|\nu(i)|}\mathcal{E}_i\{\sum_{\forall j \neq i} \omega_j\} = m$, and equation (2.22) holds. Therefore, the regular interaction case admits the same isotropic equilibria as the Brock–Durlauf mean field case. Summarizing results from Brock and Durlauf (2001a), I have the following: if $\varpi\beta > 1$ and $h = 0$, then the function $\tanh(\varpi h + \varpi \beta m)$ is centered at $m = 0$ and equation (2.22) has three roots: a positive one ("upper") (m_+^*), zero ("middle"), and a negative one ("lower") (m_-^*), where $m_+^* = |m_-^*|$. If $h \neq 0$ and $\beta > 0$, then there exists a threshold H^*, which depends on ϖ and β, such that if $\varpi h < H^*$, equation (2.22) has a unique root that agrees with h in sign. In other words, given a private utility difference h, if the dispersion of the random utility component is sufficiently large, the random component dominates choice. If, on the other hand, $\varpi h > H^*$, then equation (2.22) has three roots: one with the same sign as h and two others with the opposite sign. That is, given a private utility difference, if the dispersion of the random utility component is small, then the social component dominates choice and is capable of producing multiplicity in conformist behavior. If $\beta < 0$, then there is a unique equilibrium that agrees with h in sign. In other words, economic fundamentals that drive private decisions and social norms play complementary roles. When three equilibria exist, I will refer to the middle one (m^*) as *symmetric* and to the upper and lower ones as *asymmetric* (m_-^*, m_+^*). See figure 2.1.

I note that the model exhibits nonlinear behavior with respect to parameters h and β. Conditional on a given private utility difference between choices 1 and -1, there exists a level that the interaction effect must reach in order to produce multiple self-consistent mean choice behavior. However, as ϖh increases in magnitude, the importance of the conformity effect ϖJm diminishes in a relative sense, and thus becomes unable to produce a self-consistent mean with the opposite sign. Even if private incentives favor a

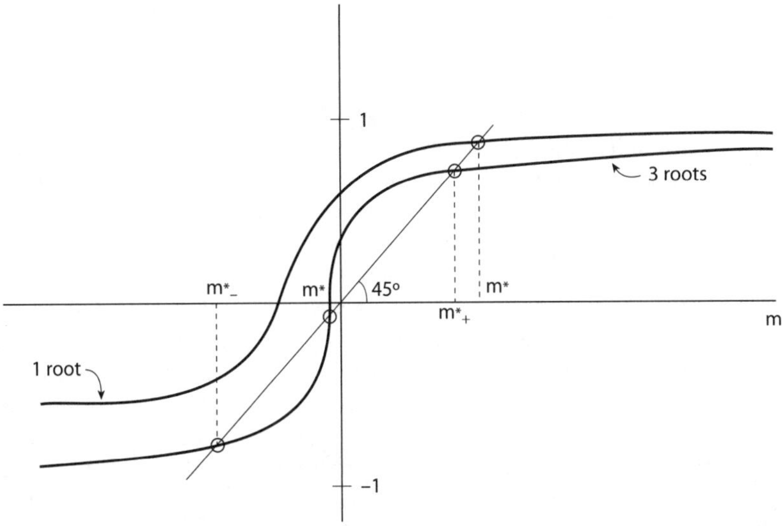

Figure 2.1. The Brock–Durlauf model.

particular decision, sufficiently strong social conformity effects can offset it. I return below in section 2.4.2 to empirics with variants of the Brock–Durlauf model.

Brock and Durlauf (2007) go beyond extreme-value distributed shocks and examine the identifiability of parameters of binary choice with social interactions models when the distribution of random payoff terms is unknown. They show that such models are identified (up to scale) under standard assumptions about the various distributions, provided that assignment to groups is random and there are no group-level unobservables. When they allow for group-level unobservables, they establish partial identification of endogenous social interactions in some interesting special cases. As a motivation, consider the case of teenage smoking: a recent survey reports that 10.0 percent of black teenagers have smoked a cigarette in the last 3 years, whereas 29.4 percent of white teenagers have. Since many contextual factors, such as family income, would likely make the black teenage smoking rate higher than the white rate, and ethnicity is a natural social group, this type of behavioral pattern is hard to understand without considering endogenous social interactions. This type of pattern reversal, which Brock and Durlauf refer to as a reversal between comparisons of group characteristics and endogenous outcomes, requires that the endogenous social effect be strong enough to generate multiple equilibria. Brock and Durlauf also establish that the model is identified (up to scale) if group assignment is based on observables. The model is partially identified if group assignment is based on unobservables, provided that matching of individuals to groups is assortative; that is, individuals with "better" characteristics are assigned to groups with "better" contextual effects. These results have not yet been used in empirical work.

The Brock–Durlauf classes of models have helped generate as well as structure analyses of a broad range of economic phenomena involving decisions subject to social interactions. For example, such diverse phenomena as diffusion of innovations (Brock and Durlauf 2010), herding and adoption of norms, like medical practices (Burke, Fournier, and Prasad 2010), cigarette smoking, or of other institutions by a population involve ideas that are conceptually related to social interactions. Although it is typically presumed that the endogenous social interactions coefficient β is positive, suggesting that individual and group-mean outcomes are strategic complements, it is logically possible for β to be negative, which would suggest that individual and group-mean outcomes are strategic substitutes. For example, consider that the development of adjacent parcels of land in exurbia may confer benefits to an individual owner if proximity to others is desired but also generate costs because of congestion and environmental degradation. Analogously to the case of correlated effects, heterogeneous characteristics that vary over space may cause spatial correlation of land use decisions. If such effects are unobservable, they would make land development decisions of adjacent parcels appear to be correlated even if they are not. Irwin and Bockstael (2002) estimate negative net social interaction effects in exurban land use development.

2.4.2 Estimations with the Brock–Durlauf Model

The linear-in-means model (2.1), a workhorse of empirical research, is a very special case. Nonidentification is specific to it when there is a one-to-one correspondence between individual and contextual effects. If the dependence of outcomes on their determinants is inherently nonlinear, then full identification may be possible. This is particularly clear in the case of binary outcomes (Brock and Durlauf 2001a, 2001b, 2007) and multinomial outcomes (Brock and Durlauf 2002, 2006; Durlauf and Ioannides 2010). I proceed with applications along the lines of the work by Brock and Durlauf (2001a, 2001b).

Brock–Durlauf social interactions models have been adopted by numerous researchers in extending a wide range of social interactions theories, though empirical investigations based on them have been many fewer. They include studies by Sirakaya (2006), Soetevent and Kooreman (2007), Li and Lee (2009), Krauth (2005), and Nakajima (2007). Nakajima uses a dynamic adaptation of the Brock–Durlauf model and estimates it at the steady state using youth tobacco surveillance data on smoking by middle-school and high-school students collected by the Centers for Disease Control and Prevention in the United States. Nakajima's findings strongly support the notion that the probability that an individual smokes is positively related to the fraction of smokers in his or her peer group. Interestingly, such peer effects are found to be stronger within the same gender and within the same race than across gender and race. Their results imply that taxes reduce youth smoking through a multiplier effect of a magnitude at least 1.5.

Soetevent and Kooreman (2007) use the study by Brock and Durlauf (2001a) to estimate an interactions model within small groups of given sizes. Their model roughly follows (2.18) but assumes normally distributed shocks (probit). Soetevent and Kooreman model binary outcomes as one-shot pure Nash equilibria of the associated noncooperative game. They estimate the model as a system of simultaneous equations by means of simulation methods. That is, the likelihood of a choice pattern in a group of I agents, $\tilde{\omega} = (\omega_1, \ldots, \omega_I)$, is the product of I individual likelihoods for events:

$$\begin{aligned} \epsilon_i &> \alpha x_i + \theta \mathbf{z}_{\nu(i)} - \frac{\beta}{I-1} \sum_{j \in \nu(i), j \neq i}^{I} \omega_j, \quad \text{if } \omega_i = 1; \\ \epsilon_i &\leq \alpha x_i + \theta \mathbf{z}_{\nu(i)} - \frac{\beta}{I-1} \sum_{j \in \nu(i), j \neq i}^{I} \omega_j, \quad \text{if } \omega_i = -1. \end{aligned} \tag{2.23}$$

Note that the outcomes in the social interactions term are specified as the actual decisions of others rather than the expected ones. This introduces a wrinkle. Unlike the Brock–Durlauf model, if one studies the predicted outcomes of the model as the values of the explanatory variables vary, one can identify *regions* of the parameter space that are consistent with multiple outcomes. By definition, in (2.23), the identifying feature of the model is the set of parameter values that satisfy inequality restrictions on regressions. Similar problems of multiplicity have also been studied in the industrial organization literature [see (Tamer 2003)]. This nonuniqueness problem affecting estimation is different from equilibrium multiplicity occurring in nonlinear models like the Brock–Durlauf model. For example, for given values of parameters, expected average choice among one's neighbors, $\mathcal{E}\{\omega_{\nu(i)}\}$, and data, each agent has a unique strategy profile in the Brock–Durlauf model.

Soetevent and Kooreman deal with the nonuniqueness problem affecting estimation, for parameter values for which it occurs, by assuming that all multiple equilibria are equally likely. Simulation of the model over different regions of the parameter space allows them to calculate the expected number of equilibria. The empirical application examines the individual behavior of high school teenagers in almost 500 school classes from 70 different schools using data from the National School Youth Survey (NSYS) of the Netherlands. In their baseline model, endogenous social interaction effects are strong for behavior closely related to school (truancy), somewhat weaker for behavior partly related to school (smoking, cell phone ownership, and moped ownership), and absent for behavior far away from school (asking for parents' permission for purchases). Intragender interactions are generally much stronger than cross-gender interactions. When school-specific fixed effects are allowed, social interaction effects are insignificant, with the exception of intragender interactions for truancy. The fact that they do find significant social interaction effects for truancy, a type of behavior closely related to school-based interactions, and do not find such effects for behaviors that might not be school-based, suggests (the authors argue) that the model measures genuine endogenous social interaction effects rather than unobserved social group effects. This estimation does not allow for contextual effects: $\theta = 0$ in equation (2.23).

Individuals' expectations of the actions of others in their social milieu is a key element of the Brock–Durlauf model. The study by Li and Lee (2009) is the only one I am aware of that uses both subjective data on expectations and inferences on expectations. Li and Lee model voting behavior and use a survey of voters in the 1996 U.S. presidential election that includes information on voting by the main respondents as well as on those individuals' perceptions of how their social acquaintances would be likely to vote. This study follows equations (2.17) and (2.18) and allows, in addition, for individual and contextual effects by specifying $2h$ in (2.18) as $\alpha x_i + \theta \mathbf{z}_{\nu(i)}$. The contextual effects do not perform well empirically and are ignored in the final regressions. These authors adapt equation (2.21) to compute respondents' rational expectations of their acquaintances' voting behavior. They reject the null hypothesis that reported subjective expectations coincide with computed rational expectations and show that they perform better empirically than rational expectations. Overall, social effects improve significantly the predictive power of the voting model. Individual characteristics such as gender, religion, and age play an important role in the formation of subjective expectations beyond what is captured by the computed rational expectations based on the model.

Sirakaya (2006) uses a national U.S. sample to identify the risk factors for recidivism among female, male, black, white, and Hispanic felony probationers. Unlike the Glaeser–Sacerdote–Scheinkman approach discussed earlier, Sirakaya's approach assumes that individual i's hazard function, the probability that probationer i will recidivate, depends on individual, $\mathbf{x}_i$, and neighborhood characteristics, $\mathbf{z}_{\nu(i)}$, as well as on social interactions among probationers in i's neighborhood, expressed through i's subjective expectation of the proportion of probationers who recidivate by some duration in i's neighborhood, $\mathcal{E}_i[m|\nu(i)]$, and the mean time until recidivation among them, $\mathcal{E}_i[t|\nu(i)]$. That is,

$$\begin{aligned} &m_i(t, \mathbf{x}_i, \mathbf{z}_{\nu(i)}, \mathcal{E}_i[m|\nu(i)], \mathcal{E}_i[t|\nu(i)]) \\ &\quad = \epsilon_0(t) \exp\left[\alpha_0 + \mathbf{x}_i\alpha + \mathbf{z}_{\nu(i)}\theta + \beta_m \mathcal{E}_i[m|\nu(i)] + \beta_t \mathcal{E}_i[t|\nu(i)]\right], \end{aligned} \tag{2.24}$$

where $\epsilon_0(t)$ denotes a baseline hazard function. Since a probationer is required to live in the jurisdiction that passed the probation sentence, the neighborhood of probationer i, $\nu(i)$, is assumed to be that jurisdiction. In other words, probationers do not self-select into neighborhoods. In selecting the covariates from a set of potential candidates, Sirakaya uses Bayesian model averaging both to account for model uncertainty and for the subsequent inference.

Sirakaya's results point to social interactions as one of the most significant factors affecting recidivism among all gender, ethnic, and race groups. The empirical results remain robust when unobserved risk factors shared by probationers within neighborhoods are allowed for, indicating negligible unobserved neighborhood-level heterogeneity. Among other significant factors are several individual characteristics, such as being male, being young, lacking employment, having a drug abuse history and prior felony convictions, and living in neighborhoods with high serious violent crime rates per capita for blacks, and a similar set of characteristics and, in addition, living in Republican neighborhoods for whites.

2.4.2.1 *Other Nonlinear Models: Drewianka's Marriage Market Application*

Drewianka (2003) draws attention to the fact that nonlinearities that are inherent in a particular phenomenon may further aid in identification. In his study of social effects in marriage markets, Drewianka argues that a higher marriage rate in a community may induce the propensity of unmarried people to marry (an endogenous social effect), ceteris paribus. But by also leaving fewer people unmatched, it hampers the search and reduces the marriage prospects of others and thus causes additional variation. Therefore, the net of these two effects, the endogenous social effect, is ambiguous. Contextual effects may also be present. For example, a woman might be more apt to marry if she lives in a community of wealthier men because such men are more likely to marry and will make more attractive spouses.

Let y_{ij} in equation (2.1) denote the propensity to marry in a given time period for individual i of gender j, $j \in \{\text{male, female}\}$. People in i's community, which is defined by their demographic characteristics $\Psi_{\nu(i)}$, who hold marriage in high regard are more likely to marry, but this is not known to the econometrician. That is, $\mathcal{E}[\epsilon_i|\Psi_{\nu(i)}] = \Psi_{\nu(i)} D \neq 0$: the correlated effect is nonzero and would appear as bias in the error in (2.1), where D is a vector of parameters, as I will clarify shortly.

Drewianka considers explicitly the two sides of the marriage market in each residential community as separate but interrelated "communities" where membership is exogenous. The marriage rate is

$$2\frac{\text{no. }|\text{matches}|}{\text{no. }|\text{male}| + \text{no. }|\text{female}|} = \left(\frac{\text{no. }|\text{matches}|}{\text{no. }|\text{group}_j|}\right)\left(\frac{\text{no. }|\text{group}_j|}{\text{no. }|\text{male}| + \text{no. }|\text{female}|}\right)$$
$$= y_j r_j, \quad j \in \{\text{male, female}\},$$

where r_j denotes the fraction of the marriage market attributed to group j. Taking the expectations of both sides of (2.1) by considering it separately for each group j, using the above expression for the group-specific marriage rate, which is the endogenous social effect here, and solving for the expectation of the endogenous social effect yield

$$\mathcal{E}[y_j|\mathbf{z}_j, \Psi_j] = \mathcal{E}[\mathbf{x}_j]\alpha + \frac{1}{1 - 2\beta_j r_j}\left(\alpha_0 + \mathcal{E}[\mathbf{z}_j]\theta + \Psi_j D\right), \tag{2.25}$$

where I have simplified notation and denoted by Ψ_j the vector of characteristics of individual i's group, by $\mathcal{E}[\mathbf{x}_j]$ the mean characteristics of group j, and by

$\mathcal{E}[\mathbf{z}_j]$ the mean contextual effect. When I substitute back into equation (2.1), the resulting model is identified because r_j varies across markets.

What is different here is that the logic of the model introduces in two sides of the market an additional source of variation in the form of a marketwide effect: the greater the number of potential marriage partners, the lower the probability that a match will occur. The opportunity cost of getting married is larger when it is easier to search for potential alternative partners. In communities where most people are single, marriage rates are lower—not just algebraically but also causally. Such an effect may help explain both the persistence of differences in marriage rates across places and groups (across which the underlying fundamentals vary) and the explosiveness with which marriage rates have changed over the last several decades. There is an inherent multiplier effect at work here. The likelihood of marrying depends on the rate at which other people match up, the endogenous social effect.

Drewianka uses data from the 5 percent Public Use Microsample (PUMS) of the 1980 U.S. census. His results show that an increase in the fraction of the population that is unmarried by 10 percent causes the marriage rate of never-married men to fall by 10 percent, and that of never-married women by 7 percent. The results are not sensitive to the definition of the marriage market, which is quite arbitrary in this application anyway and is dictated by data availability, but do vary a bit across ethnic groups. Naturally, this method applies more generally to circumstances involving search.

2.5 WHY EXPERIMENTAL DATA CAN HELP

The principal identification problem with the canonical social interactions setting is that because of such factors as endogenous explanatory variables, self-selection, omitted variables, and group unobservables, the random shock on the right-hand side of (2.1) may not be independent of the other regressors. This of course originates in the data-generating process. Experimental data allow additional options for getting around econometric identification problems. If experimental subjects are randomly assigned, placed deliberately under experimental conditions, and observed, the exogeneity of at least some unobservables is ensured. The social interactions literature has utilized experimental evidence that comes from two types of experiments, *natural* and *controlled* experiments.

Unique settings, like the administrative practice of randomly assigning roommates at Dartmouth College (see section 2.5.1 below), result in social arrangements that may be considered natural experiments. Observational data from such settings lend themselves to studying the impact of proximity on academic outcomes, provided that the intended outcome is not undone by individual actions ex post, such as individuals who dislike their original assignments succeeding in changing them. Other data come from instances where the physical layout of workplaces involves sharply different patterns allowing some workers to see only certain other workers. Mas and Moretti (2009) exploit such a setting; see section 2.5.2.

2.5.1 Observational Data from Natural Experiments

Sacerdote (2001) studies peer effects among people in close contact: freshman-year roommates and dormmates who are randomly assigned at Dartmouth College. Sacerdote estimates equation (2.1) with an individual's grade point average as a dependent variable, as a function of their own academic ability prior to college entrance, of their own social habits, and of the academic ability and grade point average of their roommates. Sacerdote finds that peers have an impact on each others' grade point averages and on decisions to join social groups such as fraternities. He does not, however, find residential peer effects on other major decisions made by college students, such as choice of a college major. He finds peer effects on grade point average at the individual room level—you keep up with your roommates! He finds that peer effects on fraternity membership occur both at the room level and at the entire dorm level—dorms are conformist! These data provide strong evidence for the existence of peer effects on student outcomes, even among highly selected college students who may be otherwise quite homogeneous but are in close proximity to one another. Peer effects are smaller, the more directly a decision is related to labor market activities.

A natural experiment is offered by the Dutch Postcode Lottery. As Kuhn, Kooreman, Soetevent, and Kapteyn (2011) analyze, a postal code (which in the Netherlands consists of 19 households on average) is randomly selected weekly, and prizes (consisting of cash and a new BMW) are awarded to lottery participants living in that postal code. On average, this generates a temporary, unexpected but substantial income shock equal to about 8 months of income for about one-third of the households in a typical winning code. The incomes of the remainder of neighboring households are unaffected. Still, the close proximity (and publicity) and the fact that the shock is unanticipated provide a setting for studying spillover effects on neighbors from the main effects on the winners. These authors document that most winners of a BMW convert it to cash, eat out significantly more 6 months after the shock, and spend more on durables and cars. They do find that individuals' winnings have social effects on their neighbors but only on two types of durable (and visible) consumption: cars and exterior home renovations. Having won the lottery does not make winners happier 6 months after the event, nor do their neighbors' winnings reduce their own happiness. This is in contrast to the fact that there is, in their data, a strong cross-sectional association between (nonlottery) income and self-reported happiness.

2.5.2 Observational Data with Unusually Detailed Features

Comprehensive data sets with unusual features also lend themselves to estimations of neighborhood effects. I review a representative number of such studies.

Aizer and Currie (2004) examine "network effects" in the utilization of publicly funded prenatal care. Using data from more than 3.5 million birth certificates from California, they find that pregnant women are most likely to be influenced in their use of public prenatal care programs by new mothers from the *same* area and ethnic group. Such use is highly correlated within groups defined using race, ethnicity, and residence in the same neighborhoods (defined as five-digit zip code areas) and persists even after accounting for unobserved characteristics by including zip code–year fixed effects. When Aizer and Currie introduce fixed effects for the hospital of delivery interacted with the year of delivery, their estimates of network effects are then either reduced or eliminated. This casts doubt on the idea that the observed correlations can be interpreted as evidence of information sharing originating in ethnic and geographic proximity. They interpret this finding as pointing instead to differences in the behavior of the low-income women involved, and of the institutions serving them, as the primary explanation for group-level differences in the use of publicly provided prenatal care. They examine the role of institutions by comparing the behavior of foreign-born with that of native-born Hispanic women. They find that such network effects are quite similar for both foreign-born and native-born Hispanic women. They conclude that it is a difference in the behavior of institutions and not information sharing that explains the established correlations between neighborhood and ethnic group membership in prenatal care use.

Cohen-Cole and Zanella (2008) study how usage of public assistance is influenced by one's neighbors' behavior. Their study builds on the earlier work by Bertrand, Luttmer, and Mullainathan (2000) by trying to disentangle an information exchange effect from preference interdependence. These authors examine whether individual outcomes covary because individuals *share information* about eligibility, application procedures, and other bureaucratic details or because higher welfare use in one's community reduces the *stigma* associated with such outcomes. The authors' identifying assumption is that information sharing occurs only within racial and ethnic groups, whereas the stigma operates across other groups as well. In other words, whereas *social* proximity matters for information exchanges, *spatial* proximity matters for stigma. Such extreme assumptions are promising first steps in disentangling specific mechanisms through which social interactions effects operate.

Grinblatt, Keloharju, and Ikaheimo (2004) use data on *all* residents of two large Finnish provinces to establish that automobile purchase decisions by close residential neighbors influence one another. The estimated endogenous neighborhood effects are strongest among individuals belonging to the same social class (especially when they belong to lower-income classes) or when the cars they purchase are of the same make or even the same model. Their findings suggest information sharing as a causal effect instead of keeping up with the Joneses. Excluding neighborhood means of demographics as contextual effects, the identification strategy here is reasonably plausible in this case: there is no reason why the average *age* of my neighbors should affect directly my taste in *cars*.

Mas and Moretti (2009) utilize a data set that reports supermarket employee productivity in 10-minute intervals. The data also report for each employee a set of peers whose composition, however, regularly changes exogenously with worker shifts. With the spatial orientation of workers in a store known, Mas and Moretti are able to analyze remarkably detailed aspects of social interactions in the workplace. They find strong evidence of positive productivity spillovers from the introduction of highly productive workers into a shift. A 10 percent increase in average coworker permanent productivity is associated with a 1.5 percent increase in a worker's effort. Most of this peer effect arises from low-productivity workers benefiting from the presence of high-productivity workers, a finding that is also corroborated by Ichino and Falk (2006) in a study based on lab experiments discussed further below. Therefore, skill diversity improves productivity [cf. (Page 2007)]. They seek to explain the mechanism that generates the peer effect by examining whether effort depends on workers' abilities to monitor one another, which originate in their spatial arrangement, and whether effort is affected by the time workers have previously spent working near one another. They find asymmetric effects: a given worker's effort is positively related to the presence and speed of workers who face him but not to the presence and speed of workers whom he faces (and do not face him). Workers who frequently overlap with one another respond more to each others' presence.

2.5.3 Large-Scale Randomized Field Experiments

A number of large-scale randomized field experiments have recently provided settings that are suitable for the estimation of social interactions models. These experiments have been designed to help inform U.S. policy aimed at breaking the "vicious cycle of urban poverty" and other social ills. The Moving to Opportunity (MTO) program, conducted by the U.S. Department of Housing and Urban Development, ran in five U.S. cities (Baltimore, Boston, Chicago, Los Angeles, and New York) from September 1994 to August 1998 (HUDUSER 2004). The program involved a randomly selected group of 4,608 families from among residents of high-poverty public housing projects. Of these, 3,169 randomly selected families in turn were randomly allocated between two subgroups: 1,349 were given *unrestricted "Section 8" vouchers*; the other 1,820 were given vouchers that could be used *only* in census tracts with poverty rates below 10 percent and were referred to as the *experimental group*. Finally, 1,310 were assigned to a *control group* and were given (together with the other two groups) logistic and counseling assistance through nongovernmental organizations should they wish to relocate to "better" neighborhoods. This process of random assignment provides an almost unique opportunity to separate the role of neighborhood context from the selection bias that may arise from residential mobility decisions. However, not all subjects chose to take up the experimental treatment: only 860 families in the experimental group and 816 in the section 8 group moved. Thus, assessing the effect of treatment per se is based on the subpopulation of compliers.

Several studies based on data from the MTO experiments show that outcomes after relocation have improved for children, and primarily for females, with respect to education, risky behavior, and physical health, but the effects on male youth were adverse. Regarding outcomes for adults, such as economic self-sufficiency and physical health, the picture is more mixed. Kling, Liebman, and Katz (2007) report that 4–7 years after relocation, families (primarily female-headed ones with children) lived in safer neighborhoods with lower poverty rates than those of a control group that was not offered vouchers. Generally, the housing voucher treatment caused otherwise similar groups of families to reside in very different neighborhoods. These authors investigate the effects on outcomes for adults and teenage youth of moving out of some of the highest-poverty neighborhoods in the United States. Their findings have three important implications. First, housing mobility by itself does not appear to be an effective antipoverty strategy, at least over a 5-year horizon. Second, even in the absence of broader economic gains, policies that move families out of distressed public housing projects using rental vouchers are likely to have benefits that significantly exceed their costs anyway. It is cheaper to provide a unit of subsidized housing with vouchers than a unit in a public housing project. Notably, the MTO intervention produced large mental health improvements. And third, important neighborhood effects do exist but only for some outcomes. The evidence that effects of housing vouchers appear to accrue from changes in neighborhood characteristics rather than from moves per se suggests that interventions that substantially improve distressed neighborhoods could have effects at least as large as those observed from moving to lower-poverty neighborhoods. It is a strength of the identification strategy with MTO-based data that it relies on subjects' being assigned randomly to different groups.

There is controversy in the literature over the validity of these findings in the context of policy design for actual large-scale policy interventions (Sobel 2006; Clampet-Lundquist and Massey 2008). Sobel (2006) worries about *interference* among MTO program participants. This occurs when different respondents' potential outcomes can depend on the treatment assignments of other subjects. This can occur even in the absence of social interactions. Using the MTO demonstration as a concrete context, Sobel proposes a framework for causal inference when interference is present and defines a number of causal estimands of interest. He characterizes the properties of the usual estimators of experimental treatment effects, which are unbiased and/or consistent in randomized studies without interference. When interference is present, the difference between a treatment group mean and a control group mean does not estimate an average treatment effect but rather the difference between two effects defined on two distinct subpopulations. This result raises concerns: a researcher who fails to recognize it could easily infer that a treatment is beneficial when in fact it is universally harmful. This calls for an examination of possible interference.

Kling, Liebman, and Katz (2007) reject the criticism of interference by pointing, inter alia, to the fact that 55 percent of household heads who signed up for the MTO program had no friends and 65 percent no family in their baseline neighborhoods. However, only one-quarter of eligible families signed up for the MTO program, which also suggests that decisions are influenced by unobservables. Durlauf (2004) argues that moving large numbers of poor families to more affluent communities will induce general equilibrium effects in terms of the location decisions of other families and strain the ability of schools in these neighborhoods to provide needed services. The commitment of affluent families to public schools could be strained by a massive influx of poor families into their communities. In the Final Impacts Evaluation of the MTO, Sanbonmatsu et al. (2011, 259), acknowledge that interference "cannot be tested directly" (with existing MTO data) and report "some suggestive evidence against its practical importance." Blume, Brock, Durlauf, and Ioannides (2011, 933–934) underscore the difficulties of drawing inferences about social interactions from treatment effects based on MTO data. Still, they acknowledge the value of MTO data-based studies "in thinking about alternative policies."

2.5.4 Laboratory Experiments

In view of the staggering increase in laboratory-based experimental economics research, it is somewhat surprising that relatively little direct attention has been paid to social interactions. I review some notable exceptions and refer the reader to the work of Blume, Brock, Durlauf, and Ioannides (2011, 923–931) for a more extensive discussion. Ichino and Falk (2006) report results from an experiment involving workers who are assigned in pairs to stuff envelopes, with the control group being subjects working alone in a room. These authors find that standard deviations of output are significantly smaller within pairs—subjects conform—than between pairs, and that social interactions raise productivity: the average output per person is greater when subjects work in pairs. They also show that social interactions are asymmetric: low-productivity workers are more sensitive to the behavior of high-productivity workers as peers.

Falk, Fischbacker, and Gächter (2009) test endogenous social interactions in a laboratory experiment where each subject is simultaneously a member of two randomly assigned and economically identical groups but has different "neighbors." In both groups subjects decide how much to contribute to a public good. These researchers define as social interactions circumstances where subjects make group-specific contributions that depend on the contribution by the subjects' respective neighbors at the same time. They find that most of the subjects' contributions are strongly influenced by the contributions of their neighbors, while only about 10 percent of the subjects exhibit no social interactions.

2.6 ENDOGENOUS SOCIAL STRUCTURE REVISITED: DYNAMICS

I develop next a dynamic model of individual decision making where the individual is aware of influences from the actions of others. I start with a given social structure and then address, in section 2.6.5 below, the deliberate choice of connections. Following Ioannides and Soetevent (2007), I introduce a behavioral model that can accommodate a broad range of instances of social interactions, such as consumption activities, human capital accumulation, and more generally income-generating activities that may be subject to neighborhood and peer effects. Some of the effects this formulation allows are relevant for neighborhood choice but are not present when one works only with outcomes.

I assume that individual i derives utility U_{it} from an activity y_{it} in period t and incurs costs in terms of utility for maintaining her social connections. The utility function U_{it} is assumed to be increasing and concave in y_{it}. It depends on the actions and characteristics of i's neighbors (in the sense of the social structure) and on the mean action and characteristics of the entire economy. I discuss these further after I introduce additional notation as follows.

$\mathbf{y}_t := (y_{1t}, y_{2t}, \ldots, y_{I,t})^{\mathrm{T}}$: a column I-vector with the actions of all individuals in $\mathcal{I}$ at time t as elements.

$\mathbf{x}_i$: a row K-vector with i's own characteristics as elements, such as the number and ages of children in a household. Matrix $\mathbf{X}$, an $I \times K$ matrix, stacks characteristics for all individuals.

$\mathbf{x}_{\nu_t(i)}$: a row K-vector with the mean characteristics of i's neighbors at time t, $j \in \nu_t(i)$, $\mathbf{x}_{\nu_t(i)} = \frac{1}{|\nu_t(i)|}\boldsymbol{\Gamma}_{it}\mathbf{X}$. This stands for the influence of the aggregate characteristics of one's neighbors, such as mean income, age, education, and other demographic and life cycle characteristics. They can be either a matter of taste directly (I like socializing with others of similar age to mine who also have children) or indirectly because such characteristics are determinants of other variables of interest, such as taxes in the community of one's residence.

I use ι to denote a column I-vector of 1s, $\mathbf{I}$ the $I \times I$ diagonal matrix of 1s, and ϕ, θ, α and ω column K-vectors of parameters.

In specifying individual preferences, I borrow and combine key features from the formulation of social interactions by Weinberg (2007), whose model is static, and by Binder and Pesaran (1998, 2001), whose models are dynamic. I assume that individual i at time t enjoys socializing with others with specific characteristics. I express this through taste for the *average characteristics*[14] of i's neighbors $j \in \nu(i)$, $\frac{1}{|\nu_t(i)|}\boldsymbol{\Gamma}_{i,t}\mathbf{X}\phi$, which I call a *level local contextual* effect. The marginal utility of one's own activity depends on one's own neighbors' mean characteristics and is expressed through the term $\frac{1}{|\nu_t(i)|}\boldsymbol{\Gamma}_{i,t}\mathbf{X}\theta y_{it}$, which may be referred to as a *marginal local contextual* effect and separately, on agent i's own characteristics, through the term $\mathbf{x}_i\alpha y_{it}$.

With interactions being at first symmetric, individual i at time t is affected by her neighbors' actions in two ways. One may be thought of as *conformism*: individual i suffers disutility from a gap between her own current action and the mean action of her neighbors in the previous period,[15] $y_{it} - \frac{1}{|\nu_{t-1}(i)|}\boldsymbol{\Gamma}_{i,t}\mathbf{y}_{t-1}$. This formulation allows the effect of neighbors' actions to depend on individual socioeconomic characteristics. For example, younger people may experience a greater disutility than older people from living in a high-income neighborhood. It expresses *endogenous local interactions*. Modifying the adjacency matrix to allow for $\gamma_{ii} \neq 0$ would introduce *own-conformity*, that is to say, a *habit formation* effect, such as when one dislikes changing one's own action from period to period.

I allow for a *global conformity* effect, through the gap between an individual's current action and the mean action among all individuals in the previous period, $y_{it} - \bar{y}_{t-1}$. This expresses *endogenous global interactions* albeit with a lag.[16] Expressing the effects in relation to neighbors' lagged actions while keeping the contemporaneous neighborhood structure is analytically convenient but not necessary and will be relaxed below when I discuss tools of spatial econometrics.

Individual i incurs a (utility) cost for maintaining her connection with individual j at time t, which is a quadratic function of the "intensity" of the social attachment, or of the synergistic effort, as measured by γ_{ij}, that is, $-c_1\boldsymbol{\Gamma}_{i,t}\iota - c_2\boldsymbol{\Gamma}_{i,t}\boldsymbol{\Gamma}'_{i,t}$, with $c_1, c_2 > 0$. This component of the utility function is critical when I come to consider weighted adjacency matrices in section 2.6.5. Finally, I allow for an individual's own marginal utility to include an additive stochastic shock, ε_{it}.

Representing all these effects by means of a quadratic utility function, I have

$$\begin{aligned} U_{it} = {} & \boldsymbol{\Gamma}_{i,t}\mathbf{X}\phi + (\alpha_0 + \mathbf{x}_i\alpha + \boldsymbol{\Gamma}_{i,t}\mathbf{X}\theta + \varepsilon_{i,t})\, y_{it} - \frac{1}{2}(1 - \beta_g - \beta_\ell)y_{it}^2 \\ & -\frac{1}{2}\beta_g\,(y_{it} - \bar{y}_{t-1})^2 - \frac{1}{2}\beta_\ell\left(y_{it} - \frac{1}{|\nu_t(i)|}\boldsymbol{\Gamma}_{i,t}\mathbf{y}_{t-1}\right)^2 \\ & +\frac{1}{|\nu_t(i)|}\boldsymbol{\Gamma}_{i,t}\mathbf{y}_{t-1}\mathbf{x}_i\omega - c_1\boldsymbol{\Gamma}_{i,t}\iota - c_2\boldsymbol{\Gamma}_{i,t}\boldsymbol{\Gamma}'_{i,t}. \end{aligned} \tag{2.26}$$

Terms on the right-hand side of (2.26) that do not involve y_{it} do not affect individuals' reaction functions. The corresponding social effects are relevant for the endogenous neighborhood choice process which rests on total utility comparisons.[17]

2.6.1 A Dynamic Model of Individual Decision Making

At the beginning of period t, individual i augments her information set Ψ_{it-1} with information about her own contemporaneous preference shock, ϵ_{it}, and with public information that has become available during period $t - 1$. This includes the period t adjacency matrix $\boldsymbol{\Gamma}_t$, which is assumed to be exogenous, her neighbors' actual past actions, $\mathbf{\Gamma}_{i,t}\mathbf{Y}_{t-1}$, and the mean lagged action for the entire economy, $\bar{y}_{t-1}$. She chooses an action plan $\{y_{it}, y_{it+1}, \ldots | \Psi_{it}\}$ so as to maximize expected lifetime utility conditional on Ψ_{it},

$$\mathcal{E}\left\{\sum_{s=t} \delta^{s-t} U_{i,s} \,|\Psi_{it}\right\}, \tag{2.27}$$

where δ, $0 < \delta < 1$, is the rate of time preference and individual utility is given by (2.26). Individual i recognizes that y_{it} enters her next period utility $U_{i,t+1}$ only if $\beta_g \neq 0$, that is, only if endogenous global interactions are present. This reflects the fact that there is no habit formation effect, $\gamma_{ii,t+1} = 0, \forall t$, in which case the term $\mathbf{\Gamma}_{i,t+1}\mathbf{y}_t$ does not contain y_{it}.

The first-order condition with respect to y_{it}, given the social structure, is

$$y_{it} = \frac{\beta_\ell}{|\nu_t(i)|}\mathbf{\Gamma}_{i,t}\mathbf{y}_{t-1} + \beta_g \bar{y}_{t-1} + \delta\frac{\beta_g}{I}\mathcal{E}\left\{(y_{i,t+1} - \bar{y}_t)\,|\Psi_{it}\right\} + \alpha_0 + \mathbf{x}_i\alpha + \mathbf{\Gamma}_{i,t}\mathbf{X}\theta + \varepsilon_{it}. \tag{2.28}$$

The interdependencies between individuals' reaction functions are clearer when the first-order conditions for all individuals are put concisely in matrix form:

$$\left[\mathbf{I} + \delta\frac{\beta_g}{I}\bar{\mathbf{I}}\right]\mathbf{y}_t = \mathcal{A}_t + \left[\beta_\ell \mathbf{A}_t + \frac{\beta_g}{I}\bar{\mathbf{I}}\right]\mathbf{y}_{t-1} + \delta\frac{\beta_g}{I}\mathcal{E}\left[\mathbf{y}_{t+1}|\Psi_t\right] + \boldsymbol{\varepsilon}_t, \tag{2.29}$$

where $\bar{\mathbf{I}}$ is an $I \times I$ matrix of 1s, $\mathbf{D}_t$ is an $I \times I$ diagonal matrix where the elements are the inverses of the size of each individual's neighborhood, $D_{ii,t} = 1/|\nu_t(i)| = 1/(\mathbf{\Gamma}_t\mathbf{\Gamma}_t)_{ii}$, and

$$\mathbf{A}_t \equiv \mathbf{D}_t\mathbf{\Gamma}_t \tag{2.30}$$

is the row normalized adjacency matrix, an $I \times I$ positive matrix.

Defining the conformist effect relative to the mean action of an individual's neighbors in the current period, $y_{it} - \frac{1}{|\nu_t(i)|}\mathbf{\Gamma}_{i,t}\mathbf{y}_t$, modifies the above system to yield

$$\left[\mathbf{I} + \delta\frac{\beta_g}{I}\bar{\mathbf{I}}\right]\mathbf{y}_t = \mathcal{A}_t + \beta_\ell \mathbf{A}_t\mathbf{y}_t + \frac{\beta_g}{I}\bar{\mathbf{I}}\mathbf{y}_{t-1} + \delta\frac{\beta_g}{I}\mathcal{E}[\mathbf{y}_{t+1}|\Psi_t] + \boldsymbol{\varepsilon}_t. \tag{2.31}$$

The simultaneous presence of the vectors of current and of lagged individual decisions, $\mathbf{y}_{t-1}, \mathbf{y}_t$, and of the expectation of future ones, $\mathcal{E}[\mathbf{y}_{t+1}|\Psi_t]$, complicates dealing with this model considerably.[18]

The consequences of allowing for a global effect become evident by comparing (2.31) with (2.29). If both β_ℓ, β_g are zero, that is, all social effects are absent, then the vector of individual outcomes simply equals individuals' own effects plus the contemporaneous random shock, $\mathbf{x}_i\alpha + \varepsilon_{it}$. Otherwise, in the presence of social effects, the left- and right-hand sides of (2.29) denote marginal lifetime utility costs and benefits for each individual from an additional unit of the respective outcome. An additional unit of $\mathbf{y}_t$ increases marginal costs now by $\mathbf{y}_t$ and marginal costs next period via the conformism effect, which when discounted to the present is equal to $\delta\frac{\beta_g}{N}\bar{\mathbf{I}}\mathbf{y}_t$.

By setting $\beta_g = 0$ and thus excluding endogenous global interactions, the system of equations determining the endogenous variables becomes

$$\mathbf{y}_t = \mathcal{A}_t + \beta_\ell \mathbf{A}_t \mathbf{y}_{t-1} + \boldsymbol{\varepsilon}_t, \tag{2.32}$$

where $\boldsymbol{\varepsilon}_t \equiv (\varepsilon_{1t}, \varepsilon_{2t}, \ldots, \varepsilon_{It})^{\mathrm{T}}$ is the I-vector of shocks, and

$$\mathcal{A}_t \equiv (\ldots, \alpha_0 + \mathbf{x}_i\alpha + \boldsymbol{\Gamma}_{i,t}\mathbf{X}\theta, \ldots)^{\mathrm{T}}$$

is a column I-vector of individual and contextual effects.

The evolution of the state of the economy, defined by $\mathbf{Y}_t$, the vector of individuals' actions, is fully described by (2.32), a VARX(1, 0) model, given the information set $\Psi_t = \bigcup_i \Psi_{i,t}$ and provided that the sequence of adjacency matrices $\boldsymbol{\Gamma}_t, t = 0, 1, \ldots,$ is specified. Intuitively, the economy evolves as a Nash equilibrium system of social interactions that adapts to external shocks of two types, deterministic ones, as denoted by the evolution of the social structure $\boldsymbol{\Gamma}_t$, and stochastic ones, as denoted by the vectors of shocks $\boldsymbol{\varepsilon}_t$.

To fix ideas, let us assume that the random vectors $\boldsymbol{\varepsilon}_t, t = 1, \ldots,$ are independent and identically distributed over time and drawn from a multivariate normal distribution with mean $\mathbf{0}$ and variance covariance matrix $\mathbf{Q}$, $\boldsymbol{\varepsilon}_t \sim \mathcal{N}(\mathbf{0}, \mathbf{Q})$. Then, by a standard derivation from stochastic systems theory of the t-step transition probability, the distribution for $\mathbf{y}_t$ at time t is characterized as follows. Given the initial state of the economy, $\mathbf{y}_0$, and under the above assumption about the shocks, the distribution of the state of the system at time t, $\mathbf{y}_t$, is normal,

$$\mathbf{y}_t \sim \mathcal{N}\left(\beta_\ell^t \prod_{s=1}^{t} \mathbf{A}_s \mathbf{y}_0 + \sum_{j=0}^{t-1}\left(\beta_\ell^{t-j-1} \prod_{s=j+1}^{t} \mathbf{A}_s\right)\mathcal{A}_j, \boldsymbol{\Sigma}_{t|0}\right), \tag{2.33}$$

where $\mathbf{A}_t$ is the row-normalized adjacency matrix defined in (2.30) and the variance-covariance matrix $\boldsymbol{\Sigma}_{t|0}$ above is given iteratively from

$$\boldsymbol{\Sigma}_{k+m|k} = \beta_\ell^2 \mathbf{A}_{k+m-1} \boldsymbol{\Sigma}_{k+m-1|k} \mathbf{A}'_{k+m-1} + \mathbf{Q}, \quad m > 1; \quad \boldsymbol{\Sigma}_{k|k} = [0]. \tag{2.34}$$

$\boldsymbol{\Sigma}_{k+m|k}$ is the matrix of mean-squared errors of the m-step predictor for $\mathbf{y}_t$.

2.6.2 Evolution of Interactions at the Steady State

Having established the mathematical existence and uniqueness of the mean and the variance-covariance matrix of the set of individually optimal outcomes, I turn next to their economic properties. Suppose first that the social structure is totally disconnected and consists of isolated nodes, in which case the adjacency matrix is a matrix of zeroes. In that case, the mean outcome is the vector of contextual effects, $\mathbf{y}^* = \mathcal{A}$, and its variance-covariance matrix is simply the variance-covariance matrix of individual shocks. Generalizing somewhat, we can allow for a factor-analytic structure for the shocks. That is, let $\boldsymbol{\varepsilon}_t = \mathbf{G}\mathbf{w}_t$, where $\mathbf{G}$ is an $I \times M$ mixing matrix and $\mathbf{w}_t$ is a random column M-vector that is independently and identically distributed over time and obeys a normal distribution with mean $\mathbf{0}$ and variance-covariance matrix $\mathbf{R}$, $\mathbf{w}_t \sim \mathcal{N}(\mathbf{0}, \mathbf{R})$. This case is of particular interest because it allows us to express the contemporaneous stochastic shock in a factor-analytic form of contemporaneously interdependent components, and therefore shocks to different individuals may be correlated. The variance-covariance matrix of $\boldsymbol{\varepsilon}_t$ at the steady state is given by $\mathbf{GRG}'$. If the social structure is arbitrary but connected, then the normalized adjacency matrix $\mathbf{A}$ is nonsingular. This allows us to solve for the variance-covariance matrix of social outcomes:

$$\boldsymbol{\Sigma}_\infty = \beta_\ell^2 \mathbf{A} \boldsymbol{\Sigma}_\infty \mathbf{A}' + \mathbf{GRG}'. \tag{2.35}$$

This yields

$$\boldsymbol{\Sigma}_\infty = \left[\mathbf{I} + \beta_\ell^2 \mathbf{A}^2 + \beta_\ell^4 \mathbf{A}^4 + \cdots\right] \mathbf{GRG}'. \tag{2.36}$$

The properties of the power series on the right-hand side of (2.36) depend on the spectral properties of the respective normalized adjacency matrix for the social structure. They are discused in the literature for a great variety of classes of social topologies of interest (Cvetković, Doob, and Sachs 1995; Ioannides 2006). The social structure affects both the mean and the variance-covariance matrix. When the social interactions topology is not connected and the adjacency matrix is singular, (2.35) still applies but (2.36) does not.

Given a vector of starting actions, $\mathbf{y}_0$, the mean vector of individuals' actions after t periods reflects the full sequence of contextual effects, $\{\mathbf{A}_0, \ldots, \mathbf{A}_{t-1}\}$, weighted by the respective adjacency matrices. The dispersion of individual actions, on the other hand, reflects the compound effect of weighted interactions as they modify dispersion of the underlying shocks.

2.6.3 An Application to the Income Distribution

As an application, I propose to think of the agents' actions as their incomes. As incomes evolve over time, with different individuals "reacting" to the incomes of others, a steady-state distribution emerges for the vector of individual incomes. This yields a statistical model of the cross-sectional income distribution. For the model in section 2.6.1, I assume that the underlying shocks are normally distributed and that there is no global effect. Thus, given a time-invariant adjacency matrix, the vector of individual incomes at the steady state obeys a multivariate normal, $\mathcal{N}(\mathbf{y}^*, \boldsymbol{\Sigma}_\infty)$, where $\mathbf{y}^* = [\mathbf{I} - \beta_\ell \mathbf{A}]^{-1} \mathbf{A}$ and $\boldsymbol{\Sigma}_\infty$ is given by (2.36). I consider next the distribution of the y_{it}'s, $i = 1, \ldots, I$, when I do not distinguish to *whom* they accrue. That is, I derive the distribution of y's along one dimension as t tends to ∞, under the assumption that they are drawn from the same distribution. This is obtained by recognizing that, in general, the probability that the value of y_i^* falls in an interval (z, dz) may be conditioned on the values of all other incomes in the previous period.

Let $\mathbf{y}_{-i}$ denote the subvector of $\mathbf{y}$ resulting from partitioning out y_i, $\mathbf{y} = (y_i, \mathbf{y}_{-i})$. The density of the cross-sectional distribution of income satisfies

$$g(z) = \frac{1}{I}\sum_{i=1}^{I}\int f_{i|_{-i}}(z|\mathbf{y}_{-i})f(\mathbf{y}_{-i})d\mathbf{y}_{-i}. \tag{2.37}$$

The densities in the above integral may be written in terms of the mean and the variance-covariance matrix in the standard fashion (Anderson 1958, 27–30). Since the mean of the conditional distribution $f_{i|_{-i}}$ of individual i's conditional on $\mathbf{y}_{-i}$, may be written as a linear function of the individual components of $\mathbf{y}_{-i}$, $\mathcal{E}(y_i|\mathbf{y}_{-i}) = y_i^* + \mathbf{\Sigma}_{i,-i}\mathbf{\Sigma}_{-i,-i}^{-1}(\mathbf{y}_{-i} - \mathbf{y}_{-i}^*)$. Its variance is given by $\sigma_i^2 - \mathbf{\Sigma}_{i,-i}\mathbf{\Sigma}_{-i,-i}^{-1}\mathbf{\Sigma}_{-i,i}$, where $\mathbf{\Sigma}_{i,-i}\mathbf{\Sigma}_{-i,-i}^{-1}\mathbf{\Sigma}_{-i,i}$ are partitions of $\mathbf{\Sigma}_{\infty}$. It is thus possible to express each of the terms in the sum on the right-hand side of (2.37) in terms of $(\mathbf{y}^*, \mathbf{\Sigma}_{\infty})$ and the respective partitions of $\mathbf{\Sigma}_{\infty}$. Thus, the density of the cross-sectional distribution of income is obtained as a mixture of normally distributed variables. The mixture need not be symmetric with respect to individuals, as their relative positions may differ. Finally, in the special case of isolated individuals, there is no interdependence, and (2.37) reduces to the average of the N independent densities. Different relative positions in the social network imply different patterns of interdependence, and all these are reflected via the variance-covariance matrix $\mathbf{\Sigma}_{\infty}$ and the associated submatrices defined above.

I note that there is direct empirical support for the notion that people have preferences for their neighbors' incomes. Luttmer (2005) uses data from the U.S. National Survey of Families and Households augmented with contextual information from census data from the Public Use Microdata Areas (PUMA). Luttmer regresses self-reported well-being against average earnings in the area of a respondent's residence defined by PUMA (see section 2.13.2), individual-specific controls that proxy for her earnings, basic demographics, and other PUMA characteristics such as its racial composition. Luttmer shows, after controlling for an individual's own income, that higher earnings of neighbors are associated with lower levels of self-reported happiness in terms of a variety of measures. In contrast, Knies, Burgess, and Propper (2007) do not find a negative association between people's life satisfaction and their relative income position in the neighborhood. These authors use data from the German Socio-economic Panel Study (SOEP) that are matched with population characteristics. In fact, when they control for own income and for neighborhood income at the zip code level (which in Germany amounts to roughly 9,000 people), they find positive associations between neighborhood income and happiness. This finding is robust to a number of tests, including adding in more controls for neighborhood quality and interacting neighborhood income with indicators that proxy the extent to which individuals interact with their neighbors. Naturally, the results reported by both these studies depend critically on the notion of neighborhood employed.

2.6.4 Choice of Social Group

In the context of the basic model of individual decision making above, I pose the question of whether or not an individual wants to interact socially with others. This involves a comparison between utility in social isolation (*autarky*) with that in the presence of social interactions. The value of autarky is obtained by setting all the γ's equal to 0 in individual i's utility function or, equivalently, the reaction function (2.29). This yields $y_{it} = \frac{1}{1-\beta_g}(\alpha_0 + \mathbf{x}_i\alpha + \epsilon_{it} + \bar{y}_{t-1})$. There is no social context other than the lagged global effect, $\bar{y}_{t-1}$, which is transmitted independently of specific connections. Whether or not connecting with others would benefit an individual depends on a comparison of the value of expected remaining utility with and without connections. I refer to the latter as the *value of autarky*. It would pay an individual to initiate connections with others if the value of utility given connections with others exceeds the value of autarky.

In addressing the initiation of connections, additional issues arise. So far I have assumed that connections are bilateral and exogenous. Generally, I may choose to be influenced by the actions of others, but nothing compels others to make their actions observable to me; it might not be advantageous to them. In many social situations, one can think of different intensities of interactions. I may regularly interact socially with many others, but I might be close to only some of them. Clearly, these thoughts lead to notions of strategic behavior regarding connections. The benefit to an individual from initiating connections depends on the actions of others. Similarly, in what sense are interconnections among individuals an appropriate model for a social group? What ties members of social groups together? One may think of group formation in terms of comparisons of optimal utilities ex ante and ex post. With many individuals, there are too many possibilities for the composition of groups.

A particularly influential model of social connections is developed by Jackson and Wolinsky (1996) that introduces pairwise stability as an equilibrium concept. This concept captures the notion that at equilibrium connections must be bilaterally agreeable: no agent can become better off by unilaterally severing a link with another person, and no two agents can be better off by adding a link connecting them. I do not adopt this strategic viewpoint in the exposition that follows. Instead, I provide an algebraic treatment that serves as an analytical foundation for the empirics of social networks that follow. In the remainder of this section I assume that individuals are eponymous, that is, recognizable entities within their social milieus.

2.6.5 Endogenous Networking

How do social network connections come about? I explore the notion that individuals initiate network connections so as to benefit in terms of expected utility by doing so. I adopt the approach of Ioannides and Soetevent (2007) and model endogenous networking as a choice of *continuous weights* by individuals to apply to connections with each of all other individuals by whose actions they wish to be influenced. Such an approach assuages the analytical difficulty of dealing with discrete endogenous variables expressing whether or not connections exist. It also makes sense in its own right. The intensities of individuals' social attachments do differ: they vary from close friendships to mere acquaintances. Accordingly, weighted adjacency matrices are used widely in the social sciences literature.[19]

It is appropriate to expand definition (2.10) and allow for *directed*, possibly time-varying connections. That is, the adjacency matrix $\mathbf{\Gamma}_t$, is now *weighted*; its elements are intensities of social attachment defined as

$$\Gamma_{ij,t} \begin{cases} \neq 0, & \text{if } i \text{ is influenced by } j \text{ in } \mathcal{G}_t; \\ = 0, & \text{otherwise.} \end{cases} \tag{2.38}$$

This formulation combines the notion of an adjacency matrix in graphs with the notion of varying intensities of social contacts and at the same time allows for the network to be directed. The adjacency matrix is no longer symmetric.[20]

I work next with a finite horizon, T, version of the typical individual's problem and consider the networking decision prior to setting the period T outcome.[21] Treating the choice of y_{iT} as conditional on $\mathbf{\Gamma}_{i,T}$ allows me to express the indirect utility function given a network topology. For simplicity, I exclude a global effect by setting $\beta_g = 0$. Individual i chooses y_{iT} so as to maximize the expected period T utility given by

$$\begin{aligned} U_{iT} &= \mathbf{\Gamma}_{i,T}\mathbf{X}\phi + (\mathcal{A}_{iT} + \varepsilon_{iT})\, y_{iT} - \frac{1}{2}(1-\beta_\ell)y_{iT}^2 \\ &\quad - \frac{\beta_\ell}{2}(y_{iT} - \mathbf{\Gamma}_{i,T}\mathbf{y}_{T-1})^2 + \mathbf{\Gamma}_{i,T}\mathbf{y}_{T-1}\mathbf{x}_i\omega - c_1\mathbf{\Gamma}_{i,T}\iota - c_2\mathbf{\Gamma}_{i,T}\mathbf{\Gamma}'_{i,T}. \end{aligned} \tag{2.39}$$

With utility maximizing choice as function of $\mathbf{\Gamma}_{i,T}$,

$$y_{iT} = \beta_\ell \mathbf{\Gamma}_{i,T}\mathbf{y}_{T-1} + \mathcal{A}_{iT} + \varepsilon_{iT},$$

the indirect utility function for agent i is

$$\begin{aligned} \tilde{U}_{iT}(\mathbf{\Gamma}_T; \mathbf{y}_{T-1}) &\equiv \mathcal{E}_{\varepsilon_t}\left[\max_{y_{iT}} : U_{iT} \mid \Psi_{i,T-1}\right] \\ &= \mathbf{\Gamma}_{i,T}\mathbf{X}\phi + \frac{1}{2}\mathcal{A}_{iT}^2 + (\beta_\ell\mathcal{A}_{iT} + \mathbf{x}_i\omega)\,\mathbf{\Gamma}_{i,T}\mathbf{y}_{T-1} \\ &\quad - \frac{1}{2}\beta_\ell(1-\beta_\ell)(\mathbf{\Gamma}_{i,T}\mathbf{y}_{T-1})^2 - c_1\mathbf{\Gamma}_{i,T}\iota - c_2\mathbf{\Gamma}_{i,T}\mathbf{\Gamma}'_{i,T} + \frac{1}{2}\sigma_\varepsilon^2. \end{aligned} \tag{2.40}$$

I assume that individual i seeks to maximize expected period T indirect utility, given by (2.40), by choosing

$$\mathbf{\Gamma}_{i,T} = (\gamma_{i1,T}, \ldots, \gamma_{ij,T}, \ldots, \gamma_{iI,T}), \quad \text{with } \gamma_{ij,T} \geq 0, \; j = 1, \ldots, I,$$

and conditional on her information set Ψ_{it}, while taking all others' decisions as given. If $c_2 > 0$, the marginal cost of a connection is increasing with intensity. This has an interpretation in terms of opportunity cost: short and superficial encounters, such as at parties, bear a lower opportunity cost than spending "quality time" with others.

The first-order conditions for $\mathbf{\Gamma}_{it}$ may be solved explicitly and after they are put in matrix form become

$$\mathbf{\Gamma}'_{iT} = \left[\beta_\ell(1-\beta_\ell)\left[\mathbf{y}_{T-1}\mathbf{y}'_{T-1}\right] - \beta_\ell \mathbf{X}\theta + 2c_2\mathbf{I}\right]^{-1}\left[\mathbf{X}\phi + (\beta_\ell + \mathbf{X}\omega)\mathbf{y}_{T-1} - c_1\iota\right]. \tag{2.41}$$

Given this explicit solution for the adjacency matrix, individual i's optimal action, given by (2.32), now becomes:

$$\mathbf{y}_T = \alpha_0\iota + \mathbf{X}\alpha + \mathbf{\Gamma}_T\mathbf{X}\theta + \beta_\ell\mathbf{\Gamma}_T\mathbf{y}_{T-1} + \boldsymbol{\varepsilon}_T. \tag{2.42}$$

They characterize individual i's optimum provided that the second-order conditions hold. It is interesting to summarize the properties of the solution.

The solution, equations (2.41) and (2.42), is an autonomous system of equations with only a contemporaneous stochastic shock, the vector ε_T. It is recursive in terms of $\mathbf{y}_{T-1}$. If we substitute for $\mathbf{\Gamma}_T$ from (2.42) into (2.41), we are left with a first-order system of difference equations for $\mathbf{y}_T$ in terms of $\mathbf{y}_{T-1}$ that is *cubic* in the y_i's. The analytical similarity to section 2.3 is evident; this model contains the earlier one as a special static case. In principle, (2.41) and (2.42) are amenable to the usual treatment for dynamic systems. The multiplicity of equilibria with respect to $\mathbf{y}_{T-1}$ is transmitted to $\mathbf{\Gamma}_T$ as well.

A number of additional remarks are in order. First, for many applications, it may be important that the entries in the adjacency matrix be positive (and can be normalized to sum up to 1). Restricting $\mathbf{\Gamma}_{i,T}$ so that it lies in the positive orthant of R^I, $\Gamma_{ij,T} \geq 0$, $j = 1, \ldots, I$, a convex set, is straightforward but requires additional restrictions on values of the preference parameters. While some of the contextual effects are constant, others may depend on the actual state of the economy as of the preceding period, $\mathbf{y}_{T-1}$. In the standard fashion for dynamic programming, the solution for $\mathbf{y}_T$ accumulates past values of stochastic shocks and is therefore random. Consequently, endogenous weighted networking implies that in setting their period $T-1$ decisions agents must take into consideration that $\mathbf{\Gamma}_T$, the adjacency matrix in period T, is an outcome of individuals' uncoordinated decisions and is stochastic.

Second, endogenous determination of the social adjacency matrix introduces intertemporal linkages in an individual's decision making: period $T-1$ decisions affect the period T adjacency matrix $\mathbf{\Gamma}_T$; and the diagonal terms of the adjacency matrix may well be nonzero, $\Gamma_{ii,t} \neq 0$. Therefore, habit formation may be an individually optimal outcome. From a psychological perspective, one can argue whether positive $\gamma_{ii,t}$'s should be interpreted as the result of willful acts or as an expression of addiction. Similarly, the dynamic nature of the problem prompts one to think of social connections as assets whose values are given by the marginal impacts of increased intensities on expected lifetime utility.[22]

The endogenous adjacency matrix need not be symmetric, let alone constant, over time. Also, an individual's choice to network with others is directed. The people I choose to be influenced by are not affected by my networking initiatives and need not reciprocate. The interactions that are initiated here are not being evaluated from the viewpoint of being mutually advantageous. This is, of course, in contrast to the pairwise stability concept (Jackson and Wolinsky 1996). Similarly, endogenous networking does not necessarily imply that social interactions assume the form of the mean field case. In general, one may seek conditions on behavioral parameters, characteristics, and all underlying determinants, including parameters of stochastic shocks, that imply specific properties of the endogenous social adjacency matrix. For example, under what conditions would particular patterns in $\mathbf{\Gamma}_t$, such as a block diagonal structure with many small blocks and only a few connections between the blocks (being reminiscent of "small worlds") emerge endogenously?

2.7 ECONOMETRICS OF SOCIAL INTERACTIONS IN SOCIAL NETWORKS

The social interactions applications that I have discussed so far presume that individuals interact in groups and thus are affected by the social context in a like manner. The social structure in real life is more complex. Sections 2.3 and 2.6.5 discuss how one can model the emergence of social structure from uncoordinated actions of individuals. Econometric models of social interactions in social networks allow researchers to examine richer patterns of interactions among individuals than those examined in the chapter so far. With few exceptions these models assume the network structure as exogenous, even when it is clearly endogenous.

Bramoullé, Djebbari, and Fortin (2009) and Lee, Liu, and Lin (2009) consider network-based versions of the linear-in-means model where each individual has her own specific reference group modeled as a social network. I express their model by adapting equation (2.1) so as to generalize the expressions of contextual and endogenous effects by means of the notation of section 2.6 in a static version of (2.42):

$$\mathbf{y} = \alpha_0 \iota + \mathbf{X}\alpha + \mathbf{\Gamma}\mathbf{X}\theta + \beta_\ell \mathbf{\Gamma}\mathbf{y} + \boldsymbol{\varepsilon}. \tag{2.43}$$

These authors assume that the vector of shocks $\boldsymbol{\varepsilon}$ is orthogonal to individual characteristics, $\mathcal{E}(\boldsymbol{\varepsilon}|\mathbf{X}) = 0$, and that its variance-covariance matrix $\mathcal{E}(\boldsymbol{\varepsilon}\boldsymbol{\varepsilon}'|\mathbf{X}) = \mathbf{\Sigma}$ is unrestricted so that arbitrary stochastic structures may be accommodated. Assuming no isolated individuals allows us to write $[\mathbf{I} - \beta_\ell \mathbf{\Gamma}]^{-1}$ in terms of its power series representation $[\mathbf{I} - \beta_\ell \mathbf{\Gamma}]^{-1} = \sum_0^\infty \beta_\ell^k \mathbf{\Gamma}^k$.[23] Using it in solving from

(2.43) for the reduced form yields

$$\mathbf{y} = \frac{\alpha_0}{1-\beta_\ell} + \mathbf{X}\alpha + \sum_{k=0}^{\infty} \beta_\ell^k \mathbf{\Gamma}^{k+1}\mathbf{X}(\alpha\beta_\ell + \theta) + \sum_{k=0}^{\infty} \beta_\ell^k \mathbf{\Gamma}^k \boldsymbol{\varepsilon}. \tag{2.44}$$

The reduced-form solution looks forbidding but can be quite simple in special cases. Consider a model of a network in which individuals interact in nonoverlapping groups of sizes $\nu(i)$ and the individual's own outcome is excluded when computing the group mean outcome. In other words, the endogenous social effect for individual i is $\beta_\ell \frac{1}{|\nu(i)|-1}\sum_{j,j\neq i} y_j$, and correspondingly for the contextual effect, $\mathbf{x}_{\nu(i)}$. Let $\mathbf{X}$ be a vector of scalars for simplicity. The reduced form for this model is (Bramoullé, Djebbari, and Fortin 2009, 45):

$$y_i = \frac{\alpha_0}{1-\beta_\ell} + \left(\alpha + \frac{\beta_\ell(\alpha\beta_\ell+\theta)}{(1-\beta_\ell)(|\nu(i)|-1+\beta_\ell)}\right)x_i$$

$$+ \frac{\alpha\beta_\ell+\theta}{(1-\beta_\ell)\left(1+\frac{\beta_\ell}{|\nu(i)|-1}\right)} x_{\nu(i)} + \varepsilon_i. \tag{2.45}$$

The reduced form reveals how social interactions are transmitted. First, regarding α, the coefficient of x_i, the direct effect is augmented by the indirect effect due to feedback from the rest of the group. The latter diminishes as the group grows in size. Second, regarding θ, the indirect effect, and the coefficient of $x_{\nu(i)}$, in (2.43), the influence of an individual's own effect diminishes as the mean effect of others grows with the size of the group: the coefficient of $\mathbf{x}_{\nu(i)}$ in the reduced form increases as the size of the group increases. The dependence of the reduced form of y_i on $|\nu(i)|$ is quite critical for econometric identification of the social interactions model.

2.7.1 Econometric Identification

Bramoullé, Djebbari, and Fortin show that if $\alpha\beta_\ell + \theta \neq 0$, that is, if the presence of some social effect is not excluded, social effects are fully identified if the matrices $\mathbf{I}, \mathbf{\Gamma}, \mathbf{\Gamma}^2$ are linearly independent. If these matrices are linearly dependent and no individuals are isolated, then social effects are not identified. This follows by using (2.44) to express the expected outcomes for each neighborhood, that is,

$$\mathcal{E}(\mathbf{\Gamma}\mathbf{y}|\mathbf{X}) = \frac{\alpha_0}{1-\beta_\ell}\iota + \mathbf{\Gamma}\mathbf{X}\alpha + \sum_{0}^{\infty} \beta_\ell^k \mathbf{\Gamma}^{k+2}\mathbf{X}(\alpha\theta + \beta_\ell). \tag{2.46}$$

When $\mathcal{E}(\mathbf{\Gamma}\mathbf{y}|\mathbf{X})$ is not collinear with regressors $(\iota, \mathbf{X}, \mathbf{\Gamma}\mathbf{X})$, then the network structure is rich enough to make the variables $(\iota, \mathbf{X}, \mathbf{\Gamma}\mathbf{X}, \mathbf{\Gamma}^2\mathbf{X})$ serve as appropriate instruments that allow endogenous and exogenous effects to be identified. Of course, identification may fail for some particular structures, but generally it is network interactions that ensure identification. More complete networks are less likely to allow identification of social interactions. If individuals do not interact in groups, defined as complete components, the network is transitive, and the matrix $\mathbf{\Gamma}^2 \neq \mathbf{0}$, then social effects are identified. Even if individuals interact in groups, the model is identified provided that groups are of different sizes and individuals are not included in their own peer groups (Lee 2007; Davezies, d'Haultfoeuille, and Fougère 2009). In many networks, identification originates from natural exclusion restrictions induced by the structure. For example, identification is ensured if for an individual there is a friend's friend who is not his own friend (i.e., the network has an intransitive triad[24]); see section 2.12. The intuition is that the characteristics of his friend's friend do not directly affect the individual's own outcome but affect it indirectly through their effects on his friend's outcome.

These authors extend their results to the case of correlated effects in the form of network (graph) component-specific terms in the unobservables $\boldsymbol{\varepsilon}$, the stochastic structure of (2.43), by proposing "within" transformations similar to the ones used in panel data models. However, many transformations can be used for this purpose. For example, one such transformation, the "local" in their terminology, involves averaging over the structural equations of all of each individuals' direct social contacts and subtracting from each individual's own equation. Differencing involves loss of information, and it is therefore not surprising that a necessary and sufficient condition for the identification of all social effects in the presence of correlated effects is that the matrices $\mathbf{I}, \mathbf{\Gamma}, \mathbf{\Gamma}^2, \mathbf{\Gamma}^3$ be linearly independent. So it is still network topology that is responsible for identification.

This is further underscored from an additional set of results discussed by Bramoullé et al. on how network structure affects the *strength* of identification by using Monte Carlo methods. For example, the more complete the network of interactions, the less likely identification is. Identification may fail for some network structures, while it is ensured when the network of interactions is transitive. Using Monte Carlo simulations for Erdös–Renyi graphs (see section 2.3.3), they find that precision of estimation decreases with the probability that any two individuals in each component are connected. This is intuitive because the resulting graphs become more similar. When this probability becomes equal to 1, individuals interact in groups and social effects are not identified. Because this probability indexes both density of connections and intransitivity, these authors seek to disentangle them by working with more complicated graph topologies. They divide a population into components of equal size, each of which is a complete subgraph, and by "rewiring" at random each connection with a given probability, they generate realizations of small-world graphs (Watts and Strogatz 1998). This data generation process keeps the expected number of links constant but varies the intransitivity via the probability of rewiring. As the latter increases, so does intransitivity. Correspondingly, one can hold intransitivity constant and vary density. For a given level of intransitivity, the precision of the estimates is everywhere a decreasing function of density. When density is low, precision is an increasing function of intransitivity; for intermediate to high levels of density, the relationship is nonmonotonic. Starting from the case of group interactions, a slight increase in the level of intransitivity holding density constant greatly improves identification. These Monte Carlo results underscore how sensitive to network structure econometric identification is.

The empirical framework proposed by Bramoullé, Djebbari, and Fortin (2009) is increasingly being adopted in empirical studies of social networks. They include those by Bramoullé, Djebbari, and Fortin (2009), Boucher, Bramoullé, Djebbari, and Fortin (2011), and Lin (2010), which involve an application with the Add Health data set that I discuss immediately below. I consider further below the work of Calvó-Armengol, Patacchini, and Zenou (2009), which also involves the Add Health data set, and several studies by Christakis and Fowler, which make very clever use the Framingham Heart Study data.

Bramoullé, Djebbari, and Fortin (2009) seek to explain recreational outcomes for students, measured by an index of participation in educational, artistic, and sports organizations and clubs, in terms of individual effects, contextual effects, and endogenous social effects, defined as the mean recreational index among one's friends at the same secondary school. Each school is assumed to be a different social network with a stochastic but strictly exogenous interaction matrix $\mathbf{\Gamma}_l$, and the large network made up of all schools is described by a block diagonal matrix $\mathbf{\Gamma}$. By suitably redefining $\mathbf{y}$, premultiplying (2.43) by $\mathbf{\Gamma}$, and subtracting from the original form, one obtains

$$[\mathbf{I} - \mathbf{\Gamma}]\mathbf{y} = [\mathbf{I} - \mathbf{\Gamma}]\mathbf{X}\alpha + [\mathbf{I} - \mathbf{\Gamma}]\mathbf{\Gamma}\mathbf{X}\theta + \beta_\ell[\mathbf{I} - \mathbf{\Gamma}]\mathbf{\Gamma}\mathbf{y} + [\mathbf{I} - \mathbf{\Gamma}]\boldsymbol{\epsilon},$$

which eliminates the group-specific effects. Their instrumental estimation approach is applied with this formulation; see (Bramoullé, Djebbari, and Fortin 2009, 50) for details. Specifically, even though the set of contextual effects employed by the authors is the neighborhood means of one's own characteristics, which is a cause of identification failure in the linear-in-means model, the model can be estimated and many coefficients are significant. For example, regarding components of $\hat{\alpha}$, the recreational activities index decreases with age and with being white but rises with being female and with parents' participation in the labor market. Correspondingly, regarding estimated components of $\hat{\theta}$, participation decreases with the mean age of respondents' friends but rises with their mean parents' participation in the labor market. The estimated endogenous social effect, $\hat{\beta} = 0.466$, is significant at the 10 percent level.

These econometric approaches take the social network as given. Bramoullé, Djebbari, and Fortin (2009) propose ideas for estimation when the social network itself is endogenous, but the error structures in the resulting social interactions models are likely to be quite complex.

2.7.2 Empirics of Social Interactions in Social Networks

I next review a number of recent empirical studies that utilize data from Add Health and explore patterns in interactions and associations within social networks. Add Health is a U.S. nationally representative study designed to facilitate exploration of the causes of health-related behaviors of adolescents in grades 7–12 and of the structure of adolescent friendship networks. For more details, see section 2.13.5 below.

While my discussion below emphasizes econometrics applications with social networks in social interactions settings, there are other instances where the topology of interactions matters in explaining economic outcomes and is fortuitous rather than a result of individuals' deliberate actions. In fact, in a recent application by Cohen-Cole, Kirilenko, and Patacchini (2010), spatial networks emerge as a by-product of the computerized placement of buy and sell orders in financial markets. The returns to trades among groups of traders may be written exactly according to (2.43). Interestingly, these authors find that network topology allows them to identify precisely both the relevance of network structure and endogenous network spillovers, which take the place of endogenous social effects. They show that network positioning on the part of traders leads to remarkable spillovers in returns: the impact of a one-standard-deviation improvement in network position (measured by Bonacich centrality) translates to a 450 percentage point annualized increase in returns. They also estimate that the implied average multiplier is as large as 20! That is, a gain of \$1 for a trader leads to an average of \$20 in gains for all traders and much more for well-connected ones. Financial markets are zero-sum markets, and so advantageous network positioning is associated with large reallocations of returns. It is precisely because of the fact that network topology in this case is decided automatically by computers, and is therefore exogenous to traders, that utilizing the methods proposed by Bramoullé, Djebbari, and Fortin (2009) is solid grounds for inference. Similarly, social networks are exogenous in the data used by Laschever (2009), who examines the effects on a veteran's employment from the employment status of the members of his military company in World War I.

2.7.2.1 *General Patterns in Social Interactions*

Fryer and Torelli (2010) use academic achievement as a definition of "acting white" by nonwhite students to examine its relationship to popularity. They measure popularity in terms of a network-specific spectral popularity index that identifies the popularity of the members of a group with the intensity of the social connections among the members of that group. Their measure, originally developed by Echenique and Fryer (2007), is the maximal eigenvalue of the social interactions matrix associated with the connected component modeling each social group, $\mathbf{\Gamma}$ in equation (2.43). The Add Health data allow them to construct the full adjacency matrix for school-based social groups. Their analysis involves a simplified version of (2.43) for academic achievement where, instead of the full system of simultaneous equations, popularity proxies network topology.[25] They demonstrate that there are large racial differences in the relationship between popularity and academic achievement.

Conley and Udry (2010) use unusual data features to study social learning in technology adoption in pineapple cultivation in Ghana. The authors measure individuals' information neighborhoods directly by tracing individual farmers' social networks. They argue that these are distinct from geographic neighborhoods that characterize the extent of common growing conditions. The challenge, again, is how to distinguish social learning from patterns of covariation in agents' actions because of common unobservable shocks or attributes. The authors obtain evidence confirming their prediction of social learning in the form of farmers' choices of inputs that imitate only those of surprisingly *successful* information neighbors. In contrast, applying the same method to choices of inputs of known technology for another crop suggests the absence of social learning effects.

Weinberg (2007) tests a number of propositions that emanate from the endogeneity of the social structure, "endogenous associations" in his terminology. Not surprisingly, in view of section 2.2.2, it is the endogeneity of association that facilitates identification in what is otherwise a linear-in-means model. Individuals choose their associations in a model that is conceptually similar to the static version of utility function in section 2.6.5 by optimizing with respect to individual elements of $\mathbf{\Gamma}_{\nu(i)}\mathbf{X}$, associates' characteristics.[26] The resulting regression equations relate mean group outcomes and contextual effects to individual characteristics, adjusted for the cost of association. Weinberg's approach in effect presumes that individuals can fashion desirable associations within social space by means of their choices of endogenous social and contextual effects, unlike the choice of neighborhoods in section 2.2.2 which is conceptualized as a choice among discrete objects. Weinberg explores a notable new feature, namely, that interactions may occur at a lower level than where groups are formed and may vary across different behaviors. Group size matters because larger groups offer more opportunities to associate with like-minded people, and this reinforces behavior through social interactions effects.

In examining how endogenous association affects behavior, Weinberg tests whether the difference in associations and behaviors between people with high and low predicted behaviors is hump-shaped in the share of the group with a predicted level of high behavior. Weinberg predicts that the relationship between average behavior in the population and the share of the group with the high characteristic is nonlinear, even if the random shock is uniformly distributed. For normally distributed shock, in particular, the differences between associations and actions of people with high and low characteristics as a function of the share of the group that has the high characteristic are hump-shaped in the share of the group with the high characteristic. Weinberg argues that the hump shape that he finds is evidence of assortative matching. As the share of a social group with high (predicted) behavior increases, the mean behavior among their friends who have a high (predicted) behavior increases relative to that of others initially and then declines as most of the macro group has a high (predicted) level of that behavior.

2.7.2.2 *Social Networks and Education Outcomes*

Calvó-Armengol, Patacchini, and Zenou (2009) estimate, using the Add Health data set, individual school performance in relation to the topology of friendship networks, while controlling for individual characteristics. They use this information to estimate a reduced form for individual educational achievement broadly along the lines of (2.44). Specifically, they assume that the part of observed individual educational outcomes not explained by individual characteristics is made up of network-component fixed effects, denoted by the vector $\boldsymbol{\eta}_\nu$, and spatially autocorrelated errors, $\boldsymbol{\varepsilon}$. That is, in my notation (Calvó-Armengol, Patacchini, and Zenou 2009), equation (9) becomes

$$\mathbf{y} = \alpha_0 \iota + \mathbf{X}\alpha + \mathbf{\Gamma X}\theta + \eta_\nu + \boldsymbol{\varepsilon}; \tag{2.47}$$

$$\boldsymbol{\varepsilon} = a\mathbf{\Gamma}\iota + \phi\mathbf{\Gamma}\boldsymbol{\varepsilon} + \boldsymbol{\epsilon}, \tag{2.48}$$

where $\mathbf{y}$ are educational attainments and $\boldsymbol{\epsilon}$ is a vector of independent and identically distributed shocks. Since the error structure is a residual that represents the portions of individual outcomes that are not explained by individual characteristics, $\mathbf{X}$, and contextual effects, $\mathbf{\Gamma X}$, it combines correlated effects and peer effects. So their estimation of the stochastic structure of (2.47) and (2.48) subsumes peer effects, that is, endogenous social effects, into the estimation of (a, ϕ) in (2.48), the effect on a school performance index of the number of each individual's friends and of the peer effects subsumed into the error structure. This is not a standard treatment of peer effects. Their assumption of the additive separability of utility in terms of own-effort and peer-effort effects leads them to identify $\frac{\phi}{a}$ as a proxy of the effect of Bonacich (1987) centrality. This concept is discussed in section 2.3.2. Their computed Bonacich measures range from 0.32 to 3.48, with an average of 1.65 and a standard deviation of 2.79. They find that a one-standard-deviation increase in the Bonacich index translates into roughly 7 percent of a standard deviation in education outcomes.

These authors' estimates of (a, ϕ), $(0.0314, 0.5667)$, are obtained with high precision and change little, becoming $(0.0323, 0.5505)$, respectively, if social interactions are allowed to be directional, with the adjacency matrix no longer being symmetric (Calvó-Armengol, Patacchini, and Zenou 2009, Table 3). A whole range of individual sociodemographic variables, family background controls, residential neighborhood variables, contextual effects, and school fixed effects are included, and a very good overall fit is obtained using 2,079,871 observations on 11,491 pupils belonging to 181 networks. Testing alternative measures of network connectedness, that is, centrality as measured by each individual's degree (how many friends one has), closeness (the inverse of the sum of each individual's shortest graph distance to every other individual), and betweenness (the number of shortest paths that involve an individual in her own network as a proportion of the number of all shortest paths), shows that only the centrality with respect to degree is significant.

2.7.2.3 Social Networks and Health Outcomes

Consider now the possibility of social interactions in habits like eating, drinking, and so on. Without detailed information on an individual's characteristics, choices, preferences, and environment, it is difficult to discern whether two friends who gain weight simultaneously do so because they are influenced by one another's habits or because they are exposed to a common environmental factor. Christakis and Fowler (2007, 2008) and Fowler and Christakis (2008a, 2008b) use a remarkable data set, the Framingham Heart Study (FHS-Net; see section 2.13.5.2), that provides evidence for the spread of obesity, smoking, drinking, happiness, and other phenomena through social networks. Cohen-Cole and Fletcher (2008) point to the potential pitfalls of estimating an equation like (2.43) while leaving out contextual effects, $\mathbf{\Gamma X}\theta$. They replicate the Christakis–Fowler results by using Christakis and Fowler's specifications with Add Health data. Cohen-Cole and Fletcher find that point estimates of the endogenous social effect [the "social network effect" described by Christakis and Fowler (2008a, 2008b)] are reduced and become statistically indistinguishable from zero once standard additional econometric techniques relevant to social interactions models are implemented, that is, by suitably further accounting for contextual effects in addition to detailed information on individuals' characteristics, choices, preferences, and environment. For example, if not corrected, Cohen-Cole and Fletcher argue, Christakis and Fowler's techniques suggest that self-reported acne, height, and headaches are also socially contagious (although they accept p-values above the customary level of 0.05 in their paper).[27]

In their response, Fowler and Christakis argue that Cohen-Cole and Fletcher make an error in interpreting their own results because they are focused on whether they can reject the null hypothesis of zero regarding whether weight gain in a social contact can cause weight gain in an individual. Yet, in three of their five specifications, they actually do replicate the approximate magnitude and the significance of the result from FHS-Net. Moreover, the Christakis–Fowler Framingham estimates actually fall inside the confidence intervals of the Cohen-Cole–Fletcher results for all five specifications. That is, Fowler and Christakis argue that Cohen-Cole and Fletcher cannot reject the null hypothesis that the Framingham estimates are the true values.

Fowler and Christakis also argue, based on their own estimations with Add Health data, that it is critically important to recognize that the effects they themselves obtain with their FHS-Net data are directional. One, a person is influenced by the behaviors of those she names as friends, but those named are not influenced by those who name them. Christakis and Fowler argue that this directionality of the effect provides an identification strategy [similar to arguments made by Bramoullé, Djebbari, and Fortin (2009)], helping to exclude a shared environment as a confounder, and they show that this directionality is found in the Add Health data just as in the FHS-Net data. Fowler and Christakis (2008a, 1403) also argue that the relationships in the FHS-Net data are social, whereas in Add Health they are physically proximate, all being based on attendance at the same school. They emphasize that their findings of obesity effects do not decay with physical distance, while they do not involve a relationship in obesity behaviors between individuals and their immediate neighbors who are not friends. That is, unlike the Add Health students who all lived in the same location, the FHS-Net friends could be (and typically were) geographically far apart. Christakis and Fowler show that there is no detectable attenuation of the coefficients with geographic distance, helping to exclude the possibility of a shared environment (e.g., local wealth or infrastructure or policies) in explaining the association between outcomes in connected individuals (this did not apply, however, to emotional contagion, which increased with geographic proximity).

With respect to the acne, height, and headache results, Christakis and Fowler (2010) respond that, among other things, Cohen-Cole and Fletcher must rely on self-reported data in Add Health, and that it is not at all implausible that adolescents might be influenced in their reporting of symptoms or height by the existence of similar symptoms in their friends or by the height of their friends (a short person with tall friends might indeed overestimate his or her height when asked). In the FHS-Net study, symptoms and height and weight were objectively measured. Newer criticism, in particular by Lyons (2011), has renewed the controversy about the statistical underpinnings of the Christakis and Fowler results.

The significance of these research findings is underscored by the extraordinary attention they have received not only in the popular press (Belluck 2008) but also in the scholarly literature. Christakis and Fowler (2011) in a comprehensive review call for additional methodological research to help establish causal effects with network data. Once again, differences in the results may be of paramount importance in designing policy. They point to the importance of model specification and the consequences of assumptions about the routes of transmission of social interactions and their scope in social space.

2.8 SPATIAL ECONOMETRICS MODELS AS SOCIAL INTERACTIONS MODELS

Recently researchers recognized the close relationship between social interactions and spatial econometrics models. By working with a static version of system (2.31), assuming no global effects, $\beta_g = 0$, and dropping time subscripts, we have $\mathbf{y} = \mathcal{A} + \beta_\ell \mathbf{A}\mathbf{y} + \boldsymbol{\varepsilon}$. This coincides with the classic Cliff–Ord model of spatial autocorrelation (SAR) with one spatial lag, $\mathbf{A}\mathbf{y}$, but no spatial error structure [see (Cliff and Ord 1981)].

Harry Kelejian and Ivar Prucha and Lung-fei Lee have helped advance the frontier on asymptotic properties of spatial econometric models. Kelejian and Prucha (2008) offer a modern treatment of spatial models of econometrics. Lee, Liu, and Lin (2009) and Lin (2010)[28] study the econometric properties and estimate a more general version of the social interactions problem with a network structure, and their approach helps bridge the gap with spatial econometrics models. They specify the model in terms of groups $g = 1, \ldots, G$:

$$\mathbf{y}_g = \beta \mathbf{A}_g \mathbf{y}_g + \mathbf{X}\alpha + \mathbf{A}_g \mathbf{Z}\theta + \alpha_{0g}\iota_g + \boldsymbol{\varepsilon}_g, \quad \boldsymbol{\varepsilon}_g = \rho \bar{\mathbf{A}}_g \boldsymbol{\varepsilon}_g + \boldsymbol{\epsilon}_g, \qquad (2.49)$$

where $\mathbf{y}_g$ is the column n_g-vector of outcomes for each member of group g, n_g is the group's size, $\mathbf{A}_g, \bar{\mathbf{A}}_g$ are the group g-specific weighted adjacency matrices, ι_g is a column n_g-vector of 1s, $\boldsymbol{\varepsilon}_g, \boldsymbol{\epsilon}_g$ are column n_g-vectors of shocks (the latter being independent and identically distributed shocks), and α_{0g} is a group-specific fixed effect. The adjacency matrices are row-normalized. This is a generalization of the typical SAR model because it allows for contextual effects, $\mathbf{A}_g \mathbf{Z}\theta$, and group unobservables, α_{0g}, and constitutes, in an intuitive sense, a generalization of approaches based on differences in group sizes. Spatial autocorrelation in the unobservables may be due to endogeneity of the social network structure itself—individuals who end up in the group have unobservables in common—and therefore the Lee–Liu–Lin approach offers a partial remedy for this problem.

2.8.1 Empirical Applications of Spatial Econometrics Models

Lin (2010) estimates the model by Lee, Liu, and Lin (2009) using Add Health data with student academic achievement as the endogenous variable and finds strong evidence for both endogenous and contextual effects, even after controlling for school-grade fixed effects, and significant spatial autocorrelation in the disturbances. The estimation results differ greatly with or without school-grade fixed effects, which suggests that omitted variable bias can be severe. Such differences may also be due to selection bias as well, in that individuals choose their peers. Lin also explores a variety of alternative network specifications, such as accounting for reciprocity in friendship specifications and excluding isolated nodes (individuals reporting no friendships in the Add Health data) in the estimation of endogenous social effects. She also accounts for spatial autocorrelation in the residuals, obtains estimates of ρ in (2.49) that range over $(-0.257, -0.237)$ and shows, as predicted by Lee, Liu, and Lin (2009), that controlling spatial autocorrelation in the residuals makes a big difference by raising the estimates of the endogenous social effects to $(0.473, 0.495)$.

Boucher, Bramoullé, Djebbari, and Fortin (2010) report estimation results along the lines of (2.49). For each group, the respective adjacency matrix is composed of elements $a_{gij} = \frac{1}{n_g - 1}$ if $i \neq j$, and $a_{gij} = 0$ otherwise. These authors use maximum likelihood and instrumental variable methods with data from the Quebec Government Ministry of Education, Recreation and Sports, with 194,553 individual test scores for 116,534 fourth- and fifth-grade students. Groups are classes in each school. The variation in class size is substantial and allows estimation of the endogenous peer effects on individual test scores for three different subjects, which are positive when significant and range from 0.438 to 0.779. Individual and contextual effects are also significant.

Head and Mayer (2008) study the spatial patterns of names in France by using data on the incidence of given names across the major administrative divisions of France (*départements*). They estimate a model of binary choice by parents of, alternatively, Christian saints', Arabic, and American names for their children. Their model follows equation (2.18), the generic version of the Brock–Durlauf model, but is effectively linearized because their assumption of a uniform distribution for the idiosyncratic component of utility yields linear cumulative functions. Such linearization makes the model vulnerable to the reflection problem. They adopt as instruments the composition in terms of average social class and ethnic origin of geographically contiguous *départements*. Under the assumption that locations are independent of name choice, they estimate the model, which encompasses idiosyncratic tastes, group preferences, and the influences of spatially proximate agents, by means of two-stage least squares. They find that social class and national origin matter, as do decisions of other parents. The evidence of spatial interactions is strong. In contiguous *départements*, the respective coefficients for the share of saints' names decline from 1.23 to 0.19, for the share of Arabic names they decline from 0.15 to −0.27, and for the share of American names they grow from 0.04 to 0.50, respectively, in 1962 and 1999. A 10 percentage point increase in the popularity of a saint's name or an American name in neighboring *départements* increases local shares of those name types by 3.4 and 3.5 percentage points, respectively. In contrast, Arabic names seem to be transmitted only through ethnic channels and do not diffuse spatially into areas with low levels of immigration.

2.8.1.1 Empirical Results with Strategic Interactions as Spatial Econometrics Models

As "large" agents, governments are aware of the direct influence their policies have on location decisions of individuals and firms and may rely on it strategically. Interaction among local and state governments in the United States is studied by means of spatial econometrics models. Brueckner (2003) reviews the literature.

Case, Rosen, and Hines (1993) formalize and test the notion that expenditures by U.S. states depend on the spending of neighboring states. They find that even after allowing for state fixed effects, year effects, and common random shocks among neighbors, a state government's level of per capita expenditures is positively and significantly affected by the expenditure levels of its neighbors: ceteris paribus, a 1 dollar increase in a neighboring state's expenditures increases a state's own expenditures by more than 70 cents. Brueckner (1998) examines interactions among local governments with respect to urban growth controls. In general, reactions by neighboring cities may be strategic substitutes or complements. Let $\mathbf{y}_g$, equation (2.49), denote the vector of measures adopted by the cities under study. Brueckner defines the growth measures variable as the sum of {0, 1}-valued variables indicating nine specific growth control policies adopted by each of the California cities in the survey. These include population growth and housing permit limitations, greenbelt limitations, square-footage limitations for commercial and for industrial construction, and others (Brueckner 1998, 448). City characteristics used include population size and demographic and educational characteristics, density and household demographic and economic characteristics, industrial composition, political preferences, city spending and taxes, and geography. Brueckner does not allow for contextual effects, that is, $\theta = 0$ in equation (2.49). He estimates the model with alternative definitions of proximity; that is, the adjacency matrix $\mathbf{A}_g$ is defined, alternatively, as $a_{ij} = 1$ (global interactions) or $a_{ij} = 1/d_{ij}$, where d_{ij} denotes the distance between cities i and j, and with the same specifications but weighted by the neighbor's population, P_{ij}, $a_{ij} = P_{ij}$ and $a_{ij} = P_{ij}/d_{ij}$.

The estimated interactions coefficient β is positive, less than 1, and statistically significant, implying that different cities' decision variables are strategic complements: an increase in the competing controls variable elicits a smaller increase in a given city's own control efforts. These findings confirm the existence of strategic interactions, "growth controls games," taking place among California cities. In addition, a large population, high educational and skill levels, a liberal political stance, and high house prices increase a city's preference for controls. Conversely, dense, high-income cities that contain many one-person households have a weaker preference for controls. Brueckner tests for and excludes spatial autocorrelation in the residuals. Interdependence due to a nonzero ρ in equation (2.49) would not be evidence of strategic interdependence. Brueckner's model and findings that neighboring policies matter are consistent with different causes of policy interdependence arising, such as cities' naively following localized antigrowth "fads." Policy interdependence due to such a common factor as tightness of the regional housing market is an instance of correlated effects. I note that one could formalize, along the lines of papers by Dennis Epple and coauthors discussed in chapter 3, section 3.7.1, the notion that individual voting patterns regarding growth controls may be subject to intercity social interactions.

2.9 SOCIAL LEARNING IN URBAN SETTINGS

Analysts typically do not observe whether individuals in close physical or geographic proximity do actually interact. Therefore, it behooves the literature to explore, if possible, interactions with others in physical, cultural, or geographic proximity that do in fact rest on actual instead of presumptive evidence. Information transmission among individuals in proximity is an important part of the urban fabric and therefore warrants attention.

Charlot and Duranton (2004) propose that workplace communication among individual workers may serve as a pathway for the transmission of interactions among individuals' human capitals. These authors find empirically that in larger and more educated cities, workers do communicate more, and this turns out to have a positive effect on wages. They utilize data from *Changements organisationnels et informatisation*, a survey conducted in 1997 in France[29] on 8,812 workers randomly drawn from the labor force in manufacturing, retail (do-it-yourself chains only), and business services accounting. Selected workers were individually interviewed, and information on working conditions, organization of work, workplace communication, and information technologies was matched with firm-level data and location data on earnings, industry, establishment size, and workplace location (rural, suburban, or urban for the city population) from the French labor force survey. Depending on the estimates, they find that 13 percent to 22 percent of the effects of a more educated and larger city on wages is due to this channel.

Weinberg, Reagan, and Yankow (2004) and Bayer, Ross, and Topa (2008) document that individual market outcomes are influenced contemporaneously by the labor market status of their neighbors. Conley and Topa (2002) are unusual in seeking to identify the actual information transmission routes in social space, arguing that socioeconomic characteristics (and, in particular, ethnic and occupational distance) explain a substantial component of the spatial dependence in unemployment and therefore are of particular importance in defining social interactions. I discuss this research more extensively in chapter 5, section 5.8, below.

There is a broader question of what types of information are transmitted among individuals residing in urban areas and whether it matters if it is deliberate or fortuitous. In general, empirical work has yet to really answer these questions and, in many cases, even to pose them. As suggested by Gaspar and Glaeser (1998), a lot can be obscured in electronic communication; what is being communicated can be much more strategic, and it is hard to "read" people as to what and if things are being hidden. One idea is that electronic and face-to-face communications are complements.

2.9.1 Graph Theory and Urban Interactions

Network-based modeling in the analysis of urban and spatial cases has had a long tradition, especially in transportation and land-use planning and economic geography. Literature on urban planning investigates patterns in urban street networks in relation to the historical roots and origins of cities. Graph-theoretic notation, introduced in section 2.3.1 above, can also describe the physical attributes of cities. This *space syntax* (Porta, Crucitti, and Latora 2006a, 2006b; Crucitti, Latora, and Porta 2006) involves primal and dual graph models. *Primal* graph models depict city streets as edges, and intersections as nodes. Distances between intersections are edge lengths. Alternatively, *dual* graphs represent streets as nodes, and intersections as edges. The *primal* representation highlights the centrality of intersections through the degrees of nodes. The *dual* representation underscores the importance of "main drags," which become nodes, whose degrees denote the number of other streets they intersect with. This discussion opens the possibility of formal modeling of urban landscapes and of the urban character. In this connection, the discussion of research on identifying cultural buzz in chapter 5 is also very promising.

Space syntax and its primal and dual representations of urban landscapes lend themselves readily to measures of accessibility, proximity, integration, and connectivity [see (Jackson 2008, 34–43, chap. 2) for definitions] which can express that some places (or streets) are more central than others. These and other studies deal with such questions as how to handle distance metrics, what kind of graph representation to use, what kind of measures to investigate, how to interpret the correlation between measures of the structure of the network and measures of the dynamics on the network, and how to link with the Geographic Information Systems (GIS) literature and related tools. Primal representations accord the additional advantage that they are compatible with international standards for geospatial data sets, including the Topologically Integrated Geographic Encoding and Referencing (TIGER) files of the U.S. Bureau of the Census. [30]

The networks representing actual cities can have degree distributions typical of "scale-free" networks—their degree distributions are power laws—and exhibit small-world properties as well. Rosvall, Trusina, Minnhagen, and Sneppen (2005) propose information-theoretic measures for quantifying the complexity of city organization, that are based on a dual representation of the city. Porta, Crucitta, and Latora (2006a) underscore how very different Ahmedabad and Venice, on the one hand, are from Richmond, California, and Walnut Creek, California, on the other. These authors take the view that Ahmedabad exhibits the imprint of "self-organization," and so does Venice, except that Venice's layout is obviously skewed by the dominance of the Grand Canal. Richmond and Walnut Creek are clearly planned cities.

2.10 CONCLUSIONS

Social interactions are ubiquitous. They provide the overarching theme of this book, which progresses from decisions by individuals and firms, through the multitude of facets of interdependence among key magnitudes describing a city's economy, up to an economy made up of cities treating social interactions as key determinants. Scholarly interest in estimating social interactions effects is expanding rapidly in numerous areas of economics and is motivating important methodological advances. For econometricians, key challenges include social interactions effects on market outcomes coexisting with feedback from the characteristics of individual market participants via their impacts on prices, consequences of self-selection, and the attendant role of the presence of individual and group unobservables. In the light of ever-improving data availability, social interactions empirics will rely increasingly critically on careful theorizing that involves precise definitions of social interactions, possibly by calling on psychology and sociology to define appropriate social spaces, and must facilitate the use of data from different sources. This will become increasingly likely as spatial and social interactions econometrics are now practically integrated. The likely payoff will be enormous: better understanding of social forces in the modern economy, with individuals sharing information while self-selecting into social groups and living and working in close proximity to one another as in firms and cities, the hallmarks of modern economic life.

2.11 HIGHLIGHTS OF THE LITERATURE AND FURTHER STUDY

Social aspects of consumption have been noted by at least as far back as Veblen (1899). However, a particularly influential precursor of the modern literature on social interactions in economics is the article by Becker (1974), and to a lesser extent the empirically oriented formulation by Pollak (1976). The most recent study on private versus social consumption goods is that of Arrow and Dasgupta (2009). Manski (1993) introduced the by now canonical typology of social effects and articulates the econometric identification problem of linear-in-means models. Manski (2000) presents a particularly informative review that encompasses broader applications of the literature. Durlauf (1997) provides foundations in terms of the statistical mechanics literature, and Brock and Durlauf (2001a) supply firmer links to economics. Ioannides (2006) extends their model to more general graph topologies. Moffitt (2001) offers an intuitive link of the conceptual origin of the identification problems of social interactions models with the classic identification in simultaneous equations models. Soetevent (2007) provides a concise review of the empirical literature with a classification of typical identification problems. Durlauf (2004) presents an exhaustive review of a variety of social effects associated with consumption as analyzed by theoretical and empirical studies. More recent reviews of theory and estimation results include those by Ioannides and Topa (2010), who emphasize labor market applications, Durlauf and Ioannides (2010), who present concisely recent progress regarding econometric issues associated with social interactions models, and Blume, Brock, Durlauf, and Ioannides (2011), who offer a comprehensive and very detailed review of the identification problems in social interactions models. Their review encompasses an exhaustive presentation of such problems in the linear-in-means model, including issues of group unobservables, variance-based methods, self-selection, social multipliers, hierarchical models and dynamic settings, and its extension to social networks and spatial models of social interactions, where it offers several new results regarding identification including the case of unknown social interactions topology. It also covers discrete choice models, binary as well as multinomial, and their respective identification problems, duration models, and experimental and quasi-experimental models.

Bramoullé, Djebbari, and Fortin (2009) report a key study on the econometric properties and empirics of the social networks version of social interactions problems along with an application based on Add Health. They build on the work of Lee (2007) and Davezies, d'Haultfoeuille, and Fougère (2009).

Lee, Liu, and Lin (2009) offer a general treatment of social interactions in networks in a manner that helps in its integration with the spatial econometrics literature.

There is a vast amount of ongoing theoretical research that is likely to change how social scientists view and model social networks. In addition to the continuing influence of the newest books, that is, studies by Goyal (2009), Jackson (2008), Newman (2010), and Vega-Redondo (2007), many papers are probing the fundamental underpinnings of social network formation, including notably those of Cabrales, Calvó-Armengol, and Zenou (2011) and others. The *Handbook of Social Economics*, edited by Alberto Bisin, Jess Benhabib, and Matthew O. Jackson (2011), will likely help establish social economics firmly as a mainstream economics field. One of the biggest challenges is to develop econometric models for handling strategic network formation. Particularly promising is further development of the links between networks and markets. Ghiglino and Goyal (2010), whose work is discussed in section 2.3.2 above, present some fundamentals, and Jackson (2008, chap. 10) offers further insights into networked markets. Ioannides (2004b) provides further background into the subject of section 2.3.3.1 by also drawing on the mathematical sociology, engineering, and computer science literatures. Kirman (1983) is a prescient piece on applications of random graph theory in economics.

There is a vast literature on graphs and networks in mathematics and statistics. The basic concepts that are most relevant to applications in mathematical sociology are presented by Wasserman and Faust (1994). Jackson (2008, chap. 2) reviews measurement aspects of networks and concisely presents, in the appendices (Jackson 2008, 43–51, chap. 2) the essential mathematics of graph theory. A brief exposition follows below.

I am conscious of neglecting many areas where the social interactions approach has been applied fruitfully. Very notable among them are individuals' decisions about asset holdings; see Brown, Ivkovich, Smith, and Weisbenner (2007). Alleged herding behavior in financial decisions is also an interesting area of research.

2.12 APPENDIX: BASIC FACTS OF GRAPH AND NETWORK THEORY FOR SOCIAL NETWORK MODELING

This appendix collects in one place some basic terminology about graphs and networks. To start with, the terms "graphs" and "networks" are synonyms for my purposes, although the former appears to be used more frequently by mathematicians and both terms are used almost interchangeably in other fields. Social interactions among individuals are defined by means of a *social structure* (or *topology*—the two terms are used interchangeably in the literature and here) that takes the form of a network whose mathematical description is a graph with the vertices representing individuals and the edges representing links between them. Network vertices and population members are thus identical concepts.

Let the elements of a set $\mathcal{I} = \{1, \ldots, I\}$ represent individuals or firms, but for concreteness I refer to individuals here. Established communication, social relations, or social interactions between any two individual members of $\mathcal{I}$ are defined by an *undirected* graph $(\mathcal{V}, \mathcal{E})$, where $\mathcal{V}$ is the set of vertices (nodes), $\mathcal{V} = \{v_1, v_2, \ldots, v_I\}$, a one-to-one map of the set of individuals $\mathcal{I}$ onto itself (the graph is labeled), and $I = |V|$ is the number of vertices (nodes), also known as the *order* of the graph; $\mathcal{E}$ is a proper subset of the collection of unordered pairs of vertices, and $|\mathcal{E}|$ is the number of edges, also known as the *size* of the graph. We say that agent i interacts with agent j if there is an edge between nodes i and j. Let $\nu(i)$ define the local neighborhood of agent i: $\nu(i) = \{j \in \mathcal{I} | j \neq i, \{i,j\} \in \mathcal{E}\}$. The number of i's neighbors is the *degree* of node i: $d_i = |\nu(i)|$. A graph is *balanced* if the degrees of all nodes are equal. The geometric properties of $(\mathcal{V}, \mathcal{E})$ are referred to as its *topology*.

For some applications, i interacts with j, as in looking up to j or imitating j, but j does not interact with i. In that case, the social interactions graph is referred to as *directed*, and it allows for a richer set of social relations. In that case, a social network is a graph $(\mathcal{V}, \mathcal{E})$, where the directed edges in $\mathcal{E}$ signify social influence: (i, j) is in $\mathcal{E}$ if and only if j influences i. A *component* of the graph $(\mathcal{V}, \mathcal{E})$ is a subgraph that is connected and maximal with respect to inclusion. The distance between any two nodes is the length of the shortest path between them.

Graph $(\mathcal{V}, \mathcal{E})$ may be represented equivalently by its *adjacency matrix* (also known as its *sociomatrix* in the mathematical sociology literature) $\mathbf{\Gamma}$, an $I \times I$ matrix, with one row and one column for each individual in $\mathcal{V}$, whose (i, j) element Γ_{ij} is equal to 1 if there exists an edge connecting agents i and j, and equal to 0 otherwise. For undirected graphs, matrix $\mathbf{\Gamma}$ is symmetric and positive, and thus its spectral properties, that is, the properties of its set of eigenvalues and eigenvectors, are well understood. For more on this see below. The adjacency matrix $\mathbf{\Gamma}$ may also be defined as a random matrix with generic realization $\tilde{\mathbf{\Gamma}}$. The entries of the adjacency matrix $\tilde{\gamma}_{ij}$ are binary random variables whose probability laws may be interdependent; see chapter 2, section 2.3.3. Alternatively, a probability measure may be defined in terms of the realizations of the matrix $\tilde{\mathbf{\Gamma}}$ itself.

Since the graph is supposed to represent social connections, it is natural to assume that no agent i is connected to himself; in other words, there are no loops: $i, \Gamma_{ii} = 0, \forall i \in \mathcal{I}$. Still $\Gamma_{ii} \neq 0$ is useful in representing habit formation in dynamic settings; see section 2.1. A *path* from i to j is a sequence of individuals $i_0, \ldots, i_K$ such that $i_0 = i, i_K = j$, and for all $k = 1, \ldots, K-1$, there is an edge from i_{k-1} to i_k. Such a path is said to have length K. If there is a path from i to j of length exceeding 1, then i *indirectly influences* j. The adjacency matrix $\mathbf{\Gamma}$ displays all paths of length 1. The K-fold product $\mathbf{\Gamma}^K$, the Kth power of $\mathbf{\Gamma}$, counts all paths of length K; if the *ij*th element of $\mathbf{\Gamma}^K$ is n, then there are n paths of length K from i to j.

By suitably ordering the vertices, the adjacency matrix of a graph $(\mathcal{V}, \mathcal{E})$ can be written as a block diagonal matrix where the rows (columns) of each block correspond to a weakly connected component. A graph $(\mathcal{V}, \mathcal{E})$ is *complete* if for each pair i and j in $\mathbf{\Gamma}$ there is an edge from i to j. Its adjacency matrix is a square matrix of 1s.

Some particular network topologies are important in the social networks literature. A *star network* is an undirected graph in which one individual, the center, is connected to all other individuals while all other individuals are connected only to the center. A *group*, also known as a *complete network*, is one that contains an edge between each two of its vertices.

In the mathematical sociology literature, social relations like friendship may exhibit *homophily*—the property where "the friend of my friend is my friend, too." Quantitatively, homophily is denoted by the prevalence of transitive triads. Triads are connected subgraphs consisting of three nodes. Transitivity is the property that the existence of an edge from node i to j and an edge from j to k implies the existence of an edge from i to k. A graph is *transitive* if it contains no intransitive triads. The linear-in-means model is specified by assuming $\mathbf{\Gamma}$ is symmetric, that edges are bidirectional, and that the graph is transitive. If this is true, then the graph is the union of completely connected components. The nodes of the component containing i constitute i's group.

A richer set of social interactions is possible by allowing the elements of adjacency matrices to be arbitrary real numbers. The adjacency matrix becomes *weighted*, and the magnitude of the number γ_{ij} measures the degree of influence j has on i; the sign expresses whether that influence is positive or negative. Most of the applications in the book are associated with nonnegative γ_{ij}'s.

For positive adjacency matrices, a number of theorems associated with their spectral properties offer powerful algebraic tools. A scalar λ and a nonzero I-column vector $\mathbf{z}$ that satisfy $\mathbf{\Gamma z} = \lambda \mathbf{z}$ are, respectively, an eigenvalue of $\mathbf{\Gamma}$ and its corresponding eigenvector: $[\mathbf{\Gamma} - \lambda \mathbf{I}]\mathbf{z} = \mathbf{0}$. It thus follows that since $\mathbf{z}$ is nonzero, the matrix $[\mathbf{\Gamma} - \lambda \mathbf{I}]$ must be nonsingular. That is, λ is a root of $\det[\mathbf{\Gamma} - \lambda \mathbf{I}] = 0$. By the Perron–Frobenius theorem, for example, $\mathbf{\Gamma}$ has a positive maximal eigenvalue, that is, an eigenvalue whose absolute value is greater than those of all other eigenvalues, and a positive corresponding eigenvector. Moreover, there is no other nonnegative eigenvector for $\mathbf{\Gamma}$. This maximal eigenvalue is bounded below (above) by the minimum (maximum) sum of the entries of its rows. Thus, if $\mathbf{\Gamma}$ has rows that sum to 1, perhaps by normalization, its maximal eigenvalue is 1.

Most of the applications of graph-theoretic models of social interactions in the book involve using linear algebra to express concisely the mean of one's neighbors' decisions (the endogenous social effect) or the mean of one's neighbors' characteristics (the contextual effect). Still, graph theory is also helpful when social structures emerge from the salience of spatial positioning when individuals differ. As I discuss in chapter 2, section 2.3.4, and in more detail in chapter 3, section 3.6, with two types of individuals, black and white, who choose locations on a *lattice* (a graph represented by the points on a plane with integer coordinates where each individual has a fixed number of neighbors) and who have preferences as to how many of their neighbors have the same skin color as themselves, and for a particular parsimonious specification of preferences, it turns out that social welfare is maximized when the *number* of edges connecting whites is *maximized*. As I discuss in more detail in section 3.6, this implies segregation of whites from blacks.

2.13 APPENDIX: SURVEY OF MICRO DATA SOURCES WITH RICH CONTEXTUAL INFORMATION

Continuing popularity of social interactions research will depend critically on a reliance on increasingly available large microdata sets that offer rich contextual information. Some of these data sets are even more attractive if they can be linked with rich publicly available sources of microgeographic data. This appendix surveys some of the most popular sources of data, especially those that have been used by works reviewed in the book. The survey includes data sources from the United States as well as from outside the United States.

2.13.1 Geocoded Data of the Panel Study of Income Dynamics

The Panel Study of Income Dynamics (PSID),[31] begun in 1968, is the longest continuing longitudinal study of a representative sample of U.S. individuals (men, women, and children) and the family units in which they reside. It started from, and continues to be based on, two independent samples: a cross-sectional national sample and a national sample of low-income families. The latter is restricted to Standard Metropolitan Statistical Areas (SMSAs) in the northern regions and non-SMSA's in the southern regions of the United States. The survey's design aims at capturing the dynamic aspects of economic and demographic behavior, but its content is broad, including sociological and psychological measures. The basic data set has also been enhanced by means of special samples, like 511 immigrant families that were added in 1997–1999. From 4,800 families that were interviewed in 1968 the sample has grown to more than 9,000 families and 22,000 individuals. The study is conducted at the Survey Research Center, Institute for Social Research, University of Michigan. The PSID data were originally collected in face-to-face interviews from 1968 and 1972. Thereafter, the majority of interviews have been conducted over the telephone, annually from 1968 to 1997 and biennually since then.

Of particular usefulness to research on socioeconomic phenomena with a spatial dimension, including social interactions and neighborhood effects, has been the availability of geocodes for the PSID. The Geocode Match Files contain the identifiers necessary to link the main PSID observations with the census tracts where the respondents reside. These links allow the addition of data on neighborhood characteristics for the geographic areas thus identified, enabling research to tap into an increasing variety of measures of the social environment. The Geocode Match Files are highly sensitive, and in order not to jeopardize the anonymity of respondents, the PSID conditions the supply of geocodes on stringent contractual obligations and allows only certain uses of them.

As of November 25, 2011, www.scholar.google.com listed 417 studies that rely on geocoded data from the PSID. By utilizing the neighborhood data, which are defined in terms of census tracts of the U.S. Bureau of the Census and link to the rich family and individual information collected in the PSID, researchers have been able to study effects of community on the life cycle. With the geocodes, it is straightforward to link with U.S. census data and other sources of data, like the American Community Survey (see below) at different levels of aggregation, such as municipalities, counties, states, and regions. A particularly noteworthy application of these data is that by Kremer (1997).

2.13.2 Public Use Microdata

A Public Use Microdata Area (PUMA)[32] is a decennial census area for which the census bureau provides specially selected extracts of raw data from a small sample of "long-form" census records that are screened to protect confidentiality. These extracts are referred to as *public use microdata sample* (PUMS) files. The 5 percent PUMAs comprise areas that contain at least 100,000 people. The 1 percent PUMAs, the super PUMAs, comprise areas of at least 400,000 people. For the 2000 census, PUMAs were not in more than one state or statistically equivalent entity. The larger 1 percent PUMAs are aggregations of the smaller 5 percent PUMAs.

The Public Use Microdata Samples (PUMS) is a popular source of contextual information for researchers using microdata sets, including the PSID. They are made available through the Integrated Public Use Microdata Series (IPUMS).[33] They consist of more than 50 high-precision samples of the U.S. population drawn from 15 U.S. censuses, from the American Community Surveys of 2000–2006, and from the Puerto Rican Community Surveys of 2005–2006. Some of these samples have existed for years, but others were created specifically for this database. The IPUMS help overcome potential inconsistencies by assigning uniform codes across all the samples.

The sources of these data are the long forms of the decennial U.S. census. Every census from 1960 to 2000 asked about one in six U.S. households to fill out a long-form census questionnaire. The long form consisted of more than 50 questions, while the short form contained only 7. The unpopularity of the long form and the increasing need for annual data have led the U.S. Bureau of the Census to develop the American Community Survey (ACS) [www.census.gov/acs/]. The ACS provides an annual snapshot of the U.S. population similar to that provided by the decennial census long form. The 2000 ACS is an approximately 1-in-750 public use sample consisting of 372,000 person records. The 2001–2006 ACS samples each represent approximately 0.4 percent of the population, with plans to increase up to 1 percent. While prior to 2004 the ACS samples contained no geographic information below the state level, increasingly detailed geographic identifiers have become available since.

The Integrated Public Use Microdata Series International (IPUMS-International)[34] is an integrated series of census microdata samples from 1960 to the present. The series includes 111 samples drawn from 35 countries, with more scheduled for release in the future.

2.13.3 Geocoded Data from the National Longitudinal Survey of Youth

The National Longitudinal Surveys (NLS) are conducted by the Bureau of Labor Statistics of the U.S. Department of Labor. They are designed to gather information at multiple points in time on labor market activities and other significant life events of several groups of men and women. One of these surveys, the 1979 National Longitudinal Survey of Youth (NLSY79), is a nationally representative sample of 12,686 young men and women who were 14–22 years old when they were first surveyed in 1979. These individuals have been interviewed annually through 1994 and are currently interviewed biennially. Information collected about the NLSY79 respondents' geographic locations have been made available separately to researchers under agreements that ensure confidentiality. The geocode data tapes contain county and state (or country if outside the United States) at birth, at age 14, at the 1979 interview data, and at each county lived in since January 1, 1978; county and state location of current job; state of residence of parents if respondent is still "attached" to the parental home; and selected environmental variables for county of residence. See Weinberg, Reagan, and Yankow (2004) for a recent example of the use of these data.

2.13.4 Confidential Data through the U.S. Bureau of the Census

Since 1994, the U.S. Bureau of the Census has operated a number of Research Data Centers (RDCs) where researchers with approved projects can access confidential census bureau and administrative data. The RDCs are operated by the census bureau in cooperation with partner institutions (academic and nonprofit organizations) such as the National Bureau of Economic Research (NBER). The conditions of use are very stringent. All RDCs must have a census bureau employee present and comply with strict federal government, census bureau, and Internal Revenue Service (IRS) information technology and physical security guidelines.[35]

All researchers accessing data at an RDC must have special sworn status. Researchers have used these facilities for a variety of purposes. One is to access confidential IRS data on plant-level data from the Longitudinal Research Database (LRD),[36] which provides such details as plant output in terms of annual production, total hours worked, materials used in annual production, and in addition, beginning-of-year book values of machines, equipment, and buildings, and many others including detailed statistics on research and development activities. Henderson (2003) uses it to study Marshall's scale economies.

Another use of this arrangement is to link public data microdata sets with their confidential counterparts that the census bureau uses to produce them. A case in point is the work of Ioannides and Zabel (2008), who link the neighborhood clusters subsample of the American Housing Survey,[37] a public data set, with the confidential version of the national sample of the American Housing Survey (AHS).

2.13.5 Other Data Sets

2.13.5.1 Neighborhood Change Data Base

Of particular significance for spatial-based research on neighborhood dynamics in the United States has been the availability of a new database from the Urban Institute[38] in cooperation with www.Geolytics.com, a private firm. This data set, the Neighborhood Change Data Base (NCDB),[39] contains matched census tract information from the U.S. censuses for 1970, 1980, 1990, and 2000. The database covers metropolitan areas and does not include rural areas. It combines tract-level data from the 1970–2000 decennial censuses. This is quite crucial because tracts approximate neighborhoods with populations typically ranging from 2,500 to 8,000, and the NCDB offers tract boundaries that are consistent. This is made possible by remapping of earlier data to a standardized set of census tract boundaries from 2000.

2.13.5.2 Add Health

Research on social networks has relied substantially on a variety of new data sources that detail behavior and code social relationships. A particularly popular data set is the National Longitudinal Study of Adolescent Health (Add Health),[40] a nationally representative study that explores the causes of health-related behaviors of adolescents in grades 7–12 and their outcomes in young adulthood. Its in-school questionnaire offers social network data for most students in 140 schools. Add Health seeks to examine how social contexts (families, friends, peers, schools, neighborhoods, and communities) influence adolescents' health and risk behaviors. Students were asked to identify up to five male and five female friends, to locate and record their student numbers, and to indicate which of five activities they had shared with each of these friends during the past week. For each respondent, friendship networks can be determined and a respondent's peer group, as well as his or her position within it, can be described in detail. Multiple measures of the strength of friendship ties are available. Patterns of association within the school community, the density and centralization of the social network, and the role of race, gender, or behaviors within school-based social networks can be examined.

Add Health has become the standard data source for empirical social network applications. Noteworthy studies that rely on Add Health have been done by Fryer and Torelli (2010), who construct objective measures of social status, instead of self-reported ones, based on friendship patterns (see section 2.7.2), Calvó-Armengol, Patacchini, and Zenou (2011), and Weinberg (2007).

Information from social networking sites and from electronic communication devices, more generally, are amounting to a torrent of data and will become increasingly accessible to investigators. Already a number of studies from mobile telephone data have helped establish patterns in individuals' movements that are interesting in the context of understanding the nature of social interactions. I discuss this further in chapter 10, section 10.1.1, below by referring to the studies of González, Hidalgo, and Barabási (2008). Data collected on the basis of use of communication technologies are subject to choice-based sampling, and therefore care is needed to purge them of endogeneity.

A number of particularly innovative studies in the social networks area involve linking data from social networking sites with administrative data. Mayer and Puller (2008) document the structure and composition of individuals' social networks using a large data set that identifies students in their social network (defined as "Facebook friends") on university campuses in Texas. Further depth is made possible by linking the facebook.com data to Texas A&M University records for each student's demographic and school outcome characteristics. Ioannides (2007) explores the connections between segregation, as measured by the spectral segregation index first introduced by Echenique and Fryer (2007), and student characteristics in the Texas A&M University–based data. He finds evidence that students who have been widely exposed to other students from their own racial group prior to entering college and those of lower socioeconomic status have significantly higher levels of segregation. He also shows that there is tremendous diversity in how white, Asian, Hispanic, and black students experience segregation once in college.

As researchers will increasingly come to rely on linking different sources of data, it is important to bear in mind that such combined data require careful econometric handling. For example, one data set may provide information on outcomes and instruments, with which a reduced form for the social interactions model may be estimated, and another data set will have information on additional variables.[41] When the second data set contains information on endogenous variables and potential instruments, two-sample instrumental variable estimators are particularly handy in facilitating estimation of structural forms and thus vastly widen the scope of instrumental variable estimation to situations where information on dependent variables, instruments, and endogenous variables of interest may not be available in a single data set. See Angrist and Pischke (2009, 147–150) for an insightful presentation of two-sample instrumental variable estimators.

The study of social interactions effects on a variety of health-related behaviors has been substantially enriched by the clever use of a long-standing data set known the Framingham Heart Study. This epidemiological study has been surveying individuals who were originally residents of Framingham, Massachusetts, in 1948 for the purpose of understanding cardiovascular disease. When it was initiated, two-thirds of the adult population of Framingham signed up to be examined by doctors every 2 years, and those who are still alive continue to be examined, although some of them have moved elsewhere in Massachusetts and the United States. Their children and grandchildren also signed up for follow-up studies initiated in 1971 and 2001. Christakis and Fowler (2009, 107) found "quite by chance" that there exist meticulously kept records with detailed information about the friends, relatives, coworkers, and neighbors of each participant. They used these records to reconstruct the social networks of all the subjects, which amounted to more than 50,000 social ties (not counting connections to neighbors), by focusing on a key group of 5,124 people within a larger network composed of a total of 12,067 people. They were also able to reconstruct how the social networks have changed since 1971 and to link the data with weight, height, and other important attributes. The large number of studies that this data set, which these authors refer to as FHS-Net, have made possible may be accessed from the authors' web sites, http://christakis.med.harvard.edu/ and http://jhfowler.ucsd.edu/, and a version of the data is accessible at www.ncbi.nlm.nih.gov/projects/gap/cgi-bin/study.cgi?study_id=phs000153.v3.p3. See section 2.7.2.3 for a presentation of some of their findings.

2.13.6 Microgeographic Data

In recent years we have witnessed the increasing application of Geographical Information Systems (GIS) in conjunction with economic analysis. This may involve combining socioeconomic data from different spatial units. GIS bring the flexibility of allowing the user to define their own concordances between different geographic units of observation when faced with data from different sources. The spatial nature of GIS data facilitates accessing and allows distances between observations or between observations and other features of interest (transportation systems, etc.) to be computed easily. These distances can be physical distances or network distances (e.g., along a transport network) or even more general concepts of social distance. The proximity of economic activity to rivers, coasts, woodlands, roads, railway lines, and airports and the use of satellite or aerial photography or digitized geologic maps can provide a huge amount of data on the earth's surface. Overman (2010) offers a concise review of the increasing importance of GIS in economics.

A vast amount of fine-grained data on cities, transportation systems, and how individuals interact in their economic and social lives, with much of these data referenced geospatially and temporally, is increasingly becoming available. They come from merging various data sources linked to communications technologies (voice and text communications, email, Twitter, etc.), and they offer tremendous opportunities for learning about the role of space (physical, economic, and social) in economies. Developments along the lines of social networks integrated with general equilibrium models will likely prove useful in learning from such data. See Miller (2010) for a review of the problems such data pose to the analyst.

Exciting opportunities are being opened up by the use of remote-sensing satellite data merged with census or survey data in defining globally consistent settlement concentration, that is, urban agglomerations. Uchida and Nelson (2008) implement an agglomeration index that combines three factors: population density, the population of a "large" urban center, and travel time to that large urban center. This concept has already been implemented in the World Development Report (2009); see section 8.5.5 below.

2.13.7 Geocoded Data from outside the United States

The statistical services of various countries have given access to geocoded data in varying degrees. I review next particularly noteworthy data sets from outside the United States and representative studies based on them.

The U.K. Office of National Statistics (ONS)[42] offers access to a number of restricted microdata for research purposes through its Virtual Microdata Laboratory (VML) facility.[43] Essentially, anything with a U.K. postcode can be georeferenced using the U.K. national postcodes directory. Data sets available include the U.K. Labour Force Survey, the Annual Population Survey (which provides detail down to the local authority level), several business surveys, and many others. Researchers have to comply with stringent access and use requirements.

A particularly rich U.K. data set is the Annual Respondent Database (ARD), an exhaustive establishment-level data set. They contain the data underlying the Annual Census of Production in the United Kingdom. The ARD contains information about all U.K. establishments [see Griffith (1999) for a detailed description of these data]. For every establishment, information is given on its postcode, five-digit industrial classification, and number of employees. The CODE-POINT data set from the Ordnance Survey of the United Kingdom (OS) gives the spatial coordinates for all U.K. postcodes, the most precise postcode georeferencing data available for the United Kingdom. These data can be merged with the ARD to generate very detailed information about the geographic location of all U.K. manufacturing establishments. See Griffith (1999) for a very detailed description of the data, and Duranton and Overman (2005) for an interesting application.

Another U.K. data set that also allows geocoding is the National Child Development Study (NCDS), a continuing longitudinal study that seeks to follow the lives of all those living in Great Britain who were born in one particular week in 1958. The aim of the study is to improve understanding of the factors affecting human development over the entire lifespan. Geocoding allows researchers to merge data from the level of Small Area Data Sets, which contain information from a 10 percent sample survey of the U.K. census for 300–400 residents. Patacchini and Zenou (2011), whose work I discuss in chapter 6, section 6.5.6, use contextual data at the *ward* level, which roughly corresponds to U.S. census tracts. Full details may be found at http://www.esds.ac.uk/longitudinal/access/ncds/l33004.asp.

The National Institute for Statistics and Economic Studies (INSEE),[44] the official French government entity handling statistics, offers a variety of microdata sets.[45] See Goux and Maurin (2007) for an application with French Labor Force Survey (LFS) data that allows effects among close neighbors to be studied. This is possible because of the nature of data collection: the basic sampling unit consists of groups of 20–30 adjacent households, known as *aires*, which serves as the researchers' concept of a neighborhood. A typical LFS consists of a representative sample of about 3,500 *aires*; within each *aire*, all the households are surveyed and within each household all persons aged 15 or more are interviewed.[46]

Researchers with access to data from Statistics Norway[47] have used administrative data, which covers all people resident in Norway, linked with data from the national censuses of 1960 and 1970 using an unique personal identifier given to all Norwegian residents by the national population register. Household and census tract identifiers in the census identify families and place of residence during childhood. The administrative data provide information from the censuses about taxable income (excluding capital gains) and educational attainment, along with a variety of family background variables. These types of data have made possible the completion of numerous studies, some of which follow up individuals over time. Norway's census tracts are defined by voting areas and are smaller than those of the United States. There are about 9,000 census tracts and about 540 municipalities. They are much closer in size to U.S. census block groups, a subdivision of census tracts and block numbering areas, which contain between 600 and 3,000 people, generally, with an optimum size of 1,500 people. See Raaum, Salvanes, and Sørensen (2006) for a particularly interesting use, and Møen, Salvanes, and Sørensen (2003) for a detailed description of the data. A more detailed discussion of this study is in chapter 6, section 6.5.1.

CHAPTER 3

Location Decisions of Individuals and Social Interactions

3.1 INTRODUCTION

When my neighbors add to their house by remodeling it, or simply keep up its maintenance in ways that shame me, they give me an incentive to keep up, too. My children's hearing about academic, sports, and other accomplishments of other children in the neighborhood motivates them to imitate them or even to react in a nonconformist way. These types of effects are known as *endogenous* social effects because they originate in deliberate decisions by other members of one's reference groups.

Individuals may value the actual characteristics of others in their social and residential milieus and deliberately seek particular configurations of such characteristics. Effects that emanate in this fashion from the characteristics of members of one's reference groups are known as *exogenous* or *contextual* effects and are also *social* effects. When different individuals tend to act similarly because they have similar characteristics (or face similar institutional environments), we say that they are subject to *correlated* effects. When the coexistence of these effects cannot be excluded on theoretical grounds, challenging problems may be posed for those wishing to distinguish among them. As I discuss in chapter 2, there are good reasons for wanting to know their respective magnitudes.

For example, how can policy affect social outcomes at the urban neighborhood or community level? How can it affect educational outcomes in schools? Specifically, in the context of the urban economy, could we engineer improvements in living conditions for the residents of "depressed" or disadvantaged areas by encouraging the relocation of individuals with particular characteristics? Two actual policy options are worth contemplating in this context and operate on the supply and the demand, respectively. Increasing the supply of affordable housing within otherwise high-housing cost communities is one such policy option. Residents who value proximity to demographically more diverse groups would be better off, but others might be worse off. The net effect depends on neighborhood effects. Another policy is subsidizing the relocation of low-income households out of disadvantaged and into more prosperous communities. Again, neighborhood effects in the form of role models may confer benefits on relocated households, but they may impact adversely incumbent households. Related conceptually is what determines the character of urban communities, their ambience, and even what determines favorable or unfavorable socioeconomic outcomes for entire communities. Whether policy can affect urban ambience may depend on neighborhood effects. If such effects are absent, those policies may have effects only through prices.

Individuals decide about joining gated communities, or other types of residential communities to which access is controlled by existing covenants (like New York City co-ops) in order to avail themselves of the services being offered and to enjoy being in such environments. Individuals value belonging to clubs precisely because it accords them some control over the types of other individuals they are likely to interact with. Individuals sort themselves across such organizations. Those choosing public communities and neighborhoods avail themselves of access to community-based and typically shared amenities. When many amenities of communities are open to the public, regardless of residence, there is a lesser degree of control over whom one will likely come into contact with.

The cost of housing and community-based taxes serves as an (indirect) admission price. Since housing prices thus help ration access to public communities, it follows that market prices themselves reflect and therefore may also proxy for attributes that characterize communities, including "social" effects. Precisely because individuals take the price of a good, housing in this instance, as given and beyond their control, and make their decisions according to the personal gain they expect to derive from different alternatives, equilibrium prices come to reflect aggregate information about the characteristics of all market participants. It is also information about those particular individuals who choose not to participate in a particular market that helps describe it terms of the distributions of individual characteristics.

In deciding whether or not to locate in a particular city or neighborhood, individuals weigh numerous factors forming expectations about what these effects are likely to be. When individuals do locate by pursuing optimizing strategies, their individual characteristics define the values of prices and the distribution of characteristics by location that will prevail at a *social equilibrium* across communities. It is in this sense that housing prices are hedonic prices associated with a social equilibrium, a concept that I seek to define more precisely in this chapter.

Some of the sorting of individuals across communities is sorting on observable information. For example, families consider information on the quality of publicly provided education, recreation, and other such amenities, which is often widely available, before deciding where to locate. As Rosen (2002) underscores, it is important to assess such sorting in order to understand, inter alia, the social valuation of neighborhood amenities when individuals differ in terms of preferences. For example, if neighborhood safety is valued differently by different people, those who value it less sort to less safe neighborhoods.

Estimating the average value to society of neighborhood safety based on valuations by those who sort to less safe neighborhoods would bias it downward, and if based on valuations by those who sort to safer neighborhoods would bias it upward. With sorting, we are likely to see different types of neighborhoods differing with respect to neighborhood safety.

The tools developed in this chapter aim at elucidating what particular factors are the most important in individuals' decisions, especially when some of them are unobservable or involve social interactions. Sorting on unobservables makes it difficult to determine which factors are responsible for sustaining neighborhoods and communities that differ significantly in terms of attributes. Are they due to the attraction of local synergies (or anticipated spillovers from locational decisions of other individuals) or to underlying and possibly only partly unobservable natural advantages? It is an important premise of the chapter that such factors work to bring and hold people together. There is an inherent difficulty in distinguishing among alternative factors that drive individuals' location decisions. This is where theory is helpful.

The chapter emphasizes the role of social interactions in the choice of a neighborhood or a community by individuals in spatial settings with distance to a city center, to transportation links, and the like, being only one of many considerations. Chapter 5 below employs the canonical urban model, with distance from a central business district (CBD) being a central element of the analysis. While housing prices, local taxes, and other attributes help ration memberships, there is otherwise free entry, where in effect social interactions function like local public goods.

Social interactions are important for location decisions because proximity to others is a key attribute of housing decisions. Neighbors typically know one another and may acquire intimate knowledge of each others' habits. The composition of urban neighborhoods in terms of the socioeconomic characteristics of their residents and the mix of economic and social activities is an important element of their attractiveness. Different communities differ in terms of density of settlement, quality of amenities and public services, and distance to employment centers and to transportation systems. The internal variety of these features also contributes to the character of communities. Such differences are important in determining the fabric of large cities and metropolitan areas. When individuals choose where to live, they take into consideration many such attributes of neighborhoods in addition to specific features of the dwelling units.

While some of the location decisions examined in the present chapter are quite closely related to group choice, as examined for example by Brock and Durlauf (2002), there are two important differences. One is allowing a continuous decision, like one about the size of a dwelling unit, and a discrete decision, like one about where one wants to live, to be joint decisions. I treat this joint decision as emanating from a single optimization problem. That is, there are alternative discrete sets of opportunities within each of which individuals may select a continuous quantity of interest. While the present chapter emphasizes the choice of housing in relation to social interactions, the approach applies equally well to choice of place of employment and, very interestingly, to joint housing and job location.

The highlights of the chapter are, first, models of individual location decisions that rely on the characteristics approach in the presence of contextual effects and use individual dwelling units as the object of choice. Since this particular approach, which originates in the industrial organization literature but is widely applied to housing markets, blurs the distinction among endogenous social effects, contextual effects, and correlated effects, the chapter also presents examples of sorting models that allow for choice of neighborhood with endogenous contextual effects. These are followed by models and associated empirical results for neighborhood choice and housing as a joint decision that allow for social effects and are motivated by utilizing available data. Models of location decisions that emphasize the influence of racial preferences and of reactions of neighbors are also discussed. They have been famously proposed by Thomas Schelling and are paradigmatic of the importance of social interactions. The last class of models examined involve a formal structure of ordered, or *hierarchical*, choice models, where individuals choose over communities defined as governmental jurisdictions.

3.2 ASPATIAL MODELS OF LOCATION WITH SOCIAL INTERACTIONS

I start with choice of location within an urban area via choice among dwelling units. Bayer, McMillan, and Rueben (2009) and Bayer, Ferreira, and McMillan (2007a, 2007b) model preferences for characteristics of other residents either directly or indirectly via the package of public services.

3.2.1 Models of Choice among Individual Dwelling Units

The models I discuss here share the feature that different dwelling units are seen as differentiated commodities, with differentiation occurring in a multitude of dimensions. The models apply with some modifications to housing markets the differentiated products approach, typically referred to as the Berry–Levinshon–Pakes (BLP) approach (Berry 1994; Berry, Levinsohn, and Pakes 1995). It is a natural approach to housing decisions, precisely because dwelling units are neither homogeneous nor standardized commodities. In the studies by Bayer, Ferreira, McMillan, and Rueben, by choosing among individual dwelling units, households also indirectly choose neighborhoods. They take into consideration the exogenous characteristics of neighborhoods in which units lie as well the characteristics of neighbors, in other words, contextual effects. Starting from the basic model of Bayer, Ferreira, and McMillan (2007a, 2007b) and Bayer, McMillan, and Rueben (2009), I consider the description of individual characteristics $\mathbf{Z}^j$, $j \in \mathcal{J}$, and of all dwelling units $\mathbf{X}_h$, $h \in \mathcal{H}$, in terms of distributions $F_{\mathbf{Z}}$ and $F_{\mathbf{X}}$, respectively. Individual j, $j \in \mathcal{J}$, evaluates a dwelling unit h in terms of a vector, $\mathbf{X}_h$, of characteristics which include dwelling size, age, type, tenure status, and neighborhood characteristics such as crime, school quality, socioeconomic composition of the neighborhood, and geography. Dwelling unit h carries a price p_h. Individual j chooses from a discrete choice set of options, $h \in \mathcal{H}^j$, so as to maximize

$$V_h^j = \alpha_X^j \mathbf{X}_h - \alpha_p^j p_h + \xi_h + \varepsilon_h^j, \ h \in \mathcal{H}^j, \tag{3.1}$$

where the quantities α_X^j, α_p^j are defined shortly below, ξ_h is a random variable specific to dwelling unit h and common to all households that consider that unit, which captures the unobserved (to the analyst) quality of the unit and its neighborhood, ε_h^j denotes a random variable that household j draws from a specified distribution, and α_X^j is j's evaluation of the respective characteristic in $\mathbf{X}_h$.

The quantities (α_X^j, α_p^j) are specified as functions of individual j's own socioeconomic characteristics, such as income, race, age, education, and so on, and of parameters as follows:

$$\alpha_q^j = \alpha_{0q} + \sum_{r=1}^{R} \alpha_r Z_r^j, \ q \in X, p, \tag{3.2}$$

where r indexes the components of the vector of observable characteristics $\mathbf{Z}^j$.[1] Rewriting V_h^j from (3.1) so as to distinguish a unit h-specific utility term, mean indirect utility δ_h,

$$\delta_h = \alpha_{0X}\mathbf{X}_h - \alpha_{0p} p_h + \xi_h, \tag{3.3}$$

from a term, λ_h^j, that contains interactions of unit-specific with individual-specific variables,

$$\lambda_h^j = \left(\sum_{r=1}^{R} \alpha_{rX} Z_r^j\right) \mathbf{X}_h - \left(\sum_{r=1}^{R} \alpha_{rp} Z_r^j\right) p_h,$$

we have

$$V_h^j = \delta_h + \lambda_h^j + \varepsilon_h^j. \tag{3.4}$$

It is straightforward to express the probability that individual j will choose dwelling unit h from her choice set $h \in \mathcal{H}^j$, once that choice set and the distribution from which the ε_h^j's are drawn have been specified.[2] If the ε_h^js obey extreme-value distributions of type II, with mean zero, variance $\frac{\pi^2}{6\varpi^2}$, and mode $-\underline{e}/\varpi$, then their cumulative distribution function has the form

$$F(\tilde{\varepsilon}) = \exp[-\exp[-\varpi(\tilde{\varepsilon} + \underline{e}/\varpi)]], \tag{3.5}$$

where $\underline{e} = 0.5772$, Euler's constant. I normalize by setting $\varpi = 1$. The choice probabilities are of the conditional logit model (here with interactions):

$$\text{Prob}_h^j = \frac{\exp[\delta_h + \lambda_h^j]}{\sum_{k \in \mathcal{H}^j} \exp[\delta_k + \lambda_k^j]}, h \in \mathcal{H}^j; \tag{3.6}$$

see (McFadden 1978) and section 3.9.1 for additional details on extreme-value distributions. This does not result in loss of generality in a regression-like framework. Given observable characteristics of dwelling units, $\mathbf{X}_h, h \in \mathcal{H}^j$, and of individuals, $\mathbf{Z}^j$, $j \in \mathcal{J}$, and a specification of the distribution of unobservable characteristic ξ_h, estimation of the discrete choice model by means of maximum likelihood naturally *forces* the probabilities that each unit will be occupied to sum up to 1 [Bayer et al., McFadden 1978, eq. (12)]. An important property of the choice probabilities from (3.6) is that they depend on the relative number of alternatives. Let f_h denote the proportion of dwelling units of type $h \in \mathcal{H}^j$. Then (3.6) becomes $\text{Prob}_h^j = \frac{f_h \cdot \exp[\delta_h + \lambda_h^j]}{\sum_{k \in \mathcal{H}^j} f_k \cdot \exp[\delta_k + \lambda_k^j]}$, $h \in \mathcal{H}^j$.

The estimation process delivers estimates of δ_h, that is, the unit-specific component of the valuation, defined in (3.3). Note also that all of the data that enter the problem bear upon the estimation of the δ_h's. Also estimated are the $(\alpha_{rX}, \alpha_{rp})$'s. It is then possible, in principle, to estimate parameters $(\alpha_{0X}, \alpha_{0p})$ and the distribution of the ξ_h's along the lines of (3.3) by using the estimated unit-specific δ_h's as dependent variables in a second-stage regression.

Although ξ_h itself may be specified stochastically to be independent of the other regressors, the values of the variables that are associated with a particular unit h, $(\mathbf{X}_h, p_h)$ are themselves subject to selection bias. This applies particularly to the price that is appropriate for each unit.

Bayer et al. recognize this endogeneity and follow the original BLP literature by instrumenting p_h by means of attributes of houses and neighborhoods beyond the immediate neighborhood where a particular household has chosen to live. Such instruments contain information about feasible alternatives but are assumed to be uncorrelated with the realizations of the specific random shocks (ξ_h, ε_h^j) that determine choice by individual j in the immediate vicinity of unit h.[3] The actual implementation of this procedure involves using a predicted vector of market-clearing prices calculated for an initial estimate of the parameter values, with the unobservable components (the ξ_h's) being set equal to zero and the probabilities being evaluated at the means of the exogenous features of locations for units $h \in \mathcal{H}_j$.

3.2.2 Self-Selection Effects in Hedonic Price Indices

So far I have addressed the valuation of dwelling units by different individuals. What does the model imply about the *market valuations* of different dwelling units? A simple way to start is by excluding the individualized component of utility, λ_h^j, from the definition of unit-specific utility (3.4). This forces the estimates of δ_h to be equal for all units, and I may therefore set it equal to 0, $\delta_h = 0$. With λ_h^j excluded, equation (3.3) can be solved for the price p_h of a unit h:

$$p_h = \frac{1}{\alpha_{0p}} \alpha_{0X} \mathbf{X}_h + \frac{1}{\alpha_{0p}} \xi_h. \qquad (3.7)$$

This is like a standard hedonic price regression that relates dwelling unit price p_h to the unit observable characteristics $\mathbf{X}_h$ and to unobservable characteristics of its neighborhood, ξ_h. However, suppression of the individualized component λ_h^j removes contextual effects from the model of housing demand. Consequently, regressors in $\mathbf{X}_h$ controlling for attributes that are positively correlated with the vector of indirect utilities will have coefficients that will be downward biased. This bias needs to be corrected (see Bayer et al.).

There is another noteworthy aspect of hedonic regressions when one conditions on characteristics of occupants. That is, units chosen by a particular group of the population will be associated, by revealed preference, with higher utility attributed to them by that group, according to the term δ_h in equation (3.4). Omitting such terms from the estimation would lead to understating the willingness to pay of such a group for dwelling-unit characteristics.

I account systematically for these effects by means of the value to an individual from the choice process. That is, the expected value of the *maximum* utility from the choice process for individual j, $\tilde{V}_j^{\mathcal{H}^j}$, is obtained by using the properties of the multinomial choice model.[4] By writing

$$\mathcal{E}\left\{\max_{h\in\mathcal{H}^j}: \ \tilde{V}_j^{\mathcal{H}^j}(\mathbf{X};\mathbf{Z}^j)\right\} = \ln\left(\sum_{h\in\mathcal{H}^j}\exp[\delta_h+\lambda_h^j]\right)$$

$$= \ln|\mathcal{H}^j| + \ln\left(\int \exp[\delta_h+\lambda_h^j]\cdot f_h d F_{\mathbf{X}|h}\right), \quad (3.8)$$

where $F_{\mathbf{X}} = |\mathcal{H}^j|\cdot f_h \cdot F_{\mathbf{X}|h}$ denotes the exogenous distribution of dwelling-unit characteristics, $\mathbf{X} = \{\mathbf{X}_h\}_{h\in\mathcal{H}}$.

In a dual fashion, I define the market valuation of each unit h as the outcome of bidding among the set of individuals, $j\in\mathcal{J}$ (Ellickson 1981). Under my assumptions, the maximum valuation of a particular unit h among all individuals in the sample, defined as

$$\tilde{V}_h^{\mathcal{J}}(X_h;\mathbf{Z}) \equiv \max_{j\in\mathcal{J}}: \ \tilde{V}_h^{\mathcal{H}^j}(\mathbf{X}_h;\mathbf{Z}^j),$$

has a probability distribution given by

$$\text{Prob}\left[\max_{i\in\mathcal{J}}: \ \delta_h+\lambda_h^j+\varepsilon_h^j \le v\right] = \exp\left[-e^{-v}\sum_{i\in\mathcal{J}}\exp[\delta_h+\lambda_h^j]\right].$$

This expression may be simplified by defining $\tilde{v}_h \equiv \ln\left[\sum_{j\in\mathcal{J}}\exp[\delta_h+\lambda_h^j]\right]$, to become

$$\text{Prob}\left[\max_{j\in\mathcal{J}}: \ \delta_h+\lambda_h^j+\varepsilon_h^j \le v\right] = \exp\left[-e^{\tilde{v}_h-v}\right].$$

It follows from the properties of extreme-value random variables that the expected value of the maximum valuation of unit h is given by $\tilde{v}_h$:

$$\mathcal{E}\left\{\tilde{V}_h^{\mathcal{J}}(\mathbf{X}_h;\mathbf{Z})\right\} = \tilde{v}_h = \delta_h + \ln\left(\int\exp[\lambda_h^j]\cdot dF_{\mathbf{Z}}\right), \quad (3.9)$$

where $F_{\mathbf{Z}}$ denotes the cumulative distribution function of the vector of characteristics of all individuals $\mathbf{Z} = \{\mathbf{Z}^j\}_{j\in\mathcal{J}}$.

A number of remarks are in order. First, note that the above derivation of the hedonic price index, equation (3.9), includes as a special case the standard definition of a hedonic index as the outer envelope of individual expenditure functions, where they are parameterized by income. Indeed, it does not depend on any particular individual's income but does depend on unit characteristics $\mathbf{X}_h$ and on the characteristics of all individuals $\mathbf{Z}$. Second, note the symmetry between the expected value of maximum utility attained by a particular individual j and the maximum valuation of unit h generated by the market, given by (3.8) and (3.9), respectively. Both involve averaging over characteristics, the former averaging over characteristics of dwelling units, $\mathbf{X}_h$, and the latter over characteristics of individuals, $\mathbf{Z}^j$. However, averaging over individual characteristics obscures the role of the number of different individuals over the range of characteristics. Let f_j denote the proportion of individuals of type j, $|\mathcal{J}| f_j$ their number, and $F_{\mathbf{Z}|j}$ the conditional distribution of their characteristics. Then the right-hand side of (3.9) becomes

$$\delta_h + \ln|\mathcal{J}| + \ln\left(\int \exp[\lambda_h^j]\cdot f_j \cdot dF_{\mathbf{Z}|j}\right),$$

which reflects the fact that the distribution of the maximum of evaluations of a particular unit by all individuals $\mathcal{J}$ depends, not surprisingly, on the numbers of different types.[5]

I stress the importance of selection bias that may underlie hedonic calculations by comparing the expected maximum valuation of unit h with the average valuation of unit h, (3.9), by the entire population of individuals. The latter is obtained by averaging the right-hand side of (3.4) over the entire population of individuals:

$$\tilde{\mathcal{V}}_h = \int \left[\delta_h + \lambda_h^j + \varepsilon_h^j\right] dF_{\mathbf{Z}} = \delta_h + |\mathcal{J}| \sum_{i\in\mathcal{J}} \lambda_h^j \cdot \text{Prob}_h^j \cdot f_j \cdot dF_{\mathbf{Z}|j}. \quad (3.10)$$

Recall from the clarification of (3.6) that the dwelling-unit choice probabilities reflect the relative numbers of types of units. Thus, $\tilde{\mathcal{V}}_h$ increases with the number of individuals who consider it and decreases with the number of units of the same type.

By the convexity of the exponential function and the definition of the choice probabilities (3.6), one can prove that the average valuation by the entire population, given by (3.10), understates the actual valuation, that is, the expectation of the maximum for each unit h, as implied by the choice model and given by (3.9). Therefore, it is the expression derived in (3.9), the outcome of a bidding process for dwelling units, that should be the basis for the hedonic function associated with models of housing decisions involving choices of individual units.

The opportunity cost of resources for supplying unit h to a particular market sets the value, at equilibrium, of the left-hand side of (3.9) above.

Then, solving it in terms of p_h yields a hedonic price index for dwelling units with associated characteristics $\mathbf{X}_h$, given a population characterized by $\mathbf{Z}$. Again, note that dwelling unit characteristics are interacted with the distributions of individual characteristics in arriving at the hedonic price function. Consider, for simplicity, that in (3.2), $\alpha_{rp} = 0, r = 1, \ldots, R$. Then, (3.9) may be solved to yield a hedonic price:

$$p_h = \frac{1}{\alpha_{0p}} \mathcal{E}\left\{\tilde{V}_h^{\mathcal{J}}(\mathbf{X}_h; \mathbf{Z})\right\} = \frac{1}{\alpha_{0p}} \ln\left(\sum_{i \in \mathcal{J}} \exp[\delta_h + \lambda_h^j]\right)$$
$$= \frac{1}{\alpha_{0p}} \left[\alpha_{0X}\mathbf{X}_h + \xi_h + \ln \int \exp[\lambda_h^j] \cdot dF_{\mathbf{Z}}\right]. \tag{3.11}$$

Therefore, the bias on unit valuation caused by excluding the individualized component of utility, as in (3.7), is given by the last term in the above expression for the hedonic price index, $\frac{1}{\alpha_{0p}} \ln \int \exp[\lambda_h^j] \cdot dF_{\mathbf{Z}_j}$.

Conditional on $\mathbf{Z}^j$,(3.6) gives the probability of individual j's choosing different types of units. Therefore, intuitively, the expected demand for different types of units by the entire population of individuals, whose number is normalized to 1, is given by

$$D_h(\mathbf{X}_h) = \int \text{Prob}_h^j \cdot dF_{\mathbf{Z}}. \tag{3.12}$$

3.2.3 Overview of Bayer et al. Empirical Findings

Bayer, McMillan, and Rueben (2004a) use the BLP approach, by specifying utility from occupying a dwelling unit, as in (3.1) and (3.2) above, as a function of its price, of its characteristics, and of the characteristics of its neighborhood. They individualize the corresponding coefficients, and the coefficient of price, in particular, by defining them as explicit functions of individual characteristics, as in equation (3.2) above. Their concept of neighborhood is census blocks in the San Francisco Bay area. Census blocks comprise groups of about 100 dwelling units each. Their data come from six counties in the San Francisco Bay area, that encompass about 650,000 individuals in 244,000 households who reside within 1,100 census tracts containing almost 39,000 census blocks. The authors obtain household data from 1990 U.S. census long forms and use confidential data to identify their locations down to the census block level. The authors thus avail themselves of a vast amount of information, available in the long census forms but unavailable in other census-based data sets, which includes incomes from a variety of sources as well as sociodemographic characteristics. The authors link the restricted-access census data with data from all housing transactions in the San Francisco Bay area between 1992 and 1996. The transactions data are based on county-level public records and involve every housing unit sold during that period, along with the exact transaction price and the exact street address. Additional data from Home

Mortgage Disclosure Act (HMDA) forms allows the authors to investigate the robustness of their findings.

The authors incorporate the boundary discontinuity design (BDD)[6] in their estimation of hedonic price regressions by including fixed effects defined over school attendance zone boundaries to control for the correlation of school quality with unobserved neighborhood quality. Their hedonic price regressions show that the inclusion of boundary fixed effects reduces the magnitudes of the coefficients on the income and education of one's neighbors by 25 percent and 60 percent, respectively. Thus higher-income and better-educated households select into neighborhoods with better amenities. They also find that the coefficient on the fraction of black neighbors declines to zero, in sharp contrast to the negative correlation of housing prices with the fraction of black neighbors typically observed and reported systematically in the previous literature. These authors argue that this is due to the correlation of race and unobserved neighborhood quality captured by the boundary fixed effect.

Generally, these authors find that hedonic price regression coefficients are very close to mean preferences for housing and neighborhood attributes that vary more or less continuously throughout the metropolitan area, including school quality, neighborhood income, and education. In contrast, they find that estimated mean preferences for black neighbors differ markedly from hedonic estimates and are significantly negative. This underscores the power of their method, since for blacks, who make up less than 10 percent of the population, mean and marginal households are far apart. Their analysis implies that, conditional on neighborhood income, households prefer to self-segregate on the basis of both race and education.

Such detail allows the authors to examine in greater depth patterns of residential segregation (Bayer, McMillan, and Reuben 2004a, 2004b, 2009) and to estimate the full equilibrium effects of preferences for educational quality. These effects include the direct valuation of educational quality as well as the indirect valuation. The latter comes from preferences for peers and neighbors who in turn, because of sorting, themselves value education more than the average individual. Bayer, Ferreira, and McMillan (2007b) use general equilibrium simulations based on the estimates reported by Bayer, Ferreira, and McMillan (2007a) to explore the size of social multiplier effects associated with increases in school quality as households re-sort. Such a social multiplier property of preferences for neighborhood amenities, for school quality in this particular case, is akin to the role of endogenous social effects more generally and has been overlooked in the literature.

3.3 AN EXACT SOLUTION FOR HEDONIC PRICES IN A MODEL OF SORTING

Next I discuss and extend an exact solution to a model of sorting, originally due to Nesheim (2002), that allows for contextual effects, own income effects, and endogenous choice of neighborhood. Consequently, one can use it to study properties of entire neighborhoods when individuals self-select. Unlike in the hedonic analysis of section 3.2.2, here contextual effects depend on the characteristics of individuals who self-select into neighborhoods.

Following Nesheim (2002), I assume that individuals choose their residential location from among a continuum of locations indexed by ℓ. Individuals consume one unit of housing each and value nonhousing consumption and their own child's expected schooling. Locations differ in terms of an attribute, average neighborhood schooling among adults, which is assumed to contribute to a child's educational outcome. Each individual allocates her income Υ to nonhousing consumption, $\Upsilon - R(\ell)$ and to unit housing rent $R(\ell)$ at location $\ell, \ell \in R_+$.

I describe each household in terms of a vector of attributes, $\mathbf{z} = (z_1, z_2, z_3, z_4, z_5)$, whose components are defined, respectively, as log of parental schooling, $s_0 = e^{z_1}$, log of parent income, $\Upsilon = e^{z_2}$, log of the child's ability in school, $a = e^{z_3}$, log of a preference parameter, $\beta = e^{z_4}$, that weights a child's schooling outcome in the utility function, and a random shock to schooling outcome, z_5, which will be assumed to be uncorrelated with all other components. That is,

$$\mathbf{z} = (\ln s_0, \ln \Upsilon, \ln a, \ln \beta, z_5).$$

Households trade off rent for the expected schooling outcomes for their children so as to maximize utility by choosing a location, ℓ. Utility is additively separable in nonhousing consumption, $\Upsilon - R(\ell)$, and in expected schooling for a child, conditional on parental characteristics and location, $\mathcal{E}(s_1|\ell)$:

$$\max_{\ell} : \left\{ \frac{1}{\gamma} \left[1 - e^{-\gamma(\Upsilon - R(\ell))} \right] + e^{z_4} \mathcal{E}(s_1|\ell) \right\}, \quad \gamma \geq 0. \tag{3.13}$$

A child's schooling outcome produced at location ℓ is described by an educational production function as a function of average schooling at ℓ, $S(\ell)$, parent's own schooling, e^{z_1}, the child's ability, e^{z_3}, and the random shock, e^{z_5}. That is,

$$s_1 = (S(\ell))^{\eta_1} e^{\eta_2 z_1 + z_3 + z_5}, \tag{3.14}$$

where η_1 and η_2 are positive parameters. The random shock z_5 is the only quantity that is unobservable by the household when it chooses a location and is assumed to be independent of the location. Average schooling at each location, $S(\ell)$, and the housing rent, $R(\ell)$, are both endogenous. They are determined consistently with equilibrium sorting of households across locations.

The sorting equilibrium is defined in terms of, one, a mapping $F(\mathbf{z})$ that assigns household types $\mathbf{z}, \mathbf{z} \in \mathbf{Z}$, to locations, $F(\mathbf{z}) : \mathbf{Z} \to R_+$, and two, a housing rent function $R(\ell)$ that equilibrates the housing market in each location, $\ell \in R_+$. The average schooling of parents who choose to locate in neighborhood ℓ, the location-specific input into the education production function (3.14), is defined as $S(\ell) = \mathcal{E}\left[e^{z_1} | z \in F^{-1}(\ell)\right]$.

Provided that monotonicity holds at equilibrium, it is convenient to proxy for location in the utility maximization problem in terms of the characteristics of interest, $S(\ell)$, a contextual effect. The housing rent function is accordingly defined as the price $p(S)$ for the contextual effect S, that is, in the place of rent at location ℓ, $R(\ell)$.

Nesheim (2002) shows that, when $\gamma \neq 0$, in (3.13), the differential equation that the hedonic price function must satisfy is not amenable to an analytical solution and can be solved only numerically. Nesheim does establish several general results, such as the existence of a unique equilibrium rent function, provided that groups of individuals with higher average willingness to pay for education are willing to pay more for high-quality locations with better education (Nesheim 2002, theorem 5.1). However, it is possible that the average education of people who choose a location with a given quality index may decline with the value of the quality index. In that case, Nesheim's result (Nesheim, 2002, Theorem 5.2) ensures the existence of a nontrivial equilibrium rent function with a discontinuous slope. Accordingly, there will be concentrations of individuals of finite mass at the points of discontinuity. Nesheim shows that this more general model is econometrically fully identified.

3.3.1 Income Effects in the Nesheim Sorting Model

By modifying a single assumption in (Nesheim 2002), namely, that component z_2 of the vector of individual characteristics $\mathbf{z}$ is the *level* of parental income, not its *log*, I obtain an analytical solution for the hedonic price $p(S)$. The first-order condition for maximizing utility (3.13) with respect to S is

$$-e^{-\gamma[z_2-p(S)]}p_S(S) + A_0\eta_1 S^{\eta_1-1}e^{\eta_2 z_1+z_3+z_4} = 0. \qquad (3.15)$$

Rearranging and taking logs yields

$$\eta_2 z_1 + \gamma z_2 + z_3 + z_4 = \Theta(S), \qquad (3.16)$$

where $\Theta(S)$, defined as

$$\Theta(S) \equiv \gamma p(S) + \ln[p_S(S)] - \ell n(A_0\eta_1) + (1-\eta_1)\ln S, \qquad (3.17)$$

with $A_0 = \mathcal{E}(e^{z_5})$, denotes the marginal quality index. $\Theta(S)$ expresses the marginal utility of neighborhood quality given its price. The left-hand side of (3.16) expresses the marginal willingness to pay for neighborhood quality. Let φ denote a vector of parameters:

$$\varphi^{\mathrm{T}} = (\eta_2, \gamma, 1, 1, 0). \qquad (3.18)$$

Next I define average neighborhood schooling, the average schooling of an adult who chooses location S, conditional on her characteristics, which satisfies the first-order condition (3.16), as

$$S = \mathcal{E}\left\{e^{z_1}|\varphi\mathbf{z} = \Theta(S)\right\}. \qquad (3.19)$$

If $z \sim N(\mu, \Sigma)$, then the log education of parents who choose location S, $\left(z_1|\varphi^{\mathrm{T}}\mathbf{z} = \Theta(S)\right)$, is normally distributed, $N\left(\widetilde{\mu}_1, \widetilde{\sigma}_1^2\right)$, with the mean $\widetilde{\mu}_1$ and the variance $\tilde{\sigma}_1^2$ given by

$$\tilde{\mu}_1 = \mu_1 + \frac{\varphi^{\mathrm{T}}\Sigma e_1}{\varphi^{\mathrm{T}}\Sigma\varphi}\left[\Theta(S) - \varphi^{\mathrm{T}}\mu\right], \; \tilde{\sigma}_1^2 = \sigma_{11}^2(1 - \tilde{\rho}_1^2),$$

with $e_1^{\mathrm{T}} \equiv (1, 0, 0, 0, 0)$, where $\tilde{\rho}_1^2 = \frac{(\varphi^{\mathrm{T}}\Sigma e_1)^2}{\sigma_{11}(\varphi^{\mathrm{T}}\Sigma\varphi)}$, denotes the square of the correlation coefficient between the log education of parents and their willingness to pay for neighborhood quality. Clearly, because of sorting, the variance of the log education of parents, conditional on the willingness to pay for neighborhood quality, is less than in the entire population.

Using (3.19) with the first-order condition for utility maximization (3.15), I obtain a differential equation for $p(S)$. That is, defining the auxiliary variables L_0, L_1 as functions of preference parameters and of the parameters of the joint distribution of vector z,

$$L_0 \equiv e^{\mu_1 - L_1[\ln(\eta_1 A_0) + \varphi^{\mathrm{T}}\mu)] + \frac{1}{2}\tilde{\sigma}_{11}^2}, \; L_1 \equiv \frac{\varphi^{\mathrm{T}}\Sigma e_1}{\varphi^{\mathrm{T}}\Sigma\varphi},$$

allows me to write

$$S = L_0\,[p_S(S)]^{L_1}\, S^{L_1(1-\eta_1)} e^{\gamma p(S)}. \tag{3.20}$$

Integrating and using the initial condition that a zero-quality neighborhood must have a zero price,[7] $p(0) = 0$, yield the equilibrium price function

$$p(S) = \frac{L_1}{\gamma}\ln\left[1 + \frac{\gamma}{L_1}L_0^{-1/L_1}\left(\eta_1 + \frac{1}{L_1}\right)^{-1} S^{\eta_1 + 1/L_1}\right]. \tag{3.21}$$

I note that L_1 would be the regression coefficient from the regression of the log education of parents on the willingness to pay for neighborhood quality (Nesheim, 2002, 33).

3.3.2 Properties of the Hedonic Price Function

For large values of S, the second term within the brackets on the right-hand side of (3.21) dominates the first, thus allowing an approximation:

$$p(S) \approx \frac{L_1}{\gamma}\ln\left[\frac{\gamma}{L_1}L_0^{-1/L_1}\left(\eta_1 + \frac{1}{L_1}\right)^{-1}\right] + \frac{1 + \eta_1 L_1}{\gamma}\ln S. \tag{3.22}$$

Generally, the equilibrium price function is increasing in S. From the sign of its second derivative,

$$p_{SS}(S) = L_0^{-1/L_1} S^{\eta_1 + (1/L_1) - 2}\frac{\eta_1 + \frac{1}{L_1} - 1 - \frac{\gamma}{L_1}L_0^{-1/L_1}\left(\eta_1 + \frac{1}{L_1}\right)^{-1} S^{\eta_1 + 1/L_1}}{\left[1 + \frac{\gamma}{L_1}L_0^{-1/L_1}\left(\eta_1 + \frac{1}{L_1}\right)^{-1} S^{\eta_1 + 1/L_1}\right]^2}, \tag{3.23}$$

it follows that the equilibrium price function is convex for low values of S and up to a threshold point, and concave thereafter, provided that $\eta_1 + \frac{1}{L_1} > 1$, $\gamma > 0$. The equilibrium rent function exhibits a key property of social interactions models: the equilibrium rent is a sigmoid function of average neighborhood quality.

From the definition of L_1 above, the condition for $p(S)$ to be sigmoid in S requires restrictions on parameters:

$$\eta_1 + \frac{\phi^{\mathrm{T}}\Sigma\phi}{\eta_2\sigma_{11} + \gamma\sigma_{21} + \sigma_{31} + \sigma_{41}} > 1.$$

As expected, an individual's marginal valuation of neighborhood quality, the hedonic demand equation (3.16), depends on the *individual's* income, but the equilibrium rent function (3.20) depends, via the auxiliary functions L_0, L_1, only on the *statistics* of the income distribution and its joint distribution with the other characteristics of interest.

Average neighborhood quality, that is, schooling, chosen by an individual with characteristics (z_1, z_2, z_3, z_4) follows by using solution (3.21) in (3.15). That is,

$$\left[1 + \frac{\gamma}{L_1} L_0^{-1/L_1} \left(\eta_1 + \frac{1}{L_1}\right)^{-1} S^{\eta_1 + 1/L_1}\right]^{L_1 - 1} S^{1/L_1} = \tilde{A}_0 e^{\eta_2 z_1 + \gamma z_2 + z_3 + z_4},$$

where $\tilde{A}_0 \equiv A_0 \eta_1 L_0^{1/L_1}$. The choice of S for an individual with characteristics (z_1, z_2, z_3, z_4) is implicitly determined by the roots of the above equation. Let the roots S of (3.21) be denoted by $\mathcal{S}(z_1, z_2, z_3, z_4)$. Then a child's education follows from (3.14),

$$\ln s_1 = \eta_2 z_1 + z_3 + z_5 + \eta_1 \mathcal{S}(z_1, z_2, z_3, z_4).$$

The dependence of a child's education on z_2, parental income, is brought in via $\mathcal{S}$, which from (3.19) depends on parental characteristics.

The magnitude of L_1 affects the sensitivity of S with respect to the willingness to pay for neighborhood quality. If $L_1 < 1$ and $\eta_1 + \frac{1}{L_1} < 1$, then there will, in general and subject to feasibility conditions, exist two solutions. For only one of them, the smaller in magnitude, it will be the case that neighborhood education increases with willingness to pay for it and with income, in particular. This is also the case if $\eta_1 + \frac{1}{L_1} > 1$ and provided the value is not too large. Both solutions are in principle acceptable, but they have different properties. For example, the larger of the two solutions implies that individuals with more own schooling choose neighborhoods with lower average schooling, which in turn implies lower schooling for their children. In other words, depending upon parameter values, the model allows for schooling at equilibrium to be either a normal or an inferior good.

The distribution of income, conditional on location choice S, is normal:

$$\left(z_2 | \varphi^{\mathrm{T}} z = \Theta(S)\right) \sim N(\widetilde{\mu}_2 \widetilde{\sigma}_{22}),$$

with the mean and the variance given by

$$\widetilde{\mu}_2 = \mu_2 + \frac{\varphi^{\mathrm{T}}\Sigma e_2}{\varphi^{\mathrm{T}}\Sigma\varphi}\left[\Theta(S) - \varphi^{\mathrm{T}}\mu\right], \quad \widetilde{\sigma}_2 = \sigma_{22}(1 - \widetilde{\rho}_2^2),$$

where $\widetilde{\rho}_2^2 = \frac{(\varphi^{\mathrm{T}}\Sigma e_2)^2}{\sigma_{22}(\varphi^{\mathrm{T}}\Sigma\varphi)}$ denotes the square of the correlation coefficient between the income of parents and their willingness to pay for neighborhood quality, and solution (3.21) is used in obtaining the expression for $\Theta(S)$,

$$\Theta(S) \equiv -\ln(\tilde{A}_0) + \frac{1}{L_1}\ln S + (L_1 - 1)\ln\left[1 + \frac{\gamma}{L_1}L_0^{-1/L_1}\left(\eta_1 + \frac{1}{L_1}\right)^{-1} S^{\eta_1 + 1/L_1}\right].$$

The distribution of education of parents who choose S is lognormal, $(z_1|\varphi^{\mathrm{T}}z = \Theta(S)) \sim N(\widetilde{\mu}_1, \widetilde{\sigma}_{11})$, and

$$\widetilde{\mu}_1 = \mu_1 + \frac{\varphi^{\mathrm{T}}\Sigma e_1}{\varphi^{\mathrm{T}}\Sigma\varphi}\left[\Theta(S) - \varphi^{\mathrm{T}}\mu\right], \quad \widetilde{\sigma}_1 = \sigma_{11}(1 - \widetilde{\rho}_1^2),$$

where $\widetilde{\rho}_1^2 = \frac{(\varphi^{\mathrm{T}}\Sigma e_1)^2}{\sigma_{11}(\varphi^{\mathrm{T}}\Sigma\varphi)}$ denotes the square of the correlation coefficient between the log education of parents and the willingness to pay for neighborhood quality.

3.3.3 The Special Case of No Income Effects

Setting $\gamma = 0$ in (3.21) yields the hedonic price of housing obtained by Nesheim:

$$p(S) = L_0^{-1/L_1}\left(\eta_1 + \frac{1}{L_1}\right)^{-1} S^{\eta_1 + 1/L_1}. \tag{3.24}$$

The elasticity of the equilibrium rent function with respect to neighborhood quality S in the absence of income effects, $\eta_1 + \frac{1}{L_1}$, is intuitive. The larger η_1, the larger price differentials must be to segregate individuals into their preferred locations. The larger L_1, the regression coefficient of the log education of parents on the willingness to pay for neighborhood quality, the less parents are willing to pay directly for neighborhood quality since they contribute indirectly through their own education and therefore the smaller price differentials are required to maintain segregation of households at equilibrium. The equilibrium price function (3.24) is convex (concave) if $\eta_1 + \frac{1}{L_1} > (<)1$. Again, the endogenous distributions of interest, of education, and of income of parents who choose neighborhood education S readily follow. Neighborhood quality as a function of S now becomes $\Theta(S) \equiv -\frac{1}{L_1}\ln L_0 - \ln(A_0\eta_1) + \frac{1}{L_1}\ln S$. Thus:

$$S = A_0^* e^{L_1(\eta_2 z_1 + z_3 + z_4)}, \quad A_0^* \equiv L_0^{-1/L_1}(A_0\eta_1)^{L_1}.$$

The log of average neighborhood schooling *chosen* by an individual with characteristics z is linear in $L_1(\eta_2 z_1 + z_3 + z_4)$, where the effect of individual characteristics is moderated by L_1. The larger L_1, the more neighborhood quality parents are willing to purchase directly since this makes their own education more effective in ensuring greater segregation of households at equilibrium.

Also interesting is the relationship between a child's education and household characteristics. That is, from (3.14), using the solution for S yields

$$\ln s_1 = a_0 + \eta_2(1 + \eta_1 L_1)z_1 + (1 + \eta_1 L_1)z_3 + \eta_1 L_1 z_4 + z_5, \tag{3.25}$$

where a_0 is a function of parameters. The intergenerational evolution of schooling is determined by $\eta_2(1+\eta_1 L_1)$, the coefficient of the log of the parents' schooling.

This example demonstrates how restrictive the typical hedonic price literature approach is, whereby estimates are sought for arbitrary functional forms for the relationship between the (marginal) valuation of neighborhood amenities as a function of observables and unobservables. In contrast, Nesheim's theory determines the equilibrium rent exactly as a function of contextual characteristics, and this in turn characterizes sorting. As Nesheim (2002) shows in detail, this model is not entirely identified, although groups of parameters may be identified by means of data on observable educational outcomes as a function of parental education, neighborhood school quality, and income.

If individuals value the characteristics of their neighbors, then as an outcome of their choice of location their neighbors' characteristics are correlated with their own. Similarly, if certain individual outcomes that households care about, like educational attainment of children, depend on the characteristics of neighbors, then unobservable characteristics of individuals are likely to be correlated with neighborhood characteristics. If children's ability increases the productivity of neighborhood quality in producing education, then people who know they have high-ability children will move to high-quality neighborhoods. This leads to sorting: higher-quality neighborhoods will have higher unobserved ability.

Neighborhood effects due to schooling have been posited as stylized facts and addressed by typically atheoretical papers, such as (Brooks-Gunn, Duncan, Klebanov, and Sealand 1993), which emphasizes the importance of sorting bias, and (Kremer 1997), who estimates schooling as a function of parental schooling and neighborhood schooling and assesses the implied role of sorting in inequality. Ioannides (2003) shows empirically that nonlinearities in the general relationship, whose special case is estimated by Kremer (1997), may alter Kremer's key results. These findings are discussed further in chapter 6, section 6.5.3.[8] Below in section 3.7.2, I discuss broadly related results obtained by means of an Epple-type model (Calabrese, Epple, Romer, and Sieg 2006).

Nesheim (2002) reports estimation results with data from the U.S. National Educational Longitudinal Survey for 1998. He demonstrates the key difficulty in estimating the model, the dependence at equilibrium between marginal price and neighborhood quality. However, the use of different data sets, which can allow controlling for additional determinants of housing price, can facilitate identification. For example, the confidential version of the Panel Study of Income Dynamics that links individual and parental characteristics to the characteristics of the neighborhoods where respondents grew up allows for additional information on housing price determinants to be brought to bear on the estimation. Alternatively, regression discontinuity designs, like that employed by Black (1999), can also be helpful precisely because they allow for exogenous instruments.

3.4 A DISCRETE LOCATION PROBLEM WITH ENDOGENOUS AND CONTEXTUAL EFFECTS

Bayer and Timmins (2005, 2007) extend the BLP approach to models of location decisions in the presence of endogenous social effects. Their method applies to residential and industrial location decisions and is particularly interesting when endogenous social effects coexist with natural advantages of locations, making it hard to distinguish their separate roles while using observations on patterns of location decisions and their covariates.

In order to disentangle the impact of unobservable local factors, Bayer and Timmins explore a source of potential instruments that is similar to those used in the Bayer et al. work on housing decisions (see section 3.2.1). That is, they use functions of characteristics of other locations that individuals could have chosen but did not, which are correlated with the fractions and characteristics of individuals who do choose particular locations but are uncorrelated with unobserved fixed attributes of those locations. However, their approach also serves to demonstrate the subtlety of the housing choice problem in the presence of neighborhood effects. From section 3.3 above, a key difficulty of the housing decision is the fact that equilibrium housing prices themselves are functions of contextual effects and as endogenous variables in their own right also reflect the distributions of underlying characteristics, that is, social effects.

I use a model similar to the one in section 3.2.1 with ℓ now indexing locations instead of dwelling units. I define the utility individual j derives from location ℓ, (3.1), to also include an endogenous social effect, α_{ϕ}^{j}, where Prob_{ℓ} denotes the share of agents who choose location ℓ:

$$V_{\ell}^{j} = \alpha_{X}^{j} X_{\ell} + \alpha_{\phi}^{j} \text{Prob}_{\ell} + \xi_{\ell} + \varepsilon_{\ell}^{j}. \tag{3.26}$$

The remainder of the notation is adapted in the obvious way from section 3.2.1. Individual j chooses location ℓ with probability

$$\text{Prob}_{\ell}^{j} = \mathcal{G}_{i\ell}(\mathbf{Z}^{j}, \mathbf{X}, \mathbf{Prob}, \xi), \ \ell \in \mathcal{L}, \ i \in \mathcal{J}, \tag{3.27}$$

where $\mathbf{Z}^{j}, \mathbf{X}, \mathbf{Prob}, \Xi$ are the matrix and vector counterparts of the respective variables. By aggregating over all individuals, we have $\text{Prob}_{\ell} = \sum_{i \in \mathcal{J}} \int \mathcal{G}_{i\ell}(\mathbf{Z}^{j}, \mathbf{X}, \mathbf{Prob}, \Xi) df(\mathbf{Z})$, from which we may write for all locations, $\ell \in \mathcal{L}$:

$$\mathbf{Prob} = \mathcal{G}(f(\mathbf{Z}, \mathbf{X}, \mathbf{Prob}, \Xi)). \tag{3.28}$$

This system of equations maps $[0, 1]^L$ into itself, where $L = |\mathcal{L}| = |\bigcup_\ell \mathcal{L}_j|$ is the size of the union of all individuals' discrete choice sets, $\mathcal{L}_j$. It defines **Prob** as a fixed point of (3.28).

Note that in moving from the individual decision, denoted by (3.27), to the aggregate (3.28), I assume in effect that all agents' location decisions form a static simultaneous move game whose Nash equilibria are represented by the fixed points of (3.28). The game assumes that agents have full information about each other's unobserved components in the preference structure, $\bar{\varepsilon}^j = (\ldots, \varepsilon_h^j, \ldots)$. Alternatively, we may assume that agents form expectations about those components of the preference parameters. This is conceptually like the social interactions problem (chapter 2, section 2.4.1), now with a full complement of covariates.

Similarly to the housing estimation problem discussed above, Bayer and Timmins propose a two-stage estimation. In the first stage, one estimates the vector of location-specific effects, $\mathcal{D} = (\ldots, \delta_\ell, \ldots)$, where following the notation introduced above I define the arrays $(\ldots, \alpha_{rX}, \ldots)$ and $(\ldots, \alpha_{r\phi}, \ldots)$,

$$\delta_\ell = \alpha_{0X} X_\ell + \alpha_{0\phi} \text{Prob}_\ell + \xi_\ell. \tag{3.29}$$

The ε_ℓ^j's, the stochastic shocks in equation (3.26) above, are assumed to be independent and identically distributed across individuals according to a distribution $F(0, \Sigma)$, where the covariance is defined over locations. One may estimate, at a first stage, $\mathcal{D}$ and a stochastic structure for the ε_ℓ^j's. At the second stage, the estimated vector of location-specific effects, $\hat{\mathcal{D}}$, is regressed against attributes of locations X_ℓ and ϕ_ℓ. However, the logic of the location decisions implies that $\mathbf{Prob}_\ell$ and ξ_ℓ are correlated and, therefore, conditions that would allow us to readily recover parameters of interest by regressing the estimated fixed effects are not satisfied.

Location choice is a special case of group choice. The system of equations (3.28) may admit a multiplicity of equilibria, but as Brock and Durlauf (2001a, 2007) emphasize, one should worry about their consequences for the estimation. Bayer and Timmins (2004a, props. 2 and 3) propose conditions that ensure uniqueness. When such conditions are implausible, one will need to deal carefully with the associated identification issues (Bisin, Moro, and Topa 2011). In particular, recall the discussion of Brock and Durlauf (2007) (see chapter 2, section 2.4.1), who develop partial identification results for binary choice models under what they argue are weak assumptions about the distribution of the unobserved group effects. Their results rest on an important difference between endogenous effects and unobserved group effects: only endogenous effects can produce multiple equilibria. Hence, if there exists qualitative evidence of the presence of multiple equilibria, it is prima facie evidence of endogenous social interactions. A case in point considered by Brock and Durlauf is "pattern reversals" in group-level outcomes. A pattern reversal occurs when the rank order of the average outcomes between two groups is the reverse of what one would predict given the observed individual and contextual effects for the groups. That is, if an analyst can predict that some equilibrium outcomes are more likely, but the reverse is actually observed, we have a case of pattern reversal, and its occurrence constitutes prima facie evidence of endogenous social interactions. Brock and Durlauf actually demonstrate that under various shape restrictions on the probability density of the unobservables, pattern reversals can occur only because of multiple equilibria and hence endogenous social interactions are present. For example, if the distribution of unobservables shifts monotonically in observables, then pattern reversals cannot occur without social interactions.

3.5 ENDOGENOUS NEIGHBORHOOD CHOICE AND CONTEXTUAL EFFECTS IN HOUSING DECISIONS

In the context of housing and other decisions, close physical and social proximity is likely to be associated with individuals' caring about the actual or expected behavior of their neighbors. Such individual decisions are likely to be associated with endogenous social effects. Sorting into neighborhoods implies that characteristics of neighbors are likely to be correlated. Results by Kiel and Zabel (2008) do confirm this intuition using data from the national sample of the American Housing Survey (NAHS), a data set discussed in more detail in chapter 2, section 2.12, and further below. The correlation coefficients between a nonwhite household head and the percentage of nonwhite heads in the immediate neighborhood and in the census tract are 0.749 and 0.677, respectively; the correlation coefficient for the percentage of nonwhite heads within small neighborhoods with that in the tract to which they belong is 0.885. Similarly, the corresponding estimates for shares of household heads who have completed high school are 0.331, 0.276, and 0.591, and for permanent income, 0.648, 0.451, and 0.607, respectively.

To accommodate such a breadth of outcomes, I augment the utility function for an individual j who is assumed to care about housing services jointly produced by a vector of characteristics of unit h such as size, number of rooms, number of baths, age, and so on, which are to be denoted by $\mathbf{x}_h$ and referred to as *dwelling attributes*, and by attributes $\mathbf{x}_{\ell(h)}$ of the neighborhood, which include location within an urban area, typically (in U.S. settings) via identification of the census tract ℓ or the community (governmental jurisdiction) in which it is located, to be referred to as *neighborhood attributes*. These may include summary statistics for the $\mathbf{x}_h$'s of dwelling units belonging to neighborhood ℓ and, in addition, housing quality attributes of the immediate neighborhood itself comprised of next-door neighbors, and so on, to be denoted by $\mathbf{x}_k$, as well as other characteristics of the census tract, $\mathbf{g}_\ell$, in which unit h lies. In addition, individual j is assumed to care about observable and unobservable demographic characteristics among her immediate neighbors in k, $\mathbf{z}_{k(j)}$, and/or in

$\ell(i)$, the tract where she resides. These are referred to as *contextual* (or *exogenous social*) *effects*. Individual j is also assumed to care about the vector of housing consumptions in her immediate neighborhood, $\mathbf{Y}_{k(j)}$, which generates an *endogenous social effect*. A utility function $V_{\ell kj}$ is specified accordingly as

$$V_{\ell kj} = U(c_j, (\mathbf{x}_h, \mathbf{x}_k, \mathbf{g}_\ell); \mathbf{z}_j; \mathbf{Y}_{k(j)}, \mathbf{z}_{k(j)}). \tag{3.30}$$

I assume that each of the vectors of dwelling and of neighborhood attributes may be partitioned into two subvectors, one corresponding to size (scale)-related attributes and the second to potentially scale-free attributes (like ambience, reputation, etc.) that characterize neighborhood quality. I posit a scalar measure of housing services, defined as a function $\mathcal{Y}\left(\mathbf{x}_{stru(h)}, \mathbf{x}_{\ell(h)}\right)$, the vectors of scale-dependent dwelling unit h and neighborhood attributes of its location, $\ell(h)$, respectively. It is appropriate to think of such a scalar measure of housing services as an *index*, and I return to such an interpretation below.

Appealing to a theorem of Samuelson and Swamy (1974) on consistent aggregation [see also (Sieg, Smith, Banzhaf, and Walsh 2002)], I posit that the size-related attributes of dwelling units enter preferences through a separable function for housing services $\mathcal{Y}(\cdot)$ that is homogeneous of degree one in all inputs.[9] I specify $\mathcal{Y}(\cdot)$ as follows:

$$Y_h = \mathcal{Y}\left(\mathbf{x}_{stru(h)}, \mathbf{x}_{\ell(h)}\right) \equiv x_{stru(h)}^{1-\vartheta} x_{\ell(h)}^{\vartheta}, \quad 0 < \vartheta < 1, \tag{3.31}$$

where inputs $x_{stru(h)}, x_{\ell(h)}$ are scalar, for simplicity, and ϑ is a parameter. The corresponding subexpenditure function for housing, defined as the minimum cost necessary to obtain Y_h units of housing services, is given by

$$E_Y = (1-\vartheta)^{-(1-\vartheta)} \vartheta^{-\vartheta} P_{stru}^{1-\vartheta} P_{\ell,nej}^{\vartheta} \cdot Y_h. \tag{3.32}$$

A definition of a price index for housing services from a dwelling unit in ℓ readily follows:

$$P_\ell \equiv (1-\vartheta)^{-1+\vartheta} \vartheta^{-\vartheta} P_{stru}^{1-\vartheta} P_{\ell,nei}^{\vartheta}, \tag{3.33}$$

where P_{stru} and $P_{\ell,nei}$ are the components of the price index corresponding to housing structure x_{stru} and to neighborhood ℓ. Here P_{stru} varies by metropolitan area, and P_ℓ varies across neighborhoods within its metropolitan area. I discuss further details of the housing price index (3.33) in section 3.5.3.1 below. Using (3.31) in (3.32) and taking logs of both sides of (3.32) above yield a regression-like equation

$$\ln E_Y = \ln P_\ell + (1-\vartheta) \ln x_{stru(h)} + \vartheta x_{\ell(h)}.$$

Suppose that for a sample of dwelling units in different locations (such as neighborhoods or communities), housing expenditure E_Y and $x_{stru(h)}$ are observable, but not $x_{\ell(h)}$. Sieg, Smith, Banzhaf, and Walsh (2002) argue that neighborhood-specific housing prices P_ℓ, as defined in (3.31), are identified (up to scale) by the tract- or community-specific fixed effects in the regression model. More generally, $\mathbf{X}_{stru(h)}$ can be a vector of observable housing characteristics, instead of the scalar $x_{stru(h)}$ above, and all unobservable attributes are included in the error. This definition may be used to get around the difficulty that the quantity of housing services is inherently unobservable[10] and work instead with the housing expenditure E_Y, which is observable, and with the components of the price index, which may be estimated.[11] I pursue this approach further in section 3.5.4 (see also section 3.9.3).

3.5.1 The Ioannides–Zabel Model of Neighborhood Choice and Housing Demand as a Joint Decision

Ioannides and Zabel (2008) develop a model of housing structure demand with neighborhood effects and of neighborhood choice as a joint decision. The estimation exploits a household-level data set augmented with contextual information at several levels of aggregation. One is the immediate-neighborhood level, consisting of about 10 neighbors, using data from the neighborhood clusters subsample of the American Housing Survey. A second level is the census tract to which these dwelling units belong.[12] A third level is the metropolitan area in which the census tract lies.

3.5.1.1 *The Preference Structure*

I follow Ioannides and Zabel (2008) and assume household j chooses among dwelling units that belong to neighborhood cluster k, $k = 1, \ldots, K_s$, in tract ℓ, $\ell = 1, \ldots, \mathcal{L}$, in a given metropolitan area and specify the utility function $\Omega_{\ell kj}$ as a variation of (3.30) to be made up of two multiplicative components. The first component, $V_{\ell kj}$, is a *conditional* indirect utility function that is specified below as a function of prices, income, and additional observable and unobservable characteristics of individuals residing in neighborhood cluster k and in the census tract ℓ in which k lies. The second, $\exp[\epsilon_{\ell kj}]$, is a random component of utility, drawn from a distribution to be specified below, that affects neighborhood choice and is assumed to be observable by the individual and unobservable by the econometrician.[13] I specify the conditional indirect utility function, $\exp[\zeta_j \mathbf{g}_\ell] \cdot \omega_{\ell kj}$, as consisting of a term containing tract-specific characteristics, $\mathbf{g}_\ell$, and of a component reflecting the value to household j from nonhousing consumption and consumption of housing services, $\omega_{\ell kj}$. That is,

$$\Omega_{\ell kj} = V_{\ell kj} \cdot \exp[\epsilon_{\ell kj}] = \exp[\zeta_j \mathbf{g}_\ell] \cdot \omega_{\ell kj} \cdot \exp[\epsilon_{\ell kj}]. \tag{3.34}$$

The term $\omega_{\ell kj}$ is defined as the maximum value of a direct utility function with respect to nonhousing consumption, c_j, and consumption of housing services, Y_j, subject to a budget constraint, $c_j + P_\ell \cdot Y_j = \Upsilon_j$, where Υ_j

denotes household income and P_ℓ is the housing price, as defined in (3.33): $\omega_{\ell kj} = \exp\left[\frac{\Upsilon_j^{1-\delta}-1}{1-\delta}\right] \cdot \exp\left[-\frac{B_{kj}P_\ell^{\mu+1}-1}{\mu+1}\right]$. That is,

$$\Omega_{\ell kj} \equiv \exp[\zeta_j \mathbf{g}_\ell] \cdot \exp\left[\frac{\Upsilon_j^{1-\delta}-1}{1-\delta}\right] \cdot \exp\left[-\frac{B_{kj}(\mathbf{Y}_k, \mathbf{Z}_k)P_\ell^{\mu+1}-1}{\mu+1}\right] \cdot \exp[\epsilon_{\ell kj}], \tag{3.35}$$

where

$$B_{kj}(\mathbf{Y}_k, \mathbf{Z}_k) = \exp\left[\bar{\alpha} + \xi z_j + \beta \mathcal{E}\left[B_y(\mathbf{Y}_k)\right] + \gamma \mathcal{E}\left[B_z(\mathbf{Z}_k)\right] + \upsilon_k + \eta_j\right], \tag{3.36}$$

$y = \ln Y$, $\delta > 0$, $\mu < 0$, $\mathbf{Y}_k$ and $\mathbf{Z}_k$ denote the vectors of individual j's neighbors' demands and of their demographic characteristics in neighborhood cluster k, and $\mathcal{E}[B_y(\mathbf{Z}_k)]$ and $\mathcal{E}[B_z(\mathbf{Z}_k)]$ denote scalar functions of neighbors' demands and of characteristics, with expectations being taken conditional on k, and preference parameters $\zeta_j, \bar{\alpha}, \xi, \beta, \gamma$ are unrestricted. The demand for housing services follows from (3.35) by Roy's identity, which after taking logs yields

$$y_{\ell kj} = \mu P_\ell + \delta \Upsilon_j + \bar{\alpha} + \xi z_j + \beta \mathcal{E}\left[B_y(\mathbf{Y}_k)\right] + \gamma \mathcal{E}\left[B_z(\mathbf{Z}_k)\right] + \upsilon_k + \eta_j.$$

I note that the slopes of the "indirect indifference curves" in (g_ℓ, P_ℓ) space, assuming that g_ℓ is a scalar,

$$-\frac{\frac{\partial V_{\ell kj}}{\partial g_\ell}}{\frac{\partial V_{\ell kj}}{\partial P_\ell}} = \frac{\zeta_j}{B_{kj}P_\ell^{\mu}},$$

are positive and increasing in price (given that $\mu < 0$) and in the parameter ζ_j that evaluates the tract-specific attributes g_ℓ. Therefore, other things being equal, tracts with better amenities are more attractive.[14] The term υ_k on the right-hand side of (3.36) denotes an idiosyncratic characteristic of neighborhood cluster k, a random variable that is assumed to be independent and identically distributed across neighborhood clusters within each census tract. It is assumed to be unobservable to households when tract and cluster choices are made, but its value is revealed once households have chosen a particular cluster k. It is thus common among all households that reside in the same cluster. The term η_j is a random household taste parameter that is observable by individual j but unobservable by the analyst; it is assumed to be independently and identically distributed over all individuals. The model implies that random variables (υ_k, η_j), which are unobservable by the analyst, make up the error component of the housing demand equation, with υ_k being a cluster-specific random effect in housing demand and η_j an independent and identically distributed stochastic shock.

The tract-specific term $\zeta_j \mathbf{g}_\ell$ in (3.34) can be specified to include tract characteristics interacted with individual characteristics. For example, this can express that households with children may assign a different weight for school quality than households with no children (see section 3.7.2 below) or that households might value the presence of neighbors of the same ethnic background or race differently than those from other ethnic backgrounds or races.

Housing price P_ℓ, according to (3.33) an index that is homogeneous of degree one in its components, is constructed as follows. The neighborhood amenities component $P_{\ell,nei}$, which *does vary* over tracts ℓ within a given metropolitan area, is standardized relative to an overall mean for the entire economy. The price per unit of housing services component P_{stru} associated with a dwelling's structure, which *does not vary* across tracts within a metropolitan area (the market for housing construction materials is assumed to be competitive at the level of the metropolitan area) and is standardized relative to an MSA-specific intercept. The price index P_ℓ expresses a key characteristic of housing markets in that both components of the good "housing services" are bundled together.

Consistently with this composite price index, housing consumption is defined as the continuous flow of services that come from the dwelling structure and neighborhood amenities. Empirically, the dwelling structure can be measured through characteristics such as a dwelling's age, its number of bedrooms and baths, the availability of a garage, and various structural quality features. Neighborhood amenities are proxied by the socioeconomic characteristics in the tract where a dwelling unit lies.

The demand for housing structure, $y_{stru,\ell,k,j}$, conditional on neighborhood choice, follows from the conditional utility function $V_{\ell kj}$ using Roy's identity[15] with respect to price P_{stru}. After taking logarithms, this yields

$$\begin{aligned} y_{stru,\ell kj} &= \alpha + \vartheta p_{\ell,nei} + [\mu(1-\vartheta) - \vartheta] p_{stru} + \delta \ln \Upsilon_j + \xi z_j \\ &\quad + \beta \mathcal{E}\left[B_y\left(\mathbf{y}_{stru,k}\right)\right] + \gamma \mathcal{E}\left[B_z\left(\mathbf{z}_k\right)\right] + \upsilon_k + \eta_j, \end{aligned} \tag{3.37}$$

with $\alpha \equiv \bar{\alpha} + \ln(1-\vartheta)$, a parameter, and lowercase p's indicating the natural logarithm of the respective price variable, $p_{\ell,nei} = \ln P_{\ell,nei}$, $p_{\ell,stru} = \ln P_{\ell,stru}$.

Again, invoking the terminology of Manski (1993), I refer to the term $B_y\,(\mathbf{y}_k)$ on the right-hand side of equation (3.37) as an *endogenous social effect*: a person's behavior depends on the actual *behavior* of her neighbors. I refer to the term $B_z(\mathbf{z}_k)$ as a *contextual effect*, a social effect that reflects tastes concerning the characteristics of one's neighbors, such as their race, ethnicity, and income. The unobserved stochastic components on the right-hand side of equation (3.37) may reflect a conditional version of what Manski calls a correlated effect: similar individuals are likely to make similar choices of dwelling units and neighborhoods and therefore have unobserved characteristics in common.

The logic of the endogenous social effect (a "keeping up with the Joneses" effect here) leads to an equation like (3.37) for each of the members of neighborhood cluster k. Thus, solving these equations simultaneously allows the analyst to obtain an instrument for $B_y(\mathbf{Y}_k)$, the endogenous social effect on the right-hand side of equation (3.37). This has implications for identification, to which I return in detail in section 3.5.2 below.

3.5.1.2 Neighborhood Choice

I assume that households limit their searches to the metropolitan area in which they are observed to live. The probability that household j chooses tract ℓ_j, from among tracts $\ell = 1, \ldots, \mathcal{L}$, and neighborhood cluster k_j, from among clusters $k = 1, \ldots, K_\ell$, is given by the probability that the (logarithm of) actual utility from this choice exceeds the utilities from all other choices:

$$\begin{aligned} \text{Prob}_{\ell_j k_j j} &= \text{Prob}\left\{\ln \omega_{\ell_j k_j j} - \ln \omega_{\ell k j} + (\zeta_j \mathbf{g}_{\ell_j} - \zeta_j \mathbf{g}_\ell)\right. \\ &\geq -(\epsilon_{\ell_j k_j j} - \epsilon_{\ell k j}); \quad \left.\forall(\ell, k) \neq (\ell_j, k_j)\right\}. \end{aligned} \tag{3.38}$$

This can be computed once the stochastic structure in equation (3.34) has been specified. It follows from equation (3.38) that, when comparing utility between any two tracts, the term $\frac{\Upsilon_j^{1-\delta}-1}{1-\delta}$ cancels out. However, income and other individual characteristics are still present through the specification of $\zeta_j g_\ell$, the household-specific terms interacting with tract characteristics and the terms $\exp\left[-\frac{B_{kj} P_\ell^{\mu+1}-1}{\mu+1}\right]$, introduced in equation (3.35) above. In view of the definition of B_{kj} in (3.36), when comparing utilities across tracts, households are assumed to have expectations with respect to v_k, which is assumed to be independent of other variables and unobservable at that point in the choice process. Therefore, the choice probabilities (3.38) are expressed as the probabilities of the events:

$$\left\{\zeta_j \mathbf{g}_{\ell_j} - \zeta_j \mathbf{g}_\ell - \frac{P_{\ell_j,stru}^{(1-\vartheta)(\mu+1)}}{\mu+1}\left(\bar{B}_{k_j j} P_{\ell_j,nei}^{\vartheta(\mu+1)} - \bar{B}_{kj} P_{\ell,nei}^{\vartheta(\mu+1)}\right) e^{v_k+\eta_j}\right.$$
$$\left.\geq -(\epsilon_{\ell_j k_j j} - \epsilon_{\ell k j}); \ell \neq \ell_j, k \neq k_j\right\}, \tag{3.39}$$

where $\bar{B}_{kj} \equiv \exp[\bar{\alpha} + \xi z_j + \beta \mathcal{E}[B_y(\mathbf{Y}_k)] + \gamma \mathcal{E}[B_z(\mathbf{Z}_k)]]$.

Condition (3.39) has the intuitively appealing implication that the larger the value of the unobserved taste parameter η_j [the independent and identically distributed shock in the demand equation (3.37)], that is, the larger the dwelling a household wants given all observables, the smaller the neighborhood price it wishes to pay. Therefore, variation of price across tracts, as expressed by component $P_{\ell,nei}$ in the composite price index (3.33), is a key element of the interaction between the discrete choice of a neighborhood and the continuous choice of a housing structure.[16]

Under the assumption that the $\epsilon_{\ell k j}$'s in equations (3.38) and (3.39) are independently and identically extreme-value distributed across all census tracts in an MSA and in all neighborhood clusters within them, the choice probabilities are given by the multinomial logit model (MNL):

$$\text{Prob}_{\ell_j k_j j} = \frac{\omega_{\ell_j k_j j} e^{\zeta_j g_{\ell_j}}}{\sum_{\ell=1}^{\mathcal{L}} \sum_{k=1}^{K_\ell} \omega_{\ell k j} e^{\zeta_j g_\ell}}. \tag{3.40}$$

A drawback of applying the MNL model is that it stretches the plausibility of the stochastic structure, as the $\epsilon_{\ell k j}$'s are unlikely to be independent across alternative residential choices. In particular, evaluating alternative clusters within the same census tract will involve common tract-level unobservables that will cause the error terms to be correlated. One can account for this possibility via a nested logit model or by more general models. See section 3.9.1.

The expected value of the maximum utility associated with the neighborhood choice problem (3.38), when the $\epsilon_{\ell kj}$'s are assumed to obey a generalized extreme-value (GEV) distribution (McFadden 1978), may be written as

$$\mathcal{E}\left\{\max_{k\in K_\ell,\ell\in\mathcal{L}} : \Omega_{\ell kj}\right\} = \sum_{\ell=1}^{\mathcal{L}}\sum_{k=1}^{K_\ell}\Omega_{\ell kj}\cdot \mathrm{Prob}_{\ell_j k_j j}$$
$$= \ln G\left[\left(\Omega_{11j}\right)^{-1},\ldots,\left(\Omega_{\ell kj}\right)^{-1},\ldots,\left(\Omega_{\mathcal{L}K_{\mathcal{L}}j}\right)^{-1}\right], \qquad (3.41)$$

where the $\Omega_{\ell kj}$'s are defined in (3.34) and the function $G[\cdot]$ satisfies McFadden's conditions for a generating function for a GEV distribution $F(\epsilon) = e^{-G[e^{-\epsilon_1},\ldots,e^{-\epsilon_N}]}$. See section 3.9.2.

The analyst typically does not know which particular neighborhoods households have considered before they choose to locate where they are observed. Ioannides and Zabel assume individuals choose over census tracts. They utilize a suggestion of McFadden (1978)[17] that the discrete choice model may be estimated by generating a random sample of alternatives from the full choice set, which may be unobserved.[18]

Ioannides and Zabel work with the neighborhood cluster subsample of the public NAHS data and rely on *confidential* U.S. census data to identify the census tract each dwelling unit observed lies in. They choose randomly 10 other tracts from among the universe of tracts in the respective metropolitan area and assume that the 11 tracts constitute the opportunity set. They approximate the expressions in the choice probabilities above by using as regressors tract-level characteristics, on their own and also interacting with individual characteristics. They also include individual variables interacted with statistics of the joint distributions of tract-level variables to proxy for the inclusive value, an auxiliary function that is included in the second stage of the nested logit model and which captures the heterogeneity of clusters within the tract. See (Ioannides and Zabel, 2008) and section 3.9.2. Their approach does fall short of a full structural estimation of the discrete choice model.

3.5.2 Housing Demand with Neighborhood Effects

The demand for housing structure equation by individual j in metropolitan area m, conditional on residing in census track ℓ_j, cluster k, is

$$y_{stru,m\ell kj} = \alpha + \vartheta p_{m,\ell,nei} + \vartheta' p_{m,stru} + \delta \ln \Upsilon_j + \beta\mathcal{E}\left[y_{stru,k(j)}\right] + \gamma\mathcal{E}\left[z_{k(j)}\right] + \upsilon_k + E[\eta_j|\ell=\ell_j] + \psi_j, \qquad (3.42)$$

where $\vartheta' \equiv \mu(1-\vartheta)-\vartheta$, a parameter, and $k(i)$ denotes the neighborhood cluster where individual i resides. Note that the endogenous and contextual effects have been specified as the means of the neighbors' housing demand and of a vector of neighbor characteristics, that is, $B_y(\mathbf{Y}_k)=\mathcal{E}\left[y_{k(j)}\right]$ and $B_z(\mathbf{z}_k)=\mathcal{E}\left[\mathbf{z}_{k(j)}\right]$, respectively.

The conditional mean correction in equation (3.42), $E[\eta_j|\ell=\ell_j]$, the Heckman correction term (Heckman 1979), accounts for the fact that the error term on the right-hand side of the demand equation (3.37) is likely to be correlated with the other regressors in the model. The correction requires 11 terms, one for each of the 10 census tracts not chosen and the one that is chosen, in the neighborhood choice model. The correction terms can be estimated using the results from the neighborhood choice equation (3.40) in the standard fashion for sample selection bias.[19] While inclusion of both components of the price index $(p_{m,stru}, p_{m,\ell,nei})$ as regressors readily follows from the model, allowing unconstrained estimation of their coefficients may determine whether neighborhood demand is a substitute or a complement to housing structure demand.

The mean of the neighbors' housing demands in equation (3.42) is correlated with the error term in equation (3.42) since it includes the unobserved cluster effect, v_k. In order to identify the model, one needs an instrument, a variable whose neighborhood average is not included in the causal model (e.g., is *not* a contextual effect). As shown by Brock and Durlauf (2001b), the selection correction terms are valid instruments in this setting. Identification is an issue even in the absence of social interactions. In order to identify the model of housing demand, conditional on residential choice, the selection correction terms, which compute $E[\eta_j|\ell=\ell_j]$, must not be collinear with the other regressors in equation (3.42). One way of achieving identification is by ensuring that one or more variables in the neighborhood choice model be excluded from the housing structure demand equation. Given that we are modeling housing structure demand, there are variables that affect neighborhood choice but not structure demand and thus qualify. Thus, the housing structure demand equation is identified via such exclusion restrictions.

Identification of the endogenous neighborhood effect, the mean of the neighbors' housing demands, $\mathcal{E}\left[y_{stru,k(i)}\right]$, rests on solving for $\mathcal{E}\left[y_{stru,k(i)}\right]$, the housing structure demand equations for all members of a cluster as a simultaneous system. The reduced form corresponding to (3.42) includes the cluster means of all Heckman correction terms $\mathcal{E}[\eta_j|\ell=\ell_j]$. Each of the 11 (in this application) sample selection bias correction terms *vary within* the cluster, as they depend on individual variables via the interaction terms in the neighborhood choice model.[20] This variation is key to identification of the endogenous neighborhood effect. Intuitively, one's neighbors' selection bias correction terms are excluded from one's own demand for housing structure equation because one's neighbors' tastes in housing (in contrast to their observed characteristics) do not directly affect one's own demand for housing. These preferences do have an indirect effect, though, through the endogenous neighborhood effect.

3.5.3 Estimation Results for Neighborhood Choice and Housing Structure Demand with Neighborhood Effects

Ioannides and Zabel (2008) decompose continuous housing demand into two components: structure demand and neighborhood demand. They model the former component in terms of a continuous scalar quantity that represents the flow of housing services. Neighborhood demand may be either a substitute or a complement to housing structure, and including both components of the price index, that of the housing structure and that of the neighborhood price, in the demand for structure equation allows the data to resolve the issue.

3.5.3.1 *The Components of the Housing Price Index*

Ioannides and Zabel estimate an ad hoc hedonic house price function, $P_{m\ell ht}$, for each unit h as a function of its structural characteristics $\mathbf{x}_{m\ell ht}$, location in MSA m, and in census track ℓ, with characteristics $\mathbf{g}_{m\ell t}$, at time t, using the noncluster NAHS data. These data offer two advantages: First, they make up approximately 90 percent of the NAHS data, a much larger data set than the neighborhood clusters subsample of the NAHS. Second, the price estimates thus obtained come from a different data set than the one used to estimate the housing structure demand equation.

There are 140 MSAs in the noncluster subsample of the NAHS. Requiring that there be at least 10 observations in an MSA in a given year for observations in that MSA to be included in the regression leaves 8,603, 10,083, and 8,283 observations for 1985, 1989, and 1993, respectively. Their hedonic equation is specified as follows:

$$\ln P_{m\ell ht} = \sum_{m=1}^{M} a_{0mt} MSA_{mht} + a_1 \mathbf{x}_{m\ell ht} + a_2 \mathbf{g}_{m\ell t} + u_{m\ell ht}, \tag{3.43}$$

where h indexes dwelling units, $i = 1, \ldots, N_m$; $\ell = 1, \ldots, \mathcal{L}_m$, census tracks in MSA m; and $m = 1, \ldots, M$ MSAs for each of the same three waves of the NAHS data for which data on clusters are also available, $t = 1985, 1989, 1993$; MSA_{mht} is a dummy variable equal to 1 if unit h is in metro area m in period t, and equal to 0 otherwise. Based on (3.43), Zabel (2004) defines a price index for the average (structure) quality dwelling unit in tract ℓ in MSA m and wave t as

$$P_{m\ell t} = \frac{\exp(\hat{a}_{0mt} + \hat{a}_1 \bar{\mathbf{x}} + \hat{a}_2 \mathbf{g}_{m\ell t})}{\exp(\hat{a}_{011} + \hat{a}_1 \bar{\mathbf{x}} + \hat{a}_2 \bar{\mathbf{g}})}, \tag{3.44}$$

where the index is relative to MSA = 1 in time period 1 (Denver in 1985) and q and g are evaluated at fixed mean values, $\bar{x}$ and $\bar{g}$, respectively. Note that $p_{111} = 1$. This price index is decomposed into

$$P_{m\ell t} = \frac{\exp(\hat{a}_{0mt} + \hat{a}_1 \bar{\mathbf{x}})}{\exp(\hat{a}_{011} + \hat{a}_1 \bar{\mathbf{x}})} \cdot \frac{\exp(\hat{a}_2 \mathbf{x}_{m\ell t})}{\exp(\hat{a}_2 \bar{\mathbf{g}})} = P_{m,stru,t} \cdot P_{m,\ell,nei,t}, \tag{3.45}$$

Table 3.1.
Multinomial Logit Model for Choice of Census Tract or Residence: Census Tract- and Individual-Level Variables

Variable[a]	Coefficient (1)	Standard Error (2)	Coefficient (3)	Standard Error (4)
Price	0.0009**	0.0004	0.0012***	0.0004
Median tract income	−0.0112**	0.0033		
Median tract income × income in 1st quartile			−0.0447**	0.0052
Median tract income × income in 2nd and 3rd quartiles			−0.0221**	0.0041
Median tract income × income in 4th quartile			−0.0030	0.0046
Median tract rent	−0.0011**	0.0003		
Median tract rent × income in 1st quartile			−0.0008	0.0006
Median tract rent × income in 2nd and 3rd quartiles			−0.0014**	0.0004
Median tract rent × income in 4th quartile			−0.0008	0.0006
Median age of house	0.0048**	0.0016		
Median age of house × income in 1st quartile			0.0124**	0.0029
Median age of house income in 2nd and 3rd quartile			−0.0029	0.0024
Median age of house income in 4th quartile			0.0147**	0.0030
Fraction of vacant units	−2.9517**	0.4040		
Fraction of vacant units × income in 1st quartile			−1.0985	0.6856
Fraction of vacant units × income in 2nd and 3rd quartile			−3.4039**	0.5890
Fraction of vacant units × income in 4th quartile			−7.8333**	1.0788
Fraction owners	1.9387**	0.1543		
Fraction owners × income in 1st quartile			2.6062**	0.2521
Fraction owners × income in 2nd and 3rd quartile			2.0889**	0.1918
Fraction owners × income in 4th quartile			1.2589**	0.2371
Fraction non-white in tract	0.5054**	0.1412		
Fraction non-white in tract × white			−0.6533**	0.1751
Fraction non-white in tract × nonwhite			4.4078**	0.2946
Dominant race	0.2732**	0.0873		
Dominant race × HH head white			−0.1862	0.1182
Dominant race × HH head nonwhite			0.5681**	0.1893
Fraction with HS degree in tract	0.2863	0.2199		
Fraction with HS degree × no HS degree			−3.9459**	0.3479

Fraction with HS degree × HS degree			−0.2363	0.2642
Fraction with HS degree × college degree			4.0347**	0.3570
Median number of bedrooms	0.0772*	0.0371		
Median bedrooms × HH size in 1st quartile			−0.2141**	0.0555
Median bedrooms × HH size in 2nd and 3rd quartiles			0.0507	0.0834
Median bedrooms × HH size in 4th quartile			0.0139	0.0776
Median bedrooms × HH head married			0.2347**	0.0629
Median age of residents	−0.0113**	0.0035		
Median age of residents × age HH head in 1st quartile			−0.0399**	0.0083
Median age of residents × age HH head in 2nd and 3rd quartile			−0.0197**	0.0064
Median age of residents × age HH head in 4th quartile			0.0125*	0.0063
Median age of residents × HH head married			−0.0051	0.0061
FML5Y	−0.0663	0.2035		
FML5Y × age HH head in 1st quartile			0.9450**	0.3216
FML5Y × age HH head in 2nd and 3rd quartiles			−0.0984	0.2619
FML5Y × age HH head in 4th quartile			0.5558	0.3271
Fraction with commute <20 min	1.0514**	0.1533	1.6299**	0.2831
Fraction with commute <20 mins × HH head male			−0.5985	0.3251
Fraction unemployed	−5.8221**	0.7005	−8.3819**	0.7578
Fraction in poverty	−2.3356**	0.3416	−3.4528**	0.3773
Natural log of tract size	−0.0253	0.0300	−0.0146	0.0311
Observations	70,092		70,092	
Log likelihood	−14, 154.6		−12, 791.7	
χ^2 Significance, all variables	0.000		0.000	
Pseudo R^2	0.0736		0.1628	

Source: Ioannides and Zabel (2008)

Robust standard errors are in parentheses. * Significant at 5%; ** significant at 1%.

[a] HH, household; HS, high school; FML5Y, family moved in last 5 years.

where $P_{m,stru,t}$, the component of a price that corresponds to structure and is invariant within MSA m, and $P_{m\ell,nei,t}$ that corresponds to neighborhood (tract) ℓ. The prices will be referred to in logs, $p = \ln P$.

Housing structure services, in logs, for an individual j living in unit $h(j)$ are defined as

$$y_{m,\ell,k,j,stru} = \ln r + \hat{a}_{0mt} + \hat{a}_1 \mathbf{x}_{m\ell ht} - p_{m,t,stru}. \tag{3.46}$$

Once the hedonic equation (3.43) is estimated, the demand for structure, according to equation (3.46), and the structure and neighborhood prices $p_{m,t,stru}$, $p_{m,\ell,t,nei}$, according to equation (3.45), can be computed.

3.5.3.2 *Estimation of Neighborhood Choice*

Ioannides and Zabel (2008, table 4) estimate the model of neighborhood choice according to equation (3.40).[21] Their results are reproduced here for convenience in table 3.1. As the discussion below confirms, their results strongly suggest that individuals like to live with others like themselves.

The structural characteristics of unit $m\ell ht$, $\mathbf{x}_{m\ell ht}$, include the age of the unit and its square; the number of full baths, bedrooms, and total rooms; whether or not there is a garage; and the number of additional structural quality variables (such as whether the enumerator saw cracks in walls or ceilings, broken pipes, etc.). The neighborhood characteristics of tracts, $\mathbf{g}_{m\ell t}$, include a dummy variable that indicates whether or not the unit lies in the central city of the MSA, the respective property tax rate, and tract-level variables that include median household income, the percentage of residents over 25 years of age who graduated from high school, and the percentage of the tract population that is nonwhite.

A benchmark model that contains only tract-specific characteristics of individuals and dwellings in the tract of current residence is reported in column 1, in table 3.1. It shows that higher price, median age of dwellings, median number of bedrooms, fractions of owners and nonwhites in the tract, and fractions of residents in the tract with a high school degree, as well as a commuting time of less than 20 minutes, all increase the likelihood of choosing a tract. On the other hand, higher median income, median rent, median age of tract residents, vacancy rate, poverty rate, and unemployment rate decrease the likelihood of choosing a tract. The fraction of residents who moved in within the last 5 years is not significant.

When income quartile dummies are thus interacted with tract median income, median rent, median age of the house, and fractions of vacancies and owners in the tract, the results show that the valuation of median tract income increases with individual income and that the valuation of vacancy rates declines with income although it increases in an absolute sense. While individuals value neighborhood homeownership rates positively, this valuation declines with income.

Interacting the tract-level race variables with the individual race variables shows that an increase in the percentage of nonwhites will decrease the likelihood of choosing a tract, with no additional effect if the tract is at least 50 percent nonwhite. For nonwhites, an increase in the percentage of nonwhites will increase the likelihood of choosing a tract, with an additional positive effect if the tract is at least 50 percent nonwhite. While there exists a strong positive relationship between individual and tract education, an increase in the fraction of residents in the tract with a high school degree reduces the probability of choosing to reside in the tract for individuals with no high school degree and increases this probability for those with a college degree. Similarly, results show that increasing the median age makes those in the first quartile of the age distribution less likely to choose the tract compared to older individuals. It also makes married household heads less attracted to the tract. When a full complement of 74 explanatory variables are included, the pseudo-R^2 rises from 0.0736 to 0.1628, and the additional variables included compared to those in the model reported in column 3 of table 3.1 are jointly statistically significant.

3.5.3.3 *Estimation of Housing Structure Demand with Neighborhood Effects*

Table 3.2, reports the estimation results for the housing structure demand equation (3.42). The regressors include the logs of the structure and neighborhood prices, and in addition the log of income, the number of persons in the household, and dummy variables that indicate if the owner has graduated from high school, is married, is white, and has moved in the last 5 years as individual variables and their cluster averages as contextual effects, and the endogenous social effect.

The first set of results, with one observation per cluster and no neighborhood effects, serves as a benchmark representing the conventional housing demand. The results, given in column 1 in table 3.2, exclude the 11 sample selection bias correction terms; those in column 2 include them. These terms are statistically significant as a group at the 1 percent level. In column 2, the estimated price elasticities for structure and neighborhood, respectively, are -0.1784 and 0.2086. The signs suggest that structure and neighborhood quality are substitutes. The income (where Ioannides and Zabel follow standard practice in housing research and use proxies for permanent rather than current income) elasticity is positive and significant: 0.2106. Household size has a positive and significant effect on the demand for housing structure.

Estimation of the structure demand equation with neighborhood effects and random effects in the stochastic structure, where the actual mean of neighbors' structure demand is included as a regressor, yields an endogenous neighborhood effect of 0.8395, which is large and very significant; the instrumental variable estimates of structure demand are reported in column 4 in table 3.2. The structure price elasticity is now much smaller than when the

Table 3.2.
Estimation Results for Structure Demand Equation

Variable[a]	One Member per Cluster		All Cluster Members Included		
	(1)	(2)	(3)	(4)	(5)
Year is 1989	0.0275	0.0347	0.0165**	0.0231	0.0369
	(0.0246)	(0.0247)	(0.0064)	(0.0232)	(0.0224)
Year is 1993	−0.0046	0.0004	0.003	0.0007	0.0038
	(0.0226)	(0.0229)	(0.0055)	(0.0142)	(0.0141)
Mean of observed demand by neighbors			0.8395**		
			(0.0141)		
Mean of predicted demand by neighbors				0.8504**	0.7254**
				(0.1748)	(0.1639)
Log of price	−0.1808**	−0.1784**	−0.0644**	−0.0772	−0.1319
	(0.0284)	(0.0292)	(0.0133)	(0.0756)	(0.0714)
Log of neighborhood price	0.2445**	0.2086**	0.0254*	−0.0624*	−0.0443
	(0.0382)	(0.0386)	(0.0111)	(0.0312)	(0.0299)
Log of income	0.2058**	0.2106**	0.0459**	0.0790**	0.0806**
	(0.0278)	(0.0277)	(0.0070)	(0.0073)	(0.0073)
Household size	0.0290**	0.0292**	0.0248**	0.0243**	0.0242**
	(0.0074)	(0.0074)	(0.0017)	(0.0020)	(0.0020)
Completed high school	0.0057	0.008	0.0178*	0.0221**	0.0209**
	(0.0297)	(0.0298)	(0.0072)	(0.0078)	(0.0077)
Changed hands in last 5 years	−0.0365	−0.0356	0.0054	−0.0033	−0.0036
	(0.0202)	(0.0203)	(0.0049)	(0.0055)	(0.0055)
White	−0.0612*	−0.0647*	−0.0115	−0.0227*	−0.0240*
	(0.0283)	(0.0320)	(0.0095)	(0.0099)	(0.0095)
Married	−0.1209**	−0.1200**	−0.0150*	−0.0137	−0.0131
	(0.0295)	(0.0290)	(0.0069)	(0.0077)	(0.0077)

Mean of neighbors' log income			0.0211	0.002	0.0609
			(0.0149)	(0.0796)	(0.0752)
Mean of neighbors' HH size			−0.0212**	−0.0188*	−0.0184
			(0.0042)	(0.0095)	(0.0095)
Percentage of neighbors completed HS			−0.0194	−0.0195	−0.0181
			(0.0173)	(0.0389)	(0.0387)
Percentage of neighbors who moved in last 5 years			−0.0179	−0.0148	−0.0288
			(0.0114)	(0.0301)	(0.0295)
Percentage of neighbors nonwhite			0.0142	−0.0185	0.0048
			(0.0126)	(0.0348)	(0.0334)
Percentage of neighbors married			0.0188	−0.0023	0.0003
			(0.0173)	(0.0399)	(0.0397)
Constant	−4.3003**	−4.3919**	−0.4949**	−0.2659	−0.7045
	(0.3182)	(0.3466)	(0.1044)	(0.6222)	(0.5887)
Observations	764	764	6372	6372	6372
Mean Observations per cluster	1	1	8.3	8.3	8.3
Heckman correction	No	Yes	Yes	Yes	No
P-value, Heckman terms		0.0004	0.4059	0.0409	
P-value, own socioeconomics	0.0000	0.0000	0.0000	0.0000	0.0000
P-value; neighbor socioeconomics			0.0000	0.3163	0.2120
R^2 overall	0.2388	0.2652	0.6155	0.4007	0.3993
Standard error of random effect				0.1355	0.1345
Standard error of regression	0.2434	0.2409	0.0460	0.1584	0.1586
Percent variance due to random effect				0.4232	0.4197

Source: Ioannides and Zabel (2008).
Robust standard errors are in parantheses. * Significant at 5%; ** significant at 1%.
[a] HH, household; HS, high school.

neighborhood effects were not included and is not significant. The neighborhood price elasticity is now negative, small in magnitude, and only marginally significant. Clearly, the neighborhood price is positively correlated with the neighborhood effects, and hence there is a positive bias when the latter are excluded from the demand equation. The negative coefficient for the neighborhood price indicates that structure and neighborhood are complements. The income elasticity is also much smaller in magnitude, though it is still positive and significant. When instrumental variables are used, the coefficient estimate for the mean of the neighbors' structure demands is 0.8504. The contextual effects are not jointly significant, and only one variable is individually marginally significant, the mean of neighbors' household sizes (p-value $= 0.048$). The sample selection bias correction terms are marginally significant as a group (p-value$=0.041$). These terms are more significant in the regressions without neighborhood effects. This is also true for the price and income elasticities. Clearly, these terms are picking up some of the omitted neighborhood effects. The estimation results for the model with neighborhood effects and without the sample selection bias correction terms are presented in column 5 in table 3.3. Generally, the results are similar to those in column 4 that include these terms. The biggest difference is that the estimated coefficient on the mean of the neighbors' structure demands falls from 0.8504 to 0.7254.

The estimates of the housing structure demand therefore do confirm that endogenous neighborhood effects are important and are strengthened when neighborhood choice is accounted for. Further, the own-price elasticity nearly doubles in magnitude (-0.1319 versus -0.0772) but remains insignificant. The regressions reported in columns 4 and 5 in table 3.2 include random cluster-specific effects, which explain a large part of the total variance of the regression. Endogenous effects are smaller when cluster-specific random effects are included. Therefore, the unobservable effect for individuals in the same neighborhood remains important, even after neighborhood choice has been accounted for.

3.5.4 Neighborhood Information in Hedonic Regressions

In view of these empirical results, one would expect contextual and endogenous social effects to be important in hedonic regressions. Next I draw from Kiel and Zabel (2008) and report their empirical hedonic results with social effects, that rely on the same data as that used by Ioannides and Zabel (2008). These authors estimate housing hedonics with neighborhood information that correspond neatly to the Ioannides–Zabel model and empirical approach. Using the same data as Ioannides and Zabel, Kiel and Zabel estimate a conventional hedonic function with a rich set of regressors, $\Pi(\mathbf{x}_h, \mathbf{x}_k, \mathbf{g}_\ell; \mathbf{z}_k; \mathbf{z}_{\ell(k)})$, whose arguments are attributes of the dwelling, cluster, tract, $\mathbf{x}_h$, $\mathbf{x}_k$, $\mathbf{g}_\ell$, respectively, and contextual effects associated with the occupants of the dwelling units in the cluster and tract of unit h, $\mathbf{z}_{kj}$, $\mathbf{z}_{\ell(k)}$, while accounting for a base MSA-specific price.

Table 3.3.
Hedonic Regression with Neighborhood Information: Log of Owner's Valuation

Variable	(1) Cluster Variables: Yes	(2) Cluster Variables: Yes	(3) Cluster Variables: No
Log of price	0.677**		1.022**
	(0.083)		(0.064)
Log of tax	−0.248**		−0.240**
	(0.031)		(0.032)
Central city	0.061		0.0005
	(0.044)		(0.044)
Age of house	0.006		0.007
	(0.004)		(0.004)
Age of house, squared	−0.007		−0.008*
	(0.004)		(0.004)
Garage	0.047		0.072
	(0.047)		(0.050)
Number of bedrooms	0.046		0.047
	(0.024)		(0.025)
Number of full baths	0.100**		0.123**
	(0.023)		(0.023)
Number of rooms	0.021		0.022
	(0.015)		(0.015)
Air conditioning	−0.076		−0.067
	(0.042)		(0.043)
Length of tenure	−0.012**		−0.012**
	(0.004)		(0.004)
Length of tenure, squared	0.026**		0.026**
	(0.009)		(0.009)
Log of lot size	0.053*		0.045*
	(0.022)		(0.022)
Log of unit ft, squared	0.202**		0.233**
	(0.055)		(0.057)
Variable at Cluster, Tract	**Cluster**	**Tract**	**Tract**
Log of permanent income	0.372**	0.354**	0.520**
	(0.066)	(0.108)	(0.103)
Log of median age of owner	0.168	0.175	0.172
	(0.161)	(0.150)	(0.151)
Proportion nonwhites	0.029	−0.263	−0.282
	(0.121)	(0.145)	(0.083)
Proportion over 25, completed high school	−0.054	0.302	0.414
	(0.122)	(0.224)	(0.227)
Proportion vacant	0.063	0.221	0.208
	(0.194)	(0.513)	(0.532)
Proportion changed hands last 5 years	0.125	−0.302	−0.276
	(0.097)	(0.278)	(0.284)

Table 3.3.
Continued.

Variable at Cluster, Tract	Cluster	Tract	Tract
Proportion owned	0.097	−0.471*	−0.486*
	(0.125)	(0.198)	(0.202)
Observations	764		764
Number of houses	392		392
R^2 within	0.469		0.467
R^2 between	0.699		0.681
R^2 overall	0.707		0.687

Source: Kiel and Zabel (2008).
Robust standard errors are in parentheses. * Significant at 5%; ** significant at 1%.

The Kiel and Zabel (2008, 184, table 3) hedonic estimates, reproduced here in table 3.3, are obtained with cluster random effects and robust standard errors. They confirm the notion that cluster, tract, and MSA ("location, location, location," three L's in their words) variables are generally highly significant in the house price hedonic equation (columns 1 and 2, which report a single regression). When the attributes of these different aspects of location are alternatively excluded from the regression, the percentage increases in the standard error are quite similar: 2.2 percent, 2.3 percent, and 2.7 percent, respectively. This indicates that each of the three L's is similarly important in determining house price. Kiel and Zabel also report results when data on clusters are excluded, column 3, which are after all a very special feature of the AHS. Doing so does not affect the estimates for the coefficients of dwelling attributes much (reported in column 3, upper panel), nor those for the census tract attributes (reported in column 3, lower panel). Yet, it is particularly noteworthy that the coefficient of the MSA-specific price index increases from 0.677 to 1.022. This indicates that the cluster variables are important in housing values and relevant for the construction of house price indices.

These results suggest that the concept of neighborhood is multifaceted. Individuals indeed care about the quality of neighborhoods at several levels ("scales"). The information at the levels of cluster, tract, and MSA can be highly correlated, but there is also independent information at those different levels each of which has a significant impact on the willingness to pay for a house in a given location. This accords with the notion that different small neighborhoods have different characters, and that their uniformity and/or diversity confers character on higher-level neighborhoods. These facts are of course very hard to measure directly, but arguably the approaches discussed here constitute a start.

While the use of the hedonic price function here is empirically well grounded, recalling the generalization of the Nesheim model in section 3.3.1 suggests that hedonic estimations are not separable from the estimation of structural parameters. This is the import of the Ekeland, Heckman, and Nesheim (2002, 2004) critique of standard hedonic estimations. Chapter 3, section 3.9.3, below, proposes a conceptual extension of the modern hedonic approach of Ekeland, Heckman, and Nesheim to housing in the presence of contextual and endogenous neighborhood effects and briefly discusses the pitfalls of misspecification. The requirements imposed on the existence of hedonic price functions make it difficult to obtain hedonic price functions for arbitrary preferences in closed form. Nonetheless, Bayer and Ross (2009) demonstrate a notable use of the monotonicity of the nonlinear relationship between neighborhood housing price and neighborhood quality as an empirical control function for neighborhood unobservables.

3.6 SPATIAL CLUSTERING AND DEMOGRAPHIC CHARACTERISTICS: SCHELLING'S MODELS

Social interactions play a central role in Thomas Schelling's models of neighborhood location decisions and neighborhood tipping (Schelling 1969, 1971, 1972, 1978).[22] Schelling (1978, 147), proposes a location model, which he refers to as a "self-forming neighborhood model," where individuals choose among locations on a lattice (checkerboard) on the basis of their preferences as to the skin color of their neighbors. His location model is explicitly spatial and aims at explaining spatial equilibrium patterns in residential segregation across neighborhoods. His results understandably attract attention: even if people have only a very mild preference for living with neighbors of their own color, much more pronounced segregation may result as an equilibrium outcome in his models. Schelling (1978, 155), proposes a second model, a "bounded-neighborhood model," commonly known as Schelling's neighborhood tipping model, that looks at features of the process of neighborhood dynamics as neighborhood composition "tips" in favor of particular groups and produces clustering of racial groups. Schelling's self-forming neighborhood model underlies the generic location model in this chapter. Both of Schelling's models are considered precursors of the social interactions literature because of their paradigmatic emphasis on the direct impact of characteristics of neighbors on individuals' decisions and their consequences for social outcomes. In Schelling's (1978, 13) own words, "[t]hat kind of analysis explores the relationship between the behavior characteristics of the *individuals* who comprise some social aggregate, and the characteristics of the aggregate." Schelling makes evocative use of such ideas along with the mechanics of self-organization to probe deeper into how social outcomes that may well be unintended reflect the magnification of individual propensities.

3.6.1 Schelling's Location Model

Let a number of black and white counters representing black and white households, respectively, be arbitrarily placed on a checkerboard, leaving some free places. Let us say that whites prefer the configuration where at least half of their eight nearest neighbors are also white to the configuration where less than half are white, and that blacks are color-neutral. From the households who are unhappy with their locations one is chosen at random and allowed to move to a preferred location. This model, when simulated, may yield *complete* segregation in spite of the fact that individuals' preferences for being with people of their own color might not be very strong. Zhang (2004) employs the tools of the theory of stochastic stability, a rigorous equilibrium concept in evolutionary game theory (Young 1998), to prove the following results: in the long run, residential segregation prevails most of the time (probabilistically speaking), vacancies are more common in black than in white neighborhoods, and whites pay more for equivalent housing.

I follow Zhang (2004) and adopt his particular specification of individuals' preferences. That is, I index utility functions for white and black households, respectively, by w and b:

$$u_{jw\ell_j} = \Upsilon_j + \theta|W_{\ell_j}| - P_{\ell_j},\ u_{jb\ell_j} = \Upsilon_j - P_{\ell_j},$$

where Υ_j denotes income, ℓ_j is individual j's location, P_{ℓ_j} is the price of housing at location ℓ_j, $|W_{\ell_j}|$, $|B_{\ell_j}|$ is the number of white and black neighbors abutting location ℓ_j, and θ is a positive parameter. Zhang assumes a simple spatial arbitrage rule according to which the price of housing is linear and decreasing in the vacancy rate, defined as $\frac{\bar{\ell}-|W_\ell|-|B_\ell|}{\bar{\ell}+1}$, where $\bar{\ell}$ denotes the number of neighboring locations at each location. This implies, when all locations have the same number of neighbors and incomes are defined net of the fixed component of the price of housing at every location ℓ, that $P_\ell = |W_\ell| + |B_\ell|$ (see Zhang, 2004, 149–150). This in turn yields reduced-form utility functions for the two types of agents:

$$u_{jw\ell_j} = \Upsilon_j + (\theta - 1)|W_{\ell_j}| - |B_{\ell_j}|,\ u_{jb\ell_j} = \Upsilon_j - |W_{\ell_j}| - |B_{\ell_j}|. \tag{3.47}$$

Note that any positive value of θ expresses a white household's preference for white neighbors.

Zhang defines the set of locations $\mathcal{L}$ as a torus with a local neighborhood structure in the form of Moore neighborhoods (each location has eight neighbors). Individuals' locations is a mapping $\iota : \mathcal{J} \to \mathcal{L}$, where $\mathcal{J}$ is interpreted more broadly to encompass individuals' characteristics. This mapping is not necessarily onto, as there may be vacant locations. However, particular attributes of the graph associated with ι are also used. Specifically, let L_w, L_b, and L_v denote the number of locations in $\mathcal{L}$ occupied by whites, occupied by blacks, and are vacant, respectively, and $E_{\ell',\ell''}$ the total number of edges connecting locations occupied by agents that are white or black or are vacant, $\ell', \ell'' \in \{w, b, v\}$. Given this notation, when summing up individuals' utilities, one recognizes that the sum of all $|W_{\ell_j}|$'s over all white households is equal to $2(\theta - 1)E_{w,w}$, the sum of all $|W_{\ell_j}|$'s over all black households is equal to $2E_{bb}$, and correspondingly the sum of all $|W_{\ell_j}|$'s over all black households plus the sum of all $|B_{\ell_j}|$'s over all black households is equal to $2E_{bw}$. The resulting expression for the sum of all utilities is

$$\sum_{i \in \mathcal{J}} u_j = |\mathcal{J}|\bar{\Upsilon} - 2E_{bb} - 2E_{bw} + 2(\theta - 1)E_{ww}, \qquad (3.48)$$

where $\bar{\Upsilon}$ denotes average income. An alternative expression for the sum of individual utilities is very helpful and is as follows. Graph topology implies that summing up all edges emanating from all white-occupied locations, $8L_w$ in all, yields

$$2E_{ww} + E_{wb} + E_{wv} = 8L_w.$$

The enumeration of edges linking black-occupied and vacant locations produces similar equations for the two other categories. For a moment assume that no locations are vacant.[23] Then, summing up the relationships among the $E_{\ell',\ell''}$'s that follow from the enumeration of white- and black-occupied locations yields $E_{w,w} + E_{w,b} + E_{b,b} = 4(L_w + L_b)$. This then allows one to express the sum of all agents' utilities, as in (3.48), alternatively in terms of the numbers of different types of edges as follows:

$$\sum_{i \in \mathcal{J}} u_j = |\mathcal{J}|\bar{\Upsilon} - 8(L_w + L_b - L_v) + 2\theta E_{ww}.$$

The sum of individuals' utilities is maximized, given (L_w, L_b, L_v), when the number of edges connecting whites is maximized. Thinking in terms of the properties of the graph describing individuals' allocations to locations, it is evident that maximizing the number of edges connecting whites amounts to segregation. But how does a particular economy reach such a state of segregation?

Zhang assumes that the economy may transition from one to another configuration as a result of moves by one or two agents at a time. Such moves may be mutually advantageous, may be advantageous to one but not the other, or may end up harming both. They may still occur because of random miscalculations, what the evolutionary game theory literature refers to as perturbations in best responses (Young 1998).[24] The probability that agents prefer allocation ι' over ι'' is given by the probability that the sum of total utilities plus the shock expressing the perturbation under one allocation exceeds that under the other. That is, assuming extreme-value-distributed perturbation shocks, this probability is

$$\text{Prob}(\iota'|\varpi) = \frac{e^{\varpi[\sum_{i\in\mathcal{J}} u_j(\iota')]}}{e^{\varpi[\sum_{i\in\mathcal{J}} u_j(\iota')]} + e^{\varpi[\sum_{i\in\mathcal{J}} u_j(\iota'')]}}, \qquad (3.49)$$

where $\varpi > 0$ is the dispersion parameter that denotes the degree of precision in the group's response[25] to randomness due to perturbations. The larger (smaller) ϖ, is the more (less) pronounced the effect of comparisons of utility magnitudes upon outcome probabilities is and the less (more) important the perturbation is.

The probabilities $\text{Prob}(\iota'|\varpi)$ given by (3.49) define a Markov process over allocations of individuals to locations. Since this process is irreducible, aperiodic, and recurrent, it has a unique stationary distribution $\pi(\cdot|\varpi)$. By Young's (1998) definition of stochastic stability, a state ι is stochastically stable relative to the process defined by (3.49) if $\lim_{\varpi\to\infty} \pi(\iota|\varpi) > 0$. That is, allocation ι may be reached if utility magnitudes that favor segregation are sufficiently influential.

Schelling's work has generated a large literature, although (interestingly and until very recently) only a small part of it has been cast in terms of formal economics, let alone formal econometric approaches. Noteworthy exceptions are studies by Miyao (1978a, 1978b), whose theoretical model is motivated by the Schelling model, Pancs and Vriend (2007), whose simulation-based approach probes the robustness of the properties of the Schelling model, and Vincović and Kirman (2006), who recognize that the essence of the Schelling model involves action at the boundaries of the areas occupied by different groups. Vincović and Kirman analyze the process of segregation by linking with the physics of clustering, which is driven by the surface tension force. The basic model in this physical analog of the Schelling model is well known to physicists and shows clearly how the "internal energy" (utility) of individuals who are on the boundaries of their own groups drives the tendency to cluster, while the rules governing mobility determine the precise form that the segregated clusters will take. These authors also discuss a range of related physical phenomena and speculate that the physical analog may provide a useful framework for studying many spatial economic phenomena where individuals' choices are affected by the characteristics and choices of their neighbors.

3.6.1.1 *Empirics with Schelling's Location Model*

The only empirical examination of the Schelling model in regard to residential choices of individuals and aggregate segregation patterns in their communities that I am aware of is that of Bruch and Mare (2006). These authors show computationally that high levels of segregation occur only when individuals' preferences incorporate a threshold function. Bruch and Mare's (2006, table 1) results for Detroit Area Studies (DAS) data show a marked increase in racial tolerance by whites between 1976 and 1992 but a less pronounced decrease in racial tolerance by blacks. Data from the Los Angeles and Boston modules of the 1992–1994 Multi-City Study of Urban Inequality (MCSUI) and the 1976 and 1992 DAS suggest that individuals do not react to the racial makeup of neighborhoods in terms of a threshold value fashion and that their responses instead follow nonlinear and approximately continuous functions that are different for whites and blacks. Their estimation results suggest that models based on individual racial preferences alone may be insufficient to account for the high levels of segregation observed in U.S. cities, although the Schelling model performs well in the aggregate. This contrasts with the Card, Mas, and Rothstein (2008a) results I discuss in section 3.6.2.1 below and must be traced in both the models and the data that Bruch and Mare employ. The extent to which neighborhoods are homogeneous or mixed may also throw light on the usefulness of the Schelling model. Section 3.6.3 below turns to a brief review of a small literature on neighborhood income distributions.

3.6.2 Schelling's Model of Neighborhood Tipping

Next I turn to a description of Schelling's bounded-neighborhood model, better known as the neighborhood tipping model. I start with an intuitive description that follows Easterly (2009) and then return to elaborate on its properties by means of a model due to Zhang (2011). Consider a single neighborhood and suppose that individual j is white and would choose to live in a neighborhood provided that the percentage of whites neighbors, $o \in [0, 1]$, is at least $\tilde{o}_j$, $o \geq \tilde{o}_j$, where $\tilde{o}_j$ is j's threshold, a preference characteristic. Otherwise, individual j would exit. The higher $\tilde{o}_j$ is, the less tolerant individual j is. Individuals differ in terms of their thresholds $\tilde{o}_j$, which are assumed to be distributed in the neighborhood in question according to $F(\tilde{o})$ when the analysis starts. For any neighborhood with a share of white residents equal to o, the percentage of white individuals who would find it acceptable to live there are those with thresholds exceeding their own preference characteristic $\tilde{o}_j$.[26] Their share is given by the value of the cumulative distribution function at o, $F = F(o)$, whose support is $[0, 1]$.

Consider the fixed points of

$$o = F(o). \tag{3.50}$$

By definition, since $F(\cdot)$ is a cumulative distribution function, $o^* = 0$ and $o^{**} = 1$ are fixed points of $F(\cdot)$. As long as $o > F(o)$, whites have an incentive to exit the neighborhood when the percentage of whites is o. This leads to fewer individuals with high values of o, and the process continues until the percentage of whites becomes equal to the lower fixed point $o^* = 0$. If, on the other hand, $o \leq F(o)$, additional whites have an incentive to enter, and this process continues until the neighborhood becomes all white, $o^{**} = 1$. I refer to these extreme equilibria as lower and upper, respectively. The process may have additional fixed points. If the two extreme equilibria, either a maximum number of blacks or no blacks, are stable and a third, mixed equilibrium, with a share of $\check{o}$, $0 < \check{o} < 1$, whites in the neighborhood, is unstable, then the mixed equilibrium defines the *tipping point*. See figure 3.1.

As an example, let the logarithms of individuals' thresholds $\ln o$ have a logistic distribution with mean and variance $\left(\bar{o}, \frac{1}{3}\frac{\pi^2}{\varpi^2}\right)$. The corresponding cumulative distribution is $F(o) = \left(1 + e^{-\varpi(\ell no - \bar{o})}\right)^{-1} = \frac{1}{2} + \frac{1}{2}\tanh\left(\frac{\varpi(\ell no - \bar{o})}{2}\right)$. Let $o^*, \check{o}, o^{**}$ denote each of the potential three fixed points. The likelihood that a mixed equilibrium exists rests on the maximum value of the corresponding density function being sufficiently high. The lower the dispersion, the higher the density at its peak and the steeper the cumulative distribution making it more likely that a mixed equilibrium exists.[27] On the other hand, the larger

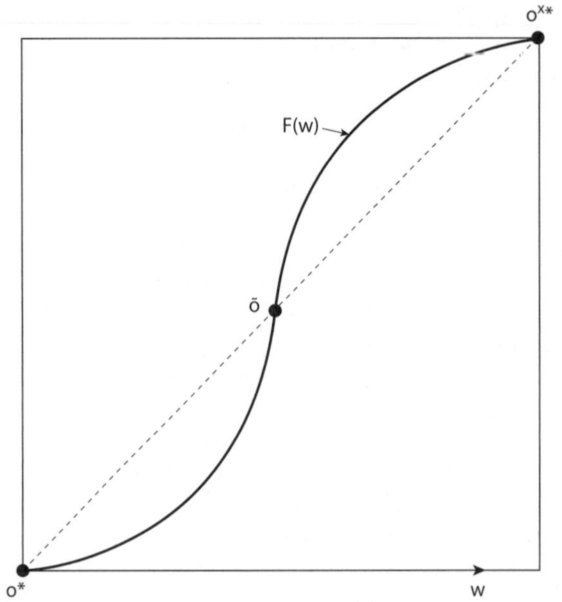

Figure 3.1. The Schelling neighborhood tipping model. *Source*: original.

the dispersion, the more likely it is that a single stable equilibrium exists. The magnitude of the mixed equilibrium point is determined by the strength of white tolerance regarding contact with blacks, relative to the dispersion in the distribution of preferences. It is higher when whites are more tolerant of minority neighbors. Although this model is cast in terms of tolerance toward members of another racial group, it is straightforward to extend with such considerations as gender, age, and income (Schelling 1978, chaps. 4 and 5, respectively) so as to account for the multifaceted nature of neighborhoods. There is nothing in the logic of neighborhood tipping that prevents it from being relevant for segregation with respect to income, religion, and other variables.

Zhang (2011) takes off from an earlier work (Zhang 2004) and offers a theoretical formulation of Schelling's neighborhood tipping model that follows logically from Schelling's model of residential segregation. It aims at unifying Schelling's two models and analyzes the notion of tipping also in terms of the concept of a stochastically stable equilibrium. Zhang shows that the property of residential location patterns that are most resistant to tipping is equivalent to a stochastically stable equilibrium. An equilibrium state is defined as being more resistant to tipping if it takes fewer expected periods for the system to return to a stochastically stable equilibrium given that it starts there. The full details of Zhang's mathematical tools go beyond the scope of the present chapter. However, there is an intuitive elegance in the basic concepts employed, and this is why I touch upon them briefly.

Individual j's utility function is defined as a piecewise linear function of the number of neighbors of the *same* color, $u_j(\iota_j)$, plus a stochastic shock, ϵ_j. Individuals may exchange neighborhoods, and in each period a pair of them is randomly chosen and allowed to switch neighborhoods. They do so if the *sum* of their individual utilities would increase, presuming that they can redistribute among themselves a net total gain in utility. Zhang again defines $\mathcal{L}$ as a torus with $L \times L$ locations, each with a local neighborhood structure in the form of Moore neighborhoods with each individual having $2\bar{\ell}$ neighbors. By referring to the sum of individuals' 1 and 2 utilities if they switch versus if they do not by $u_1(\iota') + u_2(\iota') + \epsilon_1' + \epsilon_2'$ and $u_1(\iota'') + u_2(\iota'') + \epsilon_1'' + \epsilon_2''$, respectively, and redefining the random shocks so as to be extreme-value-distributed, equation (3.49) gives the probability of a switch. The larger is ϖ, the more important utility comparisons in whether or not a switch occurs are.

For any allocation ι of individuals to locations, let a function $\varrho : \iota \to \mathbf{N}$ be defined as the number of all unordered black-white neighbor pairs. By definition, this is a natural index of segregation: the higher the value of ϱ is the more members of different races are located next to one another and the lower the segregation. It turns out that for any two individuals in different neighborhoods, the difference in the value of ϱ between switching and not switching is proportional to the change in the moving individuals' utilities (Zhang 2011, lemma 1). Switches that increase the value of total net utility will increase the number of individuals of the same color in adjacent locations and thus indicate an increase in segregation. However, moves are not ruled by total utility gain only since random perturbations also play a role.

Zhang works with the choice probabilities that emanate from the perturbed model, as defined by (3.49), and with utility functions as defined above. The implied Markov process for allocations of individuals to locations is, again, irreducible, aperiodic, and recurrent. That is, it is irreducible, because the process may move from any state to every other state, aperiodic because the process may return to every state after a finite time, and recurrent because starting from any state, the process will return to that state sometime in the future with probability 1. By Zhang's (2011, 16) theorem, for sufficiently large ϖ and after sufficient time has elapsed, the residential pattern of complete segregation that prevails is *most resistant* to tipping and is observed almost all the time. An equilibrium state most resistant to tipping is defined as the one for which it takes the least expected length of time for the system to return to it, given that it starts there and is perturbed by a sequence of "mistaken" switches. Zhang (2011, lemma 3) also shows that the stationary distribution associated with the Markov process assigns to any state ι probability given by

$$\pi(\iota) \sim e^{-\varpi \frac{\bar{u}}{2\bar{\ell}} \varrho(\iota)},$$

where $\bar{u}$ denotes the value of utility when an individual is surrounded by $\bar{\ell}$ others of the same color. The greater the value of $\varrho(\iota)$, the less the segregation and the smaller the invariant probability of that state is. Alternatively, note that $\frac{\bar{u}}{2\bar{\ell}}\varrho(\iota)$ measures utility associated with having neighbors who are racially different; the higher that utility, the less likely the respective state. Finally, the local interactions structure assumed is critical for the result. If the social interactions graph is complete—all individuals are neighbors to one another—then ϱ is invariant across states with respect to different allocations and thus all states are observed with equal probability.

3.6.2.1 *Empirics with Schelling's Neighborhood Tipping Model*

Noteworthy empirical works testing the Schelling model of neighborhood tipping are those of Card, Mas, and Rothstein (2008a, 2008b) and of Easterly (2009). Card, Mas, and Rothstein (2008a) use regression discontinuity methods and census tract data from 1970–2000 to test for discontinuities in the dynamics of neighborhood racial composition. They show that white population flows exhibit tippinglike behavior in most cities, with a distribution of tipping points ranging from 5 percent to 20 percent of the minority share. They use the Neighborhood Change Database, a panel of census tracts matched from 1970 to 2000, as their primary data source and seek to identify tipping points, which are unobservable, by selecting the point that yields the best-fitting model for tract-level white population changes. They find large, significant discontinuities in the white population growth rate at the identified tipping points. These estimates are robust to the inclusion of flexible controls for other neighborhood characteristics, including poverty, unemployment, and housing attributes. Similar tipping patterns are present in larger and smaller cities in all regions of the United States and in both suburban and central city neighborhoods. Interestingly, the authors do not find systematic evidence that rents or housing prices exhibit nonlinearities around the tipping point. They fit a flexible model for tract-level changes in white population shares in each city and find the minority share with a predicted change equal to the citywide average change. The methods yield very similar tipping points for most cities. The estimated tipping points are also highly correlated across the three decades in their sample. These authors regress the estimated tipping points against information (from the General Social Survey [GSS]) on the attitudes of white residents in different cities. The cities with the highest index values (indicating more strongly held views against racial contact) are Memphis (1.44) and Birmingham (1.31). The cities with the lowest values are San Diego (−1.06) and Rochester (−1.05). The inclusion of income controls slightly strengthens the attitude effect. The results obtained by these authors are the first direct evidence of the nonlinear dynamic behavior predicted by social interaction models of the Schelling type. It supports that model's prediction that segregation is driven, at least in part, by preferences of white families regarding the (endogenous) racial and ethnic composition of neighborhoods.

Easterly (2009) uses the same census tract–based data as Card, Mas, and Rothstein (2008a) for metropolitan areas of the United States from 1970 to 2000 to test predictions of the Schelling model. He finds that there is more "white flight" out of neighborhoods with a high initial share of whites than out of more racially mixed neighborhoods. The dynamics of neighborhood composition, as seen through these data, do not suggest instability characterizing social interactions ("strategic interdependence" in Easterly's terminology). This result is corroborated by Card, Mas, and Rothstein (2008b), who examine the racial dynamics of census tracts in major metropolitan areas over the period from 1970 to 2000. They seek to determine whether tipping is "two-sided" or "one-sided." Two-sided tipping refers to situations where neighborhoods may move to segregated equilibria, either because of white flight or because of minority flight. These correspond to Schelling's original prediction and are denoted by o^*, o^{**} in section 3.6.2 above. The mixed (integrated) equilibrium is inherently unstable. In contrast, a one-sided tipping model pertains to situations in which neighborhoods with a minority share below a critical threshold are potentially stable, but those that exceed the threshold rapidly shift to high minority composition and are thus unstable. This corresponds to the instance of the model in section 3.6.2 with a single stable fixed point. These authors argue that tipping behavior is one-sided and that neighborhoods with minority shares below the tipping point attract both white and minority residents.

Understanding fully the implications of the phenomena Schelling directed attention to is critically important for the feasibility of urban policies aiming at creating stable, economically and racially mixed neighborhoods. Understanding conditions under which Schelling's prediction holds is relevant for maintaining mixed communities. This might demand constant vigilance in terms of such policy tools as zoning and mandates of mixed income housing while market forces work in favor of segregation.

3.6.3 Neighborhood Income Distributions

Despite the elegance of Schelling's model, empirics show neighborhoods are overall quite mixed. A number of papers document both significant income mixing in the majority of U.S. urban micro neighborhoods and considerable income mixing even within neighborhoods of concentrated poverty. Hardman and Ioannides (2004) use the neighborhood clusters of the American Housing Survey (the same data set as that one used by Ioannides and Zabel; see section 3.5.1 above), standardized by metropolitan area income and household size, to explore income distributions within neighborhoods at a scale much smaller than the census tract (a representative sample of households or "kernels" and their 10 closest neighbors). Joint and conditional distributions portray neighbors' characteristics conditional on the kernel's housing tenure, race, and income. Ioannides (2004a) examines patterns of correlation among neighbors' incomes, and neighbor selection using the same data. He finds that the correlation coefficient between the incomes of a randomly chosen individual and of her neighbors is, at around 0.3, moderate but statistically very significant. Both those studies document that sorting is imperfect even in small neighborhoods, in other words, there is income mixing.

Specifically, in describing income distributions within and across neighborhoods, it is interesting to associate a typical member of each neighborhood, the kernel household in the AHS data, with statistics for the income distribution in its immediate neighborhood. For example, Hardman and Ioannides (2004, fig. 2) plot the cumulative distribution of median neighborhood income for kernel households in a given income category. On the one hand, if income mixing were complete, kernels at every income level would live in neighborhoods with the same median income, one that would match that of the entire population. The curve for every kernel income would then jump from 0 percent to 100 percent at the population's median income. On the other hand, if individuals were perfectly sorted into neighborhoods in terms of income, the median income of neighbors would be identical to the kernel's income, concentrated in each type of neighborhood. The cumulative distribution for each (segregated) income group would jump from 0 percent to 100 percent for the corresponding income category. In fact, we see neither extreme. Neighbors' median incomes are dispersed for each kernel income level, but the distribution of neighbors' median incomes rises as the incomes of kernels rise.

Another way to do this graphically is by means of a full nonparametric estimation of neighborhood income distributions conditional on the incomes of the kernels. The three-dimensional figure, figure 3.2B [reproduced here from (Ioannides 2004a, 452, fig. 2)] depicts the entire family of conditional distributions. This figure is to be read as follows. The intersection of the surface drawn by a plane perpendicular to the axis marked "kernels" yields the neighborhood income distribution conditional on the respective value of income for the kernel. Different such planes trace distributions of neighbors' incomes conditional on the incomes of their kernels. The contours picture, Fig. 3.2A [from (Ioannides 2004a, 452, fig. 3)] gives the contours of the surface of conditional distributions and is to be read in the standard fashion for map contours. Both the three-dimensional kernel and the two-dimensional contours help clarify the pattern of neighborhood sorting in U.S. neighborhoods. The two hypothetical extreme cases of perfect mixing and perfect sorting, may be examined in these figures. If U.S. neighborhood income distributions reflected perfect mixing, then the stochastic kernels would have their peaks lined up vertically and parallel to the kernel income axis. If U.S. neighborhood income distributions reflected perfect sorting, then the stochastic kernels would have their peaks lined up along the 45 degreee line. As the contour pictures clarify, the peaks of the conditional distributions line up along a line that is steeper than 45 degrees (or flatter than 45 degrees if seen against the axis of kernel incomes). This suggests imperfect sorting. The mode of the distribution of neighbors' incomes increases less than proportionately, though not linearly, with those of their kernels'. Careful observation of the contour maps suggests that, generally, the dispersion of the incomes of neighbors conditional on the incomes of kernels, originally increases but ultimately declines with kernel income. Also, the lower end of the distribution shows considerable irregularities.

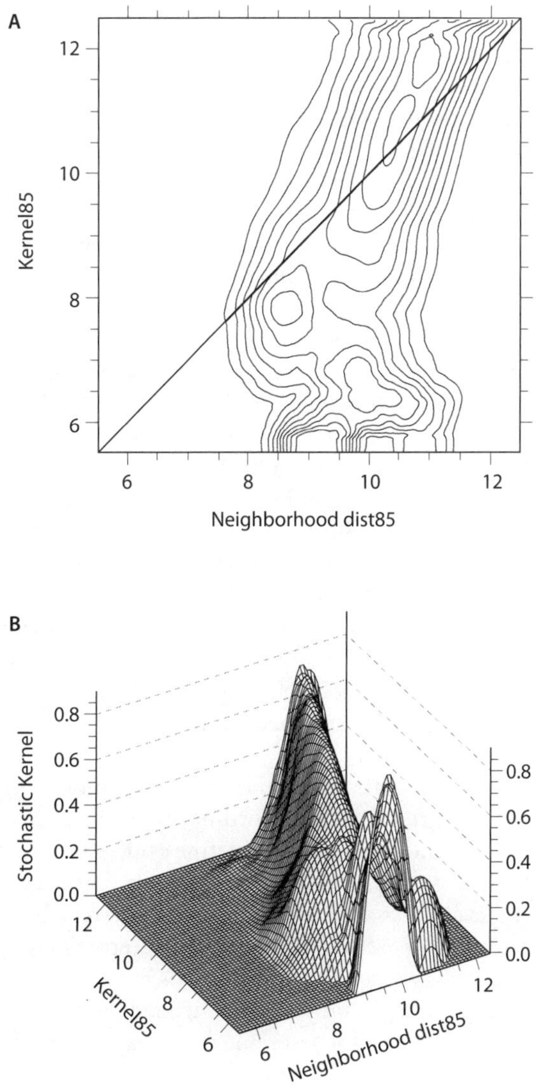

Figure 3.2. Neighborhood income distributions, American Housing Survey, 1985. *Source*: Ioannides (2004a).

These results survive even if one accounts for choice-based sampling and heterogeneity across the sample and are not affected substantially by defining neighborhoods in terms of census tracts rather than micro neighborhoods. Sorting according to income and education are similar—property values are even more sorted than incomes—but sorting in terms of age is much less pronounced. Neighborhoods of renters are more sorted than neighborhoods of owners. Metropolitan areas are much less sorted than small neighborhoods, a fact that provides an additional perspective on our findings.

Wheeler and La Jeunesse (2008) follow an approach similar to that of Hardman and Ioannides but are interested in documenting trends in the spatial decomposition of income inequality in terms of such measures as between-neighborhood and within-neighborhood differences—rather than segregation—measured as the ratio of between to total, and conduct this analysis at both the census block group and tract levels. They confirm that most income inequality within urban areas in the United States is driven by within-neighborhood differences rather than between-neighborhood differences: between 80 percent and 90 percent of a city's overall income variance is tied to the income heterogeneity within its neighborhoods. When Wheeler and La Jeunesse examine some basic correlates of inequality, they find that some of them increase inequality through a between-neighborhood channel, others through a within-neighborhood channel, and others through both. For example, they see that the business cycle and decreasing unionization influence workers in certain neighborhoods more than others. Increasing numbers of foreign-born individuals in a metropolitan area's population, on the other hand, appear to increase income heterogeneity within but not between neighborhoods. Similarly, although rising educational attainment seems to influence both measures of inequality, its association is stronger with income variation within neighborhoods. Several individual outcomes are heavily influenced by several additional characteristics of the neighborhoods in which households reside, including education, the rate of unemployment, and the prevalence of criminal behavior, and these are strongly correlated with income.

I note that the findings of Hardman, Ioannides, Wheeler, and La Jeunesse taken together clarify the extraordinary performance of the clustering models used by Badel (2009a, 2009b) to define synthetic neighborhoods, discussed in chapter 6, section 6.6, below, and the fact that they perform equally well at different levels of spatial aggregation. As micro neighborhoods, census tracts, and entire metro areas exhibit greater heterogeneity within than across, aggregation into synthetic neighborhoods may be done much more effectively. Badel's models can supply a much needed overarching theme and thus help provide a benchmark for assessing the determinants of neighborhood income distributions.

3.7 HIERARCHICAL MODELS OF COMMUNITY CHOICE WITH SOCIAL INTERACTIONS

Next I turn to models of choice of communities, defined as governmental jurisdictions that set taxes and provide public goods. This approach accounts, indirectly via the package of local public services, for preferences for characteristics of residents and the sorting that they generate, or directly via "peer effects," defined in this literature as the average income in a community relative to that in the entire economy. This class of papers are characterized by a formal structure of ordered, or *hierarchical*, choice. Individuals first choose communities and then choose housing within a community. The analytics of these models in effect rest on a single unobservable (typically a preference parameter) and its variation with income together with a single-crossing property that determine individuals' choices and their self-organization into distinct communities. In contrast to those in previous sections, these models are designed to employ data aggregated at the community level as well as distributions of characteristics within communities.[28]

3.7.1 The Epple–Sieg Class of Models

This class of models includes those by Epple and Sieg (1999), Epple, Peress, and Sieg (2010), Epple, Romer, and Sieg (2001), and Calabrese, Epple, Romer, and Sieg (2006). Their approach seeks to explain how members of a given total population, defined in terms of the distribution of individuals' demographic characteristics, allocate themselves via the housing market to distinct communities. Each community is characterized by a community-specific public good which is financed through local taxation of housing. The covariation of preferences and income induces sorting. In terms of the Manski typology, such sorting is sustained by correlated effects. Individuals who are similar in terms of preferences and incomes tend to cluster in the same community, with housing prices reflecting all available information and helping to ration access to communities. However, sorting is imperfect in these models: individuals with identical incomes may be found in different communities. These models are estimated using data aggregated at the community level.

I assume that all individuals make decisions at the same time about where to locate among $\ell = 1, \ldots, \mathcal{L}$ communities. Individuals' preferences are defined in terms of their indirect utility functions, as functions of individual income Υ, of the price of housing in community ℓ, P_ℓ, an observable quantity in principle, of the tax price for a local public good, g_ℓ, and of $\epsilon > 0$, an individual characteristic. Housing and tax prices are observable. Households differ in terms of (Υ, ϵ), which are assumed to be jointly distributed across the population according to a given distribution prior to sorting. Following Epple and Sieg (1999), I assume a utility function for a household with income Υ residing in neighborhood ℓ of the form

$$\Omega(\Upsilon, P_\ell, g_\ell; \epsilon) \equiv \left[\epsilon g_\ell^{\psi} + \left[\exp\left(\frac{\Upsilon^{1-\delta} - 1}{1-\delta} \right) \exp\left(-B \frac{P_\ell^{\mu+1} - 1}{1+\mu} \right) \right]^{\psi} \right]^{1/\psi}, \tag{3.51}$$

where $\psi < 0$, $\mu < 0$, $\delta > 0$, and $B > 0$ are parameters. By Roy's identity, this implies a housing demand that is loglinear in price and income, with elasticities being given by μ and δ, respectively.

To see how the assumption about preferences according to (3.51) serves to sustain sorting across neighborhoods, one may think of "indirect indifference" curves in (P_ℓ, g_ℓ) space. Their slopes are given by

$$\left.\frac{\partial g_\ell}{\partial P_\ell}\right|_{\Omega=\text{const}} = \frac{\left[\exp\left(\frac{\Upsilon^{1-\delta}-1}{1-\delta}\right)\exp\left(-B\frac{P_\ell^{\mu+1}-1}{1+\mu}\right)\right]^{\psi-1} B P_\ell^{\mu}}{\epsilon g_\ell^{\psi-1}} > 0. \tag{3.52}$$

Since indifference curves are monotonic in Υ and ϵ, they satisfy the single-crossing property with respect to income, Υ, and to the taste parameter, ϵ, given Υ. This property is crucial for obtaining separating equilibria with respect to both income, Υ, and the taste parameter, ϵ. To see this intuitively, consider the indirect indifference curves for two values of income, $\Upsilon', \Upsilon'', \ \Upsilon' < \Upsilon''$, with the same value of ϵ. As the indifference curve for Υ'' cuts the one for Υ' from below (has a greater slope), individuals with incomes equal to Υ'' are willing to bid a higher value to locate in a community with a higher value of P_ℓ, holding g_ℓ constant, which would thus be populated by households with higher incomes.

The $\mathcal{L}$ neighborhoods in individuals' opportunity sets may be indexed uniquely as $g_\ell < g_{\ell+1}, \ell = 0, \ldots, \mathcal{L} - 1$. This and the preference structure imply that $P_\ell < P_{\ell+1}$. According to Epple and Sieg (1999, 651), there must be an ordering of communities that must be confirmed at equilibrium.[29] I assume that this indexing coincides with the equilibrium ordering. I clarify the specifics of sorting that is likely to emerge under preferences (3.51). Next I seek to characterize the (endogenous) marginal density function for income in each community ℓ, $f_\ell(\Upsilon)$, according to the sorting model and given joint distribution of preference characteristics and income, $f(\Upsilon, \epsilon)$, across the population of the entire metropolitan area.

The set of individuals $j \in \mathcal{J}_\ell$ who reside in community ℓ are those with characteristics (Υ_j, ϵ_j) who are best off in that community:

$$V(\Upsilon_j, P_{\ell-1}; g_{\ell-1}; \epsilon_j) < V(\Upsilon_j, P_\ell; g_\ell; \epsilon_j) \leq V(\Upsilon_j, P_{\ell+1}; g_{\ell+1}; \epsilon_j). \tag{3.53}$$

I follow Epple and Sieg (1999) but simplify by assuming a unitary elasticity of housing, $\delta = 1$, in which case $\lim_{\delta=1} : \left(\frac{\Upsilon^{1-\delta}-1}{1-\delta}\right) = \ln \Upsilon$. In that case, the boundary of communities ℓ and $\ell + 1$ in $(\ln \Upsilon, \ln \epsilon)$ space is the straight line given by $\ln \epsilon - \psi \ln \Upsilon = C_\ell$, where the C_ℓ's are auxiliary variables defined by

$$C_\ell(g_\ell, P_\ell; g_{\ell+1}, P_{\ell+1}) \equiv \ln\left(\frac{\exp\left[\frac{-\psi}{\mu+1}(BP_{\ell+1}^{\mu+1} - 1)\right] - \exp\left[\frac{-\psi}{\mu+1}(BP_\ell^{\mu+1} - 1)\right]}{g_\ell^{\psi} - g_{\ell+1}^{\psi}}\right),$$

$$\ell = 1, \ldots, \mathcal{L} - 1. \tag{3.54}$$

Conditions (3.53) are transformed into

$$C_{\ell-1} + \psi \ln \Upsilon_j < \ln \epsilon_j \leq C_\ell + \psi \ln \Upsilon_j, \tag{3.55}$$

Note that C_ℓ is increasing in (g_ℓ, P_ℓ) and decreasing in $(g_{\ell+1}, P_{\ell+1})$. The assumptions about the ranking of the $\mathcal{L}$ neighborhoods imply that the C_ℓ's satisfy $C_{\ell+1} > C_\ell$. For completeness, let $C_0 = -\infty$ and $C_{\mathcal{L}} = \infty$. Therefore, all information that is relevant for the sorting of individuals into communities

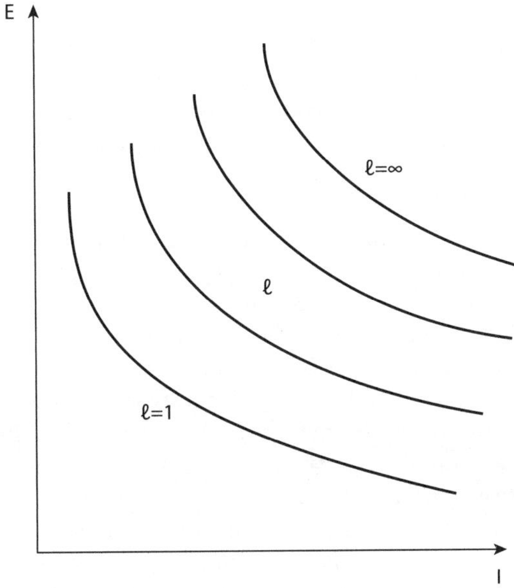

Figure 3.3. Equilibrium stratification of population across communities. *Source*: original.

is encapsulated in the auxiliary variables C_ℓ, $C_\ell = 1, \ldots, \mathcal{L} - 1$. It is in this sense that this class of models is referred to as hierarchical.

The properties of the Epple–Sieg sorting model, as demonstrated by (3.55), are summarized as follows: first, for the same value of the taste parameter ϵ, individuals are perfectly stratified across communities in terms of income; and second, given income, individuals are perfectly stratified across communities in terms of taste. See figure 3.3. Consequently, individuals' tastes and incomes are *positively correlated* across communities, that is, as we move along a 45 degree line away from the origin. Individuals' tastes for the community attribute and incomes are negatively correlated within communities, that is as we move within each of the strips that define communities. Higher-income people must have a lower taste for the community attribute than lower-income people who reside in the same community.

The number of individuals who reside in community ℓ, as a percentage of the total population of the metropolitan area, is given by the probability that $(\ln \Upsilon, \ln \epsilon)$ satisfy (3.55). This turns out to be a function of $(C_{\ell-1}, C_\ell)$, of the joint distribution of the income and taste parameter, $f(\Upsilon, \epsilon)$, and of the parameters (ψ, μ).

The Epple–Sieg estimation method matches observed community populations with those predicted by the sorting model. Epple and Sieg use community-level data on population size, number of households, mean income, median income, education expenditure, property tax rate, median property value, median gross rent, and fraction of renters for all communities in the Boston metropolitan area. They estimate all behavioral parameters and the joint distribution of income with the behavioral parameter that indexes heterogeneity, ϵ. The estimation approach rests on an index for a community-level public good (services), measured by spending on education and community crime rates, and an instrument for a community-specific housing price that may be estimated from data on housing expenditures, incomes, and property tax rates.

The model determines a joint distribution of incomes and taste parameters for every community. At the correct parameter values, the difference between the empirical quantiles of the income distributions observed in the data and the quantiles predicted by the model should be small. Heterogeneity in tastes and incomes in the metropolitan population, together with self-selection of households into communities, means that income distributions will differ across communities in the metropolitan area. This allows the authors to estimate the parameters of the income distribution, the correlation of income with the taste parameter, the ratio $\psi/\sigma_{\ell n \epsilon}$, and the income elasticity of housing demand. The remaining parameters of the model are estimated by matching the observed distribution of community-level tax rates, expenditures, and imputed rents. The baseline model with no neighborhood effects fits reasonably well but overstates expenditures in lower-income communities and understates them in higher-income communities. The model overpredicts rents in the lower-income communities and underpredicts them in higher-income communities.

Epple and Sieg find that 89 percent of the total variance of income in the Boston metropolitan area is accounted for by within-community variance.[30] They interpret this as evidence of substantial unobserved heterogeneity in preferences for local public goods, in their case a linear combination of school quality and crime. All of the parameters of the model are identified, although the price elasticity of housing demand is identified "from nuances of the functional form" rather than from information on housing expenditures. Their estimates of μ are in the range of -0.30 to -0.50.

Epple, Romer, and Sieg (2001) test the political economy part of the model, that is, whether observed levels of public expenditures satisfy necessary conditions implied by majority rule in a general equilibrium model of residential choice. Again, the model determines a joint distribution of income and taste parameters for every community. The first stage of the estimation strategy is similar to that of Epple and Sieg (1999). At the second stage, their location equilibrium estimator matches the levels of public good provision implied by the first-stage estimates with those observed in the data conditional on differences in housing prices. These authors estimate the structural parameters of the model using, again, 1980 data from the Boston MSA. A key contribution here is to show that it is in fact possible to estimate consistently the underlying parameters using orthogonality conditions derived from majority rule. They extend the analysis to estimate jointly the orthogonality conditions for majority rule and the orthogonality conditions for locational equilibrium. The empirical findings reject myopic voting models, according to which voters believe that the distribution of households across communities is not affected by a change in public good provision. More sophisticated voting models based on utility taking provide a potential explanation of the main empirical regularities.

3.7.2 Community-Specific Neighborhood Effects

The model in the previous section explains how individuals with similar preferences will seek to reside in the same communities, an instance of correlated effects at work. Yet individuals may be attracted to communities because they also value the characteristics of other individuals who choose those same communities. Calabrese, Epple, Romer, and Sieg (2006) specify g_ℓ, the community-specific attribute in (3.51) as a neighborhood effect, defining it by its physical quantity, $\bar{g}_\ell$, weighted by the mean income of community ℓ, $\overline{\Upsilon}_\ell$, relative to that of the entire economy, $\overline{\Upsilon}$:[31]

$$g_\ell \equiv \bar{g}_\ell \left(\frac{\overline{\Upsilon}_\ell}{\overline{\Upsilon}} \right)^{\phi}, \tag{3.56}$$

where $\phi \geq 0$ is a parameter. In each community, provision of the public good is financed by a proportional tax on housing expenditure, which is decided by voting.

These authors' empirical approach allows them to impose simultaneously all restrictions that arise from locational equilibrium models with myopic voting. The inclusion of neighborhood effects ameliorates a severe underprediction (in the benchmark model) of tax rates in poorer communities and overprediction in higher-income ones. Their estimates imply that relative income as a neighborhood effect is 2.5 times as important as spending. The model with neighborhood effects explains not only expenditures but also tax rates and tax bases (rents) reasonably well. In fact, the correlation between actual and predicted tax rates is 0.747 instead of -0.67 in the baseline model.

Where the public good is determined through voting, Epple, Romer, and Sieg (2001) find that the parameter estimates from the locational equilibrium and voting equilibrium components of the model lead to different results that are difficult to reconcile. The results of Calabrese, Epple, Romer, and Sieg (2006) eliminate the apparent inconsistency. Clearly, neighborhood effects enhance the versatility of the model. Lower income communities may have a lower tax base but also face a lower quality of the public good on account of lower relative income.

Specifying the quality of the local public good as a contextual effect as relative income explains things statistically, but what social mechanism does it reflect and proxy for? It could proxy for either production or consumption externalities, peer effects operating through local schools, or even endogenous social effects. In that case the model as estimated could be considered a reduced form. If peer effects through schools are the primary mechanism for neighborhood effects (as in the Nesheim model), then one would expect that parents of school-age children would tend to locate where the peer variable is higher, and households without children would locate where the peer variable is relatively low. Mean household income has a correlation coefficient of 0.57 with the fraction of households with children, 0.32 with school enrollment per household, and −0.38 with the fraction of the population over 65 years of age. To the extent that peer effects operate through the education of children, education of the adult population may provide a measure both of the value attached to education and the resources available to facilitate student learning. The authors investigate this by regressing, across communities, the logarithm of mean household income on a constant, the fraction of the population with a high school education and the fraction with more than a high school education. All estimated coefficients are highly significant, and $R^2 = 0.83$. Thus, the neighborhood effect, mean community income, is strongly related to the educational attainment of the community population. It thus also lends support to the Nesheim model.

Epple, Peress, and Sieg (2010) discuss identification and estimation of hierarchical equilibrium models in semiparametric frameworks. Individuals differ in terms of income and preferences (Υ, ϵ) and value a composite private good and a differentiated product whose quality ℓ is chosen from a discrete set of alternatives, $\ell \in \mathcal{L}$, and whose quantity is endogenous given its price P_ℓ. The slope of the indirect indifference curves in quality-price space satisfies the single-crossing property in terms of both income and taste.

These authors examine identification, given data on the shares, $n_{i\ell}$, of each consumer type who chooses the "differentiated" (housing) product ℓ, on the joint density of income and the quantity of each consumer type, and on prices and neighborhood qualities. They show that the indirect utility function is not fully identified unless it is separable (as in the earlier Epple–Sieg models) and a number of other conditions are satisfied. See Epple, Peress, and Sieg (2010), prop. 2.

These authors apply the model to community choice and housing demand using data on 93,763 properties in about 150 communities (which include the wards of the city of Pittsburgh) in Allegheny County, Pennsylvania. The data include detailed price and quality characteristics for dwelling units. In addition, they use data on community characteristics based on educational standards, crime, and travel time to the city center. They estimate housing prices using dwelling unit data, and the parameters of housing demand using census data aggregated at the community level. One of their particularly interesting findings is that households with children are more responsive to differences in housing prices (and local public good provision) than those without children. The sorting of households with children exhibits more stratification by income than that of households without children. They also find that households with children and income levels below the mean metropolitan income are more likely to live in cheaper communities than households without children. High-income households with children have stronger preferences for high-price (and high-amenity) communities than households without children.[32]

I dwell extensively on the Epple–Sieg approach and its applications because I regard it as a robust way to evaluate how the attractiveness of communities may be related to social interactions within communities, even when the nature of the interactions is not spelled out in detail. The housing price again does double-duty, by pricing housing and determining admission to living in the respective community. In the case of the earlier Epple–Sieg approach, the discreteness of the choice set limits the identification of the model, whereas in the hedonic approach of the latest Epple and Sieg-type application just discussed, the first-order conditions are exploited in order to estimate the hedonic model.

3.7.3 Combining Aggregate and Microdata

The use of data at different scales by Ioannides and Zabel (2008) rests on access to confidential data. Epple, Sieg, and their associates, on the other hand, typically work with publicly available community-based aggregate data. Ioannides and Schmidheiny (2006) aim at bridging the gap between the Ioannides–Zabel approach, on the one hand, and the Epple–Sieg approach, on the other, by combining microdata with aggregate data. Their approach demonstrates how the use of two sources of public data may circumvent the need for hard-to-access confidential data. Their approach also demonstrates the potential for use of additional information in the form of additional moment conditions associated with the distributions of observable household characteristics.

Ioannides and Schmidheiny develop a model of community choice as a discrete choice by combining features of the differentiated goods-based approach of Berry, Levinsohn and Pakes (1995, 2004) with the approach of Epple and Sieg (1999), Epple, Romer, and Sieg (2001) and Epple, Peress, and Sieg (2010). Their work rests on an iterative procedure consisting of two stages. At the first stage, they use information on the *joint* distribution of household characteristics in a metropolitan area, which in their case is obtained from the AHS Boston MSA microsample, to predict population shares and moments of household characteristics. They match these predicted shares with population shares and moments by community, which are observed in the Boston MSA 1980 census data, by means of a generalized method of moments procedure. Their approach circumvents the fact that the AHS Boston MSA sample contains *no* individual location information (which particular community a particular household resides in). Given preference parameter values β and community-specific intercepts $\mathcal{D} = (\delta_1, \ldots, \delta_{\mathcal{L}})$, the model can be used to calculate a series of predictions for the endogenous variables of interest.

In particular, let $\iota_{j\ell}$ be equal to 1 if household j lives in ℓ, and equal to 0, otherwise. The predicted share of households who live in community ℓ is

$$\hat{s}_\ell = \mathcal{E}(\iota_{j\ell}|\beta, \mathcal{D}) = \frac{1}{J}\sum_{j=1}^{J} \text{Prob}_\ell^j, \;\; \ell = 1, \ldots, \mathcal{L}, \tag{3.57}$$

where Prob_ℓ^j, the probability household j chooses community ℓ, is defined by a discrete choice model such as (3.38). Summation over j can be interpreted as numerical integration using the observed microsample from the metropolitan area as Monte Carlo draws from the true joint distribution (i.e., the universe).

This stage uses estimates of effects reflecting interactions between individual and community characteristics and estimates of community-specific intercepts $\mathcal{D} = (\delta_1, \ldots, \delta_{\mathcal{L}})$. Ioannides and Schmidheiny perform the optimization in two loops. The inner loop solves for $\mathcal{D}$ via a contraction mapping

$$\mathcal{D}_{t+1} = \mathcal{D}_t - \ln\left(\frac{\hat{s}_\ell(\beta, \mathcal{D}_t)}{s_\ell^{\text{obs}}}\right), \tag{3.58}$$

where s_ℓ^{obs} denotes the observed share of households in community ℓ, $\hat{s}_\ell$ denotes the predicted share as defined in (3.57), based on the community choice problem, and t indexes the iteration given the unknown preference parameters β. In the outer loop they search over the preference parameters.

The community-specific intercepts $\mathcal{D}$ serve as sufficient statistics for the estimation, at the second stage, of coefficients expressing the effects of community-specific characteristics by regressing them on the marginal distributions of household characteristics of the different communities in the Boston MSA in 1980. The latter is the same data set from the U.S. census that Epple et al. have also used in their earlier studies, but is augmented by means of community-specific housing prices, which are obtained from the records of all real-estate transactions. This approach is particularly promising because it does not rest on the use of confidential information.

3.8 CONCLUSION

This chapter aims at a unified view of approaches economists have used in empirically studying location decisions of individuals in the presence of social interactions. The chapter looks constructively at neighborhood effects and focuses on what we have learned empirically about their role by observing locational decisions or patterns along with individual and group characteristics. It takes the concept of neighborhood effects literally as arising in residential neighborhoods. Although many of the models presented in this chapter may seem very special, they provide, I think, the building blocks for a full understanding of neighborhood effects in housing markets.

The first class of models I examine involves models of choice over discrete sets of individual dwelling units that allow for multidimensional bundles of characteristics and lead naturally to hedonic models that account for sorting. In the context of the neighborhood effects literature, these models allow for endogenous contextual effects. I also examine an approach that endogenizes social effects, in the sense that when individuals choose neighborhoods, they recognize that their neighbors' characteristics along with their own determine educational outcomes for their children. This approach leads to equilibrium housing price functions that are consistent with hedonic valuation of neighborhood attributes.

The chapter discusses aspatial models of neighborhood choice that utilize individual- and community-level data. One class of models accounts for endogenous and contextual neighborhood effects in neighborhood choice and housing demand (with housing measured as a scalar) as a joint decision. It emphasizes a model designed to utilize individual- and neighborhood-level data at several levels of aggregation. The chapter also discusses a class of location decisions proposed by Thomas Schelling that articulate the role of racial preferences and decisions of neighbors. These models give rise to particularly interesting clustering predictions and thus merit special attention. The chapter discusses another class of models that work through the equilibrium distribution of individuals across communities. Individuals are assumed to evaluate the attractiveness of communities in relation to local public goods and to social interactions in the form of contextual effects. When considered against hedonic-type models, the housing price again does double-duty, by pricing housing and by determining "admission" into a community.

The chapter is predicated on the notion that individuals are present at a single location. Technically speaking, this is an important restriction on the general equilibrium model. It amounts to an nonconvexity restriction; unlike the basic assumption of modern economics that individuals can mix among bundles of goods, individuals are not allowed to be at different places at once. Except for vacation homes, or the special circumstances of households whose working members are not all located in the same area, this restriction is reasonable. It does have an important implication, however. As Berliant and Yu (2009) emphasize, this leads to rational expectations equilibria, which if they exist they are not fully revealing, in that they do not reveal the valuations held by those who were not successful in bidding at particular locations. Intuitively, this follows directly from the notion that housing units go to those who most value them and their characteristics. In contrast, in general equilibrium, aggregate excess demand depends on every household's demand. Housing prices reflect valuations of different neighborhoods, that is, the particular concentrations in which individuals self-organize because they find it mutually advantageous to be in close proximity to others with desirable characteristics.

3.9 APPENDICES

3.9.1 Appendix A: Generalized Extreme-Value Distributions and Their Applications to Discrete Choice Problems

The extreme-value distribution of type II, with mean zero, variance $\frac{\pi^2}{6\varpi^2}$, and mode $-\frac{\underline{e}}{\varpi}$ has as a cumulative distribution function the well-known double exponential form

$$F(\omega) = \exp\left[- \exp[-\varpi(\omega + \underline{e}/\varpi)]\right],$$

where $\underline{e} = -\int_0^\infty e^{-g} \ln g dg \approx 0.5772156649$, Euler's constant. For a mean other than zero, the respective distribution function may be obtained by the standard transformation. The extreme-value distribution of type II is a special case of the generalized extreme-value (GEV) distribution (McFadden 1978).

I draw from a truly vast literature and review here a number of particularly noteworthy developments of the GEV family of models. First, Bierlaire, Bolduc, and McFadden (2003) review succinctly the properties of GEV distributions. Specifically, let function $H(\omega_1, \ldots, \omega_K)$ in (3.61) be a nonnegative function of $(\omega_1, \ldots, \omega_K) \geq 0$, which is homogeneous of degree $\varpi > 0$, differentiable, with its mixed partial derivatives for $\ell = 1, \ldots, K$, satisfying $(-1)^\ell \frac{\partial^\ell H}{\partial \omega_1, \ldots, \partial \omega_K} \leq 0$. The corresponding cumulative distribution function is given by

$$F(\omega_1, \ldots, \omega_K) = e^{-H\left(e^{-\omega_1 + v_1}, \ldots, e^{-\omega_K + v_K}\right)}, \tag{3.59}$$

where $(v_1, \ldots, v_K)$ are location parameters. Bierlaire, Bolduc, and McFadden (2003, theorem 1) prove the following properties.

The ω_ℓ's for $\ell = 1, \ldots, K$, have univariate extreme-value distributions with common variance $\frac{\pi^2}{6\varpi^2}$ and means $v_\ell + \varpi^{-1} \ln H(\mathbf{1}_\ell) + \underline{e}\varpi^{-1}$, where $\mathbf{1}_\ell$ stands for the unit vectors for $\mathbf{C} = \{1, \ldots, K\}$ and $\underline{e}$ is Euler's constant defined above.

The maximum among the K random variables associated with the set of alternatives $\{1, \ldots, K\}$, $\omega_0 = \max_{\ell = 1, \ldots, K} : \omega_\ell$ has an extreme-value distribution with mean

$$\varpi^{-1} \left[\ln(H(e^{v_1}, \ldots, e^{v_K})) + \underline{e}\right],$$

variance $\frac{\pi^2}{6\varpi^2}$, and moment-generating function $(H(e^{v_1}, \ldots, e^{v_K}))^{\frac{t}{\varpi}} \Gamma(1 - \frac{t}{\varpi})$, where $\Gamma(\cdot)$ denotes the gamma function.

The probability that alternative ω_{ℓ_j} maximizes ω_ℓ, $\ell = 1, \ldots, K$, is given by

$$\text{Prob}(\ell_j) = \frac{e^{v_{\ell_j}} H_{\ell_j}(e^{v_1}, \ldots, e^{v_K})}{\varpi H(e^{v_1}, \ldots, e^{v_K})}, \tag{3.60}$$

where H_{ℓ_j} denotes the partial derivative of $H(\omega_1, \ldots, \omega_K)$ with respect to ω_{ℓ_j}.

The nested multinomial logit (MNL) structure may be described in terms of a particular specification of the generating function of the GEV distributions:

$$H\left(e^{\tilde{\omega}_{\ell 1j}}, \ldots, e^{\tilde{\omega}_{\ell kj}}, \ldots, e^{\tilde{\omega}_{\ell K_\ell j}}\right) = \left[\sum_{k=1}^{K_\ell} e^{\frac{1}{1-\varsigma}\tilde{\omega}_{\ell kj}}\right]^{1-\varsigma}, \quad 0 < \varsigma < 1, \tag{3.61}$$

where $\tilde{\omega} = \ln \omega$. This leads in turn to a concise description of the overall indirect utility function, as the optimum value of utility associated with the discrete decision problem (McFadden 1978, 538, theorem 1, corollary), which in this case encompasses the continuous part as well. I make use of this result.

McFadden (1978) shows that nested MNL models may be defined up to an arbitrary level of fineness. For example, at the highest level, different census tracts are represented as alternatives $\ell \in \{1, \ldots, \mathcal{L}\}$, different neighborhood clusters within tract ℓ as alternatives $k \in \{1, \ldots, K_\ell\}$, and different dwelling units within cluster k as alternatives $h \in \{1, \ldots, A_{\ell k}\}$. The corresponding generating function for a three-level nested MNL model is

$$H(w_1, \ldots, w_K) = \sum_{\ell=1}^{\mathcal{L}} \left[\sum_{k=1}^{K_\ell} \left[\sum_{h \in A_{\ell k}} w_h^{\sigma'_\ell \sigma_k} \right]^{\frac{1}{\sigma_k}} \right]^{\frac{1}{\sigma'_\ell}}$$

where $A_{\ell k}$ partitions the set of alternatives $\{1, \ldots, K\}$, and $\sigma_k, \sigma'_\ell \geq 1$. The larger σ_k or σ'_ℓ, the more substitutable are the alternatives in $A_{\ell k}$ and the more sharply the choice probabilities respond to differences in the location parameters within partition sets. The above function still generates a GEV distribution even if the sets $A_{\ell k}$ are possibly overlapping and not necessarily a partition. In this case, the choice process is described by a *directed graph* (not just a tree) where terminal nodes may be reached by one or more possible paths. This gives rise to the *network GEV model* and is in contrast to the tree-type choice process underlying the nested MNL model.

Another noteworthy property of the model establishes that GEV families of distributions are closed under location shifts. This property has particular application to properties of choice models estimated from stratified samples and/or when analysis is restricted to alternatives sampled from the full set of alternatives faced by a decision maker. Ioannides and Zabel (2008) make use of this property, which is extended to semiparametric and nonparametric estimation by Fox (2007).

A particularly interesting *spatial* case of the GEV model is when the function H is specified as

$$H(w_1, \ldots, w_K) = \sum_{\ell=1}^{K-1} \sum_{\ell'=\ell+1}^{K} \left[(\alpha_{\ell,\ell\ell'} w_\ell)^{\frac{1}{1-\varsigma}} + (\alpha_{\ell',\ell\ell'} w_{\ell'})^{\frac{1}{1-\varsigma}} \right]^{1-\varsigma},$$

where $0 < \alpha_{\ell,\ell\ell'} < 1, \forall \ell, \ell', 0 < \varsigma \leq 1, \; w_\ell > 0, \forall \ell$, and $\sum_{\ell'} \alpha_{\ell,\ell\ell'} = 1$. The parameter ς denotes dissimilarity. If it is equal to 0, the generating function $H(\cdot)$ reduces to that for the multinomial logit with all ω_ℓ's being independent.

This function satisfies the conditions for GEV distributions and yields the *spatially correlated logit* model (SCL); see Bhat and Guo (2004). The multivariate cumulative extreme-value distribution corresponding to this function is

$$F(\omega_1, \ldots, \omega_K) = \exp\left\{ - \left[\sum_{\ell=1}^{K-1} \sum_{\ell'=\ell+1}^{K} \left[\left(\alpha_{\ell,\ell\ell'} e^{-\omega_\ell}\right)^{\frac{1}{1-\varsigma}} + \left(\alpha_{\ell',\ell\ell'} e^{-\omega_{\ell'}}\right)^{\frac{1}{1-\varsigma}} \right]^{1-\varsigma} \right] \right\},$$

which implies a marginal cumulative distribution for each of the ω_ℓ's:

$$F(\omega_\ell) = \exp\left\{ - \sum_{\ell \neq \ell'} \alpha_{\ell,\ell\ell'} e^{-\omega_\ell} \right\} = e^{-e^{-\omega_\ell}}.$$

Suppose that ℓ, ℓ' represent different spatial units such as census tracts. If they are nonadjacent, then the corresponding utilities are independent, and their bivariate cumulative distribution function is given by

$$F(\omega_\ell, \omega_k) = \exp\left\{ -\sum_{\ell' \neq \ell} \alpha_{\ell,\ell\ell'} e^{-\omega_\ell} - \sum_{\ell' \neq k} \alpha_{k,\ell\ell'} e^{-\omega_k} \right\} = e^{-e^{-\omega_\ell} - e^{-\omega_k}},$$

the product of two univariate ones. If, on the other hand, ℓ, ℓ' index adjacent tracts, then the marginal bivariate distribution is given by:

$$F(\omega_\ell, \omega_k) = \exp\Bigg\{ -(1 - \alpha_{\ell,\ell k})e^{-\omega_\ell} - (1 - \alpha_{k,\ell k})e^{-\omega_k} - \left[\left(\alpha_{\ell,\ell k} e^{-\omega_\ell}\right)^{\frac{1}{1-\varsigma}} + \left(\alpha_{k,\ell k} e^{-\omega_k}\right)^{\frac{1}{1-\varsigma}} \right]^{1-\varsigma} \Bigg\}.$$

If the dissimilarity parameter ς is less than 1, then the correlation coefficient between any two spatial units cannot be written in closed form but can be computed numerically. The numerical results, as tabulated by Bhat and Guo (2004, table 1), underscore two important aspects of the properties of the correlations between the stochastic elements of two adjacent spatial units ℓ and ℓ' for different values of the dissimilarity parameter ς and for different numbers of spatial units adjacent to spatial units ℓ and ℓ'. That is, first, the greater the number of spatial units that ℓ' is adjacent to, the less the correlation between ℓ and ℓ'. Second, if spatial unit ℓ is adjacent to several alternatives, the impact of a change in ℓ is spread out across its many adjacent alternatives. This leads to a smaller correlation between ℓ and any of its adjacent alternatives. Given any pattern of spatial units adjacent to ℓ and ℓ', the correlation between them decreases as the dissimilarity parameter increases, becoming zero when $\varsigma = 1$, the MNL model. The corresponding choice probabilities are obtained by applying the formula (3.60) above. Specifically, the probability given by equation (3.60) is computed in terms of the deterministic component of utility, v_ℓ in $\omega_\ell = v_\ell + \epsilon_\ell$.

The homogeneity across individuals of the choice model associated with the SCL model may be generalized in the standard way by specifying interaction effects of observable individual-related variables with appropriate spatial-unit attributes. To account for unobserved heterogeneity, Bhat and Guo (2004) propose a mixed SCL—one with random coefficients—whereby the parameters of the SCL vary according to a prespecified distribution. Bhat and Guo (2004) report estimation results with a homogeneous SCL and a mixed SCL (MSCL), where the mixing distributions are normal, using data from a 1996 Dallas–Fort Worth MSA survey of 4839 households, augmented with land use–demographic coverage data, zone-to-zone travel data, school-rating data, census data, and PUMS data. The final sample used comprises 236 households. The dissimilarity parameter is estimated at $\hat{\varsigma} = 0.358$ and is significantly different from 1 (with a t-statistic of 3.541). Its magnitude relative to 1 suggests a high level of spatial correlation in residential location choice. Failure to account for heterogeneity leads to an incorrect inference regarding elasticities to exogenous variables and nonlinear responsiveness to exogenous variables.

3.9.1.1 *The Extreme-Value Distribution of Type II as an Asymptotic Model*

An elegant theory of extreme-order statistics examines the asymptotic properties of the maximum value of large samples of independent and identically distributed random variables drawn from different distributions. Gnedenko (1943) shows that the only limits of such extreme values once they have been suitably normalized are of three types depending upon whether the support of the distribution function $F(\omega)$ from which they are drawn has a finite upper bound or is infinite. In the latter case, a distinction is drawn between the power law tail, $1-F(\omega) \sim a\omega^{-c}$, as $\omega \to \infty$, and the exponential tail, $1-F(\omega)$ tending to 0 exponentially fast as $\omega \to \infty$. The latter case is of particular interest, as it is the case that yields the extreme-value distribution of type II as its limit.

Specifically, let $\frac{d}{d\omega}\frac{1-F(\omega)}{f(\omega)} \to 0$ as $\omega \to \infty$; then the standardized variable $\tilde{\omega}_n = \frac{\omega_{nn}-a_n}{b_n}$, with $a_n = F^{-1}(1-\frac{1}{n})$, $b_n^{-1} = nf(a_n)$, has an extreme-value distribution with probability distribution and density functions given by $e^{-e^{-\omega}}$ and $e^{-\omega-e^{-\omega}}$, respectively. Interestingly, the three types of limiting extreme value distributions are all related by simple transformations to the exponential distribution, as reported by Gnedenko (1943) and Cox and Hinkley (1974, 473).

Ellickson (1981) was the first to recognize that competition for land sites ushers in, under certain conditions, a distribution of random variables that asymptotically obeys an extreme-value of type II distribution, thus obviating the need to make an explicit assumption about stochastic shocks. Horowitz (1986) extends the bidding model for housing markets to account for some institutional characteristics of housing markets. Jaïbi and ten Raa (1998a, 1998b) revisit these asymptotic theory equivalence results and affirm the logit model as the limiting distribution, where both the systematic part of utility and the taste shocks contribute to choice. These authors link extreme-value theory explicitly with the choice model and show the following. First, if the upper tail of the underlying probability function $F(\omega)$ is thin, that is, $1-F(\omega)$ decays very fast, then the deterministic components of utility dominate choice. Second, if it is thick, uncertainty dominates the deterministic components, and choice is determined by relative sample sizes and is random. Third, if $1-F(\omega)$ decays exponentially, then the choice probabilities are given by the logit model and express a trade-off between the systematic and random components of utility. This area deserves additional attention and, in particular, the normalization necessary for the asymptotic results, too, must be embedded in the choice model. And, as an asymptotic theory it requires appropriately large samples.

3.9.2 Appendix B: A Simplified Neighborhood Choice Model

3.9.2.1 *Stochastic Specification of Unobservables in the Neighborhood Choice Problem*

This appendix provides details about the neighborhood choice model. The specification of the stochastic structure of $\epsilon_{\ell kj}$ in equation (3.34) allows one to model the choice of neighborhood as a discrete choice [McFadden (1978)]. I assume that households limit their housing search to the metropolitan area in which they are observed. The probability that individual j chooses tract ℓ_j from among tracts $\ell = 1, \ldots, \mathcal{L}$, and neighborhood cluster k_j from among clusters $k = 1, \ldots, K_\ell$, is given by the probability of the event:

$$(\zeta_j g_{\ell_j} - \zeta_j g_\ell) - \frac{1}{\mu+1}\left(\exp[\tilde{B}_{k_j j}]\exp[\upsilon_{k_j}]P_{\ell_j}^{\mu+1}\right.$$
$$\left. - \exp[\tilde{B}_{kj}]\exp[\upsilon_k]P_\ell^{\mu+1}\right) e^{\bar{\alpha}+\xi z_j+\eta_j} \geq -(\epsilon_{\ell_j k_j j} - \epsilon_{\ell kj}); \quad \forall(\ell, k) \neq (\ell_j, k_j), \tag{3.62}$$

where I allow for the more general case with households observing a cluster-specific term υ_k. I note that neighborhood choice is affected by υ_k, and this introduces dependence among observations for individuals who choose to locate in the same neighborhood cluster. Under the assumption that individuals do not observe the υ_k's, we may take expectations of the choice probabilities. This step is facilitated by the assumption that the υ_k's are uncorrelated with the other random variables in these expressions.

I acknowledge that such sorting on unobservables is not accounted for directly in the neighborhood choice model estimated by Ioannides and Zabel and discussed in the main body of the chapter. Here I explore the consequences of the model in its generality before I return to clarify the shortcuts employed in estimating the model. The interdependence of neighbors' demands, however, does receive a lot of attention in estimating the continuous housing demand part of the model.

If the $\epsilon_{\ell kj}$'s are independent and have identical extreme-value distributions across all census tracts in an MSA and in all neighborhood clusters within them, the choice probabilities are given by the multinomial logit model. A problem with this MNL model is that the $\epsilon_{\ell kj}$'s are unlikely to be independent across alternative residential choices within the same neighborhood. That is, alternative cluster choices within the same census tract will include common tract-level unobservables that will cause their error terms to be correlated. In order to capture this dependence, define the set C_ℓ, $\ell = 1, \ldots, \mathcal{L}$, to be the set of clusters in census tract ℓ and let $K_\ell = |C_\ell|$. One can think of a hierarchical structure where the C_ℓ's constitute one level and the census tracts another. At the lower level, that is, conditional on a tract, characteristics of clusters within a tract that are reflected in the $\epsilon_{\ell kj}$'s are assumed to be correlated. At the higher level, characteristics of clusters across census tracts are assumed to be uncorrelated. Also, conditional on the choice of a census tract, the cluster choices are assumed to be independent. Such a structure is the basis for the nested multinomial logit model.

Under the assumption of a nested MNL structure for the $\epsilon_{\ell kj}$'s, the dependence of choices over a set of $k=1,\ldots,K_\ell$ clusters within tract ℓ may be described in terms of a parameter ς, $\varsigma\in[0,1]$, which denotes the degree of similarity as reflected in the unobserved component of the evaluation of alternative clusters within each tract. If $\varsigma=0$, then the model implies that alternatives within each tract are independent, and the MNL model applies within each tract as well. In that case, the choice probabilities are given by equation (3.40). If $\varsigma\to 1$, the other extreme holds, and alternatives within a tract are perceived as identical. The model then implies that the choice is made in terms of the maximum value of the utility function, a deterministic quantity.

The first stage of the standard estimation strategy for the nested MNL model is to estimate the cluster choice model conditional on census tract choice using the MNL structure. Let $\mathcal{T}_\ell$ denote the tract-specific *inclusive* value associated with the choice process over K_ℓ neighborhood clusters within tract ℓ by individual j:

$$\mathcal{T}_{\ell j}=\ln\left(\sum_{k=1}^{K_\ell}\frac{1}{K_\ell}\exp\left[\frac{1}{1-\varsigma}\exp\left[-\frac{P_\ell^{\mu+1}}{\mu+1}\exp\left[\bar{\alpha}+\xi z_j+\eta_j\right]\right.\right.\right.$$
$$\left.\left.\left.\times\exp\left\{\beta B_y(\mathbf{Y}_k)+\gamma B_z(\mathbf{Z}_k)+\upsilon_k\right\}\right]\right]\right). \tag{3.63}$$

The probability of individual j's choosing tract ℓ_j from her choice set, $\ell=1,\ldots,\mathcal{L}_j$, becomes

$$\mathrm{Prob}_{\ell_j}=\frac{\exp\left[(1-\varsigma)\ln K_{\ell_j}+\zeta_j g_{\ell_j}+(1-\varsigma)\mathcal{T}_{\ell_j}\right]}{\sum_{j=1}^{\mathcal{L}_j}\exp\left[(1-\varsigma)\ln K_\ell+\zeta_j g_j+(1-\varsigma)\mathcal{T}_j\right]}. \tag{3.64}$$

Since the analyst does not observe multiple clusters in a tract, one cannot estimate the first stage of the nested MNL model, and hence we cannot calculate $\mathcal{T}_\ell$. As part of the neighborhood choice model one should estimate the inclusive value based on the results of the cluster choice model and use it in the tract choice equation (3.64). In view of the data, with an average of 500 clusters in a typical tract, it is appropriate to treat summing over k on the right-hand side of equation (3.63) as taking expectations. Hence one can proxy for $\mathcal{T}_\ell$ by using statistics of the joint distributions of tract variables that are included in the decennial censuses interacted with individual variables. This generalizes the approximation suggested by McFadden (1978, 550) and captures some of the heterogeneity in the tract in relation to individual characteristics. Alternatively, one can see the role played by K_ℓ, the number of alternatives evaluated.

3.9.2.2 Selection Correction Terms

I draw from the study by Dubin (1985) and report here for completeness the specific form of the sample selection bias correction terms included in the housing structure demand equation (3.42). The formulas were first used by Dubin and McFadden (1984). The mean of $\epsilon_{\ell kj}$, conditional on alternative ℓ_j being chosen according to the MNL model, is given by

$$E[\epsilon_\ell | \ell = \ell_j] = -\frac{\varpi\sqrt{3}}{\pi}\ln[\text{Prob}_{\ell_j}], \tag{3.65}$$

$$E[\epsilon_\ell | \ell \neq \ell_j] = \frac{\varpi\sqrt{3}}{\pi}\frac{\text{Prob}_\ell}{1-\text{Prob}_\ell}\ell n[\text{Prob}_\ell],\ \ell = 1, \ldots, \mathcal{L}_j, \ell \neq \ell_j, \tag{3.66}$$

where Prob_ℓ is the probability of choosing tract ℓ, given by equation (3.40), and the distribution of ϵ_ℓ, given by

$$\text{Prob}\{\epsilon_\ell \leq \varepsilon\} = e^{-e^{-\varepsilon\frac{\pi}{\varpi\sqrt{3}}-\underline{e}}}, \tag{3.67}$$

has an unconditional mean of zero and an unconditional variance equal to $\frac{\varpi^2}{2}$, and $\underline{e} = -\int_0^\infty e^{-g}\ln g dg = 0.5772156649\ldots$, is Euler's constant. These formulas must be modified if the nested MNL model is assumed. See (Dubin 1985, 229, theorem B.2.2).

The unconditional mean and variance of the stochastic shock in the continuous equation for housing demand, η_j, are 0 and σ_η^2, respectively. The distribution of η_j conditional on $(\epsilon_1, \ldots, \epsilon_{\mathcal{L}_j})$ has mean $(\sqrt{2}\frac{\sigma_\eta}{\varpi})\sum_{m=1}^{\mathcal{L}_j}\text{CC}_m\epsilon_m$ and variance $\sigma^2(1-\sum_{m=1}^{\mathcal{L}_\ell}\text{CC}_m^2)$, where CC_m is the correlation coefficient of η_j and ϵ_m. The CC_m's satisfy $\sum_{m=1}^{\mathcal{L}_j}\text{CC}_m = 0$, and $\sum_{m=1}^{\mathcal{L}_j}\text{CC}_m^2 < 1$.

The mean of η_j conditional on choice ℓ_j is given for the case of the MNL model by

$$E[\eta_j | \ell = \ell_j] = \frac{\sigma_\eta\sqrt{6}}{\pi}\left[\sum_{\ell=1}^{\mathcal{L}_j}\text{CC}_\ell\frac{\text{Prob}_\ell}{1-\text{Prob}_\ell}\ln[\text{Prob}_\ell] - \text{CC}_{\ell_j}\frac{\ln[\text{Prob}_{\ell_j}]}{1-\text{Prob}_{\ell_j}}\right], \tag{3.68}$$

where CC_{ℓ_j} is the correlation coefficient of η_i and $\epsilon_{\ell_j j}$. Therefore, consideration of the dependence between the random shock determining tract choice and the individual shock affecting housing demand, $(\epsilon_{\ell kj}, \eta_j)$, introduces the correlation coefficients, $(\text{CC}_1, \ldots, \text{CC}_{\mathcal{L}_j})$, between those shocks as additional unknown parameters to be estimated. The conditional second moments for the entire family of generalized extreme-value distributions (see section 3.9.2) exist in closed form and are given by Dubin (1985, app. A). Dubin's formulas can be applied to the special case of the nested MNL model.

3.9.2.3 *Treatment of Cluster-specific Effects*

Since υ_k is a random variable assumed to be uncorrelated with the other cluster-specific variables, $B_y(\mathbf{Y}_k)$ and $B_z(\mathbf{Z}_k)$, I simplify this step by assuming that individuals do not observe the value of υ_k until after they have actually chosen a particular tract. For any set of parameter values and observed tract-specific frequencies for $B_y(\mathbf{Y}_k)$ and $B_z(\mathbf{Z}_k)$, the respective terms on the right-hand side of equation (3.63) may be computed. However, these considerations do not eliminate η_j from the right-hand side of equation (3.63), an individual's unobservable characteristic. Neither does it factor out in the definition of the tract choice probability (3.64). Thus, tract choice induces a correlation between the unobservable individual characteristic in the continuous demand equation (3.42) and the unobservable shock in the tract choice equation (3.62) or the more general equations (3.64) and (3.63). This correlation may depend on various observable individual and tract characteristics and cannot be handled formally by the approach of Ioannides and Zabel (2008).

3.9.3 Appendix C: Modern Hedonic Theory and Housing Decisions

Hedonic theory applies naturally to housing. Different dwelling units are differentiated by space and by numerous other characteristics. Applying the hedonic theory of Ekeland, Heckman, and Nesheim (2004) to housing raises some formidable issues and at the same time helps firm up numerous loose ends. The arguments of utility and production functions are indexed by location, ℓ, and at the spatial equilibrium utility and profit must be invariant to location. An additional layer of complexity is introduced by social interactions. The notion that the hedonic function cannot be specified arbitrarily and independently of preferences extends naturally to the case where individuals value not only structural characteristics of dwelling units but also attributes of the neighborhoods in which they lie. As the solution to the Nesheim model of sorting in section 3.3 shows, social interactions impose stringent conditions on the solutions of endogenous quantities of interest as functions of observables. A number of papers by Ekeland, Heckman, Matzkin, and Nesheim, with the one by Heckman, Matzkin, and Nesheim (2009) being the most recent, revisit the conceptual foundations of general hedonic models but without social interactions. These authors show that the logic of hedonic models poses serious issues of misspecification, which have been systematically overlooked, and that commonly made assumptions in many applications with hedonic models imply very specific functional forms for the dependence of endogenous quantities of interest on observables. Arbitrary assumptions made in order to carry out hedonic regressions would be consistent with those conditions only by coincidence.

I sketch how the work of Ekeland, Heckman, and Nesheim (2004) may be applied to housing decisions in the presence of social interactions. I define the utility function as a function of vectors of characteristics of housing (which could include spatial variables), $\mathbf{X}$; of nonhousing consumption, c; of observable and unobservable characteristics (to the econometrician) of the individual, $(\mathbf{Z}, \epsilon)$; and of preference parameters common across all individuals, A: $\Omega(c, \mathbf{X}; \mathbf{Z}, \epsilon; A)$. Let $p(\mathbf{X})$ denote the hedonic price function, a function of observable housing characteristics, and Υ an individual's income. Both the utility and the hedonic price functions are assumed to be twice differentiable. From the budget constraint, we have that $c = \Upsilon - P(\mathbf{X})$. I substitute into the utility function,

$$\Omega(\Upsilon - P(\mathbf{X}), \mathbf{X}; \mathbf{Z}, \epsilon; A),$$

and maximize with respect to $\mathbf{X}$. The first-order conditions for an individual's utility maximization problem with respect to characteristics $\mathbf{X}$ are

$$\Omega_{\mathbf{X}}(\Upsilon - P(\mathbf{X}), \mathbf{X}; \mathbf{Z}, \epsilon; A) - P_{\mathbf{X}}(\mathbf{X})\Omega_c(\Upsilon - P(\mathbf{X}), \mathbf{X}; \mathbf{Z}, \epsilon) = 0. \qquad (3.69)$$

These are the familiar conditions (in vector form) that express equality of the marginal rate of substitution between any two characteristics to the respective price ratios, where the latter are understood as marginal prices.

The second-order conditions require that $\Omega_{\mathbf{XX}}(\Upsilon - P(\mathbf{X}), \mathbf{X}; \mathbf{Z}, \epsilon; A)$ be negative definite when evaluated at the optimum. This restriction also involves the hedonic price function, which is of course endogenous. Given an individual's characteristics, $(\mathbf{Z}, \epsilon)$, one may conceptually solve the utility maximization conditions (3.69) for the optimal housing attributes. Alternatively, for each location in the characteristics space, these conditions characterize the set of individuals who choose that location.

On the supply side, firms choose attributes $\mathbf{X}$ so as to maximize profits, $P(\mathbf{X}) - \Gamma(\mathbf{X}, q, \eta, B)$, where (q, η) denote observable and unobservable characteristics of firms and B denotes cost parameters common across firms. The first-order conditions with respect to the vector $\mathbf{X}$ for firms are

$$P_{\mathbf{X}}(\mathbf{X}) - \Gamma_{\mathbf{X}}(\mathbf{X}; q, \eta; B) = 0. \qquad (3.70)$$

Again, these are in vector form the familiar conditions that express equality of the marginal revenues to the marginal costs for each characteristic. The second-order conditions require that $P_{\mathbf{XX}}(\mathbf{X}) - \Gamma_{\mathbf{XX}}(\mathbf{X}; q, \eta; B)$ be negative definite at the optimum. As Ekeland et al. indicate, the second-order conditions are assumed to hold as strict inequalities, $\Gamma_{\mathbf{XX}}\mathbf{X}\eta'$ is negative definite and $\Omega_{\mathbf{X}\epsilon'} - P_{\mathbf{X}}\Omega_{\mathbf{X}\epsilon}$ positive definite. These conditions guarantee positive sorting on unobservables in the sense that, in equilibrium, $\frac{\partial \eta}{\partial \mathbf{X}}$ and $\frac{\partial \epsilon}{\partial \mathbf{X}}$ are positive definite.

For equilibrium, the quantities of characteristics must be equated at every value of $\mathbf{X}$. That is, the density of the quantity demanded must be equal to the density of the quantity supplied at every value of $\mathbf{X}$, which are characterized by (3.69) and (3.70), respectively. In order to express the equilibrium conditions, the unobservables must be obtained as functions of observables, $(\mathbf{X}, P(\mathbf{X}))$:

$$\epsilon = \epsilon(\mathbf{X}, P(\mathbf{X}), P_{\mathbf{X}}(\mathbf{X}), Z, A), \quad \eta = \eta(\mathbf{X}, P(\mathbf{X}), P_{\mathbf{X}}(\mathbf{X}), q, B). \qquad (3.71)$$

The implicit function theorem, applied locally, guarantees that the first-order conditions (3.69) and (3.70) may be solved as above. The stochastic assumptions about the unobservables, ϵ and η, whose densities are denoted by $f_{(\epsilon)}$ and $f_{(\eta)}$, respectively, along with the exogenous densities for observable characteristics of individuals and firms, $(\mathbf{Z}, q)$, $f_{(\mathbf{Z})}$, and $f_{(q)}$, over their respective supports, $\mathcal{Z}$ and $\mathcal{Q}$, induce densities for the characteristics demanded and the characteristics supplied.

Thus, using the standard change of variable and integrating over the exogenous densities $f_{(\mathbf{Z})}$ and $f_{(q)}$, I equate quantities of characteristics demanded with characteristics supplied and have

$$\int_{\mathcal{Z}} f_{(\epsilon)}(\epsilon(\mathbf{X}, P(\mathbf{X}), P_{\mathbf{X}}(\mathbf{X}), z, A)) \det \left[\frac{\partial \epsilon(\mathbf{X}, P(\mathbf{X}), P_{\mathbf{X}}(\mathbf{X}), z, A)}{\partial \mathbf{X}'} \right] f_{(\mathbf{Z})}(\mathbf{Z}) d\mathbf{Z}$$

$$= \int_{\mathcal{Q}} f_{(\eta)}(\eta(\mathbf{X}, P(\mathbf{X}), P_{\mathbf{X}}(\mathbf{X}), q, B)) \det \left[\frac{\partial \eta(\mathbf{X}, P(\mathbf{X}), P_{\mathbf{X}}(\mathbf{X}), q, B)}{\partial \mathbf{X}'} \right] f_{(q)}(q) dq. \tag{3.72}$$

Equation (3.72) is a partial differential equation in the unknown hedonic price function $P(\mathbf{X})$, that is very difficult to solve, in general. In addition, boundary conditions are provided by the feasibility conditions for participants. Individuals must receive at least their reservation utilities, and firms must earn nonnegative profits. It is therefore clear that an arbitrary specification for $P(\mathbf{X})$ would only by chance coincide with the actual solution to (3.72).

Some very special cases may be solved. In particular, linear quadratic specifications of $\Omega \equiv \Upsilon - P(\mathbf{X}) + \epsilon' - \frac{1}{2}\mathbf{X}'\mathbf{A}\mathbf{X}$ and $\Gamma \equiv \eta' + \frac{1}{2}\mathbf{X}'\mathbf{B}\mathbf{X}$ allow one to guess that the hedonic price function is quadratic in the characteristics $\mathbf{X}$, $P(\mathbf{X}) = p_0 + \Pi_1'\mathbf{X} + \frac{1}{2}\mathbf{X}'\Pi_2\mathbf{X}$, where p_0, Π_1, Π_2, are a scalar, a vector, and a matrix of parameters, respectively. The first-order conditions for individuals and firms are linear in $\mathbf{X}$. With additional assumptions on the distribution of the unobservables ϵ and η, identification and estimation of the unknown parameters may be established. Equilibrium is characterized by solving for a vector Π_1 and a matrix Π_2 that equate demand and supply at all $\mathbf{X}$. If vectors ϵ and η are normally distributed, this only requires equating the mean and the variance of supply and demand. These conditions lead to implicit relationships in Π_1, Π_2, which along with initial conditions (free entry for firms and equilibrium utility for individuals) that determine the price function in terms of $\mathbf{A}$, $\mathbf{B}$ and the parameters of the distributions of the shocks. Clearly, a hedonic price function thus determined is very different from an arbitrary regression of prices on observed characteristics. Finally, observations on $(P(\mathbf{X}); \mathbf{X})$ allow, in principle, inference on unknown parameters $(\mathbf{A}, \mathbf{B})$ and the parameters of the distributions of stochastic shocks, $f_{(\epsilon)}(\cdot)$, $f_{(\eta)}(\cdot)$.[33] While guessing a quadratic solution is natural in this application, it would rarely work in general.

The preference structure and the other particulars of individuals' decisions mentioned in section 3.5 add considerable complications. To appreciate them, in the remainder of this section I abstract from supply-side endogeneity and assume that individuals restrict their choices among census tracts in a given set of tracts, $\ell \in \mathcal{L}$. For each of these tracts (or communities), the distributions of housing and neighborhood attributes are given, $f(\mathbf{x}_h|\ell)$, which amounts to an assumption of a given housing stock, and so are the distributions of neighbors' consumptions of housing attributes and of neighbors' own demographic characteristics, $f(\mathbf{x}_{n(h)}|\ell)$ and $f(\mathbf{z}_{n(h)}|\ell)$, respectively. At equilibrium, individuals' choices must give rise to distributions that coincide with those taken as given.

The housing market clears by allocating households to tracts so as to equate demand with supply of all attributes in each tract and to confirm that the distribution functions $f(\mathbf{x}_{k(h)}, \mathbf{z}_{k(h)})$ are consistent with equilibrium decisions. I start from a given distribution of individuals' demographic characteristics in the population, $f(\mathbf{Z})$ and $\mathcal{Z}$ their support. These individuals allocate themselves via the housing market to a given number of distinct census tracts in a location, say a particular metropolitan area. Let P_ℓ denote a tract-specific price index that also allows for pricing of dwelling and neighborhood attributes, and $\mathbf{P}$ the vector of all such prices in the choice set $\mathcal{L}$. That is, of course, the hedonic function defined over tracts in the opportunity set.

A neighborhood selection model, based on comparing indirect utilities along the lines of (3.38), yields a probability, $\text{Prob}_s^j(P)$, that individual j will choose tract ℓ. That is,

$$\text{Prob}_\ell^j(P) = \text{Prob}\left\{\Omega\left(\mathbf{g}_\ell; \mathbf{X}, \mathbf{Z}; P\right) \geq \Omega\left(\mathbf{g}_{\ell'}\mathbf{X}, \mathbf{Z}; P\right), \forall \ell' \in \mathcal{L}\right\}. \tag{3.73}$$

At equilibrium, it must be the case that each individual is accommodated within the given urban area,

$$\int_{\mathcal{Z}} \sum_{\ell \in \mathcal{L}} \text{Prob}_\ell^j(P) \cdot f(\mathbf{Z}) d\mathbf{Z} = 1. \tag{3.74}$$

The demand for housing attributes, which is obtained schematically by expressing the unobservables in terms if observables and parameters, must be equal to the supply of housing attributes in each tract,

$$\int_{\mathcal{Z}} \text{Prob}_\ell^j(P) \cdot f(\mathbf{Z}) d\mathbf{Z} = f(\mathbf{x}_{k(h)}, \mathbf{z}_{k(h)}|\ell), \quad \forall \ell \in \mathcal{L}. \tag{3.75}$$

These conditions, understood as functional equations, determine the hedonic price function invoked above.

If, as Ioannides and Zabel (2008) state, individuals' utility functions also depend on their neighbors' housing consumptions, the distribution of neighbors' housing consumptions that individuals take as given in making their neighborhood selection and consumption decisions should match the one that results from individuals' choices in every tract, that is the "demand" matches the "supply" for endogenous neighborhood effects in each tract. Thus (3.75) should be rewritten as

$$\int_{\mathcal{Z}} \text{Prob}_{\ell}^{j}(P) \cdot f(z_j) dz_j = f(y_{k(h)}|s), \quad \forall \ell \in \mathcal{L}. \tag{3.76}$$

Equation (3.74) is satisfied automatically, given the properties of the choice functions Prob_{ℓ}^{j} and of the distribution function $f(z_j)$, provided that the demand for housing attributes equals the supply [equation (3.75), (3.76]. These equations determine the tract-specific price P_{ℓ}. One needs to show that these prices and associated distributions are well defined. In view of the complexity of the general case demonstrated here, the results of section 3.5 represent remarkable progress.

CHAPTER 4

Location Decisions of Firms and Social Interactions

4.1 INTRODUCTION

This chapter aims at understanding location decisions of firms as decisions in the presence of social interactions, thus unifying a number of approaches economists have used in studying such decisions and in measuring patterns of industrial agglomeration. It is a salient fact that firms' evaluations of alternative locations depend *directly* on where other firms locate and that this makes these approaches most interesting within a social interactions framework. To assess such direct effects, this chapter uses as a benchmark outcomes where firms compete for scarce land sites that have differential effects on their own profitabilities but no other interactions.

Firms may benefit from proximity to low-cost suppliers of manufactured inputs and resources and from proximity to their customers. Because suppliers and customers may be other firms or workers, location decisions of firms and of individuals are interdependent. Benefits from agglomeration are taken as given by any individual firm, but agglomerations result from an aggregate of actions of all firms. This simultaneity suggests that agglomerations can be studied fruitfully as equilibrium outcomes. For agglomerations to prevail, the benefits must be sufficiently strong to compensate firms for the higher prices that follow from competition for land, the key scarce input to be allocated at sites hosting agglomerations. The configuration of economic forces should be such that alternative location patterns are stable in the presence of shocks. As in chapter 3, I highlight models that allow us to learn the most from empirical investigations.

Of course, beneficial interactions among firms and among firms and individuals in the context of the urban economy are not new concepts. Economists credit Smith (1776) and Marshall (1920) for recognizing that productivity and wages are higher in larger cities. This phenomenon lies at the heart of modern modeling of the urban economy and has been explored empirically in numerous studies. Of the two most influential works in the modern theoretical literature, that by Henderson (1974) explores the consequences of the urban productivity premium for the urban structure of an economy made up of trading cities. The study by Krugman (1991a) offers a framework for thinking simultaneously about trade and the location of people and firms across space and derives the production and consumption interactions that are the hallmark of new economic geography. New economic geography combines the role of increasing returns at the level of the firm along with the value consumers attach to variety of goods and the benefits firms obtain from access to workers with suitably diverse skills (Fujita, Krugman, and Venables 1999). The integration that new economic geography accomplishes often yields results that are qualitatively different from those of the earlier literature. But, most importantly, it brings together elements that were treated as disparate prior to its advent while involving a relatively small number of parameters. A most noteworthy of the qualitative differences is the possibility of multiple equilibria. Alternative patterns of location are possible, with agglomerations prevailing if they are stable and uniform distribution of economic activity if they are unstable.

Marshall's typology of benefits firms confer on one another continues to be apt. First, labor market pooling for workers with specialized skills favors both workers and firms; second, the quantity and variety of nontraded inputs (including natural amenities) is valuable to all firms in an industry; and third, information exchanges, possibly deliberate but also inadvertent, benefit firms in closer proximity more than those located farther away.

The present chapter aims at providing an overarching framework for expressing location decisions of firms. Questions of particular interest are whether the effect of proximity to other firms in the same industry may be separately identifiable from other factors such as proximity to firms in *other* industries, the size of the total urban economy, and the availability of a suitable labor force. Still, as in chapter 3, pleasant weather and other physical amenities may be forces that individuals and firms consider attractive in common. At the same time, individuals' and firms' evaluations may diverge in other dimensions.

In the remainder of this chapter I proceed as follows. First, I address the simplest possible problem of firm location in a context where space is construed simply as land parcels of equal size that have differential effects on the productivity of firms that locate there. There are no other geographic features. I explore the role of site rents in guiding location decisions and the difficulties that site rents encounter when more complex geography is introduced. I expand the model to allow for randomness in firms' evaluations of alternative sites and for interdependence among firms' location decisions. Next I extend the model to a framework for defining empirical measures of agglomeration and review their application to a broader set of determinants of location decisions of firms. These include physical and geographic amenities and the prices of inputs used by firms. I examine a class of empirical works that allow us to explore such critical aspects of interactions among firms as localization and urbanization economies, including the role of physical proximity measured by distance between firms. I relegate to chapter 5 the study of firms' location decisions in urban space in relation to an urban center, whether predetermined or endogenous.

4.2 MODELS OF LOCATION OF FIRMS

When deciding on their locations firms need to deal with several concerns: one, availability of inputs, either directly through access to primary resources or indirectly through access to transport systems; two, availability of a suitably skilled workforce; and three, access to a suitable market or customer base. Economists start by describing hypothetical "worlds" where all these objectives are readily and simultaneously amenable to market-based solutions. Market prices are the signals that guide location decisions. The market wage rates for different types of workers, market land rents for different types of land sites in different geographic locations, and the prices of different inputs are all used by firms in making their decisions, of which location is of course a key one. Economic reality, however, is more complex than that. Prices may not contain all the information that is necessary for location decisions. For one, they do not convey information on market sizes that could proxy for the variety of inputs and worker skills that may be available in different areas.

4.2.1 Location Decisions When Land Sites Are Differentiated: The Koopmans–Beckmann Model

Let firms, indexed by k, $k = 1, \ldots, L$, engage in an activity of a fixed size, like operating a plant at only one of a discrete number of sites, $\ell = 1, \ldots, L$. Let parameters $a_{k\ell}$ denote the gross profit (revenue) that firm k would earn if it were at location ℓ. I array these parameters as entries in $\mathbf{A}$, an $L \times L$ matrix. Suppose the sites are privately owned and firms compete with each other for locating at these sites. The firm that offers the highest rent for each site wins. How would firms locate?

This simple model highlights the role of differences among alternative sites and their significance for firms' location decisions. I note also that the definition of the location problem is meaningful if each firm locates its entire plant at a single location, that is, that the allocation of firms to sites, and vice versa, is an integer one. Fractional locations may also be defined, of course, and I return to them below. I note that the problem may be posed symmetrically in principle, that is, in terms of sites' owning the technology and competing among themselves in attracting plants by posting plant rentals.

If a location ℓ earns rent ϱ_ℓ, then firm k would choose site k^* so as to maximize its net profit, profit minus rent. That is,

$$a_{kk^*} - \varrho_{k^*} \geq a_{k\ell} - \varrho_\ell, \;\; k, \ell = 1, \ldots, L. \tag{4.1}$$

Alternatively, if sites compete for firms, firms earn rentals, q_k, $k = 1, \ldots, L$. In that case, site ℓ would choose firm ℓ^* if it would maximize its net profit, that is, profit minus rent, by doing so:

$$a_{\ell^*\ell} - q_{\ell^*} \geq a_{k\ell} - q_\ell, \;\; k, \ell = 1, \ldots, L. \tag{4.2}$$

An additional consequence of this symmetry is that the sum of firm and site rents is exactly equal to the gross profit for the *optimal* assignment of plants to sites and falls below it in all other cases. Koopmans and Beckmann (1957) prove that the optimal assignment or, alternatively, the competitive allocation of firms and sites, admits a unique solution. I incorporate this result into the statement of the problem by relabeling firms so that so that firm ℓ at site ℓ is the optimal assignment. That is, there exist site and firm rents, (ϱ_ℓ, q_ℓ), $\ell = 1, \ldots, L$, such that

$$a_{\ell\ell} = q_\ell + \varrho_\ell, \quad \ell = 1, \ldots, L. \tag{4.3}$$

$$a_{ki} \leq q_k + \varrho_i, \quad k, \ell = 1, \ldots, L. \tag{4.4}$$

It is straightforward to show that the site rents and plant rentals are not unique although their respective sums are. That is, subtracting any amount from site rents and adding it to firm rents does not change the optimal allocation.

I follow Koopmans and Beckmann (1957) and pose the problem of allocation of plants to sites as a problem of optimal assignment. That is, a planner chooses the locations of all firms such that the sum total of all gross profits resulting from the assignments of firms to locations is maximized. Clearly, while this is an interesting question for a large firm that chooses locations for its different plants, a more interesting question for a modern economy is how independent firms' location decisions are facilitated by markets, in this instance markets for sites. Although I am not interested in fractional, that is, noninteger, assignments, the social planner's problem is easier to pose in terms of fractional assignments. Following Koopmans and Beckmann, I formulate the optimal assignment of all firms to all available sites in terms of finding a set of fractions, with $p_{k\ell}$ denoting the "fraction" of firm k located at site ℓ, $0 \leq p_{k\ell} \leq 1$. These fractions are conveniently arrayed in a permutation matrix, a square positive matrix $\mathbf{P}$ of dimension $L \times L$. This formulation includes the integer assignments of firms to locations as special cases: each row and column has only a single nonzero element equal to 1 and all other elements are equal to 0.

The problem of optimal assignment is then stated as finding a permutation matrix $\mathbf{P}$ such that the total value from all assignments of firms to sites,

$$\sum_{k}^{L} \sum_{\ell}^{L} a_{k\ell} p_{k\ell}, \tag{4.5}$$

is maximized. This maximization problem, subject to the constraints defining the permutation matrix, is a linear programming problem. Its generic set of feasible solutions contains integer assignments as special cases that correspond to the "corners" of the feasible set. It is a key result of Koopmans and Beckmann that the *optimal* solution to the maximization of (4.5) assumes the form of a corner solution, an integer assignment. Associated with the optimal assignment are a set of site rents and a set of plant rents, that coincide with the Lagrange multipliers corresponding, respectively, to the constraints that each site is fully occupied, $\sum_\ell p_{k\ell} = 1$, and each plant is entirely assigned, $\sum_k p_{k\ell} = 1$, and that satisfy (4.3) and (4.4) and thus make it possible for the optimal assignment to be implemented as a decentralized equilibrium. The system of rents for all firms and all locations, (q_k, ϱ_ℓ), is such that the optimal assignment profits equal the sum of the respective rents and fall short of the sum for all other assignments.

The optimal assignment‘ may be sustained as a market outcome in the following sense. If locations earn rents, ϱ_ℓ, then firm k would choose site k^* if it could maximize its net profit, profit minus rent, by doing so, that is, if

$$a_{kk^*} - \varrho_{k^*} \geq a_{k\ell} - \varrho_\ell, \quad k, \ell = 1, \ldots, L. \tag{4.6}$$

In this fashion, firms are seen as bidding for locations. Alternatively, sites could be bidding for firms, in which case firms earn rents, q_k, $k = 1, \ldots, L$. In that case, site ℓ would choose firm ℓ^* if it would maximize its net profit, profit minus rent, by doing so, that is, if

$$a_{\ell^*,\ell} - q_{\ell^*} \geq a_{k\ell} - q_{k\ell}, \quad k, \ell = 1, \ldots, L. \tag{4.7}$$

It is an important property of the optimal solution, and correspondingly of the market mechanism that implements it, that each firm (alternatively, each site) needs to know only the site (alternatively, firm) rents and its own gross profits at each location. It does not need any other data on firms' characteristics. The location rents may be seen as condensing the information available in the matrix of gross profits **A**, at least as it pertains to determining firms' locations at equilibrium. Rewriting the above conditions yields that $a_{k\ell} - \varrho_\ell \leq a_{kk^*} - \varrho_{k^*}$ or

$$a_{k\ell} - a_{kk^*} \leq \varrho_\ell - \varrho_{\ell^*}. \tag{4.8}$$

In other words, the increment in profitability that firm k would experience by moving to another location $\ell \neq k^*$, is not more than the increment in site rent that it would face. Therefore, the appropriate rents sustain the optimal assignment. The location problem makes sense only if firms face different production possibilities at different sites that are otherwise homogeneous, say from the viewpoint of geography (first nature).

4.2.2 Firm Interdependence and Location Decisions

I introduce next a modicum of interdependence along with geography by expressing the cost consequences of commodity flows among firms. Following Koopmans and Beckmann, let $b_{kk'}$ denote shipments from firm k to firm k' per unit of capacity, c_{ij} denote transportation costs per unit shipped from location i to location j, and **B**, **C** be the $L \times L$ matrices defined with $b_{kk'}$ and c_{ij} as their elements. As before, a location pattern of all firms is denoted by a matrix **P**, whose properties I specify above. Firm k's revenue net of its interfirm transportation costs is

$$\sum_i a_{ki} p_{ki} - \sum_{k'} \sum_{i,j} b_{kk'} p_{ki} c_{ij} p_{k'j} = \mathbf{A}_k \mathbf{P}_k^T - \mathbf{B}_k \mathbf{P}_k \mathbf{C} \mathbf{P}_k, \tag{4.9}$$

where p_{ki}, $p_{k'j}$ denote the fraction of firm k, k' assigned to sites i, j, respectively.

The total profits associated with a location pattern **P** are expressed by summing up the expressions in (4.9) over all firms:

$$\sum_{k,i} a_{ki} p_{ki} - \sum_{k,k'} \sum_{i,j} b_{kk'} p_{ki} c_{ij} p_{k'j}. \tag{4.10}$$

Koopmans and Beckmann show that the presence of transportation costs precludes the existence of rents that will sustain an *integer* assignment, optimal or otherwise, for the problem of maximizing (4.10), a quadratic assignment problem, subject to constraints that the assignment matrix must satisfy, that is, $0 \leq p_{ki}, p_{k'j} \leq 1$, and that each row and each column sum up to 1. Therefore, no *integer* locational equilibrium exists in the sense that it does for a model without transportation costs. This points to a critical role that indivisibility plays in assigning activities to locations. Insisting on integer assignments is, of course, essential in representing the intuitive condition that a plant or, even more so, an individual locates only in one location. This is a nonconvex condition, and the culprit in the nonexistence result.

Specific features that must be introduced into the model in order to obtain more realistic locational outcomes have attracted the attention of economists. As I discuss shortly, the fact that each firm's location depends upon the location of other firms introduces a strategic element that may not be resolved via market prices alone.[1] We will see shortly that prices may not be sufficient to guide the location decisions of firms when there is interdependence among them.

4.3 LOCATION OF FIRMS UNDER UNCERTAINTY

In empirical investigations of firms' location decisions, it is important to be able to be assess whether observed patterns differ from what one would expect from pure randomness. Therefore, it is important to allow for uncertainty. Let firm k inspect site ℓ and determine the value it would realize if it were to choose it, that is, gross profits, $\pi_{k\ell} \equiv a_{k\ell} - \varrho_\ell$, plus a random quantity ϵ_ℓ. Thus, firm k's profit at location ℓ, net of site rent, will be

$$\pi_{k\ell} + \epsilon_\ell. \tag{4.11}$$

How would firms locate so as to maximize their expected payoffs? How does uncertainty change the most likely location pattern? How does this compare with the deterministic problem of firm location examined above?

I assume that sites first post deterministic rents. Then firms allocate themselves to sites in order to maximize expected profits. Firm k wishes to locate at site ℓ if

$$a_{k\ell} + \epsilon_\ell - \varrho_\ell \geq a_{k\ell'} + \epsilon_{\ell'} - \varrho_{\ell'}, \ \forall \ell' \neq \ell, \ \ell = 1, \ldots, L, \tag{4.12}$$

and provided that it is prepared to overbid all other firms, which would occur with probability equal to that of the event

$$a_{k\ell} + \epsilon_\ell - \varrho_\ell \geq a_{k'\ell} + \epsilon_{\ell_{k'}} - \varrho_\ell, \ \forall k' \neq k, \ \ell = 1, \ldots, L, \tag{4.13}$$

where the ϵ_ℓ's are independent and identically distributed random variables and $\epsilon_{\ell_{k'}}$ is the firm k' draw when evaluating site ℓ. Next, I allow for interdependence among firms' location decisions, and finally I also introduce stochastic dependence among the ϵ_ℓ's and examine its role along with interdependence among firms' decisions.

4.3.1 A Logit Model of Firms' Location Decisions

If the ϵ_ℓ's are independent and identically distrubuted extreme-value random variables, then the probabilities that firm k, $k = 1, \ldots, L$, will choose site ℓ, $\ell = 1, \ldots, L$, are multinomial logit. If ϖ denotes the dispersion parameter, which is assumed to be common among all firms, firm k will choose site $\ell = 1, \ldots, L$, given deterministic site rents $(\varrho_1, \ldots, \varrho_\ell, \ldots, \varrho_L)$, with probability given by

$$p_{k\ell} = \frac{e^{\varpi(a_{k\ell} - \varrho_\ell)}}{\sum_{j=1}^{L} e^{\varpi(a_{kj} - \varrho_j)}}, \ \ell = 1, \ldots, L. \tag{4.14}$$

I simplify these expressions by assuming the following decomposition of gross profits. I define gross profit for firm k at location ℓ as made up of a component $\bar{a}_{k.}$ that is specific to firm k, a component $\bar{a}_{.\ell}$, that is specific to location ℓ, and a random residual. That is,

$$a_{k\ell} = \bar{a}_{k.} + \bar{a}_{.\ell} + \varepsilon_{k\ell},$$

where $\bar{a}_{k.} = \frac{1}{L}\sum_\ell a_{k\ell}$, $\bar{a}_{.\ell} = \frac{1}{L}\sum_k a_{k\ell}$ are the average gross rents over all locations for each firm and over all firms for each location. It is the residual $\varepsilon_{k\ell}$ that is independent and identically extreme-value-distributed. In the case of this decomposition, expression (4.14) become

$$p_{k\ell} = \frac{e^{\varpi(\bar{a}_{.\ell} - \varrho_\ell)}}{\sum_{j=1}^{L} e^{\varpi(\bar{a}_{.j} - \varrho_j)}}, \ \ell = 1, \ldots, L. \tag{4.15}$$

The location choice probabilities depend only on site ℓ–specific quantities, $\bar{a}_{.\ell}$, and on rents, ϱ_ℓ. Symmetrically, if sites were to choose firms, that they would depend only on firm-specific quantities, $\bar{a}_{k.}$, and on rents.

If uncertainty is very important, which we can represent by the variance of the ϵ_ℓ's in (4.11) tending to infinity, then $\varpi = 0$, the deterministic components of profits associated with different sites are irrelevant and the resulting choice is purely random: the probability of choosing any of the sites is equal to

L^{-1}. If, on the other hand, uncertainty is unimportant, that is, if the variance of the ϵ's is zero, $\varpi \to \infty$, and the location choice is entirely determined by net profits: firm ℓ chooses a site so as to maximize its profit, site ℓ^*: $a_{\ell\ell^*} - \varrho_{\ell^*} \geq a_{\ell\ell} - \varrho_\ell$. This leads back to the deterministic Koopmans–Beckmann model examined above.

Location choice probabilities determine competitive equilibrium outcomes when rents assume their equilibrium values. A set of site rents $(\varrho_1, \ldots, \varrho_\ell, \ldots, \varrho_L)$ would be an equilibrium set if, for each site ℓ, the probabilities that firms will choose it sum up to 1:

$$\sum_{k=1}^{L} \frac{e^{\varpi(a_{k\ell}-\varrho_\ell)}}{\sum_{j=1}^{L} e^{\varpi(a_{kj}-\varrho_j)}} = 1, \ \ell = 1, \ldots, L. \tag{4.16}$$

This yields L equations for the L unknown site rents. However, there is dependence among these equations: summing them up yields an identity. That is, because the choice model (4.14) implies that the probability that a firm will locate somewhere is 1 [the choice probabilities (4.14) sum up to 1]. Recall that such nonuniqueness is a feature of the Koopmans–Beckmann model, too.

Two special cases for the values of gross rents provide benchmarks that are thus particularly interesting. Consider first that gross rents are firm-specific and thus independent of the site: $a_{k\ell} = a_{k.}, \forall \ell$. In that case, location characteristics are inherently irrelevant, and therefore location choice is purely random. The above site equilibrium equation (4.16) implies that choice probabilities are simply equal to L^{-1}, and therefore rents are equal across all sites. Consider next that gross rents are only site-specific and independent of firms: $a_{k\ell} = a_{.\ell}, \forall k$. Again, the above site equilibrium equations (4.16) imply that choice probabilities are simply equal to L^{-1}, which in this case requires that $a_\ell - \varrho_\ell = a_j - \varrho_j$. Therefore, it is the covariation between site- and firm-specific profits that gives rise to differential site rents, just as in the Koopmans–Beckmann model. For the purpose of estimation, it would be important that data allow for such covariation.

The general properties of competitive equilibrium rents,[2] the solutions to (4.16), follow easily. After we normalize with respect to one of the rents, say ϱ_1, and express that all other rents are relative to it, $\varrho'_\ell \equiv \varrho_\ell - \varrho_1$, the $\ell = 2, \ldots, L$ equations (4.16) are independent. It is straightforward to establish that the left-hand side of equation (4.16), $\ell > 1$, is monotone decreasing in ϱ'_ℓ, and monotone increasing in ϱ'_k, $k \neq \ell$. As $0 \leq \varrho'_\ell \leq 1$, the function on the left-hand side ranges from a finite value that is greater than 1 to 0.

The competitive equilibrium set of site rents $(0, \varrho'_2, \ldots, \varrho'_\ell, \ldots, \varrho'_L)$ naturally reflects all the data, summarized by $(\mathbf{A}, \varpi)$, associated with the firms' decisions. The problem of identifying $(\mathbf{A}, \varpi)$, may be posed formally in terms of data on site rents and of location decisions for a sample of firms. Typically, gross profits are not observed, and therefore one needs to specify gross profits in terms of observable economic fundamentals that enter firms' decisions.

4.3.2 A Logit Model of Firms' Location Decisions with Direct Firm Interdependence

I extend the model of firms' location choices to account for interdependence among the firms by assuming that the gross profit of firm k is given by (4.9). I interpret p_{ki} on the right-hand side of (4.9) as the probability that firm k will locate at site i. Let $\mathbf{P} = [p_{k\ell}]$ denote the $L \times L$ matrix of location choice probabilities, and $\mathcal{E}\left\{p^k_{k'j}\right\}$ denote firm k's expectation of the probability that firm k' will locate at location j. Then the probability that firm k will locate at site ℓ is the probability of the event

$$a_{k\ell} - \sum_{k'}\sum_{j} b_{kk'}c_{\ell j}\mathcal{E}\left\{p^k_{k'j}\right\} + \epsilon_\ell - \varrho_\ell \geq a_{k\ell'} - \sum_{k'}\sum_{j} b_{kk'}c_{\ell' j}\mathcal{E}\left\{p^k_{k'j}\right\}$$
$$+ \epsilon_{\ell'} - \varrho_{\ell'}, \ \forall \ell' \neq \ell, \ \ell = 1, \ldots, L. \tag{4.17}$$

This generalizes the definition in (4.14) above to:

$$p_{k\ell} = \frac{e^{\varpi\left(a_{k\ell} - \sum_{k'}\sum_j b_{kk'}c_{\ell j}\mathcal{E}\left\{p^k_{k'j}\right\} - \varrho_\ell\right)}}{\sum_{i=1}^{L} e^{\varpi\left(a_{ki} - \sum_{k'}\sum_j b_{kk'}c_{\ell' j}\mathcal{E}\left\{p^k_{k'j}\right\} - \varrho_i\right)}}, \quad k, \ell = 1, \ldots, L. \tag{4.18}$$

Considering equation (4.18) for all firms and locations as a system of equations, we see that each firm's probabilities of locating at different sites depend on the firm's expectations of the location probabilities for all other firms with which a firm interacts. I proceed further by assuming that each firm k expects that firm k''s likelihood of locating at location j is equal to its probability of doing so according to (4.18), $\mathcal{E}\left[p^k_{k'j}\right] = p_{k'j}$. Equations (4.18) may be considered a simultaneous system of equations with $\mathbf{P}$ as the unknowns, given site rents ϱ_ℓ, $\ell = 1, \ldots, L$. The adding-up constraints for the location probabilities of each firm are satisfied by construction: for each firm k, $\sum_\ell p_{k\ell} = 1$, that is, each firm locates somewhere with probability 1. Therefore, we have $L^2 - L$ independent equations for the $L^2 - L$ unknown firm location probabilities. By appealing to Brouwer's fixed-point theorem, it is straightforward to show that a positive solution exists for the location probabilities. The solution might not necessarily be unique, but a simple example with two locations and two firms suggests that it is for a broad range of parameter values. While an estimation problem along theses lines may be embedded in the classic treatment of multinomial choice models by Brock and Durlauf (2006), firms' objectives are more complicated than that of their proposition 1, and therefore I believe that the identification of the present model is still an open question.

The set of rents at equilibrium may be determined in a similar manner as above. That is, for each site, we may adapt (4.16) by using the expressions for the location probabilities of each firm for each site as functions of the site rents, $p_{k\ell}(\varrho_1, \ldots, \varrho_L)$, given by (4.18), to require that each site will be occupied with probability 1:

$$\sum_{k=1}^{L} p_{k\ell}(\varrho_1, \ldots, \varrho_L) = 1, \ \ell = 1, \ldots, L. \tag{4.19}$$

This system of L equations yields $L - 1$ independent equations for the $L - 1$ unknowns, $\varrho'_\ell = \varrho_\ell - \varrho_1, \ell = 2, \ldots, L$. Although the mechanics of the determination of location probabilities and rents are similar to those in the simpler case examined in section 4.3.1 above, the analytics are considerably more complicated.

4.3.3 Localization and Urbanization Externalities: Definitions

With an eye toward applying this framework to structure empirical investigations, I interpret the above choice probabilities more broadly. First, I partition the set of firms into industries and interpret the arrays of parameters **B**, **C** so as to express patterns of interdependence among firms in the same or in different industries. Firms from any industry can locate anywhere. Second, there are no capacity constraints at locations. Location at site ℓ takes the form of a fraction of employment at site ℓ.

I use (4.18) to define a *localization externality effect*, or *Marshall–Arrow–Romer effect*, on firm k's location decision from the total presence of other firms in the *same* industry, the $\hat{p}^k_{k'j}$'s, as the shares of employment at locations j for different firms in the same industry, $k' \in \mathcal{K}_j$, that have already located when firm k makes a decision. I use (4.18) to define an *urbanization (Jacobs) externality* as the advantage conferred upon a firm by greater diversity in local economic activity and express it through the shares of employment at location j for *all other* industries, $k' \in \mathcal{K}_j$.

A number of remarks are in order. First, since productivity effects may be generated by other attributes of locations, such as total size, as measured by population, or density, of economic activity in an urban area, these definitions need to be adjusted accordingly. The effects on a firm's location decision from those by other firms may be considered instances of the generic framework of social interactions. The localization and urbanization externalities are akin to endogenous social effects, with the former being an own-industry effect and the latter a cross-industry effect. Such endogeneity is a source of econometric issues, just like individuals' decisions, which are addressed farther below. An example is whether one can distinguish empirically the extent to which firms' location decisions are driven by localization or urbanization effects or both. Second, the logit-based discrete choice framework provides an overarching analytical theme within which many of the specific measures of agglomeration may be nested.

4.4 TESTING FOR AGGLOMERATION

Given data on different types of firms and their locations in space, how could one detect whether there are, indeed, tendencies toward clustering or dispersion, let alone explain what they might be due to? In addressing this question, a number of issues arise naturally. For example, how are locations in space measured? It is often convenient to work with different sites' being defined as political or administrative units, such as cities, metropolitan areas, counties, regions, and states. However, in other applications, the actual geographic or traveling distance between locations also matters. The additional detail provided by distance may proxy for important economic interactions.

With an eye toward reducing what may be attributable to random factors, I allow for a general specification of gross profit functions. Let $\pi_{kg\ell}$, the profit function[3] for firm k in industry g located at site ℓ, be decomposed in terms of a component that depends only on a vector of observables, $\mathbf{z}_{g\ell}$, associated with industry g, and site ℓ, and parameters θ, a term that depends only on the industry, $\eta_{g\ell}$, and a random term, $\epsilon_{kg\ell}$:

$$\pi_{kg\ell} = \theta \mathbf{z}_{g\ell} + \eta_{g\ell} + \epsilon_{kg\ell}. \tag{4.20}$$

For example, wages would have a higher weight for textiles than for chemicals, and small-vessel manufacturing would depend less on proximity to the ocean than tanker building.

A probabilistic location model for firms that is more precise than (4.17) above follows once the stochastic structure in (4.20) has been specified. I assume that, one, the industry-specific term, $\eta_{g\ell}$, is a random effect, a quantity that is common to all firms belonging to industry g and is independent and identically distributed across all industries and drawn from a distribution to be specified shortly; and, two, the term $\epsilon_{kg\ell}$ is an independent and identically distributed draw across firms, industries, and locations that obeys an extreme-value distribution. Conditional on the random effect $\eta_{g\ell}$, the choice probabilities for firms in each industry g become

$$P_{kg\ell}(\eta_{g\ell}) = \frac{e^{\varpi[\theta \mathbf{z}_{g\ell}+\eta_{g\ell}]}}{\sum_{j=1}^{L} e^{\varpi[\theta \mathbf{z}_{gj}+\eta_{gj}]}} = \frac{\lambda_{g\ell} e^{\varpi \eta_{g\ell}}}{\sum_{j=1}^{L} \lambda_{gj} e^{\varpi \eta_{gj}}}, \quad \ell = 1, \ldots, L, \ g = 1, \ldots, G, \tag{4.21}$$

where the terms

$$\lambda_{gj} \equiv e^{\varpi \theta \mathbf{z}_{gj}}$$

express the impact of measured location and industry characteristics and $e^{\eta_{g\ell}}$ reflects industry location–specific random effects.

I complete the location theory by specifying the distribution of the random effects. Under the assumption that each of the terms $e^{\varpi \eta_{g\ell}}$ are independent and identically gamma-distributed with parameters $(\delta_g^{-1}\lambda_{gj}, \delta_g^{-1}\lambda_{gj})$, where the δ_g's are industry-specific parameters, then, first, each of the random variables $e^{\eta_{g\ell}}$ has a mean equal to 1 and a variance equal to $\delta_g \lambda_{gj}^{-1}$, and second, the terms $\lambda_{g\ell} e^{\eta_{g\ell}}$ also follow independent gamma distributions with parameters

$(\delta_g^{-1}\lambda_{g\ell}, \delta_g^{-1})$. Then, under these assumptions, the location choice probabilities for firms in each industry $(p_{g1}, p_{g2}, \ldots, p_{gL})$ follow multivariate Dirichlet (or beta) compound distributions with parameters $(\delta_g^{-1}\lambda_{g1}, \delta_g^{-1}\lambda_{g2}, \ldots, \delta_g^{-1}\lambda_{gL})$, which are given in closed form by[4]

$$f_{DM}\left(p_{g1}, p_{g2}, \ldots, p_{gL-1}\right) = \frac{\Gamma\left(\delta_g^{-1}\sum_{\ell=1}^{L}\lambda_{g\ell}\right)}{\prod_{\ell=1}^{L}\Gamma\left(\delta_g^{-1}\lambda_{g\ell}\right)}\prod_{\ell=1}^{L}\left(p_{g\ell}\right)^{\delta_g^{-1}\lambda_{g\ell}-1},$$

$$p_{gL} = 1 - \sum_{\ell=1}^{L-1} p_{g\ell}. \tag{4.22}$$

The expected location probabilities are given by the same expressions as (4.21), provided we set $\eta_{g\ell} = 0$, in which case the multinomial logit model follows. That is,

$$\mathcal{E}(p_{g\ell}) = \frac{\lambda_{g\ell}}{\sum_{\ell=1}^{L}\lambda_{g\ell}}. \tag{4.23}$$

However, it is the variances that differ. Specifically, for the mean and the variance for the number of industry g firms at different sites $(n_{g1}, \ldots, n_{g\ell}, \ldots, n_{gL})$, conditional on the total number of firms, n_g, in industry g, we have

$$\mathcal{E}(n_{g\ell}|n_g) = n_g\mathcal{E}(p_{kg\ell}) = n_g\frac{\lambda_{g\ell}}{\sum_{j=1}^{L}\lambda_{gj}}; \tag{4.24}$$

$$\mathcal{V}(n_{g\ell}|n_g) = n_g\mathcal{V}(p_{kg\ell}) = n_g\frac{\lambda_{g\ell}}{\sum_{j=1}^{L}\lambda_{gj}}\frac{\sum_{j\neq\ell}^{L}\lambda_{gj}}{\sum_{j=1}^{L}\lambda_{gj}}\frac{\sum_j\lambda_{gj} + n_g\delta_g}{\sum_j\lambda_{gj} + \delta_g}. \tag{4.25}$$

The last factor on the right-hand side of (4.25), which is greater than 1, measures "overdispersion" caused by the industry-specific random effects structure.

The variance of $n_{g\ell}$, the number of firms in industry g at location ℓ, is greater than under the multinomial distribution by an industry-specific factor. As δ_g tends to zero (the variance of the industry-specific random effect tends to zero), the variance of $n_{g\ell}$ tends to that of a binomial distribution, the marginal distribution of the multinomial for each of its L random variables. Since the probability density function is available in closed form, one may in fact use maximum likelihood estimation methods to test for overdispersion.

In general, the marginal for any of the variables is the beta binomial distribution. The total number of firms at each location would be described by the sum of n_g equicorrelated Bernoulli random variables, with a correlation coefficient given by

$$\frac{\delta_g}{\sum_{\ell=1}^{L}\lambda_{g\ell} + \delta_g}.$$

If there is no unobservable component in common for firms in the same industry, that is, no random effect $\eta_{g\ell} = 0, \delta_g = 0$, then the locations of such firms are uncorrelated.

This model may be estimated by means of maximum likelihood with data on counts of firms for each industry at different locations and the attributes of the locations,

$$(n_{g1}, \ldots, n_{g\ell}, \ldots, n_{gL}), \mathbf{z}_{g\ell}, \quad g = 1, \ldots, G, \quad \ell = 1, \ldots, L.$$

The respective likelihood function, based on the Dirichlet multinomial (DM) distribution, is obtained from the marginal of (4.22) with respect to $(p_{g1}, p_{g2}, \ldots, p_{gL-1})$ and is given by

$$\prod_{g=1}^{G} \frac{n_g!\Gamma(\delta_g^{-1} \sum_{\ell=1}^{L} \lambda_{g\ell})}{\Gamma(\delta_g^{-1} \sum_{\ell=1}^{L} \lambda_{g\ell} + n_g)} \prod_{\ell=1}^{L} \frac{\Gamma(\delta_g^{-1}\lambda_{g\ell} + n_{g\ell})}{\Gamma(\delta_g^{-1}\lambda_{g\ell})n_g!}. \tag{4.26}$$

This model reduces to the conditional logit model if there is no heterogeneity, either because the variance of the random effects is zero or only one firm is observed for each industry.

Guimarães and Lindrooth (2005) show that this same likelihood function may be obtained via a different route. That is, under the same assumptions the counts of firms in each industry by location, conditional on the respective random effect, are distributed as negative binomial type 1. The total counts for each industry also have negative binomial type 1 distributions. The joint likelihood, obtained by conditioning on the total count for each industry, is the same as the one above, (4.26). This translates into an estimation method that is particularly useful when the size of choice sets is large. This holds, of course, for the case of the conditional logit model, whose estimation bears an observational equivalence to the maximum likelihood estimation of Poisson-type regressions.[5] This approach has a distinct advantage when the size of the choice set is large. In such cases, researchers may use a suggestion of McFadden (1978) (see also chapter 3, sections 3.5.1.2 and 3.9.1), whereby the model may be estimated by using smaller choice sets randomly selected from the full set. The Poisson-equivalent model, on the other hand, is not hampered by the size of the choice set.

Guimarães, Figuerdio, and Woodward (2003) estimate a model of location choice of new foreign-owned manufacturing plants in Portugal over the period of March 1985 to March 1992 among 275 alternative spatial locations. They compare the McFadden model, with different alternative runs with up to 40 randomly selected locations from among the 275. The explanatory variables are total manufacturing; industry-specific, foreign-specific, and service agglomeration; labor costs; elementary and secondary education; population density; distance to Porto and to Lisbon; and location in Porto or in Lisbon. The authors do not supply information on regression fit, but the estimated coefficients are qualitatively very similar (with a few exceptions).

4.4.1 Ellison–Glaeser Indices

This basic statistical theory in the previous section underlies the statistical foundations of the Ellison–Glaeser class of indices (Ellison and Glaeser 1997). Essentially, the Ellison–Glaeser spillover model links the source of overdispersion to the presence of other plants in the same industry, or in another industry, as in the case of coagglomeration [see (Ellison, Glaeser, and Kerr 2007)].

The above development allows researchers to examine determinants of firms' location decisions by means of estimating models of firms' profit functions. In view of the definitions in section 4.3.3, it can be used to highlight the extent to which they are driven by agglomeration forces, either of the localization or of the urbanization type, and to provide a succinct measure for such forces. Intuitively, the fact that different sites generate different advantages to firms in different industries ought to be reflected ultimately in the pattern of employment. But these locational advantages may be natural characteristics of sites (and in their relation to physical and economic geography) or be due to spillovers from the presence of other firms, in the same or in other industries. There exist many indices that may be used to measure employment concentration. Many of these have axiomatic foundations, may be decomposable (Bourguignon 1979; Shorrocks 1982) and suit different settings. A number of studies seek to establish the relative importance of localized industry-specific spillovers, natural advantages, and pure random chance in contributing to geographic concentration of industry.

The Ellison and Glaeser (1997) classes of indices of geographic concentration measure the extent to which firms' location decisions deviate from pure randomness. They do so by means of a simple assumption about spillovers, namely, that firms "imitate" other firms that have already located at a site with probability γ^s; they choose their locations independently of those of others with probability $1-\gamma^s$. Parameter γ^s measures the respective endogenous social effect. Ellison and Glaeser (1997, 1999) and Dumais, Ellison, and Glaeser (2002) develop specific tests for whether observed levels of concentration are greater than would be expected to arise randomly and motivate new indices of geographic concentration and of coagglomeration. These tests are based on simple principles that go to the heart of the importance of interactions in the behavior of firms and thus deserve specific attention.

Let $\pi_{k\ell}$ denote firm k's restricted profit function (4.11) conditional on its locating its single plant at ℓ, $\ell = 1, \ldots, L$. Ellison and Glaeser (1997) specify $\ln \pi_{k\ell}$ as additively separable with respect to $\ln \bar{\pi}_\ell$, a random variable that reflects observed and unobserved characteristics and is solely a function of the characteristics of location ℓ, to $g_\ell = g_\ell(\upsilon_1, \ldots, \upsilon_{k-1})$, a term that captures the effects of spillovers from firms $1, \ldots, k-1$ that have already located at $\upsilon_1, \ldots, \upsilon_{k-1}$, respectively, when firm k makes its own decision, and $\epsilon_{k\ell}$ is a random component reflecting factors that are idiosyncratic to firm k. That is,

$$\ln \pi_{k\ell} = \ln \bar{\pi}_\ell + g_\ell(\upsilon_1, \ldots, \upsilon_{k-1}) + \epsilon_{k\ell}. \tag{4.27}$$

Larger variances in firms' propensities to locate across different areas imply differences in firms' profitabilities across locations. For example, shipyards need access to large bodies of water.

How should we specify the random variables that enter firms' choices? Under the assumption that the $\epsilon_{k\ell}$'s are independent and identically extreme-value–distributed and independent of the $\tilde{\pi}_\ell$'s, in the absence of spillovers, $g_\ell(\upsilon_1, \ldots, \upsilon_{k-1}) = 0$, and conditional on a realization of $(\tilde{\pi}_1, \ldots, \tilde{\pi}_\ell, \ldots, \tilde{\pi}_L)$, firm k maximizes expected profits by choosing location ℓ with probability

$$\text{Prob}\,(\upsilon_k = \ell|\tilde{\pi}_1, \ldots, \tilde{\pi}_\ell, \ldots, \tilde{\pi}_L) = \frac{\tilde{\pi}_\ell}{\sum_\ell \tilde{\pi}_\ell}.$$

Ellison and Glaeser (1997) assume that the probabilities, given above, that a plant locates at $(1, \ldots, \ell, \ldots, L)$ have Dirichlet distributions with expectations being equal to the share of total manufacturing employment by area ℓ, x_ℓ, that is,

$$\mathcal{E}_{\tilde{\pi}_1,\ldots,\tilde{\pi}_\ell,\ldots,\tilde{\pi}_L} \frac{\tilde{\pi}_\ell}{\sum_\ell \tilde{\pi}_\ell} = x_\ell, \; \ell = 1, \ldots, L. \tag{4.28}$$

This follows specification (4.23) above. Therefore, on average across industries, the model is specified to reproduce the overall distribution of manufacturing. In addition, they assume that the joint distribution of natural advantages is such that the variance of location decisions at each site ℓ may be parameterized by a single parameter $\gamma^{na} \in [0, 1]$,

$$\text{Var}\left(\frac{\tilde{\pi}_\ell}{\sum_\ell \tilde{\pi}_\ell}\right) = \gamma^{na} x_\ell(1 - x_\ell). \tag{4.29}$$

In this counterpart of specification (4.25) above, γ^{na} takes the place of $\frac{\sum_j \lambda_{gj} + n_g \delta_g}{\sum_j \lambda_{gj} + \delta_g}$. A value of $\gamma^{na} = 0$ implies that unobserved location characteristics have no effect on profitability; a value of $\gamma^{na} = 1$ implies that location characteristics overwhelm firm-specific characteristics and that the location with the best endowments attracts all firms. This corresponds to the maximum value that the variance can have in the model where location probabilities are described by a Dirichlet distribution.

A particularly convenient specification of $\tilde{\pi}_\ell$'s is to assume that they are independent random variables scaled so that the quantity $2[(1 - \gamma^{na})/\gamma^{na}]\tilde{\pi}_\ell$ has a χ^2 distribution with $2[(1 - \gamma^{na})/\gamma^{na}]x_\ell$ degrees of freedom. In this case, $\mathcal{E}\{\tilde{\pi}_\ell\} = x_\ell$, $\mathcal{V}\{\tilde{\pi}_\ell\} = [\gamma^{na}/(1 - \gamma^{na})]x_\ell$. This specification underscores that unobserved location effects have negligible effects on average profitability levels when γ^{na} is small and vary a lot when γ^{na} is large. In that case, the quantity $\sum \tilde{\pi}_\ell$ has a Dirichlet distribution with parameters $2[(1 - \gamma^{na})/\gamma^{na}]\sum_\ell x_\ell$, and the quantities $\frac{\tilde{\pi}_\ell}{\sum_\ell \tilde{\pi}_\ell}$ obey a Dirichlet distribution with parameters

$$\left(\frac{1 - \gamma^{na}}{\gamma^{na}} x_1, \; \ldots, \; \frac{1 - \gamma^{na}}{\gamma^{na}} x_\ell, \; \ldots, \; \frac{1 - \gamma^{na}}{\gamma^{na}} x_L\right).$$

Ellison and Glaeser extend the model to account for spillovers between pairs of plants. Let γ^s be the probability that a potentially valuable spillover exists between each pair of plants or the fraction of pairs of firms between which a spillover exists. They define $g_\ell(v_1, \ldots, v_{k-1})$ in (4.27) as $\sum_{j\neq k} e_{kj}(1 - u_{j\ell})(-\infty)$, where the e_{kj}'s are Bernoulli-distributed random variables, which are equal to 1 with probability γ^s, that indicate whether a spillover exists between each pair kj of plants, and $u_{j\ell}$ is an indicator of whether plant j is located in area ℓ. Equation (4.27) now becomes

$$\ln \pi_{k\ell} = \ln \tilde{\pi}_\ell + \sum_{j\neq k} e_{kj}(1 - u_{j\ell})(-\infty) + \epsilon_{k\ell}. \tag{4.30}$$

The factor $-\infty$ assigns a severe penalty: an optimizing firm always chooses the location where the spillovers exist, regardless of the area size or random plant-area shocks, that is, the first and third terms above.

In this more general model, the two parameters of interest (γ^{na}, γ^s) measure the extent of natural advantage, and the strength of spillovers (social interactions) affecting any pair of firms, respectively. If an industry is more concentrated relative to the entire manufacturing, then we are interested in identifying the separate role of those two forces. Ellison and Glaeser (1999) go further and seek to explain "excess" concentration, that is, over and above what is explained by observable characteristics of locations. This subject is discussed further later.

Ellison and Glaeser characterize the probability distribution of an index G, defined over all locations ℓ, of an industry's share of employment, S_ℓ, relative to the total share of manufacturing employment x_ℓ:

$$G \equiv \sum_\ell (S_\ell - x_\ell)^2, \quad \ell = 1, \ldots, L. \tag{4.31}$$

In evaluating G, the Ellison–Glaeser index, x_ℓ is exogenous data, but S_ℓ is related to actual location decisions of firms and is given by $S_\ell = \sum_k z_k u_{ki}$, where z_k is the kth firm's share of industry employment; $u_{k\ell} = 1$ if k is located at ℓ and $u_{k\ell} = 0$ otherwise. The larger the value of index G, the greater the concentration of an industry relative to manufacturing employment. Ellison and Glaeser (1997, prop. 1) prove that the expectation of G may be expressed in terms of the distribution of manufacturing employment and of the industry plant size distribution in a way that does not identify the two forces of geographic concentration separately from one another. That is,

$$\mathcal{E}(G) = \left(1 - \sum_\ell x_\ell^2\right)[\gamma + (1-\gamma)H], \tag{4.32}$$

where H denotes the industry's Herfindahl index of industry firm (plant) size distribution, $H = \sum_j z_j^2$, where z_k is firm k's share of the industry's employment, and parameters γ^{na} and γ^s are reflected in γ:

$$\gamma \equiv \gamma^{na} + \gamma^s - \gamma^{na}\gamma^s.$$

A feature of this result helps sharpen our intuition. The Herfindahl index shows up in G to correct for the inherent lumpiness of plant location when plants are large.[6] Still the most important consequence of this result is that it establishes an observational equivalence between the effects of natural advantages and spillovers on expected concentration levels. An analysis of the mean concentration of industries will allow us to estimate only γ, a function of both parameters of interest. Any estimated $\gamma \in [0, 1]$ is compatible with a pure natural advantage model ($\gamma^s = 0$), a pure spillover model ($\gamma^{na} = 0$), or models with various combinations of the two factors.[7]

This proposition allows Ellison and Glaeser to define an index of concentration in the form of an unbiased measure of the combined effect of unobserved natural advantages and localized spillovers. That is, from (4.32), using the sample value for the concentration index $\sum_\ell (S_\ell - x_\ell)^2$ in place of $\mathcal{E}(G)$ and solving for γ, we have

$$\hat{\gamma} \equiv \frac{G - \left(1 - \sum_\ell x_\ell^2\right) H}{\left(1 - \sum_\ell x_\ell^2\right)(1 - H)} \equiv \frac{\sum_\ell (S_\ell - x_\ell)^2 - \left(1 - \sum_\ell x_\ell^2\right) \sum_j z_k^2}{\left(1 - \sum_\ell x_\ell^2\right)\left(1 - \sum_j z_k^2\right)}. \quad (4.33)$$

Intuitively, the index starts from the raw index of concentration, the modified Herfindahl index (4.31), and reduces it by a term that is proportional to the Herfindahl index of plant sizes. This reduction is more important the more lumpy the geographic distribution of plant sizes. If firms locate according to the null hypothesis above, then the index defined in (4.33) is an unbiased estimate of $\gamma^{na} + \gamma^s - \gamma^{na}\gamma^s$. If there are neither natural advantages nor spillovers, then $\mathcal{E}(G) = 0$.

Equation (4.32) conveys a particular advantage of the Ellison–Glaeser index in that it is invariant to spatial aggregation. That is, instead of accounting firm locations separately for areas 1 and 2, we can aggregate them. Then the distribution of the $L - 1$ quantities $\frac{\pi_\ell}{\sum_\ell \pi_\ell}$ obeys a Dirichlet distribution with parameters

$$\left(\frac{1-\gamma^{na}}{\gamma^{na}}(x_1 + x_2), \ldots, \frac{1-\gamma^{na}}{\gamma^{na}} x_\ell, \ldots, \frac{1-\gamma^{na}}{\gamma^{na}} x_L\right).$$

Ellison and Glaeser [see also (Ellison, Glaeser, and Kerr 2007)] extend this index to the study of coagglomeration, that is, the extent to which a number of plants, each belonging to a given number of industries within an industry group, tend to colocate. Let N_j, w_j, H_j, and H be, respectively, the number of plants in the jth industry, the jth industry's share of total employment in the r industries that comprise the industry group, the Herfindahl index of the jth industry, and the Herfindahl index of the industry group. Under the assumption that the indicator variables $\{u_{k\ell}\}$, for whether a plant k locates in area ℓ, satisfy $\mathcal{E}(u_{k\ell}) = x_\ell$ and $\text{corr}(u_{k'\ell}, u_{k''\ell}) = \gamma_j$, if plants k', k'' both belong to industry j, and $\text{corr}(u_{k'\ell}, u_{k''\ell}) = \gamma_0$, otherwise. Here, the γ_j's reflect the influence of natural advantages and spillovers. If G is defined in terms of S_ℓ, x_ℓ is area ℓ's share of the aggregate employment of r industries in the group, and $H = \sum_j w_j^2 H_j$ is the plant-level Herfindahl index of the aggregate of the of r industries, then

$$\mathcal{E}(G) = \left(1 - \sum_{\ell} x_\ell^2\right) \left[H + \gamma_0 \left(1 - \sum_{k=1}^{r} w_k^2\right) + \sum_{k=1}^{r} \gamma_j w_k^2 (1 - H_k)\right].$$

Working just as with (4.32) and (4.33), Ellison and Glaeser derive a coagglomeration statistic, a variation of (4.31),

$$\gamma^c \equiv \frac{\left[G \big/ \left(1 - \sum_{\ell=1}^{M} x_\ell^2\right)\right] - H - \sum_{\ell=1}^{M} \hat{\gamma}_\ell w_\ell^2 (1 - H_\ell)}{1 - \sum_{k=1}^{N} w_k^2}. \tag{4.34}$$

Under the null hypothesis of proposition 2, Ellison and Glaeser (1997), γ^c is an unbiased estimate of parameter γ_0. An estimate of $\gamma^c = 0$ implies that there is no more agglomeration of plants in the group than that attributable to plants' tendencies to locate near other plants in the same industry and where aggregate manufacturing employment is high. Also, it is helpful to rescale the index in terms of the weighted industry-specific indices, $\lambda = \frac{\gamma^c}{\sum_j w_j \hat{\gamma}_j}$.

This index implies as a special case the no coagglomeration benchmark. That is, $\mathcal{E}(G) = 0$ if the data are generated by the rock-bottom model of purely random locations with no natural advantage or industry-specific spillovers. Its additional advantages are that it is normalized and consequently is comparable across industries with different-sized distributions of firms. It is also comparable across industries that differ in terms of the aggregation at which employment data are available and is applicable when the data are combined into larger aggregates before the index is computed.

4.4.2 Empirical Findings with the Ellison–Glaeser Index

Computation of the index requires data availability for employment for a set of industries and total manufacturing employment (S_ℓ, x_ℓ) across a set of geographic areas and the Herfindahl index for plant employment shares, respectively, for each site ℓ. Ellison and Glaeser, using the 1987 U.S. Census of Manufactures, compute $G = 0.74$, and $(1 - \sum_k x_k^2)H = 0.27$, with the sites being U.S. states. The difference, the numerator of (4.33), suggests substantial localization, with the raw concentration index G exceeding what would be expected to arise randomly in 446 out of 459 industries. A similar calculation based on population shares instead of manufacturing employment shares as the size of the state gives very similar results. Computation of the γ associated with each of the 469 industries yields a distribution for the implied γ that has a lot of mass at low values of γ, implying little concentration, and a very thick right tail. Correction of the portion of observed agglomeration due to random agglomeration turns out to be very important (Ellison and Glaeser, 1997, table 2). These patterns are reinforced by consideration of different spatial disaggregations, as by U.S. state and region.

What do the data say about patterns of coagglomeration among industries in similar standard industrial classification (SIC) codes, specifically, how does the location of plants belonging to different four-digit industries within the same three-digit class compare with the location of plants belonging to their own four-digit industries? What is the separate role of natural advantages as opposed to localized industry-specific spillovers? The latter question is taken up by Ellison and Glaeser (1999), and we discuss their approach and results further below.

Ellison, Glaeser, and Kerr (2007) take up the measurement of coagglomeration. They use data from the Longitudinal Research Database (LRD) of the U.S. Bureau of the Census (see chapter 2, Section 2.13.4) from 1972 to 1997 to compute pairwise coagglomeration measurements for U.S. manufacturing industries. Industry attributes are used to construct measures of the relevance of each of the forces in Marshall's typology of industry agglomeration to each industry pair. They assess the importance of these forces via regressions of coagglomeration indices on the measures of labor market pooling, of proximity to input suppliers or final consumers, and of intellectual spillovers. Data on the characteristics of corresponding industries in the United Kingdom are used as instruments. They find evidence to support each mechanism. The results suggest that input-output interdependence is the most important factor, followed by labor pooling.

Ellison and Glaeser (1999) extend the specification (4.30) by first introducing, a random effect $\eta_{j\ell}$, exactly as in (4.21), which is an unobserved random component of profitability common among all firms in industry j that locate in the same area and reflects the natural advantage of location ℓ. Recall specification (4.27) along with condition (4.28). The expected share of employment in a particular industry j located at location ℓ satisfies $\mathcal{E}(S_{j\ell}) = \hat{S}_{j\ell} = \frac{\bar{\pi}_{j\ell}}{\sum_{\ell'} \bar{\pi}_{j\ell'}}$ when the additive errors are extreme valued–distributed. As we saw earlier in section 4.4, the importance of the unobserved natural advantages is reflected in the variance of $S_{j\ell}$. That is, they assume that the distribution of $\eta_{j\ell}$ is such that $2\,[(1-\gamma^{na})/\gamma^{na}]\,\bar{\pi}_{j\ell}e^{\eta_{j\ell}}$ has a χ^2 distribution with $\mathcal{E}\left(\bar{\pi}_{j\ell}e^{\eta_{j\ell}}\right) = \bar{\pi}_{j\ell}$, and variance $\mathcal{V}\left(\bar{\pi}_{j\ell}e^{\eta_{j\ell}}\right) = [\gamma^{na}/(1-\gamma^{na})]\,\bar{\pi}_{j\ell}$.

They adapt (4.33) by using $\hat{S}_{j\ell}$ in place of x_ℓ. That is,

$$\hat{\gamma} \equiv \frac{\sum_\ell (S_\ell - \hat{S}_\ell)^2/(1 - \sum_\ell \hat{S}_\ell^2) - H}{1 - H}. \tag{4.35}$$

Again, the concentration index $\hat{\gamma}$ combines the effect of unobserved natural advantages and spillovers. The observable effects of natural advantages on industry location shares explain some of the variation. It is natural to expect the index of concentration defined in (4.35) to be smaller.

Ellison and Glaeser find that about 20 percent of observed geographic concentration can be explained by a small set of measurable advantageous factors and conjecture that at least half is generally due to natural advantages.

They proceed by specifying $\ln \pi_{j\ell}$ in (4.11) as

$$\ln \pi_{j\ell} = \alpha_0 \ln(\text{pop}_\ell) + \alpha_1 \ln(\text{mfg}_\ell) - \delta_j \sum_{j'} \varpi_{j'} c_{j'\ell} \iota_{jj'}, \tag{4.36}$$

where pop_ℓ and mfg_ℓ, the shares of national population and manufacturing employment in state ℓ, respectively, control for urbanization economies, j' indexes productive inputs used by industry j, $c_{j'\ell}$ is the cost of input j' at location ℓ, and $\iota_{jj'}$ is the "intensity" of use of input j' at that location. If industry j were to locate according to (4.36), then the predicted shares could be computed from the logit formula:

$$E(S_{j\ell}) = \frac{(\text{pop}_\ell)^{\alpha_0} (\text{mfg}_\ell)^{\alpha_1} \exp\left[-\delta_j \sum_{j'} \zeta_{j'} c_{j'\ell} \iota_{jj'}\right]}{\sum_{\ell'} (\text{pop}_{\ell'})^{\alpha_0} (\text{mfg}_{\ell'})^{\alpha_1} \exp\left[-\delta_j \sum_{j'} \zeta_{j'} p_{j'\ell'} \iota_{jj'}\right]}. \tag{4.37}$$

Note the similarity to (4.18).

Ellison and Glaeser report estimates (obtained by nonlinear least squares) of the shares, according to equation (4.37), using as dependent variables the 1987 state employment shares for four-digit manufacturing industries in the United States. The independent variables that measure a U.S. state's natural advantages in natural resources are the prices of electricity, natural gas, coal, agricultural products, livestock products, and lumber, all interacted with variables measuring their use. These variables perform very well in the regressions and are associated with some of the largest estimated coefficients. The measures of labor input used are manufacturing wage interacted with wages as a share of value added, the fraction of industry output that is exported, and the fraction of U.S. consumption of the output good that is imported. Interacting the first of these with exports as a share of output and with imports as a share of U.S. consumption allows the authors to examine whether industries that are more competitive internationally are more wage-sensitive. Yet, the authors find no such evidence.

Another group of labor input variables have strong positive effects. They are the share of the adult population in the state without a high-school degree interacted with the share of workers in the industry who are unskilled; the unionization rate in the state (to proxy for the presence of skilled workers) interacted with the fraction of employees in the industry who are precision production workers; and the share of the adult population in the state with bachelors' degrees or more education interacted with the fraction of industry workers who are executives or professionals. Also included are group variables measuring transportation costs. Of these, a coast dummy interacted with heavy goods exported and a coast dummy interacted with heavy goods imported measure whether industries are import-intensive or export-intensive. Neither of these has positive and significant coefficients. Finally, the share of the industry's output that is sold to consumers interacted with population density and with the difference between a state's share of income and its share of manufacturing employment are both significantly and positively related to employment.

How well do these measured natural advantage variables explain agglomeration defined at the U.S. state level? The simplest possible model with no regressors other than share of manufacturing employment, a pure urbanization effect, for which (4.37) predicts $E(S_{j\ell}) = \text{mfg}_\ell$ and (4.35) implies a mean value of $\hat{\gamma} = 0.051$. The fact that 28.1 percent of the sample has $\hat{\gamma} > 0.051$ suggests "substantial" agglomeration. For the automobile industry, this estimate is 0.127, while 12.8 percent of manufacturing industries have $\hat{\gamma} > 0.10$. Allowing for effects from the 16 cost-intensity interacted terms without industry-specific weights reduces the estimate of $\hat{\gamma}$ to 0.048. The explanatory power of the model is even greater when multiplicative industry-specific dummies are allowed. In the latter case, $\hat{\gamma} = 0.041$ and about 20 percent of the measured geographic concentration may be attributed to the few observed natural advantages that are being measured. While it is encouraging that the explanatory variables used do reduce the explained portion of agglomeration, there is plenty that is due to intraindustry spillovers and not to observable intrinsic characteristics of locations.

4.4.2.1 *Empirical Characteristics of Industries and the Ellison–Glaeser Agglomeration Index*

From among numerous applications of the Ellison–Glaeser index a particularly noteworthy one is that used by Rosenthal and Strange (2001), who use zip code–, county-, and state-level employment data for manufacturing industries and three different definitions of industries based on two-, three-, and four-digit SIC codes for the fourth quarter of 2000 in order to compute the Ellison–Glaeser index at those different levels of aggregation. The data, from the Dun and Bradstreet database, are aggregated up to zip code level. The agglomeration measure $\hat{\gamma}$ is then regressed against two groups of industry characteristics. One group proxies for natural advantages associated with proximity to inputs and includes energy, natural resources, water, and inventories, all per dollar of shipment. If industries do concentrate in order to be close to energy sources and natural resources, then these variables should have positive coefficients. The last variable is an indirect way to control for transport cost per mile of shipping. Industries that do not produce perishable goods experience lower shipping costs and are thus more likely to agglomerate. A second group proxies for the importance of the Marshall typology. The first group is measured by means of manufactured and nonmanufactured inputs (such as legal, accounting, and financial services, and insurance and communication) per dollar of shipment. Manufactured inputs are more likely to be important for agglomeration. The second group is measured by innovations per dollar of shipment, and is likely to have a positive effect on agglomeration. The availability of labor market pooling is harder to measure. Rosenthal and Strange propose three alternative proxies of labor skill, that is, net productivity per worker, the share of supervisory and support labor in production, and the percentage of workers with doctorates, master's degrees, and bachelor's degrees. They expect the effects on agglomeration of these variables to be positive.

Rosenthal and Strange find that these factors play different roles in explaining the Ellison–Glaeser index. Variables that proxy for physical input and product shipping costs, including reliance on natural resources, manufactured inputs, and production of nonperishable output, all positively affect state-level or finer lower levels of geography. The geographic scope of these effects suggests that state-level transportation modes, that is, train, truck, and barge transport, may play an important role in the location patterns of industries sensitive to shipping costs. At the other extreme, knowledge spillovers positively affect agglomeration only at the zip code level, possibly because such spillovers attenuate rapidly across space.[8] Finally, reliance on skilled labor positively affects agglomeration at all geographic levels. This latter result is particularly robust and may reflect spillover benefits that arise when skilled workers can seek out new job opportunities without having to move out of the county or out of the state of the their residence. Together, these patterns explain an important share of the variation in state- versus county-level agglomeration across industries up to 30 percent. Rosenthal and Strange also find that employment in newly formed establishments is much less systematically related to underlying determinants of agglomeration than employment in existing establishments. This could reflect a dynamic selection mechanism where only establishments that choose locations conducive to agglomerative spillovers and to benefits from natural advantages survive. But their results could also reflect a fundamental change in the nature of establishment location decisions. These authors' utilization of existing data is ingenious and elucidates factors underlying the Ellison–Glaeser index, but their estimations with the Ellison–Glaeser index as a dependent variable are not obviously justifiable in terms of an underlying model. Yet, the tradition of running regressions of indices against explanatory variables is long-standing.

4.5 OTHER APPROACHES TO STUDYING AGGLOMERATION ECONOMIES

Recall the definition of localization and urbanization externalities (effects) given in section 4.3.3 above. Different theories have different implications about localization versus urbanization effects. Still, it is hard to use evidence to distinguish among competing theories, that is, whether a site's attractiveness originates in, one, natural advantages, two, interfirm production externalities, which may be due to either localization or urbanization externalities, or three, economic geography forces.

Next I review a number of studies that look at changes in industrial concentration in relation to firms' entries and exits. An in-depth analysis of a particular industry, marketing, provides a view of particularly important localization effects. Next, studies that rely on distance-based measures avoid the loss of information on correlates of localization when one aggregates over spatial units. Last, I examine information-theoretic approaches.

4.5.1 Dynamics of Industrial Concentration When Firms Enter and Exit

In an effort to assess how different factors may contribute to *changes* in geographic concentration over time, Dumais, Ellison, and Glaeser (2002) decompose the changes in industrial agglomeration, measured by the Ellison–Glaeser index, into components attributable to births of new plants, expansions or contractions of existing plants, and closures. Looking at dynamics allows them to isolate at which points over a plant "life cycle" concentration arises, how the dynamics of concentrated and nonconcentrated industries differ, and why geographic concentration has begun to decline in the last decade. For the same reason, one may distinguish between localization (Marshall–Arrow–Romer, MAR) spillovers and the urbanization (or Jacobs, in dynamic settings) by how diversity in urban environments helps attract startups. Existing theories have not addressed how externalities affect firms' decisions at different *stages* of a plant's life.

Dumais, Ellison, and Glaeser find, using the LRD of the U.S. Bureau of the Census (see chapter 2, section 2.13.4), that over the period 1972–1997 new plant locations are deagglomerating—as if within-industry spillovers are not strong enough to maintain agglomeration—and plant closures have been reinforcing agglomeration. Generally, even heavily concentrated industries exhibit considerable mobility, and therefore agglomeration is maintained by a combination of mean reversion in state industry employment shares and randomness in its growth. The authors report very different patterns in different industries and at different times, which suggests that different forces affect industries over their plants' life cycles.

A second noteworthy finding is that new plant births tend to reduce geographic concentration. The benefits from within industry spillovers for new plant formation apparently do not have a sufficiently strong effect to maintain concentration levels by themselves. The dispersion of new plants is more supportive of the Jacobs view of the importance of urban diversity in generating new businesses.

Rosenthal and Strange (2003) specify births of new establishments, $B_{\ell t}$, between periods $t-1$ and t, and total new-establishment employment, $N_{\ell t}$, at a location in zip code ℓ, expressed per square mile of area, with contextual effects at two levels of aggregation, the zip code and the metropolitan area. Specifically, plants in their data are located in 39,060 zip codes in 373 different metropolitan areas. The data come from the Dun and Bradstreet Marketplace Database, which provides information for more than 12 million establishments in the fourth quarter of 1997. New establishments are those that have been in the database 1 year or less. This study is also noteworthy for generating essentially a microgeographic data set from an existing database.

For $(B_{\ell t}, N_{\ell t})$, births between $t-1$ and t and total employment at time t in zip code ℓ, we may write

$$B_{\ell t} = b_z y_{z,\ell,t-1} + \gamma_{mb} + \epsilon_{bt}, \tag{4.38}$$

$$N_{\ell t} = n_z y_{z,\ell,t-1} + \gamma_{mn} + \epsilon_{nt}, \tag{4.39}$$

where the explanatory variables $y_{z,\ell,t-1}$ are partitioned into characteristics of each zip code ℓ and the metropolitan area m it belongs to. They include the level of employment in an establishment's industry inside a zip code and within precisely defined concentric circles outside it. The terms γ_{mb}, γ_{mn} are functions of metropolitan area controls such as fiscal policies, labor force quality, and wage rates, and of course the physical and geographic attributes of the area m, such as climate, harbors, and proximity to natural resources. Other determinants are establishments per worker (separately calculated for other industries and for own industry) that proxy for local competitiveness, and the diversity of economic activity as measured by the Herfindahl index of the concentration of 2-digit SIC industries.

Rosenthal and Strange estimate equations (4.38) and (4.39) with data on six industries that have attracted particular attention: software (SIC 7371–3,7375), food products (SIC 20), apparel (SIC 23), printing and publishing (SIC 27), fabricated metal (SIC 34), and machinery (SIC 35). Localization effects, measured in terms of own-industry employment within concentric circles of increasing radius, are generally positive when they are significant. Urbanization effects, measured in terms of other-industry employment within concentric circles of increasing radius, do not exhibit a clear pattern. Some are positive, suggesting that the respective industries prefer to be in large centers in spite of larger congestion costs while other industries prefer to locate at a certain distance from others. The average percentage change in the estimated localization effect per mile from 1 to 3 miles goes down by two-thirds to three-fourths, depending upon the particular industry, and clearly displays a nonlinear pattern. The authors obtain interesting results when they attempt to account for the size of neighboring establishments. Localization effects, both for new establishments and in relation to employment, and for five of the six industries studied, appear to be stronger for employment in smaller establishments than in larger ones. The authors interpret this as supporting Saxenian's (1994) argument that several dimensions of the local industrial presence matter. It may also be argued that, coming as it does at a time of extraordinary improvements in information technology, this evidence also favors the notion that physical interaction is complementary to other forms of communication (see chapter 9, section 9.7.2).

4.5.2 Sharp Localization Economies in the Marketing Industry

Localization effects seem to be particularly important in certain industries. The concentration of advertising in Manhattan is a case in point. Arzaghi and Henderson (2008) study patterns of births of advertising agencies across neighborhoods in southern Manhattan and seek to infer the profit function for such firms. They examine the effect on productivity and profitability of having closer advertising agency neighbors and hence better opportunities for meetings and information exchange. Their results indicate that advertising agencies trade off higher rents of clustering near where the action is against lower costs of operating farther away from other agencies.

Arzaghi and Henderson (2008) propose the following model. Let $\bar{C}_{j\ell}$ denote the fixed costs for a firm at location ℓ to make a contact with a firm at another location j (locations are defined as census tracts in Manhattan), let $V_{j\ell}$ be the level of communications from firm j measured as firm labor (which costs per unit $c(d_{j\ell})$, a function of the geographic distance between j, and ℓ), $d_{j\ell}$, and let $u_{j\ell}$ be a randomly drawn value for the match between the firms at j and ℓ. The value of the firm's contact with a firm at location j is denoted by $\left[[u_{j\ell}V_{j\ell}^{\gamma} - V_{j\ell}c(d_{j\ell})\right] - \bar{C}_{j\ell}$, where γ, $0 < \gamma < 1$, is a parameter. Once the random variable $u_{j\ell}$ has been observed, firm ℓ chooses $V_{j\ell}$ to maximize the value of a contact with a firm at j, $V_{j\ell}^{*} = [\gamma/c(d_{j\ell})]^{\frac{1}{1-\gamma}}[u_{j\ell}]^{\frac{1}{1-\gamma}}$. The ex post value of the contact,

$$(1-\gamma)\gamma^{\gamma(1-\gamma)}c(d_{j\ell})^{-\gamma(1-\gamma)}[u_{j\ell}]^{\frac{1}{1-\gamma}} - \bar{C}_{j\ell}, \tag{4.40}$$

decreases with distance $d_{j\ell}$ and the accordant communication cost $c(d_{j\ell})$. This implies, given a fixed cost $\bar{C}_{j\ell}$, that there exists a threshold distance $d_{\max}$ beyond which the value of the contact for the firm at ℓ becomes 0. For a firm at ℓ that uses land a_ℓ and communicates with several other firms, say n_j of them at each location j, expected profit may be written as

$$\Xi_\ell a_\ell^{\alpha} \exp\left[n_j\left(\sum_j^{d_{\max}}(1-\gamma)\gamma^{\gamma(1-\gamma)}c(d_{j\ell})^{-\gamma(1-\gamma)}[u_{j\ell}]^{\frac{1}{(1-\gamma)}} - \bar{C}_{j\ell}\right)\right] - R_\ell a_\ell, \tag{4.41}$$

where R_ℓ denotes rent per unit of land at site ℓ and Ξ_ℓ is a local amenities factor. A natural interpretation of $d_{\max}$ is as density. A larger $d_{\max}$ increases the range of interactions and thus expected profits as well.

Arzaghi and Henderson use census tract data (in Manhattan they coincide with city blocks) that allow them to distinguish locations in 250-meter increments. At this fine level of geographic detail, they can infer the benefits of close interactions. Their main data are interpolated rental cost per square foot of *class A* office space, the availability of commercial sites measured by the stock of private establishments, the distance measures to other advertising agencies, and the distance measures to complementary activities such as broadcasting establishments (where advertising is placed), headquarters of clients, or graphic services, which are used as inputs. They focus on the location decisions of new firms, where location is proxied by census tract, to estimate a logit model. The regressors include the total number of private establishments (including shopping centers) in the neighborhood to capture localized general agglomeration (urbanization) economies over and above headquarter locations, which are accounted for separately. Their data come from the Census Business Register (CBR), the Standard Statistical Establishment List (SSEL), and Advertising Red Books online (to generate maps). Their spatial distribution (by census tract) is linked with census data. The observed change in locational patterns between 1987 and 1992, reputedly in response to rent changes, is an important part of their identification strategy.

Arzaghi and Henderson find rapid spatial decay in the benefits from proximity to neighbors, even in the close quarters of southern Manhattan: scale externalities dissipate very quickly with distance and are gone after 750 meters. This is a new finding in the empirical literature supporting the notion that a high density of similar commercial establishments is important in enhancing local productivity for industries where information sharing plays a critical role.[9] Arzaghi and Henderson also find that the benefits of being in a better business neighborhood are capitalized into *land rents* and *not* into *wages*. This prompts questions about reliance on wage equations to estimate the benefits of urban agglomeration economies. The fact that information spillovers for advertising agencies (which may be characteristic of certain service industries) decay so quickly begs the question of what one measures with more aggregate data, such as scale effects at the MSA level. These results also pose a challenge for future work on how to distinguish among the spatial scales at which different types of agglomeration effects operate.

4.5.3 Testing for Localization by Means of Distance-based Measures

That sharp localization economies are associated with marketing, an industry that depends so much on informational interactions, is not a surprise. There is additional sporadic evidence on the importance of direct distance, and thus it is interesting to analyze the role of distance more extensively. This is particularly important for establishing localization effects since some information may be lost when one aggregates over spatial units that are often arbitrarily defined. Testing for localization by examining whether or not patterns in interfirm distances are random is a direct way when such data are available. An industry is localized if firms in it tend to be spatially concentrated relative to the distribution of overall economic activity. If an industry is localized, one would expect the firm-to-firm distances to be less for firms in their own industries than for a firm randomly chosen from the economy at large. Such an approach is not subject to bias due to aggregation nor to border effects. Information on continuous interfirm (or interplant) distances typically requires access to special and typically confidential sources of information. Duranton and Overman (2005, 2008) and Duranton, Gobillon, and Overman (2011) utilize microgeographic information for the United Kingdom based on the ARD. For more details on the data, see chapter 2, section 2.13.7.

Analyses of spatial patterns must tackle several issues. Consider, for example, establishment size. There are very small establishments whose spatial patterns are very different from those of larger establishments in the same industry. Compare boat building, in small establishments at inland locations, with shipbuilding, in much larger establishments at coastal locations. For an industry j with n_j establishments, Duranton and Overman (2005) calculate the Euclidean distance between every pair of establishments. This generates $n_j(n_j - 1)/2$ unique bilateral distances. Journey times for any given distance might differ between low- and high-density areas. At the same time, there are opposing effects at work. Roads are fewer in low-density areas (so actual journey distances are much longer than in proportion to Euclidean distances). They are more numerous in high-density areas (so Euclidean distances are a good approximation to actual distances) but are also more congested. Particular features of the geographic landscape can introduce errors: for example, the actual travel distance between two points on opposite sides of a geographic obstacle (like a river) exceeds the Euclidean distance between them.

Given noisy distance measurements, the authors use kernel methods for smoothing when estimating the distribution of bilateral distances. That is, if $d_{k'k''}$ denotes the Euclidean distance between establishments k', k'', belonging to industry j, given n_j establishments in industry j, the estimator of the density of bilateral distances (henceforth K-density) at any point d is

$$\hat{K}(d) = \frac{1}{n_j(n_j - 1)h} \sum_{k'=1}^{n_j - 1} \sum_{k''=k'+1}^{n_j} f\left(\frac{d - d_{k'k''}}{h}\right), \tag{4.42}$$

where h is the bandwidth and $f(\cdot)$ is the kernel function. Duranton and Overman calculate all densities using a Gaussian kernel with an appropriately set bandwidth.

Duranton and Overman (2005) use distance-based tests among firms in an exhaustive U.K. data set of establishments in four-digit industries. They find (at a 5 percent confidence level) that 52 percent of firms are localized, that localization mostly takes place at scales below 50 kilometers, that the degree of localization is very skewed (with a high degree of heterogeneity in locational patterns), and that industries follow broad sectoral patterns with respect to localization. Depending on the industry, smaller establishments can be the main drivers of both localization and dispersion. Three-digit sectors show similar patterns of localization at small scales as well as a tendency to localize at medium scales.

A comparison using the Ellison–Glaeser index of concentration, evaluated with the same data set, underscores the advantages of a distance-based approach. Specifically, the mean value of the Ellison–Glaeser index across 234 U.K. industries is 0.034 and the median is 0.011. These figures are larger than their counterparts for U.S. counties but below those of U.S. states. Of U.K. industries, 94 percent have a positive Ellison–Glaeser index and thus exhibit some localization. This is very close to the 97 percent, reported by Ellison and Glaeser (1997) for the United States. Lumping locations into geographic groups introduces border effects that bias downward existing measures of localization. This downward border bias may be why the Ellison–Glaeser index is consistently found to increase with the size of spatial units. Second, the relevant geographic scales for localization emerge naturally from the Duranton–Overman approach, as there is no need to define them arbitrarily ex ante. In contrast, different industries localize at different spatial scales. This problem is compounded by the fact that small scales (urban and metropolitan) turn out to be particularly important. These are obscured when using spatial units such as U.S. states, European regions, U.K. or U.S. counties, or U.K. postcode areas.

Duranton and Overman (2008) consider the location of entrants and exiters versus continuing establishments for various categories of firms, such as domestic- versus foreign-owned, large versus small, and affiliated versus independent. They also examine colocalization between vertically linked industries. Their analysis, just like that of Duranton and Overman (2005), rests on empirical estimation of equation (4.42), the density function of interestablishment distances, and provides a set of new stylized facts. For example, the empirical densities they report for four different industries, that is, dairies and cheese making, and the manufacture of ceramic household and ornamental articles, of hinges and locks, and of electric domestic appliances, differ widely. Interestingly, in contrast to Dumais, Ellison, and Glaeser (2007), who also study firm entry, Duranton and Overman find that entrants and exiters mostly follow their industry location patterns. Establishments that are affiliated with the same firm locate together. Arguably, it is only plants with similarly large and small sizes that exhibit clustering in many industries. They provide evidence of the colocalization of vertically linked industries at the regional scale, which appears to be a new stylized fact.

The same type of detailed microgeographic information, obtained by using the same ARD data set as the Duranton–Overman studies discussed above, allows Duranton, Gobillon, and Overman (2011) to examine the impact of local taxation on the location and growth of firms and thus on clustering as well. In contrast to Holmes (1998), who uses U.S. state boundaries, these authors pair neighboring establishments across *jurisdictional* boundaries, so as to control for unobserved heterogeneity in locational characteristics, in order to estimate the impact of taxation. Their results show, after controlling for unobserved location-specific effects and instrumenting for local taxation, that local taxation has a negative impact on employment growth but no effect on entry.[10]

As these authors themselves state, these facts cry out for precise theoretical hypotheses. One can, in principle, define interactions based on geographic distances in computing a market potential function, which I take up in section 4.8 below. It is unlikely, however, that very sharp predictions regarding probability distributions for interfirm distances can be obtained.

4.5.4 Information-Theoretic Measures of Industrial Agglomeration

A number of (a priori atheoretical) measures of industrial agglomerations have been proposed by Mori, Nishikimi, and Smith and presented in a number of publications (Mori, Nishikimi, and Smith 2005, 2008; Mori and Smith 2009a, 2009b, 2009c). These measures make it possible to identify agglomerations on a map in a statistically systematic fashion by using cluster analysis techniques. They may also be linked to two well-known statistical regularities, the rank-size rule and Christaller's hierarchy of cities principle, and to a new one, the number-average size. A simple way to motivate these measures is to recall that urbanization and industrial concentration is sometimes dramatized by means of pictures of the earth from space. The clustering of lights and their brightness are very suggestive. What conclusions can one draw about economic behavior from such pictures or from their geocoded data counterparts?

One of the issues is that industrial concentration may or may not observe jurisdictional boundaries. If it does, we may want to know the significance of such boundaries. The measures that I have discussed so far in the present chapter, except for the distance-based measures of localization in section 4.5.3 above, are based on data collected according to jurisdictional boundaries such as metro U.S. areas, regions, states, and their counterpart definitions elsewhere.

Mori and Smith (2009b) develop the rigorous underpinnings of an approach for defining industrial clusters. This involves the concept of a cluster scheme, a partition of space where firms are more likely to be clustered that identifies the entire set of clusters. These partitions are convexlike sets where instead of convex segments of straight lines defining the set, Mori and Smith use minimal travel distances between centers, an economically appealing adaptation. They exclude irregular shapes, in view of the spatial compactness of agglomeration, and thus reduce the number of potential clusters. They also propose a computational analysis to detect whether the observed spatial distribution of establishments is not random and may be explained best by using statistical model-selection criteria for finding the best model as a "best cluster scheme." For each of a number of statistical techniques, such as likelihood ratio tests, Akaike's information criterion, and Schwartz's Bayesian information criterion (BIC), these authors compute the differences between the particular measures based on the observed distribution and on complete spatial randomness. They define the best cluster scheme as the one that maximizes this difference. There is a difficulty: the method requires defining spatial partitions, but the number of possible partitions of the space can be enormous. For this reason, these authors propose a cluster detection procedure that starts from the most significant, in terms of the information criterion (such as the BIC) basic region (say a municipality), and then grows the system of clusters by either expanding existing clusters or creating new clusters so as to improve the BIC until a local maximum is reached. This designates a partition of the national economic space where each industry's concentration is significantly most pronounced. Mori and Smith (2009c) apply a simple version of this latest proposed methodology. However, the earliest application, reported by Mori and Smith (2009a), is quite appealing, too, and I take it up next.

I adopt the notation of Mori and Smith (2009a), according to which an economy's continuous (location) space $\mathcal{L}$ is subdivided into disjoint municipalities, $\mathcal{L}_r, \ \mathcal{L}_\ell \subseteq \mathcal{L}$, with municipalities indexed by the set $R = \{1, \ldots, k_R\}$.

The municipalities partition the economy's space: $\bigcup_{r=1}^{k_R} \mathcal{L}_r = \mathcal{L}$. Suppose that establishment locations over space $\mathcal{L}$ may be described in terms of an *industry-specific probability distribution function*. Location decisions of different establishments in an industry may be treated as independent random samples from this unknown distribution. The class of all possible location models corresponds to the set of probability measures on $\mathcal{L}$.

Suppose that we identify groups of municipalities within which an industry's locational activity is more intense, that is, possibly disjoint *clusters* of municipalities, defined by subsets of the index set R: $C_k \subset R, \ k \in C \equiv \{1, \ldots, k_C\}$. All clusters make up a cluster scheme, $\mathbf{C}$. A cluster scheme is a partition of the index set of municipalities, $\mathbf{C} = (R_0, C_1, \ldots, C_{k_C})$.

For example, let the jurisdictions be U.S. states. In that case, a cluster could be the group of New England states {MA, CT, RI, NH, VT, ME}. The areal extent of cluster C_k is the union of the areas of all of its constituent jurisdictions, $\mathcal{L}_{C_k} = \bigcup_{r \in C_k}^{k_R}$, the entire land area of New England. The probability that an establishment locates in New England is $p_C(k) = P_C(\mathcal{L}_{C_k}), \ k \in C$.

The clustering of industry over the economy's space naturally may leave areas, residual regions, where location activity might not be very intensive. This cluster scheme is a set made up of a union of groups of all urban counties in the United States and the remainder of the country's counties. Establishments may still locate in nonurban U.S. counties. They would do so with a probability equal to the probability that an establishment will be outside clusters

$$p_C(0) = P_C(\mathcal{L}_{R_0}) = 1 - \sum_{j \in C} P_C\left(\mathcal{L}_{C_j}\right) \ j \in C.$$

How do establishments locate across clusters? To answer this we need to know how establishments locate within each cluster. The simplest possible assumption is that within each cluster location is totally random over economically usable, that is, economic space. Then the relative likelihoods of locating across clusters are equal to the ratio of the respective economic areas. For example, let the economic area of municipality ℓ be a_ℓ. The total economic area of cluster C_k is the sum of the economic areas of all municipalities that make up the cluster, $a_{C_k} = \sum_{\ell \in C_k} a_\ell$. The probability that an establishment will locate in municipality ℓ, conditional on its lying in cluster C_ℓ, is given by $P_C(\mathcal{L}_\ell | \mathcal{L}_{C_\ell}) = \frac{a_\ell}{a_{C_k}}, \ell \in C_k, k \in \{0\} \bigcup C$. The probability that an establishment will locate in municipality ℓ, given these assumptions, is

$$P_C(\ell) = p_C \frac{a_\ell}{a_{C_k}}.$$

These probabilities define a cluster probability model represented by the $k_{\mathbf{C}}$-dimensional vector of cluster probabilities: $P_{\mathbf{C}} = \{P_{\mathbf{C}} : \ell \in R\}$. Mori and Smith use this model in making inferences.

I consider now a particular industry and a sample of establishments, $k = 1, \ldots, K$, in that industry, each of which may locate independently of one another at only one of the municipalities $\ell, \ell = 1, \ldots, L$. Let x denote a realization of location decisions by the sample of all K firms:

$$x = \left\{ x_\ell^{(k)} : \ell \in R, k = 1, \ldots, K \right\}.$$

However, this is not perfectly observable; that is, we may not observe which municipalities firms are located in but only the clusters that contain those particular locations. I use the cluster probability model for cluster scheme **C** to compute the likelihood of an arbitrary realization x. Let $n_j(x)$ be the actual count of firms located either in cluster c of cluster scheme **C** or in a residual region:

$$n_c(x) = \sum_{k=1}^{K} \sum_{\ell \in C_c} x_\ell^{(k)}, \quad j \in \{0\} \cup C.$$

Given the assumptions that define the cluster probability model $P_{\mathbf{C}}$, the likelihood of sample x is

$$P_{\mathbf{C}}(x | p_{\mathbf{C}}) = a_{\mathbf{C}}(x) \prod_{j=0}^{k_{\mathbf{C}}} (p_C(j))^{n_j(x)} \tag{4.43}$$

where I have used the assumption that the n firms make independent location decisions and that $a_{\mathbf{C}}$, an auxiliary variable, is defined so that the quantities in (4.43) are actual probabilities:

$$a_{\mathbf{C}} = \prod_{i=1}^{n} \prod_{j=0}^{k_{\mathbf{C}}} \prod_{r \in C_j} \left(\frac{a_r}{a_{C_j}} \right)^{x_r^{(i)}} = \prod_{j=0}^{k_{\mathbf{C}}} \prod_{r \in C_j} \left(\frac{a_r}{a_{C_j}} \right)^{n_j(x)}.$$

One can use the probabilities according to (4.43) to obtain the log likelihood of a parameter vector $p_C(j)$ of any given cluster scheme **C** given sample x of location decisions. That is,

$$\text{LLF}(p_{\mathbf{C}} | x) = \sum_{j=0}^{k_{\mathbf{C}}} n_j(x) \ln \left[p_C(j) \right] + \ln[a_{\mathbf{C}}(x)]. \tag{4.44}$$

We may obtain an estimate for the parameter vector $p_C(j)$ by maximizing likelihood (4.44) with respect to $p_C(j)$. This is a well-defined maximization problem whose solution depends only on the summation term in (4.44). That is, the auxiliary variable $a_{\mathbf{C}}(x)$ is a function of constants and of observables but not of the unknown parameter vector $p_C(j)$. The maximum likelihood estimate identifies the parameters with the frequencies observed:

$$\widehat{p_C}(j) = \frac{n_j(x)}{n}.$$

For example, this is just like tossing a coin. After 12 heads and 8 tails turn up in 20 trials, we infer that the probability of heads for this coin is 60 percent.

The associated value of the log likelihood function (4.43) may be used as a criterion for the quality of model fit. However, such a criterion would be increasing in the number of clusters used. It would attain its maximum value with the finest possible disaggregation where clusters coincide with municipalities. Therefore, to circumvent this problem, we can adopt the Bayesian information criterion, which subtracts from the right-hand side of (4.44) a term to account for the model's complexity, $\frac{1}{2}k_C \ln(n)$. Mori and Smith use the BIC to define the best cluster scheme from all arbitrary partitions of R. This admits a large number of possibilities, including gerrymandered partitions that might not obviously lend themselves to reasonable definitions of clusters, as Mori and Smith (2009a) explain in detail. In fact, the latter study compares cluster schemes obtained with the BIC to those obtained with the Akaike information criterion. See (Mori and Smith 2009a).

4.5.4.1 *The Number-Average Size Rule*

Mori and Smith (2009a, 2009b, 2009c) are interested in broader patterns in the location decisions of firms. Consider the ratio of the mean of industrial employment in an industry in all the cities included in an area where an industry is clustered to the mean of industrial employment in cities that are not in its cluster but do contain positive employment. A similar measure may be defined in terms of establishment counts instead of employment. Both these measures, when plotted, are remarkably regular. Mori and Smith also show that, over a 20-year period, industrial location decisions are subject to a lot of churning. During the period 1980/1981–2000/2001 in Japan, all of the following happen: smaller and less diversified cities tend to stay smaller and less diversified, and larger and more diversified cities tend to stay larger and more diversified; at the same time, the locations at which agglomeration of industries takes place vary quite a lot.

Mori and Smith use data for the 160 three-digit (according to the Japanese SIC) manufacturing industries from the Establishment and Enterpriser Census of Japan in 2001. Economic areas are defined by subtracting forests, lakes, marshes, and underdeveloped areas from the total area of Japan, which yields 120,205 square kilometers, 31.8 percent, of the total area of Japan.

Mori and Smith find an interesting *statistical regularity*. Across the three-digit manufacturing industries in their data set, a linear regression of the log of the average size of cities where each industry locates against the log of the number of such cities gives a negative and statistically very significant coefficient and a very good fit. They call this the number-average size (NAS) rule. They also find it to be remarkably "stable" over time. In an effort to get at its economic underpinnings, they link it to *Christaller's hierarchy principle* (Christaller 1933) and to the *rank-size rule* for city size distributions. See also (Mori, Nishikimi, and Smith 2008). These particular results are more closely related to the issue of specialization, and I return to them in chapter 8, section 8.4, below.

4.6 EMPIRICAL EVIDENCE ON URBANIZATION (JACOBS) EXTERNALITIES: A LOOK FROM THE TOTAL FACTOR PRODUCTIVITY OF FIRMS

Next I turn to a number of noteworthy studies that utilize data that either have a panel structure or otherwise still allow researchers to follow firms (and/or plants) over time and thus offer some distinct advantages as a source of evidence on agglomeration effects. The general aim of these studies is to identify localization or urbanization effects via the measurement, directly or indirectly, of total factor productivity at the plant level. This imposes severe data conditions, which are taxing even when researchers avail themselves of true panel data on plants from U.S. Census sources.

Henderson (2003) uses plant-level data on productivity for 1972–1992 from the LRD of the U.S. Bureau of the Census (see chapter 2, section 2.13.4), and data for the period 1963–1992 from the Annual Survey of Manufactures (ASM) of the U.S. census.[11] Henderson calculates various contemporaneous and historical attributes of scale and diversity of the local industrial environment within and outside the industry. Henderson's study restricts attention to five major three-digit capital goods (machinery) industries and to the four major three-digit high-tech industries. The machinery industries are construction, metal-working, special industrial, general industrial, and refrigeration machinery and equipment. The high-tech ones are computers, electronic components, aircraft, and medical instruments.

Henderson estimates plant-level production functions for machinery and high-tech industries that allow for scale externalities from other plants in the same industry locally and from the scale or diversity of local economic activity outside the own industry at the same location. Henderson expresses the log output of plant k in MSA (or county) ℓ at time t, y_{kt}, as

$$y_{kt} = X_{kt}\alpha + \sum_{s=0}^{2} \zeta \ln \Xi_{\ell}(t-s) + \delta_t + f_{k\ell} - \epsilon_{k\ell t}, \tag{4.45}$$

where X_{kt} denotes a vector of productive inputs, $\Xi_{\ell}(t - s)$ is a vector of alternative industry characteristics that serve as total factor productivity, δ_t is a time effect, $f_{k\ell}$ is a plant k fixed effect, and $\epsilon_{k\ell t}$ is a contemporaneous fixed effect. Henderson considers a variety of alternative descriptions of each plant's environment such as own-industry employment, own-industry number of plants in the county and metropolitan area, contemporaneously as well as lagged by 5 and 10 years, and measures of localization effects such as the total number of plants in the same subindustry. Henderson also considers measures of industrial diversity to capture urbanization (Jacobs) externalities, such as a modified Ellison–Glaeser index, $G_{\ell} = \sum_j \left(\frac{E_{k\ell}}{E_{\ell}} - \frac{E_k}{E}\right)^2$, where $E_{k\ell}$, E_{ℓ}, E denote, respectively, employment in industry k in MSA ℓ, total employment in MSA ℓ over the relevant group of industries, and total national employment, again for the relevant group of industries. This measure increases with specialization. Therefore, a negative effect for G_{ℓ} in regressions according to (4.45) would imply classical urbanization (Jacobs) externalities.

Estimations along the lines of (4.45) require the availability of at least two observations per plant. Henderson experiments with a variety of alternative definitions of the appropriate industries. For example, for the high-tech industries, he considers employment in sophisticated business services, such as engineering and architectural services, research and testing, computer programming, medical and dental laboratories, and private colleges and universities.

Regarding localization effects first, Henderson reports that the count of other own-industry plants has strong productivity effects for high-tech but not for machinery industries. Single-plant firms both benefit more from and generate greater external benefits than corporate plants, given their greater reliance on the external business environment. He finds evidence of dynamic externalities only in the case of high-tech single-plant firms in that they benefit from the scale of past own-industry activity. He finds little evidence of benefits from the diversity or scale of local economic activity outside the industry. In fact, nondiversity of MSA manufacturing employment and nondiversity of MSA high-tech employment both produce positive, instead of negative effects and thus do not support the Jacobs hypothesis.

4.6.1 Interfirm Interactions versus Self-Selection

What is the mechanism through which larger cities help increase productivity of the firms they host? Urban agglomeration may enhance productivity by accommodating more productive interactions through interfirm learning. Or, it may enhance firm productivity through toughening competition and thus causing self-selection of more productive firms. Combes, Duranton, Gobillon, Puga, and Roux (2009) seek to distinguish between these possibly coexisting effects by examining the distribution of firms' productivities across cities. If stronger self-selection in larger markets attracts more-productive firms, it could cause less-productive firms to exit, thus leaving the productivity distribution of surviving firms left-truncated. Stronger agglomeration, on the other hand, right-shifts and dilates the productivity distribution. That is, although agglomeration and self-selection lead to similar predictions for mean firm productivities, they have different effects on the higher moments of the productivity distribution across cities. These authors examine these predictions by using four large-scale French establishment-level data from the INSEE. [12] Their empirical findings are based on comparing the distribution of firms' log productivities in large locations (urban areas with more than 200,000 people) with the distribution of firms' log productivities in small locations (urban areas with less than 200,000 people and rural areas) for two-digit manufacturing and business service sectors.

Working with estimates of total factor productivity (TFP) for *all* French firms, they find, for most sectors, weak evidence that the strength of selection varies across locations of different size. They obtain strong evidence in favor of agglomeration for almost all sectors: they find that agglomeration economies are stronger in denser areas. A back-of-the-envelope calculation suggests that the average value of the agglomeration effect, 0.26, corresponds to a productivity increase across the board (after accounting for selection) of roughly 4 percent for a doubling of city size, which is in line with what has been found by means of very different methods described in the agglomeration literature (Rosenthal and Strange 2004; Combes, Duranton, Gobillon, and Roux 2008). The distribution of firms' productivities in denser areas (in terms of employment) are remarkably well described by taking the distribution in less dense areas, dilating it, and shifting it to the right. Firms in denser areas (i.e., those with above-median density) are thus on average 9.7 percent more productive than those in less dense areas.

4.6.2 Identifying Agglomeration Spillovers from Quasi-Experimental Settings: "The Million Dollar Plants"

A rare glimpse into agglomeration spillover effects caused by newly locating plants is given by Greenstone, Hornbeck, and Moretti (2010). This unusual view rests on two sources of information. One is public, that is, identifying 47 plants whose location decisions were reported in *Site Selection*, a corporate real estate journal, and for which the authors are able to match to existing plant-level data from the Annual Survey of Manufactures (ASM). *Site Selection*, in its regular feature titled "Million Dollar Plants" (MDP), details the circumstances of plant location decisions. These include the county that each plant chooses *and* one or two runner-up "loser" counties. The loser counties survived a long selection process and narrowly lost. The authors quantify agglomeration spillovers by estimating how the productivity of incumbent plants changes when a new large plant opens in their county.

The authors estimate Cobb–Douglas production functions with TFP assumed to depend on the presence of the new plant using plant-level data from the ASM. For 16 of the 47 openings, they identify incumbent plants in the same two-digit SIC industry in both winning and losing counties in the 8 years preceding the opening. There are 73 losing counties in the sample. The data allow them to generate 28,732 observations for MDP counties and 418,064 for all counties. This study is very noteworthy because data on alternative locations not chosen are rarely available.

To estimate a newly opened plant's spillover effects, one needs to know the characteristics of counties that are identical to the winning one but that were not chosen by new plants. The paper uses information on the reported loser counties, from *Site Selection*, as a counterfactual for the incumbents in the winning counties after controlling for prexisting trends, plant fixed effects, industry and year fixed effects, and other observable controls. The counterfactual allows a comparison of winning to losing counties prior to the opening of the new plant. The trends in many characteristics are compared to those for the rest of the United States, with winning counties having higher rates of growth in income, population, and labor participation.

The study reports estimates of Cobb–Douglas production functions where regressing plant output while controlling for inputs of labor, capital (building and machinery), and materials allows indirect inferences on TFP as a residual. Let the set of the winner and associated loser counties for each plant k be referred to as a case and denoted by c, the industry of the plant by j, the time by t, and the year of opening by τ, which is normalized for each case so that $\tau = 0$ is the year of plant opening. Then, the regression specification for TFP, Ξ_{kcjt}, is

$$\begin{aligned}\ln \Xi_{kcjt} = {} & \delta\ \mathbf{I}(\text{Win})_{kc} + \psi\ \text{trend}_{ct} + \Psi\,(\text{trend} \times \mathbf{I}(\text{Win}))_{kct} + \kappa\ \mathbf{I}(\tau \geq 0)_{ct} \\ & + \gamma\,(\text{trend} \times \mathbf{I}(\tau \geq 0))_{ct} + \theta_1\,(\mathbf{I}(\text{Win})_{kc} \times \mathbf{I}(\tau \geq 0))_{kct} \\ & + \theta_2\,(\text{trend}_{ct} \times \mathbf{I}(\text{Win})_{kc} \times \mathbf{I}(\tau \geq 0))_{kct} + \alpha_k + \mu_{jt} + \lambda_c + \epsilon_{kcjt},\end{aligned} \tag{4.46}$$

where $\mathbf{I}(\mathcal{S})$, is an indicator function, equal to 1(0) if logical statement $\mathcal{S}$ is true (false) (e.g., $\mathbf{I}(\text{Win})_{kc} = 1$, if plant k locates in winner county c), trend_{ct} is a simple time trend, α_k is a plant-specific effect, μ_{jt} is an industry-specific time-varying shock to TFP, λ_c is a case-specific effect, and ϵ_{kcjt} is a random shock. Equation (4.46) expresses each plant's TFP in terms of interactions among observables that allow for a different intercept for all observations for winning counties, δ, for a common time trend ψ and a different time trend that differs for winning counties prior to the plant opening. If significant, these time trends would validate the research design.

The estimated trends in the TFPs of incumbent plants in winning and losing counties are statistically equivalent in the 7 years before the MDP opens. After the MDP opens, incumbent plants in winning counties experience a sharp relative increase in TFP. Five years later, the MDP opening is associated with a 12 percent relative increase in incumbent plants' TFPs, a substantial and statistically significant effect. On average, incumbent plants' outputs in winning counties are \$430 million higher 5 years later (relative to those of incumbents in losing counties), holding inputs constant. This is clear evidence of meaningful productivity spillovers generated by increased agglomeration.

4.7 THE ROLE OF INPUTS AND GEOGRAPHY IN LOCATION DECISIONS OF FIRMS

I turn next to a class of studies on location decisions of firms that allow better understanding of the sensitivity of agglomeration effects on prices or quantities of productive inputs, including shipping costs, and depend critically on the specification of total factor productivity. It clarifies further how valuable it is for identification of agglomeration effects for the analyst to have information on alternative decisions, just as in the case of million dollar plants discussed in section 4.6.2 above.

Consider the framework of Carlton's (1983) study, with a firm's production function with variable inputs denoted by $\mathbf{X} = (X_1, \ldots, X_m, \ldots, X_M)$, which may include labor of different qualities, services of capital of different types, and different types of material inputs. Let the respective vector of prices at location ℓ be $\mathbf{W}_\ell$, respectively. So, output by a firm in location ℓ, $Y_\ell = Y_\ell(\mathbf{X})$, is given by

$$Y_{k\ell} = \tilde{\Xi}_{k\ell} e^{\epsilon_\ell \gamma_\epsilon} \prod_{m=1}^{M} X_{mk}^{\gamma_m}, \tag{4.47}$$

a Cobb–Douglas production function with constant returns to scale, $\sum_m \gamma_m = 1$, where $\Xi_{\ell k}$ is total factor productivity (a constant at the moment) and factor $e^{\epsilon_\ell \gamma_\epsilon}$ denotes an unobservable specific effect that firm k enjoys in location ℓ. It is advantageous in specifying regression equations to work with the profit function, whose arguments being prices are more likely to be exogenous to each firm's decisions. If input X_M is held fixed (like a local input that might not be paid for, such as amenities, climate, and the like, which may not be directly purchased at a price), the price of output is denoted are $w_{Y\ell}$, and the prices of inputs are $w_{m\ell}$, then the corresponding restricted profit function is given by

$$\pi_{k\ell}(w_{Y\ell}; \mathbf{W}_\ell) = c_0 (w_{Y\ell})^{\frac{1}{\gamma_M}} \tilde{\Xi}_{k\ell}^{\frac{1}{\gamma_M}} \prod_{m=1}^{M-1} (w_{m\ell})^{\frac{-\gamma_m}{\gamma_M}} \dot{X}_{M\ell} (e^{\epsilon_\ell \gamma_\ell})^{\frac{\gamma_\epsilon}{\gamma_M}}, \tag{4.48}$$

where $\ln c_0 \equiv \ln \gamma_M + \sum_{m=1}^{M-1} \frac{\ln \gamma_m}{\gamma_M}$. Firms' choices imply valuations for fixed factors that are intrinsic characteristics of sites. By taking logs and dividing through by $\frac{\gamma_\epsilon}{1-1-\sum_{m=1}^{M-1}\gamma_m}$, the above equation becomes

$$\frac{\gamma_M}{\gamma_\epsilon} \ln \pi_{k\ell} = \frac{1}{\gamma_\epsilon} \ln w_{Y\ell} + \frac{1}{\gamma_\epsilon} \ln \tilde{\Xi}_{k\ell} - \sum_{m=1}^{M-1} \frac{\gamma_m}{\gamma_\epsilon} \ln w_{m\ell} + \frac{\gamma_M}{\gamma_\epsilon} \ln X_{M\ell} + \epsilon_\ell. \tag{4.49}$$

The probabilities that alternative sites may be chosen by a firm can be written in terms of the observable attributes of different sites, such as prices $\mathbf{W}_\ell = (w_{Y\ell}; w_{1\ell}, \ldots, w_{m\ell}, \ldots)$, of the quantity of the fixed factor X_M, and of the probability distribution function of the firm-location specific effects ϵ_ℓ's. With a large number of diverse sites, it is appropriate to make an assumption that firm k's draws of different sites' characteristics, $\epsilon_{k\ell}$, $\ell = 1, \ldots, L$, are independent and identically distributed according to a given distribution function. In that case, it is convenient to assume that the $\epsilon_{k\ell}$'s are extreme value–distributed with a cumulative distribution function $F(\epsilon_{k\ell}|\varpi) = \exp[-\exp[-\varpi(\epsilon_{k\ell} + \frac{\underline{e}}{\varpi})]]$, where $\underline{e} \approx 0.57721\ldots$ denotes Euler's constant. See chapter 3, section 3.9.1, for more details. Let the corresponding density function be denoted by $f(\cdot)$. This distribution has mean 0 and variance $\frac{\pi^2}{6\varpi^2}$. The probability that a firm will choose site ℓ is

$$\text{Prob}(\ell_k^* = \ell) =$$

$$\frac{\exp\left[\varpi\left[\frac{1}{\gamma_\epsilon}\ln w_{Y\ell} - \sum_{m=1}^{M-1}\frac{\gamma_m}{\gamma_\epsilon}\ln w_{m\ell} + \frac{1}{\gamma_\epsilon}\ln\tilde{\Xi}_{k\ell} + \frac{\gamma_M}{\gamma_\epsilon}\ln X_{M\ell}\right]\right]}{\sum_{\ell'=1}^{L}\exp\left[\varpi\left[\frac{1}{\gamma_\epsilon}\ln w_{Y\ell'} - \sum_{m=1}^{M-1}\frac{\gamma_m}{\gamma_\epsilon}\ln w_{m\ell'} + \frac{1}{\gamma_\epsilon}\ln\tilde{\Xi}_{k\ell'} + \frac{\gamma_M}{\gamma_\epsilon}\ln X_{M\ell'}\right]\right]}. \tag{4.50}$$

A number of remarks follow from this specification. One, if any of the explanatory variables do not vary across alternative sites, they will cancel out of both the numerator and the denominator on the right-hand side of (4.50). Two, the role of the site-specific amenity factor $X_{M\ell}$ may not be identified separately from total factor productivity, $\tilde{\Xi}_{j\ell}$, unless total factor productivity may be linked to other possibly observable factors that vary by location. Three, the price of firm j's output, $w_{j\ell}$, and total factor productivity, $\tilde{\Xi}_{j\ell}$, may be related to specific characteristics of the location that may be classified as localization and urbanization effects. I note that as the price of output is endogenous to location ℓ, it also reflects that market structure may be crucial for identifying the source of agglomeration effects, be that localization externalities, urbanization externalities, or just scale effects. Distinguishing among them may be possible if one makes falsifiable specifications. For example, one could specify the exact market structure of firm j's industry.

If the price of output and the prices of all measured inputs are observable, then the elasticities of factor inputs may be inferred from the ratios of the coefficients of $\ln w_{Y\ell}$, $\ln w_{m\ell}$, $m \neq M$, respectively, and similarly for $\ln X_{M\ell}$, if it is observable. In such a case, the returns to scale may also be inferred: $\sum_{m=1}^{M}\gamma_m$.

4.7.1 Choice of a Firm's Location and Factor Demands as Joint Decisions

The demand for labor by firm k, $X_{k\ell,}^D$, follows from Sheppard's lemma, $X_{k\ell,1}^D = -\frac{\partial\pi_{k\ell}}{\partial w_{1,\ell}}$. In logarithmic form, it is given by

$$\ln X_{1k\ell}^D = \frac{1}{\gamma_M}\ln p_{k\ell} + \frac{1}{\gamma_M}\ln\tilde{\Xi}_{k\ell} + \ln X_{M\ell}$$

$$-\sum_{m=1}^{M-1}\left(\frac{1-\sum_{j=1,j\neq m}^{M-1}\gamma_j}{\gamma_M}\right)\ln w_{m\ell} + \frac{\gamma_\epsilon}{\gamma_M}\epsilon_{k\ell}. \tag{4.51}$$

Note that adding $\ln w_{1\ell}$ to both sides of the above equation yields an expression for the log of payments to labor costs. Working in a like manner for all measurable inputs allows one, in principle, to identify the corresponding elasticities in the firm's (or industry's) production function. Since industry location is not random, such estimations may be biased unless location endogeneity is accounted for in the estimation process. Location implies entry into the local industry, which is related to industry scale, which in turn depends on output price and total factor productivity.

4.7.2 Estimation Results with the Carlton Model

Carlton (1983) estimates a model of firms' location choices jointly with employment decisions along the lines of (4.50) and (4.51). He assumes no additional features about the stochastic structure. He estimates the model by maximum likelihood. The likelihood that the event that firm *k* is observed at location ℓ and its labor demand is measured as $X_{1k\ell}$ is given by $\text{Prob}(\ell_k^* = \ell) f\left(\epsilon_{1\ell} | \ell_i^* = \ell\right)$. For the distributional assumptions made, this is given by (Dubin and McFadden 1984, 352):

$$f\left(\epsilon_{k\ell}^* | \ell_k^* = \ell\right) = \varpi \exp\left[-\varpi\left(\epsilon_{k\ell}^* + \frac{\underline{e}}{\varpi}\right)\right] \exp\left[-\exp\left[-\varpi\left(\epsilon_{k\ell}^* + \frac{\underline{e}}{\varpi}\right)\right]\right], \tag{4.52}$$

where $\underline{e}$ denotes Euler's constant, and

$$\epsilon_{k\ell}^* = \left(\frac{\gamma_\epsilon}{1-\gamma_1-\gamma_2}\right)^{-1} \ln X_{1k\ell}^D - \text{Regressors}_\ell + \frac{1}{\varpi} \ln \text{Prob}(\ell_k^* = \ell),$$

$$\text{Regressors}_\ell \equiv \frac{1}{\gamma_\epsilon} \ln w_{Y\ell} + \frac{1}{\gamma_\epsilon} \ln \Xi_{k\ell} - \sum_{m=1}^{M-1} \frac{\gamma_m}{\gamma_\epsilon} \ln w_{m\ell} + \frac{\gamma_M}{\gamma_\epsilon} \ln M_\ell,$$

and $\text{Prob}(\ell_k^* = \ell)$ is given from (4.50) above.

Carlton (1983) reports estimation results for equation (4.52) using maximum likelihood estimation methods with data from the Dun and Bradstreet database (see section 4.5.1 above). The data cover location, employment, and four-digit SIC codes for new branch manufacturing plants in 1967–1971. Carlton considers the following industries: fabricated plastic products (3079), communication-transmitting equipment (3662), and electronic components (3679). Carlton assumes electricity and natural gas as inputs in addition to labor. Wages and the prices of these inputs are defined at the SMSA level, and so is location. Carlton uses as additional locational attributes the following: personal, property, and corporate income taxes, localization effects, measured by local employment (production hours) in the respective four-digit SIC industry; technical expertise, which by being measured by the number of engineers in the region proxies for skilled labor supply; the ratio of current unemployment to the normal rate of unemployment (averaged over several years), which proxies for overall demand for the products of the location, on the one hand, and the availability of large pool of labor, on the other; business climate, which is defined as an aggregate of a large number of state incentives-linked business services [see Carlton (1983, 444), for details]. Carlton finds a large localization effect. Regarding prices, that of electricity is consistently significant across models and industries. The supply of skilled workers appears to matter only for communication-transmitting equipment. The aggregate tax variable does not perform well, perhaps because its being an average makes it measure inaccurately a firm's marginal tax burden associated with locating a plant in a particular SMSA. The implied estimate of $\gamma_1+\gamma_2+\gamma_3$, partial returns to scale, varies from 0.80 to 0.77 to 0.72 (Carlton 1983, 448). This study is particularly noteworthy because of its use of a complete structural model that allows researchers to keep track of the theoretical implications of their findings.

I note that correction for self-selection in the manner employed by Carlton is not needed when one actually observes, as in the case of million dollar plants (see section 4.6.2), alternatives that were not chosen. The availability of those data is clearly a superior alternative to arbitrary assumptions about the opportunity sets from which firms choose their locations.

Conceptually related are a number of studies by J. Vernon Henderson and associates. Henderson (1994) specifies the price of output jointly with total factor productivity as a function of geographic access (measured by the distance to the nearest major urban area), city amenities and geographic location, and a quadratic function of the number of firms and of the population (in logs). This reduced-form model is appropriate when output price data are unavailable. Similarly, here discriminating between price and scale effects, under competitive conditions, rests on specifying functional forms. Henderson expresses an industry's presence in an urban area in the form of a regression equation he estimates jointly with the number of firms present and the factor shares in the urban area. Thus, the model estimates whether or not a city hosts an industry, and if it does how many firms the industry is composed of. He utilizes data for 126 Brazilian cities for 1970 with industry data for automobile components (present in 83 percent of the cities in the sample) and agricultural machinery (present in 57 percent of the cities in the sample). For cities that host a particular industry, the model predicts a relationship among the number of firms, the supply of entrepreneurs, and the share of expenditure on labor, capital, and materials. For those that do not, the model is used to predict the likelihood that the *optimum* number of firms is zero. Henderson estimates the labor, capital, and materials shares in the production function at 0.212, 0.104, and 0.412, respectively. The remainder, 0.270 out of 1.00, Henderson attributes to entrepreneurship, the supply of entrepreneurs, and the stochastic structure. The estimates imply that profits per firm peak at 3 or 4 firms for a city of 50,000, as opposed to 33 firms for a city of 5 million people.

Henderson, Kuncoro, and Turner (1995) use U.S. data from several sources, including *County Business Patterns*, *Census of Manufactures*, and the *State and Metropolitan Area Data Book*, to study employment growth rates for five traditional capital goods industries, namely, machinery, electrical machinery, primary metals, transportation equipment, and instruments. Employment growth is higher in cities with high past employment concentrations in own industry. They find that a history of industrial diversity had a significant effect only for instruments, suggesting that urbanization (Jacobs) externalities are not so important for such mature industries. For three newer high-tech industries, that is, electronic components, medical equipment, and computers, they find that the number of cities hosting them and employment in them have grown rapidly. High past urban diversity increases the probability that a city will attract a high-tech industry. Such diversity, when interacted with a dummy for significant past own employment is very significant, and so is the presence of a more highly educated labor force. Therefore, urbanization (Jacobs) externalities are important in attracting high-tech industries, whereas localization effects (MAR dynamic externalities) are critical for retaining high-tech industries. It is thus not surprising that in order to identify clear patterns in urban industrial employment growth in the United States, one has to employ careful modeling.

4.8 ECONOMIC GEOGRAPHY MODELS FOR FIRMS' LOCATION DECISIONS

A distinguishing feature of economic geography models, and arguably their most innovative feature,[13] is their reliance on monopolistic competition models for the markets in firms' inputs and outputs. If the producers of differentiated inputs operate with increasing returns to scale and there is free entry, then the variety of firm inputs and consumer goods is related to the size of the economy, and a firm that uses such inputs benefits from variety in their availability. Clearly, a similar effect operates on the side of consumers. If consumption goods are produced using differentiated inputs, then consumers also benefit from variety. This is the feature that gives rise to multiple equilibria and processes of cumulative causation. In this section, I emphasize models of firms' location decisions in terms of concepts of new economic geography. They are central to chapters 7 and 9 below.

I adopt a simplified Krugman-style new economic geography model for a firm that is considering serving many markets out of a single location and follow Head and Mayer (2004a).[14] Let $\ell = 1, \ldots, L$ denote locations (regions), E_ℓ the expenditure by consumers at location ℓ on a representative good variety manufactured at location j, $w_{\ell j} = w_j \tau_{\ell j}$, the delivery price faced by consumers in region ℓ for products from region j defined by the product of the mill price in region j and the transport cost $\tau_{\ell j}$, and $q_{\ell j}$ the corresponding demand. When consumers' utility function is a symmetric CES with elasticity of substitution σ among all varieties, the Krugman model yields that expenditures by consumers in location ℓ on a representative good variety manufactured in j satisfy

$$w_{\ell j} q_{\ell j} = \frac{w_{\ell j}^{1-\sigma}}{\sum_{k=1}^{K} n_k w_{\ell k}^{1-\sigma}} E_\ell, \quad \ell = 1, \ldots, L, \tag{4.53}$$

where n_k is the number of varieties produced at location $k = 1, \ldots, L$. Each of the manufactured varieties is produced with increasing returns to scale according to the cost function $c_j q_j + \bar{C}_j$, where c_j is the constant marginal cost and $\bar{C}_j$ is the fixed cost of producing q_j of output. Using the standard Dixit–Stiglitz price-setting arguments, the producer of each variety maximizes the gross profit associated with its operation in each market, $\pi_{\ell j} = (p_j - c_j)\tau_{\ell j} q_{\ell j}$. The resulting plant price is simply a mark-up over marginal costs:

$$w_j = \frac{\sigma}{\sigma - 1} c_j.$$

This makes the gross profit in each market ℓ for a variety produced in region j be: $\pi_{\ell j} = \sigma^{-1} w_{\ell j} q_{\ell j}$. The total value of imports (including shipping costs) from all n_j firms at location j is equal to: $n_j w_{\ell j} q_{\ell j} = n_j w_j^{1-\sigma} \tau_{\ell j}^{1-\sigma} E_\ell \left(W_\ell^*\right)^{\sigma-1}$, where

$$W_\ell^* \equiv \left[\sum_{k=1}^{K} n_k w_k^{1-\sigma} \tau_{\ell k}^{1-\sigma}\right]^{\frac{1}{1-\sigma}}, \tag{4.54}$$

denotes the *price index* at location ℓ.[15]

The intuition behind the price index (4.54) plays an important role in the model. It is a generalized "geometric mean" of the costs of delivering to location ℓ units of goods from all its suppliers. It assigns a larger weight to locations with greater numbers of suppliers, n_k, $k = 1, \dots, L$, and to good access to market ℓ by suppliers at k, in the form of lower shipping costs as measured by high $\tau_{\ell k}^{1-\sigma}$ (recall that $\sigma > 1$). A location that is served by a large number of nearby low-priced suppliers will have a low price index.

The total net profit of a firm operating out of region k, the sum of all gross profits from serving all other locations minus the fixed costs of establishing a plant at location k, is

$$\Pi_k = \frac{1}{\sigma}(c_k)^{1-\sigma} \sum_{\ell=1}^{L} \tau_{\ell k}^{1-\sigma} E_\ell \left(W_\ell^*\right)^{\sigma-1} - \bar{C}_k, \quad k = 1, \dots, L. \tag{4.55}$$

It is convenient to define the *real market potential* for a firm operating out of region k and serving the entire economy, that is, all other regions, as

$$\text{RMP}_j = \sum_{\ell=1}^{L} \tau_{\ell j}^{1-\sigma} E_\ell \left(W_\ell^*\right)^{\sigma-1}, \quad j = 1, \dots, L. \tag{4.56}$$

This real market potential modernizes the one introduced by Harris (1954). The new feature is the price index term, $W_\ell^{*\sigma-1}$.

Head and Mayer (2004b) use the definition of profit (4.55) that a firm expects to earn by locating a plant at k to structure a discrete choice of location regression. Let U_k denote the result obtained by adding back $\bar{C}_k$ to the right-hand side of (4.55), multiplying by σ, raising to the power of $\frac{1}{\sigma-1}$, and taking logs:

$$U_k = -\ln c_k + (\sigma - 1)^{-1} \ln\left(\text{RMP}_k\right).$$

This is developed further by assuming that the unit cost of production is a Cobb–Douglas function of wages, $\bar{w}_k$, and land rents, ϱ_k, $c_k = \bar{\Xi}_k \bar{w}_k^{\alpha} \varrho_k^{1-\alpha}$, where $\bar{\Xi}_k$ denotes total factor productivity. U_k now becomes

$$U_k = -\alpha \ln \bar{w}_k - (1-\alpha) \ln \varrho_k + (\sigma-1)^{-1} \ln (\text{RMP}_k) - (1-\alpha) \ln \varrho_k + \ln \bar{\Xi}_k. \quad (4.57)$$

Roughly speaking, a firm chooses among locations in order to maximize this index. Lower factor costs are advantageous for a location, obviously. However, more subtle is the effect of market potential. Tracing through the definition of the price index, we see that the price index W_ℓ^* reflects the competition that firms in location k face from rival firms in other locations in serving each export market ℓ. The competition increases with the number of rivals (which reduces the price index) and decreases with trade and production costs. As more firms choose region k, the market becomes more crowded, lowering its market potential RMP_k and thus making the firm less profitable. This is not true for all firms, however, as they may differ in terms of total factor productivity, which is location-specific.

Head and Mayer (2004b) estimate this model using plant location decisions during 1984–1995 by 452 Japanese firms in the European Union. These authors decompose the location-specific index defined in (4.57) into

$$U_\ell = \bar{u}_s + \hat{u}_\ell + \xi_\ell,$$

where $\bar{u}_s$ is a component specific to the country or state level, $\hat{u}_\ell$ is a component specific to the regional level, and ξ_ℓ is a random shock. In their setting, the $\bar{u}_s$ are functions of characteristics of E.U. states (countries), that is, national corporate tax rates and "social charges" like payroll taxes and pensions contributions as a share of total labor costs. The $\hat{u}_\ell$ stands for characteristics of E.U. regions (NUTS1[16]) such as wages, unemployment rate, objective 1 eligibility, area, number of establishments in the region in the plant's two-digit industry classification, number of Japanese firms' affiliates in the region in the plant's three-digit industry classification, and number of affiliates owned by the same Japanese parent or members of the same vertical *keiretsu*.

This decomposition suggests a natural specification for ξ_ℓ, the random shock, namely, a nested logit model for discrete choice over states and regions. As discussed in chapter 3, section 3.9.1, if ξ_ℓ follows a multivariate extreme-value distribution with parameter ς, then the probability of a firm's choosing region j conditional on choosing state s is given by $\text{Prob}_{\ell|s} = \exp[(1-\varsigma)W_\ell - \mathcal{T}_s]$, where $\mathcal{T}_s \equiv \ell = \ln\left[\sum_{\ell \in s} \exp[(1-\varsigma)W_\ell]\right]$ denotes the inclusive value for state s. The substitutability parameter ς ranges between 0 and 1. If $\varsigma \to 1$, then different regions are perceived as identical (perfect substitutes) inside state s and the choice is made in terms of the maximum value of the index. If $\varsigma = 0$, then regions within each state are perceived as independent, that is, patterns of substitution are the same between and within states, and the multinomial logit model applies.

In their analysis, Head and Mayer need to make up for two important components of the market potential function according to (4.56): trading costs, $\tau_{\ell k}^{1-\sigma}$, and the price indices, W_ℓ^*, which are not observed. Head and Mayer estimate them by means of auxiliary regressions using trade flows between countries, making up for the unavailability of information on domestic interregional trade patterns.[17] They find that market potential, that is, demand, matters for location choice: a 10 percent increase in market potential raises the likelihood of a region's being chosen by 3 percent to 11 percent, depending on the specification. Interestingly, specification of the Krugman measure of real market potential, as defined in (4.56), actually does not perform as well as the ad hoc Harris measure, which does not include the price index. Additional agglomeration measures, such as measures of preexisting Japanese plants, suggest important "path dependence," a form of social interactions. Such measures, clearly in the spirit of new economic geography, are not predicted by the particular model used. Full dynamic specifications in new economic geography settings can yield such predictions. See chapter 8.

The basic structure of the nested logit model performs well, and the estimated substitutability parameter ς ranges between 0.59 and 0.78 for the various specifications. It is not surprising that firms' location decisions are susceptible to jurisdictional boundaries; see the findings of Holmes (1998) who reports a large and abrupt increase in manufacturing activity when one crosses a U.S. state border from an "antibusiness" to a "probusiness" state. There exist qualitatively similar but more pronounced effects at international borders. The effect of discontinuity in the cost of doing business at a boundary implied by a probusiness set of policies is amplified by the combined effect of agglomeration, tariffs, and transport costs.

These results support the new economic geography model. The trading costs structure can be adapted so as to model detailed aspects of economic (and political) geography. Empirical research continues to explore additional aspects of new economic geography models. As the review by Head and Mayer (2004a) underscores, there have been findings in favor of some propositions of the theory, such as the positive relationship between market size and wages (the urban aspect of which I discuss in chapter 6 below), and the importance of backward linkages, as in the role of market potential here. There is also evidence of productivity benefits derived from location in densely populated areas, which I discuss in chapter 6, but the mechanism that drives this pattern has not been unambiguously identified yet. Evidence offered by Hanson (2005), who structures an investigation firmly based on the Helpman (1998) version of the Krugman model, suggests parameter estimates that reflect the importance of scale economies and transport costs and that demand linkages between regions (in Hanson's case, U.S. counties) are strong and growing over time but are quite limited in geographic scope. I return to the Hanson model in chapter 8 below.

A particularly noteworthy feature of economic geography models that is not often put to empirical tests is the potential multiplicity of equilibria. A rare example of such a study involves the division of Germany following World War II and the relocation of Germany's air hub from Berlin to Frankfurt. Redding, Sturm, and Wolf (2011) treat the combination of those two events as an exogenous shock to the hub's location and argue that it was Germany's *division* and *not a change* in economic fundamentals that caused the move of

Germany's air hub from Berlin to Frankfurt. They compare Germany with other European countries, examine the determinants of bilateral departures from German airports to destinations worldwide, and use information on the origin of passengers departing from each German airport. They find that Frankfurt's current dominance in German air traffic cannot be explained by its location relative to destinations worldwide or by the density of local departures originating within 50 kilometers of the airport. It is transit traffic that makes the difference. They show that the potential benefits from relocating Germany's air hub from Frankfurt to another city within Germany would be small relative to plausible values for the sunk costs of creating the hub in the first place. There is no evidence, they claim, of a return of the air hub to Berlin, which was reestablished as Germany's capital after reunification.

4.9 RISK POOLING BY FIRMS IN THE URBAN ECONOMY

Risk sharing, one of Marshall's three original forces of agglomeration, is related to both sides of the labor market. On the supply side, individuals may exchange job-related information, which in turn may be related to urban structure. On the demand side, individuals and firms may avail themselves of opportunities for risk sharing. Marshall's original argument is formalized by Krugman (1991b, 123–127, app. C). Krugman shows that agglomerations of workers and firms in the same region constitute stable (but "asymmetric") equilibria, and the "symmetric" (equiproportionate or uniform) distribution of workers and firms across locations is unstable.

Risk pooling as an agglomeration argument need not depend on risk aversion. Expected profits, and therefore expected profit-maximizing decisions as well, depend on the variance of the equilibrium wage rate, which decreases as the number of firms increases. Risk aversion would reinforce the benefits from labor pooling. Turnover and unemployment also reinforce the impact of employment fluctuations. The specification of job matching for workers and firms would naturally reflect fundamentals of the urban economy. In the remainder of this section I discuss first the most noteworthy empirical studies and then introduce a dynamic model of risk pooling in the urban economy.

The latest and most precise empirical study on the role of labor market pooling in influencing the spatial concentration of manufacturing establishments uses data from the United Kingdom (Overman and Puga 2010). Their simple model, a refinement of one by Krugman (1991b, 123–127, app. C) predicts that establishments prefer locations where local economic outcomes affecting firms even out productivity shocks and thus attenuate their impact on local wages. The benefits of labor pooling will be greater, the larger the heterogeneity of establishment-specific shocks in the sector. Establishments thus improve their ability to adapt their employment to good and bad times. Consequently, sectors across which shocks are more heterogeneous are more likely to be agglomerated. Naturally, establishment-specific shocks are more likely to be heterogeneous if the respective establishments belong to different industries. So this is an argument in favor of urbanization externalities and against localization externalities. I present below a model that accommodates such properties and in addition makes them contingent on urban economy-wide measures.

Overman and Puga use data for establishments, for which they observe the postcode of their location, four-digit industrial classification, and employment from the Annual Respondent Database, which underlies the Annual Census of Production in the United Kingdom (see chapter 2, section 2.13, for more details on the ARD). Restricting attention to production establishments in manufacturing industries, defined in terms of the Standard Industrial Classification 92 (SIC 15000 to 36639) for the United Kingdom (excluding Northern Ireland) for 1990–2004 yields 557,595 plants, with a mean of 4.16 observations per plant.

Overman and Puga measure the likely importance of labor pooling by calculating the fluctuations in employment of individual establishments relative to their sector and averaging by sector. The theory suggests that a labor pooling advantage exists if, whenever a plant expands employment (for idiosyncratic reasons), many other plants using similar workers are contracting, and vice versa. The panel structure of the data allows them to measure the idiosyncratic shock to a plant in any given year as the difference between the percentage change in the plant's employment and the percentage change in the industry's employment (in absolute value). They show that sectors whose establishments experience more idiosyncratic volatility are more spatially concentrated, as indicated by the Ellison–Glaeser index, even after controlling for a range of other industry characteristics that include a *novel* measure of the importance of localized intermediate suppliers. This measure allows the authors to qualify the role of an industry's share of intermediate purchases. For an industry to cluster in order to share intermediate suppliers, it must be the case not only that the sector makes large purchases of intermediates but also that those intermediates are supplied by industries that are themselves very spatially concentrated.

Several other studies offer additional evidence for the key arguments of Krugman (1991b). Hong (2008) uses establishment-level data in the Korean manufacturing sector to show that firms in cities with larger labor pools are likely to experience more flexible adjustments in employment. A doubling of own-industry employment within commuting distance of the area where an establishment lies increases the establishment's flexibility in employment adjustment over two years by 37 percent. Bleakley and Lin (2007) use U.S. data from IPUMS and the *State and Metropolitan Area Data Book* to show that, on average, workers change occupation and industry less in more densely populated areas. The result is robust when standard demographic controls are used and when aggregate measures of human capital and sectoral mix are included. The authors find the opposite result, that is, higher rates of occupational and industrial switching for a subsample of younger workers. These results together suggest increasing returns to scale in matching in labor markets and returns to experience in denser urban areas.

Strange, Hejazi, and Tang (2006) seek to explore agglomeration economies for firms empirically that arise from sources of uncertainty that may be due to competitiveness, to special hiring needs, and to technological innovativeness. Firms' profitabilities in such circumstances will depend on their ability to adapt by agglomerating. Firms facing more uncertainty will agglomerate in larger cities or industry clusters. Firms facing less uncertainty will be found in small cities or outside clusters. These ideas allow for the possibility that firms sort, in terms of types and sizes, into different cities that accommodate firms with different "risk mitigation" needs. These authors find that all uncertainty-related agglomerative forces matter empirically but in different ways. Whereas competitive instability and technological innovativeness affect city size, skill orientation is associated with industry clustering. High uncertainty is measured by the probability that a firm will need a particular resource, such as workers with specialized skills. Higher uncertainty makes larger city size more attractive. However, the effect of size may be due either to urbanization (think of New York and high-end fashion) or to localization (think of Silicon Valley and the information technology industry).

The empirical application reported by Strange, Hejazi, and Tang relies on Canadian firms' responses to innovation from the 1999 Survey of Innovation (SI), a survey of establishments, classified at the three-digit level of the North American Industry Classification System (NAICS),[18] and additional data from the 1998 Labour Force Survey of Canada. Industries selected are supposed to be "footloose," that is, selling in national and international markets, and consequently choose to locate where they can best serve their markets. Establishments in the SI are linked to contextual information for the metropolitan area of their location, one of Canada's Census Metropolitan Areas (CMAs) with an urban core and at least 100,000 inhabitants. This information on the local environment for each establishment's respective CMA is based on information from labour force surveys. The authors develop three alternative uncertainty indices: competitive instability, skill orientation, and innovativeness. Obtained from the SI, these indices are based on establishments' own descriptions of their competitive environments and what they consider "key strategic factors associated with success" (Strange, Hejazi, and Tang, 2006, 341, table 2). These, and some of their constituent measures, are regressed against an industry-specific dummy urbanization index and an industrial concentration (localization) index computed from each establishment's local contextual information, separately for each of six selected industries (primary metals, fabricated metals, machinery, computers and electronics, electrical equipment, and transportation equipment). They find that competitive instability, skill orientation, and innovativeness are positively associated with agglomeration. In the cases of competitive uncertainty and innovativeness, firms facing uncertainty are found in large cities but not in industry clusters.

In the case of worker skills, firms facing uncertainty are found in specialized industry clusters but not in large cities.

4.9.1 A Dynamic Krugman–Overman–Puga Model

In the model that follows I rework the Overman and Puga (2010) adaptation of the Krugman (1991b) model in order to express frictions that firms face in the labor market. I do so by using the "large-firm" version of the Pissarides model of labor market frictions. Chapter 5, section 5.7, below, introduces a full urban model with labor market frictions à la Mortensen and Pissarides (Mortensen and Pissarides 1999; Pissarides 2000), as adapted by Wasmer and Zenou (2002). It is interesting to do so because, as I argue at greater length in chapter 5, there are features of the model, such as the role of search externalities, that may be underpinned by social interactions.[19]

Let H_{kt} denote firm k's employment, V_{kt} the stock of outstanding vacancies announced by firm k, and $w_{\ell t}$ the wage rate at location ℓ, all at time t. Hiring occurs via posting vacancies, and the stock of vacancies is a firm's sole decision variable. A vacancy costs γ per period and generates a hire with probability q_t. Thus, the expected length of time until a unit of labor is hired is equal to q_t^{-1}, if q_t were constant. I define formally this probability, $q_t = q(v_t)$, in chapter 5, section 5.7, as a decreasing function of labor market tightness, the ratio of vacancies to the number of unemployed, v_t. Separations occurring in period $t-1$ are reflected in employment in period t. Each job (unit of employment) may be destroyed with exogenous probability d. The firm's period t revenue is assumed to be quadratic in H_{kt}, so that its expected cash flow from period t on is expressed as

$$(b + \epsilon_{kt})H_{kt} - \frac{1}{2} g H_{kt}^2 - w_{\ell t} H_{kt} - \gamma V_{kt} \frac{1}{1+\rho} \mathcal{E}[Re\, V_t],$$

where b, g are positive parameters, ϵ_{kt} denotes a random variable that is independent and identically distributed across all firms in each period and has zero mean and constant variance $\mathrm{Var}(\epsilon)$, and $Re\, V_t$ is the firm's remaining value. The change in employment from period $t-1$ to period t is

$$H_{kt} - H_{k,t-1} = q_t V_{kt} - d H_{k,t-1}. \tag{4.58}$$

Vacancies are posted in period t after ϵ_{kt} is realized, and hires from them affect the firm's employment in the same period.

I obtain a first-order condition for employment H_{kt} that maximizes the firm's expected discounted cash flow. By working with the value of the firm's cash flow for two successive periods, after substituting for V_{kt}, $V_{k,t+1}$ by using (4.58) for $t, t+1$, the first-order condition for firm k's optimal employment policy H_{kt} is

$$H_{kt} = \frac{1}{g}\left[b + \epsilon_{kt} - w_{\ell t} - \left(\frac{\gamma}{q_t} - \frac{1-d}{1+\rho}\mathcal{E}_t\left[\frac{\gamma}{q_{t+1}}\right]\right)\right], \tag{4.59}$$

where ρ is the time discount rate. This condition expresses the fact that the user cost of labor to the firm from an additional unit of employment equals the wage rate plus the cost of friction. This is the cost of posting vacancies necessary to hire an additional unit of labor, $\frac{\gamma}{q_t}$, minus the cost saved because a fraction $1-d$ of workers stay on with the firm in the following period (discounted to the present), $\frac{1-d}{1+\rho}\mathcal{E}_t\left[\frac{\gamma}{q_{t+1}}\right]$.

By solving for H_{kt}, assuming a large number of firms, and summing up over all N_ℓ firms' demands, I obtain a solution for the equilibrium wage rate at ℓ:

$$w_{\ell t} = b - \left(\frac{\gamma}{q_t} - \frac{1-d}{1+\rho}\mathcal{E}_t\left[\frac{\gamma}{q_{t+1}}\right]\right) - g\frac{1}{N_\ell}\bar{H}_\ell + \frac{1}{N_\ell}\sum_k \epsilon_{kt}, \tag{4.60}$$

where $\bar{H}_\ell$ denotes the supply of labor at ℓ. The equilibrium wage rate at t depends not only on the average labor supply per firm but also on labor market tightness at t. Higher labor market tightness at t makes it more expensive to hire now. Higher labor market tightness at $t+1$ is advantageous to the firm because it foregoes hiring costs to the extent that a portion $1-d$ of jobs survive into period $t+1$.

Using the solution for the equilibrium wage rate from (4.60) in the expression for the optimal employment yields

$$H_{kt} = \frac{1}{g}\left(\epsilon_{kt} - \frac{1}{N_\ell}\sum_k \epsilon_{kt}\right) + \frac{1}{N_\ell}\bar{H}_\ell. \tag{4.61}$$

The firm's expected employment is equal to labor force per firm at ℓ. The effect of risk pooling is reflected, as reported by Overman and Puga (2010) in the stochastic shock, which now declines by $\frac{1}{N\ell}\sum_k \epsilon_{kt}$.

To clarify a firm's location decision, I express optimum cash flow per period in terms of observables and shocks as follows:

$$\frac{1}{2}g\left[b + \epsilon_{kt} - w_{\ell t} - \left(\frac{\gamma}{q_{\ell t}} - \frac{1-d}{1+\rho}\mathcal{E}_t\left[\frac{\gamma}{q_{\ell,t+1}}\right]\right)\right]^2 + \frac{1-d}{q_t}H_{k,t-1}. \tag{4.62}$$

Ignoring stochastic shocks, at first, the typical firm benefits from a lower wage rate and a smaller d, lower exogenous turnover. It also benefits from a smaller γ, from lower hiring costs, and from smaller labor market tightness at t, that is, lower competition in the labor market now, but from higher labor market tightness at $t+1$ relative to t. By taking the expectation of cash flow from (4.62) at the steady state, I have

$$\frac{1}{2}g\left[\frac{1}{N_\ell}\bar{H}_\ell\right]^2 + \frac{1-d}{N_\ell}\bar{H}_\ell\mathcal{E}\left[\frac{1}{q}\right] + \frac{1}{2}g\,(\mathrm{Var}[\epsilon_k]$$
$$+\mathrm{Var}[w_\ell] + \mathrm{Var}\left(\frac{\gamma}{q} - \frac{1-d}{1+\rho}\mathcal{E}_t\left[\frac{\gamma}{q}\right]\right)\Big)$$

$$+\frac{1}{2}g\left(-\mathrm{Cov}[\epsilon_k, w_\ell] - \mathrm{Cov}\left[\epsilon_k, \frac{\gamma}{q} - \frac{1-d}{1+\rho}\mathcal{E}\left[\frac{\gamma}{q}\right]\right]\right.$$

$$\left.+\mathrm{Cov}\left[w_\ell, \frac{\gamma}{q} - \frac{1-d}{1+\rho}\mathcal{E}\left[\frac{\gamma}{q}\right]\right]\right), \tag{4.63}$$

where taking expectations is understood as of before the resolution of uncertainty and time subscripts are dropped.

The first two terms of (4.63) are what the firm's cash flow per period would be equal to in the absence of shocks. It increases as $\frac{\bar{H}_\ell}{N_\ell}$, the ratio of workers to firms, increases because this increases the firm's labor force. The second term captures the labor pooling effect. Expected profits increase with the variance of the firm-specific productivity shock, σ_ϵ^2, and with the variance of the local wage, $\mathrm{Var}(w_\ell)$, because of the convexity of profits with respect to prices, a standard property of profit functions. However, expected profits decrease with the covariance of the firm-specific productivity shock with the local wage, $\mathrm{Cov}(\epsilon_k, w_\ell)$. The reason is that if the local wage is higher when a firm wishes to expand production in response to a positive shock and lower when the firm wishes to contract production in response to a negative shock, profits become less convex in the shock and fall in expectation. This is a key intuition of the model that Overman and Puga (2010) exploit, which highlights the microeconomic foundations of labor pooling as a source of agglomeration: firms prefer locations where their productivity shocks are evened out rather than heavily reflected in local wages.

To the Overman–Puga formulation, the introduction of labor market frictions here adds two additional effects. One is that expected profits decrease with the covariance of the firm-specific productivity shock with the net cost of hiring an additional worker, $\mathrm{Cov}\left[\epsilon_k, \frac{\gamma}{q} - \frac{1-d}{1+\rho}\mathcal{E}\left[\frac{\gamma}{q}\right]\right]$. The second is that expected profits increase with the covariance of the local wage rate with the net cost of hiring an additional worker, $\mathrm{Cov}\left[w_\ell, \frac{\gamma}{q} - \frac{1-d}{1+\rho}\mathcal{E}\left[\frac{\gamma}{q}\right]\right]$, because of concavity. Finally, by using the equilibrium solutions for the endogenous variables, the expected cash flow according to (4.63) at the steady state becomes

$$\frac{1}{2}g\left[\frac{1}{N_\ell}\bar{H}_\ell\right]^2 + \frac{1-d}{N_\ell}\bar{H}_\ell\mathcal{E}\left[\frac{1}{q}\right] + \left(1 - \frac{1}{N_\ell}\right)\frac{\mathrm{Var}[\epsilon_k]}{2g}. \tag{4.64}$$

Thus, the benefits of labor pooling increase with the heterogeneity of firms, as represented by $\mathrm{Var}[\epsilon_k]$. They also increase with improvement in the effectiveness of hiring, as represented by a decrease in the expected time until a hire is made, $\mathcal{E}\left[\frac{1}{q}\right]$.

The introduction of hiring costs thus augments the richness of the model, as they depend on labor market frictions. This allows for the rate at which vacancies return employment to depend on the industry mix at a particular location because the composition of the labor force itself may reflect the industry mix at each location. The nature of shocks and their correlation with the wage rate may also depend on the industry mix. I examine these issues further in chapter 7, section 7.8.

Expressions similar to (4.60) and (4.62) are a generalization of the work of Krugman (1991b, 125–127), who argues that the symmetric allocation of workers and firms is an unstable spatial equilibrium. This holds because in the vicinity of a symmetric allocation of workers and firms, reallocating workers so that the ratio of workers to firms remains constant leaves workers indifferent but allows one location have have more of both. In Krugman's case, optimum expected profit implies that they are higher with more firms because of risk pooling. Carrying this argument to its logical conclusions implies that for reasons of risk pooling firms would agglomerate.

Two additional remarks are in order. First, it is straightforward to allow for capital and land as productive factors. It is particularly interesting in the context of assessing how economic activity is reflected in land values to consider introducing land only. In that case, let the above model be considered per unit of land. Then at the steady-state dynamic equilibrium with free entry, the optimum profit from (4.62) accrues as land rent; see the article by Lucas (2001) and a related discussion in chapter 5, section 5.5. Again, land is valued in terms of the economic value it generates. Second, the model of risk pooling developed here abstracts from fully modeling the determination of the firm's output price. Chapter 7, section 7.8, shows how the output price depends on the fundamentals driving labor market frictions and thus reflects the industrial composition of the urban economy.

4.10 CONCLUSION

This chapter starts with a simple model of location decisions of firms. A multinomial logit model of location choice by firms readily follows from this simple assignment model, matching firms with sites. Adding features that introduce interdependence among firms allows this workhorse model to clarify different roles that interfirm externalities play in the creation of urban agglomerations. Many of the models that underlie typically used measures of agglomeration, such as the Ellison–Glaeser index, result from complicating the stochastic structure of the original multinomial logit model by means of different types of unobserved attributes of different sites that coexist with the benefits from the presence of other firms in the same or different industries. Empirically, differences in observed attributes of sites, such as access to resources and prices of inputs, are important but still leave room for intraindustry spillovers. The presence of, and physical distances from, other firms are also important determinants of firms' location decisions. Physical distances are appropriate in measuring proximity and circumvent reliance on spatial aggregation. By allowing different industries to experience localization spillovers at possibly different spatial scales, one avoids biases resulting from border effects. Certain kinds of spillovers, like knowledge spillovers, seem to attenuate quite rapidly with the distance between establishments.

The literature suggests that the effects on firms' productivities are stronger when industries are agglomerated both because of the selection of firms and of direct productivity effects of agglomerations. Information-theoretic measures of industrial agglomeration also bolster the case for different spatial patterns of agglomeration across industries. Industrial agglomerations are empirically related to patterns of specialization. An empirical expression of the hierarchy principle, a counterpart of a loglinear rank-size rule, taking the form of a linear estimated relationship between the number of industries and the average size of the cities that host those industries exhibits a very good fit. Risk pooling as an agglomeration force is also shown to be important, with establishments experiencing more idiosyncratic shocks being more spatially concentrated. The evidence from the multitude of empirical studies on firms' location decisions suggests that urbanization (Jacobs) externalities alternate roles with localization economies over time, as in the case of high-tech industries, with the former being important in attracting them in the first place and the latter being critical for retaining them.

Although not explicitly treated in this chapter, there is ample room for a policy role in industrial concentration. Even in very simple settings, the price mechanism alone cannot be trusted to function adequately. Prexisting industrial development is decisive in attracting industry, while it is still possible to seed new developments by means of local industrial policies.

CHAPTER 5

Social Interactions and Urban Spatial Equilibrium

5.1 INTRODUCTION

All city dwellers experience serendipitous urban encounters. One person mentions an event, another person links it to something else, a third speculates, and as a result a theory is developed that might influence those particular people's actions and lives later on that day, and perhaps beyond too, and not just their economic lives. All this originates in random encounters facilitated by density.

In this chapter I build on the foundations laid down in chapters 2–4 to address social interactions when economic agents operate in actual physical space, measured by the distance between each other and to urban centers within cities. This allows me to draw a distinction from the treatment of individuals and firms, in chapters 3 and 4, respectively, where proximity is defined as group membership (or community). It also brings out one of the central attractive features of urban economics, that is, analysis of the urban spatial structure by means of elegant arguments that readily lend themselves to geometric depiction. I examine how the existence of direct social interactions among individuals and firms may enrich the explanation of urban spatial structure.

This chapter is organized as follows. First, I provide a benchmark, the canonical Alonso–Mills–Muth (Alonso 1964; Mills 1967; Muth 1969) spatial model of a city in its bare essentials, and examine its implications for urban density and the associated pattern of land prices in the case with a predetermined center, the central business district (CBD). All economic and noneconomic interactions are assumed to take place in the CBD, and all amenities are located there. The canonical model delivers sorting by observables when individuals differ in terms of income: individuals segregate by income.

Next, I assume that individuals and firms value interactions with others, interactions are costly, and there is *no* predetermined center. The different geometry of locational equilibrium does not show up in the location of the CBD itself because by exploiting symmetry one can conclude that activity will peak at a geometric center. Instead, it shows up in a characteristic spatial variation of density and land rents as we move away from the endogenous CBD.

Self-organization of economic activity in space when social interactions are dispersed leaves a characteristic signature, as I show later in this chapter. I highlight these findings with key empirical results. I end the chapter by examining urban spatial equilibrium when location decisions are motivated by the acquisition of job-related information. Such analyses help evaluate policy initiatives that aim at predetermining the city center relative to dispersed self-organized outcomes. The policy initiatives may improve welfare by reducing the cost of interactions. Such interventions may also interfere with the attractiveness and special character of urban areas if the attractions that emanate from interactions themselves sustain the urban fabric.

5.1.1 The Alonso–Mills–Muth Canonical Urban Model: Individuals

I deal first with location decisions of individuals; location decisions of firms are considered in section 5.3 below. I assume that the typical individual (or household, using the terms interchangeably) derives utility from consuming housing (just land, here) in quantity $h(\ell)$ and a composite nonhousing good, $c(\ell)$, when at location ℓ, indicated by the distance from a city's *not necessarily* predetermined CBD: I consider a city arranged initially along a line.[1] The utility function is denoted by $\Omega(h(\ell), c(\ell))$ and is increasing concave in both of its arguments. The budget constraint is

$$c(\ell) + R(\ell)h(\ell) = \Upsilon - \mathcal{T}(\ell), \tag{5.1}$$

where Υ denotes income, $\mathcal{T}(\ell)$ denotes transportation costs as a function of distance from the CBD, and the price of the composite good is the same throughout the urban area and thus set equal to 1. The choice of (h, c) conditional on ℓ, in order to maximize utility $\Omega(h, c)$, subject to (5.1), must satisfy the first-order condition:

$$\frac{\Omega_h(h, c)}{\Omega_c(h, c)} = R(\ell). \tag{5.2}$$

The optimal bundle $(h^*(\ell), c^*(\ell))$ follows by solving (5.1) and (5.2) for housing and consumption. In developing the locational equilibrium model, it is convenient to work with a dual representation of preferences. By substituting back into the utility function for the optimal bundle, I obtain the indirect utility function,

$$\mathcal{O}(R(\ell); \Upsilon - \mathcal{T}(\ell)) \equiv \Omega(h^*(\ell), c^*(\ell)). \tag{5.3}$$

For spatial equilibrium, the typical individual must be indifferent across all urban locations. This is ensured by requiring invariance of the indirect utility with respect to location. This gives a condition that the land rental rate must satisfy at spatial equilibrium. Using Roy's identity, $h^*(\ell) = -\frac{\mathcal{O}_1}{\mathcal{O}_2}$, the condition becomes

$$R'(\ell) = \mathcal{T}'(\ell)\frac{\mathcal{O}_2}{\mathcal{O}_1} = -\mathcal{T}'(\ell)\frac{1}{h^*(\ell)}. \tag{5.4}$$

Alternatively, $R(\ell)$, from (5.4), may be interpreted as an individual's bid per unit of land.

The intuition of condition (5.4) is simple: living farther away from the CBD increases transportation costs, and therefore land rent must decline with distance from the CBD so as to make living in different locations equally attractive to individuals. Specifying the utility function and integrating (5.4) with respect to ℓ gives a solution for the equilibrium land rental rate. Alternatively, this gives individuals' bid rent functions.

5.1.2 An Example

Let land extend along a line away from the CBD. Closing the model requires that we characterize equilibrium in the land market. That in turn will determine the constant of integration in $R(\ell)$. Alternatively, we may assume that equilibrium utility is obtained from other opportunities in the economy. Setting equilibrium utility in the city equal to what is exogenously given determines the constant of integration. An example clarifies things. Let $\Omega(h, c) \equiv c^{1-\beta}h^{\beta}$, for which $\mathcal{O} = \beta^*(\Upsilon - \mathcal{T}(\ell))R(\ell)^{-\beta}$, where $\beta^* \equiv \beta^{\beta}(1-\beta)^{1-\beta}$, a constant. This readily implies that for spatial equilibrium, $R(\ell) = R(0)\left(1 - \frac{\mathcal{T}(\ell)}{\Upsilon}\right)^{1/\beta}$.

If the city size is given, that is, if the supply of land is given, then equating it with the demand for land determines $R(0)$. Alternatively, if the opportunity cost of land is given, then equating the land rental at the edge of the city to its opportunity cost yields a condition to be satisfied by $R(0)$ and the land size of the city, $\bar{\ell}$. So, by equating demand and supply of land, all unknowns are determined. Alternatively, we could work with the level of utility, which is given to each city in an economy with many cities. Equating $\mathcal{O}$ to the level of utility exogenously given to a particular city determines directly the land rental rate and therefore, from the condition for land equilibrium, the land size of the city. This is sometimes called the open-city model (Brueckner 1987). In that case, it follows that $R(0)$ is increasing with the level of utility in a particular city, its attractiveness. Equivalently, one may work with city size in terms of population. In all cases, the housing market equilibrium along with a boundary condition determines the urban equilibrium. Taking the log of the land rental rate, $\ln R(\ell) = \ln R(0) + \frac{1}{\beta}\left[\ln(\Upsilon - \mathcal{T}(\ell)) - \ln \Upsilon\right]$, clarifies that the effect of city size, via $R(0)$, is neatly separated from the effect of the cost of accessibility to the CBD, which reflects only transportation costs and provides all spatial variation in the land rental rate within a city.

5.1.3 Dispersed Amenities

The amenity role of the CBD is reflected in the value of the distance from it, a key metric. What if residents value amenities that are dispersed over the urban area? Amenities may be exogenous, like parks and other features of the natural landscape. Or they may be endogenous, attributes conferred on locations by decisions that agents themselves make or by the characteristics of agents at different locations.

I follow Brueckner, Thisse, and Zenou (1999) and incorporate dispersed amenities into the model by introducing the density of amenities $a(\ell)$ as an additional argument in individuals' utility function $\Omega \equiv \Omega(h(\ell), c(\ell); a(\ell))$. Individuals treat it as a parameter. I adapt the definition of the indirect utility function, defined in (5.3), in the obvious way: $\mathcal{O}(R(\ell); Y - \mathcal{T}(\ell); a(\ell)) \equiv \Omega(h^*(\ell), c^*(\ell); a(\ell))$. With only a single type of household in the urban economy, locational equilibrium implies a generalization of (5.4):

$$R'(\ell) = -\frac{\mathcal{T}'(\ell)}{h^*(\ell)} + \frac{\mathcal{O}_3}{h^*(\ell)\mathcal{O}_2} a'(\ell). \tag{5.5}$$

The rent gradient now reflects an additional effect, that of the amenity. If the direct amenity effect on utility is positive, $\mathcal{O}_3 > 0$, and is nondecreasing with distance from the CBD, the total effect on the rent gradient is positive. In order for the amenity to offset the negative effect of transportation costs on the land rent gradient, $a'(\ell)$ must be positive and sufficiently large. In section 5.1.3.2, below, I take up a number of examples of how data on spatial variation in amenities within cities provide support for this key prediction.

5.1.3.1 *The Impact of Income Heterogeneity*

If two groups of individuals who differ only with respect to income, $Y_1 < Y_2$, coexist in a city and compete for land, then in the absence of an amenity effect, each group will locate in that area of the city where it outbids the other group. If a threshold point exists, $\hat{\ell}$, it comes where the land bid rent curves for the two groups become equal, where both groups face the same price: $R_1(\hat{\ell}) = R_2(\hat{\ell})$. So the difference in housing consumption at $\hat{\ell}$ is due to the difference in income net of transportation costs. If income net of transportation costs is higher for the higher-income group, then $h_2(\hat{\ell}) > h_1(\hat{\ell})$. Under the assumption that the marginal cost of transportation depends on the opportunity cost of time, then $\mathcal{T}_1' < \mathcal{T}_2'$. The locations of the two groups depend on the difference between the slopes of the bid rent curves at $\hat{\ell}$, $R_2'(\hat{\ell}) - R_1'(\hat{\ell})$. That is, from (5.5) this difference is equal to

$$- \left(\frac{\mathcal{T}_2'\hat{\ell}}{h_2(\hat{\ell})} - \frac{\mathcal{T}_1'\hat{\ell}}{h_1(\hat{\ell})} \right) + a'(\hat{\ell}) \left(\frac{\mathcal{O}_3\left(R_2(\hat{\ell}); Y_2 - \mathcal{T}_2(\hat{\ell}); a(\hat{\ell})\right)}{\mathcal{O}_2 h_2(\hat{\ell})} - \frac{\mathcal{O}_3\left(R_1(\hat{\ell}); Y_1 - \mathcal{T}_1(\hat{\ell}); a(\hat{\ell})\right)}{\mathcal{O}_2 h_1(\hat{\ell})} \right). \tag{5.6}$$

Ignore for a moment the dependence of indirect utility on amenities. Then, whether or not the higher-income group will occupy land nearer the CBD depends on the effect of income on the demand for housing: if housing demand rises less rapidly relative to unit transportation costs as income increases, then $\frac{T_2'(\hat{\ell})}{h_2(\hat{\ell})} > \frac{T_1'(\hat{\ell})}{h_1(\hat{\ell})}$, and the rich will live near the CBD and the poor in the suburbs; if, on the other hand, unit transportation costs rises less rapidly relative to housing demand as income increases, $\frac{T_2}{h_2(\hat{\ell})} < \frac{T_1}{h_1(\hat{\ell})}$, then the rich will live in the suburbs and the poor near the CBD.

In 2000, more than 14.5 percent of people living 0–10 miles from the CBD within U.S. cities were poor, but only 8.3 percent of among those living 10–25 miles from the CBD (in the "suburbs") were poor. Wheaton (1977) uses cross-sectional data from the Bay Area Transportation Study Commission to calculate these elasticities and finds them to be very similar. This undermines the notion that it is the difference in the elasticities that explains the urban spatial structure of U.S. cities. One can test the result that it is the magnitude of the income elasticity of housing consumption relative to the income elasticity of the cost of travel that explains spatial segregation by income. Glaeser and Kahn (2008) emphasize complementary evidence from the entire United States that the income elasticity of the demand for land is too small to explain the phenomenon. Using data from the 2003 American Housing Survey, they estimate income elasticities of the demand for land ranging from 0.25 to 0.50, depending on the specification. They offer compelling evidence that transportation costs are principally responsible for the concentration of poverty near the CBD. That is, subways are critical in making it more attractive for the rich to commute farther away from the CBD. They point to pronounced differences between older cities, which were large in 1900, and new cities. In older cities, income falls with distance from the CBD for the first 3 miles and then rises. In newer cities, income rises monotonically with distance from the CBD. In other words, this suggests that we are more likely to find the nonpoor living farther away from the CBD in newer cities, where commuters use only cars. In older cities, the high time cost of travel associated with subways and high central density discourages long commutes. Therefore, not surprisingly, we find the nonpoor near the center in older cities.

To obtain a prediction for land use in the presence of the amenity $a(\ell)$, one needs to assess how the term $\frac{\mho_3(\ell)}{h(\ell)}$ in equation (5.5) above varies with income. Brueckner, Thisse, and Zenou (1999) show that if the (constant) elasticity of substitution between nonhousing consumption, housing consumption, and the services of the amenity is less than 1, then the above ratio increases with income. If access to the amenity declines with distance from the CBD but the marginal effect of distance is small, then the poor will live in the center and the rich in the suburbs. If, on the other hand, the marginal effect with distance is negative and large in absolute value, then the amenity advantage of the center will draw the rich close to the CBD and the poor to the suburbs. In this case, increasing the amenity attractiveness of the CBD may reverse the location pattern. These predictions are testable. I review below a number of representative studies. Then I return to the impact on land use of joint variation in preferences and incomes in section 5.6.2 below.

5.1.3.2 *Examples of Spatial Variation in Exogenous Amenities within Cities*

In much of the United States elementary and secondary education is publicly provided along with other local public goods, such as police and education services, and financed principally by means of local property taxes. We can estimate the value that parents place on school quality by calculating how much more people pay for houses in jurisdictions with better schools. A large literature has examined this relationship, but attempts to estimate the causal effect of school quality on house prices have been complicated by the fact that better schools tend to be located in better neighborhoods (in terms of urban residents' incomes and other demographics). As a result, estimates that do not control for neighborhood characteristics will overestimate the value of better schools. However, the variation in the land rental rate as one moves across a boundary between adjacent jurisdictions with different schools is predicted to be abrupt because of the sudden change in school quality, $a(\ell)$. Black (1999) exploits this in seeking to impute the valuation by parents of elementary schoolchildren in different communities.

Black seeks to explain values of different housing units across different attendance and school districts in a number of Massachusetts towns[2] in terms of dwelling unit characteristics, neighborhood and school district characteristics, and average test scores in the respective school and attendance districts. The value of school quality is often taken to be the regression coefficient of the test score. The problem with such a regression is accounting for many neighborhood and school district characteristics that are not observed. Black eliminates this problem and the accordant endogeneity by replacing the vector of observed characteristics with a full set of boundary dummies for houses that share (on either side) an attendance district boundary. Conceptually, this methodology is equivalent to calculating differences in mean house prices on opposite sides of attendance district boundaries, while controlling for house characteristics, and relating this to differences in test scores. Her boundary dummies account for any unobserved characteristics shared by houses on either side of the boundary. In fact, in the context of such an estimation, the exogeneity of such an abrupt change across boundaries makes it particularly valuable as a source of variation. Differences in test scores across boundaries reflect differences in unobservable components of school quality such as better peers, better teachers or administrators, or more parental involvement at the school. Black finds that parents are willing to pay 2.5 percent more for a 5 percent increase in test scores.

A second example is land use in Moscow, Russia, prior to and following the collapse of Communist rule. As Bertaud and Renaud (1997) document, in Communist Moscow land use density increased with distance from the city center. Following Russia's adoption of a market economy, the land price showed a decrease in distance from the city center, and this decrease (downward rotation) had already become more pronounced from the first to the third quarter of 1992 as the market economy started developing.

Another example is the increasing adoption of markets by the People's Republic of China. Zheng and Kahn (2008) study Beijing's housing market, which had boomed over the previous 15 years. The city's population grew by 40.6 percent, and per capita income (in constant *renminbi*) by 273.9 percent from 1991 to 2005. Using two geocoded data sets, they study the real estate price gradient, the land price gradient, population densities, and building densities in Beijing. They show that the classic urban monocentric model's predictions are largely satisfied. They also document the importance of local public goods, such as access to public transit infrastructure, core high schools, clean air, and major determinants, most of which have exogenous locations, as important determinants of real estate prices. Distance from amenities reduces prices. A dummy variable indicating whether the housing project is within 3 kilometers of a university and the university's quality, as measured by its score in China's national university entrance examinations, increases prices.

5.2 URBAN SPATIAL EQUILIBRIUM WITH SOCIAL INTERACTIONS

I next examine the geometry of locational equilibrium when there is *no predetermined center* and social interactions are dispersed. Individuals anticipate that they have to travel around within an urban area to where others live in order to interact with them. I examine the corresponding problem for firms in section 5.3.1 below.

5.2.1 Individuals Value Being near Other Individuals

How do individuals locate when the city is assumed *not* to possess a *predetermined center*? I assume that individuals value being near others in the sense that they suffer disutility from greater average distance from the actual locations of all other individuals within a city. An urban center is actually implied by the locational pattern at equilibrium when individuals are motivated by a trade-off between utility for housing and nonhousing consumption and the disutility of being too far from other individuals (Beckmann 1976).[3]

Assume that the city extends over a finite segment of the real line and make its midpoint the center of the real line $(-\infty, \infty)$. An individual who locates at ℓ, $\ell \in [-\bar{\ell}, \bar{\ell}]$, and consumes housing $h(\ell)$ and nonhousing consumption $c(\ell)$ enjoys utility

$$\Omega(h, c; \ell) \equiv a \ln h(\ell) + c(\ell) - \mathcal{T}(\ell),$$

where $\mathcal{T}(\ell)$ now denotes the average distance of an individual at ℓ from all other individuals in the urban area. This is defined in terms of the density function as

$$\mathcal{T}(\ell) = \tau \int_{-\bar{\ell}}^{\ell} (s - \ell)\chi(s)ds + \tau \int_{\ell}^{\bar{\ell}} (\ell - s)\chi(s)ds, \tag{5.7}$$

where τ is a constant. (I discuss in section 5.3.2 that this assumption reflects properties of broader significance). With a budget constraint $\Upsilon = c(\ell) + R(\ell)h(\ell)$, utility maximization yields that housing consumption at any location ℓ requires that individuals spend on housing the same amount: $a = R(\ell)h(\ell)$. By defining housing demand per unit of land, $\chi(\ell) = h(\ell)^{-1}$, the indirect utility as a function of ℓ becomes $\Omega(h(\ell), c(\ell); \mathcal{T}(\ell)) = -a \ln \chi(\ell) + \Upsilon - a - \mathcal{T}(\ell)$. For locational equilibrium, the indirect utility must be equal across all locations: $a \ln \chi(\ell) + \mathcal{T}(\ell) = \bar{u}$, where the auxiliary variable $\bar{u}$ is a constant. Differentiating (5.7) with respect to ℓ twice, we have $\frac{d^2\mathcal{T}(\ell)}{d\ell^2} = 2\tau\chi(\ell)$. Using it with the locational equilibrium condition yields

$$\frac{d^2\mathcal{T}(\ell)}{d\ell^2} = 2\tau e^{\frac{1}{a}(\bar{u}-\mathcal{T}(\ell))}. \tag{5.8}$$

Integrating this equation (Beckmann 1976; Fujita and Thisse 2002) with respect to $\mathcal{T}(\ell)$ yields the equilibrium density function

$$\chi(\ell) = \frac{a}{\tau}C_A^2 \frac{e^{C_A|\ell|}}{(1+e^{C_A|\ell|})^2}, \tag{5.9}$$

where C_A is a constant of integration. C_A can be determined by imposing a housing market equilibrium given city population $\bar{N}$, city size $\bar{\ell}$, and the opportunity cost of land at $\bar{\ell}$, R_a. That is,

$$\bar{N} = 2\int_0^{\bar{\ell}} \chi(\ell)^{-1} d\ell = 2\frac{a}{\tau}C_A \frac{e^{A\bar{\ell}}-1}{e^{A\bar{\ell}}+1}.$$

Solving for C_A (Fujita and Thisse 2002, 178) yields $C_A^2 = \frac{\tau}{a^2}(\frac{\tau\bar{N}^2}{4} + 4R_a)$ and $\chi(0) = \frac{1}{a}(\frac{\tau\bar{N}^2}{16} + R_a)$.

The equilibrium density $\chi(\ell)$ from (5.9) exhibits symmetry around 0. So, the CBD will be at $\ell = 0$. Inspection of (5.9) reveals that it coincides with the expression for the derivative of the logistic function $C_A\left(1+e^{-C_A\ell}\right)^{-1}$ for $\ell \geq 0$ and is symmetrically expressed for $\ell < 0$. Therefore, the density function of individuals at equilibrium is symmetric around $\ell = 0$ and is bell-shaped, attaining a maximum of $\chi(0) = \frac{1}{a}\left(\frac{\tau\bar{N}^2}{16} + R_a\right)$ at $\ell = 0$, the inflection point of the logistic function. The equilibrium rent function given by $R(\ell) = \frac{a}{h(\ell)} = a\chi(\ell)$ is proportional to the density function and therefore inherits its properties. The peak of the density increases with $\bar{N}$ and with R_a.

Thus, decisions of individuals who value being near others, given the geometry of interaction, still generate a tendency toward centrality. Self-organization still implies a CBD. The variation in density with distance from the CBD betrays the impact of social interactions. In contrast, in the case of a predetermined center at $\ell = 0$, everybody travels to the CBD where all social interactions take place, and the cost of interacting with others is simply the cost of transportation to the CBD. In that case, spatial equilibrium yields the

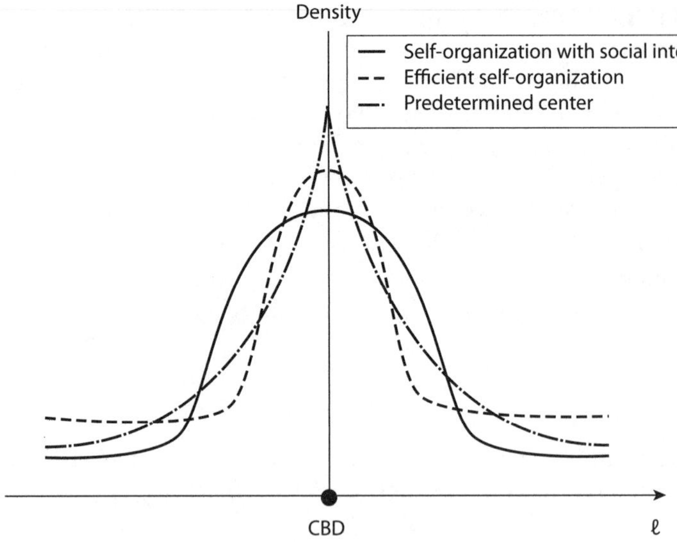

Figure 5.1. Urban spatial equilibrium with social interactions.
Source: Beckmann, (1976, fig. 8.3).

density function

$$\chi_p(\ell) = \bar{N}\frac{\tau}{2a}\left(1 - e^{-\frac{\tau}{a}\bar{\ell}}\right)e^{-\frac{\tau}{a}|\ell|}, \tag{5.10}$$

where I have solved for the value of the density function at its peak, $\chi_p(0)$, by equating supply of land with demand for land. This density is simply two negative exponential functions symmetrically set around the CBD.

We may compare the two densities (5.9) and (5.10), or equivalently the two rent functions, by setting values for $\bar{\ell}$ and C_A and computing the corresponding population and the resulting density at 0. The result is figure 5.1, which replicates that provided by Beckmann (1976, 124, fig. 8.3). The density in a city without a predetermined center, Beckmann's "dispersed city," has a smooth peak at the CBD, whereas in a city with a predetermined center at the CBD it has a discontinuous slope at the CBD,[4] and an inflection point on each site of the endogenous center.

We can see that the discontinuity in the slope of the density of individuals in the predetermined-CBD model reflects the center's role in a manner similar to the role of discontinuities in the landscape in the context of economic geography models (Fujita, Krugman, and Venables, 1999). The geometric shapes of (5.9) and (5.10) are sharply different. The density of a city without a predetermined center possesses a smooth peak at the CBD.

In Beckmann's model individuals care about the cost of visiting every other individual in the urban economy. Clearly, there could be scale economies in interaction costs as perceived by urban residents. In order to interact with individuals at a location s, an individual located at ℓ incurs transportation costs that are proportional to $|\ell - s|$ but acquires access to interactions with $\chi(\ell)$ other individuals at ℓ, which may also generate interaction costs that are a function of the density $\chi(\ell)$. The Beckmann solution (and my exposition) force the interaction costs to be proportional to the number of other individuals visited.

A dispersed city without a predetermined center at the CBD may be thought of as a competitive outcome. Its characteristics underscore the consequences of the spatial element in social interactions. Individuals impose externalities on one another when they decide where to locate independently and without taking into consideration the costs each of them imposes on all the others. It turns out that the competitive outcome produces greater dispersal than what is socially optimal (Borukhov and Hochman 1977). Interestingly, this is the opposite of the undesirable congestion we have in traditional models with a predetermined CBD. Fujita and Thisse (2002, 181–182) work out the case of the socially optimal density function for the Beckmann model. The functional forms for the densities are identical, with the socially optimal density given by (5.9), except with 2τ instead of τ and C_A defined accordingly. See figure 5.1. That is, when individuals internalize each other's interaction costs, they behave as if transportation costs are doubled and thus cluster *nearer* one another. Preference for a social life is sufficient to create a force of agglomeration but falls short of the socially optimal one. In the models described so far, proximity is desirable and no penalty for congestion is present (other than what is absorbed by housing price).

5.2.1.1 *An Application to Urban Redevelopment Projects*

The difference between the predictions of the two models, with and without a predetermined center, is seen in the properties of the rent gradients. Then one wonders whether data on rent gradients may be sufficient to empirically identify the role of social interactions in the model. The unknown parameters are the same in both cases, a and τ. The identification would rest on the particular functional properties of the rent or density functions. However, I am not aware of any direct empirical investigations along these lines. The model is a useful tool for thinking about the desirability of policy interventions. If, for example, a local government could induce everyone to interact at the CBD, then the urban economy would benefit from switching from a decentralized to the socially optimal outcome.

As Helsley and Strange (2007) document, there is a long history of urban redevelopment projects throughout the world designed to encourage social interactions in urban centers. One example is the development of the World Trade Center in New York City. The project was conceived in the context of a perceived erosion of Lower Manhattan's preeminence as a center of business in New York City as major companies moved uptown or outside New York. Less activity downtown meant less interaction among businesses. This in turn made downtown less attractive relative to midtown, completing a vicious cycle. The essence of the project was the redevelopment of a large part of Lower Manhattan that added more than 10,000,000 square feet of office space. Elsewhere in the world of urban development there has been increasing investment designed to encourage interaction. Of the designed 10 tallest buildings in the world, 8 have been built since 1990, most in fast-growing East Asian cities (Helsley and Strange 2007, 131). It is useful to recall, in this connection, ambitious redevelopment projects in Paris, where at least two French presidents, Georges Pompidou and François Mitterand, were directly involved in their promotion, especially along the ceremonial axis from the Louvre to La Defénce. Similarly, the redevelopment of London's Docklands was associated with Prime Minister Margaret Thatcher's Britain.[5]

Helsley and Strange (2007) develop a model in which individuals or firms explicitly choose the volume of interactions, in addition to space and other consumption. Consequently, the total volume of interactions is endogenous. They show that urban interactions, even when explicitly desired by individuals, are underproduced, exactly as in the Beckmann model. Increasing density at the center both adds directly to interactions there and increases interactions indirectly by encouraging visits from consumers from other locations. Their findings may justify subsidies to high-density construction at urban centers as a second-best policy to deal with an inefficient volume of urban interactions. One does not have to attribute such projects to the peculiarities of local political systems or to the notion that urban governments value such projects in their own right so as to leave their mark for posterity. In section 5.6.3.1 below, I return to the analysis of smaller-scale urban redevelopment projects, which also depend on social interactions.

5.2.2 Identifying Social Interactions as Cultural Buzz

Identifying what generates the special character of urban areas has long intrigued social scientists. Recent authors emphasize the increasing concentration of highly educated people in a small number of urban areas. Many authors focus on the United States where data are most accessible. Florida (2006) draws attention to the increased presence from 1950 to 2000 of college graduates in San Jose, California, San Francisco, California and Oakland, California, Boston, Massachusetts, Seattle, Washington, and other areas, a phenomenon that is highly correlated with increased housing prices (Gyourko, Mayer, and Sinai 2006). Studying the impact of openness to new ideas and creativity and using proxies, such as the fraction of the population that is foreign-born or gay and a coolness and a bohemian index, Florida (2002) finds that such proxies are powerful in predicting metro-based innovations.

Currid (2006) draws attention to the extraordinary *localization* of cultural and artistic activities in New York, which exceeds the localization of financial and related services, and sees it as a key explanation of New York's appeal as a global creative hub. Currid and Connolly (2008) emphasize, like Florida, the particular mix of the industrial characteristics of urban areas that is associated with increased creativity. They use geographic information systems techniques to analyze spatial autocorrelation and clustering of industries and compare the 10 most populous U.S. MSAs across several "advanced" service sectors (professional, management, media, finance, art and culture, engineering, and high technology). They use the Moran I and Getis–Ord ("hot-spot") measures (Anselin, Griffiths, and Gita 2008) and measures of spatial autocorrelation and identify three "spatial typologies of co-location" in advanced services within U.S. metropolitan areas. These are region-led (as in Miami and Detroit), central city–led (as in Chicago, New York, and Philadelphia), and specialist-led (as in Boston, Dallas, Los Angeles, Washington DC, and Houston). The typologies allow them to identify qualities of place in general and of places specifically that drive the agglomeration of advanced services.

These authors focus on New York City's art, culture, and media industries as representing key examples of geographically unique cases within advanced services. Currid and Connolly (2008, 421, fig. 1) clearly show a single regional center (a "mononucleated" cluster) in Manhattan. The special advantage of New York lies in its "walkable" built environment. The serendipity of chance encounters combines with the close proximity of curators, editors, and others on the streets of New York to produce unique outcomes. Currid (2007, 81) quotes a fashion designer: "Informal social networks are probably the most powerful driver, pretty much everyone we work with we have a personal relationship with." Culture goes to New York to be evaluated by a sophisticated cluster of specialists, just as science goes to Cambridge, Massachusetts.

In addition to these approaches, Currid and Williams (2010) use an archive of data on social activities in Los Angeles and New York, which they geocode and analyze by means of spatial statistics. What makes this research warrant attention here is that it is based on micro (individual) actions rather than demographic characteristics and industrial localization and thus distinguishes itself from demographic profiles. Currid and Williams use access to 309,414 images associated with 6,004 arts and entertainment events in Los Angeles and New York during March 2006–March 2007 from Getty Images.[6] The events are coded in terms of actual location and character, and all involve social interactions. They exclude celebrity sightings and are identified as events in fashion, film, television, and theater—magnet and hybrid (i.e., involving several industry sectors). Using the Moran I and the Getis–Ord hot-spot measures, these authors identify unique event enclaves within Los Angeles and New York. Event enclaves for different industries are found in very similar locations. For example, in Manhattan, the event enclaves are located on Fifth Avenue between Rockefeller Center and Central Park, midtown west near Lincoln Center, down Broadway, the main artery of Manhattan; South Chelsea and then into the West Village and Soho. In Los Angeles the event enclaves are primarily located in Beverly Hills and Hollywood, along Hollywood and Sunset Boulevards. On the whole, magnet events take place near overall event enclaves. The spatial depiction of the findings by these authors makes obvious sense to people familiar with those particular locales.

Events covered by Getty Images data are "buzz-worthy," and involve individuals with visible profiles. Like other industrial location decisions, deliberate choices of location for events sponsored by cultural industries are likely to involve circular causation, for example, events are held in Times Square because events are held in Times Square! A large movie theater is attractive as a particular kind of venue—say for the Oscars, it is the Kodak Theater in Westwood, Los Angeles—but it then generates a first-nature effect. (Chapter 8 returns to a fuller discussion of first and second nature.) Media attention makes these places well known. That is, repeated use creates a legacy and makes them attractive for other purposes as well, such as tourism. Once such second-nature activities arise, complementary activities can also thrive nearby, creating third-nature activities. An originally practical location acquires iconic nature over time after repeated use.

Buzz is pervasive in cities. Cities facilitate face-to-face contact. Why is this form of contact so important in many aspects of life? Storper and Venables (2004) identify buzz with the following properties of face-to-face contacts. One, it is efficient communication, especially where information is not precise, is rapidly changing, or is not easily codified; two, it helps overcome coordination and incentives problems in uncertain environments; three, it facilitates formation of in-groups; and four, it allows for direct psychological motivation. These properties are important not only in the production and appreciation of cultural products but also in productive interactions between firms and between individuals in the areas of finance and business and in influence and power. The unwritten agreements that are critical in these areas of human interactions are created and maintained through face-to-face contacts. Because trade in services and the demand for services to support international trade in goods increases with globalization, it is not surprising that buzz cities are very closely associated with globalization.

5.3 LOCATION DECISIONS OF FIRMS IN URBAN SPACE

First, I present here a simple Alonso–Mills–Muth model of firm location in the urban economy. Again, let ℓ denote the distance from the CBD, and $R(\ell)$ the rental price of land at distance ℓ. Let $k = 1, \ldots, K$ index industries. Production is constant returns to scale and uses land and labor, with unit cost functions $c_k = c_k(R, w)$, where w denotes the wage rate, which is assumed to be independent of distance from the CBD. At a competitive equilibrium with free entry, every feasible land site may qualify for a firm's location. As a result, profit per unit of production at location ℓ, $\pi_k(\ell) = p_k - \tau_k(\ell) - c_k(R, w)$, where $\tau_k(\ell)$ denotes shipping costs, is equal to zero everywhere at equilibrium.

The *rent* each firm k is willing to pay at distance ℓ, $R_k(\ell)$, is the maximum rent that producers in industry k are willing to pay per unit of land at each location without incurring losses. For a typical firm in industry k, the bid rent function is implied by equilibrium under perfect competition, where all producers make zero profits, so that the unit production cost must be equal to the price of good k minus its unit shipping cost from location ℓ to the CBD:

$$c_k(R_k(\ell), w; \Xi) = p_k - \tau_k(\ell), \tag{5.11}$$

where Ξ denotes total factor productivity. At equilibrium, industry k occupies zone k, defined by its inner, ℓ_{k-1}, and outer, ℓ_k, radii, provided that it outbids all other industries over that range:

$$R_k(\ell) \geq R_j(\ell), \ \ell_{k-1} \leq \ell \leq \ell_k, \ j = 1, \dots, K. \tag{5.12}$$

By inverting the zero profit condition for locational equilibrium for firm k, (5.11), we have the rent firm k is willing to pay:

$$R_k(\ell) = R_k(p_k - \tau_k(\ell), w; \Xi). \tag{5.13}$$

By differentiating R_k with respect to ℓ, it follows that firm k's bid rent decreases with ℓ:

$$\frac{\partial R_k}{\partial \ell} = -\frac{\tau_k'(\ell)}{h_k(\ell; w)}, \tag{5.14}$$

where $h_k(\ell; w) = \frac{\partial c_k(Rw)}{\partial R}$ is (by Roy's identity) the firm's demand for land per unit of output.

How is equilibrium in land use by firms determined in this economy? Land and labor are the only scarce resources in the model. Having assumed that firms produce with constant returns to scale, any allocation of economic activity that is consistent with equilibrium in the labor market determines urban equilibrium. Let a ring defined by boundaries ℓ_{k-1} and ℓ_k accommodate industry k and let firms be labeled by the successive rings they occupy, $k = 1, \dots, K$. Let $g(\ell)$ denote the fraction of land in a unit ring at ℓ; then the demand for labor from a ring of length $d\ell$ is $2\pi \ \mathrm{l} n_i(\ell)g(\ell)d\ell$. Equilibrium in the labor market is characterized by setting the labor demand equal to the labor supply:

$$2\pi \sum_{i=1}^{K} \int_{\ell_{i-1}}^{\ell_i} g(\ell) n_i(\ell; w) \ell d\ell = N, \tag{5.15}$$

where the firm's demand for labor per unit of land is obtained by Roy's identity and is given by

$$n_i(\ell; w) = \frac{\frac{\partial}{\partial w} c_i(R_i(\ell), w)}{\frac{\partial}{\partial R_i(\ell)} c_i(R_i(\ell), w)}. \tag{5.16}$$

This condition ignores the facts that labor may also demand land for housing and that workers do not incur transportation costs.

The description of equilibrium is complete once equilibrium in the land market is defined. The bidding process for each unit of land implies that pieces of land will be occupied by the highest bidder. That is, firm k occupies the ring of sites in the interval $[\ell_{i-1}, \ell_i]$, where

$$R_k(\ell) \geq R_i(\ell), \ i \neq k, \ i \in \{1, \dots, K\}, \ \text{and} \ R_k(\ell_k) = R_{k+1}(\ell_k).$$

With a large number of firms, the equilibrium land rent is the lower envelope of the individual firms' bid rent functions. Its mathematical description may be made more precise once the technologies of different firms have been parameterized.

5.3.1 Firms Value Being near Other Firms

Next I develop a model of firms' location decisions when firms value proximity to other firms. This is construed in the same sense as for individuals (firms derive disutility based on the average distance from other firms), and there is *no* predetermined center. This notion is central in understanding how interactions among firms allow for the effects of urban agglomeration to be realized,[7] just as in the model for individuals in section 5.2.1 above. My exposition follows that of O'Hara (1977), as adapted by Fujita and Thisse (2002).

Urban space is one-dimensional, featureless, and indexed by ℓ, $\ell \in [-\bar{\ell}, \bar{\ell}]$. Land has opportunity cost R_a. I assume that output per unit of office space, $\bar{Q}$, is independent of location, that the good is transported to markets costlessly, but that firms incur costs in order to interact with other firms in the urban area. For a firm at ℓ, this cost is denoted by $\mathcal{T}(\ell)$ and is a function of its actual location, just as in (5.7):

$$\mathcal{T}(\ell) = \tau \int_{-\bar{\ell}}^{\bar{\ell}} |\bar{\ell} - s| m(s) ds, \qquad (5.17)$$

where $m(s)$ denotes the density of firms in the urban economy and τ is a transportation cost parameter. I seek to characterize the density function $m(\ell)$, which is proxied by office space per unit of land, $m(\ell) = \mathcal{S}(\ell)$, at equilibrium. Profit per unit of office space at location ℓ is

$$\pi_o(\ell) = \bar{Q} - \mathcal{T}(\ell) - R_o(\ell),$$

where $R_o(\ell)$ denotes office rent.

Office space is supplied by construction firms using land and resources. The resource cost may be written directly in terms of a cost function, which for simplicity I assume to be an isoelastic convex function of office space per unit of land, $\mathcal{S}(\ell)^\alpha$, $\alpha > 1$. Profit that accrues to construction firms per unit of land at ℓ, as a function of office space per unit of land at ℓ, may be written as

$$\pi_c(\ell) = R_o(\ell)\mathcal{S}(\ell) - \mathcal{S}(\ell)^\alpha - R(\ell), \ \alpha > 1,$$

where $R(\ell)$ is land rent, as distinct from office rent, $R_o(\ell)$. Construction firms choose the quantity of office space per unit of land so as to maximize $\pi_c(\ell)$. The first-order condition for $\mathcal{S}(\ell)$, as a function the office rent, $R_o(\ell)$, yields $\mathcal{S}^*(\ell) = \alpha^{-\frac{1}{\alpha-1}} R_o(\ell)^{\frac{1}{\alpha-1}}$. At equilibrium, $m(\ell) = \mathcal{S}^*(\ell)$, and the density of office space is a function of office space rent. Or,

$$R_o(\ell) = \alpha m(\ell)^{\alpha-1}. \qquad (5.18)$$

This is an increasing function of the number of firms established at each location since $\alpha > 1$. At equilibrium, with free entry for the construction firms, profit $\pi_c(\ell)$ is equalized at all locations and becomes equal to 0, and the equilibrium land rent is $R(\ell) = (\alpha - 1)m(\ell)^\alpha$.

At equilibrium, profits per unit of office space,

$$\pi(\ell) = \pi^* = \bar{Q} - \mathcal{T}(\ell) - \alpha m(\ell)^{\alpha-1}, \tag{5.19}$$

are equalized across all locations. This equilibrium condition for firms defines the equilibrium density of office space per unit of land, $m(\ell)$, through a functional equation that also involves the total costs of interaction, $\mathcal{T}(\ell)$, which is the only other component that also involves $m(\ell)$. So, by differentiating (5.19) twice and using $\frac{d^2}{d\ell^2}\mathcal{T}(\ell) = 2\tau m(\ell)$, we get a second-order nonlinear differential equation in $m(\ell)$, which in general is quite cumbersome to work with.[8] In the special case of $\alpha = 2$, this equation becomes

$$\frac{d^2}{d\ell^2}m(\ell) + \tau m(\ell) = 0.$$

This second-order linear differential equation in $m(\ell)$ admits the solution for equilibrium density:

$$m(\ell) = C_A \cos(\tau^{1/2}|\ell|), \tag{5.20}$$

where C_A is a positive constant of integration. It is the segment of this curve for which the corresponding land rent lies above R_a, the exogenous opportunity cost of land, that is the equilibrium office density function. As the upper portion of a cosine function, it is roughly a bell-shaped curve, which peaks at $\ell = 0$ and is symmetric around that point, the endogenously determined center. The density function's inflection points occur at $|\bar{\ell}| = \frac{\pi}{2}\tau^{1/2}$, where the land rent is also zero. Therefore, in view of the fact that the opportunity cost of land is positive, the density function is concave over the relevant range of values of the distance from the center, ℓ.

The equilibrium office rent is given by $R_o(\ell) = 2C_A \cos\left(\tau^{1/2}|\ell|\right)$, and the equilibrium land rent is

$$R(\ell) = C_A^2 \left[\cos\left(\tau^{1/2}|\ell|\right)\right]^2. \tag{5.21}$$

For the inflection points, differentiating this function twice and setting equal to zero gives

$$\frac{d^2R(\ell)}{d\ell^2}m(\ell) = -2k^2\left[\cos\left(\tau^{1/2}|\ell|\right)\right]^2 + 2k^2\left[\sin\left(\tau^{1/2}|\ell|\right)\right]^2 = 0.$$

Therefore, the inflection points are $|\tilde{\ell}| = \frac{\pi}{4}\tau^{-1/2}$; they lie at the midpoints to the right and left of the peak. Depending upon parameter values, the rent function is initially concave over the relevant range of values of the distance from the center but may become convex, depending upon parameter values, for $|\ell| > |\tilde{\ell}|$.

The boundary of the urban area is defined by

$$R_a^{1/2} = C_A \cos\left(\tau^{1/2}\bar{\ell}\right). \tag{5.22}$$

The larger the unit transport cost, or the opportunity cost of land, the smaller the size of the city. With the boundaries of the city thus defined as a function of R_a, the number of firms in the city is given by integrating over the density, $M = \int_{-\bar{\ell}}^{\bar{\ell}} m(\ell)d\ell$, which yields

$$M = 2k\tau^{1/2} \sin\left(\tau^{1/2}\bar{\ell}\right). \tag{5.23}$$

Clearly, the higher the opportunity cost of land, the smaller the city and the smaller the number of firms in it. If the number of firms is given, equations (5.22) and (5.23) may be used to determine the value of the unknown constant of integration C_A. That is, given the number of firms, M:

$$\bar{\ell} = \tau^{-1/2} \arctan\left(\frac{M}{2}\left(\frac{\tau}{R_a}\right)^{1/2}\right), \quad C_A = \frac{R_a^{1/2}}{\cos\left(\arctan\left(\frac{M}{2}\left(\frac{\tau}{R_a}\right)^{1/2}\right)\right)}.$$

It readily follows from this that the larger the number of firms, the larger the size of the city.

Although specific assumptions have been made in developing the models for firm-to-firm interactions in the present section that are different from those for individual-to-individual interactions in section 5.2.1 above, the respective equilibrium solutions share some qualitative characteristics. They are in part shared by the Lucas and Rossi-Hansberg models, discussed further in section 5.5 below. Both models imply density and rent functions that are bell-shaped curves with peaks at 0, which by symmetry is the endogenously determined CBD. They are both concave immediately surrounding the peak. Finally, for firms, too, as for individuals' interactions, the socially optimal density is more concentrated around its peak than the competitive one. Interactions are dispersed throughout the city, and the CBD is where the density peaks.

Zenou (2009a) applies this basic approach to study joint location decisions of firms and individuals. He distinguishes between employed and unemployed individuals. Employed individuals commute to the CDB to shop and to firms' locations to work; unemployed individuals commute to the CBD to shop and to look for jobs. Land use is endogenously allocated to individuals and firms. A key feature of the model is that firms interact because they need to exchange information and engage in face-to-face contacts, and the cost of interactions for firms is defined as in (5.7). The resulting land use model (Zenou 2009a, 291, fig. 6.8) is qualitatively very similar to the one I develop in this section. However, in the most general of Zenou's models, firms locate nearer the center, employed workers surround them, and unemployed workers locate farther away. I return to Zenou's results in section 5.7.1 below.

5.3.2 Toward a General Theory of Urban Interactions

The similarities in spatial structure associated with agents' self-organization where individuals value being near other individuals and firms value being near other firms are not coincidental. As emphasized by Fujita and Smith (1990) and evidenced by equations (5.7) and (5.17), these two models are special cases of a general class of additive-interaction models. For such models, the value of interactions is additive in a term that depends only on an agent's location ℓ, $\bar{\mathcal{T}}(\ell)$, and in an interaction term that depends linearly on the cost function $\tau(s, \ell)$ and is integrated with respect to the population density, $\chi(s)$, of all other agents,

$$\mathcal{T}(\ell, \tau) = \bar{\mathcal{T}}(\ell) + \int \tau(s, \ell)\chi(s)ds. \tag{5.24}$$

Fujita and Smith show that a class of models of interactions, including those I examine above and others, such as exchanges of intermediate inputs between firms, share the property that the benefits enjoyed by an agent from her location in space are additive with respect to proximity to all other agents. Spatial accessibility, endogenous-contact and fixed-contact models are special instances of such models. A class of models can be put in formal one-to-one correspondence with one another, which makes it likely that the associated agglomeration properties they exhibit are formally identical.[9]

5.4 MONOCENTRIC VERSUS POLYCENTRIC MODELS OF THE URBAN ECONOMY

The Alonso–Mills–Muth model owes much of its elegance to the assumption that the CBD is predetermined, but it clearly continues to be useful even when social interactions are introduced and the location of the CBD becomes endogenous, just as shown. Economic and social forces combine to bring about alternative land use outcomes. Generally, there can be multiple equilibria. Fujita (1989) suggests that self-organization of urban agglomerations relies on three basic features: the heterogeneity of space, social interactions in production and/or consumption, and imperfectly competitive markets. The metric of transport costs in relation to a center is present in any configuration and generates space heterogeneity. Social interactions bind agents together in mutually sustaining ways. Moreover, imperfectly competitive markets, especially in monopolistic competition (as in the new economic geography theories discussed in chapter 4) lend themselves naturally in multiple ways to accommodate consumer and firm demands. Once properly modeled, forces that determine a CBD endogenously may in fact determine multiple centers.

The first model of a polycentric city by Fujita and Ogawa (1982) uses concepts from an article by Ogawa and Fujita (1980).[10] These authors assume that the benefit from interactions between any two firms is a negative exponential function of the distance between them. Therefore, agents wanting to be close to one another bid up rents and wages, which generates a dispersion force through land and labor markets. The agglomeration of firms increases the commuting distance for their workers on average, which in turn pushes up the wage rate and land rent around the agglomeration, and this higher cost for labor and land discourages further agglomeration of firms. When commuting costs are sufficiently high, multiple business districts are likely to form, as different agents choose the least costly of their choices. It readily follows that the equilibrium number of subcenters tends to rise with population and commuting costs.

Fujita (1989) was the first to demonstrate that pure market interactions alone can explain agglomeration of economic activities with monopolistic competition. Individuals and firms value variety in consumer and producer goods, and increasing returns at the level of individual producers along with free entry define firm size. In contrast to these agglomeration forces, transport costs provide a dispersion force. The resulting cities may be monocentric or polycentric. Their business and residential districts may be mixed. This study was decisive in ushering in the new economic geography, which emphasizes intercity transport costs more than intracity ones and predicts a greater set of possibilities. I return to this issue in section 5.5 below.

The typical image of a large city is dominated by high density downtown. We can compare this with the distribution of employment. Data on employment at place of work, by zip code, available from the U.S. Department of Commerce, allow researchers to construct exact cumulative spatial distributions of employment from the "center" of each MSA outward and to compare them with similar distributions of residential populations. These data show that for the New York Consolidated MSA employment is more concentrated than residences up to about 17 miles from the CBD. For the Los Angeles Consolidated MSA it is more concentrated only until 7 miles from the CBD. Nevertheless, overall the respective distributions are very similar to one another. In the majority of metropolitan areas, more than three-quarters of all jobs are located more than 3 miles from the CBD (Glaeser and Kahn 2001). This evidence is conceptually distinct from the existence of multiple centers, if not subcenters. For example, McMillen (1996) documents important deviations from monocentricity in Chicago land use. The area surrounding O'Hare Airport is an important employment center, and blighted areas to the south and west of Chicago's center have lower land values than monocentricity would predict.

McMillen and Smith (2003) test a basic prediction of the Ogawa–Fujita model using a Poisson model for the number of subcenters and employing data for subcenters of 62 large U.S. metropolitan areas. They find that population growth and commuting costs explain nearly 80 percent of the variation in the number of subcenters across urban areas. Areas with older housing stock tend to have more subcenters, while the median income and age of the central city do not affect the number of subcenters. Their model implies that for an area with mild congestion, a population of 2.68 million is critical for a first employment subcenter to develop, and 6.74 million for a second. More severe congestion is associated with a larger number of subcenters. It is a contribution of this article to actually empirically identify the number of subcenters. The phenomenon of suburbanization is indirect evidence that nonmonocentric land-use models are becoming increasingly relevant for describing the distribution of economic activity in urban areas. Baum-Snow (2010), for example, provides evidence that highway construction in the United States has played a major role in the within-MSA reallocation of urban populations and employment away from central cities and in favor of suburbs.

5.5 THE LUCAS–ROSSI-HANSBERG MODELS OF URBAN SPATIAL STRUCTURE WITH PRODUCTIVE EXTERNALITIES

The fact that interactions have a profound effect on urban spatial structure suggests that the spatial complexity of an urban economy is critical for the properties of its "urban externality," that is, it is the source of the distinct advantage of cities in terms of productivity. If living and working in close proximity in a city facilitates the exchange of production-related ideas, then the spatial separation between places of work in the urban economy may proxy for the difficulty of such exchanges. At a first level of approximation, such interactions can be expressed in terms of employment. This section discusses an approach, due to Lucas (2001) and Lucas and Rossi-Hansberg (2002), that serves as a basic benchmark for measuring the urban externality. Roughly speaking, the higher total factor productivity is at any location, the higher employment is in neighboring locations within the urban economy.

Firms make decisions taking into consideration the productivity advantage conferred by their location in an urban economy. At equilibrium, it is all firms' actions themselves that determine the city-level productivity advantage. Firm-to-firm interactions take place over space and are reflected in firms' location decisions and hence in land rents. Lucas (2001) sets out to examine whether the parameters of the urban externality mechanism can be identified from data on land rental functions.

Following Lucas (2001), I assume that a firm's output is given by $x(\ell) \equiv \bar{\Xi} z(\ell)^{\gamma} n^{\alpha} a(\ell)^{1-\alpha}$, where the urban externality is defined as a location-dependent component of total factor productivity, $z(\ell)^{\gamma}$, n denotes employment, $a(\ell)$ denotes land, and $\bar{\Xi}$, α, γ, are parameters. The production function exhibits constant returns to scale in employment and land. Even though the urban externality is specified arbitrarily as an isoelastic function of the productivity variable $z(\ell)$, the latter is specified as an aggregate of employment over all locations in the city, each weighted by an exponential decay function with rate δ of the direct distance from ℓ to each other location in the city.

A firm sets employment so as to maximize profit per unit of land:

$$n^*(z) = \text{argmax}_n : \{\bar{\Xi} z^{\gamma} n^{\alpha} - wn\} = \left(\frac{\alpha \bar{\Xi}}{w}\right)^{\frac{1}{1-\alpha}} z^{\frac{\gamma}{1-\alpha}}, \tag{5.25}$$

where w is the real wage and $\bar{\Xi} z$ is the total factor productivity component. Since employment anywhere depends on productivity, the function $z(\ell)$ is endogenous and location-specific. It obeys a functional equation that is simplest to derive using polar coordinates, for which the distance from $(0, \ell)$ of a location a direct distance s from (0, 0) and at an angle θ is $[\ell^2 - 2\ell s\cos(\theta) + s^2]^{1/2}$ That is

$$z(\ell) = \delta\int_0^{\bar{\ell}} n^*(z(s))s\,ds\int_0^{2\pi} e^{-\delta[\ell^2-2\ell s\,\cos(\theta)+s^2]^{1/2}}d\theta, \tag{5.26}$$

where $n^*(z(s))$ denotes employment at site s with productivity $z(s)$. In view of (5.25), the functional equation (5.26) for $z(\ell)$ becomes

$$z(\ell) = \delta\left(\frac{\alpha\,\Xi}{w}\right)^{\frac{1}{1-\alpha}}\int_0^{\bar{\ell}} z(s)^{\frac{\gamma}{1-\alpha}}s\,ds\int_0^{2\pi} e^{-\delta[\ell^2-2\ell s\cos(\theta)+s^2]^{1/2}}d\theta. \tag{5.27}$$

Important economic properties are encapsulated in this definition. The right-hand side of (5.27) aggregates the function of each firm's total factor productivity through which it affects employment. An exogenous proportional increase of 10 percent z at a particular location affects the productivity parameter everywhere by $(1.10)^{\frac{\gamma}{1-\alpha}}$. Therefore, a definition of the urban interfirm externality involves a magnification effect if $\gamma > 1-\alpha$. It is thus necessary to impose the condition

$$0 < \gamma < 1-\alpha. \tag{5.28}$$

Otherwise, the externality would swamp the effect of land prices and all activity would locate in the city center. In that case the value of z would become unbounded.[11] The stronger the urban externality, the larger γ, the elasticity of the productivity term, but α, the share of (capital-endowed) labor in output is also larger.[12] The definition of the productivity variable according to equation (5.27) is consistent with a social interactions perspective in a manner very much as in chapter 2, section 2.2, but in a nonlinear fashion. Each firm takes the productivity variable as given in setting its employment according to (5.25), which in turn reflects the total impact of employment decisions by all other firms after accounting for spatial attenuation at rate δ.

Lucas' principal interest is in examining whether equilibrium land rent functions throw light on the magnitude of production externalities associated with human capital externalities. At the spatial equilibrium with free entry for firms, the counterpart here of (5.13), land rent equals optimum profit per unit of land:

$$R(\ell) = \left\{z^{\gamma}\,\Xi(n^*(\ell))^{\alpha} - wn\right\} = [1-\alpha]\Xi^{\frac{1}{1-\alpha}}\alpha^{\frac{\alpha}{1-\alpha}}w^{-\frac{\alpha}{1-\alpha}}z(\ell)^{\frac{\gamma}{1-\alpha}}. \tag{5.29}$$

It, too, is proportional to $z(\ell)^{\frac{\gamma}{1-\alpha}}$, where $z(\ell)$ satisfies (5.27). All the properties of spatial variation in productivity are conferred on the land rental function via the spatial variation in $z(\ell)^{\frac{1}{1-\alpha}}$.

It is not possible to solve analytically for $z(\ell)$ (nor its linear city counterpart) from (5.27), and this complicates empirical investigations. Nonetheless, Lucas (2001, 252–256) provides general results for the existence and properties of the productivity variable as a function of location and city size $z = z(\ell, \bar{\ell})$, as the unique functional fixed point of (5.27). Numerical solutions he reports show the function $z(\ell, \bar{\ell})$ to be a decreasing function of the distance from the center of the axes, holding city size $\bar{\ell}$ constant. It is an increasing function of the size of the city $\bar{\ell}$ and tends to an upper envelope curve as $\bar{\ell}$ tends to ∞. The land rental functions are ordered: $\bar{\ell}' > \bar{\ell} > \ell$ implies $z(\ell, \bar{\ell}') > z(\ell, \bar{\ell})$. In other words, increased city size shifts the land rental functions upward. It is interesting that the land rental function is first convex and then concave. Its rate of decline is originally decreasing with distance from the center and then increasing when approaching the edge of the city.

Thus, in Lucas' model, the shape of the land rental function resembles those obtained in the two cases of location decisions with social interactions (endogenous amenity) and no predetermined city center that I discuss above, except very near the city center. See figure 5.1. The threshold point in the rate of decline is defined by the inflection point of $R(\ell)$. After that point the effect of the city boundary is felt by reducing sharply the weighted distances from other sites. The model does not impose a priori the assumption of a CBD, but geometric symmetry places it at the center of the axes, just as in the models in sections 5.2.1 and 5.3.1 above. As in the models of individuals' and firms' location decisions with social interactions examined earlier, the urban externality draws firms closer to each other or closer to the city center. The predicted pattern of spatial attenuation is empirically testable. In section 5.5.1 I discuss some empirical findings of spatial attenuation of human capital spillovers, although they are not based on the Lucas (2001) model.

A numerical calibration by Lucas of the magnitude of the urban externality and its interaction with human capital externalities sets bounds on its consequences for aggregate growth. Lucas considers a representative city with a total population of $N = 500{,}000$ and an area defined by $\bar{\ell} = 3$ miles and assumes the following about the economy: GDP per worker of \$ 60,000, share of land in aggregate production of 0.05, which implies a share of labor plus capital of $\alpha = 0.95$, and therefore a real wage of $0.95 \times \$60{,}000 = \$57{,}000$. He computes the remaining parameters, namely, total factor productivity, $\bar{\Xi}$, spatial attenuation rate, δ, and elasticity of the external effect, γ, as follows. Assuming no external effect, in which case workers are uniformly distributed in the city, there would be $500{,}000/28 \approx 18{,}000$ workers per square mile, and therefore $18{,}000 \times 60{,}000 \approx 1.080$ million dollars of output per square mile, which in turn implies a value for $\bar{\Xi} = 1.080 \times 10^6 \times (18{,}000)^{0.95} \approx 98$. Uniform land rents across the city would be $R = (1 - \alpha) \times \bar{\Xi} n^{\alpha} = 0.05 \times 1{,}080{,}000 =$ \$54,000 per square mile per year. By solving for the externality function $z(\ell)$ numerically from (5.27), Lucas produces a family of profiles for the distribution of employment as a function of the distance from the CBD. These results display greater richness qualitatively than solutions casually used. Most interestingly, increasing parameter γ up to its upper bound, according to the no-black-hole condition (5.28) above, of $1 - \alpha = 0.05$ raises the peak at the CBD. The fact that higher values of the elasticity parameter shift employment closer to the center suggests that as the city radius increases employment spreads out.

Lucas accounts for the residential needs of workers by introducing a residential outer periphery of the city, $[\bar{\ell}, \hat{\ell}]$. As city size increases, commuting times and/or residential land rent increases, requiring firms to pay increasing wages to attract workers. The congestion thus introduced partly offsets the desirable effects of the production externality and limits city size. In such an extended model, individuals are assumed to commute to the center and then back out to their places of work within a city's inner ring, $[0, \bar{\ell}]$. It is only commuting to the center that is assumed to be costly, however; an individual living at ℓ incurs a time cost of $\tau\ell$ to commute to the center. An individual located at ℓ has income $w(1-\tau\ell)$. With a Cobb–Douglas utility function, as in section 5.1.2, with consumption and land shares, respectively, $1-\beta$, β, demand for land is equal to $h(\ell) = \beta\frac{w(1-\tau\ell)}{R(\ell)}$. Spatial equilibrium for individuals implies that $R(\ell) = \left(\frac{1-\tau\ell}{1-\tau\bar{\ell}}\right)^{1/\beta} R(\bar{\ell})$.

With an outer radius of 10 miles and a share of residential land rents of $\beta = 0.1$ of income, total population satisfies

$$500{,}000 = \frac{2\pi}{\beta w} R(\bar{\ell}) \int_{\bar{\ell}}^{\hat{\ell}} \frac{1-\tau\ell}{1-\tau\bar{\ell}} \ell d\ell. \tag{5.30}$$

Here the land rent at the boundary between business and residential use is determined by the business sector, which takes the price of output as given. Consequently, equilibrium utility is also determined. The parameter values assumed imply that 500,000 workers live in $(10^2 - 3^2)\pi$ square miles, or 0.57×10^{-3} per worker, or approximately 129^2 square feet per worker. Solving equation (5.30) numerically yields values for τ, expressed as fractions of working time. Higher values of the externality parameter are consistent with lower values of τ. Specifically, for $\gamma = 0.01$, $\tau = 0.0384$. As γ increases, the land rent function becomes steeper as it pivots roughly around $\ell = 3$ miles. So, land rent gradients vary across cities with the same observable size characteristics, $(N, \bar{\ell}, \hat{\ell})$ and real wage rate w.

Lucas' calibration results are based on data from two Japanese cities, Hiratsuka and Yokohama. The need for the theory to reproduce the sharp peaks in rents and employment that are characteristic of the city centers of those Japanese cities pushes the estimate of γ to near its theoretical upper bound of $1-\alpha$. Lucas' results for Hiratsuka provide a better (visual) fit than those for Yokohama [see Lucas (2001, 269–270, figs. 11 and 12)]. The estimates for γ at 0.049 and 0.048 are indeed very close to their upper bound of $1-\alpha = 0.05$. The higher the value of γ, the sharper the peak around the CBD that the theory predicts.

If we define the urban externality as being propagated via the effective labor input in an urban economy and we retain diminishing returns to land, the most that the externality can do is offset the diminishing returns of effective labor in output per unit of land, resulting in something close to a constant-returns economy for the city. Thus, Lucas argues, from a growth-accounting viewpoint, the contribution of the urban externality to the U.S. rate of growth would be on the order of γ times the growth rate of effective labor. Since the latter is about 0.02, the most that this effect could be is $0.02 \times 0.05 = 0.001$, which is too small compared to the estimated Solow residual of about 0.01. Lucas (2001, 271) thus concludes that "it cannot lead to a model of increasing returns". This suggests that additional forces of endogenous technological change must be accounted for in order to establish the role of cities as engines of aggregate growth.

If industries differ with respect to the externality coefficient γ, then locational equilibrium according to the analysis in section 5.3 would imply that industries with the highest γ value, the strongest externality, would outbid other industries and end up concentrating in the center of the largest city. Goods with lower γ's could be produced further from the center of the largest city, at the center of the next rank of cities, and so on. If so, city land gradients will reflect the distribution of the γ parameters across goods, not just the average external effect. Lucas uses this argument to explain why financial services occupy the highest land values in the center of Japanese cities and manufacturing occupies lower land values farther away from the urban centers. In this case, using data on an particular city with a diversified industrial base without accounting for industrial location would bias the estimate of γ upward. The consequences of this selection bias for estimating human capital externalities, Lucas speculates, can be controlled for if we also use cross-city evidence on wages and land rents, just like Rauch (1993), who uses data on individuals and the city aggregates where they live, and Ciccone and Hall (1996), who set their empirical implementation in terms of cross-state productivity differences. Indeed, as Lucas emphasizes, it is data from the entire system of cities that must be brought to bear on estimation of the urban externality.

Lucas and Rossi-Hansberg (2002) allow land use to accommodate both consumers and producers throughout the city without imposing a particular pattern. It may be mixed, segregated, or alternating. They impose symmetry with respect to radial variations so that all variables of interest depend on distance from the city center. Individuals commute only along rays, but this does not hamper the generality of the results. The fact that productivity everywhere in the urban economy is higher the higher employment is in neighboring locations must accommodate the fact that workers' housing needs compete for land with industry use. For the same parameterization used by Lucas (2001), the fraction of land used in production in mixed areas, where employment density and residential density coexist, is given by $\theta = \frac{1-\alpha}{1-\alpha(1-\beta)}$. When commuting costs are zero, $\tau = 0$, businesses locate around the center to take most advantage of the urban externality, which is defined in terms of employment. Individuals locate beyond that zone and are compensated by the decline in land rents. Business use surrounding the center is still an equilibrium outcome if τ is small, but the rent gradient with the business sector can be made arbitrarily steep by increasing the rate of spatial attenuation of the externality.

If the commuting cost is higher by an order of magnitude, the land use is as follows: the area around the center becomes mixed; it is followed by a zone of business use and finally followed by residential use. Further increasing the commuting cost by an additional order of magnitude causes the area of mixed land use to grow almost to the entire city, followed by a narrow peripheral zone of business use. The rent gradient is now very flat over most of the city. Overall, the larger the commuting cost, the larger the area of mixed land use at equilibrium. For very high commuting costs, land use becomes in effect autarkic, producing goods that are shipped costlessly outside the city. These results could explain the stubbornness of mixed land use in cities, especially in less developed countries (LDCs), with a poor transportation infrastructure.

Baum-Snow (2010) shows that the improvement in urban transportation in U.S. metropolitan areas since 1950 has caused decentralization of both employment and population. Thus, lower transport costs allowed firms to attain the same productivity advantage of proximity as before but at greater distances. Still the fact that employment remains more centralized than residences suggests that spatial agglomeration forces of the sort modeled by Lucas and Rossi-Hansberg (2002) remain important for firms' location choices.

Another set of computational experiments conducted by Lucas and Rossi-Hansberg shows that a higher rate of spatial attenuation of the urban externality, which decreases the external effect between firms, causes localization of industry. In their case, firms outbid residential users for land near production centers, which results in multiple narrow zones of business alternating with residential use. The endogenous attractiveness of the business center is best exemplified in the Lucas–Rossi-Hansberg framework by starting with uniformly mixed land use. In that case, firms nearer the center benefit more from proximity to other firms than do firms nearer the edge, as there is no employment beyond the edge! This causes productivity to be greatest at the center, drawing more firms there and causing higher land rents there and lower land rents at the edge. But land is always needed for production, and therefore not all production can concentrate at the center. If one were to assume that people live where they work, then employment and land rents would decline as we move away from the center. Otherwise, it is possible that rents may increase and then decline again with distance from the CBD, a very interesting result of this work.[13]

Rossi-Hansberg (2004a, 2004b) examines the socially optimal location decisions when interfirm production externalities are endogenous. He shows that optimality requires greater concentration than the competitive outcome, which is in agreement with the results that I discuss earlier in sections 5.2.1 and 5.3.1. Rossi-Hansberg (2004a) examines policies like labor subsidies, land taxes, and zoning restrictions that can implement efficient allocation as an equilibrium, or close the gap between the optimal and equilibrium allocations. He shows that business land is more concentrated at the center of the city in the optimum and that higher commuting costs increase the difference between optimal and equilibrium allocations. Rossi-Hansberg (2004b) shows that the presence of interfirm externalities exaggerates the impact of such shocks as the destruction of physical capital (as by terrorist attacks) on economic activity as measured by production, employment, capital stocks, wages, and land rents, though not on the distribution of business and residential land.

5.5.1 Spatial Attenuation of Human Capital Spillovers within Cities

The results of Lucas (2001) and Lucas and Rossi-Hansberg (2002) are premised on spatial attenuation of the urban externality. Rosenthal and Strange (2008b) use 2000 Integrated Public Use Micro Sample census data (see chapter 2, section 2.13.2) to estimate the spatial pattern of human capital externalities as reflected in individual wages. They consider first the urban wage premium, that is, the phenomenon of workers' being paid more in larger cities, controlling for their characteristics, and second, the strength of human capital externalities, where the geographic proximity to more educated workers raises a worker's wage. They measure agglomeration of the employment of full-time male and female workers aged 30–65 within concentric rings whose boundary radii are 0–5 miles, 5–25 miles, 25–50 miles, and 50–100 miles from each respondent's place of work. The place of work is defined in terms of place-of-work PUMA (PWPUMA), of which there are many in a typical metropolitan area. (See chapter 2, section 2.13.2 for details on PUMAs.) Productivity is measured by wages.

A particularly noteworthy feature of the study by Rosenthal and Strange (2008b) is its use of data on geologic features (landslide hazards, seismic hazards, bedrock, and surface water) as instruments. These instruments help them address measurement error in their construction of agglomeration variables and endogeneity in the wage-agglomeration relationship. The former biases estimates of agglomeration effects toward zero. The latter is due to self-selection. That is, highly skilled workers may self-select to agglomerated areas, thus biasing upward the estimated effects of agglomeration on wages. The biases resulting from these two main sources of econometric problems work in opposite directions, making the net effect ambiguous.

Rosenthal and Strange propose an ingenious use of geologic information. The height of buildings in, say, New York is positively correlated with underlying solid geology. The observed pattern of big buildings downtown and midtown, with smaller buildings in between, reflects at least in part underlying geology. The tallest buildings are located where bedrock is relatively accessible. Rosenthal and Strange use these facts to justify employing as instruments several geologic variables that vary at the micro level of geography.[14] The geologic variables do not themselves measure human actions but are significant predictors of micro variations in density or economic activity and the presence of educated workers but do not directly affect productivity.

Rosenthal and Strange estimate an individual wage equation for individual i at location ℓ,

$$\ln w_{i\ell} = H_i \delta_{occ,MSA} + X_i \beta + g_\ell \zeta + \mu_{is} + \epsilon_{i\ell}, \tag{5.31}$$

where $\delta_{occ,MSA}$ is a vector of occupation and MSA fixed effects (with occupations measured at the three-digit level, this yields up to 24,000 fixed effects in some of their estimated models), X_i is a vector of individual observable characteristics that are available in IPUMS and includes age, education, marital status, presence of children, and years in the United States, g_ℓ is a vector of location-specific characteristics, β, ζ, are vectors of parameters, $\mu_{i\varsigma}$ represents the portion of individual i's skill that is not captured by the occupation, MSA-specific and measured effects, and $\epsilon_{i\ell}$ independent and identically distributed shocks. Self-selection into agglomerated areas is reflected in a correlation between g_ℓ and μ_{is}, and measurement error makes g_ℓ differ from the true values. Reducing the areas over which the g_ℓ's are defined limits the effects of measurement error.

Rosenthal and Strange obtain four key results. First, their estimated effect of the spatial concentration of employment on productivity shows that an increase of 100,000 in the employment of full-time workers within 5 miles is associated with an increase in wages of roughly 2 percent. Second, they distinguish the effects from different types of workers, that is, those with less than a college education from those with more. They show that the benefits of spatial concentration are driven by proximity to college-educated workers, an instance of human capital spillovers. They estimate an urbanization elasticity of 0.0516 for the college-educated and of 0.0473 for those with less than a college degree. Their estimates imply that replacing 50,000 less-than-college educated workers within 5 miles by college-educated ones would elevate a worker's wage by 10 percent. This is substantial, being roughly equivalent to the private returns from one additional year of schooling.

Third, and most important, they show that these effects attenuate with distance. The attenuation is sharp initially; the effect is $2\frac{1}{2}$ to 3 times smaller if the change in the local workforce takes place 5–25 miles away. However, the estimated effects at larger distances do not attenuate especially quickly, persisting beyond 50 miles in some models. They also examine the agglomeration effect separately on workers who are college-educated or more from that on workers who are less than college-educated. An additional 100,000 college-educated workers is associated with a wage increase of 12 percent for a worker with a college education or more and 9.4 percent for a less-than-college-educated worker. The effect from less-than college-educated workers is negative or very weak for both types of workers. Overall, the positive productivity effect outweighs the negative congestion effect for educated workers, but the reverse is true for workers with less than a college education.

5.6 NEIGHBORHOOD EFFECTS AND THE GEOMETRY OF THE CANONICAL URBAN MODEL

Correlated effects are a type of neighborhood effects that are pervasive in an urban economy. Similar people locate near one another. In order to appreciate the impact of endogenous social effects, one must understand first the impact of exogenous ones. The impact of heterogeneity on urban spatial equilibrium, first in preferences and then in incomes jointly with preferences, provides a way to demonstrate the role of correlated effects.

5.6.1 Preference Uncertainty

I introduce preference uncertainty to the urban model by means of an additive random component, φ, in individuals' indirect utility functions $\mathcal{O}$, defined in equation (5.3). I follow Anas (1990) and define space in terms of N concentric rings indexed by the distance of their inner circles from the CBD, $\ell = 0, \ell_1, \ldots, \ell_{N-1}$. Transport costs are negligible within each location (the rings are thin) and equal to τ per unit distance, across locations. Individual j, $j \in \mathcal{J}$, who considers locating in location ℓ, derives utility

$$\tilde{\Omega}_{j\ell} = \mathcal{O}(R(\ell); \Upsilon_j - \tau\ell) + \varphi_{j\ell}, \ \ell = 0, \ell_1, \ldots, \ell_{N-1}, \tag{5.32}$$

where the random variables $\varphi_{j\ell}$ are independent and identically distributed across all individuals and locations. That is, when individual j evaluates a site ℓ, she draws from a distribution that is the same for all sites; $\varphi_{j\ell}$ is unobservable to the analyst. I assume that the distribution is extreme value of type II with mean zero, variance $\frac{\pi^2}{6\varpi^2}$, and mode $-\frac{e}{\varpi}$, and with $\underline{e}$ being Euler's constant. The probability that individual j chooses location ℓ_j is given by the multinomial logit formula

$$\text{Prob}_{\ell_j} = \frac{\exp[\varpi\mathcal{O}(R(\ell_j); \Upsilon - \tau\ell_j)]}{\sum_{n=0}^{N-1}\exp[\varpi\mathcal{O}(R(\ell_n); \Upsilon - \tau\ell_n)]}, \ j \in \mathcal{J}. \tag{5.33}$$

Taste heterogeneity is characterized concisely by the dispersion parameter ϖ; the larger ϖ, the smaller the dispersion of taste. If $\varpi \to \infty$, the variance of idiosyncratic shocks is zero. In that case, only the measured component of utility determines choice. That is, if $\mathcal{O}(R(\ell_j); I_j - \tau\ell_j) > \max_{\ell\neq\ell_j}\mathcal{O}(R(\ell); I_j - \tau\ell)$, then $\text{Prob}_{\ell_j} \to 1$. If, on the other hand, $\varpi = 0$, that is, extreme taste heterogeneity, the variance of idiosyncratic shocks is infinite, and location choice is totally random and independent of utility evaluations. Each site is then chosen with equal probability: $\text{Prob}_{\ell_j} = 1/N$.

I now define equilibrium when individuals have identical incomes and each site has unit land area. Equilibrium is defined in terms of a land rental function, $R(\ell)$, and a boundary condition, $N_e \leq N - 1$, such that

$$R^e(\ell_{N_e}) = R_a, \ R^e(\ell_n) \geq R_a, \ n < N_e, \tag{5.34}$$

where R_a denotes the exogenous rental rate that land may earn in agricultural use at the city boundary. The equilibrium $R(\ell)$ is determined by setting the expected demand for land (housing) at every site equal to the supply,

$$h_\ell^*|\mathcal{J}|\text{Prob}_\ell = 1, \ \ell = \ell_0, \ldots, \ell_{N_e}, \tag{5.35}$$

where the probability Prob_ℓ that an individual chooses ℓ is given in (5.33). The maximum expected utility (see chapter 3, section 3.9.1) associated with the stochastic location model is given by

$$\overline{\mathcal{O}}_j = \varpi^{-1}\ln\left[\exp\left[\sum_{n=0}^{N-1}\varpi\mathcal{O}(R(\ell); \Upsilon_j - \tau\ell_n)\right]\right]. \tag{5.36}$$

In order to examine the impact of taste heterogeneity on the urban spatial equilibrium in more detail, we must specify the utility function. For a Cobb–Douglas utility function, $\mathcal{O} \equiv (1-\beta)^{1-\beta}\beta^{\beta}\Upsilon R^{-\beta}$, one can show that the equilibrium land rental rates obey

$$\frac{R(\ell_n)}{R(\ell_{n+1})} = \left(\frac{\Upsilon - \tau\ell_{n-1}}{\Upsilon - \tau\ell_j}\right)^{\frac{1+\frac{1}{\varpi}}{\beta+\frac{1}{\varpi}}}, n = 0, \ldots, N-1. \tag{5.37}$$

As ϖ increases, preferences become more homogeneous. The exponent on the right-hand side increases, implying that the land rent gradient falls more sharply with distance. In the case of $\varpi \to \infty$, the exponent on the right-hand side of (5.37) tends to $\frac{1}{\beta}$, and we are back in the Alonso–Mills–Muth case discussed in section 5.1.2 above. In that case, utility is equalized across all locations at equilibrium. As the variance of utility shocks decreases, rents increase within a certain distance from the CBD and decrease beyond that distance, bringing the urban structure closer to its deterministic case.

By taking logarithms of both sides of (5.37) and under the assumption that the unit transport cost τ is small relative to incomes, the above equation yields

$$\ln R(\ell_n) - \ln R(\ell_{n+1}) = \frac{\varpi + 1}{\varpi\beta + 1}\frac{\tau}{\Upsilon}(\ell_n - \ell_{n-1}). \tag{5.38}$$

It thus follows that (β, ϖ), the preference and the uncertainty parameters, may not be identified separately from regressions of the rent gradient against differences in distance from the CBD. However, individuals' preferences become more (less) diverse, that is, ϖ decreases (increases), the rent gradient is flatter (steeper), and the urban structure is less (more) compact. One can think of preference heterogeneity as a correlated effect.

A natural extension of this model is to allow for the stochastic shocks defining preference heterogeneity, $\varphi_{j\ell}$, $j \in \mathcal{J}, \ell = \ell_0, \ell_1, \ldots, \ell_{N-1}$, to be of the nested logit type, implying that individuals evaluating alternatives within a limited area draw shocks that are correlated when such alternatives are similar in specific dimensions.

5.6.2 Joint Income and Preference Heterogeneity

The next step in characterizing the equilibrium land rent function when individuals who compete for locations within an urban economy differ in terms of incomes and preferences. I assume simple Cobb–Douglas preferences and locations as defined in the previous section and that preferences are deterministic. Individuals in the urban population differ in terms of both incomes and tastes. Incomes and tastes are described by means of a joint density function of income and the preference parameter, $f(\Upsilon, \beta)$. By embedding the problem in the spatial setting of Anas (1990), as in the previous section, it is then straightforward to predict that individuals self-select across concentric rings, which are defined by their distance from the CBD, $\ell = 0, \ell_1, \ldots, \ell_{N-1}$, and that each has an area equal to 1. Self-selection of individuals across these concentric rings is similar to what is analyzed by Epple and Platt (1998). It rests on the single-crossing property of the work by Ellickson (1971), which helps define the groups in terms of income and preference characteristics, as I show shortly below. It is conceptually closely related to the treatment of hierarchical models discussed in chapter 3, section 3.7.1.

Spatial stratification of individuals prevails, if no individual has an incentive to move across rings. I define loci in (Υ, β) space, where individuals of each type are indifferent between locating in two successive rings, that is, at distances ℓ_n, ℓ_{n+1}, respectively, $n = 1, \ldots, N-1$. Let $\Upsilon = y_n\left(\frac{R_n}{R_{n+1}}; \ell_n, \ell_{n+1}; \beta\right)$ be the nth stratification envelope, that is, the income that, given rents (R_n, R_{n+1}) and distances for two successive rings (ℓ_n, ℓ_{n+1}), makes an individual with that income indifferent between locating in the two adjacent zones. That is, y_n solves $(\Upsilon - \tau\ell_n)R_n^{-\beta} = (\Upsilon - \tau\ell_{n+1})R_{n+1}^{-\beta}, n = 0, \ldots, N_e$. Rewriting this condition by solving for Y yields the functional form of stratification envelopes:

$$y_n\left(\frac{R_n}{R_{n+1}}, \ell_n, \ell_{n+1}; \beta\right) = \tau \frac{\ell_{n+1}\left(\frac{R_n}{R_{n+1}}\right)^{\beta} - \ell_n}{\left(\frac{R_n}{R_{n+1}}\right)^{\beta} - 1}, \quad n = 0, \ldots, N_e \leq N-1. \tag{5.39}$$

It is straightforward to establish by differentiation that the function $y_n\left(\frac{R_n}{R_{n+1}}, \ell_n, \ell_{n+1}; \beta\right)$ is decreasing in β and in the rent ratio R_n/R_{n+1}.[15] Since the second derivative of the stratification envelope function with respect to preference parameter β is positive, the greater importance of housing in preferences implies that the stratification loci are flatter and therefore all neighborhoods become more homogeneous with respect to income, ceteris paribus.

Since $R_{N-1} = R_{N_e} = R_a$, which is given exogenously as the opportunity cost of land, it follows that R_n declines with ℓ_n. For an equilibrium in the Nth ring, the outermost ring, the demand for land should equal the supply:

$$\int d\beta \int_{y_{N-1}}^{\infty} \beta \frac{y - \tau\ell_N}{R_a} f(y, \beta) dy = 1. \tag{5.40}$$

The left-hand side of this equation is monotonically increasing in $\frac{R_{N-1}}{R_N}$, the respective rental ratio, and the only unknown in (5.40). This allows the solution to be written as $\frac{R_{N-1}}{R_N} = \mathcal{R}_N(\ell_{N-2}, \ell_{N-1})$.

The housing market equilibrium in ring n, $n = N-2, \ldots, 0$, requires

$$\int d\beta \int_{y_{n-1}}^{y_n} \beta \frac{y - k\ell_n}{R_n} f(y, \beta) dy = 1, \; n = 1, \ldots, N-1. \tag{5.41}$$

The respective solution may be written as $\frac{R_{n-1}}{R_n} = \mathcal{R}_n\left(\frac{R_n}{R_{n+1}}; \ell_{n-1}, \ldots, \ell_N\right)$. Finally, the equation for equilibrium in ring 0 is

$$\int d\beta \int_{\min_{\Upsilon_j, j \in \mathcal{J}}}^{y_1} \frac{\beta(y - k\ell_n)}{R_1} f(y, \beta) dy = 1. \tag{5.42}$$

The left-hand side of the above equation is monotonically decreasing in R_1, and therefore (5.42) determines $\frac{R_1}{R_2}$. Working recursively, we determine the entire sequence of housing rents and the number of rings that are inhabited at equilibrium.

Once all the rents are known, the stratification envelopes for each ring (or neighborhood) are determined. I denote them by $y_n^*(\beta)$. The stratification envelopes for two successive rings, $\left(y_{n-1}^*(\beta), y_n^*(\beta)\right)$, define a region, or "strip," in (Υ, β) space, just as in figure 3.3, that characterizes the joint distribution of income and preferences within ring n, $n = 0, 1, \ldots, N-1$.

It follows from the property that the stratification envelopes $y_n(\cdot)$, defined in (5.39), are decreasing in β, that within each ring (neighborhood), incomes and housing preferences are, roughly speaking, negatively correlated. I can define the income distribution within neighborhood n readily by integrating the joint density function $f(\Upsilon, \beta)$ over the respective region. Let β_n be the inverse of the stratification envelope $n : \beta_n(y) = y_n^{*-1}(y)$. This is well defined in view of the monotonicity of $y_n^*(\beta)$. The cumulative distribution function for incomes in neighborhood n is

$$F_{n,\Upsilon}(\Upsilon) = D^{-1} \int^{\Upsilon} [F_\Upsilon(\beta_n(y)) - F_\Upsilon(\beta_{n-1}(y))] dy, \quad n = 1, \ldots, N-1, \tag{5.43}$$

where $F_\Upsilon(\cdot)$ denotes the marginal of the joint distribution $f(\Upsilon, \beta)$ and D is the percentage of the population residing in neighborhood n, the value of the numerator when the upper limit is set to infinity; it serves here as a normalizing constant.

The approach in section 5.1.3.1 above suggests that heterogeneity with respect to income can only lead to perfect stratification in terms of income. The concept of a stratification envelope (5.39) still applies, and individuals with incomes in the interval $[y_{n-1}^*(\beta), y_n^*(\beta))$ all live in ring n. If, however, individuals differ in terms of preferences but have identical incomes, then at equilibrium perfect stratification in terms of preferences emerges. The intervals of stratification are obtained by expressing the stratification loci in terms of the intervals $[B_{n-1}(\Upsilon), B_n(\Upsilon)]$, where the functions $B_{n-1}(\Upsilon)$ are defined as

$$B_n\left(\Upsilon; \frac{R_n}{R_{n+1}}\right) = \frac{\ln\left[\frac{\Upsilon - k\ell_n}{\Upsilon - k\ell_{n+1}}\right]}{\ln\left[\frac{R_n}{R_{n+1}}\right]}, \quad n = 1, \ldots, N-1. \tag{5.44}$$

Spatial equilibrium in this simple economy with joint variation in income and preferences is associated with imperfect stratification. Different concentric rings accommodate different but partly overlapping income ranges. The method I discuss here is in the spirit of Epple and Platt (1998) and of other work by Epple and associates, discussed in chapter 3, section 3.7.1. Here it is set in terms of neighborhoods rather than communities. The findings by Hardman and Ioannides and others on the properties of neighborhood income distributions that I discuss in chapter 3, section 3.6.3, also provide indirect empirical support for the role that correlated effects play in urban land use.

Finally, as Fujita (1989, 105) indicates, the recursive nature of the approach above as one moves from the outer to the inner rings is reminiscent of dynamic programming. The maximum value of the rent that land can earn at different locations, given how it is valued by different groups, is a spatial counterpart of the value function in dynamic programming.[16]

5.6.3 Endogenous Amenities in the Canonical Model

It is possible but tedious to account for endogenous amenities in the analysis of the location models for individuals in the presence of interactions (see section 5.2.1 above). Individuals may differ with respect to their valuation of characteristics of other individuals. For instance, rich individuals may like to be near other rich individuals.

Brueckner, Thisse, and Zenou (1999, 100–103) show that if this motive is sufficiently strong, it can offset the force that pushes the rich further from the CBD. Consider the special case with two zones, center and suburbs. For the rich living near the center and the poor living in the suburbs to be in equilibrium, the bid-rent curve of the poor, although steeper than that of the rich in either zone, must be entirely dominated by that of the rich in the center. This is compatible with a discontinuity at the boundary between the center and the suburbs. Such a discontinuity is of course an artifact of defining the endogenous amenity as insensitive to distance from the boundary. The position of the equilibrium rent curve is determined by the requirement that all households be accommodated within the city. Such a discontinuity gives rise to the possibility that a mixed city is an equilibrium outcome. That is, if the bid rent of the rich, when the endogenous amenity is mean neighborhood income, dominates that of the poor over the entire domain, then a city may accommodate both groups throughout. This condition is more stringent in that the rich bid rent would in this case be below that in the case of the rich alone. Moreover, the outcome is disadvantageous for the poor, who would have to pay higher rent than if they were to occupy the center on their own. Such disadvantageous desegregation is a new possibility within the canonical urban model.

This is but one of many possibilities. Miyao (1978a) shows that in the presence of negative intergroup externalities or positive intragroup externalities, the mixed-city equilibrium is always unstable, provided that land is perfectly homogeneous in the city with no differential transport cost incurred so that there is no spatial segregation for economic reasons. He also shows that a mixed-city equilibrium is not necessarily unstable in the case of a monocentric city with positive transport costs where spatial segregation occurs within the city. In fact, in the latter case the equilibrium is locally stable if the degree of externalities is sufficiently small relative to the elasticity of utility with respect to land.

5.6.3.1 *Individuals Value the Housing Consumption of Their Neighbors*

I now deal more formally with the impact on urban spatial equilibrium of the presence of endogenous neighborhood effects in the sense of chapter 3, section 3.5.1, with individuals valuing the housing consumption of their neighbors. I follow Rossi-Hansberg, Sarte, and Owens (2010) and amend the model in section 5.1.2 so as to introduce the consumption of housing services, $H(\ell)$, rather than just land. In addition, each individual also values the housing consumption of all the other city residents but in a manner that attenuates with distance. This serves as a force of local agglomeration. The housing argument in the utility function, $\tilde{H}(\ell)$, incorporates an additive endogenous neighborhood effect:

$$\tilde{H}(\ell) = \delta \int_{\underline{\ell}}^{\bar{\ell}} e^{-\delta|\ell-s|} H(s)ds + H(\ell),$$

where $[\underline{\ell}, \bar{\ell}]$ define the relevant neighborhood. Individuals rent a unit of land at ℓ for a rent $R(\ell)$ and choose nonhousing and housing consumption $(c(\ell), H(\ell))$, so as to maximize $\Omega(\tilde{H}(\ell), c(\ell)) \equiv c(\ell)^{1-\beta}\tilde{H}(\ell)^{\beta}$, subject to the budget constraint:

$$c(\ell) + R(\ell) + H(\ell) = \Upsilon - \tau\ell. \tag{5.45}$$

The first-order conditions for this problem yield $\beta c(\ell) = (1-\beta)\tilde{H}(\ell)$. Solving from the budget constraint (5.45) and substituting back into the expression for the total housing argument in the utility function yields

$$\tilde{H}(\ell) = \beta\left(\Upsilon - \tau\ell - R(\ell) + \delta \int_{\underline{\ell}}^{\bar{\ell}} e^{-\delta|\ell-s|} H(s)ds\right). \tag{5.46}$$

At spatial equilibrium, the optimum value of the utility function, $\mathcal{O}$, must be independent of location. Since $c(\ell)$ may be solved in terms of $\tilde{H}(\ell)$, it follows that $\tilde{H}(\ell)$ itself is constant at spatial equilibrium. Let that value be $\bar{H}$. Thus, $\tilde{H}(\ell) \equiv \bar{H} = \left(\frac{\beta}{1-\beta}\right)^{1-\beta}\mathcal{O}$, a value that depends on equilibrium in the entire urban economy. In other words,

$$H(\ell) = \bar{H} - \delta \int_{\underline{\ell}}^{\bar{\ell}} e^{-\delta|\ell-s|} H(s)ds, \ \ell \in [-\bar{\ell}, \bar{\ell}]. \tag{5.47}$$

This equation may be solved uniquely as a functional equation in $H(\ell)$ because the right-hand side of (5.47) is a contraction mapping. See Rossi-Hansberg, Sarte, and Owens (2010, 497–501).

To complete the discussion of urban equilibrium, I substitute from (5.47) into the budget constraint to obtain an equation for the land rental function:

$$R(\ell) = \Upsilon - \tau\ell + \delta \int_{\underline{\ell}}^{\bar{\ell}} e^{-\delta|\ell - s|} H(s)ds - \beta^{-1}\bar{H}, \ \ell \in [-\bar{\ell}, \bar{\ell}]. \quad (5.48)$$

Again, the land rental function declines with distance from the CBD, provided that the value of the externality is not strong enough. Its rate of decline reflects both transport costs and the change in the value of the externality. As before, the model is closed by using the opportunity cost of land, R_a, to define city size:

$$\delta \int_{\underline{\ell}}^{\bar{\ell}} e^{-\delta|\ell - s|} H(s)ds = R_a - (\Upsilon - \tau\bar{\ell}) + \beta^{-1}\bar{H}. \quad (5.49)$$

Again, urban equilibrium is determined by solving for $(H(\ell), \bar{\ell})$, the condition for social equilibrium, (5.47), a functional equation in $H(\ell)$, jointly with the condition for land equilibrium, (5.49). Numerical solutions of these two equations, reported by Rossi-Hansberg, Sarte, and Owens (2010, 497–501), show that housing consumption is lowest at the center and gradually increases with distance from the CBD. As the housing externality declines, housing consumption increases. The equilibrium land rental function is concave over the range of locations within the neighborhood $[-\underline{\ell}, \bar{\ell}]$. The force of agglomeration in this model again removes the sharp peak at the center that would have been present otherwise. Heterogeneity with respect to preferences or incomes, other types of shocks, or the coexistence of contextual with endogenous social interactions complicates somewhat the clarity of this picture.

Rossi-Hansberg, Sarte, and Owens (2010) use this analytical framework to evaluate local urban policy interventions of the urban renewal type both theoretically and empirically. The model suggests that subsidizing home improvements reduces private investment in the targeted neighborhood. Individuals, however, are made better off by improvements they do not have to pay for. Resources thus freed cause bidding up of the price of land. The authors evaluate the Neighborhoods-in-Bloom (NiB) program in Richmond, Virginia, which provided federally funded housing investments concentrated in a few disadvantaged neighborhoods. The impact of the program is large enough to be an exogenous shock to the attractiveness of locations that allows the identification of agglomeration effects. They find substantial effects, significantly not only in neighborhoods targeted by the programs. Neighborhoods that did not directly benefit from capital improvements experienced considerable increases in land value relative to similar sites in a control neighborhood. They find that within the targeted Richmond neighborhoods, increases in land value are consistent with externalities that fall exponentially with distance, decreasing by half approximately every 990 feet. On average, land prices in neighborhoods targeted for revitalization rose by 2 percent to 5 percent at an annual rate above those in the control neighborhood (Bellemeade). These increases translate into land value gains of between \$2 and \$6 per dollar invested in the program over a 6 year period.

5.7 TRANSMISSION OF JOB-RELATED INFORMATION AND URBAN EQUILIBRIUM

I now turn to an examination of urban equilibrium when proximity is a conduit for the transmission of job-related information. This is an instance of endogenous amenities. Evidence suggests that individuals benefit from being near others because proximity facilitates sharing information about job opportunities (Ioannides and Loury 2004; Bayer, Ross, and Topa 2008). A noteworthy feature of the resulting spatial equilibrium that I examine here is that it can also accommodate urban location decisions as an outcome of the choice between traveling to the CBD for job matching and relying on tips from social contacts at home. The transmission of job-related information affects lifetime income prospects through the impact of unemployment on permanent income. Social interactions thus make people who have characteristics in common and/or who share job information more likely to affect urban equilibrium and therefore the economy's urban structure. In chapter 7, section 7.8.1, below, I take up how such interactions can sustain urban industrial specialization or diversification when industries differ with respect to business cycle characteristics, here modeled simply in terms of the rate at which jobs are destroyed.

I draw from Wasmer and Zenou (2002), who adapt the Pissarides model of labor markets with frictions (Pissarides 1985, 2000), turning it into a job-matching model in an urban setting. In the basic Wasmer–Zenou model individuals have to engage in a search in order to make contacts with potential employers. Jobs are located in the CBD, and job matching requires costly trips to the CBD. In a notable departure from the model of Wasmer and Zenou (2002),[17] but along the lines of the Zenou (2009b) model, I assume here that individuals do *not move* each time they become unemployed; instead they choose a place to locate permanently within a city. They set their consumption in line with their permanent income. This allows me to focus on the effects on an economy's urban structure of expected income fluctuations emanating from job loss risks only.

I work first with the simplest possible model, a city inhabited by identical individuals. I then examine the implications for urban spatial equilibrium of the coexistence of individuals who differ in terms of preferences, skills, or conditions of employment. If the industries located in a city differ with respect to the rates at which jobs are destroyed, their coexistence in the same urban economy helps reduce uncertainty by means of pooling the risks. I also examine how these aspects are affected when workers choose between centralized job matching, which requires traveling to the CBD, and relying on their personal contacts. I take the behavior of firms as given, along the lines of the model in chapter 4, section 4.9, above.

I return to the model with labor market frictions as a building block for describing an economy's urban structure in chapter 7, section 7.8. There I assume that different goods are produced by combining raw labor and a range of differentiated goods, which can be interpreted as differentiated services. These services transform raw labor into skilled labor which is combined into a composite. I introduce labor market frictions by assuming that only jobs employing raw labor may be destroyed, at an industry-specific exogenous probability per unit of time. Workers who have been terminated as a result of job destruction enter the unemployed pool.

5.7.1 The Matching Model

I use ℓ again to denote locations in terms of distance from the CBD, with the urban area extending over a circle of radius $\bar{\ell}$. The urban economy is symmetric around the CBD. Each individual is endowed with a unit of raw labor. Individuals may differ with respect to their skill, i, $i = 1, 2$, interpreted here as efficiency units of labor, z_i, $z_1 < z_2$. Type-2 individuals are more highely skilled. An individual with z_i efficiency units of labor earns $w_i = \bar{w} z_i$ when employed. Alternatively, individuals may be employed by different industries whose wages, employment, and job destruction rates may differ. If unemployed, each person receives unemployment compensation at a rate b, which is assumed to be independent of a person's skill.

Let s_i be the efficiency of a job search by a type-i person when unemployed, U_i be the stock of all unemployed type-i workers in a city, V_i be the stock of vacancies for jobs for which i-types qualify, and $\bar{s}$ be the average efficiency of the search by all unemployed workers in a city. The rate of contacts between unemployed workers and vacancies per unit of time, the *Pissarides matching function* (Pissarides 1985, 2000), is denoted by

$$M(\bar{s} U_i, V_i). \tag{5.50}$$

Following Pissarides, I assume that the matching function of vacancies with unemployed workers M is increasing, is concave, and exhibits constant returns to scale with respect to both of its arguments, the effective stock of unemployed and the stock of vacancies, respectively.[18] The probability that an individual of type i who lives in location ℓ and has an efficiency of search $s_i(\ell)$ will have a contact during a small interval of time $(t, t + dt)$ is given by

$$\pi_i dt = \frac{M(\bar{s} U_i, V_i)}{U_i} \frac{s_i}{\bar{s}} dt. \tag{5.51}$$

This can be rewritten, by using the linear homogeneity property of the matching function, as a function of the effective tightness of a city's labor market for i-type individuals, υ_i, $\upsilon_i = \frac{V_i}{U_i \bar{s}}$:

$$\pi_i = \upsilon_i q(\upsilon_i) s_i, \tag{5.52}$$

where $q(\upsilon_i) \equiv \frac{M(\bar{s} U_i, V_i)}{V_i} = M(\frac{1}{\upsilon_i}, 1)$, $q' < 0$, is the rate at which vacancies are matched with unemployed workers. Therefore, the more job vacancies there are relative to the stock of unemployed workers, the greater υ_i, the tighter the labor market, and the lower the probability of contacts, q, for firms. π_i is also the job-finding rate because all job offers are accepted. It follows from the linear homogeneity of the matching function that an individual's job contact probability is increasing and concave in labor market tightness.[19]

In what follows I refer to *homogeneous cities*, inhabited by identical individuals with identical skills, and *heterogeneous cities*, inhabited by individuals representing both skill types. I define *specialized cities* as those with one type of industry; *diversified cities* host two types of industries. I simplify notation when no confusion arises by indexing with respect to i only when it becomes necessary.

5.7.2 Expected Lifetime Utility

I now develop expressions for lifetime utility in a continuous-time model at steady state under the assumption that individuals when employed risk losing their jobs and search for new jobs only when unemployed, both at constant probabilities per unit of time. Let $\Omega_{iu}(\ell)$, $\Omega_{ie}(\ell)$ denote individual i's expected lifetime income conditional, respectively, on being unemployed and employed; $\alpha_e(\ell)$, $\alpha_u(\ell)$ the commuting costs per unit of time for, respectively, an employed and an unemployed person, both assumed to be increasing functions of the distance from the nearest CBD; b the rate of unemployment compensation (or value of home production) per unit of noncommuting time; ρ the rate of interest; d_J the rate at which jobs are destroyed by a firm in industry $J = X, Y$; π_J the rate at which unemployed workers are hired by a firm in industry $J = X, Y$; $R(\ell)$ the land rental rate; and $\bar{R}$ the total land rents per capita.

Each person's demand for land (housing) is inelastic and equal to 1. Commuting is costly purely in terms of time; it reduces the labor supply and does not generate income elsewhere in the economy.

Individuals live forever. They may lend or borrow against their expected lifetime income at the constant rate ρ.[20] For an individual of type i, $\Omega_{iu}(\ell)$ and $\Omega_{ie}(\ell)$ are the expected asset values associated with the state of being, respectively, unemployed and employed. For an unemployed individual i, the expected return to being unemployed per unit of time at equilibrium must be equal to the rate of unemployment compensation adjusted for the portion of time not spent commuting, plus the expected capital gain associated with becoming employed, plus the net land rental. Similarly, if individual i is employed, the expected return to being employed per unit of time at equilibrium must be equal to the wage rate adjusted for the portion of time not spent commuting, plus the expected capital gain associated with becoming unemployed, plus the net land rental. In a continuous time framework, $\Omega_{iu}(\ell)$, $\Omega_{ie}(\ell)$ satisfy the following Bellman equations, which are linear in this case:

$$\rho\Omega_{iu}(\ell) = b(1 - \alpha_u(\ell)) + \pi_i[\Omega_{ie}(\ell) - \Omega_{iu}(\ell)] + \bar{R} - R(\ell), \tag{5.53}$$

$$\rho\Omega_{ie}(\ell) = w_i(1 - \alpha_e(\ell)) + d[\Omega_{iu}(\ell) - \Omega_{ie}(\ell)] + \bar{R} - R(\ell). \tag{5.54}$$

At the steady state, the rate of unemployment for individuals of type i in industry J must be such that flows into unemployment equal flows out of unemployment: $d_J(1 - u_i) = u_i\pi_i$. Solving for u_i yields

$$u_i = \frac{d_J}{d_J + \pi_i}. \tag{5.55}$$

An individual's steady-state unemployment rate depends on search intensity and labor market tightness, s_i, $vq(v)$, which may be city-specific. Because the job-finding rate is increasing (and concave) in labor market tightness, v_i, the steady-state unemployment rate decreases in labor market tightness.

By solving equations (5.53) and (5.54) in terms of $\Omega_{ie}(\ell)$ and $\Omega_{iu}(\ell)$ and using (5.55), I obtain an expression for the unconditional present value of the lifetime income of an individual of type i at location ℓ along a steady state of the search process: $\omega_i(\ell) = (1 - u_i)\Omega_{ie} + u_i\Omega_{iu}$. That is,

$$\omega_i(\ell) = \frac{1}{\rho}\left[\bar{R} - R(\ell) + \frac{d}{d + \pi_i} b[1 - \alpha_u(\ell)] + \frac{\pi_i}{d + \pi_i} w_i[1 - \alpha_e(\ell)]\right]. \tag{5.56}$$

The term in brackets above is the instantaneous flow of expected income net of commuting costs.

5.7.3 Spatial Equilibrium and the Land Market

For locational equilibrium within each city, individuals of the same type must be indifferent as to where to locate. I express this by imposing the equality of expected lifetime utility across all locations.[21] All individuals of the same type employ the same search intensity, so that the job-matching probability is independent of a specific location within the city. Alternatively, city populations may be computed as a function of equilibrium utility, which is common across all cities at the intercity spatial equilibrium for all individuals of the same type. For spatial equilibrium within each city, the land rental rate must vary so as to equalize expected lifetime income across all locations. Consequently, the bid rent function $R(\ell)$ reflects the value of accessibility to the CBD through its impact on the cost of an unemployed worker's making contact with a vacancy in the city at the worker's location. Considering first a single worker type, from (5.56), we have the spatial equilibrium condition

$$\omega_i(\ell) = \omega_i(\bar{\ell}), \ \ell \in [0, \bar{\ell}]. \tag{5.57}$$

Working in the standard open-city context, I anchor urban equilibrium on the opportunity cost of land, R_a, at the boundary of a typical city: $R(\bar{\ell}) = R_a$. Assuming that the opportunity value of land is 0 at the boundary, $R(\bar{\ell}) = 0$, and using it in (5.56) and (5.57), I solve for the bid rent function for individuals of type i:

$$R_i(\ell) = \frac{d}{d + \pi_i} b[\alpha_u(\bar{\ell}) - \alpha_u(\ell)] + \frac{\pi_i}{d + \pi_i} w_i[\alpha_e(\bar{\ell}) - \alpha_e(\ell)]. \tag{5.58}$$

For spatial equilibrium, the land rent must decline with distance from the CBD in order to compensate individuals for incurring commuting costs, which increase with distance from the CBD for both employed and unemployed individuals. For employed individuals, this is the full-time cost of commuting, $\alpha_e(\ell) = \bar{\alpha}_e \ell$. For unemployed individuals who may go to the CBD less frequently in order to search for jobs, $\alpha_u(\ell)$ may be related to search intensity. With search intensity at its maximum, unemployed individuals are assumed to go to the CBD as frequently as employed ones. See (Zenou 2009a, 42–58).

I complete the description of spatial equilibrium by evaluating the associated value of expected utility. It is necessary to compute the average per capita rent, $\bar{R}$, that enters (5.56). For a circular city of radius $\bar{\ell}$ and population N, this is given by $\bar{R} = \frac{1}{N}\int_0^{\bar{\ell}} 2\pi \ell R(\ell) d\ell$ and may be computed once the functions α_u, α_e have been specified. I assume $\alpha_u = \bar{\alpha}_u \ell, \alpha_e = \bar{\alpha}_e \ell$. With an inelastic individual demand for land equal to unity and the assumption of circular city geography the land (housing) market equilibrium defines the equilibrium size of the city, $\pi \bar{\ell}^2 = N$. For a homogeneous city of type i, for example, this condition is

$$\bar{\ell} = \pi^{-1/2} N^{1/2}. \tag{5.59}$$

Integrating the expression for the total land rents yields

$$\bar{R}_i = \frac{1}{3}\left(\frac{d}{d + \pi_i(\ell)} b\bar{\alpha}_u + \frac{\pi_i(\ell)}{d + \pi_i(\ell)} w_i \bar{\alpha}_e\right) \pi^{-1/2} N^{1/2}.$$

The associated expected lifetime utility, net of land rents and commuting costs and inclusive of the redistributed average land rentals, is

$$\tilde{\Omega}_i = \frac{1}{\rho}\left[\frac{1}{3}\frac{d}{d + \pi_i} b\bar{\alpha}_u \pi^{-1/2} N^{1/2} + \frac{\pi_i}{d + \pi_i} w_i \left(1 - \frac{2}{3}\bar{\alpha}_e \pi^{-1/2} N^{1/2}\right)\right]. \tag{5.60}$$

The total city labor supply, net of commuting costs, is given by

$$H_c(N) = N\left(1 - \frac{2}{3}\bar{\alpha}_e \pi^{-1/2} N^{1/2}\right). \tag{5.61}$$

I note that if $d b \bar{\alpha}_u < 2\pi_i w_i \bar{\alpha}_e$, congestion implies that an increasing population reduces welfare in this highly simplified model. This may be offset by the advantages that a large urban population makes possible, exactly as in the case with no unemployment, that I examine in chapter 7.

Wasmer and Zenou (2006) [see also Zenou (2009b)] work with a refined model with individuals being subject to relocation costs. Depending upon the magnitude of the relocation costs, workers may self-organize into different areas of the city. With positive but finite relocation costs, location depends on the employment state. At equilibrium, mobile individuals when unemployed segregate into the area immediately surrounding the CBD, while mobile individuals when employed segregate into the outermost area abutting the edge of the city. The in-between area is inhabited by immobile employed and unemployed workers who are integrated and evenly distributed in that area. With zero mobility costs, the in-between area vanishes, and individuals move each time their employment status changes. From this perspective, the model I develop in the present section is the case of high relocation costs (Zenou 2009b). The introduction of residential moves correlated with changes in employment status has the obvious consequence of making the housing and labor markets interdependent [c.f. Zenou (2009a, 26)]. Therefore, the models introduced by Wasmer and Zenou are important extensions of the canonical Alonso–Mills–Muth model of urban spatial structure.

5.7.3.1 *Location Decisions in Heterogeneous Cities*

How do differences across individuals with respect to skill or with respect to the types of jobs they hold affect location decisions within a heterogeneous city? Land use in heterogeneous cities is determined by the fact that the bid rent functions of different individual types differ. Therefore, differences in the job destruction rate for firms in different industries or, alternatively, differences in the terms of remuneration across firms imply that the respective groups of workers are segregated at equilibrium. Below I develop two examples of city equilibrium, one, where individuals are identical but may work for different industries, and two, where two different types of individuals coexist.

For persons of two different types $i = 1, 2$, employed at jobs with a destruction rate d, job-finding probabilities π_1, π_2, wages w_1, w_2, and a common rate of unemployment compensation, the switch over location $\ell = \hat{\ell}_{12}$ is where the respective bid rent functions are equalized:

$$\frac{d}{d+\pi_2} b(1-\alpha_u(\hat{\ell}_{12})) + \frac{\pi_2}{d+\pi_2} w_2(1-\alpha_e(\hat{\ell}_{12})) = \frac{d}{d+\pi_1} b(1-\alpha_u(\hat{\ell}_{12})) + \frac{\pi_1}{d+\pi_1} w_1(1-\alpha_e(\hat{\ell}_{12})). \tag{5.62}$$

Let wages satisfy $w_1 < w_2$, and let search efficiencies s_1 and s_2, satisfy $s_1 < s_2$. Under the assumption that job matching depends upon total labor market tightness, the probabilities of job contacts π_1 and π_2 satisfy $\pi_1 < \pi_2$. It follows that $R_1'(\ell) < R_2'(\ell)$ and $R_1(0) < R_2(0)$. Therefore, there exists in general a location $\hat{\ell}$ where (5.62) is satisfied, that is, the bid rents by the two types are equal. As a result, area $0 < \ell < \hat{\ell}$ is occupied by individuals of type 2; $R_1(\ell) < R_2(\ell)$ for $\ell < \hat{\ell}$. For individuals of type 1, $R_1(\ell) > R_2(\ell)$ for $\ell > \hat{\ell}$, and accordingly those locations are occupied by type-1 individuals. While this may be analyzed further in the general case, the special case of linear commuting costs yields the simple result that the group with higher job contact probability lives nearer the center. Similarly, if the two groups differ with respect to the probability of job destruction, say $d_1 > d_2$, then it can be shown that the group with the higher job breakup probability lives nearer the center. The implied segregation of individuals by type is reflected in the two segments of the land rental function, whose slopes differ. The fact that more is known in that case facilitates econometric identification.

How do individuals locate when they differ in terms of the characteristics of the jobs they hold, with only some holding permanent jobs? Let w_{pe} denote the wage rate for permanent jobs and let $(\pi_{te}, d; b, w_{te})$ be the terms of employment at jobs that may end with probability d per unit of time. If individuals are otherwise identical, there exists, in general, a unique value $\hat{\ell}_{tp}$ for which the bid rent functions associated with the two job types are equal:

$$\frac{d}{d+\pi} b(1-\bar{\alpha}_u \hat{\ell}_{tp}) + \frac{\pi_{te}}{d+\pi_{te}} w_{te}(1-\bar{\alpha}_e \hat{\ell}_{tp}) = w_{pe}(1-\bar{\alpha}_e \hat{\ell}), \qquad (5.63)$$

for $\ell > 0$. The area $0 \leq \ell \leq \hat{\ell}_{tp}$ is occupied by those with permanent jobs, and the area $\ell > \hat{\ell}_{tp}$ by those with jobs that end. Since all individuals are otherwise identical within each group, the above condition establishes that incomes net of commuting are also equalized between the two occupations. Therefore, the land rent functions reflect the differences in the terms of employment. In the special case where $b = 0$, meaning no unemployment compensation, expected earnings in industries with turnover are equal to those where employment is permanent, $\frac{\pi_{te}}{d+\pi_{te}} w_{te} = w_{pe}$. Individuals who may be unemployed are compensated for the likelihood of unemployment by means of a higher wage rate when they do work. They are all indifferent as to where they live.

The case of different types of jobs is relevant to the model of intercity trade presented in chapter 7. In a specialized city, permanent jobs coexist with one type of job associated with turnover. In a diversified city, permanent jobs that pay w_{pe} coexist with two other types of jobs in industry $J = X, Y$, with job-finding rates at π_X, π_Y, rates of job destruction at d_X, d_Y, and wages at w_X, w_Y, respectively. Condition (5.63) generalizes to

$$\frac{\pi_X}{d_X+\pi_X} w_X = \frac{\pi_Y}{d_Y+\pi_Y} w_Y = w_{pe},$$

with $b = 0$. That is, expected earnings are equalized across all employment options. These conditions imply that the land rental rate and the expected lifetime income, net of land rents and commuting costs and inclusive of the redistributed land rentals, are given by (5.58) and (5.60), respectively, with $i = X, Y$.

5.8 CHOICE OF JOB MATCHING AND SPATIAL STRUCTURE

The above results demonstrate that introducing labor market frictions in the style of the Mortensen–Pissarides model, as adapted by Wasmer and Zenou (2002) and Zenou (2009a, 2009b), enriches the model of urban spatial structure. It does so in a number of directions of current interest in social economics. A recent literature has emphasized the role of urban spatial structure for job matching. Taking cues from Helsley and Strange (1990), who were the first to highlight a matching externality in an urban setting whereby an increase in the number of agents trying to match improves the expected quality of each match, Gan and Li (2004) and Zhang (2007) model matching in specific urban settings and aim at explaining cyclicality in urban unemployment. In broadly related research that emphasizes unemployment, Gan and Zhang (2006) link city size to matching. Their model predicts that larger city sizes imply lower peak and mean unemployment rates and shorter unemployment cycles. They confirm these predictions using data for 295 U.S. Primary MSAs (PMSAs) over 1981–1997: an increase of two standard deviations in city size shortens the unemployment cycles by about 0.72 month, lowers the peak unemployment rates by 0.33 percentage point, and lowers the mean unemployment rates by 0.16 percentage point. Simon (1988) emphasizes that the short-run immobility of labor among city labor markets contributes to frictional unemployment. The more industrially diversified a city, the lower its frictional unemployment. Using data on 91 large U.S. SMSAs for 1977–1981 and ranking them in terms of their Herfindahl indices of employment, Simon finds that the 20 least and the 20 most diversified cities have frictional unemployment, respectively, at 1.4 points above and 1 point below the mean.

These and additional findings discussed at greater length in chapter 7, section 7.8, motivate my introduction of labor market frictions in the model of intercity trade in chapter 7, section 7.8.1 below.

5.8.1 Empirics

This section explores microeconomic aspects of the transmission of job-related information in urban settings. Bayer, Ross, and Topa (2008) make the strongest empirical case to date for the effects of geographic proximity on job market outcomes. They document that people who live close to each other, defined as living in the same census block, also tend to work together, defined as working in the same census block. The underlying hypothesis is that individuals interacting very locally with their social contacts exchange information about jobs.

The basic empirical framework is as follows: let i and j be individuals who reside in the same census block group but do not belong to the same household; e^b_{ij} a dummy variable equal to 1 if i and j work in the same census block, and to zero otherwise; ℓ^b_{ij} a dummy variable equal to 1 if i and j reside in the same census block, and to zero otherwise; X_{ij} a vector of sociodemographic characteristics for a matched pair (a concept to be clarified shortly below) (i, j); ϵ_g a residential block group fixed effect that serves as the baseline probability of an employment match for individuals living in the same block group, and ε_{ij} an independent and identically distributed random shock. Their hypothesis may be examined in terms of a regression:

$$e^b_{ij} = \beta' X_{ij} + (\alpha_0 + \alpha_1' X_{ij}) \cdot \ell^b_{ij} + \epsilon_g + \varepsilon_{ij}. \tag{5.64}$$

The crucial identifying assumption here is that individuals choose where to live among block groups and their characteristics, and not individual blocks. Consequently, conditional on sorting at the block group level, the assignment of individuals to specific blocks within a group can be assumed to be independent of block-specific characteristics. Thus, relative to a baseline probability, the effect of local interactions in the form of labor market referrals may be identified. The Bayer–Ross–Topa test for the presence of social interactions due to proximity reduces to testing for the statistical significance of the term ($\hat{\alpha}_0 + \hat{\alpha}_1' X_{ij}$) in (5.64). They include both the baseline probability $\hat{\epsilon}_g$ and matched pair (i, j)'s covariates in levels, $\hat{\beta}' X_{ij}$, to control for any observed and unobserved factors that may influence where individuals work at the block group level. This allows them to control for features of the urban transportation network that might induce clustering in both residence and work locations, for example. Similarly, worker characteristics might be correlated with both residential location preferences and work locations, if firms sort along the same variables. The empirical strategy of Bayer et al. addresses several additional potential pitfalls, including possible sorting below the block level and the possibility of reverse causation with coworkers giving referrals on desirable residential areas. After they estimate the social interactions effect, they consider whether the quality of the matches available in an individual's block affects employment, labor force participation, and wage outcomes.

The empirical implementation uses data from the 1990 U.S. census for the Boston metropolitan area. The authors choose individuals who do not reside in the same household, are U.S.-born, are aged 25–59, and are employed at the time of the interview. They end up with 110,000 observations. From these data, about 4 million observations are constructed on *matched* pairs by matching up individuals in a city with 2,565 block groups having an average of 10 blocks each.

Bayer, Ross, and Topa find that social interactions are stronger when a pair of individuals are more likely to interact because of education, age, or the presence of children; interactions are also stronger when one individual is strongly attached to the labor market. Interactions are weaker when both are dropouts, young people, or married females. In terms of the magnitude of the impact of match quality, an increase in referral opportunities of one standard deviation for a person raises labor force participation by 1 percentage point, weeks worked by about two-thirds of one week, hours worked per week by 0.3–1.8 hours for men, and earnings by 2.0–3.7 percentage points. For women, the effect on labor force participation and expected employment varies between 0.8 and 3.6 percentage points across specifications. Interestingly, they do not find a significant earnings effect for women, but the estimated referral effects are stronger for less educated workers, for younger workers, and for Asians and Hispanics. This study is also noteworthy for its reliance on different geographic scales for identification.

Dujardin, Peeters, and Thomas (2009) handle in a different way the potential endogeneity of location in studying the impact of neighborhood effects on the likelihood of unemployment. Starting from the census data of the 2001 Socioeconomic Survey of Belgium, they isolate 27,044 individuals, who are aged 19–25, are members of the labor force, and live with at least one parent in the Brussels area. Using a principal components analysis with

11 socioeconomic and demographic characteristics (including unemployment rates) at the neighborhood level to classify neighborhoods in the Brussels Extended Urban Area (EUA), they end up with 309 neighborhoods of which 72 are classified as deprived. The deprived neighborhoods are clustered in Brussels' urban center and contain 40.5 percent of the Brussels EUA population. Since many or most young Europeans typically live with their parents until they marry, restricting attention to individuals living with a parent arguably removes a portion of the endogeneity bias as to individuals' unemployment outcomes and so does controlling for parental characteristics. The authors show that living in a deprived neighborhood and having less educated parents who are not in the labor force or unemployed all increase the likelihood of the respondents' unemployment. Being male, older, better educated, and "less" Belgian are all associated with increased unemployment. These results survive a sensitivity analysis showing that only an "unreasonably high" selection of unobservables would render their estimates of neighborhood effects insignificant.

Weinberg, Reagan, and Yankow (2004) use a confidential version of the NLSY79 (see chapter 2, section 2.13.3) to estimate the effects of neighborhood social characteristics and job proximity on labor market activity at the census tract block group levels from the 1990 census. They also measure job proximity from the 1987 economic census. They estimate a class of models conceptually similar to equation (5.64) above, except that the endogenous variable is annual hours worked (in logs and levels). They allow for both the endogenous social effects of local employment rate and proximity to jobs (measured as the number of jobs weighted by the inverse of the distance). The study finds large contextual effects: an increase of one standard deviation in the social characteristics of a neighborhood increases annual hours by 6.1 percent. A similar increase in job proximity raises hours by 4.7 percent, but the labor activity of neighbors (the endogenous social effect) per se may not be so important. An increase in a number of neighborhood social characteristics is associated with less market work. Social interactions have nonlinear effects, with the greatest impact in the worst neighborhoods. Social characteristics are also more important for less-educated workers.

By using the panel aspects of the data, the researchers correct their estimates for neighborhood selection, using time-invariant and time-varying unobserved individual characteristics. These corrections show that the social effects of neighborhoods are indeed overstated and the effects of job access understated. Therefore, the issue of social interactions introducing reverse causation, such as via neighborhood selection (individuals moving to neighborhoods where employment rates have been growing), is indeed important and must be accounted for.

Topa (2001) tests the implications of a model of social interactions over space that assumes that agents exchange information with their social contacts about job opportunities and that hiring may occur through informal channels. He posits that individuals receive useful information about job openings from their employed social contacts but not from their unemployed contacts. Topa uses local community boundaries (as identified by residents) to distinguish local social interactions from other types of spatially correlated shocks. An increase in employment in a tract depends on the characteristics of the tract's residents and on employment in neighboring tracts, a social interactions effect. A positive local feedback implies that the stationary distribution of unemployment in a simulated city exhibits a positive spatial correlation.[22] Comparing predicted and empirical unemployment distributions over a set of contiguous census tracts allows Topa to estimate (via indirect inference using census data for Chicago in 1980 and 1990) model parameters and to test for the existence of social interactions in the form of local information spillovers and empirically measure their magnitude. Topa finds significantly positive amounts of social interaction across neighboring tracts in Chicago. The results indicate that an increase of one standard deviation in neighborhood employment increases expected employment by 0.6–1.3 percentage points. The local spillovers are stronger for areas with less-educated workers and higher fractions of minorities. They are further shaped by ethnic dividing lines and neighborhood boundaries.[23] The results point to an important asymmetry. Topa compares raising counterfactually the amount of information (as proxied by neighborhood employment) available in a disadvantaged tract and lowering it by the same amount in a well-off tract. The change yields a positive effect on expected employment in the disadvantaged tract that is roughly twice as large, in absolute value, as the negative effect in the well-off tract. Ioannides and Topa (2010) suggest that this is due to the different initial conditions in the two tracts in terms of education levels and other attributes, and to the fact that the estimated spillovers vary across these attributes. They also argue that it provides support for the notion that dispersing subsidized public housing instead of concentrating it should bring about employment benefits.

5.8.2 A Model of Job Referrals and Location Decisions

In the theoretical model so far, all job matching takes place in the CBD and requires individuals to travel to the CBD in order to work and to be matched. Next I allow individuals to choose,[24] for job-matching purposes, between traveling to the CBD and traveling to interact with others within their milieu. In the simplest possible case, where the cost of interaction is incurred in terms of travel costs, as in section 5.7 of the present chapter, the economic benefit of unemployment per unit of time for an individual located at $\ell,\ 0 < \ell < \bar{\ell}$, is given by

$$b\left(1 - \tau \int_{-\bar{\ell}}^{\bar{\ell}} |s - \ell| ds\right) = b\left(1 - \frac{\tau}{2}\left((\ell)^2 + (\bar{\ell} - \ell)^2\right)\right).$$

In this case, traveling to the CBD dominates engaging in direct social interactions. However, it is interesting to express more precisely how social interactions influence the job contact rate. I assume that individuals may also be matched with vacancies via referrals from their social contacts, located throughout the urban area.

I consider an unemployed individual who is in direct contact with k other individuals. The probability that any of her contacts is employed and hears of a vacancy is $(1-u)\frac{V}{U}u = (1-u)\upsilon u$. The probability that the individual finds a job thanks to one of her direct contacts[25] is $(1-u)\upsilon u \frac{1-(1-u)^k}{u}\frac{1}{k}$. The probability of finding a job through referral by a social contact is thus

$$\text{Prob}_{\text{ref}}(u, \upsilon; k) = 1 - \left[1 - (1-u)\upsilon \frac{1-(1-u)^k}{k}\right]^k. \tag{5.65}$$

If k is large, the right-hand side of (5.65) is approximated by $\upsilon u(1-u)k$, and the probability of finding a job is proportional to the total number of people contacted.

Unemployed individuals choose how many others to contact so as to maximize the value of unemployment. Recall that individuals consume one unit of housing each, that is, density is equal to 1. If an individual who is located at ℓ contacts others within an interval $[\ell', \ell'']$, then the probability of finding a job through one of those contacts is equal to $\text{Prob}_{\text{ref}} = \upsilon u(1-u)(\ell'' - \ell')$. The right-hand side of the counterpart of equation (5.53) now becomes

$$b\left(1 - \frac{\tau}{2}\left((\ell''-\ell)^2 + (\ell'-\ell)^2\right)\right) + (\ell''-\ell')\upsilon u(1-u)[\Omega_e(\ell) - \Omega_u(\ell)] + \bar{R} - R(\ell). \tag{5.66}$$

Maximizing with respect to (ℓ', ℓ''), the bounds defining the range of social interaction, ℓ', ℓ'', and assuming a linear city yields

$$\ell' = \ell - \frac{1}{b\tau}\upsilon u(1-u)[\Omega_e(\ell) - \Omega_u(\ell)];\ \ \ell'' = \ell + \frac{1}{b\tau}\upsilon u(1-u)[\Omega_e(\ell) - \Omega_u(\ell)].$$

The range of locations where it pays to rely on social contacts is equal to $\frac{2}{b\tau}\upsilon u(1-u)[\Omega_e(\ell) - \Omega_u(\ell)]$ and thus is explicitly dependent on ℓ. The solution for the asset values of unemployment and employment requires that the choice between job matching at the CBD versus via referral by social contacts be incorporated into the Bellman equations. That is,

$$r\Omega_{iu}(\ell) = \max\Big\{b(1 - \bar{\alpha}_u \ell) + \upsilon q(\upsilon)[\Omega_{ie}(\ell) - \Omega_{iu}(\ell)] + \bar{R} - R(\ell)\,,$$
$$b + \frac{1}{b\tau}(\upsilon u(1-u))^2[\Omega_{ie}(\ell) - \Omega_{iu}(\ell)]^2 + \bar{R} - R(\ell)\Big\}. \tag{5.67}$$

The equilibrium asset values $(\Omega_{ie}(\ell), \Omega_{iu}(\ell))$ are obtained as solutions to the system of simultaneous functional equations (5.54) and (5.67). This requires that the conditional present values of lifetime income must be recomputed, and this produces two sets of expressions for the asset value of lifetime income, one corresponding to CBD matching and the other to referral matching, respectively, for each of these quantities. However, solving for $\Omega_{iu}(\ell)$ in the case of a referral leads to a quadratic equation where both solutions are feasible in principle. These expressions do not show explicit dependence on ℓ, but do depend on $\bar{R} - R(\ell)$. By comparing over urban space, one can establish the consistency of the model and show that CBD matching is preferred by those located within the interval $[0, \ell_{ref}]$, where ℓ_{ref} corresponds to the value that equalizes the two terms on the right-hand side of (5.67) when the asset values assume their optimal solutions.

Again, spatial equilibrium requires, just in section 5.7.3.1 above, with all persons being otherwise identical within each group, that incomes net of commuting be equalized between the two respective modes of job search. The land rent functions reflect the differences in the terms of job-finding probabilities. It is also the case that the boundary depends on labor market tightness. The urban economy segregates into those who rely on CBD matching, who live *nearer* the CBD, and those who rely on referrals through social interactions, who live *farther* away from the CBD. A consequence for the model is that the job-finding rate is in this case given by

$$\text{Prob}_{\text{ref},i} = \upsilon u(1-u)\frac{2}{b\tau}\upsilon u(1-u)[\Omega_{ie}(\ell) - \Omega_{iu}(\ell)],$$

and is thus a function of distance from the CBD, changing value discontinuously at the switchover point.

Allowing for a dispersed location of firms, as in section 5.3.1 above, in the presence of labor market frictions would likely lead to results similar to those of Zenou (2009a, 286–297), discussed in section 5.3.1 above. That is, firms would cluster in a zone around the endogenously determined CBD and workers would locate around them. In his model, however, individuals change locations when their labor market status changes, with unemployed workers locating farther away from the CBD than employed workers. In contrast, in the model that I introduce in this chapter in section 5.7 and develop further here, individuals locate permanently in urban space. What corresponds here to a differential location with respect to the labor market status is location with respect to job matching at the CBD versus referral-based matching. Although it is mathematically tedious to close the model, it is conceptually straightforward to think about its implications. At the spatial equilibrium, both methods of job matching would coexist in principle. Different configurations of parameter values could make either method of job matching dominate the other.

5.9 CONCLUSIONS

The extensions of the standard Alonso–Mills–Muth model that I present in this chapter demonstrate its versatility as a depiction of urban economic and social life. While it was designed to represent a single monocentric city, its value extends to urban regions and polycentric cities. The model's versatility underscores the powers of its antecedents in the work of Von Thünen (1826) as emphasized by Samuelson (1983). Allowing for social interactions among individuals and firms in making location decisions enriches the toolkit of economists in understanding a broad range of questions from the underpinnings of the urban production externality to the incidence of unemployment across urban space. Heterogeneous cities may accommodate workers and jobs that differ with respect to turnover-related attributes of jobs. Similarly, the chapter also examines how land use reflects the pervasive role of information in the job market and the urban economy, from social learning to centralized CBD-based versus referral-based job matching. In chapter 7, section 7.8, I use the results of this section as building blocks in recasting the question of urban specialization versus diversification. Still the basic models in this chapter are limited by a very restricted view of social exchange. The rich social space within which individuals interact potentially serves as a conduit for numerous instances of reverse causation. Informal interactions, too, can be of decisive importance in individuals' actions. Urban land use is also affected extensively by the variety in the modes of land tenure, especially in a worldwide context. All these considerations offer a rich potential for future research.

CHAPTER 6

Social Interactions and Human Capital Spillovers

6.1 INTRODUCTION

Locations where the population and the economic activity are most dense are almost always the most productive. Economists explain this as the product of two forces: one, people concentrate in areas where natural amenities and resources lead to high productivity; two, people are more productive in places where they are concentrated in space. A high density of people and firms generates urban production economies that make agglomeration productive. Urban production economies are external effects that benefit producers and workers. They have been described by Marshall (1920) as technological externalities due to knowledge spillovers and to sharing of inputs at the local level. Of course, the concentration of economic activity also has costs, urban production diseconomies such as congestion and pollution, that affect both producers and consumers. Wages, prices, and rents reflect agglomeration effects (Roback 1982). In large, dispersed economies each of the high concentrations of economic activity likely has its own individual character. Some are more friendly to firms, others are nicer places to live, and some are both. Each mix of characteristics appeals to particular types of people and firms (Gabriel and Rosenthal 2004).

Some facets of these phenomena are still not fully understood, theoretically and empirically. Still we do know that relatively weak agglomeration effects can explain many of these spatial differences in productivity. Firms' investments in physical capital and choices of tradable intermediate inputs can amplify increasing returns to density as they dominate the effect of urban production diseconomies. Proximity itself can magnify these positive effects of city size by reducing shipping costs. It is inherently difficult to separate the effects of mere proximity from those of the externality due to city size, especially when economic decisions are reflected in market outcomes. Economic theory predicts and empirical work seeks to confirm that spatial concentration of economic activity actually *causes* higher productivity. Causality is generally quite hard to establish, and this chapter argues that a social interactions perspective can help to integrate many seemingly diverse approaches and findings in this area of economics.

The chapter starts by setting out basic facts about spatial patterns of wages and productivity. It begins by considering larger aggregate spatial units (states, regions, and counties) and then looks at smaller places (cities and their neighborhoods). Where do these patterns in space come from? The chapter explores approaches that rely, directly or indirectly, on social interactions approaches. These models help elucidate key problems of econometric identification of those social interactions in human capital spillovers. It links the models' empirical findings, based on the more microeconomic treatment of the previous chapters, with the aggregative city-level models that follow next in chapters 7–9.

6.1.1 Productivity Differences across States

The 2008 per capita personal income in the poorest U.S. state, Mississippi, was $30,383, and in the richest one, Connecticut, it was $56,245, with that for the entire United States being $40,166. In the same year, Mississippi had the lowest and New Hampshire the highest real gross state product (GSP) per capita, $24,403 and $56,401, respectively, while the figure for the entire United States was $37,853.[1] Bhatta and Lobo (2000) use the decomposition of factor incomes to analyze whether human capital differences explain differences in gross state product per capita levels between the richer and poorer U.S. states. They use the 1990 census and Bureau of Economic Analysis data on educational attainment, wage levels of different segments of the labor force, and compare GSP in New York, a representative rich state, with the poorest third of the states. They find that human capital differences explain at least 49 percent of the observed difference in GSP per capita between New York and the poorest third of the states.

Gross domestic product (GDP) per capita by metropolitan area is the most comprehensive measure of urban income; it has been publicly available since September 2007, when it was first provided by the Bureau of Economic Analysis of the U.S. Department of Commerce. GDP data have been available annually since 2001 in chain-indexed dollars for 363 metropolitan statistical areas, as defined by the U.S. Office of Management and Budget.[2] In 2008 the San Jose–Sunnyvale–Santa Clara (California) MSA had the highest per capita real GDP ($82,880), which was almost twice the U.S. metropolitan area average. Palm Coast, Florida had the lowest ($11,611), 72.2 percent below the U.S. metropolitan area average. (GDP and personal income per capita do not coincide.) In 2008 the Bridgeport–Stamford–Norwalk (Connecticut) MSA had the highest personal income per capita, which at $82,266 was about twice as much as the average for U.S. MSAs ($41,455). The McAllen–Edinburg–Mission (Texas) MSA had the lowest personal income per capita at $19,377.

Acemoglu and Angrist (2001) examine whether differences in educational attainments cause differences in wages across U.S. states, under the assumption that individuals do move in pursuit of opportunities. They control for the direct effect of schooling on individual wages via human capital externalities, using variation across states and over time in average secondary schooling caused by child labor laws and compulsory attendance laws, as instruments to investigate whether this relationship is causal. Using decennial census data from 1950 to 1980 at the U.S. state level, they show external returns to education about 1 percent and not significantly different from zero. Regressions using data from the 1990 census, in contrast, generate statistically significant estimates of external returns of 4 percent or more with one set of instruments. These findings may reflect the increased importance of human capital after 1980, but a full investigation suggests that the larger estimates obtained using the 1990 data are likely due to changes in the secondary schooling variable in the 1990 census. Moreover, they do not examine higher education, another variable that may have substantial external effects. Acemoglu and Angrist's findings challenge the voluminous research that either posits such effects or provides econometric evidence. Still, with the evidence on agglomeration effects being widely accepted (see section 6.9 below), the explanation may be that human capital externalities involve interactions among very skilled workers, those effects are hard to detect at the state level, and mandatory schooling laws do not really matter for such workers.

Using data for Europe and in geographic detail for France, Germany, Italy, Spain, and the United Kingdom that is finer than that available for the United States, Ciccone (2002) examines spatial differences in average labor productivity within those European countries. Average labor productivity in the manufacturing and service sectors was 140 percent higher in the five most productive German *Kreise* (roughly corresponding to U.S. counties) in 1986 than in the five least productive *Kreise*. Ciccone finds an average degree of increasing returns to the local density of economic activity between 4 percent and 5 percent. These are only slightly below estimates for the United States (Ciccone and Hall 1996). Rice, Venables, and Patacchini (2006) obtain a similar result using geographically detailed earnings data for the United Kingdom defined at the NUTS3 level.[3] Doubling of the population of working age proximate to an area is associated with a 3.5 percent increase in productivity. Their estimates take into account the scale of production in neighboring areas, weighted by travel times, and find that productivity benefits diminish quickly with travel time.

6.1.2 Productivity Differences across Regions

There are very large spatial differences in wages across U.S. counties. Average wages in the private sector, excluding agriculture and mining, in the top 50 U.S. counties in 1990 were more than three times the average wages in the bottom 50 counties. Average wages in the top 300 U.S. counties (out of 3,140) were more than twice the average wages in the bottom 300 counties. Such wide spatial differences in wages in a country characterized by few institutional impediments to geographic mobility cry out for an explanation. Why is it that in a country where individuals and capital are free to move in pursuit of better opportunities income differences are not eliminated?

6.2 SPATIAL EQUILIBRIUM

Spatial equilibrium is a powerful framework in the toolkit of urban economics, as Glaeser and Gottlieb (2009) eloquently emphasize, and constitutes the single most important difference between urban and regional economics, on the one hand, and international economics, on the other. In free market economies where cities are open economic entities, productive factors like capital and labor are free to move across space in pursuit of opportunities. As a result, in an economy without friction, differences in nominal returns to capital are eliminated across space. Individuals seeking the highest utility from living and working in different areas move between areas, and in spatial equilibrium, utility is equalized across all areas for individuals of each type. This has consequences for the returns to labor. Total factor productivity (TFP) itself may also diffuse through space. Spatial equilibrium provides a convenient way to organize such facts and develop testable hypotheses.

More formally, let ℓ denote a location at any level of spatial disaggregation. The output in unit ℓ, Y_ℓ, can be expressed as $Y_\ell = \Xi_\ell F(K_\ell, N_\ell)$, where K_ℓ is capital, N_ℓ is raw labor, and Ξ_ℓ is total factor productivity. If $F(K_\ell, N_\ell)$ is homogeneous of degree 1, per capita output as a function of the capital-labor ratio k_ℓ, can be written as $y_\ell = \Xi_\ell f(k_\ell)$. Equalization of returns to capital $\Xi_\ell f'(k_\ell)$ across all locations ℓ does not necessarily equalize the capital-labor ratios. Similarly, even if capital-labor ratios are equalized across states, spatial differences in wages, prevailing in competitive labor markets,

$$W_\ell = \Xi_\ell f(k_\ell) - \Xi_\ell k_\ell f'(k_\ell), \tag{6.1}$$

may reflect spatial differences in TFP.

Equalization of utility across all areas implies that when amenities in a particular city attract migrants, they then bid up the price of housing there. Let wages be the only source of income. Individuals supply one unit of labor each. With a simple Cobb–Douglas indirect utility function, $U_\ell = a^a(1 - a)^{1-a} W_\ell R_\ell^{-1+a}$, $0 < a < 1$, equalization of utility across cities, ℓ, ℓ', implies that wages W_ℓ and housing prices R_ℓ covary positively as follows:

$$\ln W_\ell - (1-a) \ln R_\ell = \ln W_{\ell'} - (1-a) \ln R_{\ell'}. \tag{6.2}$$

This is another way of saying that as real income (utility) is equalized, the benefits of agglomeration, as expressed by the wage rate, are reflected in the price of housing, which rations access to space. Glaeser and Gottlieb (2009) explore the power of spatial equilibrium. Population growth, availability of urban sites and their amenities, and housing supply considerations together with specification of the production structure and intercity trade can lead to a simple but remarkably powerful theory of the *wealth* of cities. I discuss their results in more detail in section 6.4 below.

It is important to bear in mind this crucial implication as I discuss the urban wage premium immediately below. I adopt the spatial equilibrium hypothesis in chapters 7–9 below. In chapters 7 and 9, equalization of utility across the urban system coexists with specialization and intercity trade. In chapter 8, spatial equilibrium drives evolution of the city size distribution.

6.2.1 The Urban Wage Premium

How do urban wages relate to populations in metropolitan areas? One way to quantify it is by the *urban wage premium*, the well-known stylized fact that people in urban areas earn more those in rural areas (Glaeser and Maré 2001, 317). A regression of the average wage against the log of the population, N_ℓ, in the respective *standard metropolitan statistical area*[4] for 1990 gives

$$W_\ell = 4{,}332 + 2{,}732 \cdot \ln N_\ell, \quad R^2 = 0.579,$$

where ℓ indexes SMSAs and the standard error of the estimated coefficient of log population is 340. The effect of city size is substantial (and is estimated with high precision): a 10 percent increase in metropolitan area size is associated with a wage that is higher by \$273 per year. An alternative specification, namely, regressing log wage against log population, gives the urban wage premium as an elasticity. Glaeser and Gottlieb (2009) report estimates ranging from 0.04 to 0.08, depending upon the instruments used, that vary from lagged populations to geologic and climatic variables. See section 6.4 below for a further discussion of their results.

Referring to (6.2), spatial equilibrium predicts that people will move to urban areas that offer higher wages if there is free mobility[5] and that this will bid up the cost of living at their destinations. The data agree. A regression of real wages, nominal wages divided by the American Chamber of Commerce Research Association (ACCRA) cost-of-living index (http://www.coli.org/) (Glaeser and Maré 2001, 320)[6] gives

$$\text{real wage}_\ell = 21{,}828 + 213 \cdot \ln N_\ell, \quad R^2 = 0.006,$$

where the standard error of the coefficient of $\ln N_\ell$ is 455. Thus, the estimate is no longer statistically significant in explaining real wages. With these data, correcting for local prices completely eliminates the city size effect on nominal wages.

A regression of the logarithm of median household incomes against median home prices, along the lines of (6.2), across U.S. metropolitan areas for 2000 is reported by Glaeser and Gottlieb (2009) and is consistent with the spatial equilibrium hypothesis:

$$\ln(\text{income}_\ell) = 5.97 + 0.34 \cdot \ln R_\ell.$$

The estimate of $1 - a = 0.34$, with a standard error of 0.02, is close to the stylized fact of the average share of expenditure on housing (Glaeser and Gottlieb 2009, 992). One has to be careful, as Glaeser and Gottlieb emphasize, when interpreting the significance of the effect of city size on wages or on individual incomes. The fact that at a spatial equilibrium housing prices reflect household incomes should not be interpreted as evidence against urban agglomeration effects. Cities with higher concentrations of skilled workers pay higher nominal wages, something I take up in further detail in section 6.4 below.

6.2.2 A Typology for Spatial Determinants of Individual Outcomes

The previous sections document key properties of per capita outcomes across different levels of spatial aggregation. The next step is a spatial decomposition for individual outcomes. Let $y_{i\nu\ell}$ denote an outcome for individual i, say human capital investment, in neighborhood (location) ν in city ℓ. Location ℓ is defined as the immediate neighborhood of i's residence ν in ℓ or the geographic area that contains it. Data unavailability may require using higher-level proxies for neighborhoods, such as counties, cities, regions, or states. I define individual i's income as the product of skill, or human capital, $h_{i\nu\ell}$, the wage per unit of human capital, $w_{\nu\ell}$, and a return to ability, $\eta_{i\nu\ell}$, which I treat as a random factor:

$$y_{i\nu\ell} = h_{i\nu\ell}\, w_{\nu\ell}\, \eta_{i\nu\ell}. \tag{6.3}$$

All three components may exhibit spatial and/or social dependence, which I specify in detail when appropriate. We first encountered the analytics of interdependence among individuals' outcomes due to spatial and/or social interactions (chapter 2, sections 2.6.1, 2.7, and 2.8). Human capital $h_{i\nu\ell}$ spatial interdependence, for example, may originate in spillovers at the level of microneighborhoods (section 6.5.1), or in self-selection and sorting at the neighborhood or city level (section 6.4), or in its acquisition via capital accumulation, which requires dynamic models (sections 6.5.2 and 6.5.3). Spatial interactions in wage rates, $w_{\nu\ell}$, may be due to spatial interactions in total factor productivity (section 6.3).

6.3 SPATIAL INTERACTIONS AND SPATIAL ECONOMIC ACTIVITY

A simple way to describe the spatial interdependence of economic activity is by means of a production function for output, in which total factor productivity reflects spatial interdependence. I start with equation (6.1) but assume that a typical firm produces with labor, human capital, physical capital, and land. The production function of a firm is specified in reference to space, indexed by location ℓ, as a Cobb–Douglas production function which is homogeneous of degree 1 in all inputs:

$$Y_\ell = \Xi_\ell \left[(H_\ell N_\ell)^\alpha (K_\ell)^\beta (M_\ell)^{1-\alpha-\beta} \right]^{1-\gamma} A_\ell^\gamma, \ 0 \le \alpha,\ \beta, \gamma \le 1,\ \alpha + \beta < 1, \tag{6.4}$$

where H_ℓ is employment-weighted average human capital, N_ℓ is employment, $H_\ell N_\ell$ denotes human capital-augmented labor input, K_ℓ is physical capital, M_ℓ is intermediate inputs, and A_ℓ is total land, all at location ℓ. The parameter γ expresses possible decreasing returns to scale for labor, capital, and intermediate inputs when holding constant the amount of land used in production. Expressing the output per unit of land, $y_\ell = Y_\ell / A_\ell$, we have

$$y_\ell = \Xi_\ell \left[(H_\ell n_\ell)^\alpha (k_\ell)^\beta (m_\ell)^{1-\alpha-\beta} \right]^{1-\gamma}, \tag{6.5}$$

where n_ℓ, k_ℓ, m_ℓ are employment, capital, and intermediate input densities per unit of land.

With free movement of physical capital and free trade in intermediate inputs across all locations in a country, and with the traded good as numeraire, firms equalize the marginal product of capital across all locations with the same rental cost of capital R. This yields capital per unit of land, $k_\ell = \beta(1-\gamma)\frac{y_\ell}{R}$, and intermediate input per unit of land, $m_\ell = (1-\alpha-\beta)(1-\gamma)\frac{y_\ell}{R_M}$, where R_M is the price of intermediate inputs. Substituting back into (6.5) yields output density in terms of $H_\ell n_\ell$, human capital–augmented labor input per unit of land at ℓ.

I examine two cases. One, following Ciccone (2008b), one can ignore the intermediate inputs in order to emphasize the specification of spatial linkages in total factor productivity Ξ_ℓ (section 6.3.1). Alternatively, I can specify the total factor productivity in terms of total output at location ℓ; see section 6.3.2. In the first case, I have that

$$y_\ell = (\Xi_\ell)^{\frac{1}{1-(1-\alpha)(1-\gamma)}} \left[H_\ell n_\ell \right]^{\frac{\alpha(1-\gamma)}{1-(1-\alpha)(1-\gamma)}}, \quad 0 \le \alpha,\ \beta, \gamma \le 1,\ \alpha + \beta < 1, \tag{6.6}$$

and the associated wage rate is given by $W_\ell = \frac{\alpha(1-\gamma)}{1-(1-\alpha)(1-\gamma)} \frac{y_\ell}{n_\ell}$. Expressed in terms of logarithms, this becomes

$$\ln w_\ell = \bar{g} + \frac{1}{1-(1-\alpha)(1-\gamma)} \left[g_\ell + \ln H_\ell - \tilde{n}_\ell \right],$$

where $w_\ell \equiv \ln W_\ell,\ g_\ell \equiv \ln \Xi_\ell,\ \tilde{n}_\ell \equiv \ln n_\ell$.

6.3.1 Spatial Interactions in Total Factor Productivity

Now assume that TFP at location ℓ is related to (spatially) lagged TFP in neighboring locations and to (time) lagged employment. The structure of the lags is exogenous. Let $\mathbf{\Gamma}$ be a row-normalized adjacency matrix (which reflects spatial interactions; see chapter 2, section 2.8) and let $\mathbf{L}_g$ and $\mathbf{L}_n$ be distributed lag structures for TFP and aggregate employment, respectively. The full specification, in vector notation, is

$$\mathbf{g}_t = \mathbf{f}_t + \mathbf{L}_n\{\tilde{\mathbf{N}}_t\} + \sigma \mathbf{L}_g\{\mathbf{\Gamma} \mathbf{g}_t\} + \mathbf{v}_t, \tag{6.7}$$

where $\mathbf{f}_t$ stands for the vector of contributions to the logarithm of TFP not related to lagged employment and to lagged own and neighbor TFP and

$\mathbf{v}_t$ stands for a vector of shocks denoting the deviations of current and past values of TFP and employment from their trends. Taking the simplest possible lagged structure, solving for the vector of log-TFP from (6.7), and substituting back into the wage equation, now stacked in vector form, yields

$$\mathbf{w}_t + \gamma^* \tilde{\mathbf{n}}_t = \mathbf{c1} + \mathbf{L}_n\{\tilde{\mathbf{N}}_t\} + \mathbf{L}_g\{\ln \mathbf{H}_t\} + \sigma \mathbf{\Gamma} \left[\mathbf{w}_t + \gamma^* \tilde{\mathbf{n}}_t - L_g\{\ln \mathbf{H}_t\}\right] + \mathbf{v}_t, \tag{6.8}$$

where $\gamma^* \equiv \frac{\gamma}{1-(1-\alpha)(1-\gamma)}$. This equation implies the following: at each location, average wages are positively related to aggregate employment if $\mathbf{L}_n > 0$; average wages are positively related to the average level of TFP in neighboring locations provided the parameter capturing the spatial diffusion of TFP is positive, $\sigma > 0$.

The key objective of estimation along the lines of (6.8) is to examine the extent of spatial differences in TFP and whether or not they are driven by spatial externalities that are themselves a function of the scale of aggregate production. The very nature of the phenomenon suggests that it might be affected by reverse causation, as is common in many social interactions settings. That is, suppose that high wages are due to high TFP, which in turn is due to externalities caused by the density of economic activity. Finding a positive correlation between average wages and employment per unit of land across counties is not solid evidence of such externalities. An alternative explanation is that individuals move to, and thus are likely to be found in, locations where TFP is high for reasons other than those controlled for. The standard remedy for identifying the effect of employment density on TFP is via instrumental variables, that is, controls that are correlated with employment density across locations, the explanatory variable of principal interest, but uncorrelated with determinants of TFP not controlled for, which would normally show up in the error.

Ciccone (2008b) works with U.S. county data and employs employment density across U.S. counties in the early nineteenth century as an instrument. Individuals and firms settled across U.S. space at that time for a variety of reasons such as transportation links, agricultural land quality, and natural resources—all different from those determining such decisions now, except perhaps coastal location or climate, which can be accounted for, and certainly on TFP outside of agriculture and mining today. Railways, highways, and airports, along with air-conditioning and heating (and the decline in the relative importance of agriculture and mining) have affected settlement patterns profoundly that now reach regions of the United States that were not developed even up to 50 years ago. Ciccone suggests a proxy for unavailable data on early nineteenth century employment densities, the total land area of each county. This measure is historically predetermined but is very highly and negatively correlated with current employment density.[7]

Ciccone's estimations suggest that the spatial distribution of TFP is driven by the aggregate scale of production and favors spatial technology diffusion. In the simplest case with no effect on a county's TFP from neighbor schooling, a high average level of schooling in neighboring locations has a negative effect on own wages when neighbors wages are held constant. That is, the lower neighbors' schooling, the lower the average TPF level of neighbors when their wages are controlled. Estimates for the full model suggest that a 10 percent increase in the TFP of a county's neighboring counties increases wages in a county by 6 percent. Doubling employment in the county increases wages by 3.6 percent. This model with externalities, which are driven by aggregate employment at the county level and with technology diffusion across neighboring counties, explains half of the large variation in wages across U.S. counties.

6.3.2 Increasing Returns to Density of Economic Activity

A strand of the literature excludes spatial interactions in TFP, by setting $\mathbf{L}_n, \mathbf{L}_g = 0$ in (6.7), and instead specifies TFP as an endogenous social effect. Ciccone and Hall (1996) specify TFP in each firm's production function (6.4) as a shifter in the form of a function of the density of total economic activity at each location: $\Xi_\ell = (\frac{Y_\ell}{A_\ell})^\lambda$. This is endogenous and is determined at the ℓ level. The implications of this assumption for the relationship between value added per firm, as a function of firm-level employment density, and county-level value added readily follow. Under the assumption that one unit of intermediate input is produced with one unit of output and given the optimal quantities of capital and of intermediate inputs as solved for before, equation (6.6) yields an expression for value added per unit of land,

$$y_\ell = (DH_\ell n_\ell)^{\frac{\alpha(1-\gamma)}{1-(1-\gamma)(1-\alpha)}} \left(\frac{Y_\ell}{A_\ell}\right)^{\frac{\lambda}{1-(1-\gamma)(1-\alpha)}}, \tag{6.9}$$

where D is a function of parameters and of the rental rate of capital (and more generally of the price of intermediate inputs as well if they are purchased in the national economy), which is treated as a constant here. Assuming that county employment N_ℓ is uniformly distributed over land within county ℓ yields a reduced form, a relationship between output density and employment density, $n_\ell = \frac{N_\ell}{A_\ell}$:

$$\frac{Y_\ell}{A_\ell} = (Dn_\ell)^{1+\frac{\lambda-\gamma}{\alpha(1-\gamma)-(\lambda-\gamma)}}. \tag{6.10}$$

Output density exhibits increasing returns to employment density. They are stronger the stronger the urban production externalities, λ, and/or the weaker the congestion effects, γ. If net urban production externalities are weak, that is, $\lambda - \gamma$ is small, then the exponent in (6.10) is approximated by $1 + \frac{\lambda-\gamma}{\alpha(1-\gamma)}$. If the share of labor in value added is about two-thirds and the share of intermediates in value added is about one-half, then the share of land in the total value of production is $\alpha(1 - \gamma) \approx 1/3$. A greater share of intermediates thus strengthen urban production externalities.[8]

How may one estimate the strength of urban production externalities?[9] Ciccone and Hall (1996) use gross state product data, the finest level of geographic detail at which value-added data were available at the time of their study. They use state-level data for labor productivity, measured as value added per person, to estimate the urban production externalities parameter θ by means of an expression, obtained by using (6.10), at the county level c and aggregating up to the state level s as follows:

$$\frac{Y_s}{N_s} = \sum_{c \in \text{state s}} \left(D \frac{N_c}{A_c} \right)^{1+\theta} \frac{N_c}{N_s}, \ \theta \equiv \frac{\lambda - \gamma}{\alpha(1-\gamma) - (\lambda - \gamma)}. \tag{6.11}$$

Ciccone and Hall work with data for 1988 and a production function like (6.11), which also includes average years of education, H_{ct} [Ciccone and Hall 1996, eq. (29)]. County-level employment densities, $\frac{N_c}{A_c}$, and the distribution of employment across counties within each state, $\frac{N_c}{N_s}$, are observable. Their estimate of θ ranges between 0.05 and 0.06. With the same parameter values as above, their estimate implies a net agglomeration effect, $\lambda - \gamma = 0.017$. Assuming a share of land in the total value of the production of $\gamma \approx 0.05$, this result implies that net agglomeration effects are magnified because of the use of mobile capital and traded intermediate inputs to yield a net elasticity of increasing returns that is twice as large. The education elasticity is not significant in their regressions.

It is possible that economic activity may self-select into areas where productivity is high, causing endogeneity bias in the estimation of equation (6.9). Ciccone and Hall argue that this endogeneity does not affect their estimates of production function elasticities because their instruments,[10] which are measures of original forces of agglomeration, have remaining influences on individuals' location decisions but do not influence productivity at present.

The Ciccone–Hall results have been reexamined in more recent studies. Chen, Weisberger, and Wong (2011) extend the Ciccone–Hall analysis and estimate the density-productivity relationship at the industry level across states while allowing for state-specific fixed and time effects. These account both for the possibility that more productive industries locate in denser states and for localization effects that are distinct from urbanization effects. Using state-specific fixed effects helps in controlling for regional amenities that are likely to affect simultaneously labor productivity (and thus wages) and the location decisions of workers (and thus density). The authors also control for regional business cycles by means of instrumenting for regional aggregate demand. This, too, may introduce an identification problem because location decisions respond to cyclical productivity variations and to contemporaneous idiosyncratic productivity shocks over and above agglomeration effects. Conditional on state, time, and business cycles, Chen et al. argue that lagged employment density is exogenous with respect to current labor productivity. They also use state differences in birthrates 20 and 25 years ago to instrument for current density. On the basis of cross sectional data for U.S. states in 1999, they find that estimates are consistent with increasing returns to scale across most one-digit SIC industries. Controlling for state-specific fixed and time effects, they estimate the total elasticity to be 0.99, but when they include cyclical controls, their estimate falls to 0.93. However, when they instrument for density using either lagged density or lagged birthrates, their estimates go up to values significantly greater than 1. So their evidence regarding the presence of net increasing returns to density is quite mixed.

Glaeser and Gottlieb (2009) (see section 6.4.2) criticize the Ciccone–Hall estimations of agglomeration economies for neglecting endogeneity of metropolitan populations due spatial equilibrium. The Ciccone–Hall approach also motivates the more macroeconomic treatment by Davis, Fisher, and Whited (2009), whose study is conceptually quite closely related to that of Rossi-Hansberg and Wright (2007) and thus is discussed in chapter 9, section 9.6.

6.3.2.1 *Agglomeration Economies and Spatial Concentration of U.S. Employment*

Another way to measure the consequences of agglomeration economies is by looking at their impact on the spatial concentration of employment. That is, one can use models of location decisions of individuals and firms in the presence of social interactions to assess how much of the observed concentration of employment is explained by agglomeration economies. Geographic variation in both productivity and other amenities results in an uneven distribution of employment over land, and it is interesting to measure the aggregate impact of agglomeration economies on the distribution of employment.

Chatterjee (2006) approaches this objective in a macroeconomic fashion using a *spatial* growth-accounting methodology.[11] Chatterjee assumes that individuals consume one transportable and one nontransportable good. The transportable good is produced using capital and labor with a Cobb–Douglas production function that reflects multiplicatively the joint effect of an economywide technology index, a locality-specific index, and an agglomeration factor that is an isoelastic function of total employment in each locality. The production of the nontransportable good is affected by a locality-specific factor and by a diseconomy (congestion) index that is exponential in employment density. There are two types of individuals, mobile ones who derive only labor incomes, and immobile ones who derive income from labor and capital. At the spatial equilibrium, mobile individuals' utilities are equalized across all locations. The combination of congestion and agglomeration economies generates an equilibrium utility that depends on density, defined as employment per unit of land. As density rises, utility may initially fall but ultimately rises, thus producing in principle three types of equilibria, two stable and one unstable.

The application with U.S. data is exhaustive of the U.S. territory in the 48 contiguous U.S. states. It includes all 17 consolidated metropolitan statistical areas, 258 metropolitan statistical areas, and 2,248 rural counties. Chatterjee calibrates the model by selecting fairly conventional values for the key parameters, including values for the elasticity of agglomeration with respect to total employment, which he sets in the range [0.1, 0.5]. He computes by how much the *concentration* of employment would decline at a counterfactual in which agglomeration economies have been eliminated. He shows that various reasonable specifications of agglomeration economies explain between 40 percent and 60 percent of the observed spatial concentration of employment in 1990 as measured by the decline of the Gini coefficient. This effect is over and above the concentration of employment that is induced by geographic differences.

6.4 THE URBAN WAGE PREMIUM AND SPATIAL EQUILIBRIUM

Rauch (1993a) examines both wages and rents for evidence of productivity gains from the geographic concentration of human capital. His simple theory predicts that, at spatial equilibrium, the average level of human capital in a city raises both wages and rents. In other words, at spatial equilibrium, wages and rents covary—see (6.2) above. Define individual utility per efficiency unit of labor as

$$V = v(R_\ell; \mathbf{Z}_\ell) W_\ell, \quad \frac{\partial v}{\partial R_\ell} < 0, \tag{6.12}$$

where W_ℓ, R_ℓ denote wage and rental rates, respectively and $\mathbf{Z}_\ell$ is a vector of characteristics of city ℓ. At spatial equilibrium, utility per efficiency unit of labor v is equalized across all cities in an open-city system of cities. If firms produce with production functions that are homogeneous of degree 1, then the unit production cost for the single tradeable good satisfies

$$C(R_\ell; W_\ell; \mathbf{Z}_\ell) = 1, \quad \frac{\partial C}{\partial R_\ell} > 0, \quad \frac{\partial C}{\partial W_\ell} > 0 \tag{6.13}$$

at spatial equilibrium, with the tradeable good being numeraire. Equations (6.12) and (6.13) determine wages and rents at spatial equilibrium given characteristics $\mathbf{Z}_\ell$. Individuals are indifferent among locations: combinations of wages and rents vary in the same direction. Firms must be compensated for higher rents with lower wages. With no spatial sorting of consumers by endowment of efficiency units, city-specific human capital per person, $\bar{h}_\ell$, is not determined by the model and therefore is treated as exogenous. Land A_ℓ in city ℓ is also exogenous.

Given $(\bar{h}_\ell, A_\ell)$, an equilibrium in land and labor determines (Y_ℓ, N_ℓ), urban output, and city size (population) associated with spatial equilibrium. That is, the demand for land by firms and individuals is equal to the supply of land:

$$Y_\ell \frac{\partial C}{\partial R_\ell} - N_\ell \bar{h}_\ell \frac{\frac{\partial v}{\partial R_\ell}}{\frac{\partial v}{\partial W_\ell}} = A_\ell;$$

the demand for human capital is equal to the supply of human capital, $N_\ell \bar{h}_\ell$:

$$Y_\ell \frac{\partial C}{\partial W_\ell} = N_\ell \bar{h}_\ell.$$

At spatial equilibrium, wages and rents reflect individual and city characteristics and therefore resemble the type of hedonic regressions that I discuss in chapters 3 and 4.

Properties of preferences and technology allow Rauch to structure the empirical analysis. If $\bar{h}_\ell$ has no amenity value for consumers but increases productivity, then a city with a higher value of $\bar{h}_\ell$ will be characterized by higher wages per efficiency unit of labor and higher rent per unit of land. The generic specification Rauch estimates for log wages, $\ln W_{i\ell}$ (and respectively, for log rents, $\ln R_{i\ell}$) of individual i in city ℓ is

$$\ln W_{i\ell} = \beta_\ell \mathbf{X}_i + \pi_h \bar{h}_\ell + \pi_e \bar{e}_\ell + \alpha_\ell \mathbf{Z}_\ell + d_\ell + d_t + u_{i\ell}, \qquad (6.14)$$

where $\mathbf{X}_i$, $\mathbf{Z}_\ell$ are vectors of characteristics of individual i and city ℓ, respectively, $u_{i\ell}$ is a random shock, and d_ℓ may be specified as $d_\ell = \bar{d} + \gamma \mathbf{Z}_\ell + \mu_\ell$, where μ_ℓ denotes a city-specific fixed effect. Notable among the individual characteristics are demographic and labor market characteristics of city residents. City-specific average years of schooling and experience $(\bar{h}_\ell, \bar{e}_\ell)$ are contextual effects.

Rauch (1993a) reports empirical results with data on 69,910 individuals and their dwellings from the 1-in-1000 Public Use Microdata Samples B (see chapter 2, section 2.13.2) of the 1980 U.S. census, which come from 237 SMSAs, and on the characteristics of the SMSAs in which the individuals live. The dependent variable in the wage regressions is the log average hourly earnings. The explanatory variables are individual schooling and labor market experience; controls for demographic characteristics such as individual gender, race, marital status, and occupational characteristics; SMSA-level averages for educational attainment and for labor-market experience; and SMSA attributes such as location, climate, and population. In the rent equations, the dependent variable is the log of monthly housing expenditures including utilities for renters and a monthly imputed rent using a discount rate of 7.85 percent for owners. The explanatory variables are size, structural characteristics of the dwelling and its lot, and mode of tenure. Rauch's estimates of the contextual effect of average human capital range from 2.8 percent to 5.1 percent for wages, and 12.8 percent to 19.9 percent for rents, and typically are highly significant.

More-productive individuals may be attracted to a city where their skills are better rewarded. The higher rewards may reflect firms' decisions based on factors that are unobservable to the analyst. In fact, over the past 30 years, the share of adult populations with college degrees rose faster in U.S. cities with higher initial schooling levels than it did in those with lower ones (Berry and Glaeser 2005). Rauch acknowledges that SMSA average human capital $\bar{h}$ may not be exogenous: controlling for the presence of universities and reasearch and development spending is not statistically significant. The estimated coefficient for culture per capita[12] is negative and significant in the wage equation and insignificant in the rent equation This result suggests that culture is an amenity that raises utility directly and that individuals trade more culture for higher wages. A milder climate reduces production costs and therefore improves productivity and makes the location more attractive. Mild climates have a positive and significant effect on rents but no effect on wages, implying that the positive productivity effect is offset by a negative amenity effect. A coastal location has a positive and significant effect in both equations, suggesting that the productivity effect dominates any amenity effects.

How then can one identify a causal effect for SMSA size while recognizing that it is endogenous? Rauch instruments city population by means of the SMSA land area A_ℓ. He argues that land area is correlated with population but does not directly affect either productivity or preferences. A first-stage regression of population against all available SMSA-level variables and land produces a significant coefficient for land and a partial correlation coefficient of 0.34, suggesting that it could serve as an instrument for size. Still, land does not perform well in second-stage regressions.

6.4.1 Self-Selection into Cities

Do individuals who self-select to move to and live in a city have above-average unobserved ability relative to the population? We can use the Roy model to analyze this question (Roy 1951). Let *unobserved* quality (ability) ψ_i for individual i take the place of human capital in determining individual income. Unobserved ability earns a return η_ℓ in city ℓ. Returning to (6.3) and ignoring variations in the wage rate, we consider two alternative cities, ℓ and ℓ', where individual i would earn incomes $y_{i\ell} = \psi_{i\ell}\eta_\ell$ and $y_{i\ell'} = \psi_{i\ell'}\eta_{\ell'}$, respectively. Under the assumption that $(\ln \psi_{\ell i}, \ln \psi_{\ell' i})$ are jointly normally distributed with means $(\mu_\ell, \mu_{\ell'})$, variances $(\sigma_\ell^2, \sigma_{\ell'}^2)$, and covariance $\sigma_{\ell\ell'}$, the mean $\psi_{i\ell}$ among those who choose ℓ over ℓ' is given by the conditional mean of $\psi_{i\ell}$:

$$\mathcal{E}(\psi_{i\ell}|i \text{ chooses } \ell) = \mu_\ell + \frac{\sigma_\ell^2 - \sigma_{\ell\ell'}}{\sigma_\psi}\text{IMR}\left(\frac{\mu_\ell - \mu_{\ell'} + \ln \eta_\ell - \ln \eta_{\ell'}}{\sigma_\psi}\right), \tag{6.15}$$

where $\sigma_\psi^2 = (\sigma_\ell^2 - \sigma_{\ell\ell'}) + (\sigma_{\ell'}^2 - \sigma_{\ell\ell'})$ denotes the variance of $\ln \psi_{\ell i} - \ln \psi_{\ell' i}$, and $\text{IMR}(\frac{\mu_\ell - \mu_{\ell'} + \ln \eta_\ell - \ln \eta_{\ell'}}{\sigma_\psi})$ the inverse Mills' ratio, IMR > 0.[13] The counterpart of this equation for city ℓ' follows by symmetry. There will be positive selection (those who choose city ℓ have a higher mean ability than average), if and only if the sign of $\sigma_\ell^2 - \sigma_{\ell\ell'}$, the coefficient of $\text{IMR}(\cdot)$ on the right-hand side of (6.15) above, is positive. Since σ_ψ^2 is positive, at least either $\sigma_\ell^2 - \sigma_{\ell\ell'}$ or $\sigma_{\ell'}^2 - \sigma_{\ell\ell'}$, or both, are positive. Therefore, there is positive selection for one or both cities. Individuals having high earnings in one city are likely to be unusually skilled and would also rank high in terms of earnings in other cities.

Suppose, for instance, that remuneration of unobserved ability is higher in SMSAs with higher average education. It is then possible that a positive coefficient for SMSA average education in the wage regression suggests positive selection rather than a causal effect of average education on individual productivity. In Rauch's basic model, SMSA average education is a site characteristic that increases firm productivity but has no amenity value. Therefore, it should raise rents as much as productivity in order to offset an increase in the cost of living and keep individuals indifferent across locations. If a selection bias is present, then the Roy model implies no such specific relationship between education and rents. Rauch uses his estimates to claim that such a finding is consistent with movement along an indifference curve and not with positive selection.

Rauch tests another implication of positive selection using an argument due to Borjas, Bronars, and Trejo (1992). Less skilled individuals may choose cities with less income inequality, so that sorting accentuates earnings inequality across regions. In other words, the selection model implies a positive association between SMSA average education and returns to ability. In that case, SMSA average education should be positively correlated with inequality in wages. Rauch computes three different measures of wage inequality: the standard deviation of "raw" log wages, the standard deviation of the residual from SMSA-specific wage regressions, and the wage regressions with only individual information (all of which are strongly correlated with one another). He finds no support for this implication of positive selection.

6.4.2 Wage Premium and Selection into Cities

Studying selection into cities by means of the Roy model, however elegant, gives only a partial view of the wage premium as compared to the full power of spatial equilibrium. Glaeser and Gottlieb (2009) develop a spatial equilibrium model in a dynamic setting that allows them to solve for city populations, wages, and housing prices [Glaeser and Gottlieb 2009, eqs. (1)–(3)] as well as for their growth rates [Glaeser and Gottlieb 2009, eqs. (1′)–(3′)]. They assume that TFP in a city's traded good sector is an isoelastic function of city population and that housing can proxy for all nontradeable goods. Their estimations control for individual characteristics, including education and age from the Census Public Use Microdata Sample (Glaeser and Gottlieb 2009, data appendix), and geographic characteristics proxying for city-level amenities (chiefly mean January temperature and precipitation, longitude, and latitude). As reported by Glaeser and Gottlieb (2009, 1003, table 4), the elasticity of the wage rate with respect to population is 0.04 [0.01], with OLS, 0.08 [0.03] when using an 1880 population to instrument for the current population (in the style of Ciccone and Hall), and 0.04 [0.02] when instrumenting for geography (standard errors are in brackets). The corresponding estimates for the house price elasticities are 0.16 [0.03], 0.06 [0.06], and 0.39 [0.09]. Finally, those for the elasticity of the real wage are not significant except when geographic instruments are used, −0.09 [0.03], suggesting that amenities are sufficiently higher in larger cities to overcome the urban wage premium. These results are generally in agreement with Ciccone and Hall. Glaeser and Gottlieb's results are particularly noteworthy, however cautious these authors are in interpreting them, because they are obtained by accounting fully for spatial equilibrium in a system-of-cities model.

6.4.2.1 *Recent Findings with U.S. Panel Data*

Glaeser and Maré (2001) show that age-earnings profiles are steeper in cities. They interpret their evidence (from both the PSID and the NLSY) as suggesting that cities accelerate the accumulation of human capital. They argue that this finding combines wage level and wage growth effects and is not simply the result of omitted ability factors. They rely on four empirical premises: one, urban residents are not much better endowed than nonurban ones with observable human capital characteristics; two, the degree of urbanization of parents' birth states also predicts higher wages; three, cross-metropolitan area variation in real wages is not strongly linked to city size; and four, migrants who come to cities experience wage gains that stay with them even after they leave the cities. These findings are strengthened by the work of Baum-Snow and Pavan (2011), who also use NLSY data and find different effects according to skill categories. That is, higher starting earnings are more important contributions to the urban wage premium for individuals with a high school education (especially in medium-size cities), while higher returns to experience in cities are more important for college graduates. However, they find that neither sorting on unobserved ability within educational categories and differences in labor market nor search frictions contribute to the observed city size wage premium.

Gould (2007) also finds that the urban wage premium differs by skill categories. He uses NLSY data to estimate a structural dynamic programming model of individuals' decisions to live in a city or in a rural area with career choice as a joint decision. This study provides the first estimates of the urban wage premium while controlling for unobserved heterogeneity and for the endogeneity of location and career decisions over time. After controlling for all sources of selection and endogeneity, Gould finds that the observed 10.8 percent wage gap between 30-year-old blue-collar workers in cities versus rural areas, by applying the model, reduces to 1.2 percent and thus is virtually fully explained. For white-collar workers, however, self-selection and endogeneity explain only one-third of the observed 17.5 percent urban wage gap, leaving 11.5 percent unexplained. His estimates also show that 5 years of city work experience increase the wage of a white-collar worker in a rural area by 8.5 percent compared to that of a similar worker without any work experience in a city. These results support the interpretation that cities make white-collar workers more productive *permanently* and imply that their moving to a city is a form of human capital investment.

Moretti (2004b) works with richer data and an equation for the wage rate of individual i in city ℓ at time t that is very similar to equation (6.14) but adapted in view of the availability of several cross sections. It is not structural, strictly speaking, but differs in terms of the error structure, where d_ℓ is the city ℓ fixed effect, d_t is the time effect, and the stochastic shock $u_{i\ell t}$ is defined as

$$u_{i\ell t} = \eta_\ell \psi_i + \nu_{\ell t} + \epsilon_{i\ell t},$$

where ψ_i is an individual-specific unobservable component of human capital, such as ability or family background, η_ℓ represents the return to ψ_i; $\nu_{\ell t}$ represents time-varying shocks to labor demand and supply in city ℓ in period and t; and $\epsilon_{i\ell t}$ is the transitory component of log wages, which is assumed to be independently and identically distributed over individuals, cities, and time.

What are the pitfalls that might affect such an estimation? The wage rate in a competitive environment reflects the marginal productivity of each type of labor, which depends on all factor inputs and on the total factor productivity of the respective establishment. Total factor productivity may itself depend on the fraction of skilled workers in city ℓ as well as on industry, city, and time characteristics. Unobservable productivity shocks correlated with the share of skilled workers would result in an overestimate of the coefficients of the spillover effects, π_h, π_e in equation (6.14).

Moretti (2004b) estimates spillovers from the college education of city residents by comparing wages for otherwise similar individuals who work in cities with different shares of college graduates in the labor force. A key issue in this comparison is the presence of unobservable characteristics of individuals and cities that may raise wages and be correlated with the share of college-educated workers. Because Moretti uses longitudinal data from the NLSY to estimate a model of nonrandom selection of workers across cities, he can allow for individual and city fixed effects. He concludes that omitted individual characteristics are not a major source of bias.

Moretti also uses census data to investigate the possibility that citywide labor demand shocks can both increase wages in a city and attract skilled workers. He estimates such shocks with an index of demand shifts while using the (lagged) city demographic structure and the presence of a land grant college as instruments. The external return estimated by using census data is remarkably similar to the external return estimated using NLSY data, with the most robust estimates of the external effect being between 0.6 percent and 1.2 percent. He finds that a 1 percent increase in the supply of college graduates raises the wages of high school dropouts by 1.9 percent, those of high school graduates by 1.6 percent, and those of college graduates by 0.4 percent. The effect is larger for less educated groups, as predicted by a conventional demand and supply model.

6.4.3 Individual Productivity and City Aggregates: The View from Data on Firms

Another approach to the identification of human capital externalities is to use data on firms. The composition of the labor force in each city and firms' productivities are determined simultaneously. More-productive firms may also be drawn to cities with a better skilled labor force. At spatial equilibrium, if firms are more productive in cities with high levels of human capital, then we expect to find that firms in those cities face higher labor and land costs.

Moretti (2004a) uses longitudinal establishment-level data from the U.S. Census of Manufacturers in 1982 and 1992 combined with individual data from the 1980 and 1990 U.S. censuses (which distinguish a three-digit industry classification) of employment and city of residence. He estimates establishment-level production functions controlling for establishment-specific permanent heterogeneity as well as time-varying industry-specific and state-specific heterogeneity. Moretti finds productivity gains from human capital spillovers: 1 percent increase in the percentage of college-educated workers raises plant productivity 0.6 percent to 0.7 percent, with higher returns for high-tech industries. The magnitude of spillovers between plants in the same city appears to depend on their "perceived economic distance" measured in terms of input-output flows, technological specialization, and patent citations. Spillovers between plants that often interact are significant, while spillovers between plants that rarely interact are much smaller. Moretti (2004a) also finds that U.S. cities where the number of college graduates as a share of the labor force increased most between 1980 and 1990 also experienced the largest wage increase for college graduates, which is consistent with human capital externalities. It is also consistent with skill-biased technological progress, particularly for high-tech industries.

6.4.3.1 *Findings with French Data*

Pierre-Philippe Combes and Gilles Duranton, working with several co-authors, explore a number of hitherto unused rich French data sets that allow them to track individuals *and* firms over time. They seek to explain wage disparities across cities in terms of spatial differences in the skill composition of the labor force, in nonhuman endowments, and in local interactions. The panel data on workers allow them to control for worker characteristics, worker fixed effects, industry fixed effects, and characteristics of local labor markets. A three-way variation in terms of individuals, firms, and time allows them to separate the effects of individual characteristics from those of places, natural endowments, and interactions-based variables.

Their studies share a common theoretical foundation. For instance, in the simplest possible setting, Combes, Duranton, and Gobillon (2008) report that the output of a representative competitive firm in area ℓ in industry j at time t is produced according to a Cobb–Douglas production function with labor and nonlabor inputs, with a total factor productivity parameter $\Xi_{\ell jt}$, and with workers differing in terms of efficiency units of labor of different types. Estimated location and time-specific effects are used as dependent variables in second-stage regressions to estimate year effects, area-specific interactions between industries, and endowment effects. Remaining residuals are characterized as local technology shocks.

Combes, Duranton, and Gobillon attribute high urban wages first to concentrations of highly skilled workers in dense local labor markets and second to local amenities. They find that individual skills account for a large fraction of existing spatial wage disparities, with strong evidence of spatial sorting by skills. Ignoring worker heterogeneity biases estimates of agglomeration economies by up to 100 percent. They also find evidence of reverse causality between agglomeration and high wages. Finally, endowments appear to play only a small role.

Combes, Duranton, Gobillon, and Roux (2010) revisit the estimation of urbanization economies using French TFP data in addition to wage data. They seek to disentangle the endogeneity of employment density by working with a new set of geologic instruments in addition to more standard historical instruments. That is, just as in the findings of Rosenthal and Strange (2008b), discussed in chapter 5, section 5.5.1, geology affects population distribution directly but also may have done so in the past. Unlike in the past, however, when the quality of soil was a factor of population concentrations through its effect on local productivity, it is no longer as important. Thus, geologic data, which are exogenous, are a possible instrument for population concentrations. In addition, past population concentrations, which are correlated with contemporaneous ones, are the outcomes of historical accidents and other factors. The availability of two such sources of instruments, geologic and historical variables, allow these researchers a variety of econometric possibilities, including overidentification tests to assess instrument orthogonality.

Using ordinary least squares (OLS), these authors find that the elasticity of mean wages and of TFP with respect to employment density in French employment areas is close to 5 percent. Instrumenting contemporaneous employment density by means of historical variables and alternatively by geologic variables reduces the estimate by up to one-fifth, so the endogeneity of employment density is only a minor issue. They find that the bias due to the endogeneity of skilled workers is larger than that of employment density. Controlling for two major sources of bias in local wage and productivity regressions still delivers evidence of significant but small agglomeration effects. Their results imply that the sorting of skilled workers across places is quantitatively more important than mere agglomeration in highly productive locations.

6.4.4 Do People in Cities Work Harder?

Rosenthal and Strange (2008a) establish that some people in cities do work harder, but why? Although these authors do not cast their study in terms of social interactions terminology, their findings can be interpreted through the lens of social interactions. Using the 1990 5 percent integrated public use microdata series (http://www.ipums.org) of the U.S. decennial census, they show that nonprofessional workers work fewer individual hours when agglomeration is higher, as measured by log population density within the part of the metropolitan area surrounding the respondent's residence (PUMA). But for professional workers agglomeration is associated with greater hours worked. Adding a measure of occupational localization, defined as the number of male and female full-time workers aged 30–65 in the same occupation per unit area of the work PUMA[14] strengthens these results. Controlling for occupational localization associates hours worked with significant, negative effects for nonprofessional workers, and very significant, positive, strong, effects for young professional workers. These effects dominate the urbanization effect, which now becomes negative. Using differencing methods, these authors find evidence consistent with the presence of both selection and productivity effects and also of an "urban rat race" effect.[15] That is, agglomeration, by encouraging hard work, magnifies the direct effect of agglomeration on incomes via the urban wage. The article's evidence of an urban rat race, where agglomeration encourages professionals to work harder, is an entirely new, social interactions–type of explanation for why cities are more productive.

Rosenthal and Strange recognize that higher productivity in urban areas, the selection of more productive workers into urban areas, and "rivalry" all imply a positive relationship between hours worked and occupational localization. If workers are motivated by rivalry, they will work longer hours in order to signal ability. This is likely to be stronger in occupations where individual productivity is harder to monitor, as in professional occupations, and weaker in nonprofessional occupations, where individual output is more readily measurable. Rivalry will lead to a stronger agglomeration market size relationship for professional occupations than for nonprofessional occupations. Another difference between the productivity, selection, and rivalry explanations concerns hours worked over an individual's life cycle. If rivalry is important, it should have a weaker effect for older workers, who no longer need to establish their reputations. The productivity and selection explanations predict no such life cycle effect.

These authors proxy the potential for rivalry broadly in terms of the number of other workers in the local labor market who may be close substitutes. They define as close substitutes the number of full-time male and female workers in an individual's age cohort and occupation who live in the same PUMA as the individual and have wages within the same 5-percentile bracket in the national wage distribution, conditional on age cohort and occupation. This variable has a positive, significant, and quantitatively large coefficient for young professionals when it is included in the regression along with the same variables, but a negative and much weaker one for older professionals. In contrast, rivalry among nonprofessionals has a negative effect that does not vary over the life cycle. Rosenthal and Strange find evidence of especially rivalrous behavior among *lawyers*. When they seek to control for a wide range of characteristics, including unobserved attributes that may be accounted for via occupation and metropolitan area interacted fixed effects (which go up to 6,000 in number), the significance of the coefficients for population density and occupational density is substantially reduced. Population density and occupational density do not vary within Work PUMAs for a given occupation, which limits their variation within MSAs. These findings are consistent with the positive selection of hard-working individuals into cities and with the high productivity of urban agglomerations. The behavior of young professionals is also consistent with the presence of keen rivalries in larger markets, a kind of *urban rat race* indeed!

6.5 SOCIAL INTERACTIONS AND HUMAN CAPITAL ACCUMULATION

A contemporary view on the acquisition of human capital is that it is driven by both private and publicly provided inputs. Individuals exercise a direct choice over the former given their resources and may be able to exercise indirect control over the latter. That is, parents may have a direct choice about inputs into the educational process, sending their children to private schools or paying for private tutors, as well as being personally involved in their education. Even households that rely on public education may choose from among the different types of communities in which they can afford to locate. This is especially true in societies where the public provision of education is locally controlled and influenced by the local political process. By locally controlled I mean that a community has at least partial control over its own inputs to educational institutions under its jurisdiction and over how they are financed.

A large class of nonlinear models typically predicts laws of motion for the intergenerational transmission of human capital often associated with multiple equilibria. They account for social interactions as important codeterminants of educational outcomes. Prominent examples include as neighborhood effects family background (Cunha and Heckman 2007; Benabou 1996a, 1996b; Durlauf 1996) and identity effects (Akerlof and Kranton 2002). All these are social effects in the sense that they influence behavior via social interactions within appropriately defined reference groups.

6.5.1 Individual Outcomes and Contemporaneous Human Capital Spillovers in Microneighborhoods

Next I explore the literature on how contemporaneous spatial proximity matters in the acquisition of skills, measured in alternative ways. For example, there is strong evidence that schooling outcomes for adolescents are correlated with those of their residential neighbors. For $h_{i\nu\ell}$ in (6.3), one may write

$$h_{i\nu\ell} = \beta_0 + \beta_\nu h_{i'\nu\ell} + \epsilon_i,$$

where individuals i, i' reside in the same neighborhood ν. Why do we see such a relationship? Is it due to social interactions or selection?

Goux and Maurin (2007), using confidential French data (see chapter 2, section 2.13.7), show that an increase of one standard deviation in the proportion of high school dropouts in the immediate residential neighborhood (a French Labor Force Survey *aire*, comprising about 20 adjacent homes; see chapter 2, section 2.13.7) increases an adolescent's probability of being held back a grade by about 10 percent of a standard deviation. The authors exploit the fact that the date of birth within the year has a significant effect on early educational outcomes. The distribution of close neighbors' months of birth affects educational outcomes but is uncorrelated with the variation not accounted for in individual educational outcomes. Thus, they use it as an instrumental variable to identify the influence of neighbors' (classmates') early outcomes on an adolescent's educational advancement at the end of junior high school. They find that when adolescents living in a neighborhood have already been held back a grade, their close neighbors are also much more likely to repeat a grade at the end of junior high school than when their neighbors have not been held back. They thus establish that an adolescent's educational advancement is negatively influenced by the proportion of noneducated families living in his or her neighborhood.

Solon, Page, and Duncan (2000) and Page and Solon (2003) use the U.S. Panel Study of Income Dynamics data to identify the statistical and causal origin of correlations between brothers' and neighboring boys' adult educational attainments and log earnings, respectively. The correlation is about 0.3 for brothers and about half that for neighbors. Thus, it originates more from growing up in the same *family* than from growing up in the same *neighborhood*. Let $h_{i\nu(i)\ell}$ denote i's educational attainment:

$$h_{i\nu(i)\ell} = \beta_0 + \beta_\nu h_{\nu(i)\ell} + \beta_f h_{f(i)\ell} + \beta_\ell h_\ell + \epsilon_i,$$

where $h_{\nu(i)\ell}$ is a neighborhood effect common among those who grew up in the same neighborhood as i, $\nu(i)$, $h_{f(i)\ell}$ is common to members of the same family, and h_ℓ varies by whether ℓ is urban or rural. Solon, Page, and Duncan argue that much of the neighbor correlation may be explained by the large earnings differentials between urban and nonurban areas and by the fact that where one has spent one's childhood helps predict their adult location. The pattern they find is subject to a variety of interpretations but is quite different from the usual view of neighborhood effects. The portion of earnings inequality linked with where one grew up has more to do with whether one grew up in a city than with which particular neighborhood one grew up in. Which part of town one grew up in seems to play a limited role in accounting for populationwide earnings variation, but it may still matter greatly for children growing up in extreme neighborhood environments or with a special sensitivity to their environments. The Solon–Page–Duncan estimates utilize a little known feature of the PSID. The PSID employs cluster sampling techniques that mean that several observations sampled in the same census tract are physically very close to one another, and such proximity is coded. These sampling clusters make the setting very similar to the French one.[16] In other words, data sampling is organized in terms of neighborhoods, and it is important to be able to account for correlations that are inherent in the sample definition.

An interesting context for these findings is provided by Raaum, Salvanes, and Sørensen (2006), in a study that is similar in spirit to that of Solon, Page, and Duncan, but which relies on a much more detailed data set from Norway. [See chapter 2, section 2.13.7.] They find neighbor correlations in years of schooling for 1946–1955 birth cohorts of 0.112 for boys and 0.103 for girls, and in log earnings of 0.059 and 0.029, respectively. When comparing the 1946–1955 with the 1956–1965 birth cohorts, clearly there is a declining effect of neighborhoods: the correlations are reduced by approximately one-half. In an effort to account for the influence of clustering of similar families in communities, the authors adjust for observed family background. As a result, the correlations drop considerably for education, down to 0.043 and 0.041 for the oldest boys and girls, respectively. For earnings of children born in 1946–1955, the correlations are reduced to 0.047 and 0.021 for boys and girls, respectively. For the younger cohorts, the neighbor correlations are about half those for the older cohorts. These authors find that the impact of families, net of neighborhood effects shared by siblings, is stable across cohorts, with 0.156 and 0.160 for the older and younger cohorts, respectively. The corresponding sister correlations are 0.127 and 0.152, suggesting a convergence between genders. Interestingly, families and neighborhoods have weaker effects on adult outcomes in Norway than in the United States, perhaps because intergenerational mobility is higher in Norway, with its Scandinavian welfare state, than in the United States. Neighborhoods explain a lower fraction of the variation in adult outcomes in the younger cohorts, perhaps because policies may be thought of as promoting equality of opportunity, such as the expansion of local government services in general and education reforms in particular.

Indirect evidence on the effect of close proximity comes from Azoulay, Graff Zivin, and Wang (2008), who estimate the spillovers generated by 137 academic "superstars" in the life sciences for their coauthors' research productivities. These superstar researchers died while still active in research. It is possible to describe such interactions in terms of the tools introduced in chapter 2, section 2.7.2. Research outcomes for research collaborators are interdependent, as described by a system of equations like (2.43). Death provides an exogenous source of variation in the structure of their collaborators' coauthorship networks: it removes a node from the social network exogenously. Comparing outcomes before and after the death of a superstar coauthor allows Azoulay et al. to determine that coauthors suffer a lasting 8 percent to 18 percent decline in their quality-adjusted publication output following the death. Their findings are surprisingly homogeneous across a wide range of coauthor and coauthor-superstar pair characteristics.

6.5.2 Linear Models of Social Interactions and Human Capital Accumulation

The dynamics of the intergenerational transmission of human capital and its accumulation in the presence of social interactions is easiest to motivate in terms of linear models. First I present results obtained by from Kremer (1997), who uses PSID data and highlights the role of neighborhood effects as contextual effects. I then turn to the work of Borjas (1995), who emphasizes human capital within individuals' ethnic groups as a contextual effect.

6.5.2.1 *Kremer's Findings on Neighborhood Effects*

Let $h_{i,t+1}$ denote human capital, measured as educational attainment in years of formal schooling, of a member of the ith dynasty in generation $t + 1$ and let $h_{it}, h_{i't}$ denote human capital at time t of her parents i, i'; $\nu(i)$ denotes the neighborhood where agents i and i' lived at the time of their offspring's upbringing, its size being $|\nu(i)|$.

Kremer (1997) postulates the following law of intergenerational transmission of educational attainment, a dynamic version of (6.2.2) applied to human capital alone:

$$h_{i,t+1} = a_0 + \frac{\alpha}{2}(h_{it} + h_{i't}) + \frac{\beta}{|\nu(i)|} \sum_{j \in \nu(i)} h_{jt} + \epsilon_{i,t+1}, \tag{6.16}$$

where a_0 denotes an exogenous intercept and $\epsilon_{i,t+1}$ a stochastic shock. Kremer uses equation (6.16) to estimate coefficients α and β and to study the intertemporal evolution of the variance in schooling (which may also be interpreted as a measure of inequality of log earnings). This estimation, as well as those by Ioannides, discussed below, are made possible thanks to confidential access to PSID geocodes allowing researchers to link respondents to the census tracts where they reside. See chapter 2, section 2.13.1.

Kremer's estimates of contextual neighborhood effect $\hat{\beta} = 0.149$ [0.072] are large especially when they are compared to the effect of parents' education $\hat{\alpha} = 0.395$ [0.051], with an estimated standard deviation of $\hat{\sigma}_\epsilon = 1.79$ years. Kremer underscores that his estimates imply that *sorting* of individuals into neighborhoods contributes little to the magnitude of the variance in schooling in a steady state. Working from (6.16), this variance is

$$\sigma_\infty^2 = \frac{\sigma_\epsilon^2}{1 - \left[\alpha^2 \frac{1+\rho_m}{2} + (\beta^2 + 2\alpha\beta)\rho_\nu\right]},$$

where ρ_m and ρ_ν denote correlation coefficients between spouses' and neighbors' educations, respectively. Correlation coefficient ρ_ν does magnify σ_∞^2. As Kremer says, "living in an educated neighborhood increases the expected education for one's child by three-quarters [as much] as marrying an educated spouse, since the effect of each parent is half the total parental effect of 0.395." These values imply that the steady-state standard deviation of education will go up by 1.7 percent (Kremer 1997, 125, n. 4) if ρ_ν doubles from 0.2 to 0.4; it will go up by only 0.9 percent (from 1.95 to 1.97 years) if ρ_m to goes up from 0.6 to 0.8.

Of course, the effects of family may not be limited to parents. Loury (2006) shows that additional years of schooling of grandmothers and grandfathers increase, respectively, college attendance rates for granddaughters and grandsons.

6.5.2.2 *Borjas' Findings on Ethnicity and Neighborhood Effects*

Borjas (1992) assumes that individuals value their own consumption and the human capital of their descendants according to a constant elasticity of substitution utility function. He assumes that a child's human capital is given by a

Cobb–Douglas function of the fraction of her own human capital a parent allocates to her child's upbringing and of a contextual social effect, represented by the mean human capital of her ethnic group. These assumptions imply a law of motion for human capital (or earnings) that relates an individual's human capital, $h_{ig,t+1}$, to those of his parents, h_{igt}, and to the mean human capital in his ethnic group g, $\bar{h}_{gt}$, as follows:

$$h_{ig,t+1} = \gamma_1 h_{igt} + \gamma_2 \bar{h}_{gt} + \xi_{igt}, \tag{6.17}$$

where all variables are measured as deviations from the mean, the shock ξ_{igt} may be decomposed as $\xi_{igt} = \epsilon_{igt} + \varepsilon_{gt}$, with the random variables ϵ_{igt} and ε_{gt} being uncorrelated, and the random variable ε_{gt} is treated as a random effect. The estimates of (6.17) with log wages data that Borjas reports vary from 0.1829 to 0.2664 for γ_1, and from 0.1455 to 0.4589 for γ_2; the estimates using schooling data vary from 0.2566 to 0.3465 for γ_1, and from 0.0990 to 0.2983 for γ_2. These results confirm that human capital in a particular generation depends not only on that in their parents' generation but also on the average within the ethnic group of their parents' generation. Again, and in view of the results of Solon, Page, and Duncan (2000) discussed in section 6.5.1 above, it follows that even a complete equalization of neighborhood backgrounds would leave inequality in educational attainment at more than 90 percent of its current level.

6.5.3 Nonlinear Models of Social Interactions and the Intergenerational Transmission of Human Capital

Nonlinear models of social interactions can deliver predictions that are qualitatively richer than those obtained with linear models, particularly because of multiple equilibria. These depend on the interplay among individual, contextual, and endogenous social effects, which in turn depends on properties of preferences in relation to the law of motion for human capital accumulation.

The following model is conceptually related to that of Azariadis and Drazen (1990) and encompasses the Borjas and Kremer models as special cases. It allows me to discuss parents' involvement in their children's education. The economy consists of a large number of agents, each of whom lives for a single period. Each parent is endowed with a given amount of human capital, which she allocates to work and to involvement in human capital acquisition by her offspring. Parents value their own consumption and the education of their children because of the economic and social success it may confer on the children.[17] In section 6.5.6 below I discuss results obtained with a similar model by Patacchini and Zenou (2011) regarding direct parental involvement in their children's education. The model is also helpful in motivating concerns about social interactions in neighborhoods expressed by households when they choose their residences. I explore this directly in section 6.5.7.

I assume a utility function with a constant elasticity of substitution (CES) between the child's human capital, $h_{i,t+1}$, measured in efficiency units, and own consumption, C_{it}:

$$U = U(h_{i,t+1}, C_{it}) \equiv \left[\zeta (h_{i,t+1})^{1-\frac{1}{\sigma}} + (1-\zeta)(C_{it})^{1-\frac{1}{\sigma}}\right]^{\frac{\sigma}{\sigma-1}}, \tag{6.18}$$

where the positive parameter σ, may be less than, equal to, or greater than 1 and denotes the elasticity of substitution between human capital stock of the child and own consumption; C_{it} serves as the numeraire. This model is also helpful below in understanding the role of parental involvement (section 6.5.6) and in presenting research that maps educational, racial, and geographic interactions across U.S. urban areas in terms of a small number of representative neighborhoods (see section 6.6 below).

Let s_{it} denote the fraction of her own human capital that a parent devotes to the production of human capital for her child, the savings rate. The remainder is allocated to paying for her own consumption, $(1 - s_{it})W_t h_{it} = C_{it}$, where W_t denotes the real wage rate per efficiency unit of labor, with consumption as numeraire. For the production of a child's human capital I assume both a parent's own input, $s_{it}h_{it}$, and a local interaction effect, υ_{it}, from the community where individual i lives. They combine through a constant elasticity of substitution production function to produce the child's human capital, $h_{i,t+1}$. My assumption of a CES function in (6.18) rather than of a Cobb–Douglas function [c.f. (Borjas 1992)], allows a richer set of predictions. For the problem at hand, it is more convenient to express this relationship in terms of C_{it} rather than with s_{it} as the unknown decision variable:

$$h_{i,t+1} = \left[\eta\left(h_{it} - \frac{1}{W_t}C_{it}\right)^{1-1/b} + (1-\eta)(\upsilon_{it})^{1-1/b}\right]^{\frac{b}{b-1}}, \tag{6.19}$$

where υ_{it} denotes a local interaction effect in the form of the average human capital stock in the community where individual i resides and b denotes the elasticity of substitution, $b > 0$. I allow for complementarity by assuming that $b, \sigma > 0$.

From the first-order conditions for the maximization of (6.18) subject to (6.19), we have

$$(h_{i,t+1})^{1/\sigma-1/b} = \frac{\eta\zeta}{(1-\zeta)W_t^{1-1/\sigma}} \frac{\left(h_{it} - \left[\frac{1}{\eta}(h_{i,t+1})^{\frac{b-1}{b}} - \frac{1-\eta}{\eta}\upsilon_{it}^{1-\frac{1}{b}}\right]^{\frac{b}{b-1}}\right)^{1/\sigma}}{\left[\frac{1}{\eta}(h_{i,t+1})^{\frac{b-1}{b}} - \frac{1-\eta}{\eta}\upsilon_{it}^{1-1/b}\right]^{\frac{1}{b-1}}}. \tag{6.20}$$

I develop the properties of the solution of (6.20) by working with its inverse, that is, with h_{it} as a function of $h_{i,t+1}$ and υ_{it}:

$$h_{it} = \left[\frac{1}{\eta}(h_{i,t+1})^{\frac{b-1}{b}} - \frac{1-\eta}{\eta}\upsilon_{it}^{\frac{b-1}{b}}\right]^{\frac{b}{b-1}} + \left(\frac{1-\zeta}{\eta\zeta}\right)^{\sigma} W_t^{\sigma-1}(h_{i,t+1})^{1-\frac{\sigma}{b}}$$
$$\times \left[\frac{1}{\eta}(h_{i,t+1})^{\frac{b-1}{b}} - \frac{1-\eta}{\eta}\upsilon_{it}^{\frac{b-1}{b}}\right]^{\frac{\sigma}{b-1}}. \tag{6.21}$$

6.5.3.1 *Law of Motion*

Conceptually, equation (6.21) amounts to a law of motion characterizing a child's human capital as an implicit function of that of her parent and of the local interaction effect, $h_{i,t+1} = \mathcal{H}(h_{it}, v_{it})$. Ioannides (2002)[18] shows that the time map associated with the law of motion (6.21) of the evolution of human capital can, depending upon the relative magnitudes of key parameters (σ, b), be either an increasing concave or increasing sigmoid function of parental human capital. In addition, the presence of the social interaction effect v_{it} in (6.21) introduces a rich set of possibilities. The lower the substitutability in consumption between the offspring's human capital and (in effect) own human capital, relative to substitutability in (home) production between own human capital and the interaction effect, the higher the relative complementarity between own and offspring human capital. As W_t changes, the dynamic system (6.21) undergoes a saddle node bifurcation (Azariadis 1993, 92). An increase in the interaction effect shifts the entire map upward. However, the exact impact of such an increase in the interaction effect upon the steady state depends on the multiplicity of equilibria and on their different stability properties.

A variety of outcomes is possible for the intergenerational evolution of human capital. Behavioral parameters and parameters of the production function for human capital combine with initial conditions to suggest possibly multiple steady-state outcomes for given (h_{io}, v_{io}). Complementarity is responsible for a very rich set of predictions.[19]

6.5.3.2 *The Role of the Topology of Interactions*

Recognizing the topology of interactions leads to a rich set of possibilities. Bala and Sorger (1998) model an economy with a social structure defined by individuals' locations on a *circle*, a lattice: each agent's peer group (neighborhood) includes herself and the two agents on either side. Bala and Sorger's model leads to a law of motion that is mathematically simpler than equation (6.21) but still nonlinear. Their model has no parental effect as such and allows for very precise effects when the local interaction effect is assumed to be of the form $v_{it} = 0.5[1 + \tanh(2\lambda[h_{it} - \frac{1}{|\nu(i)|}\sum_{j\in\nu(i)} h_{jt}])]$. That is,

$$h_{i,t+1} = a_{it}v_{it} + (1-\delta)h_{it}, \tag{6.22}$$

where a_{it}, $0 < a_{it} < 1$, denotes the learning effort. This effort is endogenous and determined from a lifetime utility maximization model with human capital being the only form of savings and the only source of income. If the social effect is nonconformist—each individual values her own human capital's distance from the mean among her neighbors, $\lambda > 0$—and λ is "small" relative to the depreciation rate of own human capital, δ, then agents with initially heterogeneous human capital stocks will converge to the same equilibrium level in the long run, which is stable. When the social effect is conformist,

$\lambda < 0$, and "large," the isotropic steady state[20] is unstable, and there exists a anisotropic steady state[21] that is stable. Introducing a global role model, a "mentor," with each individual being influenced by a mean social effect, defined as one-fourth of the sum of her neighbors' human capital plus her own plus that of the role model, affects the dynamics considerably. For example, even when only a subset of agents is affected by the role model, the effects propagate throughout the economy via the neighborhood structure. When λ is sufficiently strong, then either divergence or cyclical behavior in steady-state human capital stocks appears, depending on whether the social interactions effect is decreasing or increasing in the distance between an individual's own human capital from the mean among her neighbors.[22]

6.5.4 Estimations of Human Capital Accumulation with Nonlinear Interaction Structures

I report here two types of empirical applications with richer interaction structures. This section and the next report empirics with models that extend the Kremer and Borjas models and involve parametric and nonparametric estimations using PSID data; they are reported in sections 6.5.4.1 and 6.5.5 below. Section 6.5.6 reports estimation results that highlight the role of parental involvement. The second type of empirical application, section 6.5.7, shows that households deliberately choose neighborhoods with social interactions whose desirability depends on their own characteristics.

6.5.4.1 *Parametric Estimations with PSID Data*

I draw from my earlier work (Ioannides 2002, 2003) and report regression results according to equation (6.16). Column 1 in table 6.1 reproduces Kremer's main regression for the purpose of comparison. Columns 2, 4, and 6 report results for equation (6.16) with a similarly defined sample, based on the random subsample of the PSID. Columns 3 and 5 report estimation results with the entire PSID sample, which includes oversampling of the poor but uses the PSID weights. Columns 1 and 2 are quite similar, broadly speaking, although in my results the total effect of parents' education is numerically less important than that in Kremer's model and the opposite is true for the average education in the neighborhood.

A key prediction of the theory, outlined in section 6.5.3.1, is that parents' educations have a sigmoid effect on children's educations in the presence of an interaction effect. I test this prediction by including linear, quadratic, and cubic terms for father's education and for mother's education. The results for the polynomial structure, which are reported in columns 3 and 5 in table 6.1, respectively, for the random subsample of the PSID include both father's and mother's educations. A polynomial structure for father's education on its own is significant, but two of the regressors lose their significance when the terms for mother's education are added. The results imply a sigmoid shape

Table 6.1.
Intergenerational Transmission of Human Capital.

Model	1	2	3	4	5	6	7
Observations	880	881	1764	885	1764	881	881
$R^2_{\text{adj.}}$	0.231	0.2385	0.2212	0.2624	0.2033	0.2219	0.2411
F		70.28	126.27	32.48	62.62	63.80	35.98
LLF		−0.3463.12					
Mean dependent variable	13.18	13.96	13.75	13.96	13.75	2.62	2.62
Intercept	6.96	6.38	7.24	7.19	5.05	1.32	1.56
	(7.48)	(10.83)	(18.31)	(0.79)	(0.80)	(12.58)	(3.96)
Father's education	0.288	0.192	0.186	−0.353	−0.263	0.164	0.671
(12.11, 3.85)	(7.38)	(7.29)	(10.33)	(1.39)	(1.50)	(6.89)	(1.08)
Father's education squared	—	—	—	0.035	0.027	—	−0.436
				(1.26)	(1.44)		(1.36)
Father's education cubed	—	—	—	−0.0006	−0.0004	—	0.092
				(0.67)	(0.66)		(1.74)
Mother's education	0.154	0.166	0.139	−0.643	−1.184	0.127	−0.573
(12.9, 2.85)	(2.85)	(4.79)	(5.88)	(1.11)	(5.10)	(4.21)	(1.99)
Mother's education squared	—	—	—	0.109	0.141	—	0.483
				(2.06)	(5.84)		(2.38)
Mother's education cubed	—	—	—	−0.004	−0.004	—	−0.091
				(2.51)	(5.72)		(2.29)
Neighbors' education	0.150	0.232	0.191	1.916	3.24	0.224	0.193
(11.29, 1.53)	(2.08)	(4.46)	(5.27)	(0.71)	(1.68)	(4.91)	(4.20)
Neighbors' education, second moment	—	—	—	−0.229	−0.344	—	—
				(0.91)	(1.89)		
Neighbors' education, third moment	—	—	—	0.008	0.011	—	—
				(1.13)	(2.15)		
1970 neighbors' data	—	0.344	0.365	0.350	0.348	0.027	0.027
(0.739, 1.532)		(2.58)	(3.81)	(2.63)	(3.68)	(2.66)	(2.61)

Source: Ioannides (2002)

Dependent variable: educational attainment at 28 years of age. Sample restricted to individuals whose parents report their own educational attainment. t-Statistics are in parentheses. All regressions are weighted by the latest PSID weights.

Column 1 reports the main regression in Kremer (1997) for the purpose of comparison. Columns 2 and 4 report results from Ioannides (2002) with a similarly organized sample based on the original random sample of the PSID. Columns 3 and 5 report results with the entire PSID sample. Columns 6 and 7 report results with the same sample as that for columns 2 and 4, but the dependent variables and all regressors (except for the dummy for 1970 neighbors data) are in logs.

for the relationship between parents' educations and children's educations, with two of the terms for mother's education being statistically significant and implying an inflection point at 11.75 years. I suggest the following explanation. Mothers generally spend more time with their children, which enables them to instill more of their own values in their offspring. Moreover, mothers' own educational attainments are often seen as better proxies for "social class," especially at the time when the data were collected. Marital sorting implies that educational attainments of spouses are correlated, and such dependence may cloud the interpretation of the two different coefficients. The data reject the hypothesis that the linear terms for father's and mother's educations are equal. Nonetheless, imposing equality and including quadratic and cubic terms yields dynamics very similar to those implied by the terms for mother's education.

I test the nonlinearity of education of adults in the neighborhood where an individual was brought up by including the second and third *moments* of the distribution of education within the appropriate census tract. Their inclusion as a group is statistically significant overall. The estimated coefficients are not statistically significant for the random sample (column 4) but are more significant and do imply a nonlinear effect for neighbors' educations for the entire PSID sample (column 5). The results of this procedure are very different from those obtained when the square and the cube of the mean neighborhood educations are included as regressors.

Comparison of the signs of the coefficients of the polynomial terms for mother's education with those for the moments of neighbors' educations suggests a puzzling asymmetry. The marginal effect of mother's education, which is quadratic, attains a maximum within the range of values, is positive for most of them but is ultimately decreasing. The marginal effect of neighbors' educations, which is also quadratic, attains a minimum within the range of values and is ultimately increasing.

I explore further the significance of interactions among neighbors by using a little known feature of the PSID, namely, that cluster sampling techniques result in several observations from each census tract, which Solon, Page, and Duncan also use (see section 6.5.1 above), and in addition groupings within tracts, to be referred to as sampling clusters. There are 227 clusters with an average of 3.9 observations per cluster. The estimated coefficients differ little from those reported, but the cluster-specific random effects structure is significant and explains 11.02 percent, for column 2, and 10.83 percent, for column 4, of the variance.[23] Estimates of the model in logs, reported in columns 6 and 7, in table 6.1, are similar, but a cluster-specific random effect is significant and explains 20.48 percent, for column 6, and 18.84 percent, for column 7, of the variance.

6.5.5 Nonparametric Estimations with PSID Data

Specifying the impact of parental education and of the neighborhood distribution of educational attainment using a CES specification for interaction effects [cf. Benabou (1996b)] along the lines of equation (6.16) supports the importance of nonlinearities for both parents' education and neighbors' education. While such parametric results provide support for the nonlinear effects of parental and neighborhood educations, they depend on restricted notions of nonlinearity. I report next nonparametric estimations of stochastic kernels for various versions of equation (6.16) with the same PSID data.[24] Many stochastic kernels are estimated and reported by Ioannides (2002). A glimpse of marital sorting in terms of education is obtained by estimating the kernel of mother's education conditional on father's education. Ioannides (2002) also examines the dependence, due to selection, between average neighborhood educations (`nschup`) and average parents' educations. Figures 6.1A–B report the estimation of child's education (`maxed`) conditional on the average of father's and mother's education (`parent`), $h_{i,t+1} = G(h_{it}, \varepsilon_i)$. Figures 6.2A–B report the stochastic kernel for child's education conditional on average neighborhood's education (`nschup`), $\hat{f}(h_{i,t+1}|h_{\nu(i)t})$. This last set of estimations provides strong evidence of the presence of nonlinear effects of neighborhood education. To appreciate that, consider drawing a curve connecting the modes of the conditional densities, the "peaks" in figure 6.2B. The resulting curve exhibits increasing returns initially but decreasing returns ultimately, exactly as theory predicts.

6.5.6 The Role of Parental Involvement

Another angle of the intergenerational transmission of human capital that is amenable to empirical analysis is the role of parental *effort* as an input into the human capital of their offspring. Recall that in the model introduced in section 6.5.3, a parent's own input into offspring human capital, $s_{it}h_{it} = h_{it} - \frac{C_{it}}{W_t}$, is implicitly chosen via the selection of C_{it} as a function of parental human capital h_{it} and the local interaction effect v_{it}. Substituting for h_{it} from (6.19) into (6.18) and maximizing with respect to C_{it} yields a first-order condition, from which, in principle, the properties of $s_{it}h_{it}$ as a function of parental human capital h_{it} and the neighborhood (local interaction) effect v_{it} may be obtained. Just as with the law of motion, described in section 6.5.3.1 above, different sets of values for the key parameters, the elasticity of substitution between inputs in producing offspring human capital and the elasticity of substitution in the utility function between consumption and offspring human capital, b, σ, respectively, are consistent with a wide range of possibilities. These possibilities are again rather tedious (but elementary) to characterize unless additional specific assumptions are made. In general, they may render parental human capital h_{it} and the local interaction effect v_{it} either substitutes or complements.

Patacchini and Zenou (2011) consider this aspect more deeply by exploring the properties of parental input and of the neighborhood effect, interpreted as contributions to socialization that are internal and external to the family,

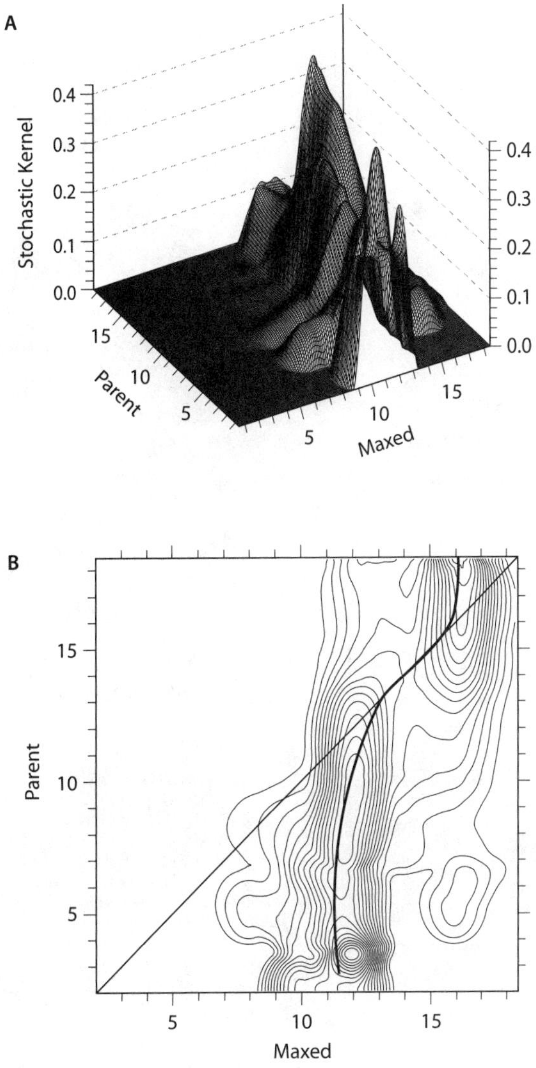

Figures 6.1A–B and 6.2A–B. Social interactions and human capital accumulation. *Source*: Ioannides (2002).

respectively. Their theoretical model is simpler than that in section 6.5.3 above and thus leads to sharper predictions. Individuals living in "good" neighborhoods with better educated parents who look after them enjoy a greater chance of reaching high educational levels. Living in "bad" neighborhoods with low-quality schools and unfavorable peer pressure and having less educated parents lower their prospects for reaching higher educational levels. Patacchini and Zenou confirm these predictions empirically.

Specifically, they employ data from the U.K. National Child Development Study, a longitudinal data set. See chapter 2, section 2.13.7, for

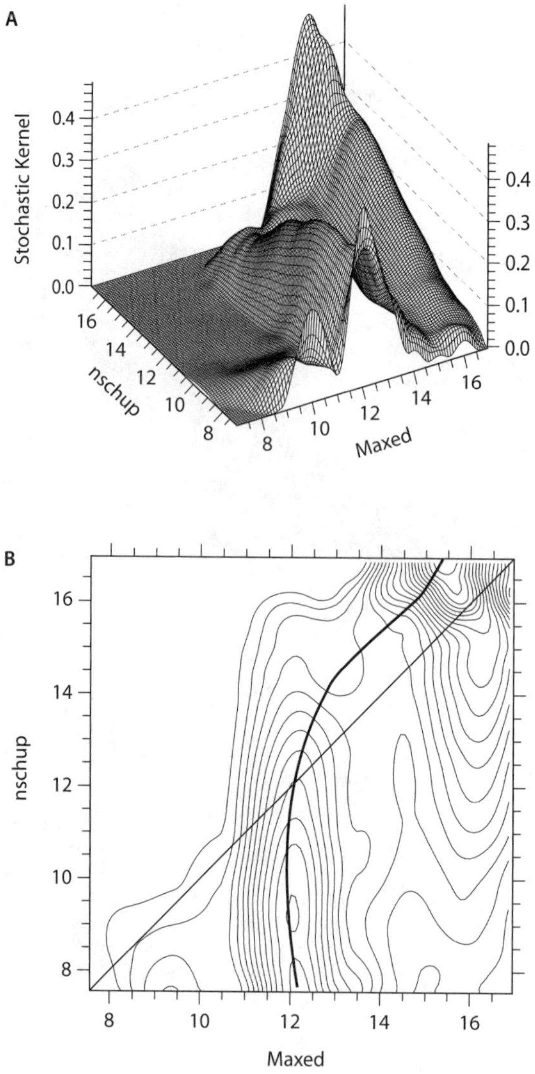

Figure 6.2A–B

details on the data. Patacchini and Zenou follow all individuals in the sample from age 7 through 33. Since these individuals were 13 years of age in 1971, obtaining contextual neighborhood information at the level of the ward from the 1971 U.K. census is appropriate. The authors use two proxies for parental time input into children's education, both defined as dichotomous variables, as follows. One proxy is based on teachers' perceptions of parental involvement, and a second on parents' self-reported information on how frequently they read to their children, both when their children are at age 7.

To offset the endogeneity bias associated with households' choices of neighborhoods, the authors work with a sample of 2,566 children and 4,897 parents, all tenants in council housing in large U.K. cities whose neighborhood choices may be considered exogenous. Like Oreopoulos (2003), the authors argue that because tenants are assigned administratively to particular council housing apartments, their assignments are uncorrelated with tenants' own educations or concern for their children's educations. The authors find evidence of sorting when regressing the mean years of education of parents who recently moved into *private* dwellings in each ward against the proportion of adults with A levels residing in that ward, with an estimated elasticity of 0.04 being highly statistically significant; they find no such correlation for those who moved into *council* dwellings.[25] While controlling for a rich set of characteristics, the authors find that the propensities of highly educated parents, estimated as a probit model, to read to their children is more sensitive to the percentage of highly skilled population in the neighborhood than that for less educated parents. Finally, they estimate the probability that individuals attain high educational levels as a function of the parents' propensities to read to their children and of the percentage of highly skilled residents in their neighborhoods of upbringing, with many other controls included. They find highly significant positive marginal effects, 0.11 and 0.07, respectively. Correspondingly, when they estimate the probability that individuals attain low educational levels as a function of their parents' propensities to read to their children and of the percentage of highly skilled residents in their neighborhoods of upbringing, again with many other controls also being included, they get highly significant negative (but numerically smaller) marginal effects, −0.02 and −0.12, respectively. Thus, parental involvement is more important than neighborhood quality for highly educated parents but less important relative to neighborhood effects for less educated parents.

These results are causal and thus can be used to guide policy. Patacchini and Zenou show that parental involvement and neighborhood quality are complements rather than substitutes and suggest that programs aimed at improving neighborhood conditions are more likely to be effective in helping the children of less-educated parents acquire education. Neighborhood improvements and social mixing policies can thus help such children.

6.5.7 Household Composition and Moving Behavior

The estimations of social interactions in education discussed above rest on associating educational outcomes for individuals with the observed educations of their parents and the mean education in their neighborhoods at the time of their own upbringing. However, parents' characteristics are not independent of those of their neighbors because households deliberately choose where to live. Parents who value social interactions that affect their children's achievements will try to avoid social contexts with attributes they think will be associated with poor outcomes. Ioannides and Zanella (2008) explore this angle by using PSID data that allow them to follow households over two successive waves of data, from 2001 to 2003, and to relate residential moves to socioeconomic characteristics $\mathbf{z}_{\nu_o(i)}$ and $\mathbf{z}_{\nu_d(i)}$, respectively, of origin and destination neighborhoods defined as census tracts, and own characteristics, $\mathbf{z}_i$. These authors estimate the propensity to move between those 2 years by means of linear and nonlinear probability models,

$$\text{Prob}_i = \alpha_0 + \alpha_{oi}\mathbf{z}_{\nu_o(i)} + \alpha_{di}\mathbf{z}_{\nu_d(i)} + \epsilon_i, \tag{6.23}$$

with a full complement of individual characteristics included. They seek to examine whether α_{oi}, α_{di} vary systematically between households with and without children. For households that do not move, origin and destination tracts coincide.

Their sample is 6,432 households from the PSID for 2001 and 2003. In addition to detailed data on individual, household, and neighborhood characteristics in both periods, at the census tract level as well as at the county level of disaggregation, thanks to access to confidential geocodes (as in sections 6.5.2.1 and 6.5.3 above), Ioannides and Zanella use U.S. census maps to identify *all* census tracts surrounding each tract in which households are originally observed. They refer to the resulting groups of census tracts as *areas*. The variables of principal interest are median household income in the tract and the percentage of the population in the tract that moved in within the last 5 years; various individual attributes such as age, home ownership, job tenure, and family size; racial and ethnic characteristics; whether foreign-born; whether receiving food stamps; and whether an individual is a high school dropout, is a high school graduate, or has some college education. The authors use tract-level counterparts of these variables as contextual effects in (6.23). Ioannides and Zanella control for endogeneity of neighborhood characteristics and of prices by extending the strategy of Bayer and Ross (2009) and using as instruments the average characteristics of neighborhoods surrounding the respondents' own. The characteristics of adjacent neighborhoods are correlated for spatial reasons, and this rank condition is easy to test. Since adjacent neighborhoods are generally substitutes, arguments similar to those of Berry, Levinsohn, and Pakes (1995), discussed in chapter 3, still apply. For other neighborhood characteristics, the characteristics of surrounding neighborhoods are valid instruments provided that, one, there are no cross-neighborhood interactions (i.e., all relevant social interactions occur within the tract), and, two, neighborhood observables and unobservables are uncorrelated. Ioannides and Zanella also assume that family composition is exogenous with respect to households' unobserved preferences for neighborhoods. They find that neighborhood effects in the form of contextual effects *do* affect significantly, and in the directions predicted, the propensity to move for households *with* school-age children but *not* for those *without* school-age children.

They find, more specifically, that mean income and the share of the population in the census tract belonging to one's own race-ethnic group who recently moved into the neighborhood increase the propensity to move in for households with children but have no effect on households without children. The percentage of residents who are foreign-born or on public assistance decreases the propensity to move in for households with children but exert no such effects for others. They find no effect of neighborhood education—although the share of educated residents has the expected sign for households with children. The share of children with poor linguistic skills in a neighborhood encourages leaving it and discourages entering it for households with children, but the corresponding effects are insignificant for those without children. The estimates for the percentage of residents who recently moved into a neighborhood, a proxy for neighborhood instability, are statistically significant and encourage moving out of a neighborhood and encourage moving into it for households with children but not for those without children, respectively. This same variable may also be interpreted as an endogenous social effect, which is identified in the case of the probit model.

A plot of the predicted probability of moving into a neighborhood as a function of the observed percentage of those who recently moved in, which in a steady state is equal to the percentage of those moving out, shows that a sigmoid function fits well through the scatter of points and suggests that there exist multiple equilibria. It also implies a "tipping point" of about 20 percent on a 2-year basis, meaning that households with children are likely to move when more than one-fifth of households leave the neighborhood in 2 years. This is a very rough estimate, of course, but is in broad agreement with the newest empirics of neighborhood tipping, documented most recently by Card, Mas, and Rothstein (2008a), that I discuss in chapter 3, section 3.6.2.1.

Ioannides and Zanella assess the likely endogeneity bias in OLS estimates by formally comparing the estimates with their instrumental variable counterparts. The OLS coefficients on contextual variables of particular interest in the baseline regression without county fixed effects are smaller in absolute value than the instrumental variable ones (when these are significant). This is consistent with a central tenet of the approach, namely, that it is precisely self-selection into neighborhoods that helps identify preferences for social interactions. The models predict correctly almost 80 percent of choices in the sample. The prediction rate is much higher for nonmovers, about 90 percent, than for movers, about 40 percent. Overall, the results of Ioannides and Zanella complement those obtained with the static data discussed in chapter 3, section 3.5.

These findings support the widely held belief that households searching for the best neighborhoods trade off social interactions that are conducive to human capital accumulation and acculturation for the cost of living in different communities. In the U.S. economy, where a large part of spending on public education is administered by local jurisdictions, demographic characteristics combine with preferences for housing and social interactions to influence the composition of communities. As children grow up and leave the parental household, its demand for housing and local public services, especially education, is impacted.

Epple, Romano, and Sieg (2009) emphasize the fact that such moves are not frictionless because of the financial and psychological costs of moving, which vary over the life cycle within a dynamic model. They embed locational choices of households in an overlapping generations model that also allows them to explore the implied dynamics for entire metropolitan areas. Their paper, which serves as a dynamic extension of Epple and Sieg's (1999) work (see chapter 3, section 3.7.1), shows that households stratify by wealth (conditional on moving costs) at equilibrium across communities. They use data from the 1970–2000 U.S. census for all Boston area jurisdictions together with Consumer Expenditure Survey data to obtain calibration results that rely on stationary equilibria in four artificial communities they construct to represent the actual ones in the Boston area. Epple, Romano, and Sieg (2009) show that changes in mobility costs have large effects on household sorting patterns and community composition. Lower moving costs reduce the variability of public education provided across communities. The findings of Ioannides and Zanella strengthen the plausibility of the conjecture by Epple, Romano, and Sieg (2009) that also allowing for households with no children would have profound effects on results in terms of the age composition of communities, their tax bases, their stratification according to wealth, and spending on education at the voting equilibrium.

6.6 SOCIAL INTERACTIONS IN SYNTHETIC NEIGHBORHOODS

The literature has come to recognize that the complexity of neighborhood interactions challenges researchers to come up with simplified ways to assess their significance. Recent research along those lines advances our ability to do so. Badel (2009a) offers a systematic approach to reducing the dimensionality of neighborhood descriptions by using clustering algorithms that allow one to map actual neighborhoods, described as census tracts, into a smaller number of *synthetic* neighborhoods. Neighborhoods are clustered based jointly on census tract–specific average human capital, racial configuration, and price of housing services, denoted by (h_ℓ, r_ℓ, p_ℓ), respectively. The census tracts clustered together into synthetic neighborhoods turn out to be in close geographic proximity to one another and are typically geographically contiguous. The resulting neighborhoods are large and look fairly homogeneous with respect to the covariation of (h_ℓ, r_ℓ, p_ℓ) within them.

Badel defines two representative neighborhoods, I and II, and obtains the following results using 2,000 U.S. census data. Of the households residing in I, 32 percent are white, while of those in II, 84 percent are white. With regard to human capital, average household earnings averages are \$33,591 in I, which amounts to 0.54 of average earnings in II (\$61,889). Household income averages \$41,747, which represents 0.55 of average income in II (\$74,577). Among black households, the ratio of average earnings in I to average earnings in II is 0.70; among white households it is 0.58 and among households in other racial categories it is 0.62. The average income of black households within neighborhood I is 0.90 of the average income of white households; the respective number is 0.74 in neighborhood II. The imputed housing price is \$10,405 in I, which represents 0.73 of the price in II (\$14,268).

These representative neighborhoods explain about one-third of the joint covariation in (h_ℓ, r_ℓ, p_ℓ), and three representative neighborhoods explain about one-half of the joint variation. Increasing the number of representative neighborhoods results in small improvements in explanatory power. Badel's results are not so surprising in view of the findings on neighborhood income distributions discussed in chapter 3, section 3.6.3 above. As reported by Hardman and Ioannides (2004), Ioannides (2004a) and Wheeler and La Jeunesse (2008), different U.S. metro areas are remarkably similar in terms of the greater relative importance of within-neighborhood as opposed to across-neighborhood differences.

Badel (2009b) uses the characteristics of the synthetic neighborhoods he defines to calibrate a equilibrium model of intergenerational transmission of human capital where heterogeneous households choose their neighborhoods. In an infinite horizon discrete time model, a typical household i in period t is defined in terms of human capital, race, and innate ability, $y_{it} = (h_{it}, r_i, z_{it})$, respectively. Individual i's state evolves over time in an autonomous manner; that is, $y_{i,t+1} = (h_{i,t+1}, r_i, z_{i,t+1})$, where race r_i is invariant, the random variable $z_{i,t+1}$ has a specified distribution that may depend on z_{it}, and $h_{i,t+1}$ is updated in a manner conceptually very similar to (6.19). That is, parental input is the portion of the parent's human capital left after paying for consumption, C_{it}, and housing, $p_{\nu(i),t}x_{\ell,t}$, and is equal to $h_{it} - \frac{1}{W_t}C_{it} - \frac{p_{\nu(i),t}}{W_t}x_{\ell,t}$. The law of motion becomes

$$h_{i,t+1} = (1-\delta)h_{it} + z_{it}A\left[\eta\left(h_{it} - \frac{1}{W_t}C_{it} - \frac{p_{\nu(i)t}}{W_t}x_{\ell t}\right)^{1-\frac{1}{\sigma}} + (1-\eta)h_{\nu(i)t}^{1-\frac{1}{\sigma}}\right]^{b^*\frac{\sigma}{\sigma-1}}, \qquad (6.24)$$

where parameter b^* denotes returns to scale. Utility per period is specified as a Cobb–Douglas function of nonhousing and housing consumption, net of a quadratic loss function of the deviation of the average race in the neighborhood, $r_{\nu(i)t}$, from a racial bliss point:

$$U_{it} = \frac{1}{1-b}\left(x_{\nu(i)t}^{1-\zeta}C_{it}^{\zeta}\right)^{1-b} - \kappa(r_{\nu(i)t} - \text{bliss})^2, \qquad (6.25)$$

where b, κ, "bliss," are positive parameters.

In calibrating the model Badel sets the percentages of white and nonwhite households at 79 percent and 21 percent, respectively, for neighborhoods I and II, the depreciation rate for human capital in (6.24) at $\delta = 0$, and both the wage rate and the housing price in neighborhood I at 1, as they play only a scaling role. He also sets parameters b, ζ in (6.25) as $b = 2.5, \zeta = 0.25$. When calibrated at the steady state, the model aims at matching the following key facts: average earnings of \$54,200, the ratio of average earnings in neighborhood I to average earnings in neighborhood II at 0.54, the variance of log lifetime earnings at 0.36, the intergenerational correlation of log lifetime earnings at 0.4, the intergenerational correlation of log consumption at 0.48, and the ratio of human capital investment to average earnings at 0.072. The last-mentioned is the value of combined public and private expenditures on primary, secondary, and college education as a share of GDP in 1999. The remaining parameters are estimated; see (Badel 2009b, table 3). The serial autocorrelation in innate ability z_{it} turns out to be equal to 0.082, the implied value for elasticity of substitution in the human capital investment function [see (6.24)] is $\hat{\sigma} = 0.56$, the share of human capital investment in the same function $\hat{\eta} = 0.027$, the returns to scale are $\widehat{b^*} = 0.769$, and $\widehat{\text{bliss}} = 0.812$.

The parameter choices made and estimates obtained by Badel allow him to replicate important facts of the U.S. economy. The calibrated model exactly replicates U.S. residential segregation by race and, in particular, explains 72 percent of the observed black-white percentage difference in household earnings. This permanent racial inequality arises not from wage discrimination or informational frictions but from residential racial segregation coupled with the effect of social interactions in the intergenerational transmission of human capital. The location decisions of households account for 86 percent of the black-white difference in average human capital investments and 97 percent of the black-white difference in average earnings. The finding of a racial bliss point of $\widehat{\text{bliss}} = 0.812$ implies strong racial preferences, a strong finding when we recall that the premise of the Schelling model, which I discuss in chapter 3, section 3.6, is that even mild racial preferences suffice for segregation.

6.7 CONCLUSIONS

This chapter looks at empirical aspects of social interactions and human capital spillovers. It shows how differences in patterns of productivity across locations and at different scales of spatial aggregation may be rationalized in terms of simple models of social interactions. The spatial units vary from small neighborhoods, for which we have data for U.S. and French cities, to entire cities or metropolitan areas, as well as counties, regions, and states (in the United States), and nations (in the European Union). Social interactions are an important source of the urban wage premium. Forces that may sustain it include individuals who work harder in cities because their neighbors work harder—an instance of social interactions par excellence—and increases in firm-specific total factor productivity associated with density of economic activity. The chapter examines forces of intergenerational transmission of human capital. While it is quite compelling to interpret spatial proximity in physical space as a conduit for social interactions, the spatial correlates of social space are of course only some of the dimensions along which social interactions take place. In particular, social interactions in neighborhoods as measured conventionally are empirically important determinants of neighborhood choice when households move.

This chapter also serves as a bridge between micro-based analyses of social interactions that impact location decisions of households and firms, examined in chapters 3 and 4, and the aggregate approach to urban structure and growth discussed in chapters 7–9. Chapter 5 augments the canonical urban spatial model to allow for social interactions while retaining the CBD-based geography of the canonical urban model. The empirical findings documenting the relationship between social interactions and outcomes at different levels of spatial aggregation reported in this chapter are key motivation for the remainder of the book, which concentrates on modeling key relationships at the city level of spatial aggregation. We see in both chapters 5 and 6 that agglomeration effects are real, even when their elasticities are quite small (a few percentage points at most), and their effects are measurable and important.

Research on social interactions and human capital spillovers so far has depended on readily available data at different geographic and spatial scales. Future research must take advantage of the fact that space is inherently continuous and that the increasing availability of microgeographic information makes it easy to merge data from different sources. The availability of information from the great variety of portable electronic devices that record the moves of individuals in urban space is particularly promising in this connection. Future research should explore the fact that phenomena at different spatial and social scales may interact in profound ways and not just via aggregation. Yet so far they have been examined by separate literatures and have developed largely independently. Finally, future research must also address cases in which proximity does not always translate into social interaction.

6.8 GUIDE TO THE LITERATURE: CHAPTERS 3–6

The first formalization of the model of demand with interdependence across individuals in chapter 3 is due to Pollak (1976), but the concept of social interactions goes at least as far back as Becker (1974). Empirical models for studying housing demand by households routinely include the socioeconomic characteristics of the communities where they live. Quigley (1985) provided the first empirical implementation in housing markets of the path-breaking article by McFadden (1978) that launched the theory of generalized extreme-value distributions. Quigley estimates a nested multinomial logit model from the work of McFadden (1978). Early treatments of neighborhood choice seen as choices among urban neighborhoods (or communities), such as that by Miyao (1978a, 1978b), emphasize dynamic properties in the presence of neighborhood effects, modeled as contextual effects, but do not go into empirics, nor do they distinguish among different types of neighborhood effects.

The challenges facing econometric identification of models of choice with social interactions was first demonstrated by Manski (1993) in an extremely influential article. Durlauf (2004) provides a comprehensive review of the theoretical and empirical literature on neighborhood effects. The interdependence among different individuals' preferences that underly the modeling of neighborhood effects and social interactions is particularly important in housing markets, where evidence of social interactions may be sought in the (implicit) price of neighborhoods. Such a price is a hedonic price that magnifies the identification problems inherent in the hedonic model. These questions are reviewed by Ekeland, Heckman, and Nesheim (2002, 2004). Nesheim (2002) makes a particularly apt application of these ideas to the choice of schooling in conjunction with neighborhood choice.

The literature on hedonic estimation has experienced an extraordinary revival underscored by the use of discrete choices involving bundles of goods that differ in terms of characteristics. Following formulations of demand for differentiated goods by Berry (1994) and Berry, Levinsohn, and Pakes (1995), a number of empirical applications to housing decisions by Bayer and a number of coauthors explore the view of choice among individual dwelling units, (Bayer, Ferreira, and McMillan 2007a, 2007b; Bayer, McMillan, and Reuben 2004a, 2004b, 2009). Bayer and Timmins (2005, 2007) discuss problems associated with estimating models of location decisions in the presence of local interactions (spillovers, in their terminology). They look at the number (and characteristics) of other individuals who choose the same or nearby locations at equilibrium. Bayer, Ross, and Topa (2008) formally include job market–related information in the range of neighborhood amenities.

Ioannides and Zabel (2008) provide the first empirical treatment of neighborhood choice and housing quantity as joint decisions in the presence of social interactions in both the discrete and continuous parts. Their study relies on the key results of Brock and Durlauf (2001b) on how self-selection aids identification. A complementary study on contextual effects in hedonic estimation is the one by Kiel and Zabel (2008).

Schelling's elegant work on segregation processes (Schelling 1969, 1971, 1972, 1978) has motivated a large literature, much of it initially outside formal economics. It was "rediscovered" as a precursor of the social interactions literature. Further studies along the lines of Schelling's ideas are those of Zhang (2004, 2011), which I rely on in the text, Young (1998), and most recently Dokumaci and Sandholm (2007), who develop a formal version of Schelling's neighborhood tipping model cast in the language of evolutionary game theory.

The models of community choice developed by Dennis Epple with a number of coauthors (Epple, Gordon, and Sieg 2010b; Epple, Romer, and Sieg 2001; Epple and Sieg 1999; and Epple, Peress, and Sieg 2005, 2007) address interesting estimation problems using aggregate community-based data with very innovative structural approaches. They have enriched our understanding of community choice and have recently served as a bridge to models using individual-based data. A notable example of the latter is that by Epple, Romano, and Sieg (2009). The sorting of individuals into communities is developed rigorously by Epple, Filimon, and Romer (1984) and Epple and Platt (1998). It utilizes the concept of the single-crossing property first articulated by Ellickson (1971).

Regarding chapter 4, formal analysis of land markets goes back to von Thünen (1930, 1826) whom Samuelson (1983) places in the pantheon. The modern literature owes a lot to Alonso (1964, 36–58) and, in particular, his formal treatment of agricultural and business firms' location decisions and the associated bid rent curves. Mills (1967) and Muth (1969) are responsible for firmly placing land use within the urban model. Koopmans and Beckmann (1957) show that the integer assignment problem of plants to sites may be decentralized as a competitive equilibrium in the absence of transport costs but not in their presence. This is important in helping to articulate the role of direct interdependence among firms in their location decisions. Schweizer (1988) presents a noteworthy survey of the treatment of the assignment problem by the general equilibrium literature for spatial economies.

In the canonical model, firms' location decisions within an urban area are motivated by firms' production decisions, where all goods are shipped to the central business district, a dimensionless point. Urban production externalities are then added. Positive externalities are a function of total urban employment and are external to the industry but internal to the urban economy (Chipman 1970; Henderson 1974, 1977b). Negative externalities, for example, pollution, are also added (Henderson 1977a) while the costs of urban congestion are implicitly a central consideration in the systems-of-cities literature.

Interfirm externalities are central in J. Vernon Henderson's work on industry location. Henderson (1994) models an ad hoc specification of total factor productivity, which in that framework is indistinguishable from output price. Interfirm externalities along with the endogenous location of firms and of land for transportation use were formally addressed first by Solow and Vickrey (1971). Borukhov and Hochman (1977) and Fujita and Ogawa (1982) impose a spatial structure on production externalities. More recently, Lucas (2001) takes up the problem of land use when firms benefit by direct interactions with other firms that attenuate with physical distance but workers travel to a predetermined CBD. Lucas and Rossi-Hansberg (2002) show the existence of equilibrium and endogenous formation of the CBD. These works emphasize the spatial structure of cities and are taken up in chapter 5. The article by Lucas (2001) is the first to seek estimation of the parameters of the urban externality via urban densities.

Carlton (1979) is a pioneering study on the empirics of firms' location decisions. The question of firm location, where space is understood in the intercity (national) sense, has been addressed by the new economic geography literature in more detail than the location decisions of individuals. The NEG literature originated with Fujita (1988, 1989) and Krugman (1990, 1991a, 1991b) and was finally synthesized in the work of Fujita, Krugman, and Venables (1999). This literature succeeds in addressing the location of firms in general equilibrium settings at a national as opposed to an intracity scale. The profitability of a location for a firm is given by the index of *market potential* at that location. The index reflects jointly proximity to consumers, degree of competition, and production costs. As a consequence of agglomeration, market potential declines as one moves away from an existing agglomeration and then starts increasing again. The range of falling profitability has been labeled the *agglomeration shadow*.

Chapter 5 emphasizes the consequences of interactions for urban spatial equilibrium where the spatial geometry of cities is modeled in terms of distances from the CBD. Chapter 6 relies on proximity as modeled by contiguity and allows for different levels of spatial disaggregation. The seminal modern works on urban spatial structure as modeled in chapter 5 are due to Beckmann (1976), Mills (1967), and Muth (1969). Mirrlees (1972) was the first to emphasize that the Alonso–Mills–Muth model rests on a fundamental nonconcavity. That is, if the services derived from different land parcels differ, we would expect a typical person to want to consume quantities from all different kinds of land. However, most people locate in just one location. With many individuals, each of whom makes optimal decisions, the problem of equilibrium in location choice and how it is sustained as a competitive equilibrium is convexified. Brueckner (1987) clarifies the unifying features of the Mills–Muth model. Ellickson (1981) pioneers bidding models of land use, and Anas (1990) introduces uncertainty into the land use model. Theoretical research by Miyao (1978a, 1978b) explores the dynamics of "mixed" cities. Fujita (1989) provides additional rigor and important extensions. Brueckner, Thisse, and Zenou (1999) explore the introduction of amenities in the urban model, and Brueckner, Thisse, and Zenou (2002) explore how consequences for skill acquisition, selection by skill, and urban specialization can be examined as properties of urban equilibrium.

Informational interactions within the urban model serve as links with job matching (and thus unemployment) and human capital acquisition and sorting. They are developed further in a book-length treatment by Zenou (2009a). Beckmann (1976) pioneers the literature on urban structure without a predetermined center. Fujita and Ogawa (1982) explore polycentric models, and McMillen and Smith (2003) provide a notable empirical investigation of that phenomenon.

The spatial patterns in productivity, wages, and income in chapter 6 are documented by numerous studies. Nevertheless, the stylized facts that wages are higher in urban areas than in rural areas, and that the urban wage premium increases with urban area size, are still not fully understood, although evidence of a causal role of the spatial concentration of economic activity in productivity is becoming increasingly persuasive. The latest and most comprehensive study is that of Glaeser and Gottlieb (2009). These authors explore the full implications of the assumption of spatial equilibrium and its application to understanding phenomena such as housing price dynamics across cities. In general, effects at different scales of aggregation have been examined by separate literatures developed largely independently. Future research in this area should aim at a decomposition of human capital spillovers in terms of causal effects of pure proximity when it is exogenous, and of selection when activities self-select and result in mutual benefits. The integrated presentation of such findings on human capital spillovers and on how proximity is central to our understanding of urban productivity premium motivates a reduction in dimensionality as I move on to studying urban structure in chapters 7–9 below, where the unit of analysis is the city. Glaeser (2008) ties together very elegantly many of the issues addressed by chapters 3–6 and also addresses issues of policy, but the manuscript for this book was already quite advanced by the time Glaeser's book appeared in 2008.

CHAPTER 7

Specialization, Intercity Trade, and Urban Structure

7.1 INTRODUCTION

Cities are high concentrations of population and thus of economic activity that punctuate the economic and geographic landscape. An uneven concentration of economic activity has been around for a long time, but the emergence of rapid urbanization signaled the beginning of economic development (Bairoch 1988). While city-rural trade has been important for urban development, De Vries (1984) and others argue that the growth of cities was due to technological advances in agriculture and transportation. The economic development of many European economies also depends on international trade, not just on cities trading with their hinterlands. Cities have risen and fallen with the military fortunes of city-states, territorial empires, and nation-states (Kim 2008).[1] An understanding of urban development requires assessing together such complex sets of forces.

The modern literature on urban structure and growth seeks to model the economic complexity of cities as entities comprising interdependent economic activities of production, exchange, and consumption. These activities choose to locate close to one another because they benefit from doing so. Social interactions are central to the functioning of the urban economy. Economists studying market economies assume that individuals choose their locations within cities so as to maximize utility by trading off the cost of traveling to jobs, shopping, entertainment, and social interactions. They also assume that individuals choose their locations among cities in order to improve their welfare. At equilibrium in market economies with freedom of movement, otherwise identical individuals should be indifferent as to where to live. This implies conditions that have important and testable consequences for resource allocation.

Firms similarly choose their locations, taking into consideration access to markets for their inputs, that is, access to workers with particular skills, costs of goods including shipping, and access to markets for their own outputs. Firms also benefit from proximity to other activities that are conducive to productivity improvements, that is, social interactions, but are not necessarily priced directly by a market. Successful cities acquire economic spheres of influence that go beyond national governmental jurisdictions.

The most influential current approach to urban structure is the system-of-cities approach, pioneered and best represented by the work of J. Vernon Henderson, of which the best known and most often quoted is (Henderson 1974). It has spawned theoretical and empirical articles and books. See in particular (Henderson 1977b, 1988).[2] The system-of-cities approach addresses urban structure by emphasizing specialization. An urban economy may produce different products that benefit from spillovers (social interactions) at the city level, are external to agents, individuals, and firms, but are internal to the industry and to the city. Many different industries may operate in the same city, but the urban economy requires people to commute to their places of work and leisure, which generates congestion and pollution costs, and so on.

Therefore, under certain conditions, it pays for cities to specialize in producing a single product or a group of related products. In this fashion, people employed by the software industry for example, are not saddled by the social costs generated by the steel industry. Urban economic activity thus leads to forces of attraction and repulsion, and the city size that results from the free movement of individuals seeking to maximize their utilities is referred to as the equilibrium city size. This is often referred to as the optimum city size but ought not to be confused with the efficient or socially optimal city size defined in terms of a planner's problem. A socially optimal city size may be defined naturally after accounting for the presence both of benefits from city size and costs of agglomeration. Whether or not the socially optimal city size is attained as the equilibrium city size in a market economy and whether public policy may improve efficiency are interesting policy questions. I refer to this source of urban specialization as specialization à la Henderson.

Whereas specialization is an advantage because of production efficiency, there are other considerations in modern economies that assign special and important roles to industrial diversification of cities, too. One such force, which goes back at least as far as Jane Jacobs (1969) and is discussed in chapter 4 above, is urbanization externalities, a collective term for the beneficial effects of the multitude of diverse activities taking place in cities, be that consumption, production, entertainment, or culture. Nowadays, this view is enriched by considering the dynamics of innovation. Duranton and Puga (2001) emphasize, and Duranton (2007) pursues further, how diversified cities act as urban "nurseries," nurturing ideas whose productive implementation is then best done in smaller specialized cities. This argues in favor of the coexistence of specialized and diversified cities, as industrial turnover ("industrial churning") continuously evolves, producing a flow of industries from one type of city to another. Another force reflects the fact that industries may differ with respect to cyclical fluctuations in their product markets that may in turn induce labor turnover. This in turn may generate a force in favor of colocation of industries that differ in terms of cyclical characteristics. A downturn for one industry is an opportunity for lucrative hiring by another industry, and this has consequences for urban industrial specialization and diversification. Krugman (1991b) formalizes this notion. I refer to this force of diversification as diversification à la Krugman.

Below I start with the evidence on urban specialization and diversification and then go on to modeling and exploring their consequences for urban structure, beginning immediately in section 7.2 with Henderson specialization. In section 7.8 I turn to labor market frictions in the presence of Krugman diversification. I discuss further the consequences of industrial turnover for urban structure in chapters 8 and 9.

7.2 EMPIRICAL EVIDENCE ON URBAN SPECIALIZATION AND DIVERSIFICATION

How can one determine whether or not a city is specialized and the industries in which it might be specialized? This is not a trivial task because even the largest relative employment shares for industrial sectors in U.S. cities are rather small in absolute terms. According to several authors, only about 20 percent of urban employment is typically sufficient to define specialization (Alexandersson 1956; Bergsman, Greenston, and Healy 1972; Black and Henderson 2003). Among U.S. cities, at least 65 percent of local labor forces are employed in "non-traded good" activities (Black and Henderson 2003). Therefore, the employment shares that suggest specialization must be treated cautiously. Bergsman, Greenston, and Healy (1972) and Henderson (1988) classify cities by type, using cluster analysis with employment data from around 1970, and find very strong "typing" by manufacturing activity. Black and Henderson (2003) report that manufacturing shares have declined since then, from more than 28 percent of U.S. nongovernmental employment to less than 19 percent, with many cities losing their manufacturing bases. The recent literature has elaborated on the nature of specialization, especially during an era of cities in transition as they are being transformed by churning and rapid relocation of industries,[3] on the one hand, and the increasing importance of services, on the other. I turn next to a modern update on the empirics of urban specialization.

Black and Henderson (2003) classify 317 metropolitan areas (cities) according to degree of specialization by two-digit standard industrial classification (SIC) activities (essentially, 80 two-digit industries) using private employment in 1992. Let $s_{J\ell}$ denote the share of industry J, $J = 1, \ldots, 80$, in total private employment in city ℓ, which belongs to city cluster c. Cities are grouped into industrial clusters according to similarities in production patterns, indicated by the shares of employment of different industries.[4] Let m_c be the number of cities in cluster c, n the number of clusters, and ι_c an indicator variable, defined as being equal to 1 if $\ell \in c$ and to 0 otherwise. Black and Henderson use Ward's criterion, which involves minimizing the distances from the share of employment in each industry in each city and cluster to the mean share of the cluster, or the error sum of squares within clusters summed across all clusters. This is written as

$$\sum_{c=1}^{n} \imath_c \left[\sum_{\ell=1}^{m_c} \sum_{J=1}^{80} \left(s_{J\ell c} - \frac{1}{m_c} \sum_{\ell}^{m_c} s_{J\ell c} \right)^2 \right]. \tag{7.1}$$

The clustering algorithm is hierarchical, and the number of clusters is set arbitrarily by the analyst.

Black and Henderson work with $n = 55$ clusters, organized into eight groups of broad product-city categories. They back this up by an F-test on whether the 55 individual clusters are distinct from one another. There are different types of manufacturing cities, service centers, and market-center cities. The eight categories are clothing and food, wood products, electronics, heavy manufacturing, oil and chemicals, market centers, health services, and other services. To appreciate their results, consider their Table 8 (Black and Henderson 2003, 365) (reproduced here as table 7.1) where cluster number 10 [see also, for more detail, Black and Henderson (2003, 369, app. 1)] includes electronics and related industries (engineering, R&D, electronics, with SIC codes 87, 35, and 36). There are three metropolitan areas in the cluster, which includes San Jose, California (part of Silicon Valley), and Huntsville, Alabama, and the computer industry share is 22 percent, with 6 percent being the respective share of the industry in national employment. Cluster 14, instruments (SIC code 38), has a share of employment which at 7.7 percent is one of the smaller ones but (characteristically) is an order of magnitude higher than its share in national employment, 0.8 percent. Sometimes, specialization is conferred by the absence of manufacturing.

These results show extraordinary diversity across cities in production (specialization) patterns, with dominant employment ranging from about 30 percent at most (28.4 percent for Jackson, Mississippi) to 4.6 percent at least (Visalia, California, and Fresno, California). Black and Henderson (2003, 365, table 8, cluster number 10; 369, app. 1) show that average sizes vary across clusters, stating that within clusters city sizes are quite similar. The share of adults with at least 4 years of higher education in 1990 is at 30 percent significantly higher for cities with high-tech centers (electronics, instruments, and computers) compared to the national average of 21.5 percent.

Considering specialization and diversification jointly provides an overview that is particularly important in understanding the entire urban structure. In emphasizing such a view, Duranton and Puga (2000) note that a city with a dominant industry and a broad base of other industries can be both diversified and specialized. By ignoring industrial clustering, one can use as a measure of diversity of city ℓ's industrial composition relative to the national average the index $\sum_J |s_{J\ell} - s_J|^{-1}$. The higher this index is, the closer city ℓ's industrial composition is to that of the national economy. In terms of the terminology introduced in chapter 4, it is natural to think of localization economies (see chapter 4, section 4.5) as supportive of specialization, and urbanization economies (see chapter 4, section 4.6) as supportive of diversification.

Table 7.1.
Examples of Clusters

Cluster	Cluster Industry	Number MSAs	MSA Size (thousands; % college +)	Share Dominant Industry (%)	Share National (%)	Comments
B	Electronics					
10	Computers (87, 35, 36) (engineering, R&D, electronics)	3	712; 27.7	22	6	San Jose CA, Huntsville AL
11	Electrical machinery (36)	2	114; 12.6	24.5	1.6	Madison County IN, Kokomo IN
12	Electronics (36)	4	159; 29.7	10.1	1.6	Binghampton NY, Bloomington IN
13	Diverse machinery (electronics)	6	232; 29.7	n.a.	n.a.	Boulder CO, Cedar Rapids IA
14	Instruments (38)	5	291; 26.4	7.7	0.8	Rochester NY, Sherman TX
G	Market centers					
40	Diverse services (health, education, engineering and management)	7	2471; 25.8	n.a.	n.a.	Boston MA, Philadelphia PA
40	Financial services (60, 62)	1	8547; 24.6	8.6	1.0	New York NY
42	Mixed-base metro areas (high tech, wholesale, transportation and bus services)	9	2673; 26.0	n.a.	n.a.	Orange County CA, Denver CO
43	New mixed-base metro areas (high tech, eating places, engineering, and management)	8	1405; 27.5	n.a.	n.a.	Phoenix AZ, San Diego CA
44	Business services (73), transportation, eating	7	1403; 24.0	9.3	5.1	Houston TX, Tampa FL
45	Diverse manufacturing	20	1285; 21.5	n.a.	n.a.	Cleveland OH, Chicago IL

Source: Black and Henderson (2003, 365, table 8).

Numbers in parentheses in column 2 represent an SIC code for which city-industry share is reported in column 5. In column 5, the number in parentheses is the national share of the industry.

Black and Henderson also note a strong correlation between changes in city size and changes in industrial composition over 1980–1990, with both the relatively fastest and slowest growing cities experiencing the greatest change in their industrial compositions. This suggests that cities change size because their types change. As I discuss below in chapter 8, Duranton (2007) underscores that industries change their locations across cities rapidly, but those changes cause rather slow movements in cities' positions up and down the urban hierarchy. Duranton and Puga (2005) draw attention to the fact that *sectoral* specialization within manufacturing (specialization à la Henderson that I emphasize so far in the present section), has declined from 1977 to 1997 in U.S. cities, as measured by the Gini coefficient of employment. In contrast, they argue that *functional* specialization of cities, which differentiates management and services from manufacturing operations, has been increasing. They (Duranton and Puga 2005, 344, table 1) report increasing functional specialization as measured by the difference in the ratio of the number of executives and managers to that of production workers (employed in precision production, fabrication, or assembly) between cities classified by size and the national average. Increasing differences persisted for larger cities from 1950 to 1990, while they diminished for smaller cities. These authors point to considerable additional evidence in favor of pronounced shifts from sectoral to functional urban specialization in the United States as well as in other economies. Section 7.6.1 below returns to this issue.

7.3 SIMPLE ECONOMICS OF URBAN SPECIALIZATION

The essential trade-off that gives rise to urban specialization may be expressed in a variety of ways. I present a model that is driven by productivity gains from the availability of a variety of intermediate inputs.[5] The effective increasing returns from a greater variety of intermediate products that are locally produced, which underlies the intuitive treatment here, are analytically equivalent, as Ciccone and Hall (1996) prove,[6] to assuming increasing returns to urban economic activity in the style of Chipman (1970) and Henderson (1974). Duranton and Puga (2004) refer to this concept as *Marshallian equivalence*.

According to the Chipman–Henderson approach, each firm in a city benefits from total factor productivity that is external to (i.e., is taken as given by) each firm and individual and assumed to be a function of some measure of aggregate economic activity in the city such as total employment or output.[7] In Ciccone and Hall's use of this concept (see chapter 6, section 6.3.2), the output per unit of land anywhere in the city enjoys an external effect from total output in the city per unit of total land. Total output is the sum of the outputs of all firms, each of which is itself a function of total output. Consequently, the value of the externality is determined at equilibrium in a manner that is conceptually similar to the canonical social interactions formulation. This is exactly what may give rise to increasing returns with respect to, say labor, which are due to the real externality conferred on production.

In the style of Dixit and Stiglitz (1977), an economy produces many final products. For each of them, let output be described by a CES production function with differentiated intermediate products as inputs. Quantity Q_J of good J is given by

$$Q_J = \left[\sum_m^{m_J} z_m^{1-\frac{1}{\sigma_J}} \right]^{\frac{\sigma_J}{\sigma_J - 1}}, \quad \sigma_J > 1,$$

where z_m is the input of intermediate variety m and $[0, m_J]$ is the range of varieties produced and used by industry J. This production function is homogeneous of degree one with respect to all inputs z_m, $m \in [0, m_J]$. Each of these inputs is in turn produced by a monopolist that uses raw labor as the only input with a linear technology with fixed costs f and unit cost c. This combination of assumptions leads to each firm's demand being isoelastic in price and its cost linear in output. In turn, these assumptions imply that price is a markup on marginal cost, itself proportional to the wage rate. Under the assumption of free entry in the production of intermediates, a symmetric monopolistically competitive environment emerges where firms enter as long as positive profits are made. At the free-entry equilibrium, the price for each intermediate is equal to the minimum average cost, and each firm supplies an amount that is independent of the total demand. This in turn implies, as I derive in detail below, that its demand for labor is a function of parameters and thus constant: $z_m = z = (\sigma_J - 1)\frac{f}{c}$. The total labor demand is equal to $m_J \sigma_J f$, which implies that $m_J = \frac{H_J}{\sigma_J f}$, where H_J denotes the amount of labor used by industry J. Therefore, the total supply of labor determines the number of firms supplying the intermediates, which makes the range (variety) of intermediates produced proportional to total labor supply, H_c. These results imply $Q_J = \bar{q}_J (H_J)^{\frac{\sigma_J}{\sigma_J - 1}}$, where $\bar{q}_J$ denotes a function of parameters, $\bar{q}_J = (\sigma_J - 1)\frac{f}{c}(\sigma_J f)^{-\frac{\sigma_J}{\sigma_J - 1}}$. The reduced form for output shows that a greater quantity of the labor supply allows a greater variety of intermediate inputs and therefore greater productivity: the elasticity of output with respect to total labor, $\frac{\sigma_J}{\sigma_J - 1}$, is greater than 1. This *pecuniary* externality is an inherent feature of the monopolistic competition model.[8] Still, it is conceptually similar to the *real* externality postulated by Henderson (1974).

In the main model I use below, the production of final goods also requires raw labor input with a Cobb–Douglas share of u_J, and thus the share of the total input from intermediates is $1 - u_J$. Not surprisingly, as I discuss in chapter 6 section 6.3.2, and derive again below, the degree of increasing returns increases with the share of intermediates.[9] It is the source of the increasing returns property that reflects the value of a variety of intermediates. The specialization argument continues to hold in such a setting, too.

The observational equivalence between the reduced forms of the two distinct approaches, the real externality in Henderson-type models, examined in chapter 6, section 6.3.2, and the pecuniary externality of the Dixit–Stiglitz monopolistic competition model, is indicative of why estimation of the sources of the urban externality is similar to problems posed by social interactions models. Both approaches may explain increasing returns to aggregate economic activity (or density) and may well coexist as forces of generating value from proximity. A moment's reflection suggests that the aggregation of outputs of monopolistically competitive firms is conceptually akin to a social effect, in this case a cross effect from the range of activity in another part of the economy. In the remainder of the chapter, I adopt the Dixit–Stiglitz model, as adapted by Krugman and Anas and Xiong (2003), as the main model. At the same time, the Anas and Xiong (2003) model also reflects key tenets of Henderson's system-of-cities approach in the definition of cities as separate entities.

7.3.1 Urban Specialization: Simple Arguments

Suppose that an economy offers a large number of potential sites for cities. Each city may accommodate simultaneously several industries producing different final goods. Production takes place in the central business district, and consequently workers who commute to work from their residences incur costs in terms of time. In the simplest possible model, commuting time is proportional to commuting distance from the central business district, and thus the labor supply net of commuting costs in a city depends upon the total population. That is, any given population requires space to be accommodated, and therefore commuting costs are involved. Services from land are consumed as housing and not used directly in production. Under the assumption that final goods are freely traded across different cities within the economy and intermediate inputs may be used within each city only, one can show by means of a simple argument that each city has an incentive to specialize in a single final good at equilibrium. I consider next the specialization argument first and then turn to an account of city geography and congestion.

Suppose, for the sake of the argument, that several final goods sectors coexist in city ℓ. Free entry implies that the total labor cost of industry J, $W_{J\ell}H_{J\ell}$, where $W_{J\ell}$ denotes the wage rate paid by industry J in city ℓ, is equal to the revenue of the industry producing good J, $P_J\, Y_{J\ell}$:$W_{J\ell}H_{J\ell} = P_J\, Q_{J\ell}$, where P_J denotes the price of industry J's output. By recalling the production function just introduced, we have that $Q_{J\ell} = \bar{q}(H_{J\ell})^{\frac{\sigma_J}{\sigma_J-1}}$. Therefore, $W_\ell = P_J\,\bar{q}(H_{J\ell})^{\frac{1}{\sigma_J-1}}$. Spatial equilibrium implies that wages are equalized for each kind of labor. Assume that such an allocation of labor prevails and consider a small perturbation of employment across sectors. It follows that sectors that gain employment experience growth in productivity because they may avail themselves of a greater range of intermediates. Workers' net incomes also go up making it easier for firms to attract workers to the city. Thus, each city is better off by specializing in a single good.

The essence of the argument survives in more complicated models and, more importantly, under different institutional and market structures. This is already evident by comparison with the classic Henderson derivation. Central to all these applications is the notion, eloquently expounded by Chipman (1970), that just as firms may treat market prices parametrically, they may also treat production functions and their determinants parametrically.[10]

A complementary perspective on specialization is offered by Duranton and Puga (2000) who emphasize the fact that specialized and diversified cities coexist in the same economy, with larger cities being more diversified but with specialized cities persisting nonetheless. In contrast to the static conceptualization of specialization that I invoke earlier in the section, Duranton and Puga emphasize that the constant industrial churning that goes on in cities is closely underpinning innovation. These authors link the high rate of plant turnover with innovations, with most of them taking place in diversified cities, while most relocations are from diversified to specialized cities. These authors seek to establish this fact by employing a novel French data set that tracks the relocation of establishments across France. Duranton and Puga (2001) further pursue this stylized fact and offer a theoretical model of diversified cities serving as innovation nurseries. Localization economies and congestion costs combine to generate advantages to urban specialization for activities that have been spawned in diversified cities. However, whereas it is attractive for innovating firms to operate in diversified cities while in their learning stages, this nursery advantage is no longer operative when firms' profitable operations depend on availing themselves of localization economies that are relevant for firms using the same process. I return to this issue in chapter 8.

7.3.2 Basic Trade-offs: City Geometry, Productivity, and City Size

I consider next the important urban fact that individuals need to travel to their workplaces from their residences. This brings into the problem congestion and the role of land and the city geometry. In the simplest possible case, each resident demands a fixed amount of land for housing, set at 1 for simplicity. If individuals commute to the CBD and the city extends circularly around it, a city of N residents has a radius of $\pi^{-1/2}N^{1/2}$. If individuals are endowed with one unit of leisure and one unit of distance traveled costs κ' units of time, then an individual who travels distance r to the CBD is left with $1-\kappa' r$ units of time to work. Therefore, the net labor supply of a city with N residents is

$$H_c(N) = \int_0^{\pi^{-1/2}N^{1/2}} 2\pi r(1-\kappa' r)dr = N\left(1-\kappa N^{1/2}\right), \qquad (7.2)$$

where $\kappa \equiv \frac{2}{3}\pi^{-1/2}\kappa'$. City geometry alone implies trade-offs. For example, given commuting cost parameter κ, a city's labor force is maximized at $N = \left(\frac{2}{3}\right)^2 \kappa^{-2}$, for which the total net labor supply is $\frac{1}{3}N$. Not surprisingly, $H_c(N)$ is decreasing in unit commuting costs.

Spatial equilibrium within the city obtains when labor income net of land rent is independent of location. This along with the assumption that the opportunity cost of land is 0, and therefore the land rent at the fringe of the city is also equal to 0, yields an equilibrium land rental function

$$R(r) = \kappa'(\pi^{-1/2}N^{1/2} - r)W. \tag{7.3}$$

It is convenient to close the model of a single city and to express all magnitudes in terms of city size. Assuming that all land rents are redistributed to city residents, total rents may be written in terms of the number of residents as follows:

$$\int_0^{\pi^{-1/2}N^{1/2}} 2\pi r R(r) dr = \frac{1}{2}\kappa W N^{3/2}. \tag{7.4}$$

This yields the per capita income, the sum of labor income net of individual commuting costs plus redistributed land rentals divided by N, as

$$\Upsilon(N) = \left(1 - \kappa N^{1/2}\right) W. \tag{7.5}$$

With a given wage rate, individual income declines with city size entirely because of congestion. At the labor supply maximizing city size, $\Upsilon(N) = \frac{1}{3}W$.

The richness of the model is underscored by recognizing that the wage rate itself depends on city size. The analysis in section 7.3.1 implies that the wge rate in industry J in city ℓ is given by

$$W_{J\ell} = P_J N_\ell^{\frac{1}{\sigma_J - 1}} \left(1 - \kappa N_\ell^{1/2}\right)^{\frac{1}{\sigma_J - 1}}. \tag{7.6}$$

It follows that the income per person is given by combining (7.5) and (7.6):

$$\Upsilon_\ell(N_\ell) = P_J N_\ell^{\frac{1}{\sigma_J - 1}} \left(1 - \kappa N_\ell^{1/2}\right)^{\frac{\sigma_J}{\sigma_J - 1}}. \tag{7.7}$$

These results express the key trade-offs associated with equilibrium city size: intracity transport costs (congestion) versus agglomeration economies. Free movement of labor leads to a city size that maximizes income per person while taking the good's price as given. This size is given by

$$N_J^* = \left(\frac{2\frac{1}{\sigma_J - 1}}{1 + 3\frac{1}{\sigma_J - 1}}\right)^2 \frac{1}{\kappa^2}. \tag{7.8}$$

This is the system-of-cities argument in favor of specialization, adapted to the case of Dixit–Stiglitz technologies. Increasing commuting costs, as reflected in κ, reduce net labor supply as a function of the city's labor force, and thus equilibrium city size. Stronger agglomeration economies, as denoted by the smaller σ_J and thus a larger elasticity of the agglomeration effect, $\frac{1}{\sigma_J - 1}$, increase it. Naturally, income maximizing city size now reflects productivity-related parameters, as well.

According to this theory, at equilibrium, cities that are smaller than this size will experience an increase in the net income of their populations if they grow by attracting additional residents. On the other hand, cities that are larger than the output-maximizing size N_J^* are adversely affected by in-migration and therefore growth in their populations, while out-migration brings them closer to the equilibrium size. By the same token, for the demand for the product of each industry to be satisfied, if it exceeds the amount produced by an optimum-sized city, there has to be more than one city of the same type. This amount may be computed by using the expression for city size from (7.8) above in the expression for net labor supply from (7.2) to obtain

$$Y_J^* = \left(\frac{4\left(\frac{1}{\sigma_J - 1}\right)^2}{\left(\frac{\sigma_J}{\sigma_J - 1}\right)^2 \kappa^2} \right)^{\frac{\sigma_J}{\sigma_J - 1}}.$$

An important consequence of this result, which was emphasized by Rossi-Hansberg and Wright (2007), albeit in a different but effectively equivalent formulation, is that introducing the margin of satisfying increased output demand by means of optimum-sized cities exhausts agglomeration economies at the city level and leads to effectively constant returns to scale at the aggregate level of the economy. Intuitively, this is exactly like a competitive industry equilibrium with free entry, when firms' cost curves are U-shaped. In a competitive industry with free entry in such a case, price is equal to minimum average cost, which is also equal to marginal cost exactly where increasing returns are offset by decreasing returns. Demand is satisfied by, in effect, firms' supplying "chunks" of output equal to the respective average-cost minimizing quantity.

How do we know that cities are in fact at their equilibrium size? Some of the parameters that determine the equilibrium value may be affected by local, regional, or national government policies. Or might be cities too large or too small? Au and Henderson (2006), who estimate (using Chinese city data), a U-shaped relationship of real income per worker as a function of employment, find that migration restrictions keep Chinese cities too small. Desmet and Rossi-Hansberg (2011) confirm this view. See chapter 8, section 8.5.7, for a more detailed discussion of their argument.

7.3.3 Equilibrium versus Socially Optimal City Size

As I discuss in chapter 1, section 1.2, the long history of preoccupation with optimum city size goes at least as far back as Plato and Aristotle (Papageorgiou and Pines 2000, 520). Plato's (ca. 360 BC) *Laws* sets optimal city size precisely at 5,040. *Laws* includes a proscription with severe penalties against these citizens being retail traders or merchants, thus putting the classical view at great variance with the modern one! Dixit (1973) poses the planner's problem for an "optimum factory town" in terms of the trade-off between economies of scale in production in the CBD and the diseconomies of congestion in commuter transport and discusses its decentralized implementation by suitable taxes and transfers. The concept was also examined by Mirrlees (1972). Henderson (1974) introduces the system-of-cities viewpoint.

7.3.3.1 *Socially Optimal Factory Towns*

I adapt the Dixit–Mirrlees approach to examine the efficient, that is, socially optimal, city size in the case of the production setting just introduced. I start with production but continue simplifying the production function by leaving out raw labor in order to emphasize the component that generates increasing returns. Each differentiated good is produced (as a result of symmetry) in the same quantity z, its production requires total labor of $H_z = f + cz$, and the number of differentiated goods is $m^* = \frac{H_c}{f+cz}$. The problem of maximizing output, given the quantity of total available labor, H_c, is

$$\mathcal{Q}_J^* = \max_z : \left[\sum_m^{\frac{H_c}{f+cz}} z_m^{1-\frac{1}{\sigma_J}} \right]^{\frac{\sigma_J}{\sigma_J-1}} = \max_z : \left(\frac{H_c}{f+cz} \right)^{\frac{\sigma_J}{\sigma_J-1}} z.$$

Solving the above maximization problem yields that, at the optimum, each differentiated good is produced at $z^* = (\sigma_J - 1)\frac{f}{c}$(requiring labor $H_z^* = \sigma f$), which coincides with the equilibrium solution in the case of an autarkic city.[11] Optimal city size coincides with the quantity that maximizes net labor supply, $N_o = \left(\frac{2}{3}\right)^2 \kappa^{-2}$, and thus is determined entirely by commuting costs that reflect city geography. This quantity exceeds the equilibrium city size N_ℓ^* derived above because it ignores the dependence of wages on net labor supply.

Allowing for intercity trade improves efficiency because of the importance of variety in production. I provide a normative framework for the analysis that follows by assuming that intermediates produced in each city are shipped to all other cities that produce the same good. Shipping is subject to iceberg transport costs—when one unit of an intermediate good is shipped from one to another city, only a fraction τ, $0 < \tau < 1$, of the quantity shipped survives while the rest "melts away" during shipping. In order to concentrate on production and avoid effects via the terms of trade, I examine the optimal production plan under the assumption that goods' prices are given as if all goods are internationally traded. Given a national population $\overline{N}$ and ignoring integer constraints, numbers and sizes of different types of cities satisfy the following:

$$\sum_J n_J N_J = \overline{N}. \qquad (7.9)$$

Given symmetry, the number of intermediates used by all cities of type J is given by $\frac{H_c}{f+cz}$, where each differentiated product is used where it is produced and in all the other $n_J - 1$ cities,

$$z = z_d + (n_J - 1)\frac{z_{d'}}{\tau}.$$

Optimal output for good J, when city populations are given, is obtained by solving:

$$\max_{z_d, z_{d'}} : n_J \left(\frac{H_c}{f + c\left(z_d + (n_J - 1)\frac{z_{d'}}{\tau}\right)} \right)^{\frac{\sigma_J}{\sigma_J - 1}} \left[z_d^{1-\frac{1}{\sigma_J}} + (n_J - 1) z_{d'}^{1-\frac{1}{\sigma_J}} \right]^{\frac{\sigma_J}{\sigma_J - 1}}.$$

From the necessary conditions for $z_d, z_{d'}$ it follows that $z_{d'} = \tau^{\sigma_J} z_d$. This simplifies the expression for each city's output, and the planner's national output maximizing problem becomes

$$\max_{z_d} : n_J \delta_J^{\frac{\sigma_J}{\sigma_J - 1}} \left(\frac{H_c}{f + c\delta_J z_d} \right)^{\frac{\sigma_J}{\sigma_J - 1}} z_d,$$

where $\delta_J = 1 + (n_J - 1)\tau^{\sigma_J - 1}$. This yields $z_d^* = \frac{1}{\delta_J}(\sigma_J - 1)\frac{f}{c}$ (requiring labor $H_z^* = \sigma f$), an expression that, as we see below, again coincides with the equilibrium solution in the case of trading cities.

I now turn to optimizing with respect to city populations, which highlights the trade-off between city production capacity and a variety of intermediates. Assuming that prices are given, the necessary conditions for choosing the sizes and numbers of cities so as to maximize the value of national production,

$$\sum_J \bar{q}_J^* n_J P_J \left[1 + (n_J - 1)\tau^{\sigma_J - 1}\right]^{\frac{\sigma_J}{\sigma_J - 1}} N_J^{\frac{1}{\sigma_J - 1}} (1 - \kappa_J N_J^{\frac{1}{2}})^{\frac{\sigma_J}{\sigma_J - 1}}, \tag{7.10}$$

where $\bar{q}_J^*$ is a function of parameters and unit commuting costs that depend on city type, subject to constraint (7.9), are obtained in the usual fashion. Let LM denote the Lagrange multiplier corresponding to (7.9). The necessary conditions for the size and number of cities of type J are, respectively, as follows:

$$\bar{q}_J^* P_J \left[1 + (n_J - 1)\tau^{\sigma_J - 1}\right]^{\frac{\sigma_J}{\sigma_J - 1}} \left[1 - \kappa_J \frac{1 + \frac{3}{\sigma_J - 1}}{\frac{2}{\sigma_J - 1}} N_J^{1/2} \right]$$
$$\times N_J^{\frac{1}{\sigma_J - 1}} (1 - \kappa_J N_J^{1/2})^{\frac{\sigma_J}{\sigma_J - 1}} = \text{LM}; \tag{7.11}$$

$$\frac{\bar{q}_J^*}{\sigma_J - 1} P_J \left(1 + \frac{n_J \tau^{\sigma_J - 1}}{1 + (n_J - 1)\tau^{\sigma_J - 1}} \right) \left[1 + (n_J - 1)\tau^{\sigma_J - 1}\right]^{\frac{\sigma_J}{\sigma_J - 1}}$$
$$\times N_J^{\frac{1}{\sigma_J - 1}} (1 - \kappa_J N_J^{1/2})^{\frac{\sigma_J}{\sigma_J - 1}} = \text{LM}\, N_J; \tag{7.12}$$

It readily follows from (7.11) that optimal city size is smaller than the income-maximizing size according to (7.8). The smaller the divergence between those two magnitudes, the higher the price. Dividing (7.11) by (7.12) yields

$$(\sigma_J - 1) \frac{1 - \kappa_J N_J^{1/2}}{1 + \frac{n_J \tau^{\sigma_J - 1}}{1 + (n_J - 1)\tau^{\sigma_J - 1}}} = \frac{1}{N_J}.$$

It thus follows that the larger the divergence, the greater the number of cities of the same type. Intercity shipments of intermediate varieties generate a force in favor of a smaller city populations so as to enhance the variety available to all cities. Given n_J, there exists a unique optimal value of N_J. The larger n_J, the smaller the respective city size. The socially optimal (in the sense of maximizing the value of national output) city size decreases with unit commuting cost κ. The presence of urban congestion ensures that there exist several cities of all types. Unfortunately, it is not possible to determine how, in general, the optimal values for the size and number of each city type vary with national population.

The national planner's problem optimizes with respect to two types of interrelated coordination problems. One, the familiar one, is inherent in the presence of agglomeration economies in the form of increasing returns to city production. The second, and newer, one rationalizes intercity spillovers as resulting from the varieties of intermediates. Can the national planner's problem be implemented? This planner's problem suggests how governments may help solve the coordination problem endemic to city formation in economies where agents may locate at several alternative destinations. The first coordination problem has been addressed by the system-of-cities literature[12] by invoking "large agents," profit-seeking entrepreneurs who subsidize factors to encourage the internalization of externalities and thereby coordinate location decisions. Grossman and Rossi-Hansberg (2010) offer an alternative mechanism for coordination. One could extend their conclusions about trade with many industries to agglomeration with many cities. As they put it, by engaging in Bertrand competition, firms recognize that by locating at a suitable site they can operate as "one-company towns." Such producers are still small in relation to the aggregate economy if the number of towns is large. Their setting is slightly different, but the coordination problem that has to do with spillovers via the variety of intermediates is a key property of the production setting and therefore does not involve additional informational assumptions. I discuss in chapter 9, section 9.8, below, the role that Henderson and Venables (2009) show is played by commitments made by forward-looking housing builders, who anticipate future city growth and rising productivity, to solving the coordination problem that is endemic to city formation.

Both city land rental and city individual income functions depend on the city-specific wage rate. This will in turn be shown to depend on whether or not a city is engaged in intercity trade. Therefore, in addition to the returns-to-scale properties at the local level, rents and individual incomes reflect economywide magnitudes as a result of the economy's urban structure.

7.3.3.2 *Socially Optimal Diversified Cities*

An alternative arrangement is for each city to host all of the industries, in which case the economy will consist of a number of identical cities. Let z_J denote the quantity of each intermediate used by industry J, $J = X, Y$, and let both industries use the same range of intermediates. Since each intermediate requires a total amount of labor $f + c(z_X + z_Y)$, the total number of intermediates produced is given by $\frac{H_c}{f+c(z_X+z_Y)}$. For comparability with the socially optimal factory towns above, I express the counterpart here of the planner's problem (7.10) as setting z_X, z_Y, so as to maximize the value of a diversified city's production as

$$\sum_J P_J \left(\frac{H_c}{f + c\sum_J z_J}\right)^{\frac{\sigma_J}{\sigma_J - 1}} z_J, \tag{7.13}$$

where prices are exogenous and play only an auxiliary role. The first-order conditions yield, for the special case of two final goods X, Y, and $\sigma_X = \sigma_Y = \sigma$, the result that $z_X + z_Y = \frac{f}{c}$. This yields $\frac{H_c}{2f}$ as the socially optimal number of intermediates to be used in production, which is different from the previous results in the present section. This implies an intermediates demand by each of the industries according to

$$z_X = \frac{f}{c} - (2-\sigma)\frac{f}{c}\frac{1}{\sigma - \frac{P_Y}{P_X}}, \quad z_Y = (2-\sigma)\frac{f}{c}\frac{1}{\sigma - \frac{P_Y}{P_X}}.$$

This solution applies under the conditions $\frac{P_Y}{P_X} < \sigma < 2$ or $\frac{P_Y}{P_X} > \sigma > 2$. I obtain the socially optimal allocation by setting the price ratio equal to the marginal rate of substitution between X and Y at the values of output per capita for each of the two goods and for the special case of the Cobb–Douglas utility function,

$$U = X^{\alpha} Y^{1-\alpha}, \tag{7.14}$$

that I employ in the remainder of the chapter. The socially optimal allocations of intermediates to the two industries are:

$$z_X^* = \frac{\alpha + (\sigma - 1)(1-\alpha)}{\alpha + \sigma(1-\alpha)}\frac{f}{c}, \quad z_Y^* = \frac{1-\alpha}{\alpha + \sigma(1-\alpha)}\frac{f}{c}.$$

This allows me to compare with the competitive outcome for a diversified, that is to say autarkic, urban economy, which I develop below in section 7.4.3. From the socially optimal quantities of output, $X^* = \left(\frac{H_c}{2f}\right)^{\frac{\sigma}{\sigma-1}} z_X^*$, $Y^* = \left(\frac{H_c}{2f}\right)^{\frac{\sigma}{\sigma-1}} z_Y^*$, per capita consumptions readily follow. The socially optimal city size maximizes utility and thus coincides here with the quantity that maximizes net labor supply per person, H_c, as per equation (7.2) above.

7.4 SPECIALIZATION, DIVERSIFICATION, AND INTERCITY TRADE

Central to market-based views of cities is the notion that urban economies are affected profoundly by the existence of intercity trade in addition to trade with their hinterlands. To the extent that they are open economic entities, cities sell goods in whose production they specialize, and they buy goods from cities that specialize in other goods. Yet, not all cities specialize. The original literature on the system-of-cities model is set in terms of international trade theory. Yet, with the notable exception of studies by Henderson (1987, 1988) and by Rossi-Hansberg and Wright (2007), which are discussed at length in chapter 9, where aspects of intercity trade are analyzed, there have been few newer in-depth developments of the theory in its original formulation that allow for intercity trade. The original system-of-cities approach overlooked the modeling of trading costs and underemphasized national space considerations.

Cities may not always be truly open economic entities for several reasons: one, the presence of outright restrictions on city economic activities, as in the communist economic systems of the former Soviet Union, Eastern Europe, and the contemporary People's Republic of China, including the latter's restrictions on intercity migration [the *houkou* system; see (Au and Henderson 2006)]. Two, professional licensing laws and associated restrictions present in interstate trade even within the United States and among the members of the European Union naturally encumber trade in services. Such restrictions may be circumvented by large firms that maintain branches in different cities, states, and countries; law firms employing lawyers licensed to practice in several U.S. states is a case in point. Thus, it appears to be important to account for trading costs within the system-of-cities approach.

Interregional trade is central to the new economic geography approach, which has emphasized intercity trading costs (Fujita, Krugman, and Venables 1999), typically in the form of iceberg shipping costs.[13] This aside, the system-of-cities and the new economic geography approaches do not differ conceptually. The system-of-cities approach has emphasized specialization due to comparative advantage in relation to congestion costs. The new economic geography approach, on the other hand, motivates trade due to desire for product diversity. A drawback of the original new economic geography approach is that it overlooked city sizes and urban structure more generally. The newer literature has more than made up for this omission as becomes clear later in this chapter. Recently, a number of works have sought to combine the two approaches. See Tabuchi (1998).

What are the properties of the urban system in light of predictions based on the theory of international trade? If cities in market economies are completely free-trading entities, with free trade in goods and factor movements, then when a city moves from autarky to intercity trade, its economy undergoes structural change. For example, when all goods must be produced within each city, productive factors may be substituted for one another according to the production function. As Ventura (2005) shows, the effective elasticity of substitution between different productive factors, such as labor and physical capital, may change dramatically from unity to infinity when a region engages in interregional trade. It is the contribution of productive factors to income, with trading prices being determined in the entire economy, that matters for regional income. Since a city is small relative to an entire economy, the prices of tradable goods and factors are given to each city. It is not obvious that similar properties apply to an economy's cities when they move from autarky to intercity trade. Spatial equilibrium is also a key feature of the urban system in free economies. See Glaeser and Gottlieb (2009). By moving to congested cities factors may exacerbate congestion. At the same time, as we have already seen, the logic of the system-of-cities model is that individual cities may effectively be subject to capacity constraints.

The chapter seeks to modernize the predictions of the system-of-cities theory in the light of new trade theory and extend the basic model of specialization and intercity trade to the case of labor turnover and labor market frictions. It accomplishes the latter by adapting features of the Pissarides matching model to the study of urban unemployment. Raw labor is subject to exogenous turnover, and firms hire by announcing vacancies that are matched with unemployed workers searching for jobs. I present in section 7.8 below key empirical facts that help motivate the development of this new model. The same basic features of the model explain urban diversification.

7.4.1 Definition of Diversification and Specialization

I adopt the main model of Anas and Xiong (2003) and assume that city dwellers have identical preferences regarding bundles of goods and consume two final goods, $J = X, Y$. Both goods are manufactured using raw (unskilled) labor and a range of manufactured intermediates. The intermediates may be either produced and used only within each city, in which case they may be interpreted as varieties of skilled services, or produced and traded among all cities within an economy's urban system or even internationally. With two final goods and ranges of varieties of intermediates that are as numerous as different cities, several patterns of what is produced and where are possible. The two final goods may both be produced within each city along with the intermediates demanded by their production, a configuration that I refer to as *full autarky* or *full diversification*. I also refer to *partial autarky*, or *partial diversification*, the configuration whereby both types of final goods are produced in each city but intermediates are traded.

I define a city as *specialized* if it produces only one of the two *final goods* and imports the other final good from other cities in the economy or from abroad. In a large economy, several cities specialize in each of the two final goods. A city may produce only *intermediate goods* and import both final goods from other cities in the economy or the international market. Or a city may produce only one final good and import the second final good and the intermediates used to produce the first final good. Thus, a greater number of possibilities exists regarding patterns of specialization than when either only raw labor is used in production or only two final goods are produced. While it is elementary but tedious to account for all these different possibilities, it is still interesting to think of them in the context of urban hierarchies. Patterns of shipping costs, and geography more generally, may in fact make it attractive for some cities to rely on only a subset of other cities for final goods or for intermediates. It is also interesting to use them in order to model functional versus sectoral specialization.

7.4.2 Production Conditions for Final Goods

The production function for each of the manufactured goods exhibits constant returns to scale with respect to all of its inputs.[14] A firm producing tradable good X in city ℓ uses raw labor H_X and a range of intermediates indexed by m, $m = 1, \ldots, m_k$, in quantities $\{z_{d_{\ell 1}}, \ldots, z_{d_{\ell j}}, \ldots, z_{d_{\ell m_k}}\}$ purchased from city ℓ, $\ell = 1, \ldots, n$, to produce final good X:

$$X = H_X^{u_X} \left[\left(\sum_{\ell=1}^{n} \sum_{m=1}^{m_k} z_{d_{\ell m}}^{1-\frac{1}{\sigma}} \right)^{\frac{\sigma}{\sigma-1}} \right]^{1-u_X}, \quad 0 < u_X < 1, \ 1 < \sigma. \tag{7.15}$$

This exhibits constant returns to scale in for inputs. When formulated in this manner,[15] the CES component of the industry production function makes all intermediates essential for production when they are available for use, even though the elasticity of substitution among them is assumed to exceed 1. That is, the marginal product of an intermediate in use is infinite when the quantity employed tends to 0, and therefore each city either produces or buys intermediates from other cities when shipping costs are not prohibitive.

With identical cities of each type (identified by the pattern of specialization and diversification) and symmetry in intermediates, each X-city produces m types of intermediates, and the above production function may be simplified to become

$$X = H_X^{u_X} m_X^{(1-u_X)\frac{\sigma}{\sigma-1}} \left[\left(z_{d_{X,\ell}}^{1-\frac{1}{\sigma}} + (n_X - 1) z_{d_{X,-\ell}}^{1-\frac{1}{\sigma}} \right)^{\frac{\sigma}{\sigma-1}} \right]^{1-u_X}, \tag{7.16}$$

where $z_{d_{X,\ell}}$ is the quantity of intermediates produced in and demanded by city ℓ and $z_{d_{X,-\ell}}$ is the quantity of intermediates produced in a city other than ℓ, of which there are $n_X - 1$, and demanded by city ℓ. An important property of the production function above is now evident: productivity increases with the range of intermediates. It is for this reason that the range is sometimes referred to as the *technology*, chosen endogenously here. Similarly, at least one of the intermediates will be essential for production in all cities and must be produced somewhere in the economy.

With iceberg transport costs at rate τ—if one unit of an intermediate good is shipped from one city to another city, a fraction τ, $0 < \tau < 1$, survives—if the price of the intermediate good is P_Z when purchased where it is produced (f.o.b. price), buyers located in other cities pay $\frac{P_Z}{\tau}$ (c.i.f.).

Since the intermediates are used in manufacturing final goods, the economy experiences pecuniary externalities associated with the availability of intermediate varieties. There is no reason for two producers to manufacture the same good because the potential range of intermediates is unbounded and all enter symmetrically into the production functions for final goods. The producer of any variety enjoys an economywide monopoly.

What pattern of specialization is likely to prevail is not well defined a priori. It may even be totally indeterminate unless we impose some structure such as an equilibrium condition. For example, what does the pattern of specialization and associated city size look like under location equilibrium when individuals are indifferent as to where to locate? In an economy of the sort that I am examining, city sizes are interdependent. Interdependence arises because of the productivity effect emanating from the range of intermediates available to each urban economy, which may also be seen as pecuniary externalities associated with monopolistic competition. Patterns of production and trade also introduce interdependence because of the impact on the sizes of respective cities and of the incentives to specialize or diversify.

7.4.3 Equilibrium in a System of Fully Autarkic Cities

I explore the significance of intercity trade by assuming first that each city is fully autarkic and produces both final goods, X and Y, and consumes all of the outputs of the two industries. Good Y is produced, just like X, by using raw labor and a range m_{aut} of intermediates that are all produced in the city. That is,

$$\mathcal{Q}_J = H_J^{u_J}\left[\left(\sum_{m=1}^{m_{\text{aut}}} z_{dJm}^{1-\frac{1}{\sigma}}\right)^{\frac{\sigma}{\sigma-1}}\right]^{1-u_J}, \quad J = X, Y,$$

where z_{dJm} is the quantity of intermediate m, $m = 1, \ldots, m_{\text{aut}}$, demanded by industry J in the city. With symmetry, of course, all types of intermediates are produced in the same quantity, z_{dJ}, and within the city itself, in this fully autarkic case. As a result, the respective production functions are simplified to become

$$\mathcal{Q}_J = m_{\text{aut}}^{\frac{\sigma(1-u_J)}{\sigma-1}} H_J^{u_J} z_{dJ}^{1-u_J}, \quad J = X, Y. \tag{7.17}$$

The firms producing X, Y maximize profits by setting H_X, H_Y while taking prices P_X, P_Y as given, so as to satisfy

$$P_X\frac{u_X X}{H_X} = W = P_Y\frac{u_Y Y}{H_Y}; \tag{7.18}$$

they also set optimally the quantities of intermediates they use, z_{d_X}, z_{d_Y}. The first-order conditions are

$$P_X\frac{(1-u_X)X}{z_{d_X}} = m_{\text{aut}}P_z = P_Y\frac{(1-u_Y)Y}{z_{d_Y}}, \tag{7.19}$$

where the last two conditions follow after accounting for symmetry in the use of intermediates. Each such intermediate is produced and supplied in monopolistically competitive markets at price $P_z = \frac{\sigma}{\sigma-1}cW$, which is equal to the marked-up marginal cost cW. Under free entry, the quantity of each intermediate supplied is $z_m = z = f\frac{\sigma-1}{c}$, and the associated demand for labor by each firm producing it is $H_z = f + cz_s = f\sigma$.

From conditions (7.18) and (7.19) I express the derived demand for each intermediate in terms of the respective amount of the raw labor demand, $z_{d_X} = H_X\frac{1-u_X}{u_X}\frac{1}{m_{\text{aut}}\frac{\sigma c}{\sigma-1}}$. This leads to a system of equations for the raw labor demands. The first expresses that the demand for raw labor by the production of intermediates equals supply (indirectly via the raw labor content of intermediates):

$$\frac{1-u_X}{u_X}H_X + \frac{1-u_Y}{u_Y}H_Y = f\sigma m_{\text{aut}}; \tag{7.20}$$

the demand for raw labor by the production of the two final goods equals the total labor supply net of the demand for intermediate production,

$$H_X + H_Y = H_c - f\sigma m_{\text{aut}}, \tag{7.21}$$

where H_c denotes the total labor supply in city c. Solving the system of equations (7.20) and (7.21) with respect to the raw labor demands by the production of final goods (H_X, H_Y) yields

$$H_X = u_X\frac{(1-u_Y)H_c - m_{\text{aut}}f\sigma}{u_X - u_Y}, \quad H_Y = u_Y\frac{-(1-u_X)H_c + m_{\text{aut}}f\sigma}{u_X - u_Y}. \tag{7.22}$$

I solve for the raw labor demands (H_X, H_Y) and the range of intermediates m_{aut} as follows. The demands for final goods X and Y satisfy $\frac{\alpha}{1-\alpha}\frac{P_Y}{P_X} = \frac{X}{Y}$. From this and (7.18), we have $\frac{H_X}{H_Y} = \frac{\alpha u_X}{(1-\alpha)u_Y}$. Substituting the latter in (7.22) yields the equilibrium value of the range of intermediates, and the demands for raw labor and for differentiated intermediates then follow:

$$m_{\text{aut}} = [\alpha(1-u_X) + (1-\alpha)(1-u_Y)]\frac{H_c}{f\sigma}; \tag{7.23}$$

$$H_X = \alpha u_X H_c, \quad H_Y = (1-\alpha)u_Y H_c. \tag{7.24}$$

The portions of raw labor allocated to the production of final goods fall below the respective quantities in the case of specialization. Solving for z_{d_X}, z_{d_Y} yields:

$$\begin{aligned} z_{d_X} &= \frac{(\sigma-1)f}{c}\frac{\alpha(1-u_X)}{\alpha(1-u_X) + (1-\alpha)(1-u_Y)}, \\ z_{d_Y} &= \frac{(\sigma-1)f}{c}\frac{(1-\alpha)(1-u_Y)}{\alpha(1-u_X) + (1-\alpha)(1-u_Y)}. \end{aligned} \tag{7.25}$$

When applied with (7.18) and (7.19), these solutions yield expressions for real price ratios in terms of city labor supply and parameters:

$$\frac{P_X}{W} = \lambda_X^{-1}[\alpha(1-u_X) + (1-\alpha)(1-u_Y)]^{-\frac{1-u_X}{\sigma-1}}(1-u_X)^{-\frac{1-u_X}{\sigma-1}}H_c^{-\frac{1-u_X}{\sigma-1}},$$

$$\frac{P_Y}{W} = \lambda_Y^{-1}[\alpha(1-u_X) + (1-\alpha)(1-u_Y)]^{-\frac{1-u_Y}{\sigma-1}}(1-u_Y)^{-\frac{1-u_Y}{\sigma-1}}H_c^{-\frac{1-u_Y}{\sigma-1}},$$

where the constants λ_X, λ_Y are defined as follows:

$$\lambda_J = \left(\frac{1-u_J}{f\sigma}\right)^{\frac{\sigma-u_J}{\sigma-1}} \left(\frac{u_J}{1-u_J}\frac{c\sigma}{\sigma-1}\right)^{u_J} \frac{f(\sigma-1)}{c}, \quad J = X, Y. \tag{7.26}$$

An interesting property of the result is that the prices of both goods, relative to the wage rate, are decreasing in the city labor supply. This economies-of-scale effect are due to the positive pecuniary externalities associated with the monopolistic competition model.

The total output for the two goods follow from (7.17):

$$X_{\text{aut}} = \alpha\lambda_X \tilde{\Lambda}^{\frac{1-u_X}{\sigma-1}} (1-u_X)^{\frac{1-u_X}{\sigma-1}} H_c^{\frac{\sigma-u_X}{\sigma-1}}, \tag{7.27}$$

$$Y_{\text{aut}} = (1-\alpha)\lambda_Y \tilde{\Lambda}^{\frac{1-u_Y}{\sigma-1}} (1-u_Y)^{\frac{1-u_Y}{\sigma-1}} H_c^{\frac{\sigma-u_Y}{\sigma-1}}, \tag{7.28}$$

where

$$\tilde{\Lambda} \equiv \alpha(1-u_X) + (1-\alpha)(1-u_Y) \tag{7.29}$$

is a constant. The indirect utility of a typical resident, $U = \left(\frac{P_X}{W}\right)^{-\alpha}\left(\frac{P_Y}{W}\right)^{-(1-\alpha)}\left[1-\kappa N^{1/2}\right]$, can now be expressed as

$$\tilde{U}_{\text{aut}}(N) = \lambda_X^{\alpha}\lambda_Y^{(1-\alpha)} \tilde{\Lambda}^{\frac{\tilde{\Lambda}}{\sigma-1}} N^{\frac{\tilde{\Lambda}}{\sigma-1}} \left(1-\kappa N^{1/2}\right)^{1+\frac{\tilde{\Lambda}}{\sigma-1}}. \tag{7.30}$$

In a system of fully autarkic cities, the equilibrium value of the price ratio is, not surprisingly, fully determined within each city and is a function of city-level magnitudes and parameters.

It is useful to think of the equilibrium size for diversified cities. Maximizing utility according to (7.30) yields

$$N^*_{\text{aut}} = \left(\frac{2\frac{\tilde{\Lambda}}{\sigma-1}}{1+3\frac{\tilde{\Lambda}}{\sigma-1}}\right)^2 \frac{1}{\kappa^2}. \tag{7.31}$$

Therefore, at the equilibrium city size, congestion costs enter the expressions for output X, Y and utility as total factor productivity terms, respectively: $\kappa^{-2\frac{1-u_X}{\sigma-1}}$, $\kappa^{-2\frac{1-u_Y}{\sigma-1}}$, and $\kappa^{-2\frac{\tilde{\Lambda}}{\sigma-1}}$. These follow from (7.27), (7.28), and (7.30), respectively, for the value of N^*_{aut} from (7.31). The difference from (7.8) is due to the fact that raw labor is also used here, thus increasing the desired size.

7.4.4 Cities Specialized in Final Goods

Let P_X and P_Y denote the prices of goods X and Y, respectively. Intermediates used in production may be produced locally in each city as well as purchased from other cities. I develop first what is a generic case when a city specializes in one of the final goods and also produces and trades intermediates. Below, I discuss further the cases where cities specialize in producing only one of final goods or only intermediates. The prices of the intermediates are endogenous because of the monopolistic market structure within which they are produced. In the development that follows, the prices of the final goods are exogenous to each city but are of course determined within the economy.

I solve for the endogenous variables by working with the profit of a firm producing good X in a particular city ℓ. The problem will be symmetric for a firm producing Y, and therefore I will not repeat it in full detail. A firm producing X chooses raw labor input H_X, and the quantities of each of all m_X varieties of intermediates available in the city, which are produced within city ℓ and imported from each of all $n_X - 1$ other cities that specialize in producing good X and trade intermediates among each other in quantities $(z_{d_\ell}, z_{d_{-\ell}})$, respectively, so as to maximize profits:

$$\max_{H_X, z_{d_\ell}, z_{d_{-\ell}}} \quad P_X X - m_X P_z z_{d_\ell} - (n_X - 1) m_X \frac{P_z}{\tau} z_{d_{-\ell}} - w_X H_X, \tag{7.32}$$

where X, as a function of all inputs, is given in (7.16).

The first-order conditions for raw labor for each of the intermediates produced within city ℓ and of intermediates imported from other cities are, respectively, as follows:

$$P_X \frac{u_X X}{H_X} = w_X; \tag{7.33}$$

$$P_X \frac{(1 - u_X) X}{z_{d_\ell}^{\frac{\sigma-1}{\sigma}} + (n_X - 1) z_{d_{-\ell}}^{\frac{\sigma-1}{\sigma}}} z_{d_\ell}^{\frac{-1}{\sigma}} = m_X P_z; \tag{7.34}$$

$$P_X \frac{(1 - u_X) X}{z_{d_\ell}^{\frac{\sigma-1}{\sigma}} + (n_X - 1) z_{d_{-\ell}}^{\frac{\sigma-1}{\sigma}}} z_{d_{-\ell}}^{\frac{-1}{\sigma}} = m_X \frac{P_z}{\tau}. \tag{7.35}$$

Each intermediate is produced with an increasing returns-to-scale technology, described in terms of a labor requirements function, $H_z = f + cz$, where f is the fixed labor requirement, c is the marginal labor requirement, and z is the output of the intermediate good. Monopoly pricing yields

$$P_z = \frac{\sigma}{\sigma - 1} c w_X. \tag{7.36}$$

Free entry into the market for each of the varieties of intermediates implies that each variety, wherever it might be produced, will be supplied at $z = (\sigma - 1)\frac{f}{c}$. The associated total demand for labor by a firm producing a variety thus is $H_z = f\sigma$. In each city, the total demand for each intermediate, which originates in city ℓ itself and in the other $n_X - 1$ cities that trade intermediates among themselves, must equal its supply,

$$z_{d_\ell} + (n_X - 1)\frac{1}{\tau} z_{d_{-\ell}} = (\sigma - 1)\frac{f}{c}. \tag{7.37}$$

By dividing equation (7.34) by (7.35), we have that $z_{d_{-\ell}} = \tau^{\sigma} z_{d_\ell}$. Consequently, from (7.37), we have

$$z_{d_\ell} = \frac{1}{\delta_X}(\sigma - 1)\frac{f}{c}, \quad z_{d_{-\ell}} = \frac{\tau^{\sigma}}{\delta_X}(\sigma - 1)\frac{f}{c}, \tag{7.38}$$

where the auxiliary variable δ_X, defined as

$$\delta_X = 1 + (n_X - 1)\tau^{\sigma-1}, \tag{7.39}$$

accounts for the combined effect of the variety of intermediates, made possible by the existence of several cities and weighted by shipping costs. For labor market equilibrium, the total labor demand by the firm manufacturing X and by the intermediates producing firms, must equal the total city the labor supply, H_c:

$$H_c = H_X + m_X H_z. \tag{7.40}$$

I show next that in each city the total labor supply is allocated as raw labor and labor employed by the intermediate-producing firms according to their respective shares in the production of good X. Consider equations (7.34) and (7.35), multiply each by z_{d_ℓ} and $z_{d_{-\ell}}$, respectively, and sum up. This yields

$$m_X \frac{\sigma}{\sigma - 1} c w_X \delta_X z_{d_\ell} = (1 - u_X) P_X X,$$

which after using (7.38) and (7.33) yields $m_X f \sigma = \frac{1-u_X}{u_X} H_X$. Consequently, $H_X = u_X H_c$ and $m_X H_z = (1 - u_X) H_c$. The range of intermediates follows:

$$m_X = \frac{1 - u_X}{f\sigma} H_c \tag{7.41}$$

and is therefore proportional to the city labor supply.

An expression for the output of good X, denoted also by X when no confusion arises, may be obtained from (7.34)–(7.36) by first solving for intermediates demands and then substituting into (7.16):

$$X = \lambda_X \delta_X^{\frac{1-u_X}{\sigma-1}} H_c^{\frac{\sigma-u_X}{\sigma-1}}, \tag{7.42}$$

where the auxiliary variable λ_X is defined as a function of parameters in (7.26). By using (7.42) and the solutions for the optimum quantities of inputs with (7.33), an expression for the wage rate may be obtained:

$$w_X = \lambda_X \delta_X^{\frac{1-u_X}{\sigma-1}} P_X H_c^{\frac{1-u_X}{\sigma-1}}, \tag{7.43}$$

which is increasing in city labor supply H_c. Note that the higher the share of intermediates in production, $1 - u_X$, the higher the degree of increasing returns. Since $\frac{\sigma-u_X}{\sigma-1} = 1 + \frac{1-u_X}{\sigma-1}$, this is true for both the output and the wage rate.

Let N_X denote the population of city ℓ specializing in X. The corresponding labor supply is given, according to (7.2), by $H_{c_\ell} = N_X(1 - \kappa N_X^{1/2})$. The output according to (7.42), the wage rate according to (7.43), and all other endogenous quantities including, in particular, individual income may be expressed in terms of the city population. For the wage rate, we have

$$w_X = \lambda_X \delta_X^{\frac{1-u_X}{\sigma-1}} P_X N_X^{\frac{1-u_X}{\sigma-1}} \left(1 - \kappa N_X^{1/2}\right)^{\frac{1-u_X}{\sigma-1}}. \tag{7.44}$$

The wage rate increases in the city population and in the number of cities. From this and (7.5) individual income in city ℓ follows as a function of (P_X, N_X):

$$\Upsilon_X(N_X) = \lambda_X P_X \left[(1 + (n_X - 1)\tau^{\sigma-1})\right]^{\frac{1-u_X}{\sigma-1}} N_X^{\frac{1-u_X}{\sigma-1}} \left(1 - \kappa N_X^{1/2}\right)^{\frac{\sigma-u_X}{\sigma-1}}. \tag{7.45}$$

To preferences defined in (7.14) there corresponds an indirect utility function, as a function of the prices of final goods (P_X, P_Y) and income Υ, given by

$$U = \alpha^{\alpha}(1-\alpha)^{1-\alpha} P_X^{-\alpha} P_Y^{-(1-\alpha)} \Upsilon. \tag{7.46}$$

Therefore, given prices for the two final goods (P_X, P_Y), the maximum utility enjoyed by a typical resident of a city of type X is

$$U_{\text{spec-}X} = \lambda_X \left(\frac{P_X}{P_Y}\right)^{1-\alpha} \left[1 + (n_X - 1)\tau^{\sigma-1}\right]^{\frac{1-u_X}{\sigma-1}} N_X^{\frac{1-u_X}{\sigma-1}} \left(1 - \kappa N_X^{1/2}\right)^{\frac{\sigma-u_X}{\sigma-1}}. \tag{7.47}$$

Not surprisingly, utility increases in the price of good X relative to that of good Y, the terms of trade for a city specializing in the production of good X. The utility enjoyed by residents of a city specializing in the production of good Y is defined symmetrically as

$$U_{\text{spec-}Y} = \lambda_Y \left(\frac{P_X}{P_Y}\right)^{-\alpha} \left[1 + (n_Y - 1)\tau^{\sigma-1}\right]^{\frac{1-u_Y}{\sigma-1}} N_Y^{\frac{1-u_Y}{\sigma-1}} \left(1 - \kappa N_Y^{1/2}\right)^{\frac{\sigma-u_Y}{\sigma-1}}. \tag{7.48}$$

It is important to review the principal effects that urban structure has on income in a city and the utility enjoyed by residents. From (7.47) and (7.48) city sizes, defined as city populations, of different city types and their numbers affect individual welfare directly. Where do these effects originate? One effect is the beneficial impact of an increased variety of intermediates, which is made possible with a larger labor supply, on the productivity of final goods. From (7.16), the greater the range, the greater the output. This reduces the effective price of city-produced goods and makes the real wage rate, from (7.44), an increasing function of city labor supply. Welfare increases with the number of cities in the economy, n_X or n_Y, because of the increased variety of intermediates being produced and traded among cities. This effect is moderated by the impact of intercity transport costs: the lower the transport costs, the greater the number of shipped goods that survive and the better off city residents are. The second effect reflects the impact of (intracity) commuting costs: as the size of the city increases, so do commuting costs, as people have to commute over longer distances. These effects are neatly expressed jointly in terms of the two factors that are functions of city population N_J, $J = X, Y$ in the expressions for utility above. I also discuss below the effects of a city's terms of trade. A larger national population has to be accommodated in a larger number of cities.

It is straightforward to obtain the value of a city's population that maximizes indirect utility, according to (7.47) for a city of type X, or to (7.48) for a city of type Y, when all effects are being accounted for while the prices and the numbers of cities are taken as given. The result is

$$N_J^* = \left(\frac{2\omega_J}{1+3\omega_J}\right)^2 \frac{1}{\kappa^2}, \quad \omega_J \equiv \frac{1-u_J}{\sigma-1}, \quad J = X, Y. \tag{7.49}$$

All the expressions involving the term $1 - \kappa(N_J^*)^{1/2}$ are simplified because its value at the optimum value of N_J^* above is simply $\frac{1+\omega_J}{1+3\omega_J}$. Therefore, commuting costs enter as a (negative) total factor productivity parameter via κ. I exploit this result further in chapter 9 below. If a J-city's population is below N_J^*, new entrants will raise utility. If, on the other hand, a J-city's population exceeds N_J^*, then current residents' pursuits of greater utility elsewhere in the economy will raise utility in the city in question. These city populations will prevail in an open-city equilibrium where the number of cities of either type is endogenous.

7.4.5 Equilibrium in a System of Partly Autarkic Cities

I highlight the significance of intercity trade in intermediates by returning to the assumption of section 7.4.3 that each city produces both final goods, X and Y, and consumes all the outputs of those two industries. However, by allowing for the manufactured intermediates to be traded within the same industry that uses them but across all cities, I may also examine the effect of trade in final goods over and above trade in intermediates.[16]

The details follow pretty much the earlier derivations, except that now I want to account for labor demand by the domestic production of intermediates, some of which are used within the city and the remainder exported. For symmetry with the fully autarkic case, I assume that there is a total of n cities. To conform with the rest of the set of possibilities, I retain $n_X + n_Y = n$ and assume that n_X of all cities trade intermediates only among each other and so do the remaining n_Y cities. For consistency with the case of specialized cities, each diversified city in the sense of this section produces two types of intermediates, one type to be used by the X-industry within the city and the remainder of the $n_X - 1$ cities, and the other to be used by the Y-industry within the city and the remainder of the $n_Y - 1$ cities.

Within a particular city among those n_X cities, each of the type X intermediates produced are demanded by the X-good industries in quantity $\frac{1-u_X}{u_X} H_X \frac{1}{m_X \delta_X c \frac{\sigma}{\sigma-1}}$. Similarly, within a particular city among the n_Y cities, each of the type Y intermediates produced is demanded by the Y-good industries in quantity $\frac{1-u_Y}{u_Y} H_Y \frac{1}{m_Y \delta_Y c \frac{\sigma}{\sigma-1}}$. In addition, each of the other $n_X - 1$ cities demands $\frac{1-u_X}{u_X} H_X \frac{1}{m_X \delta_X c \frac{\sigma}{\sigma-1}} \tau^{\sigma-1}$ and $\frac{1-u_Y}{u_Y} H_Y \frac{1}{m_Y c \delta_Y \frac{\sigma}{\sigma-1}} \tau^{\sigma-1}$, respectively.

Manipulating the first-order conditions yields the following two conditions:

$$m_X \sigma f = \frac{1-u_X}{u_X} H_X, \ m_Y \sigma f = \frac{1-u_Y}{u_Y} H_Y.$$

The condition for equilibrium in the market for raw labor now becomes

$$H_X + \frac{1-u_X}{u_X} H_X + H_Y + \frac{1-u_Y}{u_Y} H_Y = H_c. \tag{7.50}$$

A condition involving H_X, H_Y may be obtained as before. The demands for final goods X and Y satisfy $\frac{\alpha}{1-\alpha}\frac{P_Y}{P_X} = \frac{X}{Y}$. Using the first-order conditions for raw labor demands then yields $\alpha u_X H_Y = (1-\alpha) u_Y H_X$, which along with (7.50) allows us to solve for raw labor demands and ranges of intermediates:

$$H_X = \alpha u_X H_c, \ H_Y = (1-\alpha) u_Y H_c, \tag{7.51}$$

$$m_X = \alpha(1-u_X)\frac{H_c}{f\sigma}, \ m_Y = (1-\alpha)(1-u_Y)\frac{H_c}{f\sigma}. \tag{7.52}$$

I note that the allocation of raw labor to the two final goods industries in each city is the same as under full autarky, and so is the total allocation to intermediates production, although that production is shared by the two industries in the manner specified above.

Intermediates are used by the two industries in each of the n_X cities in quantities

$$z_{d_X} = \frac{f(\sigma-1)}{c}\frac{1}{\delta_X}, \ z_{d_Y} = \frac{f(\sigma-1)}{c}\frac{1}{\delta_Y}. \tag{7.53}$$

The total output for the two goods is given from (7.17):

$$X_{\text{p-aut}} = \alpha \lambda_X \tilde{\Lambda}^{\frac{1-u_X}{\sigma-1}} \delta_X^{\frac{1-u_X}{\sigma-1}} (n_X)(1-u_X)^{\frac{1-u_X}{\sigma-1}} H_c^{\frac{\sigma-u_X}{\sigma-1}}, \tag{7.54}$$

$$Y_{\text{p-aut}} = (1-\alpha) \lambda_Y \tilde{\Lambda}^{\frac{1-u_Y}{\sigma-1}} \delta_Y^{\frac{1-u_Y}{\sigma-1}} (n_Y)(1-u_Y)^{\frac{1-u_Y}{\sigma-1}} H_c^{\frac{\sigma-u_Y}{\sigma-1}}, \tag{7.55}$$

where $\tilde{\Lambda}$ is defined as above.

The indirect utility of a typical resident, $U = \left(\frac{P_X}{w}\right)^{-\alpha}\left(\frac{P_Y}{w}\right)^{-(1-\alpha)} \times \left[1 - \kappa N^{1/2}\right]$, depends upon a city's type J, which may be X or Y, and can now be expressed as

$$\tilde{U}_{\text{p-aut}}(N) = \tilde{u} \lambda_X^{\alpha} \lambda_Y^{1-\alpha} \tilde{\Lambda}^{\frac{\tilde{\Lambda}}{\sigma-1}} \delta_X{}^{\alpha\frac{1-u_X}{\sigma-1}} \delta_Y{}^{(1-\alpha)\frac{1-u_Y}{\sigma-1}} N^{\frac{\tilde{\Lambda}}{\sigma-1}} \left(1-\kappa N^{1/2}\right)^{1+\frac{\tilde{\Lambda}}{\sigma-1}}, \tag{7.56}$$

where $\tilde{u} \equiv (1-u_X)^{\alpha\frac{1-u_X}{\sigma-1}}(1-u_Y)^{(1-\alpha)\frac{1-u_Y}{\sigma-1}}$. In a system of fully autarkic cities, the equilibrium value of the price ratio is, not surprisingly, fully determined within each city. However, the outcome depends on the number of other cities because the availability of a larger variety of intermediates has advantageous welfare effects.

7.4.5.1 Full versus Partial Autarky

How do welfare outcomes under complete and partial autarky compare? Utilities at equilibrium under these alternative outcomes are given by (7.30) and (7.56), respectively. It is clear from the analytics that partial autarky with intercity trade of intermediates could easily dominate complete autarky because of the welfare effect of the greater variety of intermediates made possible by intercity trade in intermediates only.

From inspecting (7.56), it follows that the city size that maximizes the utility of city residents in the case of partial autarky coincides with that of full autarky, given in (7.31), provided that the number of cities is taken as given. At equilibrium, the number of cities is, of course, endogenous. In the absence of any intercity trade, the number of cities is simply given by the population divided by the optimum city size, given by (7.31). In the presence of intercity trade in intermediates, the number of cities is a function of the city size, $n_X = n_Y = n_{\text{p-aut}} = \frac{\overline{N}}{N}$. Let $N^*_{\text{p-aut}}$ denote the population that maximizes $\tilde{U}_{\text{p-aut}}(N)$:

$$\left(1 + \left(\frac{\overline{N}}{N} - 1\right)\tau^{\sigma-1}\right)^{\frac{\tilde{\Lambda}}{\sigma-1}} N^{\frac{\tilde{\Lambda}}{\sigma-1}} \left(1 - \kappa N^{\frac{1}{2}}\right)^{1+\frac{\tilde{\Lambda}}{\sigma-1}}. \tag{7.57}$$

It follows that $N^*_{\text{p-aut}} < N^*_{\text{aut}}$. City sizes should be smaller in the case of partial autarky, so as to allow a larger number of cities and thus a greater variety of intermediates to be traded among cities. Therefore, national urban planning that encourages intercity trade of intermediates should aim at smaller cities.

7.5 EQUILIBRIUM URBAN STRUCTURE WITH INTERCITY TRADE

I now examine urban structure when intermediates and final goods are traded among cities. There are n_X cities of type X and n_Y cities of type Y, with populations N_X, N_Y, respectively. I follow Anas and Xiong and assume that all cities of the same type trade differentiated intermediates with one another. I employ the results derived above in section 7.4.4. Final goods that are traded across cities are subject to shipping costs, with θ denoting the portion of the quantities of the final goods exported that arrives at an importing city, again an iceberg cost.

For the two city types, outputs and wage rates are

$$\begin{aligned} J &= \lambda_J \delta_J^{\frac{1-u_J}{\sigma-1}} N_J^{\frac{\sigma-u_J}{\sigma-1}} \left[1 - \kappa N_J^{1/2}\right]^{\frac{\sigma-u_J}{\sigma-1}}, \\ w_J &= P_J \lambda_J \delta_J^{\frac{1-u_J}{\sigma-1}} N_J^{\frac{1-u_J}{\sigma-1}} [1 - \kappa N_J^{1/2}]^{\frac{1-u_J}{\sigma-1}}, \end{aligned} \tag{7.58}$$

where $\delta_J \equiv 1 + (n_J - 1)\tau^{\sigma-1}$ expresses, as earlier, the combined effect of the variety of intermediates because of the availability of many cities specializing in the same final good.

Total incomes in the two types of cities are $\Upsilon_J = [1 - \kappa N_J^{1/2}] W_J$. The corresponding indirect utility functions are given by

$$U_X(N_X) = \lambda_X P_X^{1-\alpha} \left(\frac{P_Y}{\theta} \right)^{-(1-\alpha)} \delta_X^{\frac{1-u_X}{\sigma-1}} N_X^{\frac{1-u_X}{\sigma-1}} \left[1 - \kappa N_X^{1/2} \right]^{\frac{\sigma-u_X}{\sigma-1}}, \qquad (7.59)$$

$$U_Y(N_Y) = \lambda_Y P_Y^{\alpha} \left(\frac{P_X}{\theta} \right)^{-\alpha} \delta_Y^{\frac{1-u_Y}{\sigma-1}} N_Y^{\frac{1-u_Y}{\sigma-1}} \left[1 - \kappa N_Y^{1/2} \right]^{\frac{\sigma-u_Y}{\sigma-1}}. \qquad (7.60)$$

With specialized cities, spatial equilibrium requires that individuals be indifferent between living in any two cities of different types:

$$U_X(N_X) = U_Y(N_Y).$$

The national labor market must be at equilibrium:

$$n_X N_X + n_Y N_Y = \overline{N}. \qquad (7.61)$$

The national market for both final goods must be at equilibrium. The simplest way to express this is by equating the spending by X- cities on good Y to the spending by Y- cities on good X:

$$(1-\alpha) n_X X P_X = \alpha n_Y Y P_Y. \qquad (7.62)$$

Expressing the price ratio from this condition by using the solutions for output for each type of good from (7.58) above, we obtain an equation for the price ratio. A second equation is obtained by spatial equilibrium and equalizing utility across both types of cities:

$$\frac{P_X}{P_Y} = \frac{\lambda_Y}{\lambda_X} \frac{\delta_Y^{\frac{1-u_Y}{\sigma-1}}}{\delta_X^{\frac{1-u_X}{\sigma-1}}} \theta^{2\alpha-1} \frac{N_Y^{\frac{1-u_Y}{\sigma-1}}}{N_X^{\frac{1-u_X}{\sigma-1}}} \frac{\left[1 - \kappa N_Y^{1/2} \right]^{\frac{\sigma-u_Y}{\sigma-1}}}{\left[1 - \kappa N_X^{1/2} \right]^{\frac{\sigma-u_X}{\sigma-1}}}. \qquad (7.63)$$

The equilibrium price ratio is a function of the distribution of city size $(n_X, n_Y; N_X, N_Y)$. After equating the two expressions, the number of cities of each type is

$$n_X = \frac{\overline{N}}{N_X} \frac{\alpha}{\alpha + (1-\alpha)\theta^{2\alpha-1}}, \quad n_Y = \frac{\overline{N}}{N_Y} \frac{(1-\alpha)\theta^{2\alpha-1}}{\alpha + (1-\alpha)\theta^{2\alpha-1}}. \qquad (7.64)$$

How do individuals allocate themselves within a given urban system? The equilibrium level of utility is given by

$$U_{\text{spec}}(N_X, N_Y) = \lambda_X^{\alpha} \lambda_Y^{1-\alpha} \theta^{2\alpha(1-\alpha)} \delta_X^{\frac{\alpha(1-u_X)}{\sigma-1}} \delta_Y^{\frac{(1-\alpha)(1-u_Y)}{\sigma-1}}$$

$$N_X^{\frac{\alpha(1-u_X)}{\sigma-1}} \left[1 - \kappa N_X^{1/2} \right]^{\frac{\alpha(\sigma-u_X)}{\sigma-1}} N_Y^{\frac{(1-\alpha)(1-u_Y)}{\sigma-1}} \left[1 - \kappa N_Y^{1/2} \right]^{\frac{(1-\alpha)(\sigma-u_Y)}{\sigma-1}}. \qquad (7.65)$$

At the general equilibrium with a given number of cities, the equilibrium utility depends on the sizes of both city types but is separable with respect to the sizes. Maximization of the equilibrium utility $U_{spec}(N_X, N_Y)$ with respect to sizes, N_X, N_Y, while holding constant the number of cities of each type, (n_X, n_Y), defines the equilibrium city sizes. This is equivalent to maximizing, respectively, the functions

$$\mathcal{N}_{X\text{-spec}}(N_X;\kappa) \equiv H_c(N_X)^{\alpha\frac{1-u_X}{\sigma-1}}\left[1-\kappa N_X^{1/2}\right]^{\alpha},$$

$$\mathcal{N}_{Y\text{-spec}}(N_Y;\kappa) \equiv H_c(N_Y)^{(1-\alpha)\frac{1-u_Y}{\sigma-1}}\left[1-\kappa N_Y^{1/2}\right]^{1-\alpha}. \tag{7.66}$$

That is, the maximizing values are

$$N_J^* = \left(\frac{2\omega_J}{(3\omega_J+1)}\right)^2\frac{1}{\kappa^2},\quad \omega_J \equiv \frac{1-u_J}{\sigma-1}. \tag{7.67}$$

The corresponding number of cities follows from (7.64) and so does the equilibrium level of utility. If any cities are larger than the values given by (7.67), it is easy to see from the properties of (7.65) that individuals would not find it attractive to move there. On the contrary, moving to smaller cities would improve welfare. In a like manner, cities with populations larger than (7.67) would see the utility offered to their residents improve by out-migration. Still, with a given number of cities and an arbitrary population, there is no guarantee that there will always be "space for all." I eschew elaborating on the straightforward mathematical exercise for studying the various possibilities. I point to the fact that the planner's problem of the socially optimal number of cities and their sizes is also straightforward to define and would give results qualitatively similar to those obtained in sections 7.3.3 and 7.3.3.1 above.

If specialized cities were indeed of optimum size, then congestion costs would enter the expressions as total factor productivity terms for outputs of final goods and maximum utility as follows: $\kappa^{-2\frac{\sigma-u_X}{\sigma-1}}$, $\kappa^{-2\frac{\sigma-u_Y}{\sigma-1}}$, $\kappa^{-2\frac{\tilde{\Lambda}}{\sigma-1}}$. I make use of this property in chapter 9 below.

Comparing the expressions for equilibrium utility for diversified and specialized cities, (7.30) and (7.65), respectively (under the simplifying assumption that city sizes are equal), one can see that they involve the terms $\tilde{\Lambda}^{\frac{\tilde{\Lambda}}{\sigma-1}}$ and $\theta^{2\alpha(1-\alpha)}\delta_X^{\frac{\alpha(1-u_X)}{\sigma-1}}\delta_Y^{\frac{(1-\alpha)(1-u_Y)}{\sigma-1}}$, respectively, where $\tilde{\Lambda}$ is defined in (7.29). Therefore, for any set of values of preference, α, production u_X, u_Y, σ, and shipping cost τ, θ parameters, for a sufficiently large number of cities of either type, the system of specialized cities dominates (in terms of utility) the system of diversified cities. In the limit case of no shipping costs, $\theta = 1$, $\tau = 1$, and in only one of each type of city, $n_Y = n_Y = 1$, specialization dominates diversification because $\tilde{\Lambda} < 1$.

A comparison of equilibrium city sizes from (7.31) and (7.67) for autarkic and specialized cities, respectively, yields

$$N_X^* > N_{\text{aut}}^* > N_Y^*,\quad \text{if } 1-u_X > 1-u_Y. \tag{7.68}$$

That is, X-cities will be larger at equilibrium than Y-cities if the share of *intermediates* in the production of good X is greater than that in the production of good Y. I note that this comparison makes the pecuniary externality associated with the use of intermediates determine optimal city sizes, but that does not reflect the externality conferred on each type of city from the total number of cities of the same type.

With the equilibrium sizes of specialized cities given by (7.67), the numbers of the respective cities are given by (7.64). The urban structure is thus fully determined. Suppose that the economy consists of only specialized cities. Higher shipping costs for final goods, that is, a smaller θ, increase the number of cities specializing in the good for which the expenditure share exceeds one-half, and reduces that of the other type. The relative share of the total population residing in X- relative to Y-cities is equal to $\frac{\alpha}{1-\alpha}\theta^{1-2\alpha}$. It is equal to one-half when $\alpha = \frac{1}{2}$. In this special case, comparing (7.65) with (7.56) suggests the following [see Anas and Xiong (2003) for a proof]: sufficiently high intercity shipping costs for final goods reduce the attractiveness of specialization and make diversified cities more attractive. There exists a threshold value of θ for which utility is equalized across specialized and partly autarkic (or even fully autarkic) cities. This value also involves the number of cities. Alternatively, one may assume that the economy may be organized in a number of autarkic cities. Once intercity trade has become feasible, specialized cities emerge, which results in a more dispersed city size distribution. In addition, an urban system made up of diversified cities will attain a higher utility than a system of specialized cities if the share of intermediates is sufficiently low. In such a case, the productivity advantages of variety within industries are lower, generating a smaller benefit from specialization. Similarly, if the elasticity of substitution among intermediates is sufficiently high, then the value of increased variety is smaller, favoring diversification over specialization.

Summarizing, I note that the simple theory developed here implies a separability between city sizes that depend only on intracity transport costs κ and production parameters $(u_X, u_Y; \sigma)$. The intercity shipping cost for final goods, θ, affects the distribution of city sizes, while that for intermediates, τ, affects the feasibility of different configurations for the urban structure.

7.5.1 Diversified versus Specialized System of Cities: Another View

I now discuss the structure of the urban system when I do not impose location equilibrium. Instead, I take the number of cities and their populations $(n_X, n_Y; N_X, N_Y)$ as given. In some instances, it is helpful to work with equal city sizes, $N = N_X = N_Y$. This is not necessarily an optimum city size for either city type. The total number of cities now satisfies $n_X + n_Y = n = \frac{\overline{N}}{N}$.

From the trade equilibrium condition, equation (7.62), using the expressions for outputs X, Y when cities specialize, we have

$$\frac{P_X}{P_Y}=\frac{\alpha}{1-\alpha}\frac{n_Y}{n_X}\frac{\lambda_Y\delta_Y^{\frac{1-u_Y}{\sigma-1}}N_Y^{\frac{\sigma-u_Y}{\sigma-1}}\left[1-\kappa N_Y^{1/2}\right]^{\frac{\sigma-u_Y}{\sigma-1}}}{\lambda_X\delta_X^{\frac{1-u_X}{\sigma-1}}N_X^{\frac{\sigma-u_X}{\sigma-1}}\left[1-\kappa N_X^{1/2}\right]^{\frac{\sigma-u_X}{\sigma-1}}}. \tag{7.69}$$

From the expressions for equilibrium utility when cities specialize but before location equilibrium is imposed, (7.59) and (7.60), respectively, we have

$$\frac{U_X(N_X)}{U_Y(N_Y)}=\theta^{1-2\alpha}\frac{\lambda_X\delta_X^{\frac{1-u_X}{\sigma-1}}N_X^{\frac{1-u_X}{\sigma-1}}\left[1-\kappa N_X^{1/2}\right]^{\frac{\sigma-u_X}{\sigma-1}}}{\lambda_Y\delta_Y^{\frac{1-u_Y}{\sigma-1}}N_Y^{\frac{1-u_Y}{\sigma-1}}\left[1-\kappa N_Y^{1/2}\right]^{\frac{\sigma-u_Y}{\sigma-1}}}\frac{P_X}{P_Y}. \tag{7.70}$$

Therefore, the equilibrium price ratio according to (7.69) depends entirely on the number of cities of different types and so does the ratio of the respective utility levels associated with each city type. Simplifying by using (7.69) in (7.70) yields

$$\frac{U_X}{U_Y}=\frac{\alpha}{1-\alpha}\theta^{1-2\alpha}\frac{n_Y N_Y}{n_X N_X}. \tag{7.71}$$

The greater the utility in cities specializing in X relative to that in those specializing in Y, the smaller their respective share of the total population.

On the one hand, in an urban system consisting of autarkic cities, the utility at equilibrium according to (7.30) is entirely a function of parameters. In an urban system consisting of partly autarkic cities, on the other hand, the utility according to (7.56) depends on the number of cities because trade in intermediates introduces dependence on the number of cities as well. In either case, the above result suggests unequal welfare outcomes are associated with specialization in the absence of labor mobility. This is reminiscent of the findings of Matsuyama (1996), who shows that symmetry breaking in the world economy, taking the form of some countries becoming rich and other countries becoming poor, occurs because international trade induces agglomerations of different economic activities in different regions of the world. It also suggests that if individuals are free to move, increasing populations of cities specializing in one of the two goods X or Y will reduce their attractiveness, thus bringing us closer to spatial equilibrium. At spatial equilibrium, of course, (7.71) implies the same allocation for the number of cities as the one obtained in section 7.5 above, and for equilibrium utilities accordingly. Finally, the stability properties of the autarkic equilibrium are critical in understanding evolution of the urban system (Papageorgiou and Smith 1983).

7.6 RICHER URBAN STRUCTURES

The theory of urban structure that I have developed here is richer than that proposed by Henderson (1988) only because of the presence of intermediates. It is easy to extend it to the case of many final goods for which the basic separability properties that I discuss in section 7.5 above would still hold. The presence of intermediates, however, which may be produced using only labor, generates an additional set of possibilities that are worthy of further exploration. These are particularly interesting when shipping costs are also present since such costs may help sustain a multitude of trading arrangements between different cities that would otherwise be unattractive because of inefficiency.

Before motivating additional possibilities I summarize implications for the urban structures of those already examined. An economy consisting of *fully autarkic*, or diversified, cities can exhibit a structure with diverse equilibrium sizes. Such size differences reflect, as suggested by Krugman (1996) and Gabaix and Ioannides (2004), differences in geographic amenities, or in the quality of possible city locations, which in turn affect urban productivity. In the simplest possible case, they would reflect differences in urban commuting costs. *Partly autarkic cities* differ only because, in addition to producing both final goods, they benefit from economywide trade of intermediates. Differences in trading costs are thus an additional source of variation in city size. *Specialized* X- and Y-cities also produce intermediates; they import and export intermediates and trade final goods.

With intercity trade in intermediates, which are essential in production, intermediates need not be produced in every city. They may produced elsewhere and shipped to other cities as needed. So, it is possible to think of *specialized* X_0- and Y_0- cities, that is, cities that specialize in the production of *only* the final goods and purchase intermediates from elsewhere. In a like manner, there can be cities that produce only intermediates, Z-cities, and import both final goods. Similarly, X_0- and Y_0-cities can coexist with Z_0-cities and trade as is appropriate. All these logical possibilities can be explored in detail.[17]

If one were to interpret intermediates as specialized services, then the impact of economic development on urban structure may be seen in terms of the evolution of different transportation systems. Trains and planes reduce the cost of shipping final goods and thus favor specialization. However, improvements in communication technologies may be seen to favor intercity trade of intermediate specialized services and therefore generate a force in favor of diversification. I explore an additional implication of this interpretation in the following section. Urban structure is a net outcome of both forces.

A national planner in setting city sizes so as to maximize welfare would not take as given the number of cities. Just as in section 7.3.3.2, where I assume a simpler production function, a planner choosing city size N_d so as to maximize utility (7.56) would take into consideration that the number of cities, which enters the expression via the term $1+(n_J-1)\tau^{\sigma-1}$, is also affected by setting an optimum city size. This brings into the problem of determining a socially efficient city size an effect from the shipping costs for intermediates. These transport costs are not taken into consideration by setting the optimum city size at the competitive market outcome. Intercity externalities, as represented by intercity trade in intermediates, are important both for diversified cities when they import intermediates and for specialized cities that always import intermediates.

The exact relationship between the socially optimal values for diversified and specialized cities depends on parameter values. Yet, it can be shown that the socially optimal diversified city size is larger than that for a specialized city. These conditions are sufficient, as shown by Anas and Xiong (2003, prop. 3) to allow for an urban structure, which is a competitive outcome and consists of specialized cities being socially inferior relative to a system of diversified cities. This comparison is summarized by Anas and Xiong [2003, 274, eq. (5.6)]. The intuition for the comparison is the following. Intercity trade of intermediates generates externalities, which are ignored by the market equilibrium. The more important they are, the farther the competitive equilibrium is from the social optimum. In a diversified city system, each industry is smaller that in a specialized one, and therefore there is more intercity trade of intermediates. Because of this divergence, it is possible for the socially optimal setting of city sizes to make a diversified city system yield a higher level of utility than a specialized one. Xiong (1998) generalizes the prediction of the model to the case of asymmetric industries.

7.6.1 Sectoral versus Functional Specialization

Enriching the urban structure in the manner described above is not only a logical possibility but also helps in modeling the very important phenomenon of functional specialization. As mentioned in section 7.2 above, following Duranton and Puga (2005), one must recognize that manufacturing production requires inputs in the form of headquarters services and uses them along with production plants to produce outputs. Headquarters services are produced from raw labor and business services purchased from external suppliers. Such business services may be in the form of intermediates and produced by Z-cities, defined in section 7.6 above. Manufacturing firms in other cities purchase them by incurring shipping (communication) costs. Production plants themselves may use sector-specific intermediates inputs. Business service intermediates and sector-specific intermediates may be produced by means of increasing returns-to-scale technologies with different characteristics. Similarly, a firm need not colocate its headquarters with its production facilities.

All these options enhance the ability of the analyst to model modern urban economies. Duranton and Puga model functional specialization of cities by exploring the full range of logical consequences when firms are free to choose whether or not to colocate their headquarters with their production facilities. These authors show that once trading or communication costs are specified, the following configurations are logically possible. One, cities that are sectorally specialized by hosting only integrated firms (headquarters plus production facilities) in a single sector; these resemble X- or Y-cities, except that they also produce headquarters services. Two, HQ-cities, that is, cities that are functionally specialized by hosting only headquarters and their business service suppliers; they resemble X - or Y-cities but sell their output to multilocation manufacturing firms. Three, cities that are sectorally specialized by hosting only production facilities of firms in a single sector and their intermediates inputs; they also resemble X- or Y-cities. Four, cities with production plants of both multilocation firms and integrated firms in one sector. Five, cities with headquarters of both multilocation firms and integrated firms.

Duranton and Puga (2005, 356, lemma 4), rule out the coexistence of stand-alone headquarters and stand-alone production plants from different multilocation firms. Their intuition is the following. The headquarters of multilocation firms locate in a city only if it offers the lowest headquarters cost available anywhere. Similarly, the production plants of multilocation firms locate in a city only if it provides the corresponding intermediates at the lowest cost. If a city provided both the lowest headquarters cost and the lowest costs for production plants for multilocation firms in the same sector and they broke even, then multilocation firms with either headquarters or a production plant in the city would make positive profits by becoming integrated firms and thus save on shipping costs for headquarters services. It follows that, in equilibrium, headquarters and plants belonging to multilocation firms in the same sector do not coexist in the same city. Since resources used by headquarters, either directly or indirectly, can be shifted across sectors without changing given wages, headquarters and plants belonging to multilocation firms do not coexist in the same city even for different sectors. In effect, separating production from headquarters activities that contribute to manufacturing production, which multilocation firms make possible, exists to exploit the advantages of different types of cities for headquarters and production plants. The logical outcome then is for headquarters and production plants of multilocation firms to locate in different cities. Duranton and Puga (2005, 357, lemma 5) rule out the coexistence of production plants from different sectors, very much like Henderson (1974) does but as adapted in section 7.3 above. In the presence of localization economies, the final output in any given city and sector rises more than proportionately with employment in that city and sector. Duranton and Puga (2005, 358, lemma 6) rule out types four and five in the classification in the previous paragraph. That is, in equilibrium, each city hosts only final-sector manufacturing plants and intermediates suppliers, only final-sector headquarters and business service suppliers, or only integrated firms plus business services and intermediates suppliers. Finally, Duranton and Puga (2005, 360, prop. 1) define a threshold value of shipping costs for headquarters services above which firms have an incentive to integrate their headquarters with their production plants and all cities specialize by sector. Business services and intermediates suppliers would thus coexist with production plants. Otherwise, firms would locate their productions plants separately from their headquarters, and cities would specialize by function; that is, there would be headquarters cities that also host business services suppliers, and production plants cities that also host their intermediates suppliers.

7.6.2 Some Remarks on Possible Extensions

A number of remarks are in order. One, cities that produce only intermediates or only final goods involve restrictions on the range of goods produced and thus have inferior outcomes relative to the respective unconstrained cases. Still, they might become relevant in the presence of differential shipping costs, perhaps because of geography. Put differently, geography might favor the emergence of pairs of such types of cities. Still, recognizing the range of the analytical tools employed in this chapter and the multitudes of uses to which they can be put, such as by the arguments of Duranton and Puga (2005) and of others, makes it likely that they will continue serving as building blocks for additional theorizing in understanding urban structure.

Two, a natural extension would be employing the heterogeneous Dixit–Stiglitz–Fujita–Krugman–Venables model as pioneered by Melitz (2003). In chapter 9 below I take up the case with capital as a factor of production in addition to labor and intermediates. There the economy is further differentiated by adding a third stage of production where the goods considered final goods in the present chapter are used as inputs to produce in each city a composite that is in turn used for consumption and investment.

Three, it is straightforward to speculate about patterns of specialization in the presence of more than two final goods. Since labor is used as raw labor and as input in the production of intermediates, it is possible to express the total unit labor requirements for each good and convert the problem to a Ricardian setting. See Dornbusch Fischer, and Samuelson (1977). One may work in a like manner in the case of capital as an additional factor of production. See Cuñat and Melitz (2011). Such an extension is particularly interesting in the context of functional versus sectoral specialization as well.

7.7 THE ROLE OF GEOGRAPHY

So far, I have imposed uniform shipping costs associated with trade in final and intermediate goods. Next I follow Krugman (1992), but especially Matsuyama (1999), and introduce shipping costs to model arbitrary geography. Let $\mathbf{M} = [\mu_{\ell i}]$ denote a symmetric nonnegative matrix with elements $\mu_{ii} = 1$ and $\mu_{\ell i} = \tau_{\ell i}^{\sigma-1}$, where $\tau_{\ell i}$ stands for origin- and destination-specific iceberg costs, that is, the fraction of a unit of an intermediate shipped from a city at location ℓ that arrives in a city at location i. Correspondingly, the firms in city i that purchase intermediates from city ℓ pay $\frac{1}{\tau_{\ell i}} P_{z_{\ell i}}$ per unit of the intermediate they use. Let

n_{Xi}, n_{Yi}, n_{Zi}, denote the numbers of different types of cities that may occupy any of the locations $\ell = 1, \dots, L$. Consider the profit of an X-producing firm in city i:

$$P_X H_{Xi}^{u_X} \left[\sum_{\ell=1}^{L} m_\ell z_{d\ell i}^{1-\frac{1}{\sigma}} \right]^{\frac{\sigma}{\sigma-1}(1-u_X)} - W_X H_{Xi} - \sum_{\ell=1}^{L} m_\ell \frac{P_{Z\ell}}{\tau_{\ell i}} z_{d\ell i}. \tag{7.72}$$

Following this chapter's approach, I derive the following expression for the demand in city i for an intermediate produced in city ℓ:

$$z_{d\ell i} = (1 - u_X) P_X X_\ell \frac{\left(\frac{P_{Z,\ell}}{\tau_{\ell i}}\right)^{-\sigma}}{\overline{P}_{Zi}^{1-\sigma}}, \quad \forall i,$$

where $\overline{P}_{Zi}$ denotes the effective price index for intermediates in the economy from the perspective of city i:

$$\overline{P}_{Zi} = \left[\sum_{\ell=1}^{L} m_\ell \left(\frac{P_{Z,\ell}}{\tau_{\ell i}} \right)^{1-\sigma} \right]^{\frac{1}{1-\sigma}}. \tag{7.73}$$

The corresponding cost function for an X-producing firm is given by $W_i^{u_X} (\overline{P}_{Zi})^{1-u_X} X_\ell$.

An equilibrium in the market for each of m_ℓ intermediates produced in city i requires

$$\sum_{\ell=1}^{L} (1 - u_{J_\ell}) P_{J_\ell} J_\ell \frac{P_{Z,i}^{-\sigma} \tau_{i\ell}^{\sigma}}{\overline{P}_{Zi}^{1-\sigma}} = (\sigma - 1) \frac{f}{c}, \quad i = 1, \dots, L, \tag{7.74}$$

where $P_Z = \frac{\sigma}{\sigma-1} c W_\ell$ and the notation J_ℓ denotes the good in which city i at location ℓ specializes: $J_\ell = X, Y$. In the usual fashion, as long as the demand for an intermediate in city i exceeds the supply, additional firms enter.

Labor market equilibrium in city i requires

$$m_\ell f \sigma + H_{J_\ell} = H_{c_i}, \; \ell = 1, \dots, L. \tag{7.75}$$

Since $H_{J_\ell} = u_{J_\ell} H_{c_i}$, $m_\ell f \sigma = (1 - u_{J_\ell}) H_{J_\ell}$. Using this and the condition for the raw labor demand (from equation 7.33) $W_{J_\ell} = \frac{u_{J_\ell} P_{J_\ell} J_\ell}{H_{J_\ell}}$, along with the pricing condition, multiplying each of the conditions (7.74) by m_ℓ, and summing up over all i's, it follows that the equilibrium distribution of firms producing intermediates is scale-free in this model (Matsuyama 1999). That is, it does not depend on the actual magnitudes of labor supplies at different locations. Therefore, conditions (7.74) can be simplified by rewriting them in terms of cities' relative shares of intermediates and of raw labor. They may rewritten so as to express arbitrary geography by means of matrix **M**, defined earlier.

Shipping costs affecting the trade of final goods may also reflect geography. The fraction of a unit of final good shipped from city i that arrives in city ℓ may depend on both i and ℓ. Given a specific geography, as reflected in shipping costs for intermediates and final goods, one may explore alternative possibilities for cities specializing in either of the two final goods that might or might not also produce intermediates, or in intermediates. This is particularly relevant for such arrangements as specialized cities being surrounded, in the sense of patterns in shipping costs, by "satellite" cities producing only intermediates or only final goods. Special patterns of shipping costs may also make autarkic, that is, diversified, cities desirable.

Next are some examples of how geography may be expressed via the specification of **M**. First, the case I present earlier in the chapter is modeled by means of a symmetric **M**: $\mu_{\ell i} = \mu_{i\ell} = \tau^{\sigma-1}$. Suppose, alternatively, that there exist four locations around a circle. Then

$$\mathbf{M} = \begin{bmatrix} 1 & \tau^{\sigma-1} & \tau^{2(\sigma-1)} & \tau^{\sigma-1} \\ \tau^{\sigma-1} & 1 & \tau^{\sigma-1} & \tau^{(\sigma-1)^2} \\ \tau^{2(\sigma-1)} & \tau^{\sigma-1} & 1 & \tau^{\sigma-1} \\ \tau^{\sigma-1} & \tau^{2(\sigma-1)} & \tau^{(\sigma-1)} & 1 \end{bmatrix}.$$

Yet another alternative would be three locations asymmetrically placed on a line:

$$\mathbf{M} = \begin{bmatrix} 1 & \tau^{\sigma-1} & \max\{\tau^{2(\sigma-1)}, \tau^*\} \\ \max\{\tau^{2(\sigma-1)}, \tau^*\} & 1 & \tau^{\sigma-1} \\ \max\{\tau^{2(\sigma-1)}, \tau^*\} & 1 & \tau^{\sigma-1} \\ \tau^{\sigma-1} & \max\{\tau^{2(\sigma-1)}, \tau^*\} & 1 \end{bmatrix},$$

where τ^* denotes the shipping costs via a direct route between locations 1 and 3. Changes in shipping costs that affect the magnitudes of $\max\{\tau^{2(\sigma-1)}, \tau^*\}$ can have profound effects on the location of economic activity.

These modeling ideas aim at expressing a more macroscopic view of geography that has a bearing on the development of entire sites as opposed to individual firms, which I discuss in chapter 4. Very favorable conditions for economic activity, such as natural resources, rivers and navigable waterways and natural harbors, mountain ranges and passes through them, have traditionally been considered not only attractive to economic activity but also conducive to economic development itself [cf. (Matsuyama 1999)]. For example, consider the importance that Jared Diamond (1997) in his magisterial *Guns, Germs and Steel* attaches to climate and space for horizontal diffusion in the early development of economic advantages to particular locations and the cultures that happened to be located there. Eurasia benefited from such diffusion, whereas the Americas did not. A related but narrower economics-focused point was made much earlier by John Hicks (1970) in *A Theory of Economic History*, namely, that Mediterranean cultures gained a relative advantage closely related to the ease of navigation and thus development of distant trade. After improvements in ship design and ocean navigation, southern and especially Mediterranean Europe lost its advantage, relative to the north and west (Matsuyama 1999, 17). It is an interesting question how discontinuities in the physical landscape, of the type emphasized by new economic geography, may help anchor urban development (Fujita, Krugman, and Venables 1999, chap. 13). Similarly, recent research by Donaldson (2008), who uses historical data from colonial India, shows that the development of India's vast railroad network in the era of the Raj had profound effects on its economy. By allowing trade across otherwise isolated areas, the railroads of the Raj caused decreases in trade costs and interregional trade gaps and increases in interregional and international trade. They helped eliminate the responsiveness of local prices to local productivity shocks (but increased the transmission of such shocks between regions). They also increased the level of real income (but reduced that of neighboring regions without railroad access) and decreased its volatility.

7.7.1 Geography and Urban Structure: Germany's Division and Reunification

Changes in shipping costs can be quite critical as explanations of major shifts in patterns of international trade and development. One may model, for example, the impact on Germany's urban structure of the division of Germany after World War II and its reunification in 1990 by setting the fraction of intermediates shipped between two blocks of cities that were separated equal to 0. Delineating cities as being in the "West" by $\ell = 1, \ldots, \ell_W$, and as being in the "East" by $\ell = \ell_W + 1, \ldots, L$, after the division, one can write two versions of the model, one being the integrated economy, and the other being for each of the East and West components of the divided economy, by setting $\tau_{\ell',\ell''} = 0, \ell' \leq \ell_W, \ell_W + 1 \leq \ell'' \leq L$. Similarly, prohibitively high shipping costs may be assumed also for final goods. The East and the West, when separated, will reach their own independent equilibria, which may be described in terms of the tools in section 7.5. Specifically, assume for simplicity that division results in halving the economy, and city sizes in both components are at their optimum values in the sense of section 7.5, equation (7.67). Then, welfare declines because of the reduced diversity of intermediates. The asymmetric effect associated with the border may be easily expressed through geometry in specifying the matrix **M**. Matrix **M** is block diagonal during the division; it becomes fuller after reunification as links between border cities are established. Unfortunately, the resulting model with arbitrary shipping costs **M** may not be solved in closed form, leaving simulations and calibrations as the only mode of inquiry.

Another interesting feature of the German case, namely, that economic development following division in the post–World War II era proceeded under sharply different institutional settings with a market economy in the West and a planned economy in the East, may be accommodated within the model. City sizes in the model may be at values associated with spatial equilibrium in the West and at arbitrary values in the East. For the West, welfare under the model in section 7.5 may be compared with the outcome of a planning problem, which would set city populations while taking into consideration not only the net labor supply but also the value of the variety of intermediates. I return to this issue in chapter 8, section 8.8 below.

The U.S. urban system has been affected profoundly by development of the Eisenhower Interstate Highway System that connects all U.S. metropolitan areas. Duranton, Morrow, and Turner (2011) study the effects of highways in cities and between cities. Making innovative use of little known sources of data, the Commodity Flow Survey for trade in 2007 and the Highway Performance Monitoring System for highway capacity, together with employment data, population counts, and other historical data, they find that the weight and the value of bilateral trade between cities decrease rapidly with the distance between cities. They also find that increased highway capacity within cities, say by 10 percent, increases the weight of exports by 5 percent but does not appreciably affect the value of trade.

7.8 LABOR MARKET FRICTIONS IN A SYSTEM OF CITIES

With industrial specialization and diversification being important features of urbanized economies, it is natural to wonder about cyclical patterns in urban output. Starkly put, the proverbial company town is at the mercy of its industry's (cyclical) fortunes. How does that affect urban structure in an economy of company towns? Although some research has documented urban business cycles and will be discussed in more detail below, theorizing is in its infancy in this area. Similarly, cities with diversified industrial structures would likely experience business cycles differently than company towns.

The role of the urban economy in the macroeconomic business cycle is, in principle, quite fundamental though rarely addressed directly. Adherents to real business cycle theories are happy with the fact that total factor productivity growth may be generated through learning and knowledge largely created in cities. This notion is often associated with the work of Jane Jacobs (1969). More recently, it has been given additional respectability by Lucas (1988) and others, further developed rigorously by Duranton and Puga (2001), and accorded newer empirical support from a diverse group of scholars ranging from Florida (2002) to Glaeser and Maré (2001) and many others. It has been linked to the emergence of scale economies, innovations, and entrepreneurship favoring particular industries.

With intercity trade one would expect that forces of cyclical fluctuations have varying effects across industries and consequently across cities as well, as the diverse collections of industries they host may generate complex spillovers. Cyclical outcomes throughout the urban system are mediated by intercity interactions as well. These interactions may include trade, migration flows, and technological spillovers. Interactions between the urban and rural economies may also add their own dynamics.

Recent research in international trade theory has addressed the reactions of different economies to shocks as sources of comparative advantage, with the role of labor market frictions being central in this new literature. Noteworthy works are those by Davis (1998), and especially by Cuñat and Melitz (2011), Helpman and Itskhoki (2010), and Tang (2009). I return below to a detailed discussion of these studies. Dutt, Mitra, and Ranjan (2009) develop a simple model of international trade with search-induced unemployment and show empirically that trade liberalization increases unemployment in the short run but reduces it in the long run as economies adjust to a new steady state.

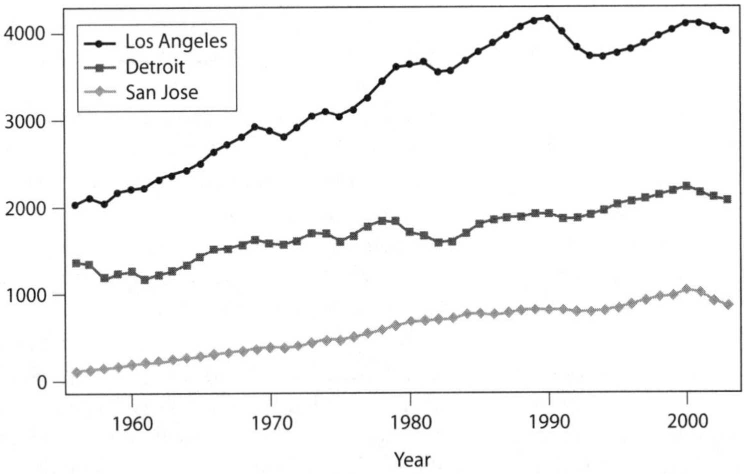

Figure 7.1. Total employment (000s) in San Jose, California, Los Angeles, California, and Detroit, Michigan. *Source*: Coulson (2006, fig. 1).

7.8.1 Evidence on Labor Turnover and Urban Structure

Recall the discussion in chapter 5, section 5.8, on job matching and spatial structure. From among the studies of urban labor markets in macroeconomic contexts, the following stand out. Diamond and Simon (1990) offer empirical insight into urban employment fluctuations. They use data from County Business Patterns and the Current Population Survey of the United States and show that urban specialization is associated with higher unemployment rates and higher weekly wages. This is broadly consistent with spatial equilibrium, as discussed below, but that article does not model the urban economy as such. Coulson (2006) examines the broad aspects of urban employment fluctuations purely empirically. As a national economy experiences business cycle fluctuations, not all of its urban or regional subeconomies rise and fall in concert. U.S. regions, states, and metropolitan areas rise and fall at different times and with different frequencies and intensities, and for different reasons. Unique characteristics of employment fluctuations of different cities are clearly related to the industrial compositions of their employment. Coulson points to a comparison of the following three MSAs, Los Angeles, California, Detroit, Michigan, and San Jose, California over the period 1956–2002 (Coulson 2006, fig. 1, reproduced here as figure 7.1). While all three of those areas experienced employment that trended upward over time during that period, the rate at which their employments did so certainly varied across cities and over time within cities. Some cities, such as San Jose, seem almost recessionproof. Unlike Detroit and Los Angeles, San Jose experienced no sustained period of job loss until about 2000. Furthermore, the downward cycles experienced by cities that are cyclically sensitive (such as Detroit and Los Angeles) were to a certain extent correlated with each other and with the national business cycle.

Owyang, Piger, Wall, and Wheeler (2008) document how important it is to look separately at high-growth and low-growth episodes. Interestingly, the usual explanatory variables employed by urban economics in explaining growth, such as human capital, industry mix, and average firm size, are particularly important for high-growth episodes. In contrast, low growth is mostly related to industry mix, specifically, the relative importance of manufacturing, but in ways that differ across cities. As they put it, happy cities are alike, and unhappy ones are so for different reasons. Finally, the frequency of the low phase appears to be related to the level of noneducation human capital but to none of the other variables mentioned above.

In the recent international trade literature that emphasizes labor market flexibility as a source of comparative advantage, Cuñat and Melitz (2011) and Tang (2009) introduce fluctuations in productivity. *Flexibility* is modeled by allowing all allocations to take place *after* the realization of uncertainty, thus reflecting that uncertainty, while *rigidity* is assumed to take the form of hiring decisions *prior* to the resolution of uncertainty. Rigidity causes ex post inefficiency that may not be offset by labor reallocation after the uncertainty is resolved. Cuñat and Melitz (2011) express the advantage of flexibility versus rigidity simply enough so that it may be incorporated into the workhorse model of Ricardian comparative advantage developed by Dornbusch, Fischer, and Samuelson (1977). That is, with one or two factors used in production, one can define a productivity advantage of each, where industries are ranked in terms of volatility or in terms of volatility and capital intensity of production, respectively. The Cuñat–Melitz model predicts that, other things being equal, countries with more flexible labor markets specialize in sectors where the ability to adapt is most important, that is, those affected by higher-variance shocks (higher volatility). These authors test the theory empirically by ranking countries in terms of labor market flexibility and availability of data on firm-level volatility and exports by sectors. Or the phenomenon of outsourcing may be simply an economy's high-volatility industries availing themselves of the comparative advantage of more flexible labor markets elsewhere. This may provide a lesson for cities in integrated economies, federal ones like the United States and Canada or like the European Union, where there are differences in mobility across cities in different countries. Helpman and Itskhoski (2010) address broadly related questions, except that their models also allow them to address unemployment by means of the Mortensen–Pissarides matching model (Mortensen and Pissarides 1999; Pissarides 1985; 2000). That is, one of the two sectors in their model produces a final good by means of a range of differentiated products that are themselves produced with raw labor and whose production is subject to Mortensen–Pissarides-type frictions. Trade integration benefits both countries but may raise their rates of unemployment. Unemployment may be higher or lower in the more flexible country, which has both higher total factor productivity and a lower price level.

Centralized matching of unemployed workers with vacancies may be considered a proxy for the role of social connections (in the close physical proximity afforded by urban living) within urban labor markets.[18] As discussed in chapter 4, section 4.9.1, firms benefit from proximity to other firms because of risk pooling, which reduces hiring costs and mitigates wage and input price fluctuations. Such proximity is also beneficial in promoting entrepreneurship.[19] However, proximity is costly in terms of congestion. In the remainder of this section I reformulate the urban model introduced in section 7.4.1 above in order to accommodate labor turnover and labor market frictions by using the model in chapter 5, section 5.7. The exposition departs from the static model and examines the urban economy in a dynamic but steady-state setting without factor accumulation.

7.8.2 Production with Labor Turnover

This basic framework extends the model employed earlier in the chapter by embedding issues of employment fluctuations and unemployment within the canonical urban model so as to accommodate labor turnover and labor market frictions. It does so in the style of the Pissarides matching model by extending the model in section 5.7, itself based on the model by Wasmer and Zenou (2002). My approach takes a very stylized view: all job matching takes place at the CBD and requires that unemployed individuals travel to the CBD in order to be matched with vacancies.

The production setting is the same as that in section 7.4.1 above. Each of two tradable goods $J = X, Y$ are produced by means of raw labor and of a composite good that is itself produced using a range of differentiated intermediates. It is output per unit of time that is now given by equation (7.15). I introduce labor market turnover by assuming exogenous job destruction (Pissarides 2000): each unit of raw labor is fired randomly when the respective job is destroyed with probability d_J per unit of time, $J = X, Y$, and becomes unemployed. I assume that firms are large enough so they may ignore stochastic fluctuations in their labor forces. I also assume that labor employed in the production of differentiated intermediates is not subject to turnover.[20] I think this is appropriate for stochastic steady states, which I assume for the purpose of the analysis below. When unemployed, workers look for jobs and are matched with vacancies via a matching mechanism located at the CBD, just as I discuss in chapter 5, section 5.8.

Consider the problem of a typical firm producing one of two tradable goods. The firm's objective is to choose employment of raw labor, H_J, which it accomplishes indirectly via posting vacancies, V_J, and quantities of intermediates, $z_{Ji}, J = X, Y$, so as to maximize present-discounted expected profit[21]:

$$\int_0^{\infty} e^{-\rho t} \left[P_J J - w_J H_J - \sum_i^m P_{zi} \dot{z}_{Ji} - \sum_i^m P_{zi} z_{Ji} - \gamma P_J V_J \right] dt, \; J = X, Y,$$

subject to a differential equation describing the dynamics of the firm's raw labor force,

$$\dot{H}_J = q_J V_J - d_J H_J, \tag{7.76}$$

for given paths of the prices P_J, P_{zi}, of wage rates W_J, and of q_J, the rate at which each vacancy returns a worker, and given the rate of output J, according to (7.15). I assume that intermediates are entirely used up in the production process so that they perform like capital that depreciates fully. An unfilled vacancy costs γ units of output J per unit of time. If $\tilde{V}_J$ denotes the costate variable associated with (7.76), then the necessary conditions for the optimality of vacancies are

$$e^{-\rho t}\left[P_J \frac{\partial J}{\partial H_J} - w_J\right] - d_J \tilde{V}_J + \frac{d\tilde{V}_J}{dt} = 0;$$

$$-e^{-\rho t}\gamma P_J + q_J \tilde{V}_J = 0.$$

The necessary conditions for the intermediates are

$$e^{-\rho t}\left[P_J \frac{\partial J}{\partial z_{Ji}} - P_{zi}\right] - P_{zi}\frac{d}{dt}\left(-e^{-\rho t}\right) = 0. \tag{7.77}$$

The pricing of intermediates continues to involve the standard markup pricing formula:

$$P_{zi} = \frac{\sigma}{\sigma - 1} c w_{ZJ},$$

where the wage rate for labor producing intermediates depends on the industry J in the case of specialization. For constant q_J, the first-order condition for H_J at the steady state is

$$u_J P_J \frac{J}{H_J} = w_J + \frac{\rho + d_J}{q_J}\gamma P_J, \; J = X, Y. \tag{7.78}$$

Rewriting this condition as

$$\frac{1}{\rho + d_J}\left(u_J P_J \frac{J}{H_J} - w_J\right) = \frac{\gamma}{q_J} P_J, \; J = X, Y, \tag{7.79}$$

makes its economic interpretation clearer. That is, the marginal revenue to the firm from an additional unit of employment, net of the wages paid, as seen in terms of the expected present value of the future net cash flow, the left-hand side of (7.79) above (which accounts for time preference and the rate of job destruction), is equal to the marginal cost of making it possible, the right-hand side above. The latter is the cost of a vacancy per unit of time, γP_J, times the average duration of the firm's search until a vacancy returns a hire, $1/q_J$. Intuitively, condition (7.79) plays the role of the demand for employment of raw labor by the respective firm. It is the counterpart here of the job creation condition (Pissarides, 2000, 70). The higher the wage rate w_J, or the expected cost of hiring, the lower employment.

The first-order condition for the intermediates (7.77) at the steady state equates the value of the marginal product of each intermediate to its price per unit of time and the associated capital cost. After using symmetry, this condition yields

$$(1 - u_J)P_J J = m z_J (1 + \rho) \frac{\sigma}{\sigma - 1} c w_Z, \quad J = X, Y. \tag{7.80}$$

For equilibrium in the market for each intermediate variety, supply must equal demand. For example, when both industries coexist in a city,

$$z_X + z_Y = (\sigma - 1) \frac{f}{c}. \tag{7.81}$$

The respective total demand for raw labor for the production of all intermediate varieties is $m f \sigma$.

7.8.2.1 Wage Setting

Wage setting in the market for raw labor recognizes the fact that firms deal with workers individually. Following a suggestion of Pissarides (2000, 68), for firms hiring many workers (as opposed to the more commonly used version of the Pissarides model of labor market frictions where a firm bargains with a single worker), it is easiest to think of the wage rate being set as if the firm bargains with each worker separately, by taking the wages of all the other workers as given, and chooses the number of jobs by taking the wage rate as given. In a departure from the studies by Pissarides (1985; 2000), Wasmer and Zenou (2002), and Zenou (2009a; 2009b), I assume that Nash wage bargaining takes the form of maximizing the product of the *expected* lifetime utilities of workers,[22] given in chapter 5 by (5.60), instead of state-dependent utility, times the marginal benefit of an additional unit of employment to the firm, given by the left-hand side of (7.79), raised to the powers of ϑ and $1 - \vartheta$, respectively, where ϑ, $0 < \vartheta < 1$, is a parameter denoting the bargaining weight for individuals. Under the assumption that each industry conducts its bargaining separately, the bargaining problem for industry J is to choose w_J so as to maximize the product of the weighted surpluses in the Nash bargaining style:

$$\left[\frac{1}{r} \left[\frac{1}{3} \frac{d_J}{d_J + \pi_J} b \bar{\alpha}_u \pi^{-1/2} N^{1/2} + \frac{\pi_J}{d_J + \pi_J} w_J \left(1 - \kappa_e N^{1/2} \right) \right] \right]^{\vartheta}$$

$$\times \left[\frac{1}{\rho + d_J} \left(u_J P_J \frac{X}{H_J} - w_J \right) \right]^{1-\vartheta},$$

where π_J are defined in the job-matching model in chapter 5, section 5.7.1, as the probabilities that individuals will have job contacts with firms in the respective industries $J = X, Y, \pi_J = \upsilon_J q(\upsilon_J)$, υ_J is labor market tightness in industry J, defined as vacancies per unemployed worker, and $\kappa_e \equiv \frac{2}{3} \bar{\alpha}_e \pi^{-1/2}$.

The result for industry J, after using the first-order condition for employment (7.79), is

$$w_J = \vartheta u_J \frac{P_J J}{H_J} = \frac{\vartheta}{1-\vartheta} \frac{\rho + d_J}{q(\upsilon_J)} \gamma P_J; \; J = X, Y. \tag{7.82}$$

That is, the wage rate for raw labor in each industry is set equal to the share ϑ of the respective value of the marginal product of raw labor. The second equality in (7.82) defines the wage rate in industry J as a function of labor market tightness, to be referred to as $w_X(\upsilon_X)$, $w_Y(\upsilon_Y)$, respectively. Recall from chapter 5 that the probability of contact by a firm decreases labor market tightness, $q'(\upsilon_J) < 0$. Consequently, equation (7.82) implies that "real" wage rates are increasing functions of tightness of the respective labor markets. This is a key intuition that follows from the Pissarides model.

7.8.2.2 *Labor Market Equilibrium*

Workers are homogeneous. Consequently, employment that exposes them to exogenous termination randomly must compensate them, ceteris paribus, for the accordant risk. The expected wage in either industry must equal the certain wage rate earned by continuously employed workers in the intermediate goods–producing sector, w_{ZJ}:

$$\frac{\pi_J}{d_J + \pi_J} w_J = w_{ZJ}, \; J = X, Y. \tag{7.83}$$

These conditions ensure, in view of the equilibrium utility derived above, spatial equilibrium within each city as well.

In a diversified (autarkic) city, for equilibrium in the labor market, labor earns equal wages in the production of intermediates, $w_{ZX} = w_{ZY} = w_Z$, and expected wages are equal across the two industries: $\frac{\pi_X}{d_X+\pi_X} w_X = \frac{\pi_Y}{d_Y+\pi_Y} w_Y$. In that case, in view of (7.82), equalization of expected wages establishes a relationship between the labor market tightness for the two industries and the relative price ratio P_X/P_Y, that must hold at equilibrium in diversified cities. This relationship is simplified, in view of the wage-setting conditions (7.82), to become

$$\frac{\frac{\pi_X}{d_X+\pi_X}}{\frac{\pi_Y}{d_Y+\pi_Y}} \frac{q(\upsilon_Y)}{q(\upsilon_X)} \frac{\rho + d_X}{\rho + d_Y} = \frac{P_Y}{P_X}. \tag{7.84}$$

By differentiation I have:

$$\frac{d\upsilon_X}{d\upsilon_Y} = \left(\frac{\rho + d_X}{\rho + d_Y} \right) \frac{\frac{d_Y}{\upsilon_Y^2} - q'(\upsilon_Y)}{\frac{d_X}{\upsilon_X^2} - q'(\upsilon_X)},$$

$$\frac{d^2\upsilon_X}{d\upsilon_Y^2} = \frac{d\upsilon_X}{d\upsilon_Y} \left[-\frac{2\frac{d_Y}{\upsilon_Y^3} + q''(\upsilon_Y)}{\frac{d_Y}{\upsilon_Y^2} - q'(\upsilon_Y)} + \frac{d\upsilon_X}{d\upsilon_Y} \frac{2\frac{d_X}{\upsilon_X^3} + q''(\upsilon_X)}{\frac{d_X}{\upsilon_X^2} - q'(\upsilon_X)} \right]. \tag{7.85}$$

Since $q' < 0$, it follows that $\frac{dv_X}{dv_Y} > 0$, which establishes the monotonicity of v_X as a function of v_Y. However, $\frac{d^2 v_X}{dv_Y^2}$ is initially decreasing and then increasing, allowing for the possibility of multiple fixed points. The counterpart of this relationship for the case of specialized cities, (7.98) below, follows from intercity spatial equilibrium. It is thus clear that the labor market tightness variables in the two industries function as counterparts of factor intensities in trade models determining the internal terms of trade.

At a steady state, equation (7.76) implies that flows into unemployment equal flows out of unemployment, and, therefore, a relationship between vacancies and employment for each industry: $V_J = \frac{d_I}{q_J} H_J$. It follows that, in a diversified city, total flow into unemployment per unit of time is $d_X H_X + d_Y H_Y$ and is equal to the rate at which vacancies are filled, $q(v_X)V_X + q(v_Y)V_Y$.

7.8.3 Cities with Two Traded-Good Industries: Diversification

I work first with the case of diversified cities. When exogenous rates of job destruction differ across the two industries, the possibility of labor pooling arises with accordant benefits to firms and individuals.

By using the first-order conditions for raw labor and for the use of intermediate goods, that is, by dividing (7.78) by (7.80) for each of the two goods, we have

$$H_J = \frac{u_J}{1 - u_J} \frac{\sigma c}{\sigma - 1} \frac{m z_J w_Z}{w_J + \frac{\rho + d_J}{q(v_J)} \gamma}, \quad J = X, Y. \tag{7.86}$$

By substituting for mz_X, mz_Y from these equations into (7.81), using the labor market equilibrium conditions (7.83), and using the pricing formula, we obtain the condition in terms of (H_X, H_Y, m) for the raw labor requirements of the intermediates sector:

$$\frac{1 - u_X}{u_X} \frac{d_X + \pi_X}{\pi_X} H_X + \frac{1 - u_Y}{u_Y} \frac{d_Y + \pi_Y}{\pi_Y} H_Y = f \sigma \vartheta (1 + \rho) m.$$

The labor market clearing condition thus becomes

$$\frac{d_X + \pi_X}{\pi_X} H_X + \frac{d_Y + \pi_Y}{\pi_Y} H_Y + m f \sigma = H_c, \tag{7.87}$$

where $H_c(N) \equiv N(1 - \kappa_e N^{1/2})$ denotes labor net of commuting costs.

With Cobb–Douglas preferences, the shares of spending within each city satisfy $\frac{P_X X}{P_Y Y} = \frac{\alpha}{1-\alpha}$. This, along with the first-order conditions for the intermediates, (7.80), and the equilibrium condition in the market for intermediates, (7.81), allows us to solve for z_X, z_Y. Using these solutions in turn in (7.86) and substituting into (7.87) allows us to solve for the range of intermediates and finally for raw labor allocations as well:

$$m = \frac{\alpha(1 - u_X) + (1 - \alpha)(1 - u_Y)}{\vartheta^*} \frac{H_c}{f\sigma};$$

$$H_X = \frac{\pi_X}{d_X + \pi_X} \frac{\vartheta(1 + \rho)\alpha u_X}{\vartheta^*} H_c, \ H_Y = \frac{\pi_Y}{d_Y + \pi_Y} \frac{\vartheta(1 + \rho)(1 - \alpha)u_Y}{\vartheta^*} H_c,$$

where

$$\vartheta^* = \alpha(1 - u_X) + (1 - \alpha)(1 - u_Y) + \vartheta(1 + \rho)(\alpha u_X + (1 - \alpha)u_Y).$$

The associated expressions for the use of intermediates by each industry are identical to those obtained for the case of complete autarky in the static model, section 7.4.3 above, and given by (7.25). The solutions for raw labor demands, H_X and H_Y, and the range of intermediates, reflect the parameters of labor market frictions via the bargaining parameter ϑ and are less than in the autarkic case. The difference reflects the need to maintain a labor force larger than employment.

Equilibrium in an autarkic urban economy is characterized fully by solving in terms of labor market tightness for each of the industries. The wage-setting equations (7.82) together with the above solutions for H_X, H_Y, m yield

$$u_{X,a} \left(1 + \frac{d_X}{\pi_X}\right)^{1 - u_X} H_c^{\frac{1 - u_X}{\sigma - 1}} = \frac{\rho + d_X}{1 - \vartheta} \frac{\gamma}{q(\upsilon_X)}, \tag{7.88}$$

$$u_{Y,a} \left(1 + \frac{d_Y}{\pi_Y}\right)^{1 - u_Y} H_c^{\frac{1 - u_Y}{\sigma - 1}} = \frac{\rho + d_Y}{1 - \vartheta} \frac{\gamma}{q(\upsilon_Y)}, \tag{7.89}$$

where $u_{X,a}$ is a function of parameters, defined as follows

$$u_{X,a} \equiv \left(\frac{\vartheta(1 + \rho)\alpha u_X}{\vartheta^*}\right)^{u_X - 1} \left(\frac{\alpha(1 - u_X)}{\alpha(1 - u_X) + (1 - \alpha)(1 - u_Y)} \frac{((\sigma - 1)f}{c}\right)^{1 - u_X}$$
$$\times \left(\frac{\alpha(1 - u_X) + (1 - \alpha)(1 - u_Y)}{\vartheta^*} \frac{1}{f\sigma}\right)^{\frac{\sigma}{\sigma - 1}(1 - u_X)}.$$

$u_{Y,a}$ is defined symmetrically. Equations (7.88) and (7.89) may be solved implicitly to obtain the respective values for labor market tightness υ_X, υ_Y as functions of $H_c(N)$. We see below that identical conditions hold separately in the case of specialized cities, (7.94) but with different parameters, $(u_{X,s}, u_{Y,s})$ instead of $(u_{X,a}, u_{Y,a})$. Solving, respectively, for υ_X and υ_Y and substituting into (7.84) yields the internal terms of trade, P_X/P_Y, as functions of city size and all parameters. Labor market tightness increases monotonically with city size for both industries. This effect is due to the presence of intermediates, which cause the marginal product of labor, the left-hand sides of (7.88) and (7.89), to increase with city size.

By dividing (7.88) by (7.89) we obtain:

$$\frac{u_{X,a}}{u_{Y,a}} \frac{\left(\frac{\pi_Y}{d_Y+\pi_Y}\right)^{1-u_Y}}{\left(\frac{\pi_X}{d_X+\pi_X}\right)^{1-u_X}} H_c^{\frac{u_Y-u_X}{\sigma-1}} = \frac{\frac{\rho+d_X}{q(\upsilon_X)}}{\frac{\rho+d_Y}{q(\upsilon_Y)}}. \tag{7.90}$$

The dependence of the labor market tightness variables (υ_X, υ_Y) on H_c varies with $u_X - u_Y$ and d_X, d_Y. It increases faster with city net labor supply H_c for the final good that is less intensive in raw labor.

It is straightforward to obtain an expression for equilibrium utility. From the wage setting conditions (7.82) and the condition for intracity spatial equilibrium (7.83) we can rewrite the indirect utility function corresponding to $X^{\alpha} Y^{1-\alpha}$,

$$\alpha^* P_X^{-\alpha} P_Y^{-(1-\alpha)} \frac{\pi_J}{d_J + \pi_J} w_J \left(1 - \kappa_e N^{1/2}\right),$$

as follows:

$$\hat{\Lambda} \left(1 - \kappa_e N^{1/2}\right) \left(\frac{\pi_X}{d_X + \pi_X} \frac{\rho + d_X}{q(\upsilon_X)}\right)^{\alpha} \left(\frac{\pi_Y}{d_Y + \pi_Y} \frac{\rho + d_Y}{q(\upsilon_Y)}\right)^{1-\alpha}, \tag{7.91}$$

where $\alpha^* = \alpha^{\alpha}(1-\alpha)^{1-\alpha}$. The effect of total net labor in the urban economy on equilibrium utility is quite different when labor market frictions are present from the case of fully autarkic cities in section 7.4.3 above. Equation (7.91) highlights the tradeoffs associated with increasing city size. Expected utility increases because of higher labor market tightness and increased wages and employment rates; it decreases because of congestion costs.

7.8.4 Cities with One Traded-Good Industry: Specialization

I characterize the urban economy when it is specialized in one of the two industries, $J = X, Y$, that produce final goods. In order to isolate the effects of specialization, I assume that each city produces its own intermediates. Each final good is traded within the system of cities, and its price is exogenous to a single city's economy. Prices of final goods are determined in the entire economy and taken as given by each city, exactly like the determination of equilibrium in the absence of labor market frictions; see section 7.5 above.

In expressing equilibrium in the labor market by setting labor demand equal to labor supply, I must account for the following: one, for the typical firm to have access to employment equal to H_J, it needs a labor force of $\frac{d_J+\pi_J}{\pi_J} H_J$; two, employment in the production of differentiated goods is not subject to turnover; and three, it is only the portion of labor net of commuting to the CBD that is available for employment, $H_c(N_J)$. That is:

$$\frac{d_J + \pi_J}{\pi_J} H_J + m\sigma f = H_c(N_J),$$

where, recalling (5.61), $H_c(N_J) \equiv N_J \left(1 - \kappa_e N_J^{1/2}\right)$.

Since the entire production of each differentiated good is used by the firm, $z_J = (\sigma - 1)\frac{f}{c}$, working with the necessary conditions and dividing (7.80) by (7.78) and imposing labor market equilibrium yield the following for the raw labor employment by industry J and the range of intermediates, respectively,

$$H_J = \frac{\vartheta(1+\rho)u_J}{\vartheta(1+\rho)u_J + 1 - u_J} \frac{\pi_J}{d_J + \pi_J} H_c(N_J), \tag{7.92}$$

$$m_J = \frac{1}{f\sigma} \frac{1 - u_J}{\vartheta(1+\rho)u_J + 1 - u_J} H_c(N_J). \tag{7.93}$$

The solution implies that $\frac{\vartheta(1+\rho)u_J}{\vartheta(1+\rho)u_J+1-u_J} H_c(N_J)$ is the labor force for industry J. This exceeds the corresponding value in autarky; not surprisingly, specialization induces greater employment of raw labor in the city industry. It does so, too, for the use of intermediates by X in the case of specialization when that industry uses them more intensively, $1 - u_X > 1 - u_Y$.

Labor market equilibrium in an urban economy specializing in $J = X, Y$ is characterized by solving in terms of labor market tightness. Substituting from the wage-setting equation (7.82) into (7.79) yields $u_J \frac{J}{H_J} = \frac{\rho + d_J}{1-\vartheta} \frac{\gamma}{q(v_J)}$. By using (7.92) and (7.93) for H_J and m in this equation, we obtain the condition that determine labor market tightness:

$$u_{J,s} \left(\frac{\pi_J + d_J}{\pi_J}\right)^{1-u_J} H_c^{\frac{1-u_J}{\sigma-1}}(N_J) = \frac{\rho + d_J}{1 - \vartheta} \frac{\gamma}{q(v_J)}, \quad J = X, Y, \tag{7.94}$$

where $u_{J,s}$, a function of parameters, is defined as

$$u_{J,s} \equiv \left(\frac{\vartheta(1+\rho)u_J}{\vartheta(1+\rho)u_J + 1 - u_J}\right)^{u_J - 1} \left(\frac{1}{f\sigma} \frac{1 - u_J}{\vartheta(1+\rho)u_J + 1 - u_J}\right)^{(1-u_J)\frac{\sigma}{\sigma-1}}$$
$$\times \left((\sigma - 1)\frac{f}{c}\right)^{1-u_J}.$$

Since the rate at which workers find jobs, $\pi(v_J)$, is increasing in labor market tightness, $\pi'(v_J) > 0$, the left-hand side of (7.94) is monotonically decreasing in labor market tightness. Since $q'(v_J) < 0$, the right-hand side is monotonically increasing in v_J. Therefore, an equilibrium value of labor market tightness exists, in general, as the unique solution to (7.94) given N_J. Several comparative statics properties follow. Notably, labor market tightness and therefore the employment rate and both wage rates, w_J, w_Z, do not depend on P_J directly. Similarly with the case of autarkic cities, greater net labor supply $H_c(N_J)$ is associated with a greater labor market tightness. In the present model, larger cities make labor more productive. They are associated with higher wages rates and lower unemployment rates. A higher job destruction rate implies lower labor market tightness and higher unemployment.

As before, preferences for final goods X and Y are assumed to be Cobb–Douglas with elasticities α, $1-\alpha$, respectively. Equilibrium utility in each type of city, given expected income per person, $\frac{\pi_J}{d_J+\pi_J} w_J \left(1 - \kappa_e N_J^{1/2}\right)$, is

$$\alpha^* \left(\frac{P_X}{w_J}\right)^{-\alpha} \left(\frac{P_Y}{w_J}\right)^{-(1-\alpha)} \frac{\pi_J}{d_J + \pi_J} \left(1 - \kappa_e N_J^{1/2}\right), \; J = X, Y. \tag{7.95}$$

I introduce again intercity trading costs of the iceberg type, that is, when a unit of a final good is shipped, only a fraction θ survives. A city specializing in X imports good Y and faces an effective price of $\theta^{-1} P_Y$. By applying (7.82) for both industries to write for P_X/w_X and P_Y/w_Y in (7.95), equilibrium indirect utility takes the form

$$\alpha^* \frac{\vartheta}{1-\vartheta} \left(\frac{P_X}{\theta^{-1} P_Y}\right)^{1-\alpha} \left(1 - \kappa_e N_X^{1/2}\right) \frac{\pi_X}{d_X + \pi_X} \frac{\rho + d_X}{q(v_X)}. \tag{7.96}$$

The counterpart of this expression for a city specializing in good Y readily follows by symmetry:

$$\alpha^* \frac{\vartheta}{1-\vartheta} \left(\frac{\theta^{-1} P_X}{P_Y}\right)^{-\alpha} \left(1 - \kappa_e N_Y^{1/2}\right) \frac{\pi_Y}{d_Y + \pi_Y} \frac{\rho + d_Y}{q(v_Y)}. \tag{7.97}$$

Expressions (7.95), (7.96), and (7.97) show the presence of a notable new effect in equilibrium utility due to labor market frictions. Greater net labor supply, $H_c(N_X)$, $H_c(N_Y)$, increases labor market tightness, and thus the employment rates of residents in either type of specialized city. It also increases equilibrium wage rates via the productivity enhancing effect of intermediates. This boosts expected utility but also increases congestion costs. Algebraically, this is indicated by the presence of the employment rate in the right-hand sides of (7.96) and (7.97) above. Other things being equal, this has the effect of increasing equilibrium city size relative to the absence of labor turnover. Other things being equal, higher final good prices P_X or P_Y have no direct effect on equilibrium size. However, with a given national population, there is, as we see shortly below, an indirect effect through the number of cities specializing in either good X or good Y that affects total supplies and thus the terms of trade.

A higher relative price of the good in which a city specializes, its terms of trade, increases welfare directly through the value of a city's exports. It also does so indirectly through the increased derived demand for labor, and through its concomitant effects in increasing labor market tightness, both wage rates, and the employment rate, which raise expected income and thus expected utility. Variations in traded goods prices at the national level thus have welfare effects on individual outcomes in different cities.

A drop in a traded good price may reduce expected utility below that offered by a diversified city and thus provide an incentive for a city to switch. Under the assumption that such a switch is costless, doing so reduces the national supply of the respective traded good and increases that of the other. Therefore, the option of diversifying industrial composition has a stabilizing effect on the terms of trade.

7.8.5 Equilibrium Urban Structure with Intercity Trade and Labor Turnover

I impose spatial equilibrium across specialized cities by equating (7.96) and (7.97). This yields

$$\frac{P_X}{P_Y} = \theta^{2\alpha-1} \frac{\left[1 - \kappa_e N_Y^{1/2}\right] \frac{\pi_Y}{d_Y+\pi_Y}}{\left[1 - \kappa_e N_X^{1/2}\right] \frac{\pi_X}{d_X+\pi_X}}. \tag{7.98}$$

The presence of the last term in the right-hand side of the above equation makes it impossible, unlike in section 7.5 above, to express the price ratio in general equilibrium in closed form as a function of (N_X, N_Y). From equation (7.94), and from its counterpart for a city specializing in good Y, the labor market tightness variables (υ_X, υ_Y) may be written implicitly as functions of N_X and N_Y, respectively.

By substituting from (7.98) back into (7.96) and (7.97), we obtain the following expression for utility at spatial equilibrium:

$$\theta^{2\alpha(1-\alpha)} \left(\left[1 - \kappa_e N_X^{1/2}\right] \frac{\pi_X}{d_X + \pi_X} \frac{\rho + d_X}{q(\upsilon_X)} \right)^{\alpha} \left(\left[1 - \kappa_e N_Y^{1/2}\right] \frac{\pi_Y}{d_Y + \pi_Y} \frac{\rho + d_Y}{q(\upsilon_Y)} \right)^{1-\alpha}. \tag{7.99}$$

The dependence of equilibrium expected utility on labor market tightness is a notable new feature of the model. As anticipated, it allows for a positive effect of city size due to improved matching which increases both wages and employment rates. Both those beneficial effects as well as adverse effects due to congestion in each type of city have spillovers in the other type of city, as well.

I characterize general equilibrium in the economy with intercity trade by equating total spending on good X by all n_Y cities specializing in producing good Y to total spending on good Y by all n_X cities specializing in good X. That is:

$$\frac{P_X}{P_Y} = \frac{\alpha}{1-\alpha} \frac{n_Y}{n_X} \frac{Y}{X}, \tag{7.100}$$

where X, Y denote the quantity of tradable goods produced by each city type. Expressing output produced for goods X, Y by using (7.92) and (7.93), I obtain the following:

$$\frac{n_Y}{n_X} \frac{Y}{X} = \frac{\hat{\Lambda}_X}{\hat{\Lambda}_Y} \frac{1-\alpha}{\alpha} \theta^{2\alpha-1} \frac{H_c^{\frac{1-u_X}{\sigma-1}}(N_X) \left(\frac{\pi_Y}{d_Y+\pi_Y}\right)^{1-u_Y} \frac{\rho+d_Y}{q(\upsilon_Y)}}{H_c^{\frac{1-u_Y}{\sigma-1}}(N_Y) \left(\frac{\pi_X}{d_X+\pi_X}\right)^{1-u_X} \frac{\rho+d_X}{q(\upsilon_X)}}. \tag{7.101}$$

Using the conditions for optimal factor use, (7.94), which in our case determine labor market tightness, in (7.101) shows that the right-hand side is equal to $u_{Y,s}/u_{X,s}$, a function of parameters only. This in turn allows us to solve for the share of the national population in the cities of each type. That is, from (7.101), (7.94), and (7.61) we obtain the counterpart here of (7.64):

$$n_X = \frac{\overline{N}}{N_X} \frac{\alpha}{\alpha + (1-\alpha)\theta^{2\alpha-1}\frac{u_{Y,s}}{u_{X,s}}}, \quad n_Y = \frac{\overline{N}}{N_Y} \frac{(1-\alpha)\theta^{2\alpha-1}\frac{u_{Y,s}}{u_{X,s}}}{\alpha + (1-\alpha)\theta^{2\alpha-1}\frac{u_{Y,s}}{u_{X,s}}}. \tag{7.102}$$

The urban structure is fully determined once city sizes (N_X, N_Y) have been determined, either via spatial equilibrium or as part of a planner's optimum. As in the model without labor market frictions earlier in the chapter, the share of population residing in either city type increases with the respective share in spending by consumers.

7.8.6 Diversified versus Specialized Cities

The solution obtained in (7.102) above for the share of population residing in either city type, or what is the same for the share of population employed in the production of the two final goods, can be readily compared with its counterpart for diversified cities. Within each diversified city, and therefore in the entire economy, the relative share of labor employed in the two industries is given by

$$\frac{\alpha(1-u_X) + \vartheta(1+\rho)\alpha u_X}{(1-\alpha)(1-u_Y) + \vartheta(1+\rho)(1-\alpha)u_Y}.$$

Suppose that all cities have the same size. Would it always pay for cities to specialize in the presence of labor market frictions? I note that the expressions for expected utility under specialization and diversification, (7.91) and (7.99), respectively, are similar, in fact identical if $N_X = N_Y$. Yet, we should bear in mind that in the case of diversification both industries in each city share the same total quantity of labor. Therefore, ceteris paribus, specialized cities would have higher employment and wage rates than diversified cities. Yet, congestion impinges upon welfare outcomes in both city types. The economy-wide terms of trade in the economy of specialized cities will in general differ from the respective value under diversification, while both are endogenous. However, the determination of the former is subject to fewer restrictions than that of the latter. With free creation of cities and free labor mobility, we would expect that new specialized cities would appear for as long they offer expected utility exceeding that of diversified cities. At spatial equilibrium, utility will be equalized across all types of cities. From (7.99), the city size that maximizes expected utility for a specialized city of either type depends on the production and labor market friction parameters associated with the other type. From (7.91), on the other hand, both sets of parameters enter the determination of equilibrium size of diversified cities. In general, intuition suggests that a larger city size must be compensated by means of higher employment rates in both industries.

The model lends itself readily to the definition of the planner's problem. Suppose there exists a given number of sites, where either specialized or diversified cities may be located. By imposing the condition that individuals should be indifferent between living in either type of city, a planner may allocate resources so as to bring about the maximum possible level of utility, while respecting the informational structure of the economy, namely that hiring takes place via matching. The solution to a planner's problem defines the socially optimal urban structure, which in general would consist of specialized and diversified cities. In addition, the planner's problem may be defined under different institutional restrictions, such as given populations in different sites.

The model of the labor market subject to frictions that I work with here although not fully stochastic allows for several interesting questions to be examined in greater depth. These include the impact of differences in the effectiveness of matching among the two industries and the importance of differences in the rates at which jobs break up in the two industries in the incidence of unemployment across the economy. It would also be interesting to examine business cycle effects across the urban system. A convenient way to do this is to assume, in a manner reminiscent of real business cycle theory, productivity shocks. These can be shocks to total factor productivity in the production of final goods, or to the productivity of the intermediate varieties. As an example, let us consider a positive shock to total factor productivity of good X. From (7.82) we have that both the wage rate and the labor market tightness increase. Employment by industry X increases, unemployment decreases and so does the unemployment rate. This increases the attractiveness of type–X cities, as well as production of good X. Ultimately, the price of good X decreases which in turn decreases the attractiveness of type–X cities. The adjustment in the economy through unemployment dynamics as total factor productivity returns to its original value traces a counter-clockwise loop along the Beveridge curve, just as in the textbook case of (Pissarides 2000, 32). This provides the basis for city-specific as well as sector-specific Beveridge curves.[23] Another possible extension is to consider the coexistence of the centralized method of search, on which this section is based, with a referral-based method, as analyzed in section 5.8 above. Different search methods can coexist in different parts of a city, as they may be chosen by individuals with different socioeconomic characteristics. Referral-based methods of search rely on social interactions. Therefore, their existence offers an additional dimension along which social interactions affect the spatial structure of the urban economy.

7.9 MODELING LESSONS FROM THE EMPIRICS OF URBAN SPECIALIZATION AND DIVERSIFICATION

In view of the evidence of the empirics of urban specialization and diversification in section 7.8.1 above, one cannot take too literal a view of specialization in a single industry. Furthermore, one can modify the model to allow for colocation of industries when there are many industries. I discuss this again further below in chapter 9, section 9.6, by introducing spillovers in the style of Rossi-Hansberg and Wright (2007).

A number of additional lessons seem particularly relevant. Since the production of nontraded goods employs the bulk of the urban labor force, it would add realism and provide better statistical fits if one were to modify the models in order to allow for nontraded goods and to include manufactured goods and services in addition to housing. The evidence on urban specialization in section 7.2 above suggests that specialization may be identified meaningfully only for groups of industries. The full power of the evidence from firms' location and industries' colocation decisions, examined in chapter 4, must be brought to bear on determining such clusters. The evidence of clustering of industries in cities may be exploited to identify industry interdependence. Of particular interest for the purpose of colocation is the risk-pooling force in agglomeration discussed in chapter 4, section 4.9. In view of the findings of Cuñat and Melitz (2011), discussed above, labor market flexibility and the accordant patterns of labor market frictions are a source of comparative advantage and therefore a motive for specialization.

A realistic theory of specialization must account for the hierarchy principle. As presented below in chapter 8, section 8.4, this principle asserts that industries found in a city of a given size will also be found in cities of a larger size. To incorporate this principle, a model must account for the colocation of industries that might be driven not only by firms' characteristics but also by those of consumers. As an intuitive explanation for the principle puts it, all cities that host gas stations need not have opera houses, too, but cities with opera houses also host gas stations. So, city types must be defined in terms of the ranges of industries that they host. In other words, this calls for examining patterns in industry colocations in diversified cities, while recognizing subtleties in the difference between specialized and diversified cities, as in the discussion in section 7.2 above.

A related matter is that the changing nature of specialization, namely, from sectoral to functional, has not been fully addressed by the empirical literature. As I discuss above in section 7.6.1, Duranton and Puga (2005) draw attention to the fact that great improvements in information and communication technologies allow headquarters of firms to locate separately from production facilities and thus for cities to specialize in terms of function, with headquarters and business services clustering in larger cities and production plants clustering in small- and medium-sized cities. Aarland, Davis, Henderson, and Ono (2007) investigate patterns in the spatial organization of firms' activities by analyzing firms' decisions to construct stand-alone central administrative offices. Using microlevel data from the U.S. census, they find that firms with such offices are much larger than those without. Firms with geographically dispersed production facilities that are industrially more diversified are more likely to have such offices. Such functional specialization is less apparent for service firms.

There are several other aspects of urban specialization versus diversification that I have not touched on. An important one is its implications for sorting of workers in terms of skills and occupations. If the technologies of producing different goods require a different occupational and skill mix of workers, then free movement of labor along with the force of specialization will confer different characters on different cities. Although the general properties of such an outcome may be studied by applying general principles of international trade theory in the manner of the present chapter, there is an additional angle. That is, larger cities may, in the spirit of Adam Smith's famous theorem that the division of labor is limited by the extent of the market, accommodate a finer division of labor. In other words, just as with the modeling of the hierarchy principle, there are indivisibilities at the worker level. So a city that hosts specialists, say brain surgeons, also hosts generalists, say pediatricians, while all cities host family physicians and car mechanics. Yet, there are cities with different types of mechanics, such as car mechanics, and so on, that do not host brain surgeons. Duranton and Jayet (2011) develop a model to study empirically the prediction that scarce specialist occupations are overrepresented in large cities. In other words, the prediction is that the division of labor is limited by the extent of the *urban* market. Duranton and Jayet test this prediction using unusually detailed data from the 1990 French census that involves more than 5 million observations. The data cover 25 percent of the French population in full-time employment in 111 three-digit French industrial sectors in 454 occupations and in 360 French urban areas (*aires urbaines*). They find that scarce occupations are better represented in large cities and that the overrepresentation increases with the scarcity of the particular occupation.

Finally, the chapter rests on spatial equilibrium, both within and across cities, which presumes that moves of households take place instantaneously. This is unrealistic, of course, because moves take time. There is almost a total absence of research in this area, but the results of Blanchard and Katz (1992), although aimed at regional evolutions, are quite suggestive. Regional shocks adjust largely by migration flows, and house prices take about 5 years to adjust. Research on the dynamics of housing prices suggests that metropolitan area housing prices may adjust after 5 years but overshoot and return to the steady state after about 10 years (Ioannides and Thanapisitikul 2008).[24] Such dynamic effects need to be addressed in more realistic versions of the models in this chapter.

7.10 SUMMARY AND CONCLUSIONS

The first part of the chapter provides the foundations for understanding urban structure and the transformational effect of intercity trade. It motivates specialization in several alternative ways. It highlights the effects of geography through the elaboration of three types of transportation costs, that is, for intracity movement of people and for intercity shipping of intermediates and of final goods. The chapter synthesizes the most prominent theories of urban structure, namely, the classical urban (system-of-cities) theory that accommodates principal stylized features of the urban structure as the outcome of very special assumptions about preferences and technology. The new economic geography literature also accommodates important features of the urban structure and has motivated research that leads directly to a robust prediction of realistic urban structures. A phenomenal amount of research has enriched theories of urban growth and development. It is also contributing to a deeper understanding of economic development more generally. I take up the empirics of urban evolution in chapter 8 next, and urban growth in chapter 9.

I rely extensively on the static model of Anas and Xiong (2003) with two manufactured goods, that are produced using raw labor and intermediates, because it lends itself nicely to the three-level production structure of chapter 9 below. The intermediates are themselves produced by means of increasing returns-to-scale technology using raw labor according to the Dixit–Stiglitz model. Allowing for specialization requires that I elaborate on alternative logically possible patterns. Cities can specialize in producing only intermediates, and thus accommodate functional specialization, or only one of the final goods. Some of these patterns might not coexist in the absence of shipping costs. At the other extreme is the canonical case of specialization in either of the final goods, where cities that specialize in the same final good also trade intermediates among themselves. At the general equilibrium with free mobility, specialization improves welfare relative to autarky.

From a broader viewpoint, the Marshallian equivalence, referred to in section 7.3 above, between different ways of specifying urban agglomeration is welcome. However, this equivalence does not facilitate empirically separating and identifying the underlying mechanisms. As Duranton and Puga (2004) point out, such identification is crucial when it comes to designing corrective policies for alternative mechanisms.

Urban specialization may also be interpreted as symmetry breaking, just as observed by Matsuyama (1996, 2008). Presence of shipping costs and particular patterns of geography may interact to make feasible a variety of patterns of specialization. For example, one may think of cities specializing in either of the final goods that benefit from importing intermediates (which could be specialized services) from "satellite" cities in their immediate vicinity. Optimum city sizes differ across these different patterns of specialization, and the model yields specific predictions about their relative frequencies at the general equilibrium of the economy. It is thus possible to compare urban structures across different economies given their fundamentals.

The chapter finally extends the basic model of specialization and intercity trade to the case of labor turnover and labor market frictions. It does so by adapting features of the Pissarides matching model, applied to the case of large firms (Pissarides 2000), and the ideas of Wasmer and Zenou (2002) to study urban unemployment. The same basic features of the model can accommodate urban specialization and diversification and the consequences of labor market turnover. Introducing labor market frictions into the system-of-cities model allows one to examine general features of urban booms and busts. In the special case examined, considerations of employment fluctuations associated with labor turnover favor diversification relative to specialization. When the national economy is hit by a macro shock, how do different cities' economies adjust? Do wages in some cities decline more than in the aggregate national economy, and why? How about unemployment and interurban migration? The model I introduce above could also be developed further in terms of its full stochastic properties. Structural change that affects urban structure in terms of diversification and specialization is also an important factor of economic dynamics. Further development of the model of urban structure in the presence of labor turnover, and of macro shocks more generally, in addition to traditional urban spatial frictions,[25] deserves attention in future research.

CHAPTER 8

Empirics of the Urban Structure and Its Evolution

8.1 INTRODUCTION

The extraordinary revival of interest in economic geography and urban economics that the economics literature has been experiencing has also registered an empirical presence.[1] A notable portion of this interest pertains to Zipf's law for city sizes. Some of the motivation for this surge in interest comes from scholars who see Zipf's law as an instance of a broader class of phenomena, many of which have been studied by physicists as well as other scientists.

Zipf's (1949) law for cities, an alleged empirical regularity that has become of considerable interest to researchers, is arguably one of the best known empirical facts in economics. In its strict version, which is also known as the rank-size rule, the law states that the second largest city is one-half the size of the largest, the third largest city is one-third the size of the largest, and so on. For instance, take the United States and order its cities by size, measured by population: New York as the largest has rank 1, and Los Angeles as the second largest has rank 2. The rank-size rule predicts that the product of each city's size times its rank is equal to a constant across all cities in an urban system.[2] Duranton (2007) refers succinctly to a broader set of empirical regularities: one, a stationary law for city size distributions that is skewed to the right, the *still*; two, churning of industries across cities as cities experience rapid changes in their industrial compositions, the *fast*; and, three, the pattern of urban size transitions, the *slow*. I take up these issues in turn. I start with Zipf's law and the vibrant exchanges both over theory and empirics pertaining to it. I then show that similar issues arise with different ways of measuring urban concentrations, including population densities over space. After I present the work of Duranton (2007), whose parsimonious model explains all three empirical regularities, I turn to the empirics of urban transitions by discussing models of urban evolution that allow for general intradistributional dependence. Such models are helpful in contemplating issues of resilience of urban systems to shocks. I discuss the U.S. experience in more detail.

The latest literature on the urban structure has a more macroeconomic flavor, seeking to establish properties of the entire urban structure in general

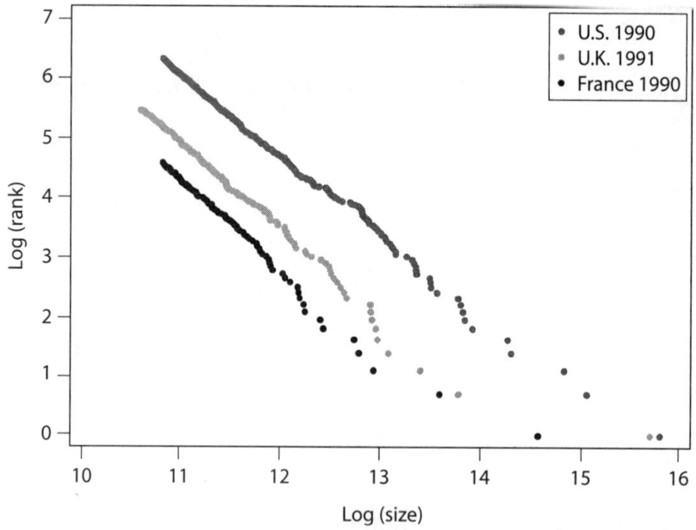

Figure 8.1. Zipf plots. *Source*: Ioannides, Overman, Rossi-Hansberg, and Schmidheiny (2008, 212, fig. B.1).

equilibrium and to characterize it via evolving size distributions of cities. I review some recent theories and clarify this further in chapter 9. There I discuss another theory, due to Rossi-Hansberg and Wright (2007), which is a dynamic system-of-cities model with capital accumulation and industry-specific shocks. That model implies Zipf's law in interesting but special cases and explains the departures from Zipf's law that we observe at each end of the city size distribution.

8.2 ZIPF'S LAW FOR CITIES

Zipf's law can be examined statistically by fitting an OLS line through the data consisting of $\{\ln[\text{Rank}_\ell], \ln S_\ell\}$, where S_ℓ denotes the normalized size of city ℓ, $S_\ell = \left(\sum_\ell N_\ell\right)^{-1} N_\ell$, $\ell = 1, \ldots, L$. That is:

$$\ln[\text{Rank}_\ell] = \bar{s}_o + \zeta \ln S_\ell + \epsilon_\ell. \tag{8.1}$$

Alternatively, one can draw a graph, known as a Zipf plot (see figure 8.1): on the vertical axis is the logarithm of the rank, and on the horizontal axis is the logarithm of the population of the corresponding city. If the rank-size rule holds, then this plot is a downward sloping line with slope equal to −1.

To a remarkable extent, statistical analyses for many different countries (Gabaix 1999a, 1999b, 2009; Gabaix and Ioannides 2004) yield estimates for ζ that are often concentrated around −1. This suggests that the size distribution of cities is well approximated by Zipf's law with coefficient −1, $\hat{\zeta} = -1$.[3] I discuss below a substantial variation in estimated Zipf coefficients across time and across countries that casts doubt on the universality and immutability of Zipf's law.

The three Zipf plots in figure 8.1 look very similar to one another, though none of the slopes of ordinary least-squares lines fitted to them equal −1. The plot for France is steeper than that for the United Kingdom, which in turn is steeper than that for the United States; the respective estimates are −1.55, −1.46, and −1.37 and are all estimated with very high precision and using 96, 232, and 552 observations, respectively. The plot for the United States is farthest to the right because U.S. cities are larger than those of the United Kingdom with the same rank, a fact that is reflected in the estimate of $\bar{s}_0$, equation (8.1). The plot for the United Kingdom in turn is farther to the right than that for France for the same reason.

Much of the theoretical literature on Zipf's law is aimed at predicting city size distributions that conform to Zipf's law, or at least to power laws for city sizes (see section 8.2 below). A more eclectic literature seeks to back out from differences across countries, like those illustrated in the above noted figure, the effects of observable country attributes and of time.

8.2.1 Basic Facts about Power Laws

Zipf's law for cities, and indeed power laws more generally, are attractive in various sciences, especially in physics, because they are *scale-free*, that is, they do not depend on definitions of units of measurement. A power law for cities states that the proportion of cities greater than a city of size S, the countercumulative of the size distribution of cities, is of the form

$$\mathrm{Prob}(s > S) = \left(\frac{S}{s_{\min}}\right)^{\zeta}, \zeta < 0, \tag{8.2}$$

where ζ and $s_{\min}$, the lower bound of the distribution, are parameters. They are, of course, functions of the deep determinants of city sizes in broader models, as I discuss further below and in chapter 9. The mean city size and the variance associated with the law, given by equation (8.2), identified as the Pareto countercumulative distribution function, are given by

$$\bar{S} = \mathcal{E}(S) = \frac{\zeta}{\zeta + 1} s_{\min}, \ \zeta < -1; \ \mathrm{Var}(S) = \frac{\zeta}{(\zeta + 1)^2(\zeta + 2)} s_{\min}^2; \zeta < -2. \tag{8.3}$$

The mean is finite if $\zeta < -1$; the variance is finite if $\zeta < -2$. Zipf's law is the Pareto law with $\zeta = -1$, in which case it coincides with the rank-size rule: since the number of cities greater than S is proportional to S, from (8.2), $\mathrm{Prob}(s > S) \times S$ is equal to $s_{\min}$, a constant. That in turn implies that the rank-size rule *cannot* correspond to a reasonable probability distribution, strictly defined; such a distribution would have neither a finite mean nor a finite variance. Still these facts do not trouble many adherents of Zipf's law, who often see it as an approximation of only the upper tail of the city size distribution along with a practical upper bound that ensures finite moments. At the same time, Eeckhout (2004) emphasizes the lognormality of city sizes when the universe of city sizes is considered.

8.2.2 Gibrat's Law

If different city sizes grow randomly with the same expected growth rate and the same variance, then Gibrat's law for the means and variances of city growth rates is consistent with Zipf's law at the upper tail of the size distribution (Gabaix 1999b).

First, let γ_t^ℓ be the gross growth rate of city ℓ, $\gamma_{t+1}^\ell = \frac{S_{t+1}^\ell}{S_t^\ell}$, where sizes are normalized by the contemporaneous average urban population. Let gross growth rates γ_t^ℓ be independently and identically distributed random variables for all ℓ's and t's with density function $f(\gamma)$. Suppose that the average normalized size stays equal to 1, that is, $\int_{-\infty}^{\infty} \gamma f(\gamma) d\gamma = 1$. Then the equation of motion of the distribution of growth rates expressed in terms of the countercumulative distribution function of S_t^ℓ, $G_t(S)$, is

$$G_{t+1}(S) = \int_0^\infty G_t\left(\frac{S}{\gamma}\right) f(\gamma)\, d\gamma. \tag{8.4}$$

Its steady-state distribution G, if it exists, satisfies

$$G(S) = \int_0^\infty G\left(\frac{S}{\gamma}\right) f(\gamma)\, d\gamma.$$

Zipf's law, expressed by a countercumulative distribution for city sizes of the form $G(S) = (S/s_{\min})^{-1}$, satisfies this condition. I note that this follows from Gibrat's law plus the condition that the average normalized size stays equal to 1. In addition, for an arbitrary Pareto law, Prob$(s > S) = (S/s_{\min})^{\zeta}$, $\zeta < 0$, to satisfy equation (8.4) at the steady state, $\mathcal{E}\left[\gamma^{-\zeta}\right] = 1$.[4]

Second, for completeness, I reproduce here, following Eeckhout (2004, 1447), the long-standing result that Gibrat's law implies asymptotically a lognormal distribution for city sizes.[5] This result follows from Gibrat's law plus the condition that the growth rates of different cities are small and independent and identically distributed random variables. Specifically, summing up the realizations of the growth rate of city ℓ from $t = 0$ to $t = T - 1$ yields

$$\sum_{t=0}^{T-1} \frac{S_{t+1}^\ell - S_t^\ell}{S_t^\ell} = \sum_{t=0}^{T-1} \gamma_{t+1}^\ell.$$

For small time intervals, the left-hand side of the above equation may be approximated by an integral, $\int_{S_0^\ell}^{S_T^\ell} \frac{dS^\ell}{S^\ell} = \ln S_T^\ell - \ln s_{\min}^\ell$ where $S_{\min}^\ell = S_0^\ell$. So the above equation becomes

$$\ln S_T^{\ell} - \ln s_{\min}^{\ell} = \sum_{t=0}^{T-1} \gamma_{t+1}^{\ell}. \tag{8.5}$$

From the central limit theorem, it follows that if the shocks γ_t^{ℓ} are small and independent and identically distributed, then their sum, the right-hand side of equation (8.5), is normally distributed given T. Thus, it follows that the city size at T, given $s_{\min}^{\ell}$, is lognormally distributed. However, as Gabaix (1999b, 261) points out, this distribution in the limit when $T \rightarrow \infty$ would have infinite variance unless it were normalized by dividing by $T^{1/2}$, or "frictions" were introduced.[6,7]

8.2.3 Zipf's Law as a Special Case of Urban Growth Following Reflected Geometric Brownian Motion

Gabaix (1999b) sets out to reconcile lognormally distributed city sizes, implied by Gibrat's law as just shown, with a power law for city sizes. He allows for growth rates of smaller cities to have larger variances or, more generally, for instantaneous means and variances of the growth rates for normalized city sizes to be size-dependent. In particular, he allows for a reflective barrier at 0.[8] Here I follow the derivation by Skouras (2009) who carries Gabaix's argument to its logical conclusion by working from first principles and not relying on the forward Kolmogorov equation.[9] Suppose that city sizes at time t vary according to the following reflected geometric Brownian motion:

$$S_t = \exp[Z_t], \; s_{\min} = \exp[z_{\min}], \tag{8.6}$$

$$Z_t = Y_t - \inf_{0 \leq \tau \leq t} : (Y_\tau - z_{\min}), \tag{8.7}$$

$$d\,Y_t = \mu dt + \sigma dB_t, \sigma > 0, \mu < 0; \tag{8.8}$$

where μ and σ denote, respectively, the instantaneous mean and variance of the growth rate of a size S_t city and B_t is a standard Brownian motion. This specification makes city size evolve as a reflected (regulated) geometric Brownian motion. That is, there exists an underlying growth rate process that evolves according to a standard Brownian motion (8.8), whose instantaneous mean is negative in order for the distribution to have a stationary asymptotic distribution. However, if city size falls below the value of $s_{\min}$, it is "reflected" back to $s_{\min}$ as specified by (8.7) above. In other words, the evolution of city sizes follows geometric Brownian motion with a constant instantaneous mean and variance as long as the size is above $s_{\min}$, so that $dZ_t = dY_t$. If city size hits the barrier $s_{\min}$, it is reset at that barrier. The reflective barrier mechanically generates positive contributions toward the mean from the lower end of the size distribution. Consequently, $\mu(S)$ has to be negative for the outcome of the process to be finite.

The density of the Z_t (the log of city size) process at time t, given its position z_0 at time $t = 0$, may be written in closed form (Ricciardi and Sacerdote 1987; Harrison 1990):

$$f(Z,t|z_0) = n\left[z_0 + \mu t, \sigma^2 t\right] + \frac{1}{\sigma\sqrt{2\pi t}}\exp\left[-\frac{4\mu t(z_0 - z_{\min}) + (Z + z_0 - 2z_{\min} - \mu t)^2}{2\sigma^2 t}\right]$$
$$-\frac{\mu}{\sigma^2}\exp\left[\frac{2\mu}{\sigma^2}(Z - z_{\min})\right]\text{erfc}\left(\frac{Z + z_0 - 2z_{\min} + \mu t}{\sigma\sqrt{2t}}\right), \qquad (8.9)$$

where $n\left[z_0 + \mu t, \sigma^2 t\right]$ is the normal density with mean $z_0 + \mu t$ and variance $\sigma^2 t$ and $\text{erfc}(u)$ is the complementary error function, $\text{erfc}(u) \equiv \frac{2}{\sqrt{\pi}}\int_u^\infty \exp[-w^2]dw = 2\left[1 - N\left(u\sqrt{2}\right)\right]$, with $N(\cdot)$ denoting the standardized normal cumulative. This solution is more general than (8.4), because it accounts for the reflective barrier and thus does not satisfy (8.4).

Following Skouras (2009), an inspection of (8.9) suggests that for values of Z far from $z_{\min}$ and small t, the last two terms above are close to 0 and the process obeys a standard Brownian motion: the density of city sizes is lognormal. However, as t grows (i.e., after a sufficiently long time), the first term tends to zero, regardless of the value of $z_{\min}$, making the standard Brownian motion component of the process negligible. The two terms reflecting the presence of the barrier are now relevant. As the argument of the complementary error function tends to $-\infty$ (recall that $\mu < 0$), its value tends to 2, and the limit of the density is

$$f_{Z_\infty}(Z) = -\zeta\exp[\zeta(Z - z_{\min})], \; \zeta = 2\frac{\mu}{\sigma^2}.$$

Integrating this limit density, the cumulative distribution function is

$$F_{Z_\infty}(Z) = 1 - \exp[\zeta(Z - z_{\min})], \; \zeta = 2\frac{\mu}{\sigma^2}. \qquad (8.10)$$

Finally, recalling (8.6), for $S \geq s_{\min}$ the limit cumulative distribution function for city sizes is

$$f_{S_\infty}(S) = -\zeta\left(\frac{S}{s_{\min}}\right)^\zeta\frac{1}{S}, \quad F_{S_\infty}(S) = 1 - \left(\frac{S}{s_{\min}}\right)^\zeta. \qquad (8.11)$$

The value of the density at $s_{\min}$ may also be obtained in closed form directly from (8.9).[10]

In sum, the limit city size distribution is quite subtle. Contrary to casual intuition, a lower barrier does not produce a truncated lognormal distribution (Skouras 2009). It produces instead a Pareto law with exponent $2\frac{\mu}{\sigma^2}$ and a lower bound $s_{\min}$.[11] Zipf's law is implied *only* as the *special case* of $-\mu = \frac{1}{2}\sigma^2$ for which $\zeta = -1$. For the mean of the limit distribution to be finite, from (8.2), $-\mu > \frac{1}{2}\sigma^2$. Intuitively, since there is a constant source of dispersion represented by the instantaneous variance, the downward tendency must be sufficiently strong to prevent the distribution from blowing up. Furthermore, changes in the underlying parameters are reflected in changes in the Zipf exponent. An increase in the absolute value of the instantaneous mean growth rate increases ζ absolutely, as does a decrease in the instantaneous variance.

The stringent parametric conditions under which power laws, including Zipf's law in particular, emerge for city size distributions are mitigated by generalizing the state dependence of the Brownian motion describing urban growth rates, which I turn to next immediately below. Several economic arguments justify the existence of a reflective barrier. For example, durable housing that decays slowly (because of physical, economic, or even political-economy reasons) may prevent existing sites from vanishing from the city size distribution.

8.2.4 Approximate Zipf's Law as a Limit When Urban Growth Follows General Geometric Brownian Motion

Instead of working with a reflective barrier, one may introduce friction by means of the births and deaths of cities as well as jumps. See Gabaix (2009, 264–266). Alternatively, a more general specification of the urban growth process as a geometric Brownian motion (Gabaix 2009, 266),

$$\frac{dS_t}{S_t} = \mu(S_t)dt + \sigma(S_t)dB_t, \tag{8.12}$$

allows for both the instantaneous mean and instantaneous variance to depend on city size. Gabaix works with the forward Kolmogorov equation whose derivation relies on Itō's lemma, the stochastic calculus counterpart of the chain rule in ordinary calculus.

Intuitively, the change in the probability distribution function $p(S, t)$ over an interval of time dt is due to a direct effect of t, $\frac{\partial}{\partial t}p(S, t)dt$, and to the effect of the change in S. The latter is obtained by working with a Taylor expansion around S_t up to the second order. Involving the second partial derivative $\frac{\partial^2}{\partial S^2}p(S, t)$ here is called for because, from (8.12), the proportional change in S_t also contains a random term, $\sigma(S_t)dB_t$, that involves the standard deviation of $\sigma(S_t)$. In these manipulations, the properties of B_t are crucial. For example, the expectation of dB_t is zero, but its standard deviation is proportional to $\sqrt{dt}$, making the instantaneous variance proportional to dt. The respective forward Kolmogorov equation becomes [Gabaix 2009, 266, eq. (26)]

$$\frac{\partial}{\partial t}p(S, t) = -\frac{\partial}{\partial S}[\mu(S)Sp(S, t)] + \frac{1}{2}\frac{\partial^2}{\partial S^2}\left[\sigma^2(S)S^2 p(S, t)\right]. \tag{8.13}$$

Integrating this partial differential equation once at its steady-state value $\frac{\partial}{\partial t}p(S, t) = 0$ and requiring that the first derivative of the right-hand side of (8.13) be equal to 0 so as to be invariant with respect to S yields

$$0 = -\mu(S)Sp(S) + \frac{1}{2}\frac{\partial}{\partial S}\left[\sigma^2(S)S^2 p(S)\right].$$

Manipulating this further[12] and using the definition of the *local* Zipf exponent, $\zeta(S) = 1 + \frac{S}{p(S)}\frac{dp(S)}{dS}$, with the invariant distribution of city sizes, $p(S)$, which satisfies (8.13), gives equation (13), in (Gabaix 1999b, 757), which is corrected in [Gabaix 2009, 266, eq. (27)]. That is,

$$\zeta(S) = -1 + 2\frac{\mu(S)}{\sigma^2(S)} - \frac{\partial \ln[\sigma^2(S)]}{\partial \ln S}, \tag{8.14}$$

where $\mu(S)$ is relative to the overall mean for all city sizes.[13] If Gibrat's law holds and the variance of the growth rate is large relative to the mean, then this equation implies that $\zeta(S)$ will be close to but absolutely larger than -1. If, on the other hand, the growth rate of the normalized city sizes is $\mu(S) = 0$ and the variance is independent of size, then the last term on the right-hand side of the equation above will be equal to 0. Then Gibrat's law holds exactly. Generally, if the instantaneous variance of the urban growth rate decreases with city size and, considering that we must have $\mu < 0$, then $\zeta(S)$ will be absolutely small for low S and will grow absolutely with size to become absolutely greater than 1. This is reinforced by the fact that the instantaneous variance of S must have an increasing elasticity with respect to S because it tends to a finite value while declining. This implies a Zipf plot that is "concave." In that case, there will be both fewer smaller and fewer larger cities than Zipf's law demands. This is in broad agreement with the data, as I discuss shortly below.

According to Skouras (2009) (see also section 8.2.7 below), Gabaix's normalization of city sizes requires dealing with conceptual problems that appear in a growing economy with increasing urbanization. City growth rates are unlikely to be independently and identically distributed, which poses problems for both Gabaix's and Eeckhout's derivations. Still, the prediction that the upper tail of city size distributions is likely to be closely approximated by a power law, which in general is a function of underlying magnitudes such as the mean and the variance of the evolution of city sizes, is a major contribution of Gabaix's work. Also significant is his articulation of the role of frictions in determining city sizes.

8.2.5 Zipf's Law from a "Spatial" Gibrat's Law

Lee and Li (2011) apply "spatially" the logic of how Gibrat's law for urban growth rates leads to a lognormal distribution of city size. They work with a simple model of a city where preferences and the production of consumption goods and of housing are all affected by different TFP functions, which in turn are defined as products of many terms, each of which is proportional to an isoelastic function of the city's population. The exponents of these isoelastic functions of city population are referred to as agglomeration parameters and are assumed to be deterministic. All the factors of proportionality are assumed to be random variables that may themselves have underlying components in common. Under their assumptions, equilibrium utility in each city itself turns out to be proportional to an isoelastic but decreasing function of city population, a feature that ensures the stability of spatial equilibrium. The solution in turn implies that, at intercity spatial equilibrium, city populations are increasing in city-specific factors of proportionality for the preference amenity and production and housing supply TFP factors. Because of the multiplicative separability of the model, the logarithm of a city's population may be written as a weighted sum of random variables, the same variables that make up the factors of proportionality mentioned earlier, where the weights are functions of the agglomeration parameters and of the parameters of the preference and production functions. Using a central limit theorem that also allows for dependence among the distributions that the summation terms obey, the authors show that city size distributions are lognormal.

Preferences and technologies are indeed subject to many random shocks, and Lee and Li's modeling of the TFP functions as isoelastic functions is quite standard. What is very innovative, however, is their assumption of many factors, which in turn naturally leads to a central limit theorem setting. These authors show by simulation that a fairly small number of factors actually suffices to explain the resulting equilibrium city size distribution, with the empirical Zipf's coefficient being related to the agglomeration parameters. The stronger the agglomeration effects, the smaller the absolute value of the Zipf's coefficient and the more dispersed the city size distribution; in fact, it does not have to be equal to -1. Lee and Li establish this step by expressing the Zipf's coefficient as the coefficient of log size in a Zipf's regression for log rank with data assumed to satisfy their equilibrium model. This simple step is quite significant in the literature, but the authors do not demonstrate that their model implies a Pareto law as such. Nonetheless, their method is very promising because it is based on assumptions that are standard ingredients of urban models, making attractive the intuitive appeal of the spatial Gibrat's law.

8.2.6 Review of Estimates for Zipf's Law for Cities

To the extent that Zipf's law for city sizes in particular, or power laws more generally, are predicted by theory, they portray limiting situations. Since no urban system is likely to be observed in a steady state, empirical research needs to deal with the fact that such specific distributions must be thought of as transitional,[14] that is, as tendencies rather than exact outcomes. The two explanations I discuss above have two features: one, dispersion forces augment urban growth throughout the size distribution; and two, a tendency for mean city sizes to decline is necessary to keep city sizes finite. The thickness of the upper tail increases with the absolute value of the mean of the instantaneous growth rate and decreases with its variance. Zipf's law is a limiting case that ensures that the mean city size is finite, that is, it is the thickest upper tail consistent with a finite mean size.

Rosen and Resnick (1980) and Soo (2005) provide notable empirical international comparative studies. These are typically conducted along the lines of equation (8.1). Rosen and Resnick examine city size distributions for 44 countries in 1970. The average Zipf's exponent is -1.13 with a standard deviation of 0.19, and in almost all countries it is between -0.8 and -1.5. Brakman, Garretsen, Marrewijk, and Van der Berg (1999) and Brakman, Garretsen, and Van Marrewijk (2001, 206–208, 220–221) show that city-proper data (i.e., for urban jurisdictions) are associated with smaller Zipf exponents (mean $= -1.13$, S.D. $= 0.19$, $N = 42$) than urban agglomeration data (mean $= -1.05$, S.D. $= 0.21$, $N = 22$). Soo (2005) finds a Zipf coefficient of -1.105 for cities but -0.854 for urban agglomerations, using data on 73 countries and two estimation methods—OLS and the Hill estimator (which reduces to the maximum likelihood estimator when a power law is the null hypothesis). With either estimator, Zipf's law is rejected far more often than one would expect based on random chance: for 53 out of 73 countries using OLS, and for 30 out of 73 countries using the Hill estimator. Soo finds that variations in the value of the Pareto exponent are better explained by political economy variables than by economic geography variables, which often have the wrong signs. The former include the Gastil index of political rights and civil liberties and measures of political stability that have an indicator variable for the time the country achieved independence, an indicator variable for whether the country had an external war between 1960 and 1985, total government expenditure as a share of GDP, and a set of continent dummies. Soo also includes scale economies, transport costs, nonagricultural economic activity, and trade as a share of GDP.

Some interpret the large dispersion of the estimates of the Zipf exponent as mixed evidence in favor of Zipf's law. Dobkins and Ioannides (2000) report OLS estimates of ζ, obtained along the lines of (8.1) with repeated cross sections of U.S. census data for metropolitan areas. Their estimates for ζ increase from -1.044 in 1900 to -0.949 in 1990. They also report maximum likelihood estimates for power law distributions along the lines of (8.2) with the same data, which increase from -0.953 in 1900 to -0.553 in 1990. When they use only the upper one-half of the sample, the estimate of ζ decreases in absolute value from -1.212 in 1900, with 56 metropolitan areas in the entire sample, to -0.993 in 1990, with 167 metropolitan areas in the sample. Gabaix (1999b) reports an estimate equal to -1.005 using the 135 largest metropolitan areas in 1990.

Despite the enticing estimates obtained with the Pareto law and U.S. metropolitan population data, doubts about the validity of Zipf's law linger. Nitsch (2005) offers a meta-analysis of 515 estimates of the Zipf exponent from 29 studies. He finds that the combined estimate of $|\zeta|$ is significantly larger than 1 and that both its mean and standard deviation generally increase over time, especially with data since 1950. This finding, which is in broad agreement with Ioannides, Overman, Rossi-Hansberg and Schmidheiny (2008), implies that city sizes are on average more evenly distributed than suggested by the strict Zipf's law. Nitsch suggests some differences across the individual point estimates that may be due to the use of metropolitan area population data instead of data for cities proper or for jurisdictions. Nitsch

(2005) also identifies problems with the rules determining the construction of data. Such problems are critical and unique to measures of urban economic activity.[15] The urban population data used should ideally measure consistently defined agglomerations, but the conventions employed by different countries make it difficult to obtain and organize the data consistently, especially over long periods of time. We should expect the exponent ζ *to be* absolutely larger for cities proper than for urban agglomerations because urban agglomerations are not bound by legal definitions of cities proper and therefore are likely to have a thicker upper tail. I use the terms "urban" and "metropolitan" as synonyms throughout this chapter. Nevertheless, the nature of the data problem is subtle and pervasive, as is underscored by the specifics of U.S. data availability. Therefore, I discuss this issue in more detail in section 8.5 below.

Nonparametric results by Dobkins and Ioannides (2000) and the finding of a significant quadratic term in a log rank regression, equation (8.1), reported by Black and Henderson (2003), raise further doubts about the validity of Zipf's law as a description of the entire distribution of city sizes for the United States. Black and Henderson (2003) regress the logarithm of city rank against the logarithm of city size and its square using twentieth century U.S. metropolitan data. Their results show that when all cities are used, the Zipf coefficient increases from -0.861 in 1900 to -0.842. It decreases from -1.01 in 1900 to -1.18 in 1990 when only the top one-third of the size distribution is used.

Inconsistencies in definitions of cities over time have been a major impediment in empirical studies of the dynamics of city size distribution. Black and Henderson (2003) and Dobkins and Ioannides (2000, 2001) use consistent definitions of metropolitan areas over time to create panel data sets. I discuss those studies below in section 8.6.3.

Ioannides and Overman (2003) use Gabaix's expression in equation (8.14) above for the local Zipf coefficient to estimate the city size distribution and thus to test directly for the validity of Zipf's law. Their nonparametric approach uses stochastic kernels and produces a three-dimensional representation of the distribution of growth rates conditional on city size. They estimate a city's growth rate as dependent on city size and estimate the mean and variance of city growth rates conditional on size.[16] Their results provide strong support for Zipf's law with U.S. data for metropolitan areas. The plot for the entire sample (Ioannides and Overman, 2003, 132, fig. 1, panels a and b), reproduced here as figure 8.2, panels a and b, suggests that, except for the very smallest cities, the conditional distribution of growth rates is remarkably stable across city sizes. The plot for the largest 110 metropolitan areas, panels c and d, is not quite as clear-cut. Growth rates for most middle-size cities appear concentrated, with some large outlying (negative) growth experiences for these cities. Growth rates for the top-size cities are fairly concentrated with a few large outlying (positive and negative) growth experiences. Panels e and f show the plot for the largest 110 cities excluding the latest two decades, and one can see that the variance of the growth rate declines for the largest cities over most of the sample period.

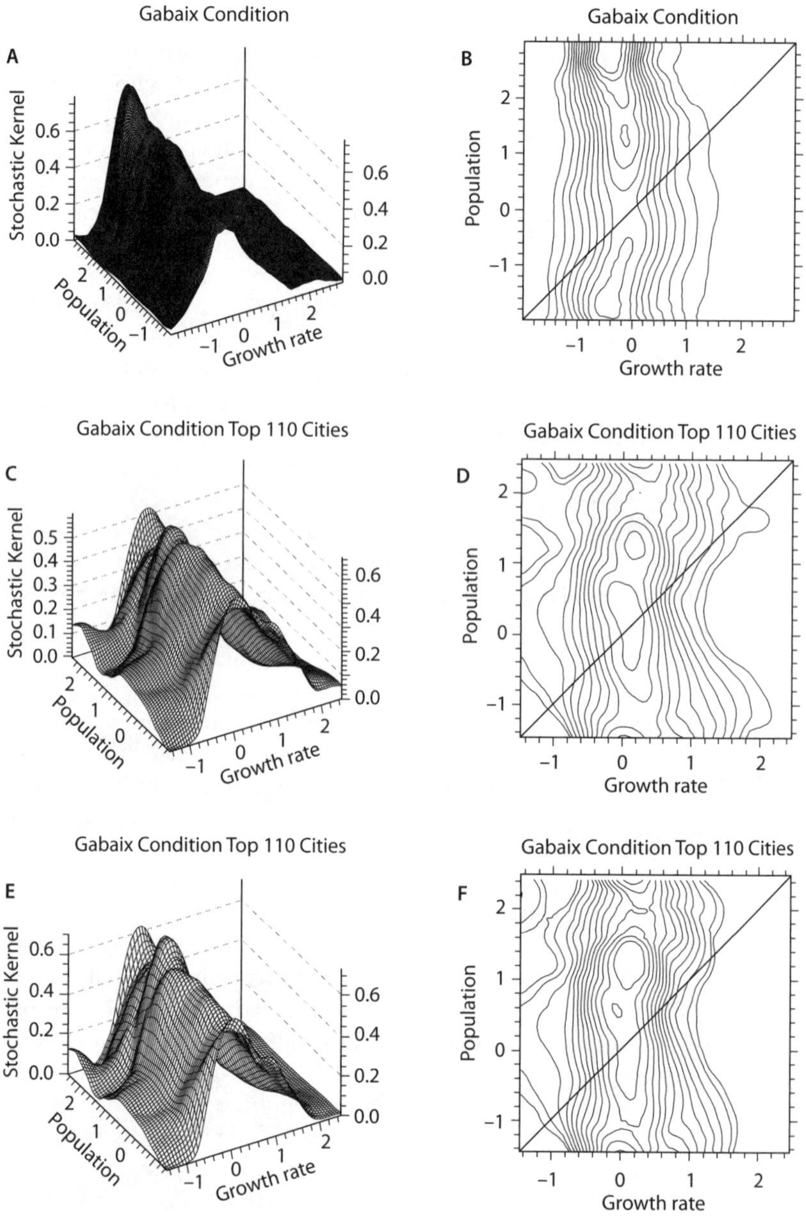

Figure 8.2. Nonlinear Zipf's law: population to growth rates. *Source*: Ioannides and Overman (2003, 132, fig. 1).

These results also help explain two interesting features of the size distribution of U.S. cities. First, estimates of $|\zeta|$ for U.S. cities decline over time. Gabaix (1999b) suggests that a declining $|\zeta|$ reflects the entry of small cities whose sizes have a lower local $|\zeta|$. Ioannides and Overman confirm this suggestion. Second, comparison of nonparametric estimates of the log rank–log size relationship to a standard parametric estimate suggests that it is roughly concave, as Black and Henderson (2003) and Dobkins and Ioannides (2000) had found. Ioannides and Overman find a local Zipf exponent that hovers between -0.8 and -0.9 for most of the range of values of city sizes and then rises and finally falls, which is consistent with this pattern. These findings confirm the importance of looking at the entire evolution of city sizes and growth rates, as the snapshot offered by 1990 data is clearly not sufficient to derive firm conclusions.

Gabaix and Ioannides (2004) offer a simple explanation for the flattening of the Zipf curve (smaller $|\zeta|$) observed for small cities, which corresponds to relatively fewer small cities. Smaller cities have growth rates with higher variance than large cities. The variance in growth rates decreases with size for small cities, and then asymptotes to a "variance floor" for large cities. This may be because large cities still have very diversified industry bases. Think, for example, of New York and Los Angeles. This pattern is what Christaller's hierarchy principle (see chapter 8, sections 8.4 and 8.4.2.1 below) would also suggest.

8.2.7 The Importance of Heterogeneity and the Skouras Model

These approaches leave open the possibility that growth rates are not independent and identically distributed random draws from the same distribution for all cities. Economic geography suggests that there exist persistent location characteristics such as physical attributes of the landscape, weather, and coastal location. Advantageous second-nature features, like market potential, are correlated with growth rates. Skouras (2009) comfortably rejects the hypothesis that city growth rates are independent and identically distributed by means of a type of Chow test. A panel variance ratio test similarly rejects homogeneity.

Skouras (2009, prop. 1), exploits the following intuition. He assumes that city sizes may obey different distributions, even a mixture of distributions, some of which can be power laws. But power laws have heavier tails than the other distributions, so if such distributions are present in the mixture, they will dominate the tail of the cross section. The large cities we observe are likely to obey power law distributions, while smaller cities are likely to be those with other distributions. This logic suggests that the upper tail will be dominated by power distributions that have the lowest *possible* power exponent, that is, the thickest tails. But this exponent cannot be larger than -1. If $\zeta > -1$, the mean would be infinite and so would the country's population. Skouras assumes that, one, average city size remains constant as the number of cities increases; two, city sizes are heterogeneous in the sense that each city obeys a distribution chosen as an independent random draw from a finite number of possible distribution functions that have power law tails or thinner; and three, one of the distributions in the mixture has density with a tail exponent equal to $-2-\epsilon^m$, where ϵ^m is a small positive number, in other words, is approximately

Zipf's law.[17] Skouras demonstrates that with those assumptions the upper tail of the distribution must be dominated by cities with distributions that are approximately Zipf.

Skouras argues forcefully that Gabaix's proposed normalization, which Ioannides and Overman follow, implies a restriction on the regulated geometric Brownian motion that is central to Gabaix's model. Skouras proposes that the normalization necessary to account for the trend needs to take into consideration how doing so interacts with key parameters of the growth process at work. Skouras suggests allowing for a general time trend in the normalized sizes and normalizing in terms of *total* population. The detrending quantity he proposes is the ratio of the total population at any time to its value at the beginning of the process, which makes the relative growth of each city proportional to its size.

Skouras assumes[18] that the heterogeneity in growth rates of suitably detrended city size data takes the form of lognormality in the body of the distribution and of Zipf's law at the upper tail. Each city's growth rate follows its own regulated geometric Brownian motion, with parameters treated as random and described in terms of a detrended lower bound (associated with the reflective barrier), which is distributed according to a lognormal distribution with parameters $(\mu^*, (\sigma^*)^2)$, for which the auxiliary parameter $2\frac{\mu^*}{(\sigma^*)^2} + 1$ has a uniform distribution over $[\gamma^*, -1.001]$. The auxiliary parameter and the lower bound are assumed to be independently distributed. This specification of a heterogeneous detrended regulated geometric Brownian motion leads to heterogeneous steady-state size distributions. It allows for Zipf's law by ensuring that the upper tail is sufficiently thin to allow for finite means of cities, whose growth leads to a Zipf steady state that dominates the tail of the cross section. The upper tail cannot be fatter than Zipf's law, mathematically speaking, because the underlying distribution will not have a finite mean (see section 8.2), and economically speaking, because the urban system is finite as a share of the economy and therefore may not be described by an infinite mean. Zipf's law arises because it possesses the thickest tail consistent with a finite mean. It also satisfies Gibrat's law and therefore implies lognormality asymptotically in the main body of the distribution, which cannot obey Zipf's law, strictly speaking, precisely because the variance of the overall distribution would be infinite. According to this explanation, large cities follow different regulated Brownian motions, but each of them obeys the parametric restriction necessary for the steady state to satisfy Zipf's law, $\mu(S) = -\frac{1}{2}\sigma^2(S)$, in the notation of equation (8.14), with a fixed effect for each city. In section (8.5.1) I discuss estimates with a mixture of distributions along the lines of Skouras's work.

A key question is whether there exists a reasonably parsimonious economic theory that would lead to such an explanation by means of a mixture of distributions for the observed facts. The results obtained by Skouras establish statistical underpinnings for a general type of intradistributional dependence, as I discuss further below. His explanation is consistent with the churning of industries across cities, which Duranton (2007) emphasizes (see section 8.3 below). Skouras points to the labor market side of churning, namely, substantial inter-MSA migration, which at 19 percent between 1995 and 2000 in the United States is nearly an order of magnitude higher than the total of net natural population growth combined with rural-urban and international immigration (Skouras 2009, 4–5). The diversified industrial base of larger cities suggests that their growth reflects the growth performances of a large number of industries. The growth performance of cities with a large number of interdependent industries is likely to be quite different from the performances of smaller, more specialized cities. So urban specialization varying with size together with heterogeneity can accommodate, in principle, the statistical requirements of the Skouras model. Because of Christaller's hierarchy principle—industries present in smaller cities are also present in larger ones—the growth performances of different-size cities can be interdependent.

8.2.8 Zipf's Law Is Not an Immutable Law

While many proponents of Zipf's law marvel at the apparent fact that it holds at many different periods of time and for countries with diverse levels of development, the theoretical approach in sections 8.2.3 and 8.2.4 above predicts that it will likely emerge as a limit. Dittmar (2008) shows empirically that Zipf's law emerged in Europe between 1500 and 1800, and later and relatively slowly in eastern Europe. Dittmar's explanations are similar to those of Gabaix (1999a), but they emphasize the role of land in the emergence of Zipf's law.

Dittmar assumes that individual utility is proportional to consumption, with a factor of proportionality (an amenity shock, $a_{it} = \epsilon_{it}(1-\tau_{it})$) that reflects the combined effect of a city-specific policy (like taxation, τ_{it}, or obstacles to intercity migration) and random shocks, ϵ_{it}. In an economy with an overlapping generations structure, output is produced with labor by young and old workers and land, according to a Cobb–Douglas production function with elasticities $\alpha, \beta, 1-\alpha-\beta$, respectively. The equalization of utility via intercity migration of young people implies that the number of young in city i, S_{it}^y, can be written as a function of the number of old, S_{it}^o, and land, L_{it}. The number of young, an endogenous variable, becomes

$$S_{it}^y = \left(S_{it}^o\right)^{\frac{\beta}{1-\alpha}} \Xi_{it}^{\frac{1}{1-\alpha}} \left(L_{it}\right)^{\frac{1-\alpha-\beta}{1-\alpha}} (1-\tau_{it})^{\frac{1}{1-\alpha}} \left(\frac{\alpha\epsilon_{it}}{u_t}\right)^{\frac{1}{1-\alpha}},$$

where Ξ_{it} and u_t denote, respectively, total factor productivity and intercity equilibrium utility.

If land is not important in urban production, that is, $\alpha + \beta \approx 1$, and if city total factor productivity and policy do not vary with city population, then city net growth rates, defined as the number of young minus the number of deaths among the old, δS_{it}^o, over the number of old, are independent of city size provided that cities are prevented from getting too small, as proposed by

Gabaix (1999b). That is,

$$\gamma_{it}^{n} = \frac{S_t^y - \delta S_t^o}{S_t^o} = \Xi_t^{\frac{1}{1-\alpha}} \left(\frac{\alpha \epsilon_{it}}{u_t}\right)^{\frac{1}{1-\alpha}} - \delta.$$

If, on the other hand, land is important in production, $\alpha + \beta < 1$, city net growth rate is written as

$$\gamma_{it}^{n} = \Xi_t^{\frac{1}{1-\alpha}} (S_{it}^o)^{\frac{\beta+\alpha-1}{1-\alpha}} (L_i)^{\frac{1-\alpha-\beta}{1-\alpha}} \left(\frac{\alpha \epsilon_{it}}{u_t}\right)^{\frac{1}{1-\alpha}} - \delta.$$

Both the mean and the variance of city growth rates decrease with city population, if land is fixed, $L_{it} = L_i$.

Dittmar suggests that initially city production depends on land in the city's hinterland being in fixed supply. He associates the case of $\alpha + \beta \approx 1$, Zipf's law, with the modern era. Technologically advanced production depends less on land because trade and agricultural productivity have relaxed the land constraint. Dittmar argues that the emergence of cities was differentially affected by the removal of legal restrictions on labor mobility and by sectoral reallocation, both of which are associated with persistent deviations from Zipf's law. As Dittmar suggests, the fact that this law emerged unevenly over time, while the physical landscape remained invariant, is not consistent with narrow geographic explanations. The emergence of Zipf's law in an era with little urban specialization is inconsistent with explanations based on theories of specialization in modern production and the consequent notion of optimal city size. Dittmar's findings instead support an important tenet of new economic geography that locational advantages are established endogenously as economic development proceeds; see section 8.5.6.

Working with the latest international data,[19] Ioannides, Overman, Rossi-Hansberg, and Schmidheiny (2008) strongly reject Zipf's law strictly construed (i.e., $\zeta = -1$). They establish a *causal* link between the evolution of Zipf's coefficient and the adoption of information technologies, thus underscoring that Zipf's law is not an immutable fact. This work employs the Rossi-Hansberg–Wright urban growth model, and I return to these studies in more detail in chapter 9, sections 9.6 and 9.7.2.

8.3 THE DURANTON MODEL OF ENDOGENOUS CITY FORMATION

Duranton (2007) proposes a model that uses ingredients from the quality ladder model of growth developed by Grossman and Helpman (1991) in an urban framework to explain how cities grow and decline as they win or lose industries following technological innovations. The model explains the three stylized facts (the still, the fast, and the slow) that were introduced earlier in section 8.1. Urban population transitions and stationary city size distributions are naturally closely related. The link between industry mobility and population transition, on the other hand, may reflect complex patterns of interdependence. At least in the context of the United States, urban evolution is characterized by different cities changing (industrial) character over time.

Duranton documents industrial churning by means of data for the urban systems of the United States and France. He uses employment data at the level of 70 two-digit industries for 277 U.S. metropolitan areas from the U.S. Bureau of the Census County Business Patterns, 1977–1997, and population data from the U.S. census. For France, he uses employment data at the level of 96 two-digit sectors for plants with more than 20 employees that are available for 217 French metropolitan areas, 1985–1993. Duranton estimates mean first-passage times, obtained from Markov transition matrices, of the evolution of city sizes across the U.S. metro areas for each sector. He uses them to show that the sectoral mobility of employment (averaged across sectors) is much faster than the mobility of metropolitan area populations: the respective mean passage times are 277 versus 1,428 years. Similar estimates, 207 versus 446 years, are obtained with broadly similar French data.

Duranton develops a Schumpeterian growth model with firms producing competitive products in a multiindustry setting. Firms invest in research in order to reap the monopoly profits associated with the highest quality. Self-sustaining and nonexplosive growth is possible since new innovations are neither more difficult nor easier than past ones. There exist J goods, and individuals value the consumption of quantities of each of the existing qualities of all goods. In each industry, there are research firms that compete for patents giving them a monopoly right to production of the next best quality. A successful innovation increases quality by a gross rate of q_m, the quality markup. Research firms may achieve an innovation in another industry, but at a propensity to innovate γ that is less than that in their own industry, β: $\beta > \gamma$. The probability that an innovation takes place in industry z is given by the sum total of the innovation probabilities of all research firms, directly and via spillovers:

$$\iota(z) = \beta \int \lambda^k(z)dk + \gamma \sum_{z' \neq z} \int \lambda^k(z')dk,$$

where k indexes research firms and $\lambda^k(z)$ denotes firm k's rate of innovation in industry z. At the steady-state equilibrium under symmetry, the above becomes $\iota(z) = \iota = (\beta + \gamma(J - 1))\lambda$. Duranton solves for the equilibrium propensity to innovate and the nominal wage rate independent of the urban structure. The value of innovating firms is, at equilibrium, equal to the expected present value of the benefit from innovation, $\upsilon = \frac{w}{\beta+\gamma(J-1)}$, where w is the wage rate. At the intertemporal equilibrium, the net return from innovating, which is the profit per period plus the capital gain, as a share of the value of the firm, is equal to the rate of discount ρ plus the cost of innovation, which is given by ι; when a firm innovates, the leader loses the advantage. There is free entry among price-setting oligopolists for quality below the new top of the quality ladder. The competition model implies that profit per period is equal to $1-q_m^{-1}$. So the condition for intertemporal equilibrium becomes $\frac{1-q_m^{-1}+\dot{\upsilon}}{\upsilon} - \iota(z) = \rho$.

These two conditions when solved simultaneously at the steady state yield the equilibrium wage rate and the rate of innovation, respectively:

$$w = \left(\frac{1}{J} + \frac{\rho}{\beta + \gamma(J-1)}\right)^{-1}, \ \lambda = \frac{1}{J}\left(1 - \frac{1}{q_m}\right) - \frac{\rho}{(\beta + \gamma(J-1))q_m}.$$

The wage rate increases with the number of industries and both propensities to innovate, β and γ. The rate of innovation also increases with both propensities.

The expected growth rate of output of the urban system g is equal to the growth in quality-adjusted output made possible by each innovation, $(\delta - 1)/J$, where δ is the gross rate of quality improvement times the instantaneous probability of innovation, ιJ:

$$g = \left(1 - \frac{1}{q_m}\right)\left[(q_m - 1)\left(\gamma + \frac{\beta - \gamma}{J}\right) - \rho\right].$$

This growth rate is increasing in the markup of quality improvements q_m, and in the rates of innovation; it decreases with the number of industries. So small innovation-driven technological shocks are the main engine behind the growth and decline of cities in Duranton's model.

Matching industries and cities depends only on the total number of industries, J, and of cities, L, with $J \gg L$, and of the number of cities of different sizes. With many more industries than cities, each city is identified by a unique immobile industry, which he defines as first nature. The remaining industries are mobile, thus appropriately called second nature. They provide a reason for the growth and decline of cities by locating in the city where the last innovation took place. Industries experience more turbulence than cities, so the growth of a given city is well defined as the sum of the industries it gains minus those it loses. This and related features of the industrial structure imply that the probability of gaining and losing industries increases less than proportionately with city size. At the steady-state equilibrium, larger cities host more industries.

Let f_S denote the number of cities of size S. Duranton's reasoning is based on economic decisions of firms and involves random assignments in a steady-state setting. The outcome lacks direct intuition but translates to a functional equation for f_S [see (Duranton 2007, app. A) for details]:

$$f_{S+1} = \frac{(2S-1)J - SL - 2S(S-1)}{S(J-S-1)} f_S - \frac{(S-1)(J-L-S+2)}{S(J-S-1)} f_{S-1}.$$

Duranton's solution to this functional equation shows that the number of cities of size S decreases as S increases. The fast holds because industries experience greater turbulence than cities: a city grows by the sum of the industries it gains minus the sum of the industries it loses. With respect to the slow, cities may move up and down the hierarchy as a result of industrial churning. Cities of size S, which by definition host S industries each, grow in number because such cities gain when research firms they host innovate.

They gain by the share of innovating firms $\frac{S}{J}$ times the probability that such an improvement occurs at a second-nature industry located in another city, $\frac{J-L-S+1}{J-1}$; they lose an industry with probability $\frac{S-1}{J-1} \times \frac{J-S}{J}$. The mean growth rate is $\mathcal{E}\left\{\frac{f_{S+1}-f_S}{f_S}\right\} = \frac{J-SL}{(J-1)JS}$, which decreases with city size, in rough agreement with the facts. The variance of the growth rate reflects the fact that the larger a city is, the more likely it is that cross-industry innovations will improve industries located there and thus do not generate increased employment. It is equal to $\frac{S(2J-L+2-2S)-J}{(J-1)JS}$, and it is decreasing and convex with respect to L. This is confirmed by Duranton and in earlier work by Overman and Ioannides (2001).

The still, persistence of the city size distribution, is characterized by obtaining an expression of the local Zipf's exponent:

$$\zeta(S) = \frac{-(L-3)S + J - 1}{J - S - 1}.$$

This implies in turn that the steady-state log rank–log size curve is concave, with a Zipf's exponent larger than -1 in the lower tail and smaller than -1 in the upper tail. This prediction is generally consistent with the facts. It also accords with the following intuition. For larger cities, the chance of losing industries increases more than proportionately with city size, while the chance of gaining industries increases less than proportionately. Because in the model an industry can be in only one location, larger cities host more industries while smaller cities are more specialized.

The model performs well empirically. It does not match Gibrat's law, but it does match, when simulated, remarkably well both the French and, even better, the U.S. city size distributions when key parameters are calibrated based on the respective fundamentals.[20] For the simulations, Duranton works with numbers for cities, $L_{\text{France}} = 232$, $L_{\text{US}} = 922$, that are equal to the number of immobile industries. He computes numbers for industries $J_{\text{France}} = 1{,}500$, $J_{\text{US}} = 12{,}820$, so as to match observed total populations at the steady state.

It is a strength of Duranton's theory that the prediction for the city size distribution follows from matching industries with cities and therefore depends only on the number of cities and industries. But the economies of France and of the United States cannot be as different as the above numbers suggest. Duranton shows that observed regularities in the city size distribution are compatible with basic building blocks derived from central notions of urban economics, such as the existence of agglomeration economies and crowding costs. These building blocks are crucial for his simulation results based on the theory. Because of its simplicity, Duranton's benchmark model lends itself to adding such features as a net propensity to innovate that increases (modestly) with size and offsets the tendency for large cities to lose more industries than they gain. Thus convexity is introduced in the upper tail. This is important for the model's ability to match the U.S. city size distribution.

8.4 THE HIERARCHY PRINCIPLE

A number of descriptive models of city size, city location, and market area based on the trade-off between increasing returns to scale in production and the cost of transporting goods from factories to homes encompass the hierarchy principle, which coincides with central place theory, practically speaking. Its modern version asserts that industries found in a city of a given size are also found in cities of a larger size. The tradition really started as an empirically motivated description of production in southern Germany, originally reported by Christaller (1933), that goes roughly as follows. Grain grown on farms was auctioned in the local markets and shipped to villages where it was milled into flour. The flour was then shipped to larger towns and was baked into bread and sold in those same towns as well as in the villages themselves. The market area of the villages was limited by the greatest distance accessible to the rural population. Recognizing that this is similar for towns vis-a-vis larger towns and cities and also depends on geography as reflected on shipping costs, a picture of interdependence emerges where urban populations form a "hierarchy." While this certainly fits the notion of a functional hierarchy, Christaller also works with an actual physical hierarchy. Commodities characterized by low transport costs but high returns to scale are provided by a smaller number of larger cities high in the hierarchy. Commodities characterized by high transport costs but low returns to scale are provided by most cities. Lösch (1944) elaborates further on this theory. Under certain assumptions about demand, the theory implies a complex of overlapping, ordered layers of hexagonal partitions of the plane corresponding to the market areas of cities in the hierarchy. It is easy to see that one can fit a hexagon over seven smaller ones, defined by the centers of the six hexagons that surround an equal-sized one at the center, and similarly at higher levels. In fact, flying over southern Germany confirms some of these observations to some extent, even down to the present day. The theory has developed beyond these basic descriptive models.[21] See discussion of Tabuchi (2009) in section 8.4.2.2 below.

Mori, Nishikimi, and Smith (2008) and Mori and Smith (2009a, 2009b, 2009c) define the hierarchy principle for empirical purposes in terms of industrial diversity: industries in cities with a given number of industries that have chosen to locate there (cities "choice" industries) will be found in all cities with greater industrial diversity. I discuss next the empirical regularity, introduced in chapter 4, section 4.5.4, that Mori, Nishikimi, and Smith refer to as the *number–average size rule*, which these authors also link to the rank-size rule and the hierarchy principle. The NAS rule asserts that there is a negative log linear relationship between the number and average population size of the cities where a given industry is present, the choice cities for that industry.[22] In other words, larger cities host industries that are present in fewer cities. Cities that host opera houses are larger and fewer. In contrast, the hierarchy principle asserts that if a city hosts gas stations, than cities that host opera houses also host gas stations.

8.4.1 Hierarchy Principle versus the Number–Average Size Rule versus Rank-Size Rule

The intuitive relationship between the hierarchy principle, the NAS rule, and the rank-size rule may also be expressed analytically (Mori, Nishikimi and Smith 2008, 192–193, theorem 1). If an economy's urban system satisfies the hierarchy principle, then the rank–size rule implies the NAS rule. Specifically, let s be a continuous index of cities, $s \in \mathbf{S} = [0, S_{\max}]$, a given *interval*. The total number of cities is $S_{\max} = \int_{\mathbf{S}} dS$. Cities are ranked by their sizes, rank$(S) = \rho(S)$; the largest city has rank 0: $\rho(S) < \rho(S')$ if $S > S'$.

Consider now a set of *industry types*, indexed by $j \in \mathbf{J}$, with industry j located in a measurable subset $\mathbf{S}_j \subset \mathbf{S}$ of the cities in $\mathbf{S}$. Let $\mathbf{S}_j$ be an interval, $\mathbf{S}_j = [0, r_j]$, where r_j denotes the rank of the smallest population units occupied by industry j. This assumption encompasses a strict version of the hierarchy principle. Let n_j be the number of cities where industry j is present (industry j's choice cities): $n_j = \int_{\mathbf{S}_j} ds$. The average size of industry j's choice cities is $\overline{S}_j = \frac{1}{n_j} \int_{\mathbf{S}_j} s\, ds$. The empirical NAS rule is expressed as

$$\ln[\overline{S}_j] = a + \zeta' \ln[n_j], \ a > 0, \zeta' < 0,$$

or equivalently, in levels as $\overline{S}_j = \alpha n_j^{\zeta'}, \alpha \equiv e^a$.

The hierarchy principle *asserts* that for each industry type $j \in \mathbf{J}$, the set of cities that host j is an *interval* $\mathbf{S}_j = [0, r_j] \in \mathbf{S}$. That is, if the smallest city in which an industry is present has rank ρ_j, then the total number of choice cities for industry j, n_j, the cities that are larger than the city of rank ρ_j, is equal to r_j. This is a critical step, as we will see shortly. The average size of cities that contain industry j is $\overline{S}_j = \frac{1}{r_j} \int_0^{r_j} \rho(S) dS$.

Let city sizes and ranks satisfy a rank-size rule, $\rho(S) = \alpha S^{\zeta}$, with scale factor α and exponent $\zeta < 0$. Then for an economy defined by $\mathbf{E} = (\mathbf{J}, \rho, n)$, Mori, Nishikimi, and Smith (2008, theorem 1), states that if the hierarchy principle holds for $\mathbf{E}$, then the rank-size rule and the NAS rule are equivalent, that is, they imply one another with appropriately defined coefficients.[23] The proof depends critically on the fact that the hierarchy principle is represented by an interval.

8.4.2 From Industrial Location Theory to a Theory of Urban Structure: Assessing the Progress toward a Unified Theory

Mori and Smith's (2009a, 2009c) careful documentation of industry location patterns and the sizes of the cities that host them confirms that localization patterns are not random and that they are firmly linked to patterns of agglomeration in Japan. Their theoretical findings (Mori, Nishikimi, and Smith, 2008) clarify the conceptual interrelationships between the NAS rule and the rank-size rule, on the one hand, and the hierarchy principle, on the other. As Ioannides (2009) argues, these relationships are very interesting and too tantalizing to ignore. But how they arise from location decisions of firms is an important question. Models like those explored in chapter 4 assign probabilities to location decisions of different firms from which one can compute probabilities for different realizations of strings of 0s and 1s associated with cities and industries. Such strings feature prominently in the graphical representations of the hierarchy principle by Mori and Smith (2009c, 194, fig. 9). Location choices that depend on industry presence and city size could provide a link from the hierarchy principle, a qualitative relationship, to the NAS and rank-size rules. In this connection, important theoretical results by Hsu (2009) and Tabuchi (2009), however special, are very promising and deserve special attention because they provide an overarching theme linking qualitative and quantitative aspects of the location of firms. I thus turn to them next.

8.4.2.1 *Central Place Theory and City Size Distribution*

Hsu (2009) proposes a theory that is consistent with the NAS rule and is based on a model of location choices of firms. He assumes a continuum of goods whose demand is inelastic, that differ with respect to fixed costs. They all are produced at equilibrium. He assumes a continuum of immobile consumers (farmers) and then extends the model to allow for workers, too. Fixed costs induce each firm to choose a single location. Firms trade off fixed costs against transportation costs in serving their markets. Firms are thus found at a discrete but infinite number of locations. Hsu's results provide the microfoundations of central place theory connecting central place hierarchy and city size distributions. He verifies the NAS rule with U.S. data (from County Business Patterns) on 77 three-digit NAICS industries [which, like the work by Mori, Nishikimi, and Smith (2009), excludes agricultural, forestry, fishing, hunting, and mining industries] for 1997 and their locations in MSAs and consolidated MSAs (CMSAs).

Hsu's theoretical result has an appealing simplicity. Products with low fixed costs are produced in many locations that are closer to one another. As we go up the fixed-cost ladder, firms locate farther and farther apart, but because of symmetry they colocate with lower-level firms. Finally, the firms producing products with the highest fixed costs are farthest apart, but their locations still obey the same logic as those in lower layers. They serve wider areas from fewer locations. In other words, again, fewer cities host opera houses than gas stations. The regularity of locations has a quality reminiscent of central place theory. It also has a *fractal structure*, albeit in one dimension. The size of a typical city in a layer is interpreted as the total production of goods whose fixed costs are at most equal to those produced only in that city. Quite significantly, Hsu (2009, 14, sec. 3.1.2) proves that under the assumption that the distribution of fixed costs is *regularly varying*, the countercumulative city size distribution has an approximate Pareto exponent given by $\frac{-1}{1+2\alpha}$, $\alpha \in (-\frac{1}{2}, 0)$, where parameter α indexes the regularly varying distribution

[Hsu, 2009, 15–16, prop. 3, (b)], and is thus absolutely larger than 1. The class of regularly varying distributions is sufficiently general to accommodate many commonly used ones. There are many dimensions in which this model can be generalized. For example, here cities are just locations of firms, and the model is strictly a partial equilibrium. Moreover, land is not priced. The essence of his results is preserved even when Hsu allows for mobile workers. The fact that city size distributions with exponents that may fall below -1 emerge in a model where firms' locations obey a central place hierarchy is a significant achievement. The number of layers in the hierarchy is increasing in the dispersion of the fixed-costs distributions.

8.4.2.2 *Central Place Theory and Christaller–Lösch Hexagons*

Tabuchi (2009) develops a model of the location of firms and their self-organization into marketplaces where firms compete not only within the marketplace but also between marketplaces. As the population increases exogenously, peripheral subcenters emerge to serve consumers who find themselves too far away from existing more centrally located marketplaces. Tabuchi studies the number, size, and locations of marketplaces that constitute central and edge cities [cf. (Garreau 1991)]. His motivation comes from evidence that in Japan's large cities the retail share in suburban areas has been rising relative to that in central areas. His results concur with the evidence. He also shows that hexagonal configurations, like those of Christaller (1933) and Lösch (1944), emerge endogenously as a self-organized equilibrium in the monopolistically competitive retail market when consumers are uniformly distributed over space. However, unlike the situation in Christaller's case, the hexagons here are not functionally nested because there is only a single good. Nonetheless, obtaining an hexagonal pattern of self-organized marketplaces in two-dimensional space is a significant achievement.

There is an interesting analogy between the spatial dispersion techniques employed by Hsu and the "temporal" dispersion associated with the dynamics of urban growth, discussed in chapter 9 below. Since the creation of cities involves fixed costs, it does not occur continuously and instead takes place sequentially. See section 9.8 in particular.

8.5 CITIES VERSUS METROPOLITAN AREAS VERSUS URBAN PLACES VERSUS DENSITIES VERSUS CLUSTERS

What are cities from a data viewpoint? A variety of administrative divisions are used by the U.S. Bureau of the Census. According to the *Geographic Areas Reference Manual* of the U.S. Census Bureau,[24] an *incorporated place* is a governmental unit incorporated under state law as a city, town (except in the New England states, New York, and Wisconsin), borough (except in Alaska and New York), or village and having legally prescribed limits, powers, and functions. The unincorporated counterpart is called a *census-designated place*;

such places lack separate governments but otherwise resemble incorporated places. The census data on places for the year 2000, whose names may be found at http://www.census.gov/geo/www/gazetteer/places.html, contains observations on 25,359 places, including cities, towns, and villages, ranging in population from 1 person to more than 8 million persons. The entire population of places is 208,735,266 out of a total U.S. population of 281,421,906 in the 2000 U. S. Census.

8.5.1 Data on U.S. Places

Defining cities as places instead of metropolitan areas makes quite a bit of difference. First, it obviates the need to work with only the upper tail of city size distributions. For example, Eeckhout (2004) uses data on 25,359 places for 2000 and reports that a lognormal fits the size distribution better than a Pareto. Moreover, for those observations for which both 1990 and 2000 data exist, Eeckhout shows that the growth rate of places defined as places is independent of city size—Gibrat's law holds. The proportionate growth process, together with the lognormality of the size distribution, establishes that, when considering all cities and not just the upper tail of the distribution, the distribution of city sizes is lognormal. The recent discussion following Eeckhout (2004), Levy (2009), and Ioannides and Skouras (2009), underscores once again that distinguishing empirically between a Pareto and a lognormal upper tail of the city size distribution is quite crucial for establishing Zipf's law. The findings of Skouras (2009), discussed above, show that while the main "body" of the distribution is "congruent" with lognormality (Eeckhout 2004, fig. 4) the upper tail most definitely is not. The lognormal tail, as plotted by Skouras, (2009, fig. 6) is considerably thinner than in the actual data for the 80 largest U.S. cities in all the 25,358 places data that he uses for demonstration.[25]

Ioannides and Skouras (2009) report estimates for a new distribution function using the U.S. places data for 2000. This new distribution function is obtained by endogenous switching between a lognormal and a Pareto distribution. The switching function $\alpha(S)$ is a normal cumulative distribution function with mean m_α and variance σ_α^2 and obviously depends on city size. That is, the specified density is

$$f_{sw}\left(S; \mathcal{E}(S), \mathrm{Var}(S), m_\alpha, \sigma_\alpha^2, \beta, \zeta\right) = \frac{\alpha(S)\beta f_{ln}(S) + (1-\alpha(S))\,p(S)}{\int_0^\infty [\alpha(S)\beta f_{ln}(S) + (1-\alpha(S))\,p(S)]\,dS}, \; S \geq 1, \tag{8.16}$$

where $f_{ln}(S)$ is a lognormal density function with mean $\mathcal{E}(S)$ and variance $\mathrm{Var}(S)$, and $p(S)$ is a Pareto density function corresponding to (8.2) with a lower cutoff $s_{\min} = 1$ (which is appropriate for the data) and exponent ζ. Parameter β normalizes the level of $p(S)$ to ensure that it is similar to that of f_{ln} where transition to the Pareto law occurs.

The estimates are obtained with maximum likelihood estimation methods. They exhibit great precision and show that since $\hat{m}_\alpha = 100{,}070$ (with

$\hat{\sigma}_\alpha = 2,580$ and standard errors, respectively, 4,057 and 1,629), the transition from lognormality to power behavior is sudden as city populations increase above 100,000. Thus, Zipf's law holds for 0.98 percent of the places but 36.9 percent of the population living in places. The estimated Pareto coefficient is $\hat{\zeta} = -1.368$ with a standard error of 0.006. The quality of fit of this estimation is visually very impressive.[26]

8.5.2 Data on U.S. Metropolitan Areas

Another issue of data consistency arises within the upper tail. U.S. cities as economic rather than governmental units are defined by the Office of Management and Budget (OMB) using data provided by the U.S. census. The OMB moved to the Standard Metropolitan Area definition in 1950, to Standard Metropolitan Statistical Areas after 1959, and, in 1983, to the Metropolitan Statistical Area, Primary Metropolitan Statistical Area (PMSA), and Consolidated Metropolitan Statistical Area classification.[27] A MSA is made up of entire counties (except in New England) and must have either 50,000 or more inhabitants or an urbanized area of at least 50,000 inhabitants, plus adjacent territory with a high degree of social and economic integration as measured by commuting and a total metropolitan population of at least 100,000 (75,000 in New England).

Dobkins and Ioannides (2000) generate data that are consistent by using the areas as defined at the time of the respective census; that is, they use the 1960 definitions for 1960 data, the 1970 definitions for 1970 data, and so on.[28] The 1900–1940 data are constructed using the 1950 definitions of SMAs according to Bogue (1953). The 1950–1980 data are consistent with the SMSA definitions in the respective years. The United States had 112 urban MSAs in 1900 and 334 such areas in 1990. New cities, defined as those "entering" in each decade, are a key feature of the U.S. urban system, with many entrants appearing in newly developed geographic areas.

Black and Henderson (2003) also generate consistent data by using the decennial population census to count urban populations by *county*, which they track over time. One problem is that some county definitions have changed over time (with most changes occurring prior to 1940). In 1990, the Black and Henderson definition of a metropolitan area, which is made up of a single or several contiguous counties, gives 282 metropolitan areas covering 695 consolidated counties (of a total of 3,043 modern counties) instead of a sample of 334 metropolitan areas in the continental United States covering 742 counties according to Dobkins and Ioannides. Their data process produces some dramatic drawbacks, as well. For example, Black and Henderson are forced to leave *out* all of Florida. They, too, use Donald Bogue's current definitions to follow the component counties in the metro areas in 1990 back to 1900. Black and Henderson's most significant data innovation is in *imposing* a relative cutoff population (instead of the absolute one of 50,000 inhabitants used by

Dobkins and Ioannides) to define what population centers are to be considered cities. For example, when does Phoenix, Arizona, which had zero population in 1900, become a city? Black and Henderson define a relative cutoff point as the smallest city whose population as a share of the mean urban population equals that for 1990. In their data, this is equal to 52,262/527,508 = 0.099.[29] This results in 194 metro areas in 1900 with a mean population size of 129,596.

8.5.3 Spatial Concentration of Economic Activity in the United States

The United States was transformed from a rural to an urban society over the last three centuries with formal economic activity spreading over the entire continent. Economic historians have provided broader historical perspectives on the spatial concentration of economic activity in the United States. Beeson, DeJong, and Troesken (1999) and Beeson and DeJong (2002) examine regional patterns of population growth at the state and county levels from 1790 to 1990. They find that state-level populations show convergence, while county-level populations show divergence. With initial tendencies in counties toward convergence lasting roughly through the 1800s, in the post–World War II period county populations have diverged. Their analysis points to the importance of *transitional dynamics* as opposed to *steady-state dynamics.* When territories opened up for settlement, growth rates were very high relative to steady states. Once such "frontier effects" are controlled for, the tendency to divergence in the postwar period is clear.

Kim (2000) emphasizes that after the 1700s, a century of little growth, the pace of urbanization rose to historically unprecedented levels between the nineteenth and early twentieth centuries. In the twentieth century, the urban population continued to increase but in a much more dispersed manner as suburban populations also increased. Kim emphasizes the impact of changes in regional comparative advantage and in economies of scale in transportation and local public goods on patterns of U.S. urban development. He finds that differences in urban sizes are associated with the role of reduced market transaction costs in coordinating greater geographic division of labor. Kim (2007) looks at the dynamic evolution of urban densities. He documents the historical changes in population and employment densities in U.S. cities and metropolitan areas and explores the causes of their rise and decline between the late nineteenth and twentieth centuries.

The role of urban density has recently attracted attention in relation to the evolution of other measures of urban size such as *employment.* In particular, Carlino and Chatterjee (2001, 2002) point to a pronounced trend toward deconcentration of employment in the United States since World War II. That is, the employment share of originally relatively dense MSAs has declined and the share of less dense MSAs has risen. Similarly, they show that such effects also apply within MSAs. They explain these trends by means of density-dependent congestion costs. They do not, however, estimate models for the pattern of transition. Still, these works challenge the view, based on population size studies, that the urban landscape is in some sort of steady state. Instead, there is considerable change.

8.5.4 Data on Population Densities

Even within such a changing environment, Holmes and Lee (2010) find fractal-type similarities in the distribution of density within and across metropolitan areas. Holmes and Lee examine population densities across the United States by looking at the distribution of population across 6 × 6 mile squares of U.S. territory (according to a grid defined in the early 1800s by the Public Land Survey System of the U.S. Government). They examine whether Zipf's law and Gibrat's law hold for densities or for additional measures of economic activity for which data are available. At the bottom tail of the distribution of 6 × 6 mile squares, the distribution is roughly lognormal. For squares with a population above 1,000, a Zipf's plot has a piecewise linear shape, with a kink at about a population of 50,000. Below the kink the slope is −0.75; above the kink, the slope is about −2. The finding is robust across different regions in the country. Gibrat's law, on the other hand, does not hold for populations of squares. Mean growth rates have an inverted U-shaped relationship with population size, and the variance in growth rates declines with size. Holmes and Lee point out that the slope of −2 in the upper tail matches what one would obtain with MSA-level data if population density were substituted for population in a Zipf's regression.[30] They note that the slope of −2 also matches what one would find by using the maximum population square in the MSA instead of average density, or by looking at 6 × 6 mile squares within MSAs at the upper tail. "All of this suggests some kind of fractal pattern in the right tail, in which the distribution of squares within MSAs looks like the distribution of MSAs across the country. This in turn looks like the distribution of squares across the country and within individual regions" (Holmes and Lee 2010, 22). Holmes and Lee's findings of a very tight fit for the Zipf's plot between 1,000 and 50,000 populations are intriguing; they suggest that further research on joint analysis of the distribution of populations of squares within metropolitan areas and across metropolitan areas would be fruitful. These results are remarkable because they go beyond the arbitrariness of MSA definitions.

Further evidence on Zipf's law with a different definition of a city is reported by Rozenfeld, Rybski, Gabaix, and Makse (2011). They construct cities "from the bottom up," as it were, by using a city clustering algorithm (CCA). That is, they cluster together populated areas obtained from high-resolution U.S. Bureau of the Census data using a fine geographic grid covering both urban and rural areas. In this view, cities are population clusters, that is, adjacent populated geographic spaces, defined in terms of one parameter (the cell size). The original U.S. data consist of 61,224 sites defined by Federal Information Processing Standards (FIPS), which are in turn associated with corresponding populations provided by the U.S. Bureau of the Census. They are then coarse-grained to a grid of 2 × 2 kilometers. These sites have populations varying between 1,500 and 8,000.

These authors find that Zipf's law holds for such sites with populations of more than 10,000 inhabitants in the United States, with ζ being estimated at -1.04 and with very high precision. For Great Britain, on the other hand, they estimate a power law for sites with more than 1,000 inhabitants (with sites being defined in terms of a finer grid of 200 meters), with ζ estimated at -0.88, again with very high precision. They find evidence that land areas themselves follow a power law with ζ estimated at -0.97. Hence, they suggest, Zipf's law appears to hold in the United States (though not for Great Britain) over a considerably larger population range than previously established. There remains a lower tail that does not follow Zipf's law. In this sense, these latest results are in broad agreement with Eeckhout (2004) and Holmes and Lee (2010). They are also consistent with the findings of Decker, Kerkhoff, and Moses (2007), who compare census data with that obtained for cluster areas of remotely sensed nighttime lights. Decker et al. estimate Zipf plots (rank-size distributions) for all populated places in the United States, all municipalities of Switzerland, and all "counties" (two administrative levels below the nation) (Decker, Kerkhoff, and Moses 2007, e934, fig. 4). The bodies of those distributions yield excellent lognormal fits over four orders of magnitude in population, but the tail of the world distribution seems to deviate from a power law, unlike the other two, which fit power laws with exponents greater than -1.[31]

8.5.5 A GIS-based Agglomeration Index

The findings of Holmes and Lee (2010) are significant in helping demonstrate that even studies based on U.S. data, which are regarded as high-quality data for cities, may suffer from the lack of a uniform measure of urbanization. A very significant recent data development is a proposed measure set out in the 2009 *World Development Report*. This is a new state-of-the-art GIS-based definition of "urban" area, *the agglomeration index* (Holmes and Lee 2010, 55, box 1.3). It imposes minimum thresholds for area population size, population density, and maximum (road) commuting time to a sizable settlement. The report uses 50,000 people for a population threshold, 150 people per square kilometer for density, and 60 minutes for travel to the nearest large city. This index produces discrepancies in both directions between the share of urbanization it implies and those implied by country-based definitions. Nonetheless, a great advantage of this measure is its consistency internationally.

Two additional remarks are in order. First, a clustering algorithm has also been used by Mori and Smith (2008), as discussed in chapter 4, section 4.5.4, to determine industry concentrations. Second, the choice of grid fineness is quite important. As Holmes and Lee discuss, very fine grids produce larger numbers of uninhabited cells, implying a smaller dispersion of the distribution. This is, in fact, confirmed by Rozenfeld, Rybski, Gabaix, and Makse (2011, fig. 2, A, B). Not surprisingly, as the grid becomes finer, the estimate of $|\zeta|$ increases.

8.5.6 What Can We Learn from Estimations of Power Laws for City Sizes?

There are several lessons to take away from estimations of city size distributions. One involves testing predictions of economic theory for city size distributions. A second type of learning, popular in econophysics, is aimed at confirming or refuting the success of power laws as statistical models in their own right. Taking again an eclectic view, I argue that estimates obtained with either motive in mind, and regardless of whether they constitute a test of theories or motivate theories that build on them, do not contribute to solid scientific progress unless they inform on models whose primitives are natural assumptions.[32] That is, models should be grounded on commonly acceptable fundamentals and must involve attractive assumptions about primitives. I would argue that one should be suspicious of attempts to characterize city size distributions as obeying immutable laws. Of course, it is perfectly possible that theories may imply laws in the limit that are in effect not only scale-free but also parameter-free, especially since the existence and stability of equilibrium outcomes may themselves provide such bounds.

The fact that the distribution of city sizes may satisfy Zipf's law even if city growth rates do not satisfy Gibrat's law poses tricky scientific questions. For example, and as suggested by Krugman (1996), the presence of Zipf's law in features of physical geography, such as sizes of rivers and other geologic objects, may be transmitted to the urban system that adapts to them. Consequently, Henderson-style systems-of-cities theories are not incompatible with Zipf's law for cities, in that Zipf's law for city sizes may originate from underlying determinants of city sizes (Henderson 1988). For example, as I discuss in chapter 7, that would be the case if the commuting cost parameter κ were assumed itself to satisfy a power law, which is then transmitted to optimum city size, as per the derivations in chapter 7, section 7.5. Yet, the persistence of a Pareto upper tail across countries at very different levels of development weakens the credibility of such explanations.

The stability of city size distributions is interesting even if the distributions do not adhere strictly to power laws. Economists find it appealing to model the fundamentals of the process that determines city size distributions. Doing so generates models that may be relied on to obtain predictions as countries undergo structural transformation or groups of countries integrate, as with the European Union. Such restructuring may unleash economic forces that reshape urban systems nationally and internationally. What is likely to happen to the sizes of different nations' larger cities and their ranks? It is a key feature of Zipf's law that it offers an unconditional prediction. But is it reliable?

Every cloud has a silver lining, however. An empirical law like Zipf's law has motivated more general and far-reaching inquiries into urban structure and growth and therefore into the determinants of city size distributions.

8.5.7 What Can We Learn from Actual City Size Distributions? Urban Accounting and Welfare

While our theories of city size distributions would not be complete unless they are validated by actual data, there is a lot that can be done even in the absence of a perfect theory. A good case in point, and a very innovative study at that, is the one by Desmet and Rossi-Hansberg (2011), who use data for U.S. MSAs and develop a number of counterfactual exercises to assess the importance of a small number of forces in accounting for city size distribution and welfare. They work with a dynamic model at a steady state, where utility per period is a standard logarithmic function of aggregate consumption and labor supply and is a city-specific urban amenity parameter. Aggregate output is produced with capital and labor using a Cobb–Douglas production function. The economy consists of many cities and is calibrated with data from a variety of sources. In each city, an urban transportation system is financed by a (distortionary) tax on labor income. Using a representative individual infinite-horizon model at a steady state and imposing spatial equilibrium allow the authors to isolate the role of the following three forces on urban welfare: efficiency as measured by TFP in aggregate production, amenities as measured by the utility function parameter, and frictions as measured by the inefficiency of public spending on urban transportation infrastructure. Their counterfactual exercises compare welfare, as measured by the equilibrium level of utility of the representative individual, and actual and predicted city size distributions under alternative values of the underlying three forces. In one set of exercises, they fix at the average level each of these forces in turn and compare the predicted and actual distributions. In another, they fix two of them, leaving only one to vary. In a third, they allow for TFP in city output production and, alternatively, for the amenity parameter to depend on city size, a form of urbanization externality.

Desmet and Rossi-Hansberg's decomposition of U.S. city size distribution in terms of these three forces is particularly revealing in the sense that eliminating any one of them implies large reallocations of people, while bringing about little change in welfare. For example, a 20 percent reduction in the TFP of aggregate production leads to a reduction in welfare between 3 percent and 4 percent, and a 20 percent reduction in amenities leads to a reduction in welfare of between 4 percent and 6 percent. The reductions in welfare would change little if instead the shocks were to be idiosyncratic but averaged to the same amount. The presence of urbanization externalities is associated with little change in welfare that does not appreciably vary when the elasticity of the externality is changed from 0.02 to 0.04. Another way to look at their results is that impeded mobility of U.S. households, because of insolvency and/or borrowing constraints, is associated with limited effects on welfare.

Lest it be thought that the results of Desmet and Rossi-Hansberg are due to particular properties of their model, their application to Chinese data reveals that Chinese cities are "too small," thus agreeing with a result of Au and Henderson (2006). That is, among several counterfactual exercises, Desmet and Rossi-Hansberg show that endowing Chinese cities with the same level of efficiency would increase welfare by 47 percent, an order of magnitude higher, and the size distribution would become much more dispersed with both more larger and more smaller cities. A particularly innovative feature of the model is that, by construction and for a particular set of parameter values, it matches exactly the observed U.S. MSA size distribution, which obviates the need to examine the predictive performance of the model. In this sense, Desmet and Rossi-Hansberg's approach to *urban accounting* by mimicking the Solow residual methods popularized by the business cycle accounting literature demonstrates amply how much we can learn from the *actual* city size distribution.

8.6 EVOLVING URBAN STRUCTURES WITH GENERAL INTRADISTRIBUTION DEPENDENCE

To what extent does the growth of cities of one size class or type, say the largest cities, have an impact on other classes and types, say medium-size cities or manufacturing-type cities, in the same region or nation? Conventional cross-sectional and panel data techniques do not allow us to look at this question (Quah 1993). Intercity trade, where medium-size cities trade manufacturing products with other cities while large cities trade specialized business services with all other cities are examples of economic forces operating within the distribution of city sizes. Making such inferences requires explicit modeling of the dynamics of the entire distribution of cities. Methods that condition means and variances on city sizes give only a partial view of such processes.

8.6.1 An Empirical Model of the Evolution of the City Size Distribution

Overman and Ioannides (2001) and Ioannides and Overman (2004) use nonlinear techniques, pioneered by Quah (1993), that posit that f_t, the frequency (density) distribution of population $S_{\ell t}$ of city ℓ at time t, evolves over time according to a first-order nonlinear autoregression:

$$f_{t+1} = \mathcal{M}(f_t, \epsilon_{t+1}), \tag{8.17}$$

where $\mathcal{M}$ is an operator that maps (f_t, ε_{t+1}) to a probability measure for f_{t+1} and ε_{t+1} is a stochastic function representing random shocks. The random growth model proposed by Simon (1955) may be considered a special case of processes consistent with specification (8.17). Overman and Ioannides (2001) obtain nonparametric estimates of a law of motion for intradistribution dynamics with U.S. metropolitan area data for 1900–1990. They estimate the probability distribution function of city i's population at time $t+1$ conditional on its population at time t, $\widehat{f}(S_{\ell,t+1}|S_{\ell,t}) = \frac{\widehat{f}(S_{\ell,t},S_{\ell,t+1})}{\widehat{f}(S_{\ell,t})}$. I discuss the results in more detail below in sections 8.6.3 and 8.6.6.1.

8.6.2 A Linear Model of Urban Evolution

Nonlinear models like that in (8.17) allow for general statistical interdependence among city populations in two successive periods. They may also admit multiple equilibria and path dependence. One of their drawbacks is that they are unwieldy when working analytically on the local dynamic properties of $\mathcal{M}$ in (8.17). It is easier to think of $\mathcal{M}$ as a linear operator, $\mathbf{M}$, in which case it could be represented as a Markov transition matrix. By assuming no random disturbances, equation (8.17) becomes $f_{t+1} = \mathbf{M} \cdot f_t$. Iterating forward for t' periods yields $f_{t+t'} = \mathbf{M}^{t'} \cdot f_t$. Invoking the terminology of Eaton and Eckstein (1997), we see in turn that divergent, convergent, or parallel growth may be ascertained in terms of the spectral properties of $\mathbf{M}$, which determine the properties of $f_\infty \equiv \lim_{t\to\infty} f_t$. If a limit distribution f_∞ exists, then by the Perron–Frobenius theorem it is given by the eigenvector corresponding to the unique unit eigenvalue of $\mathbf{M}$, the nonzero solution of $[\mathbf{M} - \mathbf{I}]f_\infty = 0]$, where $0]$ denotes a column vector of zeroes. *Parallel* growth is understood to occur if f_∞ tends to a limit with nonzero probability over the entire support; *convergent* growth occurs if f_∞ is a mass point, and *divergent* growth if f_∞ is a polarized or segmented distribution.

Dobkins and Ioannides (2000) and Black and Henderson (2003) adapt a linear version of equation (8.17) to allow new cities to enter according to a frequency distribution ε_t. If the number of entrants between t and $t+1$ is I_t^n, $I_{t+1} = I_t + I_t^n$, then

$$f_{t+1} = \frac{I_t}{I_{t+1}} \mathbf{M}_t f_t + \frac{I_t^n}{I_{t+1}} \varepsilon_t. \tag{8.18}$$

If $\mathbf{M}_t$ and $\iota_t \equiv \frac{I_t^n}{I_{t+1}}$ are time-invariant, then equation (8.18) is amenable to the standard treatment for linear systems. Letting $\mathbf{M}$ be the transition matrix, and $\mathbf{i}$ the vector of entering cities with all components equal to to ι, assuming them both to be time-invariant, and iterating equation (8.18) forward from 0 until time t yields

$$\begin{aligned} f_t &= (1-\iota)^t \mathbf{M}^t f_0 + \iota \sum_{\tau=0}^{t-1} [(1-\iota)\mathbf{M}]^{t-\tau} \varepsilon_\tau \\ &= (1-\iota)^t \mathbf{M}^t f_0 + [\mathbf{I} - (1-\iota)\mathbf{M}]^{-1} [\mathbf{I} - ((1-\iota)\mathbf{M})^t]\mathbf{i}, \end{aligned}$$

where f_0 denotes the initial distribution of city sizes and the second equality assumes that $\mathbf{i}$ is deterministic and constant.

A steady-state solution to (8.18) characterizes the distribution of city sizes in the long run with entry. In general, if there are few or no entrants, $\iota \approx 0$, then the homogeneous solution, the first term on the right-hand side of (8.18), is nonnegligible and the state of the urban system in the long run is described by the full solution above. If, on the other hand, significant numbers of new cities enter, ι is nonnegligible and $(1 - \iota)^t$ tends to 0 as t tends to infinity. In that case, the first term has a vanishing influence and the second term on the right-hand side of (8.18) may *not* be ignored. The magnitude of the largest eigenvalue of $(1 - \iota)\mathbf{M}$ is $(1 - \iota)$, and the impact of the initial conditions are of decreasing importance as $\iota\bar{\varepsilon}$, the vector of new cities that enter in a typical period, is significant. The steady-state distribution would then be $[\mathbf{I} - (1 - \iota)\mathbf{M}]^{-1}\mathbf{i}$ (Black and Henderson 2003). I discuss further below the particular use that Black and Henderson make of this formulation.

Overman and Ioannides' nonparametric estimates of stochastic transition kernels for the evolution of the distribution of U.S. metropolitan area populations for the period 1900–1990 show regional differences in the degree of mobility within the city size distribution. The distribution of city sizes is predominantly characterized by persistence. Most U.S. regions show roughly monotonic changes in their shares of larger cities, but in contrast the west south-central and west-north-central regions show a higher level of urban churning, that is, intradistributional mobility, than all the other regions. Those two regions saw their shares increase and then subsequently decrease during the study period.

8.6.3 Urban Evolution in the United States: Empirical Magnitudes

From the Dobkins and Ioannides data on metropolitan areas for 1900–1990 let us examine the numbers of entering cities in each decade, which as shares of the existing stock of cities are $|\iota|_{1910} = 0.194$, $|\iota|_{1920} = 0.067$ $|\iota|_{1930} = 0.051$, $|\iota|_{1940} = 0.019$, $|\iota|_{1950} = 0.012$, $|\iota|_{1960} = 0.229$, $|\iota|_{1970} = 0.136$, $|\iota|_{1980} = 0.245$, and $|\iota|_{1990} = 0.036$. These numbers suggest a nonstationary series for the entry pattern of new cities. Dobkins and Ioannides (2001) use reduced form models to examine determinants of the entry of new cities.

By coding the position of each city relative to others within the distribution, one can see whether or not specific cities move up or down in the distribution over time. Dobkins and Ioannides (2000) and Black and Henderson (2003) both report transition matrices.[33] Black and Henderson (2003) code the cutoff points that define five cells with frequencies of 35, 30, 15, 10, and 10 percent, respectively. They compare frequencies at different times to the steady-state solution of equation (8.18), which accounts for entry. They interpret the increasing concentration at the upper end of the distribution as a result of scale economies and changes in technology. The mean city size increased fourfold from 1900 to 1990, and the median rose fivefold, with medium-size cities growing substantially. Black and Henderson attribute this growth more to the effect of changes in national demand for the output of intercity traded services, which favors large cities, and less to the impact of technology (through local knowledge accumulation and improved commuting).

In Black and Henderson's results, only the diagonal and immediately off-diagonal entries of the transition matrices are statistically significant. In effect, cities move only up or down one empirically determined cell in a decade. They show that the stationarity of the transition matrices is never close to being rejected. They examine city mobility by means of first-passage times and find that upward mobility is much stronger than downward mobility. Most cities grow and few contract, probably because it is hard for a city to shrink once an urban scale has been established. Most big cities stay big. Black and Henderson employ a multinomial logit model to study period-to-period transitions. They then use those characteristics that are associated with moving up (down) to define superior (inferior) sites. They compute mean passage times for hypothetical superior (inferior) sites, which are defined by enhancing each site with 1.5 standard deviations from its mean value. They find that superior sites move up quickly and never move down. Inferior sites move up very slowly and down quite quickly.

The entry of new cities is an important feature of growing urban systems like that of the United States over the twentieth century, so a natural question is where do new cities arise given the existing urban system. Dobkins and Ioannides (2001) explore determinants of the location of new cities and examine spatial interactions among U.S. cities. They use such spatial measures as distance of each city from the nearest larger city in a higher-tier adjacency and location within U.S. regions. They "date" cities from the time their sites were originally settled.[34] They find that among cities that enter the system during 1900–1990, larger cities are more likely to locate near other cities rather than farther away from them. Moreover, older cities are more likely to have neighbors. Distance from the nearest higher-tier city is not always a significant determinant of size and growth.

8.6.4 Economic Geography and Market Potential

How important for urban growth are spatial features of sites where cities are located? Locational aspects can be formalized in terms of two features: *first* nature and *second* nature. Theory suggests that together these are important determinants of the extent of development at a location (Fujita, Krugman, and Venables 1999). First-nature features are intrinsic to the physical geography of a site itself. For example, coastal locations, those near navigable rivers, or those with favorable climates have first-nature features that might encourage development. Second-nature features of a location are those that derive from spatial interactions between economic agents once settlements are established.

Fujita, Krugman, and Venables (1999) add important new spatial insights to Henderson's early research on systems of cities (Henderson 1974, 1988).

The system-of-cities approach features powerful models of intrametropolitan spatial structure but neglects intermetropolitan spatial structure. Intermetropolitan spatial structure plays a key role in the new economic geography literature (Krugman 1991a; Fujita, Krugman, and Venables 1999).

8.6.5 The Hanson Model

The results discussed in the previous section provide insight into U.S. urban evolution. Still they do not offer precise information on the forces that each city exerts on other cities through its second nature. These forces may be described in terms of *market potential*, considered in sections 4.8 and 7.7. The concept was originally introduced by Harris (1954) and subsequently modernized by Krugman (1992), who cast it in a theoretically rigorous framework and enriched it with a price index of traded goods that deflates each city's demand by its price index.

Hanson (2005) was the first to make a structural estimation of an augmented market potential function based on the Krugman (1991b) model of economic geography.[35] He uses a Krugman-style economic geography model with consumers valuing a variety of goods and estimates its structural parameters. He asks if spatial interactions—in the form of regional demand linkages—contribute to spatial agglomeration via their influence on wages. He uses the conditions for locational equilibrium and for equilibrium in the housing market to derive an expression for the wage W_ℓ in a U.S. county ℓ as a function of the wage in every other county ℓ', and of the respective county income, Y_ℓ, housing stock, H_ℓ, distances $d_{\ell\ell'}$, and rate of (iceberg) shipping costs, τ. That is,

$$\ln W_\ell = b_0 + \sigma^{-1}\ln\left[\sum_{\ell'} Y_{\ell'}^{\frac{\sigma(\mu-1)+1}{\mu}} H_{\ell'}^{\frac{(\sigma-1)(1-\mu)}{\mu}} W_{\ell'}^{\frac{\sigma-1}{\mu}} e^{-\tau(\sigma-1)d_{\ell\ell'}}\right] + \eta_\ell, \tag{8.19}$$

where $1-\mu$ denotes the housing share of expenditure and σ the elasticity of substitution between varieties, each of which is produced under conditions of monopolistic competition with free entry. The housing stock H_ℓ is fixed in each county, county income Y_ℓ consists of wage income and housing rent income (under the assumption that all housing everywhere is owned equally by all), τ is transportation cost per unit distance, and $d_{\ell\ell'}$ is geodesic distance between counties ℓ and ℓ', $e^{-\tau d_{\ell\ell'}}$ defines iceberg costs, and η_ℓ is a random shock. Local congestion is expressed as housing costs. That is, the larger the housing share of income, $1-\mu$, the larger the effect of the housing stock but the smaller the effect of income in county ℓ' on the demand for labor in county ℓ. Agglomeration is advantageous because of increasing returns and the welfare effect of varieties, provided that agglomeration offsets congestion, that is, if $1 > \sigma(1-\mu)$.

Hanson avails himself of data for 3,075 counties in the continental United States for the years 1970, 1980, and 1990. He reports large implied estimates for σ ranging from 1.75 to 2.05, and for μ ranging from 0.55 to 0.75. Hanson's results suggest that demand linkages between U.S. counties are strong and growing over the study period but attenuate geographically quite rapidly. Hanson's estimates of the model's parameters are broadly consistent with theory. In this instance, the data reject the Harris market potential function in favor of the Krugman augmented market potential function. Hanson's estimates of increasing trade costs are large in value and rise in magnitude over time. The magnitude of these costs implies that demand linkages between regions are very weak for regions separated by more than 1,000 kilometers. In reality, the sizable trade between distant regions suggests that actual trade costs may in fact be much lower. For example, the cost of moving a ton by rail has declined in real terms by more than 90 percent since the late nineteenth century, and the rise in trucking has been even more dramatic (Glaeser and Kohlase 2004). Hanson's estimated increase in trade costs may reflect an ongoing secular shift in economic activity from low trade cost manufacturing to high trade cost services. A drawback in Hanson's (2005) work is that the endogeneity of outcomes in neighboring areas is not controlled for. In contrast, Head and Mayer (2004b) (see chapter 4, section 4.8) in effect control for endogeneity by relating the location decisions of Japanese firms to the prexisting presence of Japanese firms' affiliates in locations under study.

8.6.6 A Dynamic Hanson Model Adapted to Cities

I adapt the views of Krugman (1992) and Hanson (2005) and define a new economic geography system-of-cities model in a dynamic setting. Let $\mathcal{L}$ denote a set of names of all cities in a particular economy, that is, $\ell = 1$, denotes Abilene Texas, $\ell = 206$ denotes New York, New York, and so on. Let $\mathcal{L}_t$ denote the set of cities *extant* at time t: $\mathcal{L}_t \subseteq \mathcal{L}$. Let $L_t = |\mathcal{L}_t|$. Set $\mathcal{L}$ may contain unoccupied geographic *sites* as elements defined within particular geography (a two-dimensional lattice, the real line, or even the North American landscape). With this geography I associate a set of intercity transport costs of the iceberg type: each unit shipped between locations ℓ' and ℓ'', $\ell', \ell'' \in \mathcal{L}$, incurs an iceberg cost, a fraction $e^{-\tau d_{\ell',\ell''}}$, where $d_{\ell',\ell''}$ denotes the "effective" distance between any pair of locations in $\mathcal{L}$.

Let S_{it} denote the size, in terms of population (or employment), of city ℓ at time t, $\ell \in \mathcal{L}_t, 1 \leq \ell \leq L_t$, and time periods $t = 1, \ldots T$. Let $\mathbf{S}_t$ denote the vector of sizes of the L_t cities in existence in the economy at time t, $\mathbf{S}_t \in R_+^{I_t}$, and $\bar{N}_t$ the total population in the economy. I assume that not all potential urban sites are occupied at any time t and that there is plenty of space for new urban development: $\max_t$: $I_t < L$.

I take $(\mathcal{I}_t, g_t)$, the set and location of cities in each period, as given. Consumers are infinitely lived but cannot save. They take their incomes as given and maximize utility in each period. In each city i, individuals are identical in terms of human capital and preferences. Their preferences for consumption of housing services, C_{hit}, and of manufacturing goods, represented by a composite, C_{mit}, are defined by:

$$U_{it} = C_{mit}^{\mu} C_{hit}^{1-\mu}, \quad 0 < \mu < 1, \tag{8.20}$$

where μ is the share of expenditure for manufactures. The manufacturing composite C_{mit} is defined as a symmetric CES function of the quantities of all manufacturing product varieties:

$$C_{mit} = \left(\sum_{j=1}^{n_t} c_{jit}^{1-\frac{1}{\sigma}} \right)^{\frac{\sigma}{\sigma-1}}, \quad 1 < \sigma, \tag{8.21}$$

where c_{jit} is the quantity of variety j consumed in city i at time t, σ is the direct partial elasticity of substitution between any two varieties, and n_t is the number of varieties available in the entire economy. To (8.20) and (8.21), there corresponds an indirect utility function, given by $\Upsilon \overline{P}^{-\mu} R^{-(1-\mu)}$, where Υ denotes per capita income, $\overline{P}$ denotes the price index for the composite of all varieties available in each city, which I derive in equation (8.30) below, and R denotes the housing rent.

Product variety j is produced in city i in quantity C_{jit} by means of an increasing returns-to-scale technology. It requires only labor in quantity $\alpha + \beta_i C_{jit}$, where the marginal labor requirement β_i depends upon the city where production takes place. At equilibrium, each variety is produced by a single monopolistically competitive firm. With free entry, each firm produces up to the point where profits are zero. Each firm's optimum output in city i is equal to $(\sigma - 1)\frac{\alpha}{\beta_i}$, its price is equal to $\frac{\sigma}{\sigma-1}\beta_i W_{it}$, and its production requires $\alpha\sigma$ units of labor. Each variety demands the same total quantity of labor, although its price may differ because the marginal labor requirements β_i may vary across cities and so may wages W_{it}. It is a property of the Dixit–Stiglitz model that the benefits of increasing returns show up, as it were, on the demand side: the larger the elasticity of substitution, the closer the substitutes for one another the differentiated goods become (in which case variety is less important), and the nearer each good's price is to $\beta_i W_{it}$, its marginal cost of production.[36]

The number of product varieties in each city is proportional to its labor force, which is assumed to be equal to its population, $n_{it} = \frac{\lambda_{it}\overline{S}_t}{\alpha\sigma}$, where λ_{it} is city i's share of the national population, $\lambda_{it} = \frac{S_{it}}{\overline{S}_t}$. Therefore, the total number of varieties in the economy, $n_t = \sum_{i=1}^{I_t} n_{it}$, is proportional to the total population and is given by

$$n_t = \frac{1}{\alpha\sigma}\overline{S}_t. \tag{8.22}$$

The economy's total population, $\overline{S}_t$, is assumed to be equal to the total labor force at time t.

The following variables are associated with city i at time t: W_{it}, the nominal wage rate; $\overline{P}_{it}$, the price index of manufactures; R_{it}, the rental rate for housing; γ_{it}, city i's population growth rate from $t-1$ to t; Y_{it}, Υ_{it}, the total income in city i, per capita income in city i; $\mathcal{I}_t^o = \mathcal{I}_{t-1} \cap \mathcal{I}_t$, the set of old cities at time t; $\mathcal{I}_t^n = \mathcal{I}_t \setminus \mathcal{I}_{t-1}$, the set of old cities at time t; and $\bar{N}_{o,t} = \sum_{i\in\mathcal{I}_{t-1}\cap\mathcal{I}_t} \lambda_{it}\bar{N}_t$, the population of *old* cities, cities that existed prior to t.

Individuals are attracted to different cities in relation to the utilities they offer. Considerations of labor mobility lead to a *first* set of equilibrium conditions. The population growth rate for each city i in existence in $t-1$, $\gamma_{it} \equiv \frac{\lambda_{it}\bar{S}_t - \lambda_{it-1}\bar{S}_{t-1}}{\lambda_{it-1}\bar{S}_{t-1}}$, relative to the aggregate growth rate of the population in existing old cities, $\gamma_{ot} = \frac{\bar{N}_{o,t} - \bar{N}_{o,t-1}}{\bar{N}_{o,t-1}}$, is assumed to be proportional to the gap, in logarithmic terms, between real utility and average real utility across the entire economy in the previous period:

$$\gamma_{it} - \gamma_{ot} = \rho_o \left[\ln\Upsilon_{it} - (1-\mu)\ln R_{it} - \mu\ln\bar{P}_{it} - \bar{u}_{t-1}\right], \ \forall i \in \mathcal{I}_t^o, \ t = 1, \ldots, T. \tag{8.23}$$

Condition (8.23) describes the law of motion for the population of cities that continue in existence.

For each new city i, a city that comes into existence between $t-1$ and t, I define the rate at which it is first populated in terms of the difference between its growth rate with respect to the mean city size at $t-1$, $\bar{\lambda}_{it-1}\bar{P}_{t-1}$, and the growth rate of old cities $\gamma_{o,t}$ and assume again a law similar to (8.23):

$$\frac{\lambda_{it}\bar{N}_t - \bar{\lambda}_{it-1}\bar{N}_{t-1}}{\bar{\lambda}_{it-1}\bar{N}_{t-1}} - \gamma_{ot} = \rho_n \left[\ln\Upsilon_{it} - (1-\mu)\ln R_{it} - \mu\ln\bar{P}_{it} - \bar{u}_{t-1}\right], \\ \times \forall i \in \mathcal{I}_t^n, \ t = 1, \ldots, T, \tag{8.24}$$

$$\ln\Upsilon_{it} - (1-\mu)\ln R_{it} - \mu\ln T_{it} \geq \min_{j\in\mathcal{L}_t\cap\mathcal{L}_{t-1}} : \left\{\ln\Upsilon_{jt} - (1-\mu)\ln R_{jt} - \mu\ln\bar{P}_{jt}\right\}, \\ \times \ \forall i \in \mathcal{I}_t^n, \ t = 1, \ldots, T, \tag{8.25}$$

where $\bar{u}_{t-1}$ is defined as the log of the geometric average real utility across the economy at time $t-1$,

$$\bar{u}_{t-1} \equiv \sum_{j=1}^{I_{t-1}} \lambda_{jt-1}[\ln\Upsilon_{jt-1} - (1-\mu)\ln R_{jt-1} - \mu\ln\bar{P}_{jt-1}], \tag{8.26}$$

and subscripts o and n stand for old and new, respectively. Condition (8.24) describes the law according to which newly created cities are populated. New cities are born if they can offer utility at least equal to that of the least attractive city among those existing at t, condition (8.25). This condition determines the distribution of the total population into old and new cities. The appearance of a new city has a qualitative effect on the dynamics of the entire system. Thus, the *first* set of equilibrium conditions, equations (8.23) and (8.24), expresses a *bifurcation* of the dynamic system that describes the evolution of the system of cities.

The supply of housing in each city, H_{it}, is inelastic and owned communally by all members of the economy. Housing is supplied inelastically in perfectly competitive markets. The *second* set of equilibrium conditions defines total income in each city as the sum of direct income from labor and the redistribution of all housing rents:

$$Y_{it} = \lambda_{it}\bar{S}_t \left(W_{it} + \frac{1-\mu}{\mu} \sum_j^{I_t} \lambda_{jt} W_{jt} \right), \quad \forall i \in \mathcal{I}_t,\ t = 1, \ldots, T. \tag{8.27}$$

Income per capita follows readily: $\Upsilon_{it} = W_{it} + \frac{1-\mu}{\mu} \sum_j^{I_t} \lambda_{jt} W_{jt},\ \forall i \in \mathcal{I}_t,\ t = 1, \ldots, T.$

The *third* set of equilibrium conditions is equilibrium housing rent in city i at time t:

$$R_{it} = (1-\mu)\frac{\Upsilon_{it}}{H_{it}}, \quad \forall i \in \mathcal{I}_t,\ t = 1, \ldots, T. \tag{8.28}$$

Given H_{it}, the housing stock in each city, higher city income implies higher rent, which in turn decreases real welfare (the value of indirect utility) for the city's residents. Cities that are attractive from the viewpoint of geography are associated with higher wages, which from (8.27) imply higher incomes, and those cities must sustain higher housing rents. Alternatively, this condition may be seen as portraying congestion.

The *fourth* equilibrium condition expresses equilibrium in the labor market in each city (Krugman 1992). Spending by all cities on each city's products must be equal to that city's labor income, $\lambda_{it}\bar{P}_t W_{it}$. This simplifies to yield

$$W_{it} = \mu \left(\sum_{k=1}^{I_t} \Upsilon_{kt} \left(\bar{P}_{kt} \beta_i^{-1} e^{-\tau d_{i,k}} \right)^{\sigma-1} \right)^{1/\sigma}, \quad \forall i \in \mathcal{I}_t, t = 1, \ldots, T. \tag{8.29}$$

This condition is homogeneous of degree 1 with respect to the Υ_{kt}'s and the $\bar{P}_{kt}$'s. It must hold if all firms at a site are to break even, even at sites that are not yet settled. See (Fujita, Krugman, and Venables 1999, 53). This provides feasibility bounds for new locations to host cities.

Krugman emphasizes the similarity of the right-hand side of (8.29) to Harris' concept of market potential. It differs from that market potential concept only because the $\bar{P}_{kt}$'s, the manufacturing price indices for all locations, also enter each other's definition, as I show immediately below. Prices anywhere reflect the effects of competition from producers in all other locations. The value for labor is higher in locations that are "closer" in terms of transport costs to areas with high consumer demand: this expresses a notion of *backward linkages*. The larger the "purchasing power" from other locations, $Y_{k,t}\bar{P}_{k,t}$, adjusted for shipping costs, $e^{-\tau d_{i,k}}$, the larger the wage rate at any location i.

The *fifth* equilibrium condition defines the price index for manufactures in each city that is associated with the underlying model (Krugman, 1992):

$$\bar{P}_{it} = \tilde{\sigma} \bar{S}_t^{\frac{1}{1-\sigma}} \left(\sum_{k=1}^{I_t} \lambda_{kt} \left(\beta_k W_{kt} e^{\tau d_{i,k}} \right)^{1-\sigma} \right)^{\frac{1}{1-\sigma}}, \forall i \in \mathcal{I}_t,\ t = 1, \ldots, T, \tag{8.30}$$

where $\tilde{\sigma} = \frac{\sigma}{\sigma-1}(\alpha\sigma)^{\frac{1}{\sigma-1}}$ is a constant. That is, the price index reflects the price of all goods consumed each location, which is equal to $\frac{\sigma}{\sigma-1}\beta_i W_{it}$, at location i at time t and adjusted on account of shipping costs. The price index in each city is homogeneous of degree 1 for all wage rates. It is decreasing in the number of varieties available. As Krugman states, condition (8.30) can be interpreted as a notion of *forward linkages*: the lower price index in a city, the higher the share of economic activity in cities with low transport costs to that city. To clarify this further, consider that equation (8.30) implies, for large σ, the following approximate form: $\bar{P}_{it} \approx \min_{k\in\mathcal{I}_t} : \left\{ \frac{\beta_k W_{kt} e^{\tau d_{i,k}}}{\lambda_{kt}} \right\}$. However, advantageous forward linkages are in part offset by congestion costs.[37]

In this economy, general equilibrium is defined for a given total population $\bar{S}_t$ and a number of cities I_t in terms of the values of the $5I_t$ unknowns at time t, $\{\lambda_{it}, W_{it}, Y_{it}, R_{it}, \bar{P}_{it}\}_{i\in I_t}$, which satisfy the $5I_t$ independent equations (8.24) or (8.23), 8.27), (8.28), (8.29), and (8.30), the condition for equilibrium in the national labor market given the lagged values of all endogenous variables. In general, highly nonlinear systems as in the present model typically have multiple solutions, which in our dynamic setting implies a dramatic increase in the richness of the dynamics beyond what is already known from the studies by Krugman (1992) and Fujita, Krugman, and Venables (1999).

Eliminating incomes, Y_{it}, by using (8.27), and housing rents, R_{it}, by using (8.28), and substituting into the remaining equations yield a set of two simultaneous dynamic equations for wages and price indices, W_{it} and $\bar{P}_{it}$. These depend on population shares and on the conditions that define population growth rates of all cities in the economy, which involves wages and price indices and population shares. For a city that is extant at $t-1$ to maintain its population, it must offer real wages that are at least equal to the economy average in the previous period.

Here the growth of existing cities is grounded in the notion that a higher market potential implies higher growth. From (8.23), the higher a city's backward linkages, the higher its income, and thus the higher its growth. This is in part offset by higher housing (i.e., congestion) costs. Similarly, the higher the forward linkages, the lower the price index for manufactures, and thus the higher the growth rate.

Black and Henderson (2003) and Ioannides and Overman (2004) use alternative versions of such a dynamic adaptation of the Hanson model to examine the spatial characteristics of the U.S. urban system as it evolved over the twentieth century. Important features they include are actual economic geography, the tendency for all cities to grow, the gradual convergence to some kind of equilibrium in the westward expansion of the U.S. population, the movement of population toward the Sun Belt and, finally, changes in the U.S. urban system induced by shifts over the period in the industrial structure away from manufacturing and toward services. These are important features in the spatial evolution of the U.S. urban system and have not yet been elaborated in the formal theory.

8.6.6.1 *Empirical Findings by Black and Henderson and by Ioannides and Overman*

Black and Henderson (2003) emphasize the stability of U.S. city size distribution in a period when both numbers and sizes of cities increase, 1990–1990.

The relative sizes of cities change as their industrial composition changes, but the transition pattern, as I discussed earlier, remains fairly stationary. Parametric regressions for city growth rates according to

$$\ln S_{i,t+1} - \ln S_{it} = \alpha + \delta_t + \beta \mathbf{X}_{it} + \gamma \ln S_{it} + u_i + \epsilon_{it}$$

are particularly interesting. They are reported by Black and Henderson (2003, table 7) and reproduced here as table 8.1. Black and Henderson include as regressors in $\mathbf{X}_{it}$ such invariant city characteristics as superior sites (e.g., a better climate and a coastal location), which are associated with a higher growth of cities. In addition, the market potential, defined according to Harris (1954) as the sum of all other city populations divided by their distance from each city i, and its square are very significant. These results suggest that a larger market potential is advantageous, but its marginal effect diminishes as it becomes large. The autoregressive coefficient is negative and significant. These regressions do not imply convergence to a fixed city size because each city's growth rate is, via the market potential variable, related to the urban system, which is evolving over time.

Ioannides and Overman (2004) rely primarily on nonparametric estimations of stochastic kernels for the distributions of city sizes and growth rates, conditional on various measures of the market potential. Nonparametric techniques are particularly appropriate for studying the complex evolution of the urban system because they impose little structure on the analysis. The first group of findings concern the spatial pattern of the location of cities in the United States. By the end of the twentieth century, the location of cities in the United States was essentially random. This finding is partly explained by the fact that the authors pool regions with very different topographies. One possibility is that there were many good first-nature sites for cities at the end of the twentieth century. This contrasts with the nonrandom pattern at beginning of the century, as their results on city size and settlement dates show. They can also identify a role for second nature by considering the location of cities of different sizes. Large cities tend to be located close to other cities, while small cities tend to be isolated.

Their second group of findings suggest that there is no simple positive relationship between city size and the market potentials, as shown by Ioannides and Overman (2004, 145, fig. 4). See figure 8.3. This relationship appears to change substantially over time. There is evidence of a positive such relationship at the start of the century, but by the end of the century it apparently holds only for the largest cities. Overall, by the end of the twentieth century, the distribution of city sizes conditional on the market potential is nearly independent of the market potential. Similar results hold when the market potential is weighted by city wages and when the Black and Henderson county-based data are used rather than the Dobkins and Ioannides city-based data. Nonetheless, Ioannides and Overman do find a role for second nature in determining city outcomes. Spatial interactions matter for understanding when a city grows faster than its historical average. They also matter for understanding which cities pay higher wages. These spatial effects are only

Table 8.1.
The Determinants of Relative Urban Growth.

Variable	(i)	(ii)	(iii)	(iv)†
ln[Heat° days]	−0.095**	−0.102**	−0.105**	−0.113**
	(0.015)	(0.015)	(0.015)	(0.015)
ln[Precipitation]	−0.075**	−0.074**	−0.087**	−0.089**
	(0.016)	(0.015)	(0.017)	(0.017)
Coastal dummy	0.034**	0.049**	0.031**	0.046**
	(0.010)	(0.011)	(0.010)	(0.010)
Market potential			0.127**	0.141**
			(0.030)	(0.030)
(Market potential)^2			−0.027*	−0.028**
			(0.0065)	(0.0065)
ln[Population$_{it}$]		- 0.023**		−0.025**
		(0.0033)		(0.0034)
Regional and time dummies	Yes	Yes	Yes	Yes†
R^2_{adj}	0.373	0.385	0.378	0.392
	Fixed Effects		GMM	
Market potential	0.651**		0.805**	
	(0.147)		(0.055)	
Market potential^2	−0.117*		−0.085**	
	(0.024)		(0.0061)	
ln Population$_{it}$	−0.194**		−0.192**	
	(0.018)		(0.0091)	

Source: Black and Henderson (2003).
Standard errors in parentheses. * Significant at 10%; ** significant at 5%.
†Relative to the West, in column (iv), regional dummies on city growth rates for the Northeast, Midwest, and South are −1.9, −1.3, and −0.095 respectively. With time-regional dummies, the time pattern is that regional differences before 1950 are very modest, with only the Northeast growing consistently but modestly slower. From 1950 to 1970 or 1980, all regions grow much more slowly than the West, although the differential for the South is smaller. The differentials for the Northeast and Midwest are distinctly smaller for 1990.

weakly present at the beginning of the period and slowly emerge during the century.

8.7 GEOGRAPHY AND SPATIAL CLUSTERING

In section 8.5 above I note that features of the landscape (first nature) itself could give rise to power laws. As Krugman (1996, 416) points out, features of the geographic landscape, like river systems, where a river's size is measured by its flow, may follow power laws themselves. Such features are a fixed input to production or an amenity. Power laws may be transmitted to the urban system

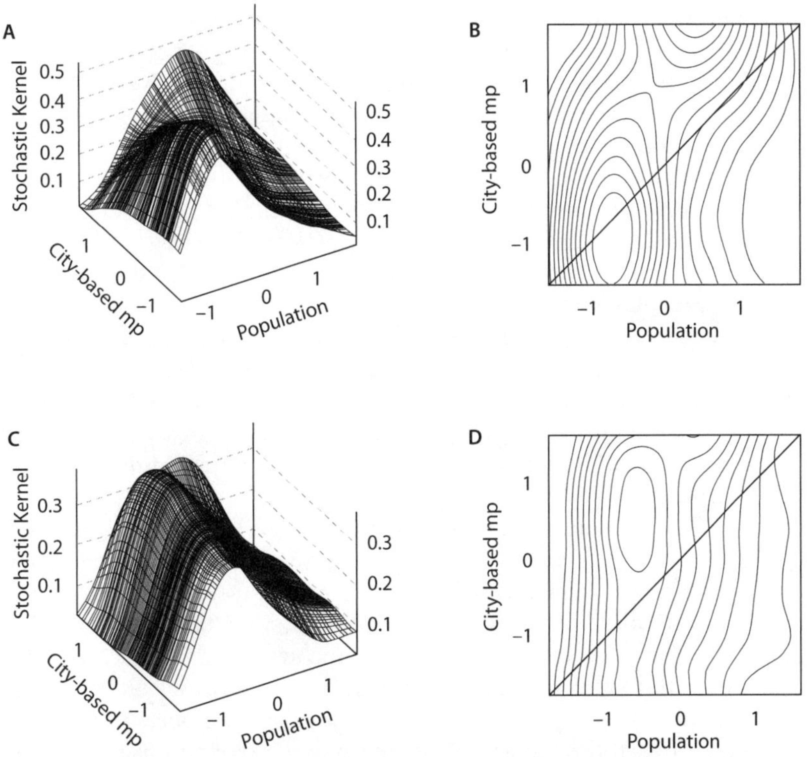

Figure 8.3. Evolution of city sizes in relation to market potential.
Source: Ioannides and Overman (2004, 145, fig. 4).

through optimizing behavior and thus may influence urban structure and its evolution. See (Gabaix and Ioannides 2004, 2361) for more details.

Since economic agglomeration is linked with higher productivity, we expect it to be linked to aggregate growth. Since inhomogeneity in location patterns may be generated by optimizing behavior, the potential exists for interdependence between agglomeration and growth as an outcome of optimizing behavior. This may give rise to a source of endogenous growth and can also explain the evolution of economic activity over time and space. I take this up in chapter 9 below.

I discuss next an approach that generates spatial clustering in one as well as in two dimensions. The dynamic Hanson model adapted to cities in section 8.6.6 can be enriched by working with very specific spatial detail. Fujita, Krugman, and Venables (1999, chaps. 10 and 17) and Chincarini and Asherie (2008) provide a series of analytical applications involving dynamical systems that describe the evolution of each city in terms of the state of other neighboring cities, or of all other cities in the urban system in the preceding period. These analyses typically describe space as a lattice. A full analysis of spatial features of models of economic geography is beyond the scope of the book.

Still, the limited description that follows offers a glimpse of the richness of dynamic spatial equilibrium models in the presence of interactions.

Chincarini and Asherie (2008) go beyond Fujita, Krugman, and Venables (1999) and Fujita and Mori (1997) and characterize *analytically* the number of clusters formed in an economy identical to that studied by Fujita et al. instead of relying on simulations. Specifically, the economy is populated by farmers, who are spread uniformly over the continuous space and are immobile, and by workers, who move to locations offering a real wage above the average real wage in the economy. Total income in each location consists of farmers' incomes plus workers' incomes, each of which are proportional to the respective densities. The price index at each location is defined as in (8.30) in terms of wages at every other location, and shipping costs depend on distance traveled. Prices of manufactured goods shipped are expressed in terms of wages. Equilibrium nominal wages at each location are expressed in terms of the market potential, which aggregates the demand for goods from all other locations, as in (8.19).

The resulting system of partial differential equations admits a uniform distribution of economic activity as a steady-state equilibrium. Starting from such a steady-state equilibrium, perturbing it spatially, and representing the perturbations in terms of Fourier expansions, Chincarini and Asherie express the spatial perturbations in economic activity by means of spatial waves at different frequencies. The different harmonics evolve independently because of the linearity and rotational invariance of the model. They obtain analytical solutions for the temporal evolution of the economy as it settles into distinct clusters for both a one-dimensional circular economy and a (previously unsolved) two-dimensional model of city formation. They also obtain closed-form solutions for the growth rates of each Fourier harmonic of the perturbed density of workers, for both a circular and a spherical economy, of the full range of harmonics that express the perturbations. The growth rate for the mth Fourier harmonic of the perturbed worker density is given by Chincarini and Asherie [2008, 258, eqs. (28) and (29)] and is reproduced here:

$$g_m = \rho \left[\frac{(1-\mu\eta)(\mu\eta - \eta^2)}{\sigma - \mu\eta - (\sigma - 1)\eta^2} - \frac{\mu\eta}{1-\sigma} \right], \quad \eta \equiv \frac{\Gamma_m(\tau r(\sigma - 1))}{\Gamma_0(\tau r(\sigma - 1)},$$

where $\Gamma_m(z)$ is defined in terms of the spherical modified Bessel function of the second kind, $i_m(z)$, $\Gamma_m = e^{-z} i_m(z)$, r is the radius of the circle, and all other parameters are as defined earlier. The growth rates are expressed in terms of preference parameters, that is, the expenditure shares in individuals' utility functions, $(\mu, 1-\mu)$, and of the elasticity of substitution across the consumption varieties, σ, iceberg shipping costs, τ, and the size of the economy.

For a circular economy, the solution for the perturbations will be dominated by the one with the numerically largest growth rate, g_{m^*} (the magnitude of the spatial harmonic of order m^*), which determines the number of clusters formed.[38] This determines the dominant frequency so that the distribution of workers is proportional to $e^{g_{m^*}t} e^{m^* \phi \sqrt{-1}}$, where ϕ denotes the angle that describes the location around a circle of radius r. Thus, economic activity is proportional to the sinusoidal term with amplitude given by $e^{g_{m*}t}$. In other words, the larger the share of workers in the economy, the more workers tend to agglomerate and the smaller the number of different clusters. In the extreme case of negligible shipping costs, there is no advantage to having more than one manufacturing agglomeration. Increasing transportation costs and economies of scale increase the number of clusters.

Chincarini and Asherie also develop a model of location on spherical surfaces. The analysis proceeds along very similar lines, with the perturbations expressed in terms of the two-dimensional analog of a Fourier series. They show that even though the harmonics are defined in terms of two indices, because of rotational invariance a single growth rate suffices to express the solution. They also show that whereas in the one-dimensional case cities are equally spaced around the circle, in two dimensions new structural features arise and involve "higher-level" symmetries[39] that could potentially fit the actual formation of economic clusters more accurately and involve a richer and perhaps more realistic set of possibilities. For example, a central city may be growing on at pole of the sphere with other cities growing around it. This resembles the phenomenon of "edge cities."[40] This is an important finding that contrasts with earlier claims, such as that by Ogawa and Fujita (1982), that one- and two-dimensional settings do not differ qualitatively.

8.8 STUDIES OF URBAN STRUCTURE BASED ON "QUASI-NATURAL EXPERIMENTS"

What happens when an established urban system experiences a major unexpected shock, such as destruction brought by war? Will it be rebuilt as a replica of its previous form, or will another form prevail? Davis and Weinstein (2002) were the first to ask these questions, followed by Bosker, Brakman, Garretsen, and Schramm (2007, 2008). These studies use as "quasi-natural experiments" the impact of the strategic bombing of Japan, during World War II,[41] in the first case, and of Germany, in the latter two cases. The studies differ, however, in their time horizons. In the study of Japan, the time span ranges over the past 8,000 years. In the study with data from Germany, the range is from the beginning to the end of the twentieth century. Redding and Sturm (2008) focus on the impact of the reunification of Germany.

Davis and Weinstein (2002) and Bosker, Brakman, Garretsen, and Schramm (2007) examine the performance of three not mutually exclusive theories of economic geography and urban development in explaining urban growth patterns following such shocks. These theories are, first, *increasing returns*; second, *random growth processes*; and third, *locational fundamentals*. Davis and Weinstein argue, looking at temporary shocks, that they predict very *different* and *testable impacts* on the size distribution.

One way to think about these shocks is as conceptual experiments along the lines of equation (8.17), augmented with entry from a stock of potential inhabitants, or of the model in section 8.6.6. We can think of destruction as setting new initial conditions for urban evolution.

Davis and Weinstein (2002) find evidence of robustness in Japan's urban system and interpret it as evidence against the increasing returns and random growth theories and in favor of the locational fundamentals theory. They also find it consistent with a hybrid theory: locational advantages help establish basic patterns of regional densities and increasing returns, or random growth helps determine the degree of concentration. Brakman, Garretsen, and Schramm (2004) estimate the impact of World War II destruction on city growth in postwar Germany and find it to be significant but temporary, both for Germany as a whole and for West German cities on their own, but not significant for East German cities. This may reflect the prevalence of central planning in East Germany, which rendered urban growth less sensitive to economic fundamentals, in contrast to the long term outcomes in the free market system in West Germany.

Bosker, Brakman, Garretsen, and Schramm (2008) use more detailed data for West Germany to study the evolution of the city size distribution and the growth of individual cities separately. Their data allow them to identify shocks from the effects of World War II associated with Germany's division and its reunification. They find that the evolution of the German city size distribution is permanently affected by the World War II shock. Cities that were hit hard did not recover from the loss in relative size. The city size distribution did not revert to its pre–World War II level and has become more evenly distributed. The impact of the partition and reunification of West and East Germany is much less pronounced. A second finding is that, once corrected for the heavy war destruction, panel unit root tests reject Gibrat's law of urban growth rates for about 75 percent of all cities. This is also confirmed by nonparametric evidence. Overall, they view their results as most consistent with theories of city growth emphasizing increasing returns to scale.

Redding and Sturm (2008) use the division of Germany during 1945–1990 and its reunification in 1990 to study the importance of market access for economic development. It is straightforward to see this in terms of the model that I discuss in chapter 7, section 7.7 above. Redding and Sturm observe that following the division, cities in West Germany, especially smaller ones close to the East-West German border experienced a substantial decline in population growth relative to other West German cities. The model accounts for the quantitative magnitude of their findings and shows a causal effect of market access on the spatial distribution of economic activity. Redding and Sturm show that, for plausible parameter values, they can predict an overall relative decline of cities on both sides of the East-West German border, with a more pronounced effect on smaller cities, and those changes cannot be explained by specialization patterns or the degree of war-related disruption. They also show that the decline of those cities is not affected by European economic integration which might have favored cities in the western part of West Germany.

The historical dimensions of these studies have clearly opened up new horizons for economic research. They are providing additional evidence on the resilience of urban systems in the large. Repeated destructions of urban settlements in Europe have been consistently followed by reconstruction along the earlier patterns. As Hohenberg (2004) emphasizes in connection with the European experience, urban systems show remarkable resilience in the light of so many technological and social changes. A major unexplored topic here is the impact of the European Union on European urban systems.

8.9 GLOBAL ASPECTS OF CITY SIZE DISTRIBUTION AND ITS EVOLUTION

The U.S.-based studies that I discuss in this chapter show little intradistributional mobility for cities, but a global view of intradistributional mobility gives a stark picture of change emerging on a slow time scale. Batty's (2006) graphical depiction superimposes Zipf plots over time and also introduces the device of "rank clocks." This ranks the largest 100 cities in the world, marked from 1, at the center of a circle, to 100, on its circumference. Then, city ranks are marked radially, from the earliest time, 430 BC, marked as $00:00+\epsilon$, to 2000 AD, marked as $11:59-\epsilon$ (Batty 2006, 594 fig. 3). Connecting the points gives rank clock paths. This graphic shows, for example, that both Rome and Chinese cities were quite dominant for much of history, having eclipsed Babylon and Benares in late antiquity. The rank volatility of the clock paths for other cities increases from the onset of the Industrial Revolution to the modern era, when the size dominance of contemporary developing world cities, like Mexico City, emerges. This is not surprising and in fact is consistent with the leapfrogging that characterizes economic growth across the world. It suggests that theories of urban primacy along with theories of urbanization combined with leapfrogging can explain global aspects of city size distribution.

It is tempting to speculate that global leapfrogging might itself be explained in terms of interactions among cities, for instance, by generalizing the models of chapter 4, section 4.8; chapter 7, section 7.7; and Chapter 8, section 8.6.6, by defining international borders and coding the patterns of trade costs and factor mobility. Head and Mayer (2011) highlight the importance of the market potential for economic development by showing that conferring Thailand's market potential on the Congo Democratic Republic would increase its GDP per capita by a factor of about 24. Similarly, he estimates that the average growth of market potential in their sample due to neighboring countries between 1993 and 2003 has raised income per capita by about 105 percent.

A contemporary view of the income counterpart of urban concentrations is telling. Consider the figure presented by Nordhaus (2006, 3513, fig. 1), reproduced here as figure 8.4, which is an economic map of Europe with heights proportional to gross domestic product per area (in millions of 1995

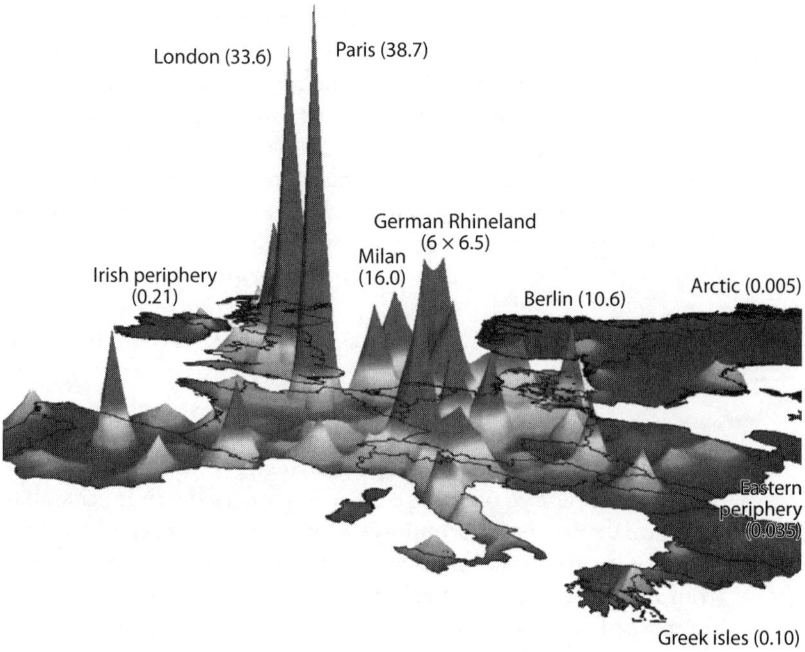

Figure 8.4. Economic map of Europe. *Source*: Nordhaus (2006, 3513, fig. 1).

U.S. dollars per square kilometer). The pronounced concentrations in the spatial distribution of income per area are irregular but qualitatively similar to the predictions of spatial clustering models of the new economic geography.[42]

8.10 CONCLUSION

A phenomenal amount of research has tried to describe and explain the evolution of city size distributions within and across countries. The theories and empirical findings in this chapter suggest a need to explore deeper phenomena whose surfaces economists have just barely scratched. The existing literature ranges from fairly simple theories aiming at statistical underpinnings of the most salient feature of city size distributions, namely, their thick upper tails (Gabaix 1999a, 1999b; Rossi-Hansberg and Wright 2007; Skouras 2009), to full-fledged theories with elaborate economic foundations, such as that of Duranton (2007) and of Rossi-Hansberg and Wright (2007). Duranton's theory, in particular, also incorporates an important and hitherto neglected attribute of modern industry, rapid industrial churning, showing how it may explain the slow upward and downward movement of cities within the urban hierarchy. Recent research has augmented the notion of urban specialization, underscoring the emergence of functional (as opposed to sectoral) specialization and showing how it is intimately related to the role of urban concentrations as cradles of innovation. Diversified cities spawn innovations and at the same time may help mitigate cyclical risks, as industries with different labor turnover properties benefit from colocation.

Other research is expanding the scope of inquiry. For example, Rose (2006a) adds tantalizing similarities between city and country size distributions. He compares city size with country size distributions, in terms of estimates of both Zipf's law and of Gibrat's law. The Zipf exponents are very similar and so are the Gibrat's coefficients.[43] Decker, Kerkhoff, and Moses (2007), referred to in section 8.5.4 above, see global patterns in city size distributions across nations. Such patterns follow, they argue, from fundamental laws related to the flow and distribution of resources within and among cities that should ultimately be explicable in ecological terms. Cities and countries are different population entities in a number of aspects. Cities within the same country are much more similar to one another than to those in different countries. Countries have more control over their policies and institutions than cities. Nevertheless, it is tempting to use theories of city size distribution to explain country sizes. Externalities, agglomeration effects, and amenity shocks may be driving the quests of ethnic groups for nationhood in the spirit of Alesina and Spolaore (2003) and in a fashion similar to the emergence of cities described by Rossi-Hansberg and Wright (2007) whose particular theory of urban growth I take up in chapter 9 below.

As Hicks argues, the great wealth and thus urban concentrations in the ancient past, such as in Mesopotamia, the Near East, Greece, and Rome, were facilitated by the ease of navigation in the Mediterranean, and similarly in the Far East. But just as understanding this role requires a geographic depiction, so can modern technology, like GIS, be used to integrate economic and microgeographic information more effectively. A shocking failure of research on this topic is the arbitrariness of commonly used measures of urban concentrations of economic activity: cities, towns, places, metropolitan areas, agglomerations, conurbations, and so on, and the associated and possibly overlapping governmental jurisdictions. It thus behooves economists to utilize the multitude of measures available for testing their theories of city formation and urban interactions. Perhaps different types of aggregation are appropriate for different phenomena of interest. Future empirical research must address the spatial distribution of economic activity in greater depth.

CHAPTER 9
Intercity Trade and Long-Run Urban Growth

9.1 INTRODUCTION

In the study of urban growth, one direction has emphasized its historical aspects. Massive population movements from rural to urban areas fueled the initial stage of urban population growth and have been associated with sustained increases in living standards. Growth is typically associated with urbanization, but the reverse does not always hold, as the evidence from Africa suggests. Innovations are closely associated with urban concentrations. A related direction focuses on the physical infrastructure of cities and how it may change as cities grow. It also focuses on how changes in commuting costs, and in the industrial composition of national output and other technological changes, have affected the growth of cities. A third direction has focused on understanding the evolution of systems of cities, that is, how cities of different sizes interact, accommodate, and share different functions as the economy develops, and what the properties of the size distribution of urban areas are for economies at different stages of development. Why is it that the properties of the system of cities and of city size distribution largely persist while the national population is growing? There is considerable contemporary interest in the conceptual link between urban growth and economic growth and in whether policies that work in one place can be transplanted and work equally well elsewhere. What economic functions are carried by cities of different sizes in a growing economy? Of course, all these lines of inquiry are closely interrelated, and none of them may be fully understood, theoretically and empirically, entirely on its own.

The concentration of population and economic activity in urban areas may increase because individuals migrate from rural areas or from other urban areas or because the national population grows, creating a demand for new cities to house people and production. Urban centers can be sustained only if agricultural productivity has increased sufficiently to allow people to move away from the land and devote themselves to non-food-producing activities.[1] Such "symmetry breaking" in the uniform distribution of economic activity is an important factor in understanding urban development (Matsuyama 1995, 1996; Papageorgiou and Smith 1983). Also important is recognizing that cities became able to sustain their populations without fresh flows from the countryside only after public health improved urban health standards sufficiently (Cairns 1997; Cutler and Miller 2005). Research on the process of urbanization spans the early modern era, with the case of Europe having been the most thoroughly studied (De Vries 1984), up to recent studies that have applied modern tools to examine urbanization in East Asia (Fujita, Mori, Henderson, and Kanemoto 2004). The new economic geography literature has emphasized how an economy can become "differentiated" into an industrialized core (urban sector) and an agricultural periphery (Krugman 1991a). These ideas have generated new lines of research; see several related papers in the handbook edited by Henderson and Thisse (2004).

This chapter starts with a basic model of the growth of isolated cities that is influenced by Ventura (2005). It allows for investment in physical capital and in urban transportation as ways to increase urban productive capacity. I follow up with a sample of growth empirics for the U.S., European, and Brazilian systems of cities with an emphasis on transportation improvements and factor accumulation. I turn next to a model of economic growth in a system of cities that leads to a precise description of the law of motion in dynamic settings of either autarkic cities or specialized cities that engage in intercity trade. The endogenous variety of intermediates allows for a combination of weak (strong) diminishing returns and strong (weak) market size effects to lead to increasing (decreasing) returns to scale in either city type. The model also allows urban growth to be influenced by local (city) governments' investment in reducing urban commuting costs. Under appropriate conditions, unceasing growth sustains a divergent or a parallel pattern in city sizes. Examining economic growth in an integrated economy, defined as intercity trade in manufactured goods and factor mobility within the urban system, is facilitated by the fact that under my assumptions, the law of motion for capital in the integrated economy has the same dynamic properties as its counterpart for an economy with autarkic cities. That is because when cities do specialize, in this model, the advantage of specialization is exactly offset by the effect of its superior performance on the terms of trade.

While cities have performed different functions in the course of economic development, a key fact, documented in chapter 8, persists for a wide cross section of countries and different time periods. That is, the size distribution of cities is roughly stable, and its upper tail is Pareto-distributed. Chapter 8 highlights a number of explanations, including those offered by Gabaix (1999b), Duranton (2007), and Skouras (2009). This chapter presents a complementary explanation due to Rossi-Hansberg and Wright (2007), who use a neoclassical growth model to derive predictions that are consistent with observed systematic deviations from Zipf's law. In particular, the actual size distribution of cities shows fewer smaller and larger cities than the Pareto distribution, and estimates of the exponent of the Pareto distribution are often different from -1. These authors identify the standard deviation of the industry productivity shocks as a key factor behind these deviations from Zipf's law.

An increasing share of national economic activity occurring in cities is driven by the goods and services provided by different kinds of cities. This fact links national and urban growth. Understanding urban growth ultimately involves understanding the basic forces that generate the real and pecuniary externalities that allow urban agglomeration to thrive, on the one hand, and that generate congestion as a consequence of agglomeration, on the other.

Reductions in commuting costs can lead to larger cities in terms of area, population, and output. Chatterjee and Carlino (2001) study how disparities in employment density across U.S. metropolitan areas have lessened substantially over the postwar period. Employment has grown faster in the initially less dense metropolitan areas compared to the initially more dense metropolitan areas. A increase in aggregate metropolitan employment leads to deconcentration because congestion costs rise faster for the initially most dense metropolitan areas than for the initially less dense ones. Another angle, offered by Ioannides, Overman, Rossi-Hansberg, and Schmidheiny (2008)—see chapter 8, section 8.2.8, and section 9.7.2 below—is that adoption of information and communication technologies may increase the geographic scope of production externalities and thus increase the proportion of smaller cities. Lower commuting costs may weaken the link between housing location choices and workplace locations. Urban growth can therefore lead to suburbanization as well as to multiple business centers [cf. (Anas, Arnott, and Small 1998; Glaeser and Kahn 2004)]. All these phenomena affect the properties of the tails of the city size distribution.

Jacobs (1969) and Lucas (1988) underscore knowledge spillovers at the city level as a main engine of aggregate economic growth. The growth literature has also argued that, in order for an economy to exhibit unceasing growth, the aggregate technology has to exhibit asymptotically constant returns to scale (Jones 1999). If not, the growth rate in an economy will ultimately either explode or converge to zero. How is this consistent with the presence of scale effects at the city level? Eaton and Eckstein (1997), motivated by empirical evidence from the French and Japanese urban systems, study the possibility of parallel city growth, which is assumed to depend critically on intercity knowledge flows together with the accumulation of partly city-specific human capital across a given number of cities. Rossi-Hansberg and Wright (2007) propose a theory in which scale effects and congestion forces at the city level balance out in equilibrium to determine the numbers and sizes of cities. Thus, the economy exhibits constant returns to scale through the number of cities increasing along with the scale of the economy. The model admits a balanced growth path along which growth is positive even in the absence of population growth. Relative to the Ventura-type model, this model allows technology to depend on human capital accumulation and makes sustained aggregate growth not a knife-edge result. By seeing balanced growth as the result of the interplay between urban scale effects and congestion costs, these theories have important implications for the size distribution of cities and the urban growth process. These implications turn out to be consistent with the empirical size distribution of cities as encapsulated in Zipf's law and in observed systematic deviations from Zipf's law.

The history of urbanization is closely related to intercity and international trade. Cities grow as they trade with their hinterlands and with other nearby as well as distant cities. Changes in the fundamentals may affect the relative sizes of cities, and this is transmitted through intercity trade. The role of trade in growth is one of the areas that have attracted the attention of both the new economic geography and the endogenous growth literature. In some of those theories, endogenous technological change is driven by specialization, which is in turn driven by the extent of the market. Openness is naturally underpinning growth in the extent of the market.

Eaton and Eckstein (1997) distinguish *parallel*, *convergent*, and *divergent* urban growth (see chapter 8, section 8.6.2). These alternative possibilities may be handled simultaneously only by a model that contains the key forces that drive urbanization. An increase in intracity commuting costs along with population growth induces the emergence of new cities. However, once cities have specialized, the taste for product variety drives the appearance of additional cities, while intercity transportation costs limit the process and act as a force of agglomeration. *Centrifugal* forces, namely, congestion, lead to wasteful commuting and to congestion costs in the form of higher rents; *centripetal* forces, favor fewer and larger cities. Generally, the earlier new economic geography works ignored the fact that cities have been growing in size and number and the reasons why very large cities have appeared. Throughout the world, cities of a wide range of sizes coexist with large, diversified cities.

The chapter finally returns to the empirics of urban structure and economic growth. One issue concerns constant returns to scale at the level of the national economy, which both main models in this chapter predict. That is, variation in the urban structure through the birth, growth, and death of cities provides a margin that eliminates local increasing returns to yield constant returns to scale at the level of the aggregate economy. A second pertains to the sequential nature of urban growth and its impact on the entire cross-sectional city size distribution. New cities do not appear instantaneously because their infrastructures need to be built first and their competition with existing cities for population has interesting implications for such key city variables as housing rents. The chapter concludes with the highlights of the latest research on spatial aspects of urban growth that relies on exhaustive data sets that also include microgeographic information.

9.2 GROWTH OF ISOLATED CITIES

In the models I used in previous chapters to examine the urban economy, I have emphasized individuals' demands for space and deemphasized that of firms. To compensate, this section follows Miyao (1977, 1981) and starts with the case of growth of an isolated city with a von Thünen production economy. Growth is possible because the population, and thus the labor force, is growing exogenously and is being accommodated by a spatially expanding city. The spatial expansion of the city is facilitated by investments to reduce unit commuting costs, which are financed by a tax on the city's output. This leads to a well-defined growth problem whose optimal solution is expressed in terms of choosing the tax rate needed to maximize net output per capita. It turns out that the optimal tax rate should be equal to the land elasticity of output.

9.2.1 Growth of an Isolated von Thünen City

Producers located in a series of concentric circles around the CBD produce goods using land and labor under constant returns to scale, and ship the goods to the CBD, from where they are sold at a fixed price, which is normalized at unity. Recall from chapter 5, section 5.3, that perfect competition and spatial equilibrium require that the profit be zero at all locations. This yields in turn that the production cost per unit of output produced at distance ℓ from the CBD, $c(R(\ell), w; A)$, as a function of land rent, $R(\ell)$, wage rate, w, and total factor productivity, A, must satisfy (5.14), reproduced here as

$$c(R(\ell), w) = 1 - \tau_{\text{rate}} - \kappa\ell, \tag{9.1}$$

where τ_{rate} is the tax rate per unit of good shipped and κ is the transportation cost per mile per unit of output. I deal with the special case of a Cobb–Douglas production function for output, which I write in terms of labor per unit of land n as $f(n) = n^{1-\gamma}$, where γ is the land elasticity of output. Unit costs become $c(R(\ell), w) \equiv (1-\gamma)^{-(1-\gamma)}\gamma^{\gamma}W^{1-\gamma}R(\ell)^{\gamma}$. The equilibrium land rental rate readily follows:

$$R(\ell) = \gamma^{\frac{1-\gamma}{\gamma}} W^{-1/\gamma}(1 - \tau_{\text{rate}} - \kappa\ell)^{1/\gamma}.$$

From Roy's identity [chapter 5, (5.16)], I express labor per unit of land $n(\ell)$ at ℓ and obtain $n(\ell) = \frac{1-\gamma}{\gamma}\frac{R(\ell)}{W}$. This together with the spatial equilibrium condition (9.1) yields the distribution of employment as

$$n(\ell) = (1-\gamma)^{1/\gamma}\gamma^{-1/\gamma}W^{-1/\gamma}(1 - \tau_{\text{rate}} - \kappa\ell)^{1/\gamma}. \tag{9.2}$$

I assume, as in chapter 7, that the opportunity cost of land at the edge of the city is 0, which allows me to solve for city size, $\bar{\ell} = \frac{1-\tau_{\text{rate}}}{\kappa}$. I ignore competition for land use by individuals and assume that a fraction b_f of land is allocated to production and that all individuals work. The full-employment condition then is

$$2\pi b_f \int_0^{\bar{\ell}} n(\ell)\ell d\ell = N.$$

I define the auxiliary variable $z \equiv \kappa \ell$ and, following Miyao (1981), rewrite the full-employment condition as

$$2\pi b_f (1-\gamma)^{1/\gamma} W^{-1/\gamma} \int_0^{1-\tau_{\text{rate}}} (1-\tau-z)^{1/\gamma} z dz = \frac{1}{k},$$

where $k \equiv \frac{1}{N\kappa^2}$, turns out to be a convenient state variable. Carrying out the integration by parts (Miyao 1981, 106) and rewriting the full employment condition yield

$$W^{-\frac{1-\gamma}{\gamma}} = w^*(1-\tau_{\text{rate}})^{-(1+2\gamma)(1-\gamma)\frac{1}{\gamma}} k^{-(1-\gamma)}, \tag{9.3}$$

where w^* denotes a constant, that does not depend on k, τ. Following Miyao, I assume that the transportation investment, which is financed by tax revenues, obtained by applying the tax rate times total city output, is spread evenly over all land devoted to transportation, again assumed to be a constant fraction, b_τ, of all city land, $b_\tau \pi \left(\frac{1-\tau_{\text{rate}}}{\kappa}\right)$.[2]

Miyao assumes that transportation investment per unit of land devoted to transportation brings about a uniform reduction in unit transport costs, with the rate of decrease in κ being an increasing monotone function of transportation investment per unit of land. Then, Miyao (1981, 106, theorem 8.1) ensures the existence of a balanced growth path along which the auxiliary state variable k grows at a constant rate. This implies from the definition $k \equiv \frac{1}{N\kappa^2}$ that along such a path the rate of decline in unit transport cost is equal to one-half the rate of population growth. Furthermore, Miyao (1981, 108, theorem 8.3) ensures that the tax rate that maximizes total gross output, net of tax and transport costs per person, is equal to the land elasticity of output, $\tau_{\text{rate}} = \gamma$. Not surprisingly, this result is reminiscent of the *golden rule* of neoclassical growth theory, namely, that the savings rate that maximizes consumption per person in a steady state is equal to the capital elasticity of aggregate output. Whereas in neoclassical growth theory savings are invested in order to augment productive capacity, here augmenting productive capacity requires expanding the space occupied by the city, which is accomplished with transportation investment. I return below to the possibility of expanding city size via investment in reducing unit transport cost.

9.2.2 Empirical Aspects of Urban Growth through Transportation Improvements

Curiously, the impact of transportation improvements on urban growth has received little empirical attention. Duranton and Turner (2010, 2011)[2] are two noteworthy and recent exceptions. Duranton and Turner (2010) work with an equilibrium model of cities where equalization of utility among cities implies that city size increases with each city's intrinsic attractiveness and decreases with unit transport cost. Allowing for the fact that a city's attractiveness is subject to stochastic shocks and that adjustment of its size is subject to frictions leads to a dynamic equation for city size. Furthermore, specifying that the unit transport cost improves with the quality and extent of a city's transportation technology apart from infrastructure, decreases with the extent of its transportation infrastructure $K_{g,i,t}$, and increases with city size leads to a regression equation for city i's population growth rate:

$$\ln N_{i,t+1} - \ln N_{it} = B_i + B_t + C_1 \ln K_{git} - C_2 \ln N_{it} + \varepsilon_{it}, \qquad (9.4)$$

where B_i, B_t denote city-specific and time-specific effects.

In estimating equation (9.4), Duranton and Turner are primarily interested in C_1, the elasticity of the urban population growth rate with respect to transportation infrastructure K_{git}. However, in every economy, but especially in that of the United States, transportation infrastructure is not an exogenous variable to city i. That is, it is likely to reflect the city's past, current, and future attractiveness and thus is likely to be correlated with ε_{it}. In other words, a city with more infrastructure today may have more tomorrow, and therefore anticipation of greater infrastructure will affect growth tomorrow. Moreover, its existing infrastructure depreciates because of a variety of random factors and is likely to depend on the city's specific characteristics. Such considerations lead the authors to adopt as instruments the following two variables: one, kilometers of interstate highways *planned* for each MSA in 1947 based on the 1947 legislation that started the U.S. interstate highway system (a controlled-access system of highways that connects all U.S. metropolitan areas); two, kilometers of 1898 railroads contained in each MSA. A political economy analysis of highway plans provided by the authors suggests strongly that the first variable would help predict kilometers of interstate highways in 1980. A historical analysis of engineering practices in relation to geographic terrain suggests that old routes often provide sites for locations for new roads. The old routes thus serve as an indicator of the extent to which the terrain lends itself to straight, level routes. Both these hypotheses are confirmed by the authors' first-stage regressions (Duranton and Turner, 2010, table 2). These variables are not direct determinants of current MSA populations and thus qualify as instruments. From a variety of regressions, reported by Duranton and Turner (2010, table 4), for the MSA population growth rates from 1980 to 2000, as a function of the 1980 stock of highways and of the population, appropriately instrumented as just discussed, the authors conclude that a 10 percent increase in a MSA's stock of roads in 1980 causes a 2 percent increase in the MSA's population over the subsequent 20 years. Alternatively expressed, an increase of one standard deviation in roads per capita causes an increase of 0.5 percent in the annual growth rate. Duranton and Turner compare this effect numerically to results obtained by others on the effect of climate (which is not a policy variable, naturally), finding it to be similar in magnitude, and to that of human capital or dynamic externalities, finding it to be stronger.

Whereas Duranton and Turner emphasize the aggregate impact of increased highways on urban growth, Baum-Snow (2007) examines the impact of U.S. highway construction on intrametropolitan population distribution. Baum-Snow argues that the interstate highway system actually *caused* a 17 percent decline in central-city populations, while the total population in U.S. metropolitan areas grew 72 percent during the same period of time, 1950–1990. Baum-Snow uses an instrumenting strategy similar to that of Duranton and Turner, employing 1947 planned highways as an instrument. His estimates imply that each new highway causes "constant-geography" central-city populations to decline, ceteris paribus, by about 18 percent. The effect is underscored by the following counterfactual that the author reports: had the interstate highway not been built, instead of declining by 17 percent, aggregate central-city populations would have grown by 8 percent. These particular estimates reflect a variety of underlying factors that have contributed to suburbanization, including the location of different types of jobs, the availability of public transit, and changing patterns for goods shipping through the interstate highway network, ports, and airports, and others.

9.2.3 Growth Due to Factor Supplies

Having examined the role of growth by investments in expanding a city's spatial size, I now turn to growth due to increased factor supplies. The essential openness of cities in market economies makes cities' growth prospects depend on their attractiveness. In an economy with free intercity factor movements, individuals can move to cities that offer higher utility, and capital can move to cities that offer higher nominal returns. Modeling sources of growth in an isolated city must heed openness but is quite straightforward, provided that one may identify sufficient factors so as to account for all measurable and appropriate factors of interest. There is considerable interest in the extent to which sources of urban growth, in terms of both observables and unobservables, may be influenced by policy.

A standard approach emulates growth-accounting exercises at the national level. I follow Crihfield and Panggabean (1995)—also recall chapter 6, section 6.3—and adapt equation (6.4) to write the output for city i as

$$Y_{it} = \Xi_{it} K_{it}^{\beta} K_{git}^{\beta_g} H_{it}^{\alpha} N_{it}^{\nu-\beta-\beta_g-\alpha}, \tag{9.5}$$

where ν denotes aggregate returns to scale that may be greater than 1. Here $\beta, \beta_g, \alpha, \nu-\beta-\beta_g-\alpha$ are the respective output elasticities of capital, K_{it}, public capital, K_{git}, human capital, H_{it}, labor, N_{it}. Ξ_{it}, total factor productivity, and N_{it}, city i labor are assumed to grow at constant rates g and g_n, respectively. Crihfield and Panggabean (1995, 160) ignore land as input and adopt the standard OMB definitions of MSAs (see chapter 8, section 8.5.2) but adjust them so as to maintain geographic consistency over time. Crihfield and Panggabean assume that out of total income, fractions s_k, s_{k_g}, s_h are saved and invested in private capital, public capital, and human capital, respectively. This allows them to solve for per capita city output along a balanced growth path in terms of savings rates, city i labor, and parameters in the standard fashion of the augmented versions of the Solow growth model (Solow 1956; Mankiw, Romer, and Weil 1992). Adapting the model to allow for incomplete adjustment of the growth of per capita output, relative to the growth gap between the balanced growth path and the initial value of per capita income, y_{i0}, yields a regression equation:

$$\begin{aligned}\ln y_{it} - \ln y_{i0} &= (1-a^*)\ln \Xi_{i0} + (1-a^*)gt + \frac{(1-a^*)\beta}{1-\beta-\beta_g-\alpha}\ln s_k \\ &+ \frac{(1-a^*)\beta_g}{1-\beta-\beta_g-\alpha}\ln s_{k_g} \\ &+ \frac{(1-a^*)\alpha}{1-\beta-\beta_g-\alpha}\ln s_h + \frac{(1-a^*)(\beta+\beta_g+\alpha)}{1-\beta-\beta_g-\alpha}\ln(\delta+g_n) \\ &-(1-a^*)\ln y_{i0} + \frac{(1-a^*)(\nu-1)}{1-\beta-\beta_g-\alpha}\ln N_{it}.\end{aligned}$$

Adjustment is complete if $a^* = 0$; there is no adjustment if $a^* = 1$; it is partial, otherwise, $0 < a^* < 1$.

This formulation allows the authors to estimate the degree of adjustment as the coefficient of income at the beginning period, $\ln y_{i0}$, and thus implicitly to test for convergence to the balanced growth path. From the sum of the coefficients of s_k, s_{k_g}, s_h, and $\ln(\delta + g_n)$, one can test the Cobb–Douglas assumption for the production function. The sum of the elasticities in the production function (9.5) should be equal to 1 if it is Cobb–Douglas with constant returns to scale. The sign of the coefficient of $\ln N_{it}$ allows one to infer whether returns to scale exceed 1.

In urban growth accounting, a critical issue is availability of data. For the United States in particular, as I discuss in chapter 6, metropolitan income (value-added) data did not become available until September 2007. Crihfield and Panggabean (1995, 160–163) report growth-accounting results for 282 MSAs in the United States, where they construct metropolitan total personal income by using state personal income per capital times area populations. They use the percentage of persons in the MSA's most populous county who are 25 years old and older and have completed 12 or more years of schooling to proxy for human capital, investment by manufacturing industries to proxy for private sector investment, all capital outlays by local governments in the MSA to proxy for public investments; and state-level depreciation rates. In addition, these authors include a number of location characteristics such as regional dummies and resource and local prices, institutional characteristics, such as unionization rates, and unemployment rates. Their results (Crihfield and Panggabean 1995, 157, table 6) suggest a moderate rate of convergence of about 6 percent per year, total returns to scale in the range of 1.049–1.054 thus slightly exceeding 1, and a perverse effect for total capital, which is negative. Their results do stand out as some of the few reported in this area. However, they are based to a considerable extent on imputed data and therefore have to be treated with caution.

9.2.4 Economic Growth in a Cross Section of U.S. Cities

Glaeser, Scheinkman, and Shleifer (1995, 122) examine the urban growth patterns of U.S. cities and metropolitan areas between 1960 and 1990 in relation to various 1960 urban characteristics. They rely on data for the 203 largest U.S. cities from the U.S. *County and City Data Books* (1950, 1960, 1970), from the 1990 census, and from a number of other sources for some socioeconomic characteristics. From an average 1960 population of 269,000, these cities grew to an average of 288,000 in 1990 (8.5 percent). Some cities shrank, like East St. Louis, Missouri (70 percent), and others grew phenomenally, like Las Vegas, Nevada (139 percent).

The authors show that income and population growth are positively related to initial median years of schooling, negatively related to initial unemployment, and negatively related to the initial share of employment in manufacturing. Interestingly, breaking up the years of schooling shows that an increase in the percentage of the population with 12–15 years of schooling is very significant relative to an increase in those with 16 years or more. They examine the effects of social and political variables, such as income and education inequality, racial composition, and segregation, but overall they are less successful in identifying strong effects associated with these variables. However, notable among them is the effect of a weighted segregation index, constructed as a Tauber–Tauber segregation index[3] times the percentage of the population that was nonwhite in 1960, which is positive for growth. When instead of such variables the authors control for the levels and composition of government receipts and expenditures in 1960, they obtain no striking results for growth.

In general, treating cities in isolation, the approach adopted by all the studies that I review in this section, misses important aspects of the openness of the urban system and therefore its effect on growth. The strong effects obtained for human capital variables is indicative of the importance of skills and growth in technology and consistent with such effects in cross-country regressions.

9.2.5 Economic Growth in a Cross Section of European Cities

A paucity of city data is a problem for students of European cities. For the period before the advent of Eurostat's *Urban Audit*,[4] the only available data for European cities were census data or regional data. Bosker and Marlet (2007) use data for 260 cities and towns, administratively defined, in 27 European countries, which were surveyed at three different points in the 1990s. They report regressions of population growth rates against birthrate, population in 1991, and population density in 1991, and in addition, groups of similar variables separately, roughly following Glaeser, Scheinkman, and Shliefer (1995), such as variables that are descriptive of general economic conditions (like GDP per capita and unemployment rates), of human capital, of the employment structure, and of weather conditions, amenities, and disamenities.

They interpret their results as suggesting that urban growth in Europe is quite persistent and, in spite of increasing European integration, largely driven by growth of the nationally born population. Nonnational European-born and non-European-born migrants contribute only marginally to urban growth differences. Differences in birthrates between cities explain a large part of the variation in cities' growth rates. This finding is less surprising given the low residential mobility in Europe and sets European city population dynamics apart from those observed in the United States. Smaller, less dense, safer, amenity-rich cities with high levels of GDP per capita are growing fastest. Overall, European city growth does not show a movement toward cities with a nice climate [unlike in the United States; see Glaeser and Gottlieb (2009)], which could be explained by low mobility and the relatively small within-country climate differences. Also, cities with higher levels of human capital do not exhibit higher population growth. Unfortunately, this study, although informative, is not directly comparable to studies based on U.S. MSA data because Bosker and Marlet were limited to data for administratively defined urban areas and the definitions of urban areas are different.

9.2.6 The Determinants of Urban Growth in Brazil

Brazil, the second most populous country in the Western Hemisphere, is highly urbanized and has a federal political structure. After rapid urbanization, its cities account, in the late 2000s, for 80 percent of its population and 90 percent of its GDP. Da Mata et al. (2007) seek to identify the determinants of city growth within Brazil's urban system in order to help understand why some Brazilian cities are more successful than others and how policy matters in explaining "urban success" stories. Designing policy interventions to stimulate urban growth depends on factors outside a city government's immediate control, such as geographic and economic location and national-level decentralization, as well as on regional policies, with local politics also playing a role. The Da Mata et al. study is based on a data set that was deliberately created to conform to a concept of urban agglomerations, for which data are not routinely collected in Brazil. The data involve the grouping of Brazilian *municípios* to form 123 urban agglomerations.

Da Mata et al. seek to identify the growth process by separately estimating demand and supply for living in a city, expressed in terms of utility, proxied by income to be enjoyed by a resident. Demand depends on city size, local cost of living, amenities, and so on; supply depends on income per worker in relation to incomes and other attributes offered by competing locales. The estimations reported also account for urban systemwide characteristics such as market potential, intercity transport costs and urban-rural interactions and therefore highlight the urban structure of individual city growth.

Results for the demand side, reported by Da Mata et al. (2007, table 2), show that income per worker depends positively and significantly on schooling and on market potential but negatively on the number of workers and on intercity transport costs. Since several of the explanatory variables are in principle endogenous, the authors use the following variables as instruments: semiarid area dummy, distance to state capital, distance to São Paolo, ratio of manufacturing to service employment, infant mortality, humidity, average years of schooling and state capital, and time dummies. Results for the supply side, reported by Da Mata et al. (2007, table 3), show that population depends positively and significantly on income per capita and on rural population market potential, and negatively on rural income opportunities market potential, for all three cross sections as well as for the pooled sample, 1980, 1991, and 2000. The instruments for the supply-side estimates used are semiarid area dummy, distance to São Paolo, market potential of agricultural land availability in 1970, port dummy, per capita capital stock in 1970, southern region, and time dummies. Equating income from the demand- and-supply equations, solving for city size, and estimating (using all instruments) the resulting reduced-form equation, reported by Da Mata et al. (2007, table 4), yield highly statistically significant coefficients. A greater rural land population supply increases city sizes, and so do market potential and average schooling. A 1 percent increase in rural population and in market potential increases city size by 2.7 percent and 1.7 percent, respectively. Improved rural income opportunities and intercity transport costs decrease it. A 1 percent decline in rural land opportunities would increase city size by 3.7 percent.

The authors' results on the decomposition of city growth, where each determinant is attributed to its estimate multiplied by the mean value of the regressor, relative to the sum of all fitted values, show that there is a strong negative effect of base period city size (−24 percent). However, increases in market potential have a strong positive effect (108 percent). Changes in educational attainment (21 percent), along with the base period's educational attainment (10 percent) also matter. The estimated effects of market potential, measured in terms of the concepts introduced in chapter 8, and technology spillovers support the new economic geography emphasis on local markets and the endogenous growth literature emphasis on human capital accumulation (Da Mata et al. 2007, 267–268, table 7).

9.3 A VENTURA-TYPE MODEL OF INTERCITY TRADE AND ECONOMIC GROWTH

I develop next a model of urban growth that builds further on the basic structure of chapter 7 and combines it with features from the model of trade and growth presented by Ventura (2005). A number of distinct cities, each of which is subject to congestion (a feature not present in Ventura's model of sites, regions, or nations), may produce one or both of two tradable goods X and Y. Each of these goods is produced using physical capital, raw labor, and intermediates. Tradable goods X and Y are not consumed directly. Instead, they are combined in each city to produce an aggregate, or composite good, by means of Cobb–Douglas production functions with shares α and $1-\alpha$, respectively.[5]

The aggregate is in turn used in each city for consumption and for investment in physical capital. In sum, there is a *three-stage production structure*: at the *first* stage, a composite of capital and raw labor is used to produce intermediates; at the *second* stage, intermediates and the same composite of capital and raw labor are used to produced goods X and Y; at the *third* stage, goods X and Y are combined in each city to produce consumption and investment.[6]

Here I am asking the reader to delve into fairly complex material. The first stage reflects a modicum of complexity that Venables (1996) was first to emphasize and that helped launch the popularity of the Dixit–Stiglitz model in international trade applications. The element of endogeneity involved in the intermediates-producing sector's buying its own output enriches the model and is technically very simple to incorporate. The second and third stages integrate results from chapter 7 in a modular fashion and underscore further the importance of diversification versus specialization and therefore intercity trade. The third stage sets up the model in a more standard macroeconomic framework and contributes to an increasingly popular urban macroeconomic literature.

I start with the case of autarkic cities and refrain from indexing the respective quantities as long as no confusion arises. A number of individuals $\bar{N}_t$ are born every period and live for two periods. The economy has the demographic structure of the overlapping generations model. I assume that individuals born at time t, work when young, consume their net labor income net of their savings, and consume again when they are old, C_{1t}, C_{2t+1}, respectively. I assume Cobb–Douglas preferences for first- and second-period consumption for the typical individual,

$$U_t = S_{\mathrm{av}}^{-S_{\mathrm{av}}}(1 - S_{\mathrm{av}})^{-(1-S_{\mathrm{av}})} C_{1t}^{1-S_{\mathrm{av}}} C_{2,t+1}^{S_{\mathrm{av}}}, \quad 0 < S_{\mathrm{av}} < 1, \tag{9.6}$$

where S_{av} is a parameter.

Net labor supplied by the young generation in a particular city at t is given by $H_t = N_t(1 - \kappa N_t^{1/2})$, with N_t the number of members of the young generation in a particular city at t, $\kappa \equiv \frac{2}{3}\pi^{-1/2}\kappa'$, and κ' the time cost per unit of distance traveled.

If W_t denotes the wage rate per unit of time, spatial equilibrium within the city obtains when labor income net of land rent is independent of location. This along with the assumption that the opportunity cost of land is 0, and therefore, that land rent at the fringe of the city is also equal to 0, yields an equilibrium land rental function as per equation (7.3), chapter 7, section 7.3.2. It declines linearly as a function of distance from the CBD and is proportional to the contemporaneous wage rate, W_t. It is convenient to close the model of a single city and to express all magnitudes in terms of city size. I again assume that all land rents in a given city are redistributed to its young residents, in which case total rents may be written in terms of the number of young residents according to (7.4) as $\frac{1}{2}\kappa W_t N_t^{3/2}$. This yields a first-period net labor income per young resident, after redistributed land rentals and net of individual commuting costs, of $(1-\kappa N_t^{1/2})W_t$. With a given wage rate, individual income declines with city size, other things being equal, entirely because of congestion. But there are benefits to urban production that are reflected onto the wage rate.

Let R_{t+1} be the total return to physical capital, K_{t+1}, in time period $t+1$, that is held by a member of the young generation at time t. To the above utility function there corresponds an indirect utility function:

$$R_{t+1}^{S_{\rm av}}\left(1-\kappa N_t^{1/2}\right)W_t. \tag{9.7}$$

I assume that capital depreciates fully in one period. The young maximize utility by saving a fraction $S_{\rm av}$ of their net labor income. The productive capital stock in period $t+1$, K_{t+1}, is equal to the total savings of the young at time t. Therefore, to preview our growth model, we have $K_{t+1}=S_{\rm av}N_t(1-\kappa N_t^{1/2})W_t$.

First I develop the case where all cities are autarkic, that is, there is no intercity trade, and cities produce both manufactured tradable goods and use them in turn to produce the composite used for consumption and investment. Each of the manufactured tradable goods, $J=X,Y$, is produced by a Cobb–Douglas production function with constant returns to scale, using a composite of raw labor and physical capital, with elasticities $1-\phi_J$, ϕ_J, respectively, and a composite made of intermediates. The shares of the two composites are u_J, $1-u_J$ respectively. There exists an industry J-specific total factor productivity Ξ_{Jt}. Production conditions for each of two industries J are specified via their respective total cost functions:

$$B_{Jt}(Q_{Jt})=\left[\frac{1}{\Xi_{Jt}}\left(\frac{W_t}{1-\phi_J}\right)^{1-\phi_J}\left(\frac{R_t}{\phi_J}\right)^{\phi_J}\right]^{u_J}\left[\sum_m P_{Zt}^{1-\sigma}(m)\right]^{\frac{1-u_J}{1-\sigma}}Q_{Jt}, \tag{9.8}$$

where Q_{Jt} is the total output of good $J=X,Y$, P_{Zt} is the price of the typical intermediate, elasticity parameters u_J,ϕ_J satisfy $0<u_J,\phi_J<1$, and the elasticity of substitution in the intermediates composite σ is greater than 1. The TFP term Ξ_{Jt} summarizes the effect on industry productivity of geography, institutions, and other factors that are exogenous to the analysis.[7]

Each of the varieties of intermediates used by industry J are produced according to a linear production function with fixed costs (which imply increasing returns to scale), with fixed and variable costs incurred in the same composite of physical capital and raw labor used in the production of manufactured goods X and Y. The shares of the productive factor inputs used are the same as ϕ_J, $1-\phi_J$, $J=X,Y$, respectively.[8] The respective total cost function is

$$b_{it}(Z_{Jt}(m))=\frac{f+cZ_{Jt}(m)}{\Xi_{Jt}}\left[\left(\frac{W_t}{1-\phi_J}\right)^{1-\phi_J}\left(\frac{R_t}{\phi_J}\right)^{\phi_J}\right],$$

and $Z_{Jt}(m)$, is the quantity of the input variety m used by industry $J=X,Y$. Its price is determined in the usual way from the monopolistic price-setting problem (Dixit and Stiglitz 1977) and is equal to the marginal cost marked up by $\frac{\sigma}{\sigma-1}$:

$$P_{ZJt} = \frac{\sigma}{\sigma-1}\frac{c}{\Xi_{Jt}}\left(\frac{W_t}{1-\phi_J}\right)^{1-\phi_J}\left(\frac{R_t}{\phi_J}\right)^{\phi_J}.$$

At the monopolistically competitive equilibrium with free entry, each of the intermediates is supplied at quantity $(\sigma-1)\frac{f}{c}$ and costs $\frac{\sigma f}{\Xi_{Jt}}\left(\frac{W_t}{1-\phi_J}\right)^{1-\phi_J}\left(\frac{R_t}{\phi_J}\right)^{\phi_J}$ per unit to produce. Its producer earns zero profits.

9.4 GROWTH IN AN ECONOMY OF AUTARKIC CITIES

The manufactured goods are not directly consumed, unlike in chapter 7. Instead, manufactured goods available in quantities $\mathcal{Q}_{Xt}, \mathcal{Q}_{Yt}$, are combined to produce a composite good that is used for consumption and investment in each city in a quantity given by

$$\mathcal{Q}_t = \mathcal{Q}_{Xt}^{\alpha}\mathcal{Q}_{Yt}^{1-\alpha}. \tag{9.9}$$

In order not to clutter up the notation, I index different cities only when it is necessary. The natural numeraire to use is, just as in the Ventura model, the composite good itself in every city. Its price is set equal to 1:

$$P_t \equiv 1 \equiv \left(\frac{P_{Xt}}{\alpha}\right)^{\alpha}\left(\frac{P_{Yt}}{1-\alpha}\right)^{1-\alpha}. \tag{9.10}$$

Therefore, $P_t\mathcal{Q}_t = \mathcal{Q}_t \equiv P_{Xt}X_t + P_{Xt}Y_t$ and

$$\mathcal{Q}_t = C_t + K_{t+1}.$$

The final-good industries X and Y receive a share of aggregate spending $\alpha, 1-\alpha$, respectively, of which fractions $1-\phi_X, 1-\phi_Y$, respectively, go to labor. Therefore, aggregate labor income as a function of output is

$$W_tH_t = W_tN_t\left(1-\kappa N_t^{1/2}\right) = (1-\phi)\mathcal{Q}_t, \tag{9.11}$$

where $\phi \equiv \alpha\phi_X + (1-\alpha)\phi_Y$ denotes the weighted share of capital in aggregate output and H_t denotes labor. Clearly, $0 < \phi < 1$.

In order to characterize economic growth by means of a law of motion for industrial capital, I express in terms of capital all endogenous quantities that would enter the law of motion. Working with the production function of each final-good industry, the output-capital ratio when the optimal quantity of each intermediate is used may be written as

$$\frac{\mathcal{Q}_{Jt}}{K_{Jt}} = \left(\frac{\sigma}{\sigma-1}\right)^{-(1-u_J)} m_{Jt}^{\frac{1-u_J}{\sigma-1}}\,\Xi_{Jt}\left(\frac{K_{Jt}}{H_{Jt}}\right)^{\phi_J-1}. \tag{9.12}$$

The range of intermediates used in the production of good J, m_{Jt}, which is referred to as the technology, is endogenously determined in the model and may be expressed as a function of the productive factors used (H_{Jt}, K_{Jt}) as

$$m_{Jt} = \frac{1-u_J}{f\sigma}\,\Xi_{Jt} H_{Jt}^{1-\phi_J} K_{Jt}^{\phi_J}.$$

This result may be interpreted as follows. Increased factor use raises incentives to specialize, allows the fixed costs of more varieties to be recouped, and thus improves productivity. Equation (9.12) now becomes

$$\frac{Q_{Jt}}{K_{Jt}} = \bar{\Xi}_{Jt} H_{Jt}^{\mu_J(1-\phi_J)} K_{Jt}^{\mu_J\phi_J-1}, \tag{9.13}$$

where the auxiliary variable μ_J,

$$\mu_J \equiv 1 + \frac{1-u_J}{\sigma-1},$$

measures the importance of market size effects (as discussed in chapter 7) and

$$\bar{\Xi}_{Jt} \equiv \left(\frac{\sigma}{\sigma-1}\right)^{-(1-u_J)} \left(\frac{1-u_J}{\sigma}\right)^{\frac{1-u_J}{\sigma}-1} f^{\mu_J}\,\Xi_{Jt}^{\mu_J} \tag{9.14}$$

is an augmented measure of industry J TFP from (9.8), a function of Ξ_{Jt}, total factor productivity in industry J, and of parameters.

I note that $\mu_J(1-\phi_J)$, the exponent of labor in (9.13) above, is positive. Intuitively, an increase in labor used raises the output-capital ratio, as the direct positive effect of making physical capital more productive is reinforced by the indirect effect of increasing input variety. Increases in physical capital, on the other hand, have an ambiguous effect on the output-capital ratio, as the sign of $\mu_J\phi_J - 1$ is ambiguous. The direct negative effect of making physical capital abundant and the indirect positive effect of increasing input variety work in opposite directions. Depending upon the magnitudes of market size effects, indicated by μ_J, and diminishing returns, ϕ_J, that is, if $\mu_J\phi_J < (>) 1$, increases in physical capital reduce (increase) the industry's output-capital ratio.

Next, in order to derive an expression for the aggregate output-capital ratio as a function of the aggregate quantities of labor and physical capital, I express industry allocations of productive factors, H_{Xt}, H_{Yt} and K_{Xt}, K_{Yt}, respectively, in terms of their respective aggregate quantities, $H_{Xt}+H_{Yt}=H_t$, $K_{Xt}+K_{Yt}=K_t$:

$$H_{Jt} = \alpha_J \frac{1-\phi_J}{1-\phi} H_t,$$

$$K_{Jt} = \alpha_J \frac{\phi_J}{\phi} K_t,$$

where $J = X, Y$, $\alpha_X = \alpha$, and $\alpha_Y = 1-\alpha$. Using these expressions on the right-hand side of (9.12), the equations for the output-capital ratio in each of the final-goods industries, we have

$$\frac{Q_t}{K_t} = \Xi_t^* H_t^{\mu(1-\phi)-\upsilon} K_t^{\mu\phi+\upsilon-1}, \tag{9.15}$$

where μ denotes a weighted market-size effects parameter defined as

$$\mu \equiv \alpha\mu_X + (1-\alpha)\mu_Y = 1 + \frac{1-(\alpha u_X + (1-\alpha)u_Y)}{\sigma - 1} > 1$$

and υ is the "covariance" between $\mu_J, \phi_J, J = X, Y$,

$$\begin{aligned}\upsilon &\equiv \alpha(\mu_X - \mu)(\phi_X - \phi) + (1-\alpha)(\mu_Y - \mu)(\phi_Y - \phi) \\ &= -\alpha(1-\alpha)\frac{1}{\sigma - 1}(u_X - u_Y)(\phi_X - \phi_Y),\end{aligned}$$

and Ξ_t^*, aggregate TFP, is

$$\begin{aligned}\Xi_t^* \equiv &\left[\alpha^{\mu_X}\left(\frac{1-\phi_X}{1-\phi}\right)^{\mu_X(1-\phi_X)}\left(\frac{\phi_X}{\phi}\right)^{\mu_X\phi_X}\bar{\Xi}_{Xt}\right]^{\alpha} \\ &\times\left[(1-\alpha)^{\mu_Y}\left(\frac{1-\phi_Y}{1-\phi}\right)^{\mu_Y(1-\phi_Y)}\left(\frac{\phi_Y}{\phi}\right)^{\mu_Y\phi_Y}\bar{\Xi}_{Yt}\right]^{1-\alpha},\end{aligned} \tag{9.16}$$

where $\bar{\Xi}_{Xt}, \bar{\Xi}_{Yt}$ are defined in (9.14). It thus follows that Ξ_t^* is proportional to $\bar{\Xi}_{Xt}^{\alpha\mu_X}\bar{\Xi}_{Yt}^{(1-\alpha)\mu_Y}$.

Equation (9.15) is the effective aggregate production function in that it gives the output-capital ratio for the entire urban economy as a reduced form after the endogeneity of the range of intermediates (technology) has been accounted for. I note that it exhibits increasing returns to scale in (H_t, K_t), since $\mu > 1$. Just as for the individual final-goods industries, increases in labor have unambiguously positive effects on the output-capital ratio because $\mu(1-\phi) - \upsilon > 0$. Increases in physical capital, on the other hand, have ambiguous effects on the output-capital ratio. If the representative industry has strong diminishing returns and weak market-size effects, $\mu\phi + \upsilon < 1$, then increasing physical capital reduces the output-capital ratio. If the representative industry has weak diminishing returns and strong market-size effects, $\mu\phi + \upsilon \geq 1$, increasing physical capital increases the output-capital ratio.

Since young individuals save a fraction S_{av} of their labor income, which aggregates to $(1-\phi)Q_t$, and given the expression for the effective aggregate function (9.15), we have the law of motion for the autarkic urban economy:

$$K_{t+1} = S_{\mathrm{av}}(1-\phi)\Xi_t^* H_t^{\mu(1-\phi)-\upsilon} K_t^{\mu\phi+\upsilon}. \tag{9.17}$$

This shows that each autarkic urban economy obeys a Solow growth model with a Cobb–Douglas production function that exhibits increasing returns to scale, as the sum of the factor share coefficients satisfies $\mu \geq 1$.

Let the set of autarkic cities in the economy at time t be indexed by i, $i \in \mathcal{I}_t$. The only modification needed in the above theory is to account for the net quantity of labor available for production, given city geometry, as a function of city population, N_{it}. That is, $H_{it} = N_{it}\left(1 - \kappa_i N_{it}^{1/2}\right)$. The law of motion (9.17) in city i becomes

$$K_{i,t+1} = (1-\phi)S_{\text{av}}\Xi_{it}^{*}\left(N_{it}\left(1-\kappa_i N_{it}^{1/2}\right)\right)^{\mu(1-\phi)-\upsilon} K_{it}^{\mu\phi+\upsilon}. \qquad (9.18)$$

It is straightforward to show that the output of city i satisfies a similar equation,

$$\mathcal{Q}_{i,t+1} = \hat{\Xi}_{it}\mathcal{Q}_{it}^{\mu\phi+\upsilon}, \qquad (9.19)$$

where $\hat{\Xi}_{i,t}$ is a function of parameters and of Ξ_t^{*}, defined in (9.16).

9.4.1 Autarkic Cities and National Economic Growth

In an autarkic setting, each city's population is given and may grow over time through an excess of births over deaths. This is, of course, consistent with our model provided that net labor supply by the young is positive, which requires that $N_{it} < \kappa_i^{-2}$. While I could allow for intercity migration, it would be more realistic to allow for capital mobility. I am interested in the ultimate conditions that the urban structure of the economy imposes on national economic growth. Toward that end, I assume that technological diffusion across cities equalizes aggregate TFP Ξ_t^{*}, defined in (9.16). I also assume that each city is populated with the number of young people that maximizes the net labor supply and that the young share housing with the old. In such a case, city i's population is given by $\frac{4}{9}\kappa_i^{-2}$ and is therefore proportional to κ_i^{-2}. It turns out that other assumptions give qualitatively similar results.[9] As we see further below, the factor multiplying κ_i^{-2} may differ, depending upon the intercity trade regime. Suppose also that commuting costs are the same[10] across all urban sites, $\kappa_i = \kappa$. The number of cities is thus equal to

$$n_t = \frac{9}{4}\kappa^2 \bar{N}_t.$$

The higher the commuting costs or the larger the national population, the larger the number of cities needed. If a country's local geographic attributes are heterogeneous, thus giving rise to increasing commuting costs, the sizes of newer cities will be increasingly smaller and their numbers may grow faster than the national population.

It is instructive to write the aggregate economy counterpart of equation (9.19), the evolution of aggregate output, for the case of homogeneous sites. The aggregate output at two successive periods is given by $\mathcal{Q}_{t+1} = n_t\mathcal{Q}_{i,t+1}$, $\mathcal{Q}_t = n_{t-1}\mathcal{Q}_{it}$. Under the assumption that Ξ_{it}^{*} is independent of i and time-invariant, $\Xi_{it}^{*} = \Xi^{*}$, equation (9.19) may be rewritten in terms of $\frac{\mathcal{Q}_t}{N_t}$. It is straightforward to establish that output per person has a steady state if $\mu\phi + \upsilon < 1$. If $\mu\phi + \upsilon \geq 1$, output per person grows along a balanced growth path at a gross rate equal to $e^{\ln[\mathcal{Q}_0](\mu\phi+\upsilon)}$.

This is, in a nutshell, the counterpart here of the case, of urban growth as analyzed by Henderson and Ioannides (1981). Unlike their case, as well as that of Ioannides (1994), in the present model sustained growth is possible even if the national population is constant, provided that the condition for a representative industry to have weak diminishing returns and strong market-size effects, that is, $\mu\phi + \upsilon \geq 1$, holds. The source of growth is consistent with endogenous growth theories.

9.4.2 Investment in Urban Transportation

An uncomfortable consequence of the above model is that geometric growth in the number of cities will outstrip a country's land area in finite time. It is thus important to examine whether the force of economic growth may be sufficient to make up for the scarcity of land, itself another instance of the important question posed first by Malthus (1798). At the same time, the empirical analysis (using international data) of transportation investment and growth by Canning and Fay (1993) reports substantial effects of transportation investment on growth, especially for developing countries, but does not distinguish urban from nonurban transportation. I return to the formulation by Miyao, which I present in section 9.2.1 above for the case of isolated cities, and assume that transportation investment has the effect of reducing κ, the unit transportation cost parameter that was defined in section 9.3 and is the only attribute of the urban transportation system, and thus helps overcome local congestion. I posit that the unit transportation cost κ may be reduced by means of investing physical capital in the transportation system.[11] I posit that

$$\kappa_{i,t+1} \equiv \bar{\kappa}_i \left(N_{it} k_{gi,t+1}\right)^{-\eta}, \quad \eta, \bar{\kappa} > 0, \tag{9.20}$$

where $(\bar{\kappa}_i, \eta)$ denote parameters and $k_{gi,t+1}$ is physical capital per young person at time t invested in the transportation system (unit transportation capital for short). Investment undertaken at time t becomes productive in $t + 1$. The unit transportation cost tends to zero asymptotically and in a convex fashion as total transportation capital tends to infinity. With this assumption, the maximum net labor supply and the young population of city i become functions of transportation investment and are given by $\frac{1}{3} n_i^* \left(N_{it} k_{gi,t+1}\right)^{2\eta}$ and $n_i^* \left(N_{it} k_{gi,t+1}\right)^{2\eta}$, respectively, where $n_i^* = \frac{4}{9} \frac{1}{\bar{\kappa}_i^2}$. Transportation capital, like production capital, is assumed to depreciate fully after one period.

I assume that transportation investment is in the form of the same composite used for consumption and investment in the production of goods. From among a number of possible ways to finance transportation investment, I assume, consistently with Miyao, discussed in section 9.2.1 above, that the government of city i levies a lump sum tax equal to $k_{gi,t+1}$ per young individual, which it uses to finance investment in transportation. Therefore, the law of motion for capital (9.17) becomes

$$K_{i,t+1} = S_{\text{av}} \left[(1 - \phi) Q_{it} - N_{it} k_{gi,t+1}\right].$$

I assume that the government of city i sets the amount of transportation investment so as to maximize the utility of the typical member of generation t, given by (9.7). At the capital market equilibrium in city i, the gross return to physical capital is equal to the marginal product of capital in producing aggregate output, with the external effects on capital being taken as given, that is,

$$R_{i,t+1} = \phi \Xi_t^* H_{i,t+1}^{\mu(1-\phi)-\upsilon} K_{i,t+1}^{\mu\phi+\upsilon-1}.$$

Since net labor supply at time $t+1$ is proportional to $\kappa_{i,t+1}^{-2}$, it may be written in view of (9.20) as a function of $k_{g,t+1}$. Rewriting the maximand from (9.7) we have

$$\left[\phi \Xi_t^* \left[\frac{n_i^*}{3}\left(N_{it}k_{gi,t+1}\right)^{2\eta}\right]^{\mu(1-\phi)-\upsilon} \left[S_{\text{av}}(1-\phi)Q_{it} - S_{\text{av}}N_{it}k_{gi,t+1}\right]^{\mu\phi+\upsilon-1}\right]^{S_{\text{av}}}$$
$$\times \left[(1-\phi)Q_{it} - N_{it}k_{gi,t+1}\right] N_{it}^{-1}. \tag{9.21}$$

Maximization of the indirect utility of a young person with respect to $k_{i,g,t+1}$ yields that the total investment in transportation, $N_{i,t}k_{g,i,t+1}$, is a *constant share* $\tilde{\eta}$ of city labor income $(1-\phi)Q_{it}$:

$$N_{it}k_{gi,t+1} = \tilde{\eta}(1-\phi)Q_{it}, \tag{9.22}$$

where $\tilde{\eta}$ is defined in terms of parameters as follows:

$$\tilde{\eta} \equiv \frac{2\eta(\mu(1-\phi)-\upsilon)}{2\eta(\mu(1-\phi)-\upsilon) + S_{\text{av}}(\mu\phi+\upsilon-1)+1}. \tag{9.23}$$

In view of the properties of all the auxiliary parameters, it follows that the quantity

$$\mu(1-\phi)-\upsilon = \frac{1}{\sigma-1}\left[\sigma(1-\alpha\phi_X-(1-\alpha)\phi_Y)+\alpha\phi_X u_X+(1-\alpha)\phi_Y u_Y\right]$$

is positive. Therefore, the numerator on the right-hand side of (9.23) is positive. For the denominator on the right-hand side of (9.23) to be positive, it is sufficient but not necessary that the returns to scale be sufficiently strong to ensure that $\mu\phi+\upsilon > 1$. Just as before, this can occur if the representative industry of the city has weak diminishing returns and strong market-size effects. Under these conditions, $\tilde{\eta}$ lies between 0 and 1. Unfortunately, this simple result does not carry over to the case of specialized cities; see section 9.5.3 below.

Therefore, with the total investment in transportation being a fraction of the total output of city i, the law of motion for productive capital becomes

$$K_{i,t+1} = (1-\phi)(1-\tilde{\eta})S_{\text{av}}Q_{it}. \tag{9.24}$$

The evolution of city income implied by the law of motion may be characterized as follows. Using the expression for productive capital in period $t+1$ from (9.24) as a function of city i output at t, and using (9.22) to express the net labor supply also as a function of city i output at t, along with the expression for the output-capital ratio from (9.15), we obtain the following law of motion for city i output:

$$\mathcal{Q}_{i,t+1} = \mathcal{Z}_{i,t+1}\mathcal{Q}_{it}^{2\eta(\mu(1-\phi)-\upsilon)+\mu\phi+\upsilon}, \qquad (9.25)$$

where

$$\mathcal{Z}_{i,t+1} \equiv \Xi^*_{i,t+1}\left(\frac{4}{27}\bar{\kappa}_i^{-2}n_i^*\right)^{\mu(1-\phi)-\upsilon}[\bar{\eta}(1-\phi)]^{2\eta(\mu(1-\phi)-\upsilon)}[(1-\phi)S_{\mathrm{av}}(1-\bar{\eta})]^{\mu\phi+\upsilon},$$

where Ξ^*_t is defined in (9.16). Clearly, because $\mu(1-\phi)-\upsilon$ is positive, a sufficient condition for the economy of city i to exhibit increasing returns to scale is $\mu\phi+\upsilon \geq 1$, which is the same condition as for the economy without transportation investment to exhibit increasing returns to scale. A necessary condition may also be obtained. The larger η is, the more effective transportation capital investment in reducing unit commuting costs is and the more likely it is that the economy of city i exhibits increasing returns to scale. I simplify by assuming that $\mathcal{Z}_{it}$ is time-invariant, which requires that TFP functions for both industries also be time-invariant. It follows then that if $2\eta(\mu(1-\phi)-\upsilon)+\mu\phi+\upsilon < 1$, city output has a steady state, whereas if $2\eta(\mu(1-\phi)-\upsilon)+\mu\phi+\upsilon \geq 1$, city output grows along a balanced growth path at a rate equal to $2\eta(\mu(1-\phi)-\upsilon)+\mu\phi+\upsilon$.

9.4.2.1 *Spatial Equilibrium with Autarkic Cities*

I examine next the consequences of spatial equilibrium in an economy of autarkic cities, where I allow for intercity movement of individuals but without assuming capital market integration. Using the result for optimum transportation investment (9.22) in the expression for indirect utility (9.21), an expression follows that is a multiplicative function of city i output times output per person, $\mathcal{Q}_{it}^{\hat{h}}\frac{\mathcal{Q}_{it}}{N_{it}}$, where $\hat{h}$ is a positive function of parameters. The first factor in the previous expression encapsulates all the effects that follow from the production structure and summarizes each city's productivity advantage. The equalization of individuals' lifetime utilities across cities determines city populations of young people. These populations depend, in view of the expressions for city output (9.15), on all city capitals as well, in addition to city-specific characteristics that enter via Ξ^*_{it}. Therefore, city populations coevolve with the entire vector of city capitals in the economy.

9.4.3 Divergent versus Convergent Autarkic Cities

How do city sizes vary over time when transportation investment is endogenous? A key result of the chapter is to characterize exactly the pattern of evolution of city sizes. With total transportation investment evolving according to (9.22), *city size*, defined as the optimal number of young at time $t+1$, is related to city output according to

$$\nu_{i,t+1} = n_i^* \left(\tilde{\eta}(1-\phi)\mathcal{Q}_{it}\right)^{2\eta}, \tag{9.26}$$

from which we have that

$$\frac{\nu_{i,t+1}}{\nu_{it}} = \left(\frac{\mathcal{Q}_{it}}{\mathcal{Q}_{i,t-1}}\right)^{2\eta}. \tag{9.27}$$

This renders endogenous the growth rate of city size and provides a direct relationship between the growth rate of city size from time t to period $t+1$ and the growth rate of city output from $t-1$ to t, which in view of (9.25) may be written in terms of city output in period $t-1$. From the law of motion for city output derived earlier (9.25), the gross growth rate for city output along the balanced growth path is given by $\frac{\mathcal{Q}_{it}}{\mathcal{Q}_{i,t-1}} = \mathcal{Q}_0 e^{2\eta(\mu(1-\phi)-\upsilon)+\mu\phi+\upsilon}$, where I have assumed that the function of parameters $\mathcal{Z}_{it}$ is time-invariant, $\mathcal{Z}_i$.

I note that $\mathcal{Z}_i$ is larger the smaller parameter $\bar{\kappa}_i$ is in unit commuting costs. So, a particular advantage of a city's urban transport system, perhaps due to local geography, is translated to a growth effect via $\mathcal{Q}_0$ for the sizes of the respective city types. Relative growth rates depend on respective output ratios. Growth rates of cities are constant, increasing or decreasing, depending upon whether city output is constant, increasing, or decreasing.

An important consequence of endogenizing urban transportation costs, and therefore city size as well, is that the number of cities is also endogenous. This implies in turn that if (9.25), the law of motion of city output, exhibits increasing returns to scale, then city sizes will grow. This follows from the fact that increasing returns to scale in city output are ensured if $\mu\phi + \upsilon$ exceeds 1, while $\mu(1-\phi) - \upsilon$ is always positive. This is due to increasing returns to scale in the urban economy, which originate, of course, in the specification of technology through the use of intermediates. Consequently, whether or not the number of cities grows depends on the rate of growth of the population relative to the (endogenous) rate of growth of city size. Furthermore, the economy here consists of a number of autarkic (i.e., independent) cities, which implies a great variety of possible outcomes.

Returning to the typology of Eaton and Eckstein (1997) and referring to (9.25) and (9.27), I note the following about urban growth rates in the long run. Parallel growth would be a knife-edge case, where parameter values allow for a steady-state (i.e., constant) city output over time. This requires decreasing returns to scale in city output:

$$2\eta(\mu(1-\phi)-\upsilon) + \mu\phi + \upsilon < 1$$

(and constant $\mathcal{Z}_{it}$). In that case, urban growth rates would be equal to zero in the long run. If parameter values give constant returns to scale, that is, if the exponent of city i output in (9.25) is exactly equal to 1, then the growth rate of city output is $\mathcal{Z}_{i,t+1} - 1$, and the corresponding growth rate in the number of cities is $(\mathcal{Z}_{i,t+1})^{2\eta} - 1$. In that case, urban growth would be parallel only if the parameters $\mathcal{Z}_{it}$ are constant and equal across all cities. In the case of increasing returns to scale, that is, if the exponent of city i output in (9.25) is greater than 1, urban growth is divergent, as urban growth rates are larger for large cities. I conclude that convergent growth is possible in the long run in this model only in the knife-edge case when the exponent of Q_{it} in (9.25) is equal to 1. Finally, imposing spatial equilibrium as per section 9.4.2.1 above, renders individual cities' growth rates dependent on each other.

To conclude, this analysis clarifies that interactions between, one, the pecuniary externalities that are intrinsic in the technological assumptions made, two, the increasing returns to scale associated with the fixed costs of the urban economy, and three, diminishing returns to other aspects of the production setting, may generate a force of sustained growth in the urban economy. Such a force may be sufficiently strong to generate divergent growth. In that case, it is possible for the growth rate of city size to exceed that of population growth and lead to increasing urban concentration. The feasibility of this full range of outcomes is logically possible here because congestion in national space and the associated matter of intercity transportation have been ignored. Intercity transportation reflects different aspects of geography and may generate diminishing returns that may offset the increasing returns I have emphasized so far. Alternatively, one may keep the number of cities constant and allow for growth on developed land that cities have access to. I take up such a model in section 9.7.3 below.

9.5 ECONOMIC INTEGRATION, URBAN SPECIALIZATION, AND GROWTH

Equation (9.18) demonstrates that cities may also differ in terms of congestion parameters κ_i and, in addition, in terms of city-specific total factor productivities, the Ξ^*_{it}'s. If individuals are free to move across cities, then spatial equilibrium requires that individuals be indifferent as to where they locate. That is, individuals' lifetime utilities are equalized across all cities. This in turn implies conditions on intercity wage patterns. Unlike the canonical case in the Ventura (2005) model, wages will typically differ across cities at spatial equilibrium. Similarly, if capital is perfectly mobile, it will move so as pursue maximum *nominal* returns and in the process equalize them across all cities.

I refer to the case where both capital and labor are free to move as *economic integration*. With economic integration, industries locate where industry productivities, the Ξ_{Jt}'s, are the most advantageous, and capital locates so as maximize its return. Unlike the consequences of economic integration as examined by Ventura (2005), where aggregate productivity is equal to the most favorable possible in the economy, here urban congestion may prevent industry from locating so as to take the greatest advantage of locational factors. Put differently, free entry of cities into the most advantageous locations may be impeded by competing uses of land at alternative urban sites at the national level. However, utilities enjoyed by city residents at equilibrium do depend on city populations, and therefore spatial equilibrium implies restrictions on the locations of individuals. I simplify the exposition by assuming that all cities have equal unit commuting costs κ.

First, I take up resource allocation under the assumption that cities specialize in the production of tradable goods. I examine the case when each specialized city also produces intermediates used in the production of the traded good. Let Q_{Xit}, Q_{Yjt} denote the total quantities of the traded goods X, Y produced by cities i, j that specialize in their production, respectively. The formulation is symmetric for the two city types, and therefore I work with a city of type X, X-city for short. I suppress redundant subscripts and write for the nominal wage and the gross rate of return to capital in an X-city:

$$W_{Xt} = (1 - \phi_X)\frac{P_X Q_X}{H_X}, \quad R_{Xt} = \phi_X \frac{P_X Q_X}{K_X}, \tag{9.28}$$

where P_X denotes the local price of traded good X, which is expressed in terms of the local price index, the numeraire, which from (9.10) is equal to 1 in all cities. I also assume initially that there are no intercity shipping costs for traded goods. With economic integration, the gross nominal rate of return is equalized[12] across all city types:

$$R_t = R_{Xt} = R_{Yt}.$$

Spatial equilibrium for individuals requires that indirect utility (9.7) be equalized across all cities. In view of free capital mobility, spatial equilibrium requires that

$$R_{t+1}^{S_{\text{av}}}\left(1 - \kappa N_{Xt}^{1/2}\right) W_{Xt} = R_{t+1}^{S_{\text{av}}}\left(1 - \kappa N_{Yt}^{1/2}\right) W_{Yt}. \tag{9.29}$$

Using the expression for net labor supply in each city yields the following condition for spatial equilibrium:

$$\frac{P_X Q_{Xit}}{P_Y Q_{Yit}} = \frac{1-\phi_Y}{1-\phi_X}\frac{N_{Xit}}{N_{Yit}}. \tag{9.30}$$

Free capital mobility requires that

$$\frac{P_X Q_{Xit}}{P_Y Q_{Yit}} = \frac{\phi_Y}{\phi_X}\frac{K_{Xit}}{K_{Yit}}. \tag{9.31}$$

Therefore, the full set of conditions for economic integration imply a proportional relationship between the ratios of capital per young person in the two types of cities:

$$\frac{K_{Xit}}{N_{Xit}} = \frac{\frac{\phi_X}{1-\phi_X}}{\frac{\phi_Y}{1-\phi_Y}}\frac{K_{Yit}}{N_{Yit}}.$$

Alternatively, since the ratio of city populations, $\frac{N_{Xit}}{N_{Yit}}$, is known at any point in time, economic integration then implies that

$$\frac{K_{Xit}}{K_{Yit}} = \frac{N_{Xit}\,\frac{\phi_X}{1-\phi_X}}{N_{Yit}\,\frac{\phi_Y}{1-\phi_Y}}. \tag{9.32}$$

The demand for good Y by a city of type X is given by the share of the income of a city of type X divided by P_Y. It suffices to work with the equilibrium conditions for intercity trade in good X, which may be simply stated as the share of spending on good X by all Y cities and is equal to the spending on good Y by all X cities:

$$\frac{\mathcal{Q}_Y}{\mathcal{Q}_X} = \frac{1-\alpha}{\alpha}\frac{n_X}{n_Y}\frac{P_X}{P_Y}. \tag{9.33}$$

Substituting into the spatial equilibrium condition (9.30) yields

$$\frac{n_X N_X}{n_Y N_Y} = \frac{\alpha(1-\phi_X)}{(1-\alpha)(1-\phi_Y)}. \tag{9.34}$$

This condition, along with the total labor supply condition, $n_X N_X + n_Y N_Y = \bar{N}$, yields the equilibrium number of cities of each type:

$$n_X = \frac{\bar{N}}{N_X}\frac{\alpha(1-\phi_X)}{\alpha(1-\phi_X)+(1-\alpha)(1-\phi_Y)}, \quad n_Y = \frac{\bar{N}}{N_Y}\frac{(1-\alpha)(1-\phi_Y)}{\alpha(1-\phi_X)+(1-\alpha)(1-\phi_Y)}. \tag{9.35}$$

Interestingly, the relative frequencies of the two types of cities differ, ceteris paribus, between the static and dynamic cases only if $\phi_X \neq \phi_Y$, that is, if the capital intensity of production differs between the two manufactured goods. The more labor-intensive good requires a greater share of the population.

I solve for capital allocations in the two types of cities by using, in addition, the condition for the total supply of capital, $n_X K_{Xt} + n_Y K_{Yt} = K_t$. Thus,

$$K_{Xt} = N_{Xt}\frac{K_t}{\bar{N}}\frac{\phi_X}{1-\phi_X}\frac{1-\alpha\phi_X-(1-\alpha)\phi_Y}{\alpha\phi_X+(1-\alpha)\phi_Y}.$$

Next I compute the real income of the two types of cities. For a city of type X this is equal to $P_X\mathcal{Q}_X$. From the definition of the numeraire, in every city, $P_X = \alpha^\alpha(1-\alpha)^{1-\alpha}\left(\frac{P_X}{P_Y}\right)^{1-\alpha}$. Using (9.30) to obtain an expression for the terms of trade, the price ratio, we obtain an expression for the real income of a type-X city:

$$\mathcal{Q}_X\alpha^\alpha(1-\alpha)^{1-\alpha}\left(\frac{P_X}{P_Y}\right)^{1-\alpha} = \alpha_X^*\mathcal{Q}_X^\alpha\mathcal{Q}_Y^{1-\alpha}\left(\frac{N_{Xit}}{N_{Yit}}\right)^{1-\alpha},$$

where $\alpha_X^* = \alpha^\alpha(1-\alpha)^{1-\alpha}\left(\frac{1-\phi_Y}{1-\phi_X}\right)^{1-\alpha}$. The real income of a city specializing in good X, $\mathcal{X}_t$, may be expressed by using (9.13) in terms of the city populations of both types of cities, (N_X, N_Y), total capital in the economy, K_t, and parameters as follows:

$$\mathcal{X}_t = \mathcal{N}_X \left(\frac{K_t}{\bar{N}} \right)^{\alpha\mu_X\phi_X + (1-\alpha)\mu_Y\phi_Y}, \tag{9.36}$$

where the auxiliary variable $\mathcal{N}_X$ is defined as a function of city sizes and parameters:

$$\mathcal{N}_X(N_X, N_Y) \equiv \alpha_X^* \widehat{\Xi}_t N_X^{\alpha\mu_X+1-\alpha} \left(1 - \kappa N_X^{1/2}\right)^{\alpha\mu_X(1-\phi_X)} \times N_Y^{(1-\alpha)\mu_Y-(1-\alpha)} \left(1 - \kappa N_Y^{1/2}\right)^{(1-\alpha)\mu_Y(1-\phi_Y)}, \tag{9.37}$$

where $\alpha_X^* \equiv \alpha^\alpha(1-\alpha)^{1-\alpha}\left(\frac{1-\phi_Y}{1-\phi_X}\right)$, and the function $\widehat{\Xi}_t$ is defined as

$$\widehat{\Xi}_t \equiv \bar{\Xi}_{Xt}^{\alpha} \bar{\Xi}_{Yt}^{1-\alpha} \left(\frac{\phi_X}{1-\phi_X} \right)^{\alpha\mu_X\phi_X} \left(\frac{\phi_Y}{1-\phi_Y} \right)^{(1-\alpha)\mu_Y\phi_Y} \times \left(\frac{1 - \alpha\phi_X - (1-\alpha)\phi_Y}{\alpha\phi_X + (1-\alpha)\phi_Y} \right)^{\alpha\mu_X\phi_X + (1-\alpha)\mu_Y\phi_Y} \tag{9.38}$$

and the TFP functions $\bar{\Xi}_{Xt}$, $\bar{\Xi}_{Yt}$ are defined in (9.14).

The TFP function $\widehat{\Xi}_t$ is the counterpart of the integrated economy of Ξ_t^* defined in (9.16) for the autarkic cities. The industry TFP functions $\bar{\Xi}_{Xt}$, $\bar{\Xi}_{Yt}$ enter $\widehat{\Xi}_t$ with the *same* exponents, α, $1-\alpha$, respectively, as in Ξ_t^*, but are multiplied by different functions of parameters. The counterpart of (9.36) for $P_Y\mathcal{Q}_Y$, the real income of a city specializing in good Y, is given by

$$\mathcal{Y}_t = \mathcal{N}_Y \left(\frac{K_t}{\bar{N}} \right)^{\alpha\mu_X\phi_X + (1-\alpha)\mu_Y\phi_Y}, \tag{9.39}$$

where $\alpha_Y^* = \alpha^\alpha(1-\alpha)^{1-\alpha}\left(\frac{1-\phi_X}{1-\phi_Y}\right)^\alpha$ and

$$\mathcal{N}_Y(N_X, N_Y) \equiv \alpha_Y^* \widehat{\Xi}_t N_X^{\alpha\mu_X-\alpha} \left(1 - \kappa N_X^{1/2}\right)^{\alpha\mu_X(1-\phi_X)} \times N_Y^{(1-\alpha)\mu_Y+\alpha} \left(1 - \kappa N_Y^{1/2}\right)^{(1-\alpha)\mu_Y(1-\phi_Y)}. \tag{9.40}$$

9.5.1 Law of Motion for an Integrated Economy

I derive the law of motion for total capital in an integrated economy by recalling that savings per person in an X-city is given by $\mathcal{S}_{av}W_X\left(1-\kappa N_X^{1/2}\right)$. This implies that total savings for both types of cities are given by the share of labor income that is saved: $n_X\mathcal{S}(1-\phi_X)P_X\mathcal{Q}_X$ and $n_Y\mathcal{S}(1-\phi_Y)P_Y\mathcal{Q}_Y$. Therefore, the law of motion for capital becomes

$$K_{t+1} = \mathcal{S}_{av}\left[n_X(1-\phi_X)\mathcal{N}_X + n_Y(1-\phi_Y)\mathcal{N}_Y\right]\left(\frac{K_t}{\bar{N}} \right)^{\alpha\mu_X\phi_X + (1-\alpha)\mu_Y\phi_Y}, \tag{9.41}$$

where $\mathcal{N}_X, \mathcal{N}_Y$ are defined in equations (9.37) and (9.40) above. Note that TFP $\widehat{\Xi}_t$ factors out from the two terms within the brackets, making the total available savings proportional to $\Xi_{Xt}^{\alpha\mu_X}\Xi_{Yt}^{(1-\alpha)\mu_Y}$.

An important result readily follows from a comparison of (9.41), the law of motion of an integrated economy, with (9.17), its counterpart for each autarkic urban economy. That is, the elasticities of total savings with respect to capital for those respective cases *coincide*:

$$\mu\phi + \upsilon \equiv \alpha\mu_X\phi_X + (1-\alpha)\mu_Y\phi_Y. \tag{9.42}$$

The intuition of this result is the following. In an integrated economy cities specialize, and thus an industry with greater economies of scale need not be "set back" and be forced to compete for resources with another industry that exhibits lower economies of scale. However, the advantage of specialization in this model is exactly offset by the effect of its superior performance on the terms of trade. In fact, it is a telling sign that this is even "mechanically" so in the above derivations. This follows from the fact that the terms of trade, P_X/P_Y, are evaluated at the general equilibrium of the national economy. This is confirmed by the fact that the TFP functions for the autarkic and the integrated economies are both proportional to the same factor $\Xi_{Xt}^{\alpha\mu_X}\Xi_{Yt}^{(1-\alpha)\mu_Y}$ and differ only with respect to a multiplicative function of parameters.

With free movement of labor, individuals seek to maximize their lifetime utilities and therefore city populations tend to their optimum sizes. It is easy to see that this is equivalent to maximizing the value of a city's output. The optimum city sizes follow from the maximization of $\mathcal{N}_X$ with respect to N_X, and $\mathcal{N}_Y$ with respect to N_Y, for X- and Y-types of cities, respectively. Note that even though $\mathcal{N}_X$ also depends on N_Y, the dependence is separable and the maximizing value of N_X does not depend on N_Y, and similarly for $\mathcal{N}_Y$ and N_Y. Again, the optimum values are inversely proportional to unit commuting costs squared:

$$N_X^* = \left(\frac{2(\alpha\mu_X + 1 - \alpha)}{2(\alpha\mu_X + 1 - \alpha) + \alpha\mu_X(1-\phi_X)}\right)^2 \frac{1}{\kappa^2}, \tag{9.43}$$

$$N_Y^* = \left(\frac{2((1-\alpha)\mu_Y + \alpha)}{2((1-\alpha)\mu_Y + \alpha) + (1-\alpha)\mu_Y(1-\phi_Y)}\right)^2 \frac{1}{\kappa^2}. \tag{9.44}$$

It is important to note that the factors that multiply $\frac{1}{\kappa^2}$ in the expressions above now depend on parameters and thus differ, in general, from $\frac{4}{9}$, the one under autarky, the alternative trade regime we examined earlier. Accordingly, the relative frequencies of the two types of cities are determined from (9.34) as functions of parameters. However, a simple comparison shows that specialized cities are larger than autarkic cities. That is, specialization confers an advantage because an increase in market size allows each industry to support a higher degree of specialization and is accommodated by larger city size. Socially optimal city sizes, however, would be different from (9.43) and (9.44), as I discuss in the next section.

In the canonical case of an integrated economy of many cities, even if goods and capital move at negligible costs, individuals might not be able to move to their preferred locations, because of "effective capacity constraints" in cities. Any geographic distribution of production and factors is possible provided that such capacity constraints are satisfied. Capacity constraints prompt the creation of new cities. In general, sites may differ in terms of efficiency, reflected in the commuting cost parameter and other factors that enter into TFP. So, unlike the canonical case examined by Ventura (2005), here it is indeed possible to determine the production or spending located in each city. This is one of the instances where the system-of-cities model differs from the standard setup of international trade theory.

It is straightforward, albeit algebraically tedious, to show that, other things being equal, specialization improves welfare relative to autarky. This follows from comparing city output under autarky and under specialization, from (9.15) and (9.36), respectively. Given the same unit commuting cost, city sizes are assumed to be equal for each type of city in the specialization case and for all autarkic cities in the autarkic case. The introduction of iceberg shipping costs for either final goods or intermediates does not change these results qualitatively.

A number of remarks are in order. This treatment of autarky in a growing economy does not assume intercity trade in intermediates. Here each city produces the intermediates its industries demand, which is still the case with intercity trade and growth, where cities of either type still produce the intermediates they demand and do not import any other intermediates from other cities of the same type. This assumption deprives cities of the benefits of a greater variety of intermediates, which over time may grow with the number of cities, but does not affect the returns-to-scale properties. It is made in order to be able to focus on intercity trade in goods. It would, however, be straightforward to introduce this feature.

9.5.2 Constant Returns-to-Scale Property at the National Economy

Factor mobility and economic integration alter the economies-of-scale properties of the model. In particular, we may write real national income as the sum total of real incomes generated in each city type, $\mathcal{X}_t$ and $\mathcal{Y}_t$, from (9.36) and (9.39), respectively, multiplied by the number of cities of each type,

$$\mathcal{Q}_t = \frac{\alpha(1-\phi_X)}{\alpha(1-\phi_X)+(1-\alpha)(a-\phi_Y)}\frac{\bar{N}}{N_{Xt}}\mathcal{X}_t + \frac{(1-\alpha)(1-\phi_Y)}{\alpha(1-\phi_X)+(1-\alpha)(a-\phi_Y)}\frac{\bar{N}}{N_{Yt}}\mathcal{Y}_t. \tag{9.45}$$

At the optimum city sizes, or alternatively given (N_X, N_Y), the right-hand side of (9.45) becomes proportional to

$$\bar{\mathcal{N}} K_t^{\alpha\mu_X\phi_X+(1-\alpha)\mu_Y\phi_Y}\,\bar{N}^{1-[\alpha\mu_X\phi_X+(1-\alpha)\mu_Y\phi_Y]}, \tag{9.46}$$

where

$$\bar{\mathcal{N}} = \nu^*_{XY} N_X^{\alpha(\mu_X-1)} \left(1 - \kappa N_X^{1/2}\right)^{\alpha\mu_X(1-\phi_X)} N_Y^{(1-\alpha)(\mu_Y-1)} \left(1 - \kappa N_Y^{1/2}\right)^{(1-\alpha)\mu_Y(1-\phi_Y)} \tag{9.47}$$

and ν^*_{XY} is a function of parameters. Therefore, the national economy exhibits constant returns to scale with respect to total capital and labor, $(K_t, \bar{N})$. This is, of course, a confirmation in a Dixit–Stiglitz-inspired setting of the results of Rossi-Hansberg and Wright (2007), itself obtained in a Lucas-inspired setting; see section 9.6 below. It is in contrast to Ventura's (2005) model, where integration alters the substitutability among factors and depends critically on the assumption that there is no congestion at the national level for sites that are suitable for urban use. The creation of new cities is the margin that eliminates local increasing returns when they are present and thus confers constant returns to scale at the level of the aggregate economy. This is exactly like the description of an industry equilibrium with free entry of firms, each operating with U-shaped average cost curves, which may be described as operating with constant returns to scale, with the unit cost being equal to the minimum average cost.

The above result allows me to derive the socially optimal city sizes. They are the values of N_X, N_Y that maximize the expression $\bar{\mathcal{N}}$ in (9.47) above:

$$N_X^* = \left(\frac{2\alpha(\mu_X - 1)}{2\alpha(\mu_X - 1) + \alpha\mu_X(1 - \phi_X)}\right)^2 \frac{1}{\kappa^2}, \tag{9.48}$$

$$N_Y^* = \left(\frac{2(1-\alpha)(\mu_Y - 1)}{2(1-\alpha)(\mu_Y - 1) + (1-\alpha)\mu_Y(1 - \phi_Y)}\right)^2 \frac{1}{\kappa^2}. \tag{9.49}$$

A comparison of (9.43) and (9.44) with (9.48) and (9.49) shows that city sizes are smaller in the integrated case than in the autarkic case. The intuition of the result is that an integrated economy made up of specialized cities enhances its productivity by availing itself of greater varieties of intermediates by having smaller cities. That economic integration favors smaller economic entities also agrees with a key result from the sizes-of-nations literature (Alesina and Spolaore 2003).

The availability of the law of motion for the autarkic case and for the intercity trade case in closed form, and the fact that they share the same returns-to-scale properties, lend our approach nicely to modeling urban business cycles by specifying TFP shocks via the industry TFP factors Ξ_{Xt}, Ξ_{Yt} introduced in (9.8) above. With industry-specific stochastic shocks, the behavior of aggregate city output is expressed succinctly in Ξ_t^* and $\widehat{\Xi}_t$ for the case of autarky versus the case of intercity trade, defined in (9.16) and (9.38), respectively. These magnitudes have in common the term $\Xi_{Xt},^{\alpha\mu_X} \Xi_{Yt}^{(1-\alpha)\mu_Y}$; they differ only in terms of multiplicative factors that depend only on parameters.

In addition, without necessarily introducing unemployment, we can use the model to study the effects of labor market pooling when the shocks to the two industries are imperfectly correlated. Such issues have not been examined in the literature. In principle, when shocks to both industries coexist, the effect on prices may be partially offset, thus conferring an advantage on autarky, which then allows for the diversification of risks relative to intercity trade.

9.5.3 Investment in Urban Transportation with Specialized Cities

Just as with diversified cities, we retain assumption (9.20) and consider how investment in urban transportation, financed out of lump-sum taxes in each type of city, may be chosen so as to maximize the utility of a typical member of a generation at each period in time. Just as in the earlier analysis in section 9.4.2, I assume that city populations are chosen so as to maximize city output for each type of city. This yields expressions (9.43) and (9.44).

Using the expressions for factor prices from (9.28) and for output-maximizing city sizes from (9.43) and (9.44) in the condition for spatial equilibrium across the two types of cities (9.29), we obtain expressions for the utilities of young members of generation t who reside in type X and type Y cities. At spatial equilibrium, they must be equal,

$$\left[\phi_X \mathcal{N}_{X,t+1}\left(\frac{K_{t+1}}{\bar{N}}\right)^{\mu\phi+\upsilon-1}\right]^{S_{\mathrm{av}}}\left[(1-\phi_X)N_{Xt}^{-1}\mathcal{N}_{Xt}\left(\frac{K_t}{\bar{N}}\right)^{\mu\phi+\upsilon}-k_{Xg,t+1}\right]$$

$$=\left[\phi_Y \mathcal{N}_{Y,t+1}\left(\frac{K_{t+1}}{\bar{N}}\right)^{\mu\phi+\upsilon-1}\right]^{S_{\mathrm{av}}}\left[(1-\phi_Y)N_{Yt}^{-1}\mathcal{N}_{Yt}\left(\frac{K_t}{\bar{N}}\right)^{\mu\phi+\upsilon}-k_{Yg,t+1}\right], \tag{9.50}$$

where, we recall from (9.42), $\mu\phi+\upsilon\equiv\alpha\mu_X\phi_X+(1-\alpha)\mu_Y\phi_Y$. As I discuss in section 9.4, this constant may be greater than or less than 1, depending upon whether the representative industry has weak diminishing returns and strong market-size effects, $\mu\phi+\upsilon\geq 1$, or strong diminishing returns and weak market-size effects, $\mu\phi+\upsilon<1$. The expressions for $\mathcal{N}_{Xt}, \mathcal{N}_{X,t+1}; \mathcal{N}_{Yt}, \mathcal{N}_{Y,t+1}$ are obtained from (9.37) and (9.40), respectively. Since equalization of the first term on each side above, the gross returns to capital, which ensures capital market equilibrium, has already been employed, it suffices for spatial equilibrium to ensure that wages, net of tax, are equalized:

$$(1-\phi_X)N_{Xt}^{-1}\mathcal{N}_{Xt}\left(\frac{K_t}{\bar{N}}\right)^{\mu\phi+\upsilon}-k_{Xg,t+1}=(1-\phi_Y)\mathcal{N}_{Yt}N_{Xt}^{-1}\left(\frac{K_t}{\bar{N}}\right)^{\mu\phi+\upsilon}-k_{Yg,t+1}.$$

The law of motion, (9.51), modified to account for investment in urban transportation, becomes

$$K_{t+1}=S_{\mathrm{av}}\left[(n_X(1-\phi_X)\mathcal{N}_{Xt}+n_Y(1-\phi_Y)\mathcal{N}_{Yt})\left(\frac{K_t}{\bar{N}}\right)^{\mu\phi+\upsilon}\right.$$

$$\left.-n_X N_{Xt}k_{Xg,t+1}-n_Y N_{Yt}k_{Yg,t+1}\right]. \tag{9.41'}$$

The maximization of utility of a typical resident in each type of city with respect to $k_{Xg,t+1}$, $k_{Yg,t+1}$ separately and subject to the spatial equilibrium constraint yields a solution via one of the roots of a quadratic equation.[13] We may specify parameter restrictions under which the solution is positive and feasible, that is, less than $(1-\phi_X)N_{Xt}^{-1}\mathcal{N}_{Xt}\left(\frac{K_t}{N}\right)^{\mu\phi+\upsilon}$, $(1-\phi_Y)\mathcal{N}_{Yt}N_{Xt}^{-1}\left(\frac{K_t}{N}\right)^{\mu\phi+\upsilon}$, respectively, that is, less than the respective wage rates.

Unfortunately, the solution in the case of specialized cities does not admit a particularly simple expression, unlike in the case of diversified cities. Still, it follows that $k_{Xg,t+1}k_{Yg,t+1}$ vary with $\left(\frac{K_t}{N}\right)^{\mu\phi+\upsilon}$ in both city types. Some qualitative properties readily follow. In view of expressions (9.43) and (9.44), both lagged transportation investments k_{Xgt}, k_{Ygt} enter via (9.37) and (9.40) in the solutions for $k_{Xg,t+1}$, $k_{Yg,t+1}$. This suggests the presence of spillovers across the two types of cities that must be accounted for when the transportation investment is set optimally. These spillovers are due, in effect, to the pecuniary externalities associated with the use of intermediates in production, which in turn makes the terms of trade depend on the sizes of both types of cities. This force is not present in the case of autarkic cities, where spillovers are internal, and it necessitates refinement of the concept of optimum city size in the presence of intercity trade. The solution may also involve complex dynamic dependence, as may be expected from the quadratic solution. Finally, for these same reasons, there is no longer an equivalence between the law of motion in growing urban economies with autarkic and with specialized cities, which I discuss in section 9.5.1 above.

9.5.4 Extensions

Numerous issues that deserve further attention may be handled by this approach. The urbanization process and its interaction with intercity economic integration, the relationship between different patterns of shipping costs and patterns of specialization, and issues of policy stand out as particularly important. Patterns of specialization among cities map to different predictions about urban hierarchies and associated city size distributions. Modeling the proximity between cities and possible competition among alternative sites is another important issue. I speculate briefly about each of these topics in turn.

It is straightforward to introduce transportation costs into the intercity shipping of tradable goods. This is reflected in the cost of producing the composite in each city. I assume, as before, iceberg shipping costs, so that if a unit of either good X or good Y is shipped, a fraction θ, $\theta < 1$, arrives. For a city specializing in good X, the price of the composite good, from (9.10), is $\left(\frac{p_{Xt}}{\theta\alpha}\right)^{\alpha}\left(\frac{p_{Yt}}{1-\alpha}\right)^{1-\alpha}$. The case for good Y is similar. This results in a modification of the respective expressions for the output of each city type, which is the same as that in equations (9.36) and (9.39) because of the presence of the additional factor $\theta^{2\alpha(1-\alpha)}$. Just as in the analysis of investment in order to reduce commuting costs, one can introduce investment in order to reduce shipping costs of tradable goods. Unfortunately, the unavailability of simple closed-form solutions for capital per person in reducing commuting costs in type-X, and type-Y cities, $k_{Xg,t+1}$, $k_{Yg,t+1}$, respectively, discussed in section 9.5.3, makes it unattractive to purse this further analytically.

A straightforward extension of this framework is to allow for more than two different tradable goods. The results would be qualitatively similar to those obtained with the Rossi-Hansberg–Wright model, discussed further below. A potentially richer extension would be to modify the model so as to account for functional specialization, which is discussed in chapter 7, section 7.6.1, as well as the Christaller hierarchy principle, which is discussed in chapter 8, sections 8.4 and 8.4.2.1, in conjunction with location decisions of firms and the evolution of the city size distribution. Hierarchical ranking of industries implies different TFP functions in higher-order cities that host a wider range of industries than in lower-order cities.

9.6 THE ROSSI-HANSBERG–WRIGHT MODEL OF URBAN STRUCTURE AND ITS EVOLUTION

Rossi-Hansberg and Wright (2007) build on ideas from the system-of-cities theory of Henderson (1974) and its urban growth application by Black and Henderson (1999) to develop a model where the urban structure emerges by eliminating local increasing returns to scale to yield constant returns to scale in the aggregate. This is accomplished by a model where local production takes place with a Cobb–Douglas production function and constant returns to scale in capital and labor services. Labor services are produced using raw labor and human capital, again with a Cobb–Douglas production function. Cities specialize completely in the production of different products.

This approach differs from that described earlier in the present chapter in that total factor productivity affecting local production, which is external to each firm, is specified [in the style of endogenous growth (Lucas 1988)] as a function of total human capital and total employment in the city under a Cobb–Douglas production function and is also affected multiplicatively by an exogenous shock. Thus, a notable feature of the approach is that it is firmly linked with a stochastic structure and aims at explaining city size distributions.

The specific ingredients of the model are as follows. Each city is described by a model similar to that presented earlier in this chapter. Total rents are given by $\frac{1}{2}\kappa N^{3/2}$, where N is city population and total commuting costs are given by $\kappa N^{3/2}$. The typical firm in industry j, $j = 1, \dots, J$, produces with Cobb–Douglas production functions $\Xi_{jt} k_{jt}^{\beta_j} h_{jt}^{\alpha_j} (u_{jt} n_{jt})^{1-\alpha_j-\beta_j}$, where k_{jt} is physical capital, h_{jt} is human capital, n_{jt} is the number of the firm's employees, each of whom spends a fraction u_{jt} of her time at work (and the remainder investing in human capital), and Ξ_{jt} is total factor productivity, that is, technology, in industry j at time t. The latter is assumed to be "produced" by human capital and labor and given by

$$\tilde{\Xi}_{jt} = \Xi_{jt}\tilde{H}_{jt}^{\gamma_j}\tilde{N}_{jt}^{\varepsilon_j}, \tag{9.51}$$

where $\tilde{H}_{jt}$ and $\tilde{N}_{jt}$ denote industry j-wide specific human capital and total employment, respectively, and A_{jt} is an independent and identically distributed productivity shock whose logarithm $\ln A_{jt}$ has mean zero and variance ν. I note that specification (9.51) of total factor productivity involves only magnitudes associated with individuals, that is, human capital and number of workers, and thus lends itself to interpretation as knowledge spillovers that are city- and industry-specific. It is efficient for cities to specialize in this model just as in Henderson (1974), as this allows agents to economize on commuting costs. I discuss below how the model can be extended to account for diversified cities.

Parameters γ_j and ε_j in (9.51) determine the importance of knowledge spillovers in the economy, which are external to firms but internal to the urban economy because of the presence of city developers. If both are equal to zero, there are no external effects and economic activity has no incentive to agglomerate in cities. The larger both of these parameters are, the more important an industry's total human capital and labor in determining city-specific total factor productivity are. If Ξ_{jt} is deterministic, we return to the formulation developed by Chipman (1970) and Henderson (1974), except that in their formulations each industry's productivity depends on its economywide human capital and employment. Still the randomness in total factor productivity is a crucial feature of the urban evolution process in this model that influences capital stocks in the long run and allows Rossi-Hansberg and Wright to characterize the long-run properties of city size distribution.

The external effects parameters are not necessarily constant. Ioannides, Overman, Rossi-Hansberg, and Schmidheiny (2008), for example, assume that these two parameters vary with the quality of information technology, ι_t, $\gamma_j(\iota_t)$, where $\partial\gamma_j(\iota_t)/\partial\iota_t < 0$ and, similarly, $\varepsilon_j(\iota_t)$ are such that $\partial\varepsilon_j(\iota_t)/\partial\iota_t < 0$.[14]

Rossi-Hansberg and Wright embed the problem of urban evolution in a representative individual infinite-horizon planning problem. The typical household diversifies risks by having its members employed in all industries. It allocates resources to physical and human capital and plans state-contingent consumption. Assuming the presence of city developers or governments that internalize citywide externalities, Rossi-Hansberg and Wright show that in this framework the unique equilibrium allocation solves the following planning problem: choose state-contingent sequences of consumption, physical capital investment, allocation of household members across industries, number of cities for each industry, share of time allocated to work, and physical and human capital for each industry, $\{C_{jt}, X_{jt}, N_{jt}, \mu_{jt}, u_{jt}, K_{jt}, H_{jt}\}_{t=0,j=1}^{\infty,J}$, in order to maximize:

$$E_0\left[\sum_{t=0}^{\infty}(1+\rho)^{-t}N_t\left(\sum_{i=1}^{J}\ln C_{it}/N_t\right)\right] \tag{9.52}$$

subject to, for all j and t, resource constraints for each industry and time period,

$$C_{jt} + X_{jt} + b\left(\frac{N_{jt}}{\mu_{jt}}\right)^{3/2}\mu_{jt},$$

$$\leq \Xi_{jt}\left(\frac{K_{jt}}{\mu_{jt}}\right)^{\beta_j}\left(\frac{H_{jt}}{\mu_{jt}}\right)^{\alpha_j+\gamma_j}\left(\frac{N_{jt}}{\mu_{jt}}\right)^{1-\alpha_j-\beta_j+\varepsilon_j} u_{jt}^{1-\alpha_j-\beta_j}\mu_{jt}, \tag{9.53}$$

labor supply available for employment (which may grow exogenously at rate g_N),

$$N_t = \sum_{j=1}^{J} N_{jt}, \tag{9.54}$$

a physical capital accumulation constraint[15],

$$K_{j,t+1} = K_{jt}^{\omega_j} X_{jt}^{1-\omega_j}, \tag{9.55}$$

and a human capital accumulation constraint[16],

$$H_{j,t+1} = H_{jt}\left[B_j^0 + (1 - u_{jt})B_j^1\right], \tag{9.56}$$

where N_{jt}, K_{jt}, X_{jt} and H_{jt} denote total labor, total physical capital, physical capital investment, and total human capital in industry j, while C_{jt} denotes total consumption of the representative household and μ_{jt} denotes the number of cities producing goods in industry j. Decision variable u_{jt} denotes the fraction of time the representative agent devotes to accumulating human capital. Thus, the maximization problem above amounts to maximizing household utility subject to a resource constraint (9.53), a labor market equilibrium condition (9.54), and the two factor accumulation equations (9.55) and (9.56).

The first-order condition with respect to the number of cities μ_{jt} becomes

$$s_{jt} = \frac{N_{jt}}{\mu_{jt}} = \left[\frac{2\left(\gamma_j + \varepsilon_j\right)}{b}\Xi_{jt}K_{jt}^{\beta_j}H_{jt}^{\alpha_j+\gamma_j}N_{jt}^{-\alpha_j-\beta_j+\varepsilon_j}u_{jt}^{1-\alpha_j-\beta_j}\mu_{jt}^{-\gamma_j-\varepsilon_j}\right]^2, \tag{9.57}$$

and so the size of a city, s_{jt}, with core industry j is then given by

$$s_{jt} = \left[\left[\frac{2\left(\gamma_j + \varepsilon_j\right)}{b}\right]^{\frac{1}{1-2\left(\gamma_j+\varepsilon_j\right)}} F_j\hat{\Xi}_{jt}H_{jt}^{\hat{\alpha}_j}K_{jt}^{\hat{\beta}_j}N_{jt}^{-\hat{\alpha}_j-\hat{\beta}_j}u_{jt}^{\hat{\phi}_j}\right]^2, \tag{9.58}$$

where the auxiliary variables $\hat{\Xi}_{jt}$, $\hat{\alpha}_j$, $\hat{\beta}_j$ and $\hat{\phi}_j$ are defined as

$$\hat{\Xi}_{jt} = \Xi_{jt}^{\frac{1}{1-2\left(\gamma_j+\varepsilon_j\right)}}, \quad \hat{\alpha}_j = \frac{\alpha_j + \gamma_j}{1 - 2\left(\gamma_j + \varepsilon_j\right)},$$

$$\hat{\beta}_j = \frac{\beta_j}{1 - 2\left(\gamma_j + \varepsilon_j\right)}, \text{ and } \hat{\phi}_j = \frac{1 - \alpha_j - \beta_j}{1 - 2\left(\gamma_j + \varepsilon_j\right)}.$$

Thanks to the loglinear specification, Rossi-Hansberg and Wright show that capital investments and consumption in each industry are time-invariant fractions of output net of commuting costs and that u_{jt} is constant over time. Taking natural logarithms yields

$$\ln s_{jt} = 2\left(\psi_{jt} + \frac{1}{1-2\left(\gamma_j+\varepsilon_j\right)}\ln\frac{2\left(\gamma_j+\varepsilon_j\right)}{b} + \frac{1}{1-2\left(\gamma_j+\varepsilon_j\right)}\ln \Xi_{jt} + \hat{\beta}_j \ln K_{jt}\right), \qquad (9.59)$$

where ψ_{jt} includes all nonstochastic variables including N_{jt} and H_{jt}.

Hence the mean and the variance of city sizes are given, respectively, by

$$\ln S_{jt} = 2\left(\psi_{jt} + \frac{1}{1-2\left(\gamma_j+\varepsilon_j\right)}\ln\frac{2\left(\gamma_j+\varepsilon_j\right)}{b} + \hat{\beta}_j E\left(\ln K_{jt}\right)\right), \qquad (9.60)$$

$$V_0\left(\ln S_{jt}\right) = 4\left(\frac{1}{1-2\left(\gamma_j+\varepsilon_j\right)}\right)^2 \nu + 4\left(\hat{\beta}_j\right)^2 V\left(\ln K_{jt}\right). \qquad (9.61)$$

Rossi-Hansberg and Wright show that, as $t \to \infty$,

$$V_0\left[\ln K_{jt}\right] = \frac{\nu}{\left(1+\hat{\beta}_j\right)^2}, \qquad (9.62)$$

so that the variance of the long-run log-city size distribution is given by

$$V_0\left[\ln s_{jt}\right] = 4\nu\left(\left(\frac{1}{1-2\left(\gamma_j+\varepsilon_j\right)}\right)^2 + \left(\frac{\beta_j}{1-2\left(\gamma_j+\varepsilon_j\right)+\beta_j}\right)^2\right). \qquad (9.63)$$

The specifications underlying this model lead to a simple result, in that the optimal city size, that is, the size that maximizes output net of commuting costs, implies that total commuting costs in each city are a constant fraction of the total city output. This implies in turn that optimal city size is proportional to the square of the average product of labor. The model admits a balanced growth path along which growth is positive even if population growth is zero. Furthermore, along a balanced growth path, the growth rate of each type of city may be written in terms of three components: one is proportional to the growth rate of human capital per person in each type of city, a second is proportional to the rate of growth of the total factor productivity shock in the city's industry, and a third is proportional to the excess of the contemporaneous total factor productivity divided by weighted sum of past realizations of total factor productivities. That is,

$$\ln S_{j,t+1} - \ln S_{jt} = \frac{2\hat{\alpha}_j}{1-\hat{\beta}_j}[g_{Hj} - g_N] + 2[\ln \hat{\Xi}_{j,t+1} - \ln \hat{\Xi}_{jt}]$$

$$+2(1-\omega_j)\hat{\beta}_j \left[\ln \Xi_{jt} - \sum_{\tau=1}^{\infty} \frac{\left(\omega_j + (1-\omega_j)\hat{\beta}_j\right)^{\tau-1}}{\left(1 - \left(\omega_j + (1-\omega_j)\hat{\beta}_j\right)\right)^{-1}} \ln \hat{\Xi}_{j,t-\tau} \right]. \quad (9.64)$$

A number of properties readily follow. Faster growth of human capital, larger g_{Hj}, leads to larger cities, while faster population growth, larger g_N, leads to smaller cities. The third term on the right-hand side of (9.64) carries the influence of the entire sequence of past shocks. Rossi-Hansberg and Wright (2007, 612, prop. 3) characterize the emergence of Zipf's law in exactly two restrictive cases. One case obtains when that third term is eliminated, which occurs when capital is not used in production ($\hat{\beta}_j = 0$) or investment may not affect capital ($\omega_j = 1$). In that case, the growth rate of the total factor productivity shock is time-invariant. Productivity shocks are permanent and produce permanent increases in the level of the marginal product of labor making its growth rate scale-independent. A second case obtains if there is no role for labor in production ($\beta_j = 1$), industry production is AK (McGrattan 1998), that is, there is no human capital and production is linear in physical capital, all capital depreciates fully after production, there is no population growth, and productivity shocks are temporary. In this case, productivity shocks have a permanent effect on the marginal product of labor through the accumulation of human capital. As Rossi-Hansberg and Wright (2007, prop. 3) state, not only must the growth process satisfy Gibrat's law *but* city sizes must be bounded below by a constant also if the invariant distribution of city sizes is to satisfy Zipf's law in the limit when the lower bound tends to 0.[17]

Rossi-Hansberg and Wright show that if neither of the above conditions is satisfied, the growth rate of cities exhibits reversion to the mean and that the standard deviation of city sizes increases with the standard deviation of industry shocks. That is, if a city is large, defined as having experienced a history of productivity shocks above average, it can be expected to grow more slowly than average in the future because of diminishing returns to capital invested in its industry. Higher than average past shocks suggest that such industries have high capital stocks. The opposite is true for small cities. Therefore, there would be relatively few small cities, and large cities would not be large enough. This is reinforced by the fact that investment technology requires investments to be higher in industries with larger capital stocks. Rossi-Hansberg and Wright (2007, 612, prop. 4) show that if productivity levels are bounded uniformly for all industries, then there exists a unique invariant distribution of city sizes with thinner tails than a Pareto distribution with coefficient −1. Recall from chapter 8 that this "concavity" result is consistent with the data for several countries and similar to that obtained by Duranton (2007). Zipf's law can be the outcome, albeit in a special case of a very important class of models, that is, those inspired by the system-of-cities approach augmented by adopting features of the endogenous growth theory. As an aside, this theory lends itself naturally to structural estimation, but I am not aware of any such research to date.

A notable feature of the model is that intercity trade is imposed on the entire economy and, unlike in the model discussed earlier in the chapter, autarky, that is, diversified cities, may not coexist with specialized cities. Autarky can be imposed by redefining total factor productivity (9.51) so that it depends on city-specific magnitudes. However, Rossi-Hansberg and Wright readily provide for an extension. In an unpublished appendix,[18] they propose two different extensions of their basic model to explain diversified cities. One is to modify the definition of total factor productivity so that it can be generated from human capital and employment across industries in groups, j^{τ}, $\tau = 1, \ldots, G_j$. Industries in such groups enjoy spillovers among themselves, as between the assembly of automobiles and auto parts manufacturing, apparel design and textile design, and so on. That is,

$$\tilde{\Xi}_{jt} = \Xi_{jt} \sum_{\tau=1}^{G_j} \left(\bar{H}_{jt^{\tau}}^{\gamma_j} \bar{N}_{jt^{\tau}}^{\varepsilon_j} \right)^{1/G_j}. \tag{9.65}$$

With this assumption, many of their results remain unchanged and carry over to the case where the industries in a group have an incentive to colocate in the same cities. A second modification that also allows for diversified cities involves introducing into the utility function consumption of a nontraded good. With the simplified assumption that the nontraded good is produced with labor only and that its production takes place anywhere in the city where its producers live, they show that the proportion of the labor force allocated to the production of the nontraded good is a (constant) function of parameters. And most importantly, both these modifications yield solutions that are proportional to those already discussed above and do not affect the urban structure.

9.7 EMPIRICAL ASPECTS OF URBAN STRUCTURE AND LONG-RUN URBAN GROWTH

None of the growth theories for systems of cities, including the specific ones that I review here, have been directly tested. They have, however, been used to motivate empirical studies of urban growth. I start with the basic underpinnings of modern growth theory. As Lucas (1988) and Jones (1999) argue, increasing returns to scale are important in understanding growth takeoffs and related phenomena but ultimately are incompatible with sustained growth, as they lead to explosive growth in the long run. It is thus particularly interesting to examine the key result of Rossi-Hansberg and Wright—that the economy at the national level exhibits constant returns to scale—in the light of data. I then turn to a specific application of the Rossi-Hansberg–Wright framework in examining the impact of information and communication technology on urban structure. This brings me to a discussion of the estimation of agglomeration effects. The chapter ends with an empirical examination of the phenomenon of sequential urban growth.

9.7.1 Constant Returns to Scale at the Level of the National Economy?

A stark conclusion of Rossi-Hansberg and Wright, which is reaffirmed earlier in the chapter above for the Ventura-type model, is that the urban structure makes the economy exhibit constant returns to scale at the level of the national economy. The emergence of cities expresses a trade-off between commuting costs and local production externalities and therefore reconciles increasing returns at the local level and constant returns at the aggregate level. As Douglas Clement (2004, 3) puts it in discussing the Rossi-Hansberg and Wright (2007) approach, "a national economy, like a living organism, shapes its internal structure so that the nation as a whole can expand on a stable course." An essential prerequisite for this result is that cities do not interact in a manner that would interfere with aggregate returns to scale, nor does the intercity transportation system.

An indirect way to examine returns-to-scale properties of the aggregate economy is by testing for the presence of scale (i.e., size) effects in growth performance. This question has been central to understanding economic growth. The direct approach to returns-to-scale properties involves estimating aggregate production functions. Duffy and Papageorgiou (2000) use international country data with a CES aggregate production function and find the returns to scale to be 0.973, that is, close to but less than 1, when labor adjusted for quality is used, but statistically insignificantly different from 1 when raw labor is used. Perälä (2008) finds that using the Cobb–Douglas approach leads to stronger evidence for aggregate increasing returns among economies in the early stages of development, but that using CES also supports aggregate scale economies for advanced economies, though at 1.038 it is not very strong.[19]

Returning to the indirect approach, generally speaking, economists have been unable to find evidence in support of the predictions of endogenous growth theory. Specifically, since Backus Kehoe, and Kehoe (1992) first examined empirically the existence of effects of scale, measured by GDP and a number of other magnitudes, on the growth rate of GDP per capita, a number of researchers have all but excluded the possibility that such scale effects exist. In fact, failure to find evidence in support of scale effects in endogenous growth has led researchers to redefine the question (Dinopoulos and Thompson 2000). Rose (2006b) presents results for scale effects on the level of income per capita and, in addition, on a variety of other measures (such as inflation, material well-being, health, education, the quality of a country's institutions, heterogeneity, and a number of different international indices and rankings, all of which are not relevant to the present chapter).

Rose (2006b, 497, table 1, panel A) reports estimated coefficients on country size (measured by log of population but instrumented by log of country area) with data for up to 208 countries and 5 years, 1960–2000. It turns out that real income per person is almost always negatively correlated (when it is significant) with size, in spite of the different sets of controls used. Sensitivity analysis, reported by Rose (2006b, 506, table A.4) shows that a statistically significant positive coefficient appears only when high-income countries are dropped. At the same time, the effect is numerically strongest (but negative) when the data are pooled and fixed effects are used, that is, for −0.62 and −0.54 for log real GDP per capita and log PPP real GDP per capita, respectively. I conclude that the evidence on scale effects is weak.

Empirical examinations of the basic prediction of the model regarding growth in the number and sizes of cities rests critically on the definition of a city. As I discuss earlier in chapter 8, section 8.5, this is far from straightforward. Still, an interesting picture emerges from several data sets. Ioannides and Overman (2004), using the Dobkins–Ioannides data set, show that while during 1900–1990 the U.S. urban population grew at an average rate of 23.3 percent per decade, the number of metropolitan areas grew at 12.9 percent and the mean city size grew at 9.3 percent. Similarly, according to the Black–Henderson data, discussed in chapter 8, section 8.5, the urban population grew at an average rate of 21.8 percent and the number of cities grew at a rate of 4.2 percent, but the mean size grew at rate of 16.9 percent. These differences make sense in view of the relative cutoff concept employed by Black and Henderson and imply that the number of urban areas grew at a considerably smaller rate than the urban population. Implicit in this difference is technological change that makes possible the accommodation of increasing populations in cities. I emphasize that these empirical observations apply only to the U.S. case. An international comparison has so far been hampered by the nonavailability of suitable data based on consistent definitions for cities across different countries.

9.7.2 Adoption of Information and Communication Technologies and Urban Structure

Ioannides, Overman, Rossi-Hansberg, and Schmidheiny (2008) use the Rossi-Hansberg–Wright framework to structure estimation of the impact of the adoption of information and communication technologies (ICT) on city size distributions. Working from (9.63) above, it follows that the variance of the city size distribution is increasing in $\gamma_j(\iota_t) + \varepsilon_j(\iota_t)$. Given that it is assumed that $\partial \gamma_j(\iota_t)/\partial \iota_t < 0$ and $\partial \varepsilon_j(\iota_t)/\partial \iota_t < 0$, the variance is decreasing in ι_t or is decreasing in the quality of ICT.

The key to an empirical investigation of the impact of ICT on city size distribution is to connect the variance of the distribution of city sizes to the Zipf coefficient and use it as a measure of dispersion. This is important because typically only data for the upper tail of the city size distribution are reliably observed. The local Zipf coefficient is given by the elasticity of the countercumulative of the city size distribution, Prob($s > S$), with respect to city size,

$$\zeta(S) = \frac{S}{\partial S} \frac{\partial \text{Prob}(s > S)}{\text{Prob}(s > S)} < 0.$$

Given the mean city size, an increasing variance is associated with shifting mass to the tails of the distribution. This implies that for S high enough (large enough city sizes), $|\zeta|$ will be smaller the larger the variance. As the variance goes to infinity, $\zeta(S) > -2$, $\lim_{S\to\infty} \zeta(S)$ converges to the Pareto coefficient. That the Zipf coefficient is related to the dispersion of the distribution should not be so surprising. In fact, the Zipf coefficient is closely related to the coefficient of variation, which is defined as the standard deviation divided by the mean.[20] Recall also that in the special case of reflected Brownian urban growth, discussed in chapter 8, section 8.2.3, the expression for the Zipf coefficient is decreasing absolutely in the instantaneous variance of the urban growth process.

Ioannides et al. estimate the Zipf coefficient for a country c in year t as the coefficient of city size in regressions like those according to chapter 8, equation (8.1), $\ln[\text{Rank}_i] = \bar{s}_o + \zeta_{ct} \ln S_i + \epsilon_i$, except that the Zipf coefficient itself is assumed to obey

$$\zeta_{ct} = \theta_c + \theta_{\text{tr}} t + \mathbf{X}_{ct}\eta + \varepsilon_{ct}, \tag{9.66}$$

where θ_c is a constant that may be country-specific, $\theta_{\text{tr}} t$ is a linear time trend, η is a vector of unknown coefficients, and $\mathbf{X}_{ct}$ of explanatory variables.

While adoption of ICT, proxied by the use of telephones and the internet, may indeed be a determinant of city size, it is possible that the effect on ζ_{ct} reflects another force affecting the dispersion of economic activity. For example, changes in the urban structure could come from increasing use of the automobile, and economies could respond to those changes by changing the number of telephone lines per capita. Then, the number of telephone lines per capita would be a function of urban structure instead of being a determinant of it, and thus endogenous. In that case, a regression would capture an association between ICT and urban structure that includes both the direct causal effect (from ICT to urban structure) and any indirect feedback effects (from urban structure to ICT). In the worst-case scenario, there may actually be no causal effect of ICT on urban structure, but one may reach the erroneous conclusion that there is an effect because regressions pick up the reverse feedback effect from urban structure to ICT.

To deal with this problem, these authors construct instrumental variables for ICT adoption based on the market structure in the telecommunications sector. Clearly, market structure in the telecommunications sector should affect the number of telephone lines, thus satisfying one of the conditions for a valid instrument. The telecommunications market structure is also unlikely to have a direct effect on urban structure (independent, that is, of its effect on ICT), thus satisfying another condition for a valid instrument. But, might the telecommunication market structure be affected if the urban structure changes for some exogenous reason? For example, the general trend toward economic liberalization and deregulation during the 1980s affected many sectors in addition to the telecommunications sector of many economies. Might reform of one of these sectors (e.g., transport) have changed urban structure, thus confounding the effect of ICT adoption? By including other measures of liberalization, these authors provide some indirect evidence that this is not the case and that their instruments are likely to be valid.

To capture the causal effect of the number of telephone lines on urban structure, these authors first predict the number of telephone lines in a given country and year on the basis of the values of the instrumental variables. The specific instruments used are public monopoly, private monopoly, time since public monopoly ended, time since private monopoly ended (all in the country's telecommunication sector), membership in the European Union, and membership in the North American Free Trade Agreement. Additional explanatory variables are road density, population, GDP per capita, trade as a share of GDP, several other variables measuring the composition of GDP, land area of country, and number of cities. After instrumenting in the above fashion, the authors report regression results with equation (9.66) that show a robust negative and statistically significant effect of the number of telephone lines per capita on the Zipf coefficient. Thus, over their study period, increasing telephone lines per capita have caused dispersion of the population across the urban structure to generate a more concentrated city size distribution. Overall, as access to telephones improves, the decreased dispersion in city size distributions implies that local production externalities decrease. That results in an urban structure that is less dependent on past shocks and hence a size distribution of cities with smaller variance. Their results are numerically substantial. For example, the share of cities with more than a million inhabitants would be reduced by 0.6 percentage points, if the number of telephone lines is increased by one standard deviation, while all other variables are set equal to zero. Since the share of world cities with populations larger than a million is about 4.3 percent, this implies about a 14 percent decrease in the number of these large cities.

Although Ioannides et al. report that the effect of internet penetration appears to be similar to that of telephones, though weaker and less statistically significant, that conclusion is based on fewer data than for telephones. As emphasized by Gaspar and Glaeser (1998), face-to-face and electronic communications may be complements or substitutes. Gaspar and Glaeser argue in favor of their being complements, which contrasts with the results of Ioannides et al. Cuberes (2010), using data on actual bilateral internet traffic between cities within and across countries finds that larger cities use the internet more intensively. Using data on internet intensiveness across U.S. cities, he finds that web-based communication decreases with distance, suggesting it is complementary to face-to-face communications. While Cuberes's data on bilateral flows are powerful, it is also true that internet-intensive economic activities concentrate in larger cities, which necessitates the use of instrumental variable techniques.

9.7.3 An Application to the Estimation of Agglomeration Effects

Davis, Fisher, and Whited (2009), motivated by the work of Ciccone and Hall (1996), develop a macroeconomic model of urban structure that broadly resembles that of Rossi-Hansberg and Wright (2007). The Davis–Fisher–Whited model enriches the literature because its scope requires them to use a broader data set in order to estimate agglomeration effects. The model's main features are as follows. The production of an intermediate good that is unique to each city benefits from a total factor productivity that combines multiplicatively an endogenous effect that depends on the density of output per unit of land, as in the Ciccone–Hall formulation discussed in chapter 6, section 6.3.2, and on an exogenous city-specific transitory shock that follows a common trend. Cities are designated by locations on a unit interval and are indexed by the stock of developed land and the exogenous city-specific productivity. The city-specific intermediate goods are produced using developed land, capital, and labor. They are aggregated into a final good by means of a CES function of all city-specific intermediate goods. The final good is used for consumption, investment in physical capital, and investment in developing land. The latter process resembles the investment function in the Rossi-Hansberg–Wright model equation, (9.55) above, in that developed land at the beginning of the period combines multiplicatively, according to a Cobb–Douglas function, with investment to produce developed land at the beginning of next period. This treatment is critical for ensuring that there is cross-sectional heterogeneity in developed land, which in turn leads to cross-sectional variation in land rents that help identify agglomeration effects. Housing services are produced in every city using developed land and physical capital. Assuming that the utility per period of a representative household is logarithmic and separable into consumption and housing and that the household uses its income from capital, labor, and profits leads to a well-defined problem where competitive markets in housing, land development, final-good consumption, and the derived demand for city-specific intermediate goods price all these commodities. The supply of land development evolves accordingly over time.

These authors examine the feasibility of a balanced growth path by decomposing the output of each city's good per worker in terms of factors of output per unit of land, land per worker, and capital per worker. This allows them to derive [Davis, Fisher, and Whited (2009, eq. (18)] that, if a balanced growth path exists, it implies that the growth rate in consumption GR_c takes the form

$$\mathrm{GR}_c = \theta_{\mathrm{reg}} \left(\mathrm{GR}_l\right)^{\frac{\lambda(1-\gamma)-1}{(1-\beta)\lambda(1-\gamma)}},$$

where θ_{reg} denotes the rate at which the city-specific productivity transitory shock regresses to the common trend, GR_l is the gross growth rate of land development costs, λ is the elasticity of the total factor productivity with respect to density, as in chapter 6, section 6.3.2, γ is the elasticity of land in the production of the city-specific good, and $\beta(1-\gamma)$ is that of physical capital.

The authors recognize, that, just as in Lucas's (2001) model, discussed in chapter 5, section 5.5, the magnitude of the elasticity of the agglomeration effect, in fact, the exponent $\frac{\lambda(1-\gamma)-1}{(1-\beta)\lambda(1-\gamma)}$ above multiplied by the inverse of the share of land in housing production, may be identified from the counterpart here of the density gradient, the ratio of land rental rates in two different cities. This can be obtained by regressing log wage ratios across different cities against log housing rental rate ratios and log city-specific price ratios [Lucas 2001, eq. (21)]. An important refinement is to account for heterogeneous labor, in which case high-density effects may be confounded with the self-selection of workers across cities.

The authors' preferred estimates are interesting. By setting the capital share in housing production at 0.85 and the gross growth rate of land development costs at $GR_l = 1.012$, the percentage increase in per capita consumption growth GR_c that may be attributed to agglomeration effects is estimated at 0.107, and the lowest one at 0.054. This is in the range of the corresponding estimates obtained by Ciccone and Hall (1996). This work is an important addition to the emerging literature on the macroeconomic aspects of urban structure, an area of research whose direct lineage to the endogenous growth literature was pioneered by Rossi-Hansberg and Wright (2007).

9.8 SEQUENTIAL URBAN GROWTH AND DECAY

The models of growth in a system of cities that I have discussed so far presume that growth in all cities occurs simultaneously. This is contrary to the experience of many countries, especially less developed countries. Typically, for cities to function, substantial sunk costs for laying down infrastructure and building public works and housing must be incurred first. This notion is supported by considerable empirical evidence, with David Cuberes being the first (in his University of Chicago 2005 doctoral dissertation) to emphasize it empirically using international data. Cuberes (2011) emphasizes the following three salient features of urban growth rates: one, right skewness in the cross section of urban growth rates; two, increasing rank of the fastest growing cities; and three, accentuation of this pattern with urban growth. Cuberes uses several data sources, namely, the Henderson–World Cities international metropolitan area data,[21] the Brinkhoff City Population data,[22] and the Lahmeyer data site.[23]

Cuberes (2011) reports results with administrative data for both urban jurisdictions and metropolitan areas from 54 countries, and with start dates for most countries falling in the period 1880–2000 although being mainly drawn from within the range 1880–1930; for the United States they start in 1790. He reports positive skewness coefficients for urban growth rates in 73 percent of the cases (which are statistically significant by a normality test). The results are weaker for metropolitan areas, with data from 115 countries since 1960, but still in the same direction. Cuberes examines increasing rank for the fastest growing cities by means of regressions for the average rank among the 25 percent fastest growing cities (or metropolitan areas) against time, while controlling for country-specific characteristics (like geography and culture) via fixed effects and for the number of cities in each country and decade. The latter controls for increasing urbanization over time. The ranks of the fastest growing cities do increase significantly over time. That is, over time, the group of fastest growing cities comes to include successively lower-ranked cities. Cuberes examines the accentuation of this pattern by regressing the growth in rank of the fastest growing 25 percent of cities against the growth rate of the urban population and the growth in the number of cities, while again using country-fixed effects. These regressions yield very significant effects for the growth rate of urban populations, even while controlling for the (growing) number of cities. The results are robust to different definitions of cities and of the set of fastest growing cities. The average rank of the 25 percent slowest growing cities, on the other hand, shows a negative trend when the number of cities is controlled for but is positive, though not as numerically strong, for the 25 percent slowest growing metropolitan areas.[24]

Although Cuberes was the first to address empirically the notion of sequential growth, several theoretical works have addressed related issues. In addition to Cuberes's (2009) article, these include those by Fujita (1978, chap.6), Henderson and Ioannides (1981) and, most recently, Henderson and Venables (2009). First I discuss results reported by Henderson and Ioannides (1981) that provide conceptual underpinnings of sequential urban growth phenomena. Part I of their paper pioneered the notion that the economy grows by generating more cities of the same type, each sized at the efficient size and with their numbers growing at the rate of growth of the population. Henderson (1987, 1988) extends this idea to cities of different types. Part II examines the case where each city is occupied only after all of its infrastructure has been laid down. In the study by Henderson and Ioannides (1981), the first city appears at the beginning of the analysis by borrowing its infrastructure capital at a fixed interest rate in the international market. Its infrastructure expresses a trade-off between the benefits of size and its congestion and costs, under the assumption of myopic behavior and irreversibility. As the population increases, the creation of a second city, and then a third, and so on, becomes attractive. As additional cities are created, spatial equilibrium calls for the repopulation of *all* cities in order for utilities to be equalized across the entire urban system. This causes some delicate positive and normative problems, in the presence of urbanization externalities, which Hadar and Pines (2004) also address, that may lead to multiplicity of equilibria and inefficient outcomes. It also introduces path dependence on public capital endowments. Henderson and Ioannides also discuss a planner's optimum where spatial equilibrium is imposed and the interest costs of infrastructure investment are financed by a redistributive poll tax on all residents. In the limit, the points in time at which cities are built get closer together, the infrastructure capitals converge to a common value, and lumpiness problems in city formation and investment are mitigated by scale. Smaller, older cities may in fact be abandoned (becoming ghost towns) so as not to be a "drag" on future urban development and thus eliminate path dependence. Ghost towns are actually also possible even with reversible investment in public infrastructure (Hader and Pines 2004, 132). When city sites differ in terms of amenities, this theory predicts that it is the sites of lowest quality (in terms of transport advantages, climate, and other amenities) that may be abandoned first.[25] The key predictions of this model have not been tested empirically.

Henderson and Venables (2009) return to these issues by adapting a powerful framework due to Fujita (1978, 199–329, chapt. 6),[26] and modernize the approach by allowing for irreversible infrastructure and housing capital investments to be chosen by forward-looking agents. The problem is first stated as that of a planner who chooses creating a sequence of cities $\{1, 2, \dots, \ell, \dots\}$ with respective populations $N_\ell(t)$ so as to maximize the present discounted value of the stream of welfare surpluses associated with each city net of housing costs. Each city's total surplus TS $(N_\ell(t))$ is defined as total output minus land rents minus commuting costs. In my notation, this may be written approximately[27] as proportional to $H_c^{\frac{\sigma}{\sigma-1}}\,(N_\ell(t))$. Housing costs involve sunk costs that are proportional to the population increase.

The cities form from scratch untill they grow to their stationary sizes within a finite length of time. The planner's optimum involves cities growing strictly in sequence and without interruption to their final sizes, which are larger than the quantities that maximize surplus per worker. If more than one city is growing at any point in time, they must be identical. The necessary condition for city ℓ yields that the social value from an additional worker entering city ℓ at a particular point in time is equal to the present value of the flow of the marginal surpluses created by the worker. Cities that are no longer growing have equal sizes. The model does not allow for declining city populations.

Henderson and Venables show that sequential growth is the only stable equilibrium. While many institutional settings can sustain this optimum, assuming suitable policy tools are provided, a competitive equilibrium setting without city governments (or "private" ones, i.e., developers) is particularly attractive. Free mobility, then, equalizes labor surplus across all cities, which in turn implies that house rents are equal to labor surplus (defined as average surplus minus average land rent) plus subsidies minus wages. Builders incur sunk costs for housing which they amortize by charging house rents to workers.

Henderson and Venables explore the following two fundamental insights. One, the fact that home-building entrepreneurs incur sunk costs in the form of capital investments solves coordination failure problems that are endemic to city formation. That is, via such commitments, forward-looking builders anticipate future city growth and rising productivity reflected by positive marginal surpluses. Interestingly, equilibrium city sizes may be smaller or larger than socially optimal, depending on the way in which externalities vary with city size. Two, housing prices adjust across different cities as growth proceeds so as to equalize individuals' utilities and thus ensure spatial equilibrium. When a new city forms, the housing prices in old cities adjust in order to maintain occupancy in both the new and old cities. Henderson and Venables argue that rental prices should be constant in growing cities, while realized incomes in those cities grow because of urban externalities becoming more mature. Existing mature cities initially have high housing prices in order to deter further in-migration. However, the emergence of a new city triggers rent declines in existing cities, but rents ultimately rise again as the new city nears the completion of its growth process. This feature of their model smooths the allocation of population within the urban system. The associated prediction lends itself to empirical testing. Price paths in more mature cities in developing countries can be compared with those in the current fastest growing city. But even in mature urban systems like that of the United States, there are instances of regions, like the Southwest, that have at times grown in population much faster than other parts of the country. According to Henderson and Venables, rapidly growing areas should experience constant rents as they absorb new inhabitants, while mature areas retain their populations through price changes.

Henderson and Venables point to evidence that new cities grow from scratch without population losses for preexisting cities. For example, from 1900 to 1990, when the United States moved from being 40 percent urban to 75 percent urban, as Black and Henderson (2003) discuss, no medium or larger metropolitan areas experienced population losses between decades exceeding 5 percent. Relying on a worldwide data set for 1960–2000 covering all metropolitan areas with more than 100,000 in population, Henderson and Wang (2007) identify 25 countries that start with just 1 metropolitan area in 1960 and have more metropolitan areas form during 1960–2000. Of these 25 initial metropolitan areas, 22 experience no population losses in subsequent decades. Of the 3 that do, none lose population during the decade when new metropolitan areas enter the picture; and each has a special circumstance (war-ravaged Phnom Penh in the 1970s, cities in Latvia and Estonia, countries that gained their independence following the breakup of the Soviet Union, where all cities lose population from 1990 to 2000).

It is interesting to contrast these predictions with the results of Glaeser and Gyourko (2005) who study urban decline. These authors show that because of the durability of housing decline is not the mirror image of growth. A simple empirical observation motivates their study. Consider a regression of median house prices across U.S. metropolitan areas against median family incomes and a representative amenity measure, median January temperatures. Both these variables have very significant coefficients. Plotting median house values against their fitted values shows "superstar cities" being associated with large residuals. The authors observe that at least one-quarter of the sample of median house prices falls below the estimated construction cost of a modest-quality home, $97,794 in 2000. Therefore, for housing prices to be low enough to allow individuals to live in low-wage, low-amenity places, houses there must sell below their construction costs. Houses that were built when it was attractive to do so in terms of construction costs and future expectations continue, because of their durability, to provide shelter in such locales as long as they stand up, keeping their cities alive as well. Contemporaneous construction costs are irrelevant in providing lower bounds. It is land values that do.

Durability of housing is responsible for a number of the Glaeser and Gyourko findings: one, city growth rates are skewed so that cities grow more quickly than they decline. Two, urban decline is highly persistent: durability means that it can take a long time for negative urban shocks to be fully reflected in urban population levels. Three, positive shocks to wages and/or amenities increase population more than they increase housing prices. Four, negative shocks decrease housing prices more than they decrease population. Consequently, the relationship between house price growth and population growth is concave. Five, if housing prices are below construction costs, then the city declines. Six, the combination of cheap housing and weak labor demand attracts individuals with low levels of human capital to declining cities. This is explained by the fact that when wages and/or amenities decline, housing costs also fall. This fall is not large enough to offset the disadvantage felt by highly skilled workers, who value high wages and high amenities, but is attractive to the poor. Concentrations of poverty may further deter growth. If low levels of human capital create negative externalities or result in lower levels of innovation, a self-reinforcing decay process may be generated, allowing an initial decline to cause a concentration of poverty.

9.9 "SPACE: THE FINAL FRONTIER?"

Krugman (1998) highlights how (at least up until the time of his writing) space had been neglected by introductory texts and mainstream economics writing alike. Fortunately, space and spatial economics are nowadays attracting increasing attention. A number of recent theoretical and empirical works are examining the static and dynamic aspects of the clustering of economic activity over the entire space rather than focusing on metropolitan areas or cities alone.

Michaels, Rauch, and Redding (2012) construct an unusually detailed data set for the United States, which exploits information on subcounty units, known as Minor Civil Divisions (MCDs), that extends from 1880 until 2000 and involves population and employment by industry. Even though their coverage is incomplete, these data show that the instability of population distribution over the U.S. land mass gives rise to increasing polarization of economic density over time. The authors show that Gibrat's law no longer holds over the entire range of population concentrations; instead, population growth initially decreases with initial density for low levels and then increases in an intermediate range of densities before it increases at higher densities. A higher variance in the density of nonagricultural employment than in that of agricultural employment suggests industrial clustering. Agricultural employment growth is decreasing, and nonagricultural employment growth is uncorrelated, with initial population density. The authors report a striking similarity in the relationship between population growth and employment structure in the United States to that in Brazil during 1970–2000.[28]

These authors rationalize these findings in terms of a model with conventional ingredients. Preferences are Cobb–Douglas over residential land and a CES index of tradable goods, an agricultural and a nonagricultural good, both of which are produced under perfect competition and are costlessly traded across locations. Output is produced with labor and land, nonagricultural output benefits from a density ("urbanization") sector- and site-specific externality, and both sectors benefit from sector-specific total factor productivity, $\Xi_{j\ell t}$, with $j = \{A, N\}$ denoting agriculture and non-agriculture, respectively, and i indexes cities. Log TFP, $\ell n \Xi_{j\ell t}$, is assumed to evolve over time according to an autoregression that also includes a time-varying secular component $\ln\bar{G}_{jt}$ and an idiosyncratic component $g_{j\ell t}$:

$$\ln \Xi_{j\ell t} = \ln \bar{\Xi}_{jt} + \ln(1 + g_{j\ell t}) + \nu_j \ln \Xi_{j\ell,t-1}, \quad j = \{A, N\}.$$

This model yields a relationship between population growth, by sector and site, and lagged density:

$$\ln\left(\frac{S_{j\ell t}}{S_{j\ell,t-1}}\right) = \bar{s}_{jt} + \bar{g}_j \ln(1 + g_{j\ell t}) - (1 - \nu_j)\ln\left(\frac{S_{j\ell,t-1}}{N_\ell}\right).$$

This model performs well in predicting a structural transformation from agriculture to nonagricultural employment. For example, a mean reversion in agricultural employment growth, $0 < \nu_A < 1$, proportional growth in nonagricultural activity, $\nu_N = 1$, an agricultural employment share that is decreasing in population density at high densities, and more rapid employment growth in nonagriculture than in agriculture explain a U-shaped relationship between population growth and initial population density.

The Michaels, Rauch, and Redding model is one of local autarky although factors may move. This is a drawback, in contrast to the model by Desmet and Rossi-Hansberg (2009), where trade across locations takes place. Desmet and Rossi-Hansberg develop a theoretical model of the distribution of two industries, manufacturing and services, over a continuum of locations. They address specifically the decline in the employment share of manufacturing and the respective increase in that of services and highlight results that they obtain computationally with U.S. macroeconomic and county-level data. Their model rests critically on endogenous innovation. Locations choose whether or not to invest in innovation, which takes the form of a shift in their production frontiers, but the outcome is stochastic. A location that draws a shift may benefit from innovation for only one period before its advantage is arbitraged away by land and labor. Since production in both industries uses land and labor, it is subject to decreasing returns to scale, which in turn works as a congestion force. The greater the incentive to innovate, the higher the density of employment, but innovations diffuse spatially and each location chooses the best technology it has access to.

Locations specializing in manufacturing innovate more, but that leads to a decrease in the share of manufacturing and a drop in the prices of its goods. The ensuing increase in the services employment share accelerates innovation in services as well, which results in accelerated productivity growth in services while manufacturing productivity growth continues. At the same time, land rents also grow, as suggested by the data. Regarding the spatial aspects, initially when services productivity is almost stagnant, manufacturing is more concentrated than services. Once innovation in services gets under way, services employment becomes spatially more concentrated. The essential geographic element of this work involves a link between location decisions of agents and their decisions to innovate, which are affected by two key parameters, transport costs for goods and the elasticity of substitution between services and manufactured goods in preferences. Higher transport costs reduce welfare by making trade more costly. However, as these authors show, theoretically increased transport costs help induce higher density and thus innovation as well, which in turn promote localized growth.

Differences in the elasticity of substitution generate nonmonotonic patterns in location and growth. A smaller elasticity of substitution induces agents to locate closer to locations that specialize in sectors in which they do not work. This in turn discourages the emergence of large service clusters and thus innovation. At the same time, this change encourages agents in manufacturing areas to increase the share of their consumption of services, which encourages services production nearby and therefore innovation as well. These authors show numerically that the first effect dominates for high values of the elasticity of substitution, whereas the second dominates for low values, in both cases with the elasticity of substitution less than 1. This finding is an important new dimension in spatial economics that enriches, via spatial diffusion of innovations, the importance of space. Geographic trade-offs, expressed by means of transport costs that affect trade, and spatial diffusion that affects innovation show how subtle spatial considerations can be.

All in all, space may have been the last frontier, but once its exploration in the context of urban, regional, and macroeconomic research has started in earnest, it is likely to lead to bountiful results. There exist interesting prospects in several dimensions. To give a few examples, improved measurement of spatial economic activity is now becoming available in the United States, through the imputations of GDP by metropolitan areas published since 2007 by the Bureau of Economic Analysis and discussed in chapter 6 above.[29] These data have yet to be really utilized. It would be interesting to combine them with microgeographic and other information available with spatial detail, as in the work of Henderson, Storeyard, and Weil (2011) (see below), who study income growth, and of Burchfield, Overman, Puga, and Turner (2006), who study sprawl, to give two very different examples. Internationally, only a few countries publish GDP by urban concentrations, with the notable exception of China. However, a number of measures of urban economic activity, some of which are discussed in chapter 8 above, and the particular definition of a GIS-based agglomeration index, proposed and explored by the World Development Report (World Bank 2009) (see chapter 8, section 8.5.5), are providing additional impetus for the further study of urban economic activity in a multitude of dimensions.

9.10 WHY DOES A CITY GROW?

Even after examining the principal explanations that economists may offer about why cities grow, numerous questions have naturally been left unanswered about why some urban areas grow faster than others and whether successes may be emulated and failures prevented. Isolated cities can grow because of growth in productive factors, like land, capital, and labor, and in their quality and because of total factor productivity growth. Transportation improvements, like the U.S. interstate highway system, have caused growth in the size of U.S. metropolitan areas and have favored their suburbanization. Equally ambitious European Union–wide infrastructure projects fuel hope for vast benefits to be reaped. However, the single most notable fact about urban growth is arguably that cities are very open economic entities, which allows them, through intercity trade as well as human capital investments, technology diffusion, and migration, to operate at the technological frontier.

In the intercity trade and growth model in section 9.5 above, it is a combination of weak (strong) diminishing returns and strong (weak) market size effects that plays the role of total factor productivity and can lead to increasing (decreasing) returns to scale. In the Rossi-Hansberg–Wright model in section 9.6 above, a balanced growth path, along which growth is positive even if population growth is zero, allows for technology to depend on human capital accumulation. In addition to specialization and human capital accumulation, the models admit a role for policy and institutions. In the former model, institutional differences in the provision of public capital in some cities can affect growth in the entire urban structure.

Throughout history, cities that have grown out of their hinterlands have continued interacting with them. In a world of rapid urbanization and continued concentration of sophisticated activities in the major urban centers of the world, the typical city in an advanced economy benefits from trading with all other cities. So, for many cities, it is intercity trade that plays the role of the hinterland. While certain types and sizes of cities continue to thrive on interacting with their hinterlands, it is hard to see this through the urban structure. As chapters 7 and 8 and the material earlier in the present chapter establish, urban structure is endogenous, and therefore studying the pattern of interactions between cities and their hinterlands econometrically requires care. A way to approach this is by examining cities in less developed countries whose economies may be more vulnerable to exogenous shocks.

Henderson, Storeygard, and Weil (2011) take this up by using modern tools of microgeographic research to establish the continuing importance of hinterlands for urban growth. Specifically, they use satellite night lights data[30] as a proxy for economic activity at temporal and geographic scales for which traditional data are of poor quality or entirely unavailable. The study relies on two sources of data for African cities, one being lights, which are measured from satellite photography and proxy for urban economic activity, and a second being annual rainfall estimates, which proxy for agricultural productivity. They define cities as contiguous lit areas and then match them with data on established cities' geographic coordinates. They measure average rainfall over all grid areas, which they treat as an exogenous cause of increase in agricultural yields. Data availability restricts them to studying 541 African cities for 18 countries over the period 1995–2003. See Henderson, Storeygard, and Weil (2011, table A.2.).

Regressing urban growth, measured in terms of lights, against rain contemporaneously as well as with several lags, shows that the effects of rainfall are large. Each standard deviation increase in rain (0.90 millimeter/day) in the current or in either of the prior 2 years, leads to a 14 percent increase in lights. The translation of this effect in terms of economic growth is made possible by this study's other findings, where it seeks to improve the estimates of income growth for countries with poor-quality data. See Henderson, Storeygard, and Weil (2011, 1–17). Such an increase in lights represents a 4 percent increase in GDP for a city. So, a sustained increase in productivity would have very strong effects on urban incomes. As Brueckner (1990) and this study both emphasize, urban-rural interactions are complex, with an important role being played by the rural–urban income ratio in thwarting rural-to-urban migration.

While this chapter does not emphasize policy tools as such, its main models rest on the key role that governments play in coordinating production at particular sites. By doing so, they help solve the equilibrium multiplicity problem that is inherent in the lack of ability of individuals with specific skills and tastes, and of firms with specific plans, to coordinate and locate in a particular city. Note, for example, that Henderson and Venables let this coordination problem be solved by considering the role of housing, as I discuss in the previous section. Henderson (1974) invokes city developers. Because of spatial interdependencies (externalities and interactions) and "bundling" (urban opportunities and amenities do not come à la carte), households and businesses need coordinated locational decisions to optimize their benefits. This in turn gives rise to mechanisms of spatial sorting or self-selection, which result in complex patterns of demographic differences (Storper 2008) within large, diversified cities, as well as in differences across more specialized cities (Florida 2002).

Thus, the forces of urban growth articulated by this chapter are not mysterious. They combine purely economic factors, on the one hand, and institutions, on the other, to generate diverse outcomes. The Manhattans, Silicon Valleys, and Route 128 settings (and their counterparts throughout the world) may not be the sort of exotic outcomes they sometimes are made out to be.

9.11 GUIDE TO THE LITERATURE FOR CHAPTERS 7–9

The Henderson (1974) system-of-cities model and key features of the new economic geography introduced by Fujita, Krugman, and Venables (1999) and their numerous refinements provide the key modeling ingredients for the basic model of specialization and intercity trade in chapter 7. The Henderson (1974) system-of-cities model, with city-level external effects on firms and adverse congestion effects, has been profoundly influential and defines a tradeoff that leads to the notion of equilibrium city size. The synthesis, in chapter 7, of the Henderson and Krugman models relies on the work of Anas and Xiong (2003). The incorporation of labor market frictions and unemployment is new and utilizes results by Pissarides (1985, 2000) and Wasmer and Zenou (2002, 2006). Chapter 8 takes a more macro viewpoint by looking at approaches aimed at explaining persistent features of city size distributions worldwide. This topic continues to also attract extraordinary attention from researchers in econophysics and others outside economics proper.

The topic of urban growth and the related issue of the urbanization process continue to attract considerable interest from economists, historians, geographers, and other social scientists. Chapter 9 aims at synthesizing the theoretical economics literature so as to facilitate further applications and to highlight the empirical understanding of urban growth processes worldwide and of spatial interactions among cities. It brings together key modeling features of the urban and international trade literature, including new trade theories, along with appreciation for the role of geography. It also addresses such questions as whether investment in local public infrastructure may cause urban growth to be divergent or convergent and why city sizes may differ systematically. Diversified and specialized cities may coexist in complex ways.

Henderson and Ioannides (1981), who provided the first paper on economic growth in a system of cities, allow for a growing population being accommodated in an increasing number of optimally sized identical cities. They also address issues of lumpiness. Henderson (1988, 67–80) discusses further an extension with two types of cities and intercity trade. Anas (1992) contrasts laissez faire and planning. Ioannides (1994) revisits the topic by embedding the growth model in an overlapping generations model, where each city specializes in a single intermediate good, cities trade intermediates, and individuals consume a CES aggregate of intermediates. There is sustained growth only when the population is increasing, in which case an increasing variety of intermediate goods is possible.

An article by Eaton and Eckstein (1997) and broadly related work by Quah (1997) helped revive interest in the persistence of city size distributions and its relationship to urban growth. They motivated several empirical papers, of which most focus on U.S. urban patterns, including notably those by Black and Henderson (2003), Dobkins and Ioannides (2000), and Ioannides and Overman (2004). Black and Henderson (1999b) propose an endogenous growth model with two types of cities and intercity trade in a numeraire good and a consumption good in an infinite-horizon dynastic setting. Henderson (2005) presents the most comprehensive recent review of research on urbanization and growth, and Ioannides and Rossi-Hansberg (2008) provide a brief overall view. A particularly interesting review of dynamic models is that by Berliant and Wang (2004), who also adapt the Jacobs–Lucas–Romer idea, as modeled in Lucas (1988), by introducing aggregate city capital to capture the

Marshallian externality. Rossi-Hansberg and Wright (2007) work with many goods which are produced using physical and human capital in completely specialized cities by means of Cobb–Douglas production functions that are subject to spillovers, which are multiplicative functions of total industry employment and city human capital. They embed the issue of urban structure in a modern optimal economic growth model with the accumulation of human and physical capital, choice of leisure time between work and human capital accumulation, and a general stochastic structure, and articulate conditions in their model for the emergence of Zipf's law for city size distributions. Another notable feature of their paper is its clarification of how the evolution of city size distribution through the birth, growth, and death of cities reconciles increasing returns at the city level with constant returns to scale at the aggregate level.

The first model in chapter 9 on intercity trade and growth is original. It is a synthesis of the work of Anas and Xiong (2003), which does not deal with dynamics, and of Ventura (2005), which neither models urban economies nor imposes spatial equilibrium. The Ventura (2005) model develops a regional and global view of economic growth by relying on the Dixit and Stiglitz (1977) model as adapted to growth and trade theory by Ethier (1982) and Helpman and Krugman (1985). Xiong's (1998) dissertation does contain a chapter on dynamics, but the approach in chapter 9 is quite different. Specifically, Xiong (1998, chap. 4), emphasizes the transient dynamics of an economy that contains different city types as well as lumpiness, timing, and population swing issues associated with new city development.

CHAPTER 10

Urban Magic: Concluding Remarks

Social interactions are fundamental in the functioning of economies at many scales. We engage in social interactions throughout our lives, though we do not label them as such, just as we speak prose without labeling it.

New technologies, from writing to steam to the internet, have facilitated new ways to interact. Nevertheless face-to-face contacts remain strikingly important to us. They are an extraordinarily efficient communications technology fundamental to the functioning of cities. They solve incentive problems, facilitate socialization and learning, and provide psychological motivation. Moreover, face-to-face contacts as a mode of social interaction are particularly valuable in environments where information is imperfect, rapidly changing, and not easily codified (all features endemic in today's economy).

The present chapter speculates about the prospect for deeper understanding, first, of social interactions in spatial settings, and second, of their significance for the functioning and future role of cities and regions. The research discussed here has identified promising tools. For instance, researchers can look at social exchange in terms of the number of interactional steps between economic agents (individuals, firms, and others). We can then ask how those interactions affect us at different scales. New tools provide foundations for exploring properties of urban networks, from the lowest microscale up to the highest levels of aggregation. Graph theory offers particularly promising tools for exploring the urban social fabric and the interactions that define it: it facilitates analysis that starts from face-to-face contacts and goes all the way up to interactions among population groups, regions, and nations. Its tools can be used to study the physical structure of cities, of aspatial social networks, and of their interaction.

The interplay between social networks in urban settings and a city's physical structure has many dimensions. Social sciences deal with social connections between individuals in ways that complement each other. While economists are increasingly using graph theory as a mathematical tool, sociologists have used it for much longer. For example, investigations of the small-world phenomenon have provided empirical evidence that randomly identified individuals surprisingly often have a common acquaintance or can reach each other through a short chain of first-hand contacts. Much attention has been paid to startling empirical findings, starting with those of Milgram (1967), who suggests, based on experimental evidence, that the average successful chain is found to have only five or six intermediate steps, hence the popular term (and movie title) "six degrees of separation."[1] Kleinberg (2000a, 2000b) uses modern algorithmic tools to characterize theoretically how individuals using local information in social network models can construct short paths to reach one another.

Although a pure social science finding, Milgram's six degrees of separation suggests how social interconnections within cities can influence urban productivity. How easily agents can find one another and exchange ideas depends critically on the properties of city-based social networks. Once one starts thinking about the problem in those terms, it is natural to wonder how the networks of a city's physical infrastructure interact with its social infrastructure and how both help influence urban productivity.

10.1 NETWORKS, URBAN INFRASTRUCTURE, AND SOCIAL INTERACTIONS

Graph-theoretic tools can model and highlight particular features of natural and social landscapes in city geography. One of the earliest problems posed in graph-theoretic terms was motivated by the geography of the city of Königsberg (Kaliningrad since 1946). The city was cut into four pieces by a river, the Pregel, and had seven bridges. Leonhard Euler asked whether it was possible to draw a walk from some point in the city that would cross each bridge exactly once and return to the starting point. The four pieces of Königsberg can be modeled as nodes of a graph, the seven bridges as edges, and Euler's walk as a problem on such a graph.[2] Euler proved there was no solution. Numerous properties of urban physical structure may be defined once graph theory is employed.

Several scholars of ancient and modern urban landscapes are tempted to think of differences in the layouts across cities as potentially related to what was accomplished in different cities historically. A fascinating case in point is the analysis by Ober (2008) in his introduction to the Kleisthenis political reforms in classical Athens. The apparently deliberate organization, designed by Kleisthenis, of groups of communities into the *demoi*, which compelled citizens who were residents of the *demoi's* rural communities to become informed on the concerns of suburban and finally of urban communities as they made their way to the *ekklesia* (the citizens' assembly in the central city), lends itself marvelously to representation by means of graph-theoretic tools. Too little appears to be known historically about the relationship between urban spatial layouts and urban "creativity."

"Meeting around the water cooler"[3] is another phrase that has also entered the popular culture and reflects ways in which the pattern of interpersonal interactions is influenced by the physical layout. In other words, the actual location of the water cooler within the workplace matters. Numerous companies seek to create social gathering spots so that staff members can learn from one another. Also telling is contemporary business interest in using social networking software tools to promote exchanges in the workplace.

As I discuss in chapter 2, section 2.9.1, research on the relationship between urban layout is facilitated by the development of appropriate analytical tools, known as space syntax, in the form of *primal* and *dual* graphs (Porta, Crucitti, and Latora 2006a, 2006b). In the context of the information measures proposed by Rosvall (2004), old, self-organized cities, like Stockholm's Gamla Stan, are harder to navigate than newer, planned cities, like New York's Manhattan. It is interesting to contemplate what can be learned by relating topological properties of urban layouts of historic cities to historic events and achievements.

The case of classical Athens, as studied in depth by Ober (2008), shows how important it was to engineer physical interactions, in the absence of telephones and other forms of distance communication, as part of political reform. It was critical to be informed by as many citizens as possible about how policy options were perceived within their communities. In a like manner, one wonders, whether Edinburgh's urban layout contributed to that city's role as the intellectual capital of the Scottish Enlightment (Buchan 2003). History is full of anecdotal evidence that cities throughout the world were fertile conduits for artistic and scientific ideas long before the emerging division of labor moved such activities into specialized spaces in universities and other institutions. When Jane Jacobs conjectured that the complexity of city life underlies its creativity (Jacobs 1969), she was scorned by economists; nowadays many of them value her ideas. The contemporary phrase regarding the importance of the location of the water cooler within an office, around which spontaneous and occasionally creative conversations often start, suggests that the topology of the urban layout has been important to what goes on in a city intellectually and otherwise. Interactions cannot be defined independently of prevalent information technology at the time.

The other side to urban living is that congestion is unpleasant; its features distract and overload the brain. Interestingly, research by Berman, Jonides, and Kaplan (2008), discussed by Lehrer (2009), suggests that such effects may be offset by patterns in the composition of the urban landscape that may be subject to design. Exactly which interactions make cities tick in either a "good" or a "bad" direction remains elusive. Interactions are also subject to a modicum of congestion, which is not always bad; after all, crowded parties are the best.

The past decade has witnessed a coming together of the technological networks that connect computers on the internet and the social networks that have always connected people since the emergence of human societies (Kleinberg 2008). Not only was the full social use of internet machinery not foreseen by its designers, but the Web itself was the first computer-based object not explicitly designed by computer scientists (Papadimitriou 2003). Interestingly, its technology generates masses of addressable data on the electronic traces of human interactions. González, Hidalgo, and Barabási

(2008) use data from 100,000 anonymous mobile telephone users whose positions are tracked over a 6-month period and show that human trajectories have high temporal and spatial regularity, with time-independent individual time paths and regular frequenting of particular locations. Once corrected for individual characteristics, paths obey a single spatial distribution. The next question is how this outcome is influenced by the physical infrastructure of the places where the subjects live. This can inform urban design. Previous research suggested that human movements follow random walks with fat-tailed displacements and waiting time distributions. Thus, quite a lot can be learned from these new data sources. Information and communication technologies mediate numerous modes of interactions that may be directly interpersonal or involve self-expression in the intellectual, scientific, or opinion sphere. Data from internet-based communications and interactivity could revolutionize our understanding of collective human behavior because they record interactions at multiple space and time scales on multifaceted aspects of individuals' lives (Watts 2007). Graph and network theory is the mathematical language that facilitates the analysis of such interactions.

10.2 GRAPHS AND THE CITY

Ironically, the set of mathematical tools that Euler was inspired to develop from his daily urban experience living in Königsberg have come, in the form of graph and network theory, to dominate thinking about the physical and social aspects of living in modern cities. How well do they depict the structure of modern urban societies? The searchability of social networks constitutes an interesting challenge. Our ability to surf the Web depends on the centrality of the Web graph (see chapter 2, section 2.3.2). Originally a core sociological concept applied to social networks (Bonacich 1987; Wasserman and Faust 1994), network centrality has received renewed attention in the internet era because of its use by the search engines that we live with. Frequently visited sites are important, but how do search engines identify them?

Search engines use assessments of the importance of different sites implied by patterns in Web users' decisions. If, for example, the importance of a site is proportional to the importance of other sites linked to it, then the spectral properties of the Web graph come in handy.[4] If importance is understood as social importance, graph theory is essential in understanding it. Google, a powerful and resourceful company, employs the PageRank algorithm,[5] with its hundreds of millions of dimensions, which exploits the spectral properties of the Web graph to locate pages with the desired contents. Individuals, even those as gregarious as Lois Weisberg,[6] do not. Yet, the second lesson from Milgram's remarkable experiments is that ordinary people with a knowledge of their own acquaintances were collectively able to forward the letter to a distant target so effectively. From a computational viewpoint, this is a statement about the ability of a heuristic *routing algorithm*, based on only local information, to find efficient paths to arbitrary destinations.

Jon Kleinberg formally poses the problem by modeling a social network with what Watts and Strogatz (1998) term the *small-world property*. Consider a social network embedded in a d-dimensional lattice where each individual is linked to her immediate neighbors within a lattice distance d. In addition, each individual is linked, in a purely random fashion, with other individuals all over the network. In such a model of a small-world social network, individuals can be on a circle, in a two-dimensional lattice, and so on. Kleinberg (2000a, 2000b) proves that, in this model with uniformly random connections to distant others, no decentralized algorithm can find short paths, even though they exist, by construction. How then, did the individuals in Milgram's experiments find the destinations?

Kleinberg (2000a, 2000b) also proves that, if instead of the long-range connections being placed uniformly at random connections they are placed between nodes of this network with a probability that decays like the dth power of their distance (in d dimensions), then efficient search is possible. Moreover, he shows that this is the only link distribution of this form for which efficient search is possible. The intuition here is that a probability decaying like the dth power of the distance is in fact uniform over all "distance scales"—an individual is roughly as likely to be connected at distances 1–10 as at distances 10–100, 100–1,000, and so on. The parts of the Manhattan topology that form a square lattice are the easiest to visualize: $d = 2$. In other words, individuals belong to an "archipelago"[7] in which, the groups they belong to are not entirely ingrown. They have both local cohesiveness and offshoots that are sufficiently far-reaching to confer searchability on the entire social network. Away from a selection connection rule, that is, if it is less than inversely proportional to 2, the social network becomes more homogeneous, and it provides less informative cues. In the limit, when long-range connections are generated uniformly at random, the result is a world in which short chains exist but individuals faced with a disorienting array of social contacts are unable to find them (Kleinberg 2000a). If it grows more than proportionately to 2, then too much clustering occurs.[8]

Urban interactions make the global local in the sense that different people who benefit from one another can easily interact, deliberately or by chance. But what appears to be conducive to innovation based on social exchange is suitably small-scale. Joshua Lederberg describes how New York played a special role in his scientific career because of its distinctive combination of richness and scale of interaction. In Lederberg's words:

> It was, and is, a communication network. New York is a super-university. Evolutionists will tell you that you get the most rapid diversification of species where you have an archipelago—where you have islands that are not totally isolated from one another but have sufficient isolation so that each one can develop a distinctive flavor and sufficient communication so that there is some gene flow between them.[9]

Perhaps the archipelago metaphor offers the best picture of the magic of cities. Those of us, and indeed it is most of us, who live in cities nowadays live within a set of networks that are superimposed on one another. There is the physical urban space and its natural representation through streets, neighborhoods, actual and mental routes, and links. There is also the pattern of social and personal interdependence. And there is the ever-changing technological framework within which all other networks merge. Education, culture, entertainment, and life itself involve the internet and the World Wide Web in a myriad of ways. The archipelago metaphor highlights urban magic in another way: the archipelago's geologic and climatic features underpin its biodiversity. The creation of cities over physical space locates the urban archipelago and its internal social and economic structures, which are man-made, adapt to each other in a never-ending pattern of interdependence.

NOTES

Notes to Chapter 1 Introduction

1. Rothenberg (1967) offers the mainstream economics view, and Gans (1968) and Marris (1974) provide sociology and urban planning critiques.
2. The repeated arguments in favor of 5,040 throughout *The Laws* include the claim that its arithmetic property of admitting 59 divisors is advantageous for the mechanics of urban government in the fictitious city of *Magnetes*, whose design *The Laws* addresses.
3. "Jane Jacobs and worse" was a notorious statement made by an eminent economist of the "Chicago School" (ca. 1971). Today it is for me a critical reminder of how economic thinking proceeds by pushing economic ideas to their logical conclusions and then renewing itself via self-criticism.

Notes to Chapter 2 Social Interactions

1. It is straightforward to define individual actions as resulting from the purposeful maximization of a utility function. If this function is quadratic, then linear decisions readily follow, as I show explicitly below. See the work by Blume, Brock, Durlauf, and Ioannides (2011, 944–947, app. A1) for a rigorous derivation and analysis of equilibria in the linear-in-means model. See also sections 2.3 and 2.6 below.
2. The work by Henderson, Mieszkowski, and Sauvageau (1978) appears to be a pioneering empirical study of peer effects in the classroom. This study employs an unusually detailed data set comprised of French-speaking students in Montreal that allows for a range of controls for family, teacher, and school effects. These authors find that peer effects are clearly present and are concave, that is, the marginal effect of an increase in mean classroom IQ is decreasing in the level of mean IQ. This finding suggests that tracking classes by IQ would be inefficient if the objective of the school were to maximize average educational achievement. It also allows analysis of distributional consequences from classroom mixing, with more able students being hurt and less able students being helped.
3. Expectations are sometimes observed. See the discussion of Li and Lee (2009), sec. 2.4.2.
4. This term as a theoretical concept was originally due to Schlicht (1981a, 1981b).
5. Specification of the neighborhood quality index as a function of observable attributes need not be arbitrary. It could be based on the same underlying utility index from which the quantity decision y_i also emanates (Ioannides and Zabel 2008). The implied cross-equations restrictions are testable. I discuss in more detail below their model of joint discrete–continuous decisions based on indirect utility functions; see chapter 3, section 3.5.1. See also Graham (2008b) for an "alternative" hedonic approach to correcting for the consequences of self-selection.

6. To demonstrate, in the simple case where $(\epsilon_i, \vartheta_{i,\nu})$ are bivariate normal, the Heckman correction term is given by $\mathrm{Cov}(\epsilon, \vartheta)\frac{n(\zeta W_{i,\nu})}{N(\zeta W_{i,\nu})}$, where $n(\cdot)$, $N(\cdot)$ denote, respectively, the standardized normal density and cumulative distribution functions.
7. Brock and Durlauf (2001b) and Durlauf (2004) provide more details on the econometric properties of the estimation process.
8. Cabrales et al. follow standard practice in this literature and define a finite number of types of players and work with an m-replica game, for which the total number of individuals is a large multiple of the number of types.
9. The solutions are given by

$$y = 2\sqrt{\frac{a}{3\beta^2_{\text{adj}}}} \cdot \cos\left[\arccos\left(-\frac{27\beta^2_{\text{adj}}}{4a^3}\right) + 120°k\right], \quad k = 0, 1, 2.$$

For the cubic equation, see http://mathworld.wolfram.com/CubicEquation.html and http://en.wikipedia.org/wiki/Cubic_equation.
10. Alternatively, the Erdös–Renyi graph is defined as a topological structure where the number of connections (edges) m is randomly distributed over all possible $\frac{1}{2}I(I-1)$ connections among agents. Then, the Erdös–Renyi graph, $\mathcal{G}^{ER}_{I,m}$, is the ensemble of graphs in which all graphs with m edges out of the possible $\frac{1}{2}I(I-1)$ occurs with equal probability. In statistical mechanics, the equivalence of the two ways of defining random graphs is exact, with the former being the canonical and the latter the grand-canonical ensemble, corresponding to the Helmholtz and Gibbs free energies, respectively. These are generating functions for moments of graph properties over the distribution of graphs, which are related by a Lagrange transform with respect to the "field" p and the "order parameter" m. See the work of Ioannides (1990, 1997, 2004) and Newman (2010) for extensive discussions and references to the random graphs literature.

    Cabrales, Calvó-Armengol, and Zenou (2011) also view the whole pattern of social interactions as a random graph, where each link ij is activated with independent probability g_{ij}, known as the multinomial random graph model.
11. See, in particular, the work of Faloutsos, Faloutsos, and Faloutsos (1999), who find that the autonomous systems of the internet obey a power law, $p_k \sim k^{-\beta}$, $k > 0$, with an exponent in the range $(2, 3)$, and that pages on the Web have (directed) hyperlinks between them whose distribution is heavily right-skewed and is well approximated by a power law with an exponent similar to that of the internet.
12. McKelvey and Palfrey (1995) and Chen, Friedman, and Thisse (1997) develop, independently of the social interactions literature, game-theoretic discrete choice models with interactive features that are also based on the logit model.
13. If two independent and identically distributed random variables, $\epsilon(-1)$, $\epsilon(1)$, obey type I extreme-value distributions, then their difference has a logistic distribution: $\mathrm{Prob}\{\epsilon(-1) - \epsilon(1) \leq x\} = \frac{\exp[\varpi x]}{1+\exp[\varpi x]}$. See chapter 3, section 3.9.1.1.
14. It is possible that the appropriate aggregation is by means other than taking an average.
15. While it is convenient for some of the analytics of the dynamic model to define this in terms of the lagged value of neighbors, I do allow contemporaneous social interactions in section 2.7 below.
16. The concept of global interactions is not very rigorous when the number of individuals is finite. Any pattern of interactions may be expressed by a suitably defined

interactions matrix with entries that are finite numbers. When the number of individuals is infinite, one may distinguish influence by a finite number of neighbors from that by a finite measure of all members of the economy. See Horst and Scheinkman (2006).

17. Binder and Pesaran (2001) assume that the social weights are constant across individuals, in contrast to an arbitrary adjacency matrix which may accommodate the full range between local and global interactions. Those authors provide an exhaustive analysis of solutions of rational expectations models for certain classes of social interactions; see below. They also address the infinite regress problem (of forecasting what the average opinion expects the average opinion to be, etc.) by conditioning on public information only. By appropriate redefinition of the adjacency matrix, it may accommodate habit persistence. It is possible that individuals may differ with respect to attitudes toward conformism or altruism, which would require a more general specification of preferences than (2.26).
In particular, following Binder and Pesaran [2001, eq. (14)], would include quadratic components of the form
$$\frac{1}{2}\left(y_{it}-\eta y_{i,t-1}\right)^2-\frac{\beta}{2}\left(y_{it}-\eta y_{i,t-1}-\left(\frac{1}{|\nu(i)|}\Gamma_i\mathbf{y}_t-\eta\frac{1}{|\nu(i)|}\Gamma_i\mathbf{y}_{t-1}\right)\right)^2,$$
with parameter $\beta>0$ measuring conformism. Conformism is expressed by a trade-off between individual-specific growth in income (or consumption), on the one hand and the gap between that growth and its counterpart among an individual's neighbors on the other. They model *altruism* by expressing a trade-off between the excess of one's own current income over a target lagged income and its counterpart among one's neighbors. Following equation (15) in Binder and Pesaran (2001) would yield the quadratic component
$$-\frac{1}{2}\left(y_{it}-\eta y_{i,t-1}+\tau\left(\frac{1}{|\nu(i)|}\Gamma_i\mathbf{y}_t-\eta\frac{1}{|\nu(i)|}\Gamma_i\mathbf{y}_{t-1}\right)\right)^2,$$
with parameter $\tau\in(0,1)$ reflecting altruism and $\tau<0$, $\tau\in(-1,0)$, reflecting jealousy. That is, growth in i's action and in mean action among neighbors are substitutes or complements, respectively. I note that in both specifications above, the necessary conditions for optimization imply contemporaneous interdependence between different agents' actions, the elements of $\mathbf{y}_t$. In a production-setting interpretation, the quadratic terms in the gap between own actions and those of one's neighbors may be interpreted as miscoordination. See Calvó-Armengol and de Martí Beltran (2009, 125).

18. See Binder and Pesaran (1997) and Ioannides and Soetevent (2007, 381–382, prop. 4) for mathematical techniques that allow one to handle such systems.

19. See Weinberg (2007) and Calvó-Armengol and Jackson (2004, 2007) for recent economics applications in a labor market context that explores the implications of exogenous information networks.

20. In the terminology of DeMarzo, Vayanos, and Zwiebel (2003), if $\gamma_{ij}>0$, then i "listens" to j. A weighted adjacency matrix may come about even when connections are indicated by either 0 or 1. This is the case when agents update their beliefs using Bayes' theorem. My approach is conceptually related to that of Goyal (2005). However, Goyal assumes a given *balanced* graph and allows agents (firms in his case) to choose the intensity of effort. All agents' efforts affect interagent link quality. All previous derivations in the chapter thus far readily apply to the case of a weighted adjacency matrix except that it is no longer necessary to normalize by the

size of the neighborhood. However, the invertibility of the counterpart of $[\mathbf{I} - \beta\alpha\tilde{\Gamma}]$ needs to be specifically established.

21. Working in a finite time horizon allows me to simplify the expression for utility by not weighting by the size of neighborhoods. The analytics employed and intuition gained by the finite-horizon approach may be used to extend the model to an infinite-horizon setting. See Bisin, Horst, and Özgür (2004) for an extension with one-sided local and global social interactions as well.
22. This concept is novel in the social interactions literature. See Ioannides and Soetevent (2007) for more details. Its relationship with the sociological concept of structural holes has not been explored. See Goyal and Vega-Redondo (2007).
23. The invertibility of $[\mathbf{I} - \beta_\ell \mathbf{\Gamma}]$ is ensured under general conditions. See Debreu and Herstein (1953, 601, theorem III).
24. A triad is a set of three nodes i, j, k such that i is connected with j, j is connected with k, and k is connected with i. A triad is said to be transitive, and a graph is transitive if it contains no intransitive triads, that is, there are no individuals where the friends of their friends are not their own friends. From such a perspective, the generic linear model in section 2.2 is specified by assuming that it is symmetric, that edges are bidirectional, and that the graph is transitive.
25. Echenique and Fryer's (2007, 455) *spatial segregation index* can be intuitively motivated as follows. Suppose each individual possesses group-specific capital $y_{i,t}$ whose growth depends on the values possessed by her social contacts weighted by the relative intensity of interaction (the matrix Γ is row-normalized): $y_{i,t} = y_{i,t-1} + \sum_{j\in\nu(i)} \gamma_{ij} y_{j,t-1}$. Then the index is defined as the asymptotic rate of growth of group-specific capital: $\lim_{t\to\infty} \frac{y_{i,t}}{y_{i,t-1}}$. This limit is independent of i and equal to the maximal eigenvalue of $\mathbf{\Gamma}$.
26. For full compatibility with Weinberg's model, one should include the following additional term in (2.26): $\frac{1}{\nu(i)}\Gamma_i \mathbf{X} \ \tilde{\mathbf{y}} \ \mathbf{x}_i$, where $\tilde{\mathbf{y}}$ is a matrix of parameters that denotes the value of associating with others with specific characteristics.
27. In this connection, see (Thompson 2009) for an entertaining (nontechnical) presentation of the issues in this area of social interactions research.
28. The work of Bramoullé, Djebbari, and Fortin (2009) complements that of Lee (2007) and of Lee, Liu, and Lin (2009), with the first emphasizing identification issues and the last two estimation and asymptotic properties.
29. http://www.enquetecoi.net/fr1997/cadre1.htm.
30. http://tiger.census.gov/.
31. http://psidonline.isr.umich.edu/Guide/Overview.html.
32. http://www.census.gov/geo/puma/puma2000.html
33. http://www.ipums.org/.
34. https://international.ipums.org/international/.
35. http://www.ces.census.gov/index.php/ces/cmsdownloads?down_key=21.
36. http://www.census.gov/econ/overview/ma0800.html. See Miranda and Jarmin (2002) for a detailed discussion of the data.
37. http://www.census.gov/hhes/www/housing/ahs/ahs.html.
38. http://www.urban.org.
39. http://www.urban.org/publications/900555.html.
40. http://www.cpc.unc.edu/addhealth. The project is designed by J. Richard Udry, Peter S. Bearman, and Kathleen Mullan Harris and funded by a grant P01-HD31921 from the National Institute of Child Health and Human Development, with cooperative funding from 17 other agencies. The data are provided by Add

Health, Carolina Population Center, addhealth@unc.edu; Moody (2000) and Weinberg (2007) offer concise descriptions of the data set.

41. An example of such a study is the one by Ioannides and Seslen (2002), where data on characteristics and incomes of neighbors from the American Housing Survey are linked to data on wealth holdings from the Panel Study of Income Dynamics. By conditioning on variables available in both data sets, these authors construct a synthetic "augmented" data set that includes household income and wealth, which allows them to compute neighborhood wealth distributions.
42. http://www.statistics.gov.uk.
43. http://www.ons.gov.uk/about/who-we-are/our-services/vml/index.html. I thank Henry G. Overman for clarifications.
44. http://www.insee.fr.
45. See http://www.webcommerce.insee.fr/index.php and http://www.webcommerce.insee.fr/index.php.
46. I thank Dominique Goux for helpful clarifications of the French data sources.
47. http://www.ssb.no/english/. I thank Kjell Salvanes for clarifications of the Norwegian data sources.

Notes to Chapter 3 Location Decisions of Individuals and Social Interactions

1. The stochastic structure in Berry, Levinson, and Pakes (1995) has an additional random shock, making it a mixed logit model.
2. While it is convenient to assume that the stochastic shock ε_h^j in (3.4) is extreme-value distributed, as Bayer et al. in fact do, in view of Ellickson (1981) it is not necessary to do so. The theory of order statistics offers conditions under which extreme-value distributions obtain as a limit of the bidding process that underlies the allocation of dwellings to individuals. See Ellickson (1981) and Jaïbi and ten Raa (1998). However, as Lerman and Kern (1983) point out, it is important to correct for the size of the sample of draws. That is, the maximum of a sample of N independent and identically distributed random draws from a Gumbel distribution with zero mean has mean $\ln N$. Section 3.9.1.1 offers additional details.
3. As they put it, such an instrumenting strategy exploits an inherent feature of the sorting process—that the overall demand for houses in a particular neighborhood is affected not only by the features of the neighborhood itself but also by the way these features relate to the broader landscape of dwelling-unit choice sets and neighborhoods in the region.
4. The actual distribution of maximum utility is also available in closed form. See Anderson, De Palma and Thisse (1992, p. 60–61) for a proof. While it is noteworthy that under the assumption of the multinomial logit model, the expected maximum utilities, conditional on choice, are all equal to the overall expected maximum utility (Anas and Feng 1998), this does not invalidate the approach. The multinomial logit model is invoked as a matter of analytical convenience here.
5. This point was first made by Lerman and Kern (1983) in their discussion of Ellickson (1981) and rests on the fundamental result of Fisher and Tippett (1928) that the distribution of the maximum of $|\mathcal{J}|$ random variables shifts by $\ln |\mathcal{J}|$.
6. See Black 1999, Lee and Lemieux 2010, and the discussion of this technique in further detail in chapter 5, section 5.1.3.2 below.
7. This presumes that there is no capacity constraint. Otherwise, $p(S)$ should be determined by the condition that a particular community offers a minimum amount of utility that depends on individuals' characteristics. The problem, in that case, is

similar to the Epple–Sieg class of models discussed in section 3.7.1 below. I thank Bob Helsley for forcing me to clarify this point.

8. Graham (2008b) seeks to identify the causal effects of parental schooling and neighborhood schooling, while recognizing that parents choose the neighborhoods where they bring up their children. His model of intertemporal optimization yields an Euler-like equation, which links the hedonic price of housing to parental schooling, neighborhood schooling, and total ability and is the counterpart of (3.17). Its integration yields a hedonic price as an isoelastic function of neighborhood schooling, an exact counterpart of (3.24), and thus is less general than my generalization of Nesheim's example (3.21).
9. I note, however, that the linear homogeneity restriction of housing services (3.32) is arbitrary in the context of the Ekeland, Heckman, and Nesheim (2002, 2004) hedonic theory and of Neisheim (2002), discussed above. Yet it is suggested by the Samuelson–Swamy requirements for consistent aggregation that imply an invariant price index. It may be treated as an overidentifying restriction that can be tested by means of techniques similar to measures of rank violations used in comparing different types of indices that Epple, Sieg, and their coauthors themselves employ.
10. This feature of housing as a commodity is well known, of course, and numerous approaches have aimed at circumventing it. The first systematic one, however, is that of Epple, Gordon, and Sieg (2010), who estimate housing decisions when the unobservability of quantity is accounted for and both housing quantities and prices are treated as latent variables. The approach rests on duality theory and utilizes the value of housing per unit of land and the price of land in order to obtain an alternative representation of the indirect profit function as a function of those observables. The empirical demonstration of their approach uses data from recently built properties in Allegheny County, Pennsylvania.
11. However, the above definition is appropriate when both components are freely variable. Once a component has been fixed, the appropriate expenditure function is the quasi-fixed one and thus different from (3.32).
12. The microdata from the American Housing Survey were geocoded by means of confidential U.S. census data. See chapter 2, section 2.13.4, on details pertaining to access to confidential sources of data more generally. The main data source used for this study is the national sample of the American Housing Survey (NAHS). The NAHS is an unbalanced panel of more than 50,000 households units that are interviewed every 2 years and contains detailed information on dwelling units through time and on their current occupants including an evaluation of the unit's market value. These authors define neighborhood selection as discrete choice over census tracts. Public census data provide information on the joint distribution of various variables within tracts, which is crucial for the estimation by Ioannides and Zabel and by Epple and coauthors, which I discuss in section 3.7.1 below.
13. This model is influenced by features of studies by Dubin and McFadden (1984) and by Epple, Romer, and Sieg (2001).
14. This model is not designed to sustain equilibrium community formation unlike that of Epple and Sieg (1999) and Epple, Romer, and Sieg (2001). Therefore, it is not a drawback that it does not satisfy the single-crossing property with respect to income. This could, of course, be accommodated but would make the error structure less transparent.
15. I acknowledge an imprecision here. This step requires that Roy's identity be taken with respect to a suitably restricted indirect utility function, where the appropriate neighborhood-specific components of the consumption bundle are held fixed,

once neighborhood is chosen. However, this approach is not structural in the econometric sense and is designed to highlight the complexities of housing as a joint discrete and continuous decision.

16. This interaction between η_h and tract-specific variables introduces heteroscedasticity in the errors of the discrete choice problem.
17. See Blackley and Ondrich (1988) and Quigley (1985) for two exceptions, and Fox (2007) for a modernization of McFadden's procedure. Bierlaire, Bolduc and McFadden (2003) show that the consistency of estimation when using a subset of the opportunity set extends to all random utility models where the errors obey a generalized extreme-value distribution.
18. This estimation is consistent, provided that: one, independence from irrelevant alternatives holds; and two, if an alternative is included in the assigned set, then it has the logical possibility of being an observed choice from that set. The first condition is ensured by their use of the MNL; the second is satisfied because random selection satisfies the "uniform conditioning property" of McFadden (1978). See also McFadden, Bierlaire, Bolduc, and McFadden (2003, 88–89), and Fox (2007).
19. The specific forms of the sample selection bias correction terms are computed using the results of Dubin and McFadden (1984) and Dubin (1985). See chapter 3, section 3.9.2, for details.
20. This feature addresses the concern regarding the identification described by Angrist and Pischke (2009, 192–197 sec. 4.6.2), in that the equation accounts for variation in ex ante peer characteristics that predate the outcome variable, as in the determinants of neighborhood choice.
21. See also section 3.9.2. and the discussion leading up to Equation (3.40).
22. Schelling (1969) presents a nontechnical exposition whereas Schelling (1971) is a technical description of both models, Schelling (1972) emphasizes the neighborhood tipping model, and Schelling (1978) discusses broader implications of earlier works on the dynamics of segregation by emphasizing how *micromotives* affect *macrobehavior*.
23. See Zhang (2004, 167–168) for the case with vacant locations.
24. Formally, this may be defined as a potential game with potential function defined as $\frac{1}{2}\sum_{i\in\mathcal{J}} u_j(\iota)$.
25. Recall that in chapter 2, section 2.4.1, this pertains to individual responses.
26. This model may be thought of as a simplification of the one by Miyao (1978b) who adapts the Schelling model as follows. Individuals belong to a number of finite types, and their evaluations of neighborhoods are randomly distributed across the population with a deterministic component that depends on the number of individuals of each type that locate at every location. Individuals choose the location they find most attractive. Equilibrium is defined as equality between the selection probability for each location and the proportion of individuals of the respective type who actually choose a location. A number of examples reveal that stability of the integrated equilibrium is ensured if and only if the intensity of the externality is sufficiently small relative to the dispersion of preferences for the different locations. Like the Brock–Durlauf model, (chapter 2, section 2.4.1) for multiple equilibria to emerge, the intensity of the externality must be sufficiently large.
27. This is qualitatively similar to the three possible equilibria depicted by Card, Mas, and Rothstein (2008a, 181, fig. II).
28. A number of noteworthy earlier papers, including several papers by Dennis Epple and coauthors (Epple, Filimon, and Romer 1984; Epple and Romer 1990), as well

as several more recent papers, (Benabou 1993, 1996a, 1996b; Durlauf 1996; Epple and Platt 1998; Epple and Romano 1998, emphasize the role of prices in bringing about rich sets of outcomes in the form of segregated or uniform equilibria. Details of these papers are summarized by Durlauf (2004, 2193–2194, table 1.)

29. This ordering must satisfy boundary indifference, income stratification, and ascending bundles. That is, if $P_\ell > P_{\ell'}$, then $g_\ell > g_{\ell'}$ if and only if community ℓ is populated by higher-income people than community ℓ'.
30. These agree with the findings of Hardman and Ioannides (2004) and Ioannides (2004a), who use data for the entire United States.
31. Although the authors refer to this as a peer effect, it is actually a contextual neighborhood effect in terms of the Manski typology.
32. Similar results are reported by Ioannides and Zanella (2008), who use PSID data for 2001 and 2003, and discussed in chapter 6, section 6.5.7, below.
33. See Ekeland, Heckman, and Nesheim (2002) and the latest generalization of this approach by Heckman, Matzkin, and Nesheim (2009).

Notes to Chapter 4 Location Decisions of Firms and Social Interactions

1. Convexity of preferences, a standard assumption in economic theory, implies here that an agent wishes to consume services at all possible sites. In view of this, as Schweizer (1988) emphasizes, an attractive reformulation of the problem would be to consider a large number of firms relative to sites and work with the densities of agents at different sites. The Koopmans–Beckmann solution is interpreted meaningfully in that case.

   Starrett (1978) examines general properties of locational equilibrium where he allows for firms to locate close to one another so as to eliminate transportation costs. A priori, in the Arrow–Debreu model where commodities are indexed by time, event, and site, there does not seem to be a problem of existence for spatial equilibrium. Still, Starrett (1978) proves a "spatial impossibility theorem," that is, if all locations are identical and transport costs are zero, then perfect competition, with constant returns to scale in production, competitive markets, and price-taking agents, implies that economic activity is uniform over space and does not involve any transportation. That is, if activities are divisible, then they will locate at all possible locations, with each location operating in autarky and being identical to every other location. In other words, there will be no urban concentrations.

   Schweizer (1988), inter alia, argues that the problem resides in the fact that firms need to be separated from each other so as to consume a positive amount of land that cannot be made arbitrarily small. This requirement introduces a tension with the need to avoid transport costs and is not imposed in the Starrett formulation. Alternatively, Ellickson and Zame (2005) argue that a more interesting implication of Starrett's theorem is to explore what competitive equilibrium says in realistic settings where locations are not identical and transportation costs are not zero! Ellickson and Zame show that perfect competition with a little bit of heterogeneity can lead to very heterogeneous outcomes. Thisse (2000) argues that in order to avoid the conceptual difficulty articulated by the spatial impossibility theorem, one needs to introduce either *heterogeneity of space*, widespread production, and consumption *externalities*, or *imperfectly competitive* markets. The first is exactly how the neoclassical theory of international trade motivates trade, including in particular, by means of the Armington assumption (namely, that goods are differentiated by the origin); the second is a hallmark of urban economics; and the third is a key feature of new economic geography. Once introduced, such features can justify spatial concentrations.

2. What if sites post rents in order to maximize the expected value of the rent they will receive? That is, site ℓ may choose rent $\hat{\varrho}_\ell$, taking all other rents as given, so as to maximize:

$$\hat{\varrho}_\ell \sum_{k=1}^{L} \frac{e^{\varpi(a_{k\ell}-\hat{\varrho}_\ell)}}{\sum_{j=1}^{L} e^{\varpi(a_{kj}-\varrho_j)}}, \qquad \ell = 1, \ldots, L.$$

Symmetrically, each of the firms could themselves post rents for different sites, so as to maximize the expected value of the profit they will earn, after locations have been determined.

3. This may be considered as a specification of (4.17) above.
4. See Kotz, Balakrishnan, and Johnson [2000, 485, eq. (49.1)]: Guimarães and Lindrooth (2005) for an application.
5. Guimarães, Figuerdio, and Woodward (2003) demonstrate that by using the observational equivalence between the maximum likelihood estimation of the logit model and that of Poisson-type regressions. Using a Poisson model, the number of firms located at each site ℓ, n_ℓ, is fully described by a Poisson parameter $\mathcal{E}(n_\ell) = \exp[\alpha + \theta \mathbf{z}_\ell]$. Maximizing the respective likelihood function with respect to α yields $\exp[\alpha] = N(\sum_{\ell=1}^{L} \exp[\theta \mathbf{z}_\ell])^{-1}$, $N = \sum_\ell n_\ell$. Substituting back into the likelihood function (a step also known as concentrating the likelihood function) yields an expression that coincides with that of the likelihood function for the logit model plus terms that are constants (Guimarães, Figuerdio, and Woodward 2003, 202). The same approach applies when the data have a group structure, in which case the number of firms in industry g located at each site ℓ, $n_{g\ell}$, is fully described by a Poisson parameter $\mathcal{E}(n_{g\ell}) = \exp[\alpha_g + \theta \mathbf{z}_{g\ell}$. The approach estimates fixed effects, however, as opposed to random effects in the case of the Dirichlet multinomial model above, which rests on maximization of the likelihood function (4.26).
6. Although the presence of the Herfindahl index for the plant size distribution in the definition of the Ellison–Glaeser index accounts for plant sizes, Holmes and Stevens (2002) see a bigger role for varying plant sizes. They point to the empirical fact that plant sizes are larger where industry concentrations are greater. Holmes and Stevens (2004a) propose a model [originally in Holmes (1999)], an "alternative" to the Dixit–Stiglitz monopolistic competition model (1977), where industry concentrations also generate positive feedback on concentrations of economic activity, especially in manufacturing. In their model, firms have monopoly power in local markets but behave competitively in export markets. The model assumes that locations differ in terms of population, but demand must be satisfied in part by local production, which gives an edge to local concentration, and the remainder may be supplied by either local production or imports. Goods differ only in terms of transportation costs, and the availability of a constant-returns backstop technology places a ceiling on prices. This is binding for goods that are not traded, and firms use the increasing-returns-to-scale technology to supply their export markets. Specialization patterns depend only upon populations at various locations.
7. This corresponds to the identification problem of social interactions in linear-in-means models, discussed in chapter 2, section 2.2.1, in that one may estimate a social interactions effect— a contextual effect, $\gamma^s = 0$, an endogenous effect, $\gamma^{na} = 0$, or both.
8. In fact, this is independently verified by Rosenthal and Strange (2003).

9. This is a key element of the work of Lucas and Rossi-Hansberg (2002), which is discussed in chapter 5, section 5.5.
10. This instance of a regression discontinuity designlike approach applied to firms' decisions is reminiscent of a study by Black (1999), where home values in adjacent jurisdictions help estimate unobservables in households' valuations of public school quality. See chapter 5, section 5.1.3.2.
11. See http://www.census.gov/mcd/asmhome.html. The ASM reports regular surveys covering years between the actual economic census—manufacturing. Among the statistics included in this survey, whose samples are drawn from all manufacturing establishments with one or more paid employees, are employment, payroll, value added by manufacture, cost of materials consumed, value of shipments, detailed capital expenditures, supplemental labor costs, fuel and electric energy used, and inventories by stage of fabrication.
12. One data set is the *Bénéfices Réel Normaux* (BRN), which allows the authors to construct value added by firm for each year for publicly traded firms. A second is the *Régime Social des Indépendants* (RSI), which contains the balance sheets of all smaller firms. Together, the BRN and RSI constitute the *universe* of French firms. Two additional data sets, the *Système d'Identification du Repértoire des Enterprises* (SIREN) and *Déclaration Annuelles de Données Sociales* (DADS), provide additional information. For each of 942,506 firms, between 1994 and 2002, these researchers know a firm's value added, the value of its assets (with and without financial assets), total employment, and detailed cost share information. For each establishment within each firm, they know its detailed location, its wage bill, and its number of paid hours by skill level.
13. New economic geography earned Paul R. Krugman, its chief proponent, the 2008 Sveriges Riksbank Prize in Economic Sciences in Memory of Alfred Nobel. The scientific background provided by the prize committee of the Royal Swedish Academy of Sciences is an excellent summary of Krugman's contributions to economics. http://nobelprize.org/nobel_prizes/economics/laureates/2008/ecoadv08.pdf.
14. This is a survey that focuses on specific contributions of new economic geography: one, the concept of market potential and its role in raising factor prices and attracting factor supplies; two, the concept of the home market/magnification effect whereby in a number of ways an increase in demand for a country's products leads to more than a one-for-one increase in production; three, the effects of trade in inducing agglomeration; and, four, instability of equilibria, persistence, and agglomeration.
15. This concept was first introduced by Krugman (1992) and was refined by Fujita, Krugman, and Venables (1999).
16. NUTS, which stands for nomenclature of territorial units for statistics (in French), is the official designation of regions in the European Union. They range from NUTS0, the E.U. member states, to NUTS5, which number in the hundreds of thousands. NUTS1 are large regions with populations ranging from 3 million to 7 million people. For example, France is divided into eight NUTS1 regions. For more details, see http://ec.europa.eu/eurostat/ramon/nuts/home_regions_en.html.
17. See Head and Mayer (2004b 962), for details of the estimation. However, it is based on using the model to specify imports $\mathrm{IM}_{\ell k}$ by consumers at location ℓ from location k, $\mathrm{IM}_{\ell k} = n_k p_k^{1-\sigma} \tau_{\ell k}^{1-\sigma} E_\ell P_\ell^{\sigma-1}$. The trading costs are proxied by a function of distance between the respective countries, $d_{\ell k}$, of a language dummy

(Lang$_{\ell k}$ = 1, if and only if ℓ, k, share a language), of a border dummy (Bord$_{\ell k}$ = 1, if and only if ℓ, k, share a border): $d_{\ell k}^{-\delta} \exp[-(b'_{\ell k} - b''_{\ell k}\text{Lang}_{\ell j})\text{Bord}_{\ell k} + \epsilon_{\ell j}]$. The distance and border effects may be refined in more general choice settings where there may also be tariff effects as well, in addition to border effects, and the two may lead different predictions. See Rossi-Hansberg (2005).

18. NAICS is the successor to SIC. Roughly, three-digit NAICS industries correspond to two-digit Standard Industrial Classification industries.
19. Chapter 7, section 7.8, below, develops a model of the firm similar to the present one to study urban specialization and diversification when different industries differ with respect to labor turnover.

Notes to Chapter 5 Social Interactions and Urban Spatial Equilibrium

1. While the notion of a circular city is arguably more realistically appealing, a number of works have underscored that analytically there is no advantage to the circular configuration. In particular, as Ogawa and Fujita (1980, 1989) show, nonmonocentric urban configurations in two-dimensional space (with circular symmetry imposed) are qualitatively essentially the same as those in one-dimensional space.
2. The choice of Massachusetts is apt because its public school districts are administered by local (city and town) governments and thus many are small and rather homogeneous.
3. Bazhanov and Hartwick (2006) reconsider Beckmann's solution and solve explicitly for $U = h^{1/2}c^{1/2}$. I adopt Beckmann's original solution here and its modernization by Fujita and Thisse (2002, 174–182), because it is easier to compare with the urban economy under a predetermined center.
4. Empirical evidence for many cities around the world agrees with this prediction. See, in particular, Bertaud (2004, 11) and other evidence in http://alain-bertaud.com on density gradients in cities around the world.
5. Prime Minister Tony Blair, too, put emphasis on the redevelopment of South East London by removing "urban blight" in the form of large housing estates, like Aylesbury Estates.
6. http://www.gettyimages.com/.
7. O'Hara (1977) works with a more general, two-dimensional model, but the results are qualitatively similar in the special case of $a = 2$. The model may be solved only numerically in the most general case.
8. This yields

$$\alpha(\alpha-1)[m(\ell)]^{\alpha} - 2\frac{d^2 m(\ell)}{d\ell^2} + \alpha(\alpha-1)(\alpha-2)m(\ell)^{\alpha-3}\left(\frac{dm(\ell)}{d\ell}\right)^2 + 2\tau m(\ell) = 0.$$

9. Fujita and Smith (1990) show that these correspondences are instances of a general class of conjugacy correspondences between convex (and concave) functions developed by Rockafellar (1970). Their mathematically rigorous concepts of accessibility and locational benefit are specific to these models but may be extended to more general settings.
10. See Mori (2008) for a brief review of this literature.
11. This is the exact counterpart of what Fujita, Krugman, and Venables (1999) call the "no black hole condition."
12. Ciccone and Hall (1996) similarly posit that the urban externality depends on total output in the metropolitan area (see section 6.3.2 below).

13. In key ways, the results of the paper are consistent with those of Fujita, Krugman, and Venables (1999), except that individuals are assumed to be fully mobile and therefore areas of no economic activity are a possible outcome. In contrast, some immobility is necessary in the Fujita et al. case in order to define regions.
14. Specifically, for those portions of each concentric ring that lie within some defined PWPUMA (and not over the ocean or the Great Lakes), they use data from the U.S. Geological Survey to compute the following four measures: the amount of the ring covered by water, the fraction of the ring underlaid by sedimentary rock, the fraction of the ring designated a seismic hazard, and the fraction designated a landslide hazard.
15.

$$\frac{\partial y_n}{\partial \beta} = -k(\ell_{n+1} - \ell_n)\ln\left(\frac{R_n}{R_{n+1}}\right)\frac{\left(\frac{R_n}{R_{n+1}}\right)^{\beta}}{\left(\left(\frac{R_n}{R_{n+1}}\right)^{\beta} - 1\right)^2};$$

$$\times \frac{\partial y_n}{\partial \frac{R_n}{R_{n+1}}} = -\beta(\ell_{n+1} - \ell_n)\frac{\left(\frac{R_n}{R_{n+1}}\right)^{\beta-1}}{\left(\left(\frac{R_n}{R_{n+1}}\right)^{\beta} - 1\right)^2}.$$

16. See Fujita (1989) for formalization of the *bid rent function*, which is particularly helpful in analyzing location decisions of different agents and carries the additional advantage of unifying analytically and conceptually the study of decisions of individuals and of firms.
17. Wasmer and Zenou (2006) generalize the model of Wasmer and Zenou (2002) in order to allow for relocation (mobility) costs but otherwise retain the setting of Wasmer and Zenou (2002). Accordingly, they modify the Bellman equations to account for incurring a fixed cost each time a labor market transition occurs. Their analysis implies residential segregation into four groups: mobile employed and unemployed workers, and immobile employed and unemployed workers. They show that immobile workers occupy space in between the mobile types and that the respective region shrinks to nonexistence when relocation costs go to 0. Zenou (2009a) develops further models of this type into a broader theory of urban labor markets.
18. Diamond (1982) assumes increasing returns to matching: the probability of a match is higher when there are larger numbers of both unemployed workers and vacancies. Helsley and Strange (1990) obtain a source of agglomeration economies rooted in job matching, in that larger labor markets may provide better matches between jobs and workers. Lagos (2000) and Stevens (2007) endogenize the Pissarides matching function. Petrangolo and Pissarides (2001) provide an excellent overview of the literature that the Pissarides matching function has given rise to.
19. By differentiating the job-matching probability with respect to υ_i one gets

$$\frac{d\pi_i}{d\upsilon} = \left[\left(\frac{1}{\upsilon_i}, 1\right) - \frac{M_1}{\upsilon_i}\right] M \quad s_i > 0, \qquad \frac{d^2\pi_i}{d\upsilon_i^2} = \frac{M_{11}}{\upsilon_i^3} s_i^2 < 0,$$

with both inequalities following from the properties of the matching function.
20. In contrast to the bold assumption I make here, Zenou (2009a, 96–97, 2009b) works with the assumption of perfect capital markets with a zero interest rate.
21. Chris Pissarides points out that normally in search models indifference across a number of possible states, which in this model also includes locations, as an

equilibrium condition is expressed as the equality of the present discounted value of entering each state. This translates into equality between the value of unemployment in each state. However, unlike Wasmer and Zenou (2002), I do not assume that people move when they become unemployed. Therefore, for consistency with the central feature of open-city models, I work with expected lifetime utility, permanent income in this instance.

22. Calvó-Armengol and Jackson (2004, 2007b) show theoretically that unemployment across socially interacting individuals is correlated contemporaneously and intertemporally. Unemployment exhibits duration dependence: the longer an individual has been unemployed, the less likely he or she is to get a job. They also show that because staying in the labor market is costly, a group that starts in an inferior position relative to another group experiences higher drop-out rates and lower employment.
23. See Ioannides and Topa (2010, 352–357) for additional details on neighborhood effects and job matching. Conley and Topa (2002) seek to identify attributes of social dimensions that serve as a conduit for social interactions.
24. I thank Chris Pissarides for urging me to examine such an aspect of the model.
25. This is derived in detail by Calvó-Armengol and Zenou (2005) and Ioannides and Soetevent (2006). It is consistent with the identifying assumptions of Topa (2001).

Notes to Chapter 6 Social Interactions and Human Capital Spillovers

1. http://www.census.gov/. Differences in gross domestic product per capita are much wider across the member states of the European Union. These reflect, in part, lower mobility due to numerous impediments in the integration of European labor markets.
2. http://www.bea.gov/newsreleases/regional/gdp_metro/gdp_metro_newsrelease.htm.
3. Named after the initials (in French) for Nomenclature of Territorial Units for Statistics, NUTS are designations of different scales of spatial aggregation in the European Union. In this study, NUTS3 refers to 133 regions that in the United Kingdom correspond to counties outside metropolitan areas. In contrast, the 96 NUTS3 in France are *départements*.
4. These are standardized county-based areas having at least one urbanized area with a population of 50,000 or more. Each metropolitan area consists of one or more counties and includes the counties containing the core urban area, as well as any adjacent counties that have a high degree of social and economic integration (as measured by commuting to work) with the urban core. *Micropolitan statistical areas* are also geographic entities defined by the U.S. Office of Management and Budget for use by federal statistical agencies in collecting, tabulating, and publishing federal statistics. A micropolitan area contains an urban core with a population of at least 10,000 (but less than 50,000). See http://www.census.gov/population/www/metroareas/metroarea.html for more details. Further use is made of these data in chapter 8 below.
5. This is a very strong assumption, and its consequences vary across demographic and occupational characteristics, in particular, age and skills, as well as across E.U. countries, and between the European Union as a whole and the United States.
6. While regressing the real wage against city population makes perfect sense in its own right, it is nominal wages that should reflect a city's greater productivity. If

workers were not more productive in larger cities, firms producing goods that are traded nationally or internationally would leave high-wage cities and relocate to low-wage cities. Firms producing traded goods face the same price everywhere in the nation, net of transport costs, so that as long as there are some firms producing traded goods in every city, average productivity has to be higher in cities where nominal wages are higher (Acemoglu and Angrist 2000; Moretti 2004c).

7. As Ciccone (2008, 4–5) discusses, this is because county boundaries were originally drawn so as to equalize populations and, second, beause county populations have been persistent.
8. Ciccone and Hall (1996) show that an observationally equivalent formulation is arrived at if one assumes that increasing returns are instead due to an endogenous variety of intermediate products. Output per unit of land is assumed to be a Cobb–Douglas function of labor per acre and of a composite good produced using a range of differentiated inputs in the Dixit–Stiglitz style, which themselves are produced using labor. See chapter 7 below.
9. Ciccone (2008b) argues that estimates should be based on city (i.e, metropolitan area) value added. He stresses that relying on the total value of production, or on value added from the U.S. Census of Manufactures, overstates value added in a city because it does not net out the value of services firms purchase from other firms and from their own headquarters. If not corrected, this might lead to double counting, when headquarters themselves are included, especially in an urban setting.
10. Specifically, their instruments are the presence or absence of a railroad in a state in 1860, population in the state in 1850, population density in 1880 and distance from the eastern seaboard of the United States.
11. There are two precursors of this approach in the macroeconomic literature. Hall and Jones (1999) compute a contemporaneous (Solow) residual across countries, thus a *spatial residual*, that accounts for a substantial portion of differences in income per capita and then seek to explain its variation across countries in terms of social infrastructure, that is, differences in institutions. They treat social infrastructure as endogenous, being determined historically by location and other factors. Chari, Kehoe, and McGrattan (2007) explore the notion that many models are equivalent to a prototype growth model except for time-varying wedges that resemble productivity, labor and investment taxes, and government consumption. I discuss a conceptually related study by Desmet and Rossi-Hansberg (2011) in chapter 8, section 8.5.7.
12. This is defined as an index based on the presence of symphony orchestras, opera companies, dance companies, public television, fine arts resources, museums and so on.
13. The inverse Mills' ratio is defined as the ratio of the value of the density over 1 minus the cumulative distribution function at some given value. Recall from chapter 2, section 2.2.2, that this expression is a key tool for correcting for sample selection bias (Heckman 1979)
14. Work PUMAs have an average of roughly 210,000 people in residence and range from just over 100,000 people present to over 3 million. See chapter 2, section 2.13.2, for more details on PUMAs.
15. Tellingly, the working paper version was titled "The Urban Rat Race."
16. They are very significant when used to identify proximity. See the work of Ioannides (2002, 2003), also discussed in sections 6.5.4 and 6.5.5 further below, for a case in point.

17. Not surprisingly, according to the General Social Survey (1987 ISSP module on social inequality), 85 percent of people in the United States think that education is essential or very important for getting ahead in life. Compare this with the 23 percent who think that family wealth is instead essential or very important.
18. Ioannides (2002 Prop. 1) explores the general properties of the law of motion and deals with properties of specific cases, many of which have been utilized by the empirical literature but have not been explored as emanating from the same general behavioral framework (Ioannides 2002, prop. 2).
19. My definition of complementarity in terms of a comparison of consumption and production elasticities partly heeds Matsuyama's point that complementarity should not be assumed but derived (Matsuyama 1995).
20. Isotropic: different agents are in similar steady states; see section chapter 2, section 2.4.1, and Ioannides (2006, 567, prop. 3).
21. Anisotropic means that successive agents alternate over the two steady states.
22. Bala and Sorger (2001) consider a similar model, except that equilibria may create different classes of agents in the society, that, is managers, who invest only in human capital, and workers, whose human capital is the (smallest) amount they are endowed. Stationary equilibria may be of different types, such as when all agents are workers trapped in self-perpetuating poverty traps. There are also spatially anisotropic ("stratified") equilibria, where there exist managers who live within clusters of locations adjacent to those of workers.
23. Additional evidence of the codependence of education of individuals who grew up in the same neighborhood is obtained by regressing an individual's education against neighborhood education and the mean education among all other individuals who grew up in the same neighborhood. The respective coefficients are 0.178 (6.92) and 0.564 (21.81), and $R^2 = .225$.
24. I use Danny Quah's tsrf program, available at http://econ.lse.ac.uk/-dquah/tsrf.html. To understand the construction of the stochastic kernel, consider the kernel showing the child's education (`maxed`) conditional on the average of the father's and mother's educations (`parent`), $h_{i,t+1} = G(h_{it}, \varepsilon_i)$, reported in figures 6.1.1 A–B. To estimate that stochastic kernel, the program first derives a nonparametric estimate of the joint distribution $f(h_{it}, h_{i,t+1})$. Then, it numerically integrates under this joint distribution with respect to $h_{i,t+1}$ to get the marginal distribution of average parents' educations $f(h_{it})$. Next the conditional distribution $f(h_{i,t+1}|h_{it})$ is estimated by $\hat{f}(h_{i,t+1}|h_{it}) = \frac{\hat{f}(h_{it}, h_{i,t+1})}{\hat{f}(h_{it})}$. Under regularity conditions, this gives us a consistent estimator for the conditional distribution for any value of parents' educations h_{it}.
25. This finding also points to the fact that U.K. neighborhoods are much less sorted than U.S. ones. From table 6.1 below, columns 7 and 8, the elasticity of individual education with respect to neighborhood education is around 0.2.

Notes to Chapter 7 Specialization, Intercity Trade, and Urban Structure

1. The evolution of the population of Constantinople is telling. From an important ancient Greek colony, Byzantium, the city rose steadily after becoming in the fourth century the new capital of the Roman Empire to a population of 500,000–800,000 people in the ninth and tenth centuries. It had fallen to 35,000 by the time it was retaken by the Byzantines after the Fourth Crusade in 1261 and grew back up to 50,000 by the time it was captured by the Ottomans. Istanbul, the modern city and no longer the capital of Turkey, has grown enormously to more

than 12 million inhabitants, thus becoming one of the largest cities proper in the world. This history is not atypical. As Batty (2006) documents via the device of "rank clocks," cities have risen and fallen with their civilizations throughout recorded history. See the discussion of city mobility in chapter 8, section 8.9, below.

2. Chapter 9, section 9.11, contains a brief guide to the literature.
3. This fact is underscored by Duranton (2007); it constitutes *the fast* in his description. See chapter 8, section 8.3.
4. See section 9.6 for a discussion of how Rossi-Hansberg and Wright (2007) model the presence of interrelated industries.
5. The discussion here follows that of Duranton and Puga (2004).
6. I thank Gilles Duranton for pointing out that this result was preceded by that of Rivera-Batiz (1988).
7. Recall from chapter 4 that this effect is also known as the effect of Jacobs or Marshall–Arrow–Romer externalities.
8. This may well be a misnomer, in that the effect is not via the price, strictly speaking, which is a constant markup on marginal cost but through the consequences of the free entry.
9. Ciccone and Hall (1996) model output per unit of land as a Cobb–Douglas function of raw labor and of the contribution from intermediates. By means of similar arguments, they show that output per unit of land is an isoelastic function of total labor supply that exhibits increasing returns to scale if the elasticity of substitution among the intermediates is high enough and the share of intermediates is sufficiently important. See chapter 6, section 6.3.2.
10. Grossman and Rossi-Hansberg (2010) pursue this notion further in working with a continuum of industries that benefit from national external economies of scale at the industry level. They show that with Bertrand competition, firms internalize the externality by setting a price below those of other firms. Such an out-of-equilibrium threat eliminates many of the pathologies of the standard approach and helps establish a unique equilibrium in line with natural comparative advantage. I return to their results below.
11. It is straightforward to show that that would still be the case if I posed the problem as choosing the quantity of one of the differentiated goods and allocating the remaining labor equally among all the other goods so as to maximize output. This naturally follows from symmetry.
12. I owe emphasis on this point to Esteban Rossi-Hansberg. Henderson (1974, 1988), and most recently Rossi-Hansberg and Wright (2007), have examined theoretically the consequences for city sizes when cities are indeed built by profit-seeking entrepreneurs. Government entities can play roles similar to those of entrepreneurs.
13. See the work of Matsuyama (2007) who generalizes shipping costs "beyond iceberg costs."
14. Abdel-Rahman (1996) also employs a similar production structure with two manufactured goods that may be traded but only one of which is used for consumption and the other only for commuting. Contrary to his claim (Abdel-Rahman 1996, 3, n. 5), this chapter succeeds in solving analytically in the case of two consumption goods. This formulation is critical for chapter 9, where the two goods are combined to produce a composite which in turn is used for consumption and investment. Abdel-Rahman and Fujita (1993) use a simpler model and internal economies of scale to address urban specialization versus diversification.

15. In contrast, following Ciccone and Hall (1996) we have to assume that production function (7.15) is for output per unit of land, the total contribution of nonland inputs (each defined as per unit of land) has an elasticity ϱ, making $1-\varrho$ the share of land in total production. The resulting elasticity of output per unit of land with respect to employment per unit of land would be $\varrho\left[1+(1-u_X)\frac{1}{\sigma-1}\right]$.
16. The model of this section is what Anas and Xiong (2003) refer to as a system of *diversified* cities.
17. The special case of one X-city "paired" with one X_o-city has been examined by Xiong (1998, pp. B). Similarly, the special case of one X-city and Z-city has also been examined by Xiong (1998, pp. B).
18. See section 5.8 for a decentralized model of job-related contacts.
19. Huang (2008) shows, using data for 600 London neighborhoods down to the level of a square mile, that a new generation of entrepreneurs is more likely to enter industries overrepresented among their residential neighbors. This effect is stronger when there is more scope for social interactions in a neighborhood as proxied by higher ethnic homogeneity, more "sociable" housing structures, or a higher entrepreneurial population density. The effect is also stronger in industries that require more informational interactions among entrepreneurs. These differential effects support those of social interactions on individual decisions.
20. This is, admittedly, a very strong assumption that serves to simplify the problem. A more general model could allow for some substitutability among different varieties of labor in production in the style of Helpman and Itskhoki (2010). Ioannides (2011) assumes that the inputs are composites of intermediate varieties, which are produced with labor hired in frictional labor markets.
21. This treatment follows Pissarides (2000, 68–70), with the model adapted for large firms.
22. I thank Chris Pissarides for pointing out that this is an important difference. It deviates from the assumption of Wasmer and Zenou (2002) in order to render the bargaining solution for the wage rate independent of location. In the present setting, it is expected lifetime utility that is equalized across locations. Associating the bargaining outcome with the increase in the expected value of employment over unemployment would make it dependent on location.
23. Equalization of labor market tightness across different city types follows from the fact that individuals are a priori identical. Ioannides (2011) develops an alternative case where workers differ in terms of skills and the production of different types of intermediates requires workers with different skills. In that case, labor market tightness differs across cities of different types, thus allowing for a greater variation of unemployment across the economy's cities.
24. Glaeser and Gyourko (2005) confirm such longer adjustment lags.
25. See Behrens, Mion, Yasusada, and Südekum (2011) for a novel framework that addresses the role of spatial frictions in determining the city size distribution, individual city sizes, and the productivity advantage of larger cities.

Notes to Chapter 8 Empirics of the Urban Structure and Its Evolution

1. Chapter 9, section 9.11, contains a brief guide to the literature.
2. Another important empirical fact about the urban structure is patterns of specialization and diversification, which I discuss extensively in chapter 7.
3. Gabaix and Ibragimov (2011) return to a known bias of the estimate of the Zipf coefficient from equation (8.1), also discussed by Gabaix and Ioannides (2004).

This bias arises from the fact that city ranks and sizes are obviously correlated by construction. The bias is strong in small samples, and the correction they propose, that is, to use ln (Rank − 0.5) in place of ln Rank as a dependent variable in equation (8.1) (Gabaix and Ibragimov 2011, theorem 1), is optimal in the sense that the proposed transformation of the dependent variable reduces the bias to leading order only. However, Ioannides, Overman, Rossi-Hansberg, and Schmidheiny (2008) employ this correction and find no discernible difference in the estimates.

4. Gabaix (2009, 260) considers this condition fundamental to random growth processes and refers to it as *Champernowne's equation*. However, the derivation of (8.4) does not acknowledge the reflective barrier; see section 8.2.3. Realizations of city sizes that hit it are not independent.
5. Eeckhout (2004, 1143–1147), offers a rock-bottom economic model where productivity is enhanced by urbanization economies, an increasing function of city size, and individuals' net labor supply is affected by congestion externalities, a decreasing function of city size. When the respective functions are isoelastic, and provided that urbanization externalities are not too strong, city sizes follow Gibrat's law.
6. I thank Gilles Duranton for emphasizing in a private communication that almost all research in this area introduces some sort of friction, such as in the form of immobile activities, durable housing, or a minimum population.
7. Reed (2002) assumes that city sizes evolve according to geometric Brownian motion, that is, they obey Gibrat's law. Under the additional assumption that new cities enter at exponentially distributed times, Reed shows that the limit marginal size distribution, that is, marginal with respect to time of entry, is a mixture of exponential distributions, where the mixing distribution is normal cumulative, whose parameters depend on those of the distribution function for initial city sizes as well as of the geometric Brownian motion. This may be transformed to a "double Pareto lognormal" distribution. Giesen, Zimmermann, and Suedekum (2010) use the 2000 U.S. urban places data and, in addition, similar data for Germany for 2006 and for several other countries to estimate the model proposed by Reed (2002).
8. Gabaix (2009) allows formally for several possibilities and updates his earlier results by a number of enhancements such as allowing for entries, exits, and jumps. The entry (and exit) of new cities is critical theoretically and empirically and does receive attention, respectively, from Gabaix (1999b, 2009) and Eeckhout (2004). Krugman (1995) adapts a model due to Simon (1955) that relates the locations of new cities to existing city sizes, though not their actual physical locations. If city sizes obey a power law, then $1 - F(N) \propto S^{\zeta}$. City sizes are measured in "lumps," understood as the minimum possible city size. Let total population N_{tot} grow by the addition of lumps at a Poisson rate. Krugman examines a steady state where $f(N)/N_{\text{tot}}$ is constant. A new lump that appears attaches itself to a city of size $N-1$, with probability $1 - p_a$, turning it to size N, or forms a new city with probability p_a. Using the assumptions made about the growth process, Krugman finds that approximately $F(N)$ is of the above form, with $\zeta = -\frac{1}{1-p_a}$. This simple model links the entry of new cities to Zipf's law. Dobkins and Ioannides (2001) explore empirically ideas that are roughly based on Simon (1955). I discuss their empirical results further below.
9. I thank Spyros Skouras for pointing out forcefully that the forward Kolmogorov equation does not hold in this instance, as derived by Gabaix. See also Skouras (2009). Intuitively, the truncation at the reflective barrier operates on the growth process itself in a manner not captured by the Kolmogorov derivation. See a further discussion below.

10. See Ricciardi and Sacerdote (1997, 363). Its limit is equal to $-2\frac{\mu}{\sigma^2}$, which confirms (8.11).
11. Gabaix (2009) also works with a geometric Brownian motion. Gabaix's (2009, 756) equation (11), for the special case of $\mu(S,t) = \bar{\mu}S$, $\sigma(S) = \bar{\sigma}S$, yields a forward Kolomogorov equation whose steady-state solution is of the form $p(S) \sim S^{\zeta-1}$, where $\zeta = -1 - \frac{2\bar{\mu}}{\bar{\sigma}^2}$. As the results relied upon above indicate, the solution for the steady state in the case of reflected Brownian motion is not just the unrestricted steady-state solution applied to the restricted support. Nonetheless, Gabaix's approach continues to be very powerful in deriving the limit distribution for another specification of the stochastic evolution of city sizes. See section 8.2.4 below.
12. Rewriting the above yields
$$-\frac{Sp'(S)}{p(S)} = S\left(-\frac{2\mu(S)}{S\sigma^2(S)} + \frac{(\sigma^2(S)S^2)'}{2\sigma^2(S)S^2}\right) = -\frac{2\mu(S)}{\sigma^2(S)} + 2 + \frac{S\,(\sigma^2(S))'}{\sigma^2(S)}$$
$$= 2 - \frac{2\mu(S)}{\sigma^2(S)} + \frac{S}{\sigma^2(S)}\left(\sigma^2(S)\right)'.$$
13. Note that here ζ is defined as the algebraic *opposite* of that defined by Gabaix (1999b). He provides a closed-form solution for ζ when the growth rates themselves are lognormally distributed (Gabaix 1999b, prop.5). Skouras (2009) insists that the derivation of (8.14) does not acknowledge the presence of the lower barrier.
14. This transitional nature is confirmed by Ioannides and Skouras (2009), who estimate a switching regressions model of the U.S. urban structure. A power law for the city size distribution emerges abruptly after about 100,000 of population. See section 8.5.1 below.
15. One may recognize that measuring activity by firms versus by their individual establishments separately raises similar issues.
16. All stochastic kernels are calculated nonparametrically using a Gaussian kernel with bandwidth set as per Silverman (1986, sec. 3.4.2). To estimate the kernel, Ioannides and Overman first derive the joint distribution of normalized population and growth rates. They then numerically integrate under this joint distribution with respect to growth rates to get the marginal distribution of population at time *t*. Finally, they estimate the marginal distribution of growth rates conditional on population size by dividing the joint distribution by the marginal distribution. Calculations were performed with Danny T. Quah's `tsrf` econometric shell. The contours work exactly like the more standard contours on a map. Any one contour connects all the points on the stochastic kernel at a certain height.
17. Skouras notes that the results of Gabaix (1999b), Rossi-Hansberg and Wright (2007), and Duranton (2007) imply that structural parameters will be consistent with this third assumption.
18. Skouras made this point independently of Levy (2009), who comments on Eeckhout's (2004) characterization of the emergence of a hybrid lognormal power law distribution for the top 0.6 percent of places (that housed more than 23 percent of the U.S. population in 2000) as "a puzzle yet to be answered." Eeckhout does not accept the criticism.
19. There are two popular international data sources nowadays. One is Thomas Brinkhoff's *City Population Project*, http://www.citypopulation.de. The second is *World Cities Data*, by the World Bank as part of documentation of the 2009 World Development Report, http://www.econ.brown.edu/faculty/henderson/worldcities.html.

20. This is important because the U.S. data imply a roughly concave Zipf's curve and the French data a visually less concave one.
21. New economic geography has provided one of several possible types of models capable of producing hierarchies of cities. Fujita, Krugman, and Mori (1998) generate something resembling central place theory in a general equilibrium framework by employing imperfect competition and increasing returns at the firm level.
22. More recently, Hsu (2009) has reported this same regularity using U.S. data. See section 8.4.2.1 below.
23. The proof is straightforward. Given a rank–size rule, then the average size of cities that contain industry j is obtained as the average size of the n_j cities that have ranks r_j and higher, $\rho(S) < \rho(S_j)$:

$$\overline{S}_j = \frac{1}{r_j}\int_0^{n_j} \rho(S)dS = \frac{1}{n_j}\int_0^{n_j} \alpha S^{\zeta} dS = \frac{\alpha}{1+\zeta} n_j^{\zeta}. \tag{8.1}$$

So, rank–size rule $\rho(S) = \alpha S^{\zeta}$ implies NAS rule $\overline{S}_j = \frac{\alpha}{1+\zeta} n_j^{\zeta}$, provided that $0 < -\zeta < 1$.

Conversely, given the hierarchy principle, the NAS rule $\overline{S}_j = \alpha n_j^{\zeta'}$, implies a rank-size rule with exponent $\zeta = \zeta'$. This follows because for any rank $r \in \mathbf{S}$, there is an industry j for which the smallest city it occupies has rank and size $r_j = n_j = r$. Then

$$\frac{1}{r}\int_0^{r} \rho(S)dS = \overline{S} = \alpha S^{\zeta}, \forall S \in \mathbf{S}.$$

24. http://www.census.gov/geo/www/garm.html.
25. This is not so surprising once one recognizes, as Mitzenmacher (2003) notes, how similar the log densities for the Pareto and the lognormal distributions are. The former is given by $(\zeta - 1)\ln S$, and the latter by

$$-\frac{1}{2}\ln[2\pi\sigma] - \ln S - \frac{(\ln S - \mathcal{E}(S))^2}{2\sigma^2} = -\frac{1}{2}\ln\left[2\pi\sqrt{\mathrm{Var}(S)}\right] + \left[\frac{\mathcal{E}(S)}{\mathrm{Var}(S)} - 1\right] \times \ln S - \frac{(\ln S)^2}{2\mathrm{Var}(S)} - \frac{(\mathcal{E}(S))^2}{2\mathrm{Var}(S)}.$$

The latter has a very thin tail. The last term for the lognormal tends to vanish when the standard deviation is large enough, making both log densities linear in the log of city size. The inference problem is compounded by the fact that at the upper tail paucity of observations hampers estimation. But Var(S) may depend on size, and its effect in a regression may not wash out.
26. Ioannides and Skouras (2011) use a slightly different (deterministic) switching model and provide additional support by means of estimates with the metropolitan-micropolitan areas data and the Rozenfeld, Rybski, Gabaix, and Makse (2011) data. Decker, Kerkhoff, and Moses (2007) also offer support, though informally, for the lognormal distribution in the main body and a power law in the upper tail. See section 8.5.4 below. Also complementary to these results are those of Malevergne, Pisarenko, and Sornette (2009, fig. 1), who report results on a uniformly most powerful unbiased (UMPU) test for the null of the Pareto distribution against a truncated lognormal using the 2000 U.S. urban places data. They plot the p-value for the UMPU test against the city rank of the cutoff for the Pareto (upper panel). The p-value becomes very low for ranks above 1,000, thus supporting the lognormal for cities below those ranks. Similar support in favor of

the Pareto for large cities is provided by plotting Hill's estimates for the inverse Pareto exponent (lower panel).

27. See http://www.census.gov/population/www/metroareas/files/00-32997.pdf.
28. This requires returning to original data sources for those years and relying on the work of Bogue (1953) for the 1900–1940 data. Most data available prior to 1950 are for populations residing within legal city boundaries. Such data are still available but ignore the real fact of suburban integration. Bogue (1953) uses the 1950 SMA definitions to reconstruct what populations would have been in those areas in each of the decennial years from 1900 to 1990. Most of the metropolitan area data identify city units by counties, but in New England, metropolitan area definitions may involve parts of counties. The U.S. Bureau of the Census redefined SMSAs as MSAs and CMSAs in 1983, which creates problems for data from the 1980 and 1990 censuses. For consistency, Dobkins and Ioannides reassembled the 1990 data according to the 1980 definitions (by county).
29. Problems with the implementation of this procedure are discussed by Black and Henderson (2003, 347, n. 3). Chiefly, the cutoff point is not monotonic in the rank of the smallest city.
30. This is consistent, they note, with the Zipf's coefficient of -1 for the population-based regression if the land elasticity of population is one-half.
31. See the findings of Henderson, Storeygard, and Weil (2011), discussed in chapter 9, section 9.10, who also use satellite night lights data.
32. This critique is not appropriate for Eeckhout's (2004) view, where shocks to total factor productivity induce population mobility that is consistent with Gibrat's law. See Eeckhout (2009).
33. De Vries (1984, chap. 7), appears to have originated the study of urban evolution by means of transition matrices.
34. The earliest date in the data set is that for Jacksonville, Florida. This data set includes the St. Augustine area and dates back to 1564. The latest is for Richland, Washington, originally the site of a nuclear facility established in 1944. See Dobkins and Ioannides 2001, 707.
35. Hanson actually uses the Helpman (1998) extension of the Krugman (1991a) model, which he considers easier to adapt to empirical use.
36. This model can be augmented to allow for individuals' demands for an agricultural good, which in turn generate demand and thus value for agricultural land.
37. The minor difference in (8.29) and (8.30) from Krugman's formula is due to the fact that I work with city-specific marginal labor requirements and therefore do not normalize so as to make the price equal to the wage rate for each good.
38. This corresponds to the maximal eigenvalue of the respective dynamical system, with much the same intuition as the social interactions model of Ioannides (2006).
39. See http://web.uniovi.es/qcg/harmonics/harmonics.html for a visualization of such symmetries.
40. Strictly speaking the model is not one of edge cities. Garreau (1991) defined edge cities as urban concentrations that form around major metropolitan cities and bring together jobs, marketplaces, and residential areas. Several examples of such edge cities are the area around Route 128 and the Massachusetts Turnpike in the Boston region, the Schaumburg area west of O'Hare Airport near Chicago, Irvine, south of Los Angeles, and many others throughout the world.
41. Imaizumi, Ito, and Okazaki (2008) provide a rare critique of this line of work by pointing out that the *strategic* bombing during World War II was by design not random. It aimed at destroying critical Japanese assets and infrastructure. They work

instead with data from the 1923 Great Kanto earthquake in Japan as an example of a truly random disaster and its implications for industrial agglomeration. Their point is well taken, but their study is too crude to be relied upon for the purpose of drawing conclusions about agglomeration.

42. These estimates are based on the Geographically Based Economic Database (http://gecon.yale.edu/) compiled from information gathered in 1990 and assembled at Yale University (Nordhaus 2006). The database provides estimates for 1990 of GDP, population, and land area of regular grid cells that at a 1° latitude by 1° longitude scale are about 100 × 100 kilometers at the equator.
43. González-Val and Sanso-Navarro (2008) provide a critique of the reliability of Rose's estimates.

Notes to Chapter 9 Intercity Trade and Long-Run Urban Growth

1. The notion that agricultural surplus is needed for urbanization goes quite far back. Many scholars associate it with Lewis (1954).
2. Duranton and Turner (2011) examine empirically the relationship between road capacity and road use. They show that traffic increases almost in exact proportion to infrastructure. They suggest that this is explained by more driving by existing residents, driving by new residents, and increased traffic due to an increase in transportation-intensive activities.
3. This is defined as the percentage of nonwhites that would have to move to achieve perfect integration (Tauber and Tauber 1965).
4. See http://www.urbanaudit.org/. Following a pilot project for the collection of comparable statistics and indicators for European cities, the first full-scale European Urban Audit took place in 2003 for the then 15 countries of the European Union. In 2004 the project was extended to the 10 new member states plus Bulgaria, Romania, and Turkey. The second full-scale Urban Audit took place between 2006 and 2007 and involved 321 European cities in the 27 countries of the European Union, along with 36 additional cities in Norway, Switzerland, and Turkey. Data collection currently takes place every 3 years, but an annual data collection is being planned for a smaller number of targeted variables.
5. In this three-tiered production setting, the production of the composite corresponds to the role that preferences play in the main model in chapter 7.
6. This specification modernizes Henderson's (1987, 1988) work for the purpose of examining urban growth in particular. It differs from that of Rossi-Hansberg and Wright (2007) because they rely on the Lucas model to generate sustained growth. It differs from both the Henderson and Rossi-Hansberg–Wright approaches because of its assumption that tradable goods are not consumed directly. It also allows a comparison between autarky and intercity trade, which helps highlight the importance of intercity trade.
7. This specification combines the ideas of Anas and Xiong (2003) and Ventura (2005).
8. This may be generalized to allow for input-output linkages by requiring [see also Fujita, Krugman, and Venables (1999), chap. 14] that each intermediate-good industry uses its own composite as an input, along with capital and labor. This is accomplished by introducing $[\int_0^{M_{it}} p_{it}^{1-\epsilon_i}]$ as an additional term on the right-hand side of the cost function $b_{it}(Z_{Jt})$.
9. For example, a local government may be assumed to maximize the utility of the typical resident by setting the city population. Therefore, I may choose a city

population that maximizes the indirect utility of the typical individual at each point in time, given by (9.7). Using (9.18), I may express $R_{i,t+1}$, the gross return to capital in terms of N_{it}, as well. Even in this case, however, the resulting optimum is inversely proportional to the square of unit commuting costs, with the coefficient of proportionality being different.

10. Differences in the κ_i's may be used to express differences in local geography across sites.
11. This assumption is visualized by Miyao as involving capital being spread evenly over the land area allotted to the transportation system and bringing about a uniform rate of reduction in unit transportation cost everywhere in the city [Miyao 1981, 103, eq. (6)]. The fact that I set density at 1 is not a substantive difference. A conceptually similar result follows from a seemingly different assumption made by Desmet and Rossi-Hansberg (2011) when working with isoelastic functions. They define government spending in terms of what is needed to build and maintain urban infrastructure for the total number of miles commuted, whereas I assume government investment improves the unit cost of commuting.
12. As Fujita and Thisse (2009, 113), emphasize, while the mobility of capital is driven by differences in nominal returns, workers move when there is a positive difference in utility (real wages). In other words, differences in living costs matter to workers but not to owners of capital.
13. Specifically, by substituting for $k_{Yg,t+1}$ from the condition that expresses equalization of wages into (9.41) and then using the resulting expression for K_{t+1} in each of the expressions for utility in (9.50), we may obtain necessary conditions for utility maximization in the form of quadratic equations. For $k_{Xg,t+1}$ specifically, this equation is

$$\begin{aligned}&(2S_{\text{av}}\eta(\alpha\mu_X+1-\alpha)+S_{\text{av}}(\mu\phi+\upsilon-1)+1)k_{Xg,t+1}^2-[(2S_{\text{av}}\eta(\alpha\mu_X+1-\alpha)\\&+S(\mu\phi+\upsilon-1))\bar{W}_{Xt}+((2S_{\text{av}}\eta(\alpha\mu_X+1-\alpha)+1)\bar{K}_{t+1}]k_{Xg,t+1}\\&+2S_{\text{av}}\eta(\alpha\mu_X+1-\alpha)\bar{W}_{Xt}\bar{K}_{t+1}=0,\end{aligned}$$

where we have ignored some inessential constants and defined the auxiliary variables $\bar{W}_{Xt}$, $\bar{K}_{t+1}$ as follows:

$$\bar{W}_{Xt}\equiv(1-\phi_X)N_{X,t}^{-1}\mathcal{N}_{X,t}\left(\frac{K_t}{\bar{N}}\right)^{\mu\phi+\upsilon},$$

$$\begin{aligned}\bar{K}_{t+1}\equiv\bar{N}^{-1}&\left[S_{\text{av}}\frac{\bar{N}}{N_X}n_X(1-\phi_X)\mathcal{N}_X+(1-S_{\text{av}})\right.\\&\left.\times\left(n_Y\frac{N_Y}{N_X}(1-\phi_X)\mathcal{N}_{X,t}-n_Y(1-\phi_Y)\mathcal{N}_{Y,t}\right)\right]\left(\frac{K_t}{\bar{N}}\right)^{\mu\phi+\upsilon}.\end{aligned}$$

A quadratic equation for $k_{Yg,t+1}$ is derived symmetrically. Inspection of the above equation shows that the solution varies less than proportionately to $\left(\frac{K_t}{N}\right)^{\mu\phi+\upsilon}$, because of the spillovers between the two types of cities, as I discuss further below.

14. One needs to impose

$$\gamma_j(\iota)+\varepsilon_j(\iota)<\frac{1}{2}$$

for all ι. Otherwise, cities would grow unboundedly. See details below.

15. The multiplicative form of the accumulation constraint, pioneered by Lucas and Prescott (1971), combines well with the loglinear model to produce closed-form solutions.

16. This form of the human capital accumulation constraint was pioneered by Lucas (1988) and constitutes a key building block of endogenous growth theory.
17. The strategy of the proof employed by Rossi-Hansberg and Wright differs somewhat from that of Gabaix (1999b). Rossi-Hansberg and Wright divide industries into groups with similar technologies to first prove that Zipf's law holds for each group. Recall that each industry can have many cities. Then they aggregate across groups to show Zipf's law for the entire economy. See Rossi-Hansberg and Wright (2007, 620–621).
18. See "Robustness Appendix," http://www.princeton.edu/˜erossi/USGrob.pdf.
19. Interestingly, Antràs (2004) in his study of the elasticity of substitution properties of the U.S. aggregate production function *assumes* constant returns to scale.
20. For a Pareto city size distribution, this may be expressed as $(\frac{\zeta}{1+\zeta})^{0.5}$. Similarly, the Gini coefficient for such a distribution is given by $-0.5\zeta + 1$.
21. http://www.econ.brown.edu/faculty/henderson/worldcities.html.
22. http://www.citypopulation.de.
23. http://www.library.uu.nl/wesp/jalahome.htm.
24. David Cuberes, in a private communication, suggests that the results are weaker for metropolitan areas possibly because the time span (1960–2000) is much smaller than that for administratively defined cities (1790–2000). Another possibility is that metropolitan areas are significantly different economic entities than cities and so the logic of sequential city growth may not be as apt. This, of course, hampers urban research more generally.
25. This result must be qualified in the presence of costs of shifting production capital or sunk costs associated with agglomeration of activity and other forms of strategic complementarity of the form examined by economic geography (Krugman 1991b; Rauch 1993b). Pritchett (2006) presents a work motivated by international trade, providing a view that sees ghost towns as an inevitable outcome of unimpeded labor mobility which confers the advantage of lower income differences across an economy.
26. Fujita (1978, chapt. 6) defines a problem of choosing positive allocations of investment to a finite number of investment projects out of the sum total of their outputs at any point in time in order to maximize total income in the *final* period. Projects have identical production functions that are characterized by variable returns to scale with respect to capital (their sole input), starting with increasing and ending with decreasing returns to scale. That is, the marginal productivity of investment exhibits a single maximum. Investment allocated to a project initially enjoys increasing marginal return; however, after it has peaked, other projects become more attractive and the planner finds it advantageous to switch to them. The optimal policy implies that no project can pass any other project that started receiving investment before it did (Fujita 1978, 225–226). The problem with urban sequential growth is thus conceptually very similar, from the viewpoint of a planner but involves functions that peak, thus implying that cities have finite capacities.
27. The difference is that the expression for per capita income from (7.7) accounts for a redistribution of rents.
28. Brazil's federal states are divided into municipalities, for which fairly stable geographic units, known as *áreas mínimas comparáveis*, may be defined.
29. http://www.bea.gov/newsreleases/regional/gdp_metro/gdp_metro_newsrelease.htm.

30. Studies by Decker, Kerkhoff, and Moses (2007), discussed in chapter 8, section 8.5.4, also use satellite night lights data. This resource is of limited direct use in very advanced countries because of top-coding of the data.

Notes to Chapter 10 Urban Magic: Concluding Remarks

1. The objective of the experiment was to determine chains of acquaintances linking pairs of people in the United States who did not know one another but deliberately tried to do their best to reach a named targeted recipient. In a typical instance of the experiment, a person in Nebraska was given a letter to be delivered to a person in Massachusetts. The person at the origin was initially told basic information about the person at the destination, including his address and occupation. The source was then instructed to send the letter to someone he or she knew on a first-name basis so as to transmit the letter to the target as swiftly as possible. Anyone subsequently receiving the letter was given the same instructions, and the chain of communication continued until the letter was received by the named recipient.
2. Such a walk is known as an Eulerian tour (Jackson 2008, 46–47).
3. See "Gathering around the Virtual Water Cooler," http://www.communities.hp.com/online/blogs/labsblog/archive/2008/06/03/test-3.aspx.
4. If the importance of site i, z_i, is proportional to the sum of the importance of the other sites, $j \neq i$, that it is connected with, then $z_i = \lambda^{-1} \sum_j \mathbf{\Gamma}_{ij} z_j$, where $\mathbf{\Gamma}_{ij}$ denotes the i-th row of the Web graph. Thus, a simultaneity arises that admits a simple mathematical expression. The importance of all sites is determined simultaneously: written as a vector, $\mathbf{z}$, the social importances of all sites satisfies $\mathbf{\Gamma z} = \lambda \mathbf{z}$. In other words, the vector of the social importance of sites, $\mathbf{z}$, and the respective coefficient of proportionality, λ, are an eigenvector and its respective eigenvalue of the adjacency matrix $\mathbf{\Gamma}$. Since the adjacency matrix is symmetric and positive, the Perron–Frobenius theorem (see chapter 2, section 2.12), guarantees the existence of a maximal positive eigenvalue and a corresponding positive eigenvector, provided that the graph is connected (or else the maximal eigenvalue would be equal to zero).
5. http://en.wikipedia.org/wiki/PageRank.
6. As the commissioner of Chicago's Department of Cultural Affairs, Lois Weisberg launched the Chicago Cultural Center, created Gallery 37, and brought Chicago the incredibly popular "Cows on Parade" exhibit. Long before her career in city government, she started a drama troupe, published an underground newspaper, founded Friends of the Parks, ran the Chicago Council of Lawyers, and managed multiple political campaigns. Her numerous careers, magnetic personality, and intricate web of friends and acquaintances inspired Malcolm Gladwell's (1999) "Six Degrees of Lois Weisberg" and http://www.wttw.com/chicagostories/loisweisberg.html.
7. This metaphor is explained further below.
8. Kleinberg (2008) presents a further evocative discussion of the newer, web-based experiments that he and others have conducted. Experiments involving paths through social networks to distant targeted individuals have been repeated by a number of groups of researchers. Most recently, Dodds, Muhamad, and Watts (2003) have studied the use of email to reach individuals within a global social network, and Liben-Nowell and Kleinberg (2008) used chain-letter data to trace the flow of information through the internet.
9. *The New Yorker* (1978). I am grateful to Tom Bender for this evocative reference.

BIBLIOGRAPHY

Aarland, Kristin, James C. Davis, J. Vernon Henderson, and Yukako Ono. 2007. "Spatial Organization of Firms: The Decision to Split Production and Administration." *Rand Journal of Economics* 38(2):480–494.

Abdel-Rahman, Hesham M. 1996. "When Do Cities Specialize in Production?" *Regional Science and Urban Economics* 26:1–22.

Abdel-Rahman, Hesham M., and Alex Anas. 2004. "Theories of Systems of Cities." In J. Vernon Henderson and Jacques-François Thisse, eds., *Handbook of Regional and Urban Economics*, Vol. 4, *Cities and Geography*, 2293–2339. Amsterdam: Elsevier North-Holland.

Abdel-Rahman, Hesham M., and Masahisa Fujita. 1993. "Specialization and Diversification in a System of Cities." *Journal of Urban Economics* 33(2):189–222.

Abel, Jaison R., and Todd M. Gabe. 2008. "Human Capital and Economic Activity in Urban America." Staff report, no. 332, Federal Reserve Bank of New York, July.

Acemoglu, Daron, and Joshua Angrist. 2000. "How Large Are Human Capital Externalities? Evidence from Compulsory Schooling Laws." In Ben Bernanke and Kenneth Rogoff, eds., *NBER Macroeconomic Annual* 2000, 9–59. Cambridge, MA: MIT Press.

Aizer, Anna, and Janet Currie. 2004. "Networks or Neighborhoods? Interpreting Correlations in the Use of Publicly Funded Maternity Care in California." *Journal of Public Economics* 88:2573–2585.

Akerlof, George A., and Rachel E. Kranton. 2002. "Identity and Schooling: Some Lessons for the Economics of Education." *Journal of Economic Literature* XL:1167–1120.

Alesina, Alberto, and Enrico Spolaore. 2003. *The Sizes of Nations*. Cambridge, MA: MIT Press.

Alexandersson, Gunnar. 1956. *The Industrial Structure of American Cities*. Lincoln, NE: University of Nebraska Press.

Alonso, William. 1964. *Location and Land Use*. Cambridge, MA: Harvard University Press.

Amiti, Mary, and Christopher A. Pissarides. 2005. "Trade and Industrial Location with Heterogeneous Labor." *Journal of International Economics* 67:392–412.

Anas, Alex. 1990. "Taste Heterogeneity and Urban Spatial Structure: the Logit Model and Monocentric Theory Reconciled." *Journal of Urban Economics* 28(3):318–335.

Anas, Alex. 1992. "On the Birth and Growth of Cities: Laissez Faire and Planning Compared." *Regional Science and Urban Economics* 22:243–258.

Anas, Alex, Richard Arnott, and Kenneth Small. 1998. "Urban Spatial Structure." *Journal of Economic Literature* 36:1426–1464.

Anas, Alex, and Cheng-Min Feng. 1988. "Invariance of Expected Utilities in Logit Models." *Economics Letters* 27:41–45.

Anas, Alex, and Kai Xiong. 2003. "Intercity Trade and the Industrial Diversification of Cities." *Journal of Urban Economics* 54:258–276.

Anderson, Theodore W. 1958. *An Introduction to Multivariate Statistical Analysis.* New York: John Wiley and Sons.

Anderson, Simon P., André de Palma, and Jacques-François Thisse. 1992. *Discrete Choice Theory of Product Differentiation.* Cambridge, MA: MIT Press.

Angrist, Joshua D., and Kevin Lang. 2004. "Does School Integration Generate Peer Effects? Evidence from Boston's METCO Program." *American Economic Review* 2004:1613–1634.

Angrist, Joshua D., and Jörn-Steffen Pischke. 2009. *Mostly Harmless Econometrics.* Princeton, NJ: Princeton University Press.

Anselin Luc, Elisabeth Griffiths, and George Tita. 2008. "Crime Mapping and Hot Spot Analysis." In R. Wortley and L. Mazerolle, eds., *Environmental Criminology and Crime Analysis*, 97–116. Collumpton, Devon: Willan Publishing.

Antràs, Pol. 2004. "Is the U.S. Aggregate Production Function Cobb–Douglas? New Estimates of the Elasticity of Substitution." *Contributions to Macroeconomics* 4(1):art. 4.

Arcidiacono, Peter, and Sean Nicholson. 2005. "Peer Effects in Medical School." *Journal of Public Economics* 89:327–350.

Aristotle. ca. 340 BC. *Politics.* http://classics.mit.edu/Aristotle/politics.mb.txt

Aristotle. ca. 330 BC. *Nicomachean Ethics.* http://classics.mit.edu/Aristotle/nicomachaen.html

Arrow, Kenneth J. 2009. "Some Developments in Economic Theory Since 1940: An Eyewitness Account." *Annual Reviews of Economics* 1:1–16.

Arrow, Kenneth J., and Partha Dasgupta. 2009. "Conspicuous Consumption, Inconspicuous Leisure." *Economic Journal* 119:F497–F516.

Arzaghi, Mohammad, and J. Vernon Henderson. 2008. "Networking off Madison Avenue." *Review of Economic Studies* 75:1011–1038.

Au, Chun-Chung, and J. Vernon Henderson. 2006. "Are Chinese Cities Too Small?" *Review of Economic Studies* 73:549–576.

Azariadis, Costas, and Alan Drazen. 1990. "Threshold Externalities in Economic Development." *Quarterly Journal of Economics* 105(2):501–526.

Azoulay, Pierre, Joshna S. Graff Zivin, and Jialan Wang. 2008. "Superstar Extinction." *Quarterly Journal of Economics* 125(2):549–589.

Backus, David K., Patrick J. Kehoe, and Timothy J. Kehoe. 1992. "In Search of Scale Effects in Trade and Growth." *Journal of Economic Theory* 58(2):377–409.

Badel, Alejandro. 2009a. "Representative Neighborhoods of Metropolitan U.S.: A Characterization of Race, Human Capital and Housing Prices." Working paper, Georgetown University, March 13.

Badel, Alejandro. 2009b. "Understanding Permanent Black-White Inequality: Neighborhood Human Capital Externalities and Residential Segregation." Working paper, Georgetown University, March 30.

Bairoch, Paul. 1988. *Cities and Economic Development.* Chicago: University of Chicago Press.

Bala, Venkatesh, and Gerhard Sorger. 1998. "The Evolution of Human Capital in an Interacting Agent Economy." *Journal of Economic Behavior and Organization* 36:85–108.

Bala, Venkatesh, and Gerhard Sorger. 2001. "A Spatial-Temporal Model of Human Capital Accumulation." *Journal of Economic Theory* 96:153–179.

Ballester, Coralio, Antoni Calvó-Armengol, and Yves Zenou. 2006. "Who's Who in Networks. Wanted: the Key Player." *Econometrica* 74(5):1403–1417.

Barukhov, Eli, and Oded Hodaman. 1977. "Optimum and Market Equilibrium in a Model without a Predetermined Center." *Environment and Planning A* 9(8):849–856.

Batty, Michael. 2006. "Rank Clocks." *Nature* 444(30):592–596.

Baum-Snow, Nathaniel. 2007. "Did Highways Cause Suburbanization?" *Quarterly Journal of Economics* 122(2):775–805.

Baum-Snow, Nathaniel, and Ronni Pavan. 2011. "Understanding the City Size Wage Gap." Working paper, Brown University. *Review of Economic Studies*, forthcoming.

Bayer, Patrick, Fernando Vendramel Ferreira, and Robert McMillan. 2007a. "A Unified Framework for Measuring Preferences for Schools and Neighborhoods." *Journal of Political Economy* 115(4):588–638.

Bayer, Patrick, Fernando Vendramel Ferreira, and Robert McMillan. 2007b. "Tiebout Sorting, Social Multipliers and the Demand for School Quality." Working paper no. 10871, NBER.

Bayer, Patrick, and Robert McMillan. 2006. "Racial Sorting and Neighborhood Quality." NBER Working paper no. 11813, NBER.

Bayer, Patrick, Robert McMillan, and Kim Rueben. 2004a. "Residential Segregation in General Equilibrium." Working paper, Yale University, March.

Bayer, Patrick, Robert McMillan, and Kim Rueben. 2004b. "What Drives Racial Segregation? New Evidence Using Census Microdata." *Journal of Urban Economics* 56:514–535.

Bayer, Patrick, Robert McMillan and Kim Rueben. 2009. "An Equilibrium Model of Sorting in an Urban Housing Market." Working paper no. 10865, NBER.

Bayer, Patrick, and Stephen L. Ross. 2009. "Identifying Individual and Group Effects in the Presence of Sorting: A Neighborhood Effects Application." Working paper no. 12111, NBER.

Bayer, Patrick, Stephen L. Ross, and Giorgio Topa. 2008. "Place of Work and Place of Residence: Informal Hiring Networks and Labor Market Outcomes." *Journal of Political Economy* 116(6):1150–1196.

Bayer, Patrick, and Christopher Timmins. 2005. "On the Equilibrium Properties of Locational Sorting Models." *Journal of Urban Economics* 57(3):462–477.

Bayer, Patrick, and Christopher Timmins. 2007. "Estimating Equilibrium Models of Sorting across Locations." *Economic Journal* 117:353–374.

Bazhanov, Andrei, and John Hartwick. 2005. "Dispersed Interactions of Urban Residents." Working paper no. 766, Munich Personal RePEc archive. http://mpra.ub.uni-muenchen.de/766/

Becker, Gary S. 1974. "A Theory of Social Interactions." *Journal of Political Economy* 82: 1063–1093.

Beckmann, Martin J. 1976. "Spatial Equilibrium in the Dispersed City." In George Papageorgiou, J., ed., *Mathematical Land Use Theory*, 117–125. Lexington, MA: Lexington Books.

Beeson, Patricia E., and David N. DeJong. 2002. "Divergence." *Contributions to Macroeconomics* 2(1):art. 6.

Beeson, Patricia E., David N. DeJong, and Werner Troesken. 2001. "Population Growth in U.S. Counties 1840–1990." *Regional Science and Urban Economics* 31(6):669–999.

Behrens, Kristian, Giordano Mion, Yasusada Murata, and Jens Südekum. 2011. "Spatial Frictions." Discussion Paper no. 8572, CEPR.

Belluck, Pam. 2008. "Strangers May Cheer You Up, Study Says." *New York Times*, December 4. http://www.nytimes.com/2008/12/05/health/05happy-web.html?_r=3

Benabou, Roland. 1993. "Workings of a City: Location, Education, and Production." *Quarterly Journal of Economics* 108(3):619–652.

Benabou, Roland. 1996a. "Equity and Efficiency in Human Capital Investment: The Local Connection." *Review of Economic Studies* 63:237–264.

Benabou, Roland. 1996b. "Heterogeneity, Stratification and Growth: Macroeconomic Implications of Community Structure and School Finance." *American Economic Review* 86(3):584–609.

Benhabib, Jess, Alberto Bisin, and Matthew O. Jackson, eds., *Handbook of Social Economics*. New York: Elsevier North-Holland.

Bergsman, Joel, Peter Greenston, and Robert Healy. 1972. "The Agglomeration Process in Urban Growth." *Urban Studies* 9(3):263–288.

Berliant, Marcus, and Chia-Ming Yu. 2009. "Rational Expectations in Urban Economics." Working paper. Washington University, January. http://mpra.ub.uni-munchen.de/12709/

Berliant, Marcus, and Ping Wang. 2004. "Dynamic Urban Models: Agglomeration and Growth." In Pieter Nijkamp and Roberta Capello, eds., *Urban Dynamics and Growth: Advances in Urban Economics*. New York: Elsevier North-Holland.

Berman, Marc G., John Jonides, and Stephen Kaplan. 2008. "The Cognitive Benefits of Interacting with Nature." *Psychological Science* 19(12):1207–1212.

Berry, Christopher R., and Edward L. Glaeser. 2005. "The Divergence of Human Capital Levels across Cities." *Papers in Regional Science* 84(3):407–444.

Berry, Steven T. 1994. "Estimating Discrete-Choice Models of Product Differentiation." *RAND Journal of Economics* 25(2):242–262.

Berry, Steven T., James Levinsohn, and Ariel Pakes. 1995. "Automobile Prices in Market Equilibrium." *Econometrica* 63(4):841–890.

Berry, Steven T., James Levinsohn, and Ariel Pakes. 2004. "Differentiated Products Demand Systems from a Combination of Micro and Macro Data: The New Car Market." *Journal of Political Economy* 112(1):68–105.

Bertaud, Alain. 2004. "The Spatial Organization of Cities: Deliberate Outcome or Unforeseen Consequence?" http://alain-bertaud.com/images/AB_The_spatial_organization_of_cities_Version_3.pdf

Bertaud, Alain, and Bertrand Renaud. 1997. "Socialist Cities without Land Markets." *Journal of Urban Economics* 41:137–151.

Bertrand, Marianne, Erzo Luttmer, and Sendhil Mullainathan. 2000. "Network Interactions and Welfare Cultures." *Quarterly Journal of Economics* 115:1019–1055.

Bhat, Chandra R., and Jessica Guo. 2004. "A Mixed Spatially Correlated Logit Model: Formulation and Application to Residential Choice Modeling." *Transportation Research B* 38:147–168.

Bhatta, Saurav Dev, and José Lobo. 2000. "Human Capital and per Capita Product: A Comparison of U.S. States." *Papers in Regional Science* 79:393–411.

Bierlaire, Michel, Denis Bolduc, and Daniel McFadden (2003) "Characteristics of Generalized Extreme Value Distributions." March. http://roso.epfl.ch/mbi/papers/mcfadden0403.pdf

Binder, Michael, and M. Hashem Pesaran. 1997. "Multivariate Linear Rational Expectations Models: Characterization of the Nature of the Solutions and Their Fully Recursive Computation." *Econometric Theory* 13:877–888.

Binder, Michael, and M. Hashem Pesaran. 1998. "Decision Making in the Presence of Heterogeneous Information and Social Interactions." *International Economic Review* 39:1027–1052.

Binder, Michael, and M. Hashem Pesaran. 2001. "Life-cycle Consumption under Social Interactions." *Journal of Economic Dynamics and Control* 25:35–83.

Bisin, Alberto, Ulrich Horst, and Onur Özgür. 2004. "Rational Expectations Equilibria of Economies with Social Interactions." *Journal of Economic Theory* 127:74–116.

Bisin, Alberto, Andrea Moro, and Georgio Topa. 2011. "The Empirical Content of Models with Multiple Equilibria in Economies with Social Interactions." New York University, September.

Black, Sandra. 1999. "Do Better Schools Matter? Parental Valuation of Elementary Education." *Quarterly Journal of Economics* 114(2):577–599.

Black, Sandra, Paul J. Devereux, and Kjell G. Salvanes. 2004. "Why The Apple Doesn't Fall Far: Understanding the Integenerational Transmission of Human Capital." Working paper no. 10066, NBER October.

Black, Duncan, and J. Vernon Henderson. 1999a. "Spatial Evolution of Population and Industry in the United States." *American Economic Review* 89(2):323–327.

Black, Duncan, and J. Vernon Henderson. 1999b. "A Theory of Urban Growth." *Journal of Political Economy* 107(2):252–284.

Black, Duncan, and J. Vernon Henderson. 2003. "Urban Evolution in the USA." *Journal of Economic Geography* 3:343–372.

Blackley, Paul, and Jan Ondrich. 1988. "A Limiting Joint-Choice Model with Discrete and Continuous Housing Characteristics." *Review of Economics and Statistics* 70:266–274.

Blanchard, Olivier J., and Laurence F. Katz. 1992. "Regional Evolutions." *Brookings Papers on Economic Activity* 1:1–75.

Bleakley, Hoyt, and Jeffrey Lin. 2007. "Thick Market Effects and Churning in the Labor Market: Evidence from U.S. Cities." Working paper no. 07–23, Federal Reserve Bank of Philadelphia, October.

Blume, Laurence E. 1997. "Population Games." In W. Brain Arthur, Steven N. Durlauf, and David A. Lane, eds. *The Economy as an Evolving Complex System II*, 425–460. Reading, MA: Addison-Wesley.

Blume, Laurence E., William A. Brock, Steven N. Durlauf, and Yannis M. Ioannides. 2011. "Identification of Social Interactions." In Jess Benhabib, Alberto Bisin, and Matthew O. Jackson, eds., *Handbook of Social Economics*, 854–964. Amsterdam: Elsevier North-Holland.

Bogue, Donald J. 1953. *Population Growth in Standard Metropolitan Areas 1900–1950*. Oxford, OH: Scripps Foundation in Research in Population Problems.

Bonacich, Phillip 1987. "Power and Centrality: A Family of Measures." *American Journal of Sociology* 92(5):1170–1182.

Borjas, George J. 1992. "Ethnic Capital and Intergenerational Mobility." *Quarterly Journal of Economics* 107(1):123–150.

Borjas, George J. 1995. "Ethnicity, Neighborhoods, and Human Capital Externalities." *American Economic Review* 85(3):365–390.

Borjas, George J. 1998. "To Ghetto or Not to Ghetto: Ethnicity and Residential Segregation." *Journal of Urban Economics* 44:228–253.

Borjas, George J., Stephen G. Bronars, and Stephen J. Trejo. 1992. "Self-Selection and Internal Migration in the United States." *Journal of Urban Economics* 32:159–185.

Borukhov, Eli, and Oded Hochman. 1977. "Optimum and Market Equilibrium in a Model of a City without a Predetermined Center." *Environment and Planning A* 9:849–856.

Bosker, Maarten, Steven Brakman, Harry Garretsen and Marc Schramm. 2007. "Looking for Multiple Equilibria When Geography Matters." *Journal of Urban Economics* 61(1):152–169.

Bosker, Maarten, Steven Brakman, Harry Garretsen, and Marc Schramm. 2008. "A Century of Shocks: The Evolution of the German City Size Distribution 1925–1999." *Regional Science and Urban Economics* 38:330–347.

Bosker, Maarten, and Gerard Marlet. 2007. "Growth and Decline of European Cities in the 1990s." Discussion paper no. 06–18, Tjalling C. Koopmans Research Institute.

Boucher, Vincent, Yann Bramoullé, Habiba Djebbari, and Bernard Fortin. 2010. "Do Peers Affect Student Achievement? Evidence from Canada Using Group Size Variation." Working paper no. 2010s-08, CIRANO.

Bourguignon, François. 1979. "Decomposable Income Inequality Measures." *Econometrica* 47(4):901–920.

Brakman, Steven, Harry Garretsen, and Charles Van Marrewijk, 2001. *An Introduction to Geographical Economics*. Cambridge and New York: Cambridge University Press.

Brakman, Steven, Harry Garretsen, Charles Marrewijk, and Marianne Van der Berg. 1999. "The Return of Zipf: Towards a Further Understanding of the Rank-Size Rule." *Journal of Regional Science* 39:183–213.

Bramoullé, Yann, Habiba Djebbari, and Bernard Fortin. 2009. "Identification of Peer Effects through Social Networks." *Journal of Econometrics* 150(1):41–55.

Bramoullé, Yann, and Bernard Fortin. 2009. "The Econometrics of Social Networks." Working paper no. 09–13, CIRPÉE, Université Laval, April.

Brock, William A., and Steven N. Durlauf. 2001a. "Discrete Choice with Social Interactions." *Review of Economic Studies* 68:235–260.

Brock, William A., and Steven N. Durlauf. 2001b. "Interaction-Based Models." In James J. Heckman and Edward Leamer, eds., *Handbook of Econometrics*. Vol. 5, 3297–3380. Amsterdam: Elsevier North-Holland.

Brock, William A., and Steven N. Durlauf. 2002. "A Multinomial Choice Model with Neighborhood Effects." *American Economic Review* 92:298–303.

Brock, William A., and Steven N. Durlauf. 2006. "Multinomial Choice with Social Interactions." In Laurence E. Blume, and Steven N. Durlauf, eds., *The Economy as an Evolving Complex System*, Vol. III, 175–206. Oxford and New York: Oxford University Press.

Brock, William A., and Steven N. Durlauf. 2007. "Identification of Binary Choice Models with Social Interactions." *Journal of Econometrics* 140:52–75.

Brock, William A., and Steven N. Durlauf. 2010. "Social Interactions and Adoption Curves." *Journal of the European Economic Association* 8:232–251.

Brooks-Gunn, Jeanne, Greg J. Duncan, Pamela K. Klebanov, and N. Sealand. 1993. "Do Neighborhoods Affect Child and Adolescent Development?" *American Journal of Sociology* 99(2):353–395.

Brown, Jeffrey R., Zoran Ivkovich, Paul A. Smith, and Scott Weisbenner. 2007. "Neighbors Matter: Causal Community Effects and Stock Market Participation." Working paper no. 13168, NBER, June.

Bruch, Elizabeth E., and Robert D. Mare. 2006. "Neighborhood Choice and Neighborhood Change." *American Journal of Sociology* 112(3):667–709.

Brueckner, Jan K. 1987. "The Structure of Urban Equilibria: A Unified Treatment of the Muth–Mills Model." In Edwin S. Mills, ed., *Handbook of Regional and Urban Economics*, Vol. II, 821–845. Amsterdam and New York: Elsevier North-Holland.

Brueckner, Jan K. 1990. "Analyzing Third-World Urbanization: A Model with Empirical Evidence." *Economic Development and Cultural Change* 38(3):587–610.

Brueckner, Jan K. 1998. "Testing for Strategic Interaction among Local Governments: The Case of Growth Controls." *Journal of Urban Economics* 44:438–467.

Brueckner, Jan K. 2003. "Strategic Interaction among Governments: An Overview of Empirical Studies." *International Regional Science Review* 26(2):175–188.

Brueckner, Jan K., Jacques-François Thisse, and Yves Zenou. 1999. "Why Is Central Paris Rich and Downtown Detroit Poor? An Amenity-Based Theory." *European Economic Review* 43:91–107.

Brueckner, Jan K., Jacques-François Thisse, and Yves Zenou. 2002. "Local Labor Markets, Job Matching and Urban Location." *International Economic Review* 41(3):155–171.

Buchan, James. 2003. *Capital of the Mind: How Edinburgh Changed the World*. London: John Murray Publishers.

Burchfield, Marcia, Henry G. Overman, Diego Puga, and Matthew Turner. "The Determinants of Urban Sprawl: A Portrait from Space." *Quarterly Journal of Economics* 121(2):587–633.

Bureau of Economic Analysis, U.S. Department of Commerce. 2007. "Gross Domestic Product by Metropolitan Area." http://www.bea.gov/regional/gdpmetro/

Burke, Mary A. 2008. "Social Multipliers." In Steven N. Durlauf and Laurence E. Blume eds., *The New Palgrave Dictionary of Economics Online*. New York: Palgrave MacMillan.

Burke, Mary A., Gary Fournier, and Kislaya Prasad. 2010. "Geographical Variations in a Model of Physician Treatment Choice with Social Interactions." *Journal of Economic Behavior and Organization* 73:418–443.

Cabrales, Antonio, Antoni Calvó-Armengol, and Yves Zenou. 2011. "Social Interactions and Spillovers." *Games and Economic Behavior* 72:339–360.

Cairns, John F. 1997. *Matters of Life and Death: Perspectives on Public Health, Molecular Biology, Cancer, and the Prospects for the Human Race*. Princeton, NJ: Princeton University Press.

Calabrese, Stephen, Dennis Epple, Thomas Romer, and Holger Sieg. 2006. "Local Public Good Provision: Voting, Peer Effects, and Mobility." *Journal of Public Economics* 90:959–981.

Calvó-Armengol, Antoni, and Matthew O. Jackson. 2004. "The Effects of Social Networks on Employment and Inequality." *American Economic Review* 94(3):426–454.

Calvó-Armengol, Antoni, and Matthew O. Jackson. 2007. "Networks in Labor Markets: Wage and Employment Dynamics and Inequality." *Journal of Economic Theory* 132:27–46.

Calvó-Armengol, Antoni, Eleonora Patacchini, and Yves Zenou. 2009. "Peer Effects and Social Networks in Education." *Review of Economic Studies* 76: 1239–1267.

Calvó-Armengol, Antoni, and Yves Zenou. 2005. "Job Matching, Social Network and Word-of-Mouth Communication." *Journal of Urban Economics* 57(3): 500–522.

Canning, David, and Marianne Fay. 1993. "The Effects of Transportation Networks on Economic Growth." Working paper, Department of Economics, Columbia University. http://academiccommons.columbia.edu/item/ac:99886

Card, David, Alexandre Mas, and Jesse Rothstein. 2008a. "Tipping and the Dynamics of Segregation." *Quarterly Journal of Economics* 123(1): 177–218.

Card, David, Alexandre Mas, and Jesse Rothstein. 2008b. "Are Mixed Neighborhoods Always Unstable: Two-Sided and One-Sided Tipping." Working paper, Princeton Industrial Relations Section, July.

Carlino, Gerald A., and Satyajit Chatterjee. 2001. "Aggregate Metropolitan Employment Growth and the Deconcentration of Metropolitan Employment." *Journal of Monetary Economics* 48(3):549–583.

Carlino, Gerald A., and Satyajit Chatterjee. 2002. "Employment Deconcentration: A New Perspective on America's Postwar Urban Revolution." *Journal of Regional Science* 42:455–475.

Carlton, Dennis W. 1979. "Why Do New Firms Locate Where They Do? An Econometric Model." In William C. Wheaton, ed., *Interregional Movements and Regional Growth*. 13–50. Washington D.C.: The Urban Institute.

Carlton, Dennis W. 1983. "The Location and Employment Choices of New Firms: An Econometric Model with Discrete and Continuous Endogenous Variables." *Review of Economics and Statistics* 65(3):440–449.

Case, Anne C., Harvey S. Rosen, and James C. Hines. 1993. "Budget Spillovers and Fiscal Policy Interdependence: Evidence from the States." *Journal of Public Economics* 52(3):285–307.

Chari, Varadarajan. V., Patrick J. Kehoe, and Ellen McGrattan. 2007. "Business Cycle Accounting." *Econometrica* 75(3):781–836.

Charlot, Sylvie, and Gilles Duranton. 2004. "Communication Externalities in Cities." *Journal of Urban Economics* 56:581–613.

Chatterjee, Satyajit. 2006. "A Qualitative Assessment of the Role of Agglomeration Economies in the Spatial Concentration of U.S. Employment." Working paper no. 06–20, Research Department, Federal Reserve Bank of Philadelphia.

Chatterjee, Satyajit, and Gerald A. Carlino. 2001. "Aggregate Metropolitan Employment Growth and the Deconcentration of Metropolitan Employment." *Journal of Monetary Economics* 48(3):549–583.

Chen, Hsiao-Chi, James W. Friedman, and Jacques-François Thisse. 1997. "Boundedly Rational Nash Equilibrium: Probabilistic Choice Approach." *Games and Economic Behavior* 18:32–54.

Chen, Yu-chin, Noah Weisberger, and Edwin Wong. 2011. "Local Labor Markets and Increasing Returns to Scale: How Strong Is the Evidence?" Working paper, Department of Economics, University of Washington.

Chincarini, Ludwig, and Neer Asherie. 2008. "An Analytical Model for the Formation of Economic Clusters." *Regional Science and Urban Economics* 38:252–270.

Chipman, John S. 1970. "External Economies of Scale and Competitive Equilibrium." *Quarterly Journal of Economics* 84(3):347–385.

Christakis, Nicholas A., and James H. Fowler, J., 2007. "The Spread of Obesity in a Large Social Network over 32 Years." *New England Journal of Medicine* 357(4):370–379.

Christakis, Nicholas A., and James H. Fowler. 2008. "The Collective Dynamics of Smoking in a Large Social Network." *New England Journal of Medicine* 358:2249–2258.

Christakis, Nicholas A., and James H. Fowler. 2009. *Connected: The Surprising Power of Our Social Networks and How They Shape Our Lives*. New York: Little, Brown and Company.

Christakis, Nicholas A., and James H. Fowler. 2010. "Examining Dynamic Social Networks and Human Behavior." *Annals of Applied Statistics*, forthcoming.

Christakis, Nicholas A., and James H. Fowler. 2011. "Social Contagion Theory: Examining Dynamic Social Networks and Human Behavior." September, arxiv.org/ftp/arxiv/papers/1109.5235.pdf; *Statistics in Medicine*, forthcoming.

Christaller, Walter. 1933. *Die Zentralen Orte in Süddeutschland*. Jena: Gustav Fischer. Translated as *Central Places in Southern Germany* by Carlisle Baskin, 1966. Englewood Cliffs, NJ: Prentice Hall.

Ciccone, Antonio. 2002. "Agglomeration Effects in Europe." *European Economic Review* 46(2):213–227.

Ciccone, Antonio. 2008a. "Technology Diffusion and the Spatial Distribution of Wages in the U.S." Working paper 500, Department of Economics, Universita Pompeu Fabra, December.
Ciccone, Antonio. 2008b. "Urban Production Externalities." In Steven N. Durlauf and Laurence E. Blume, eds., *New Palgrave Dictionary of Economics Online*. New York: Palgrave Mcmillan.
Ciccone, Antonio, and Robert E. Hall. 1996. "Productivity and the Density of Economic Activity." *American Economic Review* 86:54–70.
Ciccone, Antonio, and Giovanni Peri. 2006. "Identifying Human-Capital Externalities: Theory with Applications." *Review of Economic Studies* 73:381–412.
Clampet-Lundquist, Susan, and Douglas S. Massey. 2008. "Neighborhood Effects on Economic Self-sufficiency: A reconsideration of the Moving to Opportunity Experiment." *American Journal of Sociology* 114(1):107–143.
Clement, Douglas. 2004. "Sets and the City: Urban Growth May Seem Chaotic, but Order Lies beneath." *The Region*. Federal Reserve Bank of Minneapolis, September.
Cliff, Andrew D., and J.K. Ord. 1981. *Spatial Processes, Models and Applications*. London: Pion.
Cohen-Cole, Ethan, and Jason M. Fletcher. 2008a. "Is Obesity Contagious? Social Networks versus Environmental Factors in the Obesity Epidemic." *Journal of Health Economics* 27(5):1382–1387.
Cohen-Cole, Ethan, and Jason M. Fletcher. 2008b. "Detecting Implausible Social Network Effects in Acne, Height, and Headaches: Longitudinal Analysis." *British Medical Journal* 337:2533.
Cohen-Cole, Ethan, Andrei Kirilenko, and Eleonora Patacchini. 2010. "Are Networks Priced? Network Topology and Order Trading Strategies in High Liquidity Markets." Working papers series 1011, Einaudi Institute for Economics and Finance.
Cohen-Cole, Ethan, and Giulio Zanella. 2008. "Welfare Stigma or Information Sharing? Decomposing Social Effects in Social Benefit Use." Working paper, Department of Economics, University of Siena, November.
Combes, Pierre-Philippe, Gilles Duranton, and Laurent Gobillon. 2008. "Spatial Wage Disparities: Sorting Matters." *Journal of Urban Economics* 63:723–742.
Combes, Pierre-Philippe, Gilles Duranton, Laurent Gobillon, and Sébastien Roux. 2010. "Estimating Agglomeration Economies with History, Geology, and Worker Effects." In Edward L. Glaeser, ed., *The Economics of Agglomeration*, 15–65. Chicago: University of Chicago Press.
Combes, Pierre-Philippe, Gilles Duranton, Laurent Gobillon, Diego Puga, and Sébastien Roux. 2009. "The Productivity Advantage of Large Cities: Distinguishing Agglomeration from Firm Selection." Discussion paper no.719, CEPR; *Econometrica*, forthcoming.
Conley, Timothy, and Georgio Topa. 2002. "Socio-Economic Distance and Spatial Patterns in Unemployment." *Journal of Applied Econometrics* 17(4):303–327.
Conley, Timothy G., and Christopher R. Udry. 2010. "Learning about a New Technology: Pineapple in Ghana." *American Economic Review* 100(1):35–69.
Coulson, N. Edward. 2006. "Measuring and Analyzing Urban Employment Fluctuations." In Richard Arnott and Daniel McMillen, eds., *Blackwell Companion to Urban Economics*, 460–478. Oxford: Blackwell Publishing.
Cox, D. R., and David V. Hinkley. 1974. *Theoretical Statistics*. London: Chapman and Hall.
Crihfield, John B., and Martin P.H. Panggabean. 1995. "Growth and Convergence in U.S. Cities." *Journal of Urban Economics* 38:136–165.

Crucitti, Paolo, Vito Latora, and Sergio Porta. 2006. "Centrality Measures in Spatial Networks of Urban Streets." *Physical Review E* 73:1–5.

Cuberes, David. 2009. "A Model of Sequential City Growth." *Berkeley Electronic Journal of Macroeconomics* 9(1):art. 18.

Cuberes, David. 2010. "Are Internet and Face-to-Face Contacts Complements or Substitutes? Some Cross-Country Evidence." Working paper, University of Alicante.

Cuberes, David. 2011. "Sequential City Growth: Empirical Evidence." *Journal of Urban Economics* 69:220–239.

Cunha, Flavio, and James J. Heckman. 2007. "The Technology of Skill Formation." *American Economic Review Papers and Proceedings* 97(2):31–47.

Cuñat, Alejandro, and Marc J. Melitz. 2011. "Volatility, Labor Market Flexibility, and the Pattern of Comparative Advantage." *Journal of the European Economic Association*, forthcoming.

Currid, Elizabeth. 2006. "New York as a Global Creative Hub: A Competitive Analysis of Four Theories on World Cities." *Economic Development Quarterly* 20(4): 330–350.

Currid, Elizabeth. 2007a. *The Warhol Economy: How Fashion, Art and Music Drive New York City*. Princeton, NJ: Princeton University Press.

Currid, Elizabeth. 2007b. "How Art and Culture Happen in New York." *Journal of the American Planning Association* 73(4):454–467.

Currid, Elizabeth, and James Connolly. 2008. "Patterns of Knowledge: The Geography of Advanced Services and the Case of Art and Culture." *Annals of the Association of American Geographers* 98(2):414–434.

Currid, Elizabeth, and Sarah Williams. 2010. "The Geography of Buzz: Art, Culture and the Social Milieu in Los Angeles and New York." *Journal of Economic Geography* 10(3):423–451.

Cutler, David, and Grant Miller. 2005. "The Role of Public Health Improvements in Health Advances." *Demography* 42(1):1–22.

Cvetković, Dragoš M., Michael Doob, and Horst Sachs. 1995. *Spectra of Graphs: Theory and Applications*, 3rd ed. Heidelberg: Johann Ambrosius Barth Verlag.

da Mata, Daniel D., Uwe Deichmann, J. Vernon Henderson, Somik V. Lall, and Hyoung G. Wang. 2007. "Determinants of City Growth in Brazil." *Journal of Urban Economics* 62(2):252–272.

Davezies, Laurent, Xavier d' Haultfoeuille, and Denis Fougère. 2009. "Identification of Peer Effects Using Group Size Variation." *Econometrics Journal* 12:397–413.

Davis, Donald R. 1998. "Does Unemployment in Europe Prop up American Wages? National Labor Markets and Global Trade." *American Economic Review* 88(3):478–494.

Davis, Donald R., and David E. Weinstein. 2002. "Bones, Bombs, and Break Points: The Geography of Economic Activity." *American Economic Review* 92(5):1269–1289.

Davis, Morris A., Jonas D.M. Fisher, and Toni M. Whited. 2009. "Agglomeration and Productivity: New Estimates and Macroeconomic Implications." Working paper, University of Wisconsin, August.

De Vries, Jan. 1984. *European Urbanization: 1500–1800*. Cambridge, MA: Harvard University Press.

Debreu, Gerard, and Israel. N. Herstein. 1953. "Nonnegative Square Matrices." *Econometrica* 21(4):597–607.

Decker, Ethan H., Andrew J. Kerkhoff, and Melanie E. Moses. 2007. "Global Patterns of City Size Distributions and Their Fundamental Drivers." *Public Library of Science ONE* 9:e934.

DeMarzo, Peter M., Dimitri Vayanos, and Jeffrey Zwiebel. 2003. "Persuasion Bias, Social Influence, and Uni-Dimensional Opinions." *Quarterly Journal of Economics* 118:909–968.

Desmet, Klaus, and Esteban Rossi-Hansberg. 2009. "Spatial Development." Working paper, Princeton University, September.

Desmet, Klaus, and Esteban Rossi-Hansberg. 2010. "On Spatial Dynamics." *Journal of Regional Science* 50(1): 43–63.

Desmet, Klaus, and Esteban Rossi-Hansberg. 2011. "Urban Accounting and Welfare." Working paper, Department of Economics. Princeton University, March.

Devereux, Michael, Rachel Griffith, and Helen Simpson. 2004. "The Geographic Distribution of Production Activity in the U.K." *Regional Science and Urban Economics* 34(5):533–564.

Diamond, Charles A., and Curtis J. Simon. 1990. "Industrial Specialization and the Returns to Labor." *Journal of Labor Economics* 8(2):175–201.

Diamond, Jared. 1997. *Guns, Germs and Steel: The Fates of Human Societies*. New York: W.W. Norton.

Dinopoulos, Elias, and Peter Thompson. 2000. "Endogenous Growth in a Cross-Section of Countries." *Journal of International Economics* 51(2):335–362.

Dittmar, Jeremiah. 2008. "Cities, Institutions, and Growth: The Emergence of Zipf's Law." Working paper, Department of Economics, University of California, Berkeley, November.

Dixit, Avinash K. 1973. "The Optimum Factory Town." *The Bell Journal of Economics and Management Science* 4(2):637–651.

Dixit, Avinash K., and Joseph E. Stiglitz. 1977. "Monopolistic Competition and Optimum Product Diversity." *American Economic Review* 67(3):297–308.

Dobkins, Linda H., and Yannis M. Ioannides. 2000. "Dynamic Evolution of the U.S. City Size Distribution." In Jean-Marie Huriot and Jacques-François Thisse, eds., *The Economics of Cities*, 217–260. Cambridge: Cambridge University Press.

Dobkins, Linda H., and Yannis M. Ioannides. 2001. "Spatial Interactions among U.S. Cities." *Regional Science and Urban Economics* 31(6):701–731.

Dodds, Peter Sheridan, Roby Muhamad, and Duncan J. Watts. 2003. "An Experimental Study of Search in Global Social Networks." *Science* 301:827–829.

Dokumaci, Emin, and William J. Sandholm. 2007. "Schelling Redux: An Evolutionary Dynamic Model of Residential Segregation." Working paper, University of Wisconsin.

Donaldson, Dave. 2008. "Railroads of the Raj: Estimating the Impact of Transportation Infrastructure." Working paper, Department of Economics, MIT, November.

Dornbusch, Rudi, Stanley Fischer, and Paul A. Samuelson. 1977. "Comparative Advantage, Trade, and Payments in a Ricardian Model with a Continuum of Goods." *American Economic Review* 67(5):823–839.

Dougherty, Peter J. 2002. *Who Is Afraid of Adam Smith? How The Market Got Its Soul!* New York: John Wiley and Sons.

Doxiadis, Constantinos A. 1970. "Ekistics: the Science of Human Settlements." *Science* 170:393–404.

Drewianka, Scott. 2003. "Estimating Social Effects in Matching Markets: Externalities in Spousal Search." *Review of Economics and Statistics* 85:408–423.

Dubin, Jeffrey A. 1985. "Conditional Moments in the Generalized Extreme Value Family." App. B, In Jeffrey A. Dubin, ed., *Consumer Durables Choice and the Demand for Electricity*, 217–254. Amsterdam: Elsevier North-Holland. http://www.pacificeconomicsgroup.com/jad/Books/2041append%20b.pdf

Dubin, Jeffrey A., and Daniel L. McFadden. 1984. "An Econometric Analysis of Residential Electrical Appliance Holdings and Consumption." *Econometrica* 52:345–362.

Duffy, John, and Chris Papageorgiou. 2000. "The Specification of the Aggregate Production Function: a Cross-Country Empirical Investigation." *Journal of Economic Growth* 5:83–116.

Dujardin, Claire, Dominque Peeters, and Isabelle Thomas. 2009. "Neighborhood Effects and Endogeneity Issues." Discussion paper no. 56, CORE, Louvain-la-Neuve, Belgium.

Dumais, Guy, Glenn Ellison, and Edward L. Glaeser. 2002. "Geographic Concentration as a Dynamic Process." *Review of Economics and Statistics* LXXXIV:2, May, 193–204.

Duranton, Gilles. 2007. "Urban Evolutions: The Fast, the Slow, and the Still." *American Economic Review* 97(1):197–221.

Duranton, Gilles, Laurent Gobillon, and Henry G. Overman. 2011. "Assessing the Effects of Local Taxation Using Microgeographic Data." *Economic Journal* 121:1017–1046.

Duranton, Gilles, and Hubert Jayet. 2011. "Is the Division of Labour Limited by the Extent of the Market? Evidence from French Cities." *Journal of Urban Economics* 69(1):56–71.

Duranton, Gilles, Peter Morrow, and Matthew Turner. 2011. "Roads and Trade: Evidence from the U.S." Working paper, University of Toronto, July.

Duranton, Gilles, and Henry G. Overman. 2005. "Testing for Localization Using Micro-Geographic Data." *Review of Economic Studies* 72:1077–1106.

Duranton, Gilles, and Henry G. Overman. 2008. "Exploring the Detailed Location Patterns of U.K. Manufacturing Industries Using Microgeographic Data." *Journal of Regional Science* 48(1):313–343.

Duranton, Gilles, and Diego Puga. 2000. "Diversity and Specialisation in Cities: Why, Where and When Does It Matter?" *Urban Studies* 37(3):533–555.

Duranton, Gilles, and Diego Puga. 2001. "Nursery Cities: Urban Diversity, Process Innovation, and the Life Cycle of Products." *American Economic Review* 91(5):1454–1477.

Duranton, Gilles, and Diego Puga. 2004. "Micro-Foundations of Urban Agglomeration Economies." In J. Vernon Henderson and Jacques-François Thisse, eds., *Handbook of Regional and Urban Economics*. Vol. 4, *Cities and Geography*, chap. 48, 2063–2117. Amsterdam: Elsevier North-Holland.

Duranton, Gilles, and Diego Puga. 2005. "From Sectoral to Functional Urban Specialization." *Journal of Urban Economics* 57(2): 343–370.

Duranton, Gilles, and Matthew A. Turner. 2010. "Urban Growth and Transportation." Working paper, Department of Economics, University of Toronto, November 25. Revised 2011.

Duranton, Gilles, and Matthew A. Turner. 2011. "The Fundamental Law of Highway Congestion: Evidence from the U.S." *American Economic Review*, 101(6):2616–2652.

Durlauf, Steven N. 1996. "Neighborhood Feedbacks, Endogenous Stratification, and Income Inequality." In William Barnett, et al., eds., *Dynamic Disequilibrium Modelling*. Cambridge: Cambridge University Press.

Durlauf, Steven N. 2004. "Neighborhood Effects." In J. Vernon Henderson and Jacques-François Thisse, eds., *Handbook of Urban and Regional Economics*. Vol. 4, *Cities and Geography*, 2173–2242. Amsterdam: Elsevier North-Holland.

Durlauf, Steven N., and Yannis M. Ioannides. 2010. "Social Interactions." *Annual Review of Economics* 2:451–478.

Dutt, Pushan, Devashish Mitra, and Priya Ranjan. 2009. "International Trade and Unemployment: Theory and Cross-national Evidence." *Journal of International Economics* 78(1):32–44.

Easterly, William. 2009. "Empirics of Strategic Interdependence: The Case of the Racial Tipping Point." *Berkeley Electronic Journal of Macroeconomics: Contributions.* 9(1):art. 25.

Eaton, Jonathan, and Zvi Eckstein. 1997. "Cities and Growth: Theory and Evidence from France and Japan." *Regional Science and Urban Economics* 27:443–474.

Echenique, Federico, and Roland G. Fryer, Jr. 2007. "A Measure of Segregation Based on Social Interactions." *Quarterly Journal of Economics* 122(2):441–485.

Eeckhout, Jan E. 2004. "Gibrat's Law for (All) Cities." *American Economic Review* 94:1429–1451.

Eeckhout, Jan. 2009. "Gibrat's Law for (All) Cities: Reply." *American Economic Review* 99(4):1676–1683.

Ekeland, Ivar, James J. Heckman, and Lars Nesheim. 2002. "Identifying Hedonic Models." *American Economic Review, Papers and Proceedings* 92(2):304–309.

Ekeland, Ivar, James J. Heckman, and Lars Nesheim. 2004. "Identification and Estimation of Hedonic Models." *Journal of Political Economy* 112(1):S60–S109.

Ellickson, Bryan. 1971. "Jurisdictional Fragmentation and Residential Choice." *American Economic Review* 61:334–339.

Ellickson, Bryan. 1981. "An Alternative Test of the Hedonic Theory of Housing Markets." *Journal of Urban Economics* 9:56–79.

Ellickson, Bryan, and William Zame. 2005. "A Competitive Model of Economic Geography." *Economic Theory* 25(1):89–103.

Ellison, Glenn, and Edward L. Glaeser. 1997. "Geographic Concentration in U.S. Manufacturing Industries: A Dartboard Approach." *Journal of Political Economy* 105(5):889–927.

Ellison, Glenn, and Edward L. Glaeser. 1999. "The Geographic Concentration of Industry: Does Natural Advantage Explain Agglomeration?" *American Economic Review* 89(2):311–316.

Ellison, Glenn, Edward L. Glaeser, and William Kerr. 2007. "What Causes Industry Agglomeration? Evidence from Coagglomeration Patterns." Working paper no. 13068, NBER, April.

Epple, Dennis, Radu Filimon, and Thomas Romer. 1984. "Equilibrium among Local Jurisdictions: Toward an Integrated Treatment of Voting and Residential Choices." *Journal of Public Economics* 24(3):281–304.

Epple, Dennis, Brett Gordon, and Holger Sieg. 2010a. "A New Approach to Estimating the Production for Housing." *American Economic Review* 100(3):905–924.

Epple, Dennis, Brett Gordon, and Holger Sieg. 2010b. "Integrating Location-Specific Amenities into Multi-Community Equilibrium Models." *Journal of Regional Science* 50(1):381–400.

Epple, Dennis, Michael Peress, and Holger Sieg. 2007. "Household Sorting and Neighborhood Formation." Working paper, Department of Economics, Carnegie Mellon University, December.

Epple, Dennis, Michael Peress, and Holger Sieg. 2010. "Identification and Semiparametric Estimation of Equilibrium Models of Local Jurisdictions." *American Economic Journal: Microeconomics* 2(4): 195–220.

Epple, Dennis, and Glenn J. Platt. 1998. "Equilibrium and Local Redistribution in an Urban Economy when Households Differ in Both Preferences and Income." *Journal of Urban Economics* 43:23–51.

Epple, Dennis, and Richard Romano. 1998. "Competition between Private and Public Schools and Peer Group Effects." *American Economic Review* 88(1):33–62.

Epple, Dennis, Richard Romano, and Holger Sieg. 2009. "Life Cycle Dynamics within Metropolitan Communities." Working paper, Carnegie Mellon University, April 28.

Epple, Dennis, and Thomas Romer. 1990. "Mobility and Redistribution." *Journal of Political Economy* 99(4):828–858.

Epple, Dennis, Thomas Romer, and Holger Sieg. 2001. "Interjurisdictional Sorting and Majority Rule: an Empirical Analysis." *Econometrica* 69(6):1437–1465.

Epple, Dennis, and Holger Sieg. 1999. "Estimating Equilibrium Models of Local Jurisdictions." *Journal of Political Economy* 107:645–681.

Erdös, Paul, and Alfred Renyi. 1959. "On Random Graphs I." *Publicationes Mathematicae Debrecen*, 6:290–297.

Erdös, Paul, and Alfred Renyi. 1960. "On the Evolution of Random Graphs." *Publications of the Mathematical Institute of the Hungarian Academy of Sciences* 5:17–61.

Ethier, Wilfred J. 1982. "National and International Returns to Scale in the Modern Theory of International Trade." *American Economic Review* 72(3):389–405.

Falk, Armin, Urs Fischbacher, and Simon Gächter. 2009. "Living in Two Neighborhoods: Social Interactions in the Lab." Working paper, University of Zurich.

Fisher, Ronald A., and Leonard H. C. Tippett. 1928. "Limiting Forms of the Frequency Distribution of the Largest or Smallest Member of a Sample." *Proceedings of the Cambridge Philosophical Society, Mathematical and Physical Sciences* 24:180–190.

Florida, Richard. 2002. *The Rise of the Creative Class: And How It's Transforming Work, Leisure, Community and Everyday Life*. New York: Basic Books.

Fox, Jeremy T. 2007. "Semiparametric Estimation of Multinomial Discrete-Choice Models Using a Subset of Choices." *RAND Journal of Economics* 38(4):1002–1019.

Fowler, James H., and Nicholas A. Christakis. 2008a. "Estimating Peer Effects on Health in Social Networks: A Response to Cohen-Cole and Fletcher; and Trogdon, Nonnemaker, and Pais." *Journal of Health Economics* 27(5):1400–1405.

Fowler, James H., and Nicholas A. Christakis. 2008b. "Dynamic Spread of Happiness in a Large Social Network: Longitudinal Analysis over 20 Years in the Framingham Heart Study." *British Medical Journal* 337.

Fryer, Roland G., and Paul Torelli. 2010. "An Empirical Analysis of 'Acting White.'" *Journal of Public Economics* 94(5–6):380–396.

Fujita, Masahisa. 1978. *Spatial Development Planning: A Dynamic Convex Programming Approach*. Amsterdam: North-Holland.

Fujita, Masahisa. 1988. "A Monopolistic Competition Model of Spatial Agglomerations: Differentiated Product Approach." *Regional Science and Urban Economics* 18:87–124.

Fujita, Masahisa. 1989. *Urban Economic Theory: Land Use and City Size*. Cambridge: Cambridge University Press.

Fujita, Masahisa, Paul Krugman, and Tomoya Mori. 1998. "On the Evolution of Hierarchical Urban Systems." *European Economic Review* 43:209–251.

Fujita, Masahisa, Paul Krugman, and Anthony J. Venables. 1999. *The Spatial Economy: Cities, Regions and International Trade*. Cambridge, MA: MIT Press.

Fujita, Masahisa, and Tomoya Mori. 1997. "Structural Stability and Evolution of Urban Systems." *Regional Science and Urban Economics* 27:399–442.

Fujita, Masahisa, Tomoya Mori, J. Vernon Henderson, and Yoshitsugu Kanemoto. 2004. "Spatial Distribution of Economic Activities in Japan and China." In J. Vernon Henderson, and Jacques-François Thisse, eds., *Handbook of Regional and*

Urban Economics. Vol. 4, *Cities and Geography*, 2911–2977. Amsterdam: Elsevier North-Holland.

Fujita, Masahisa, and Hideaki Ogawa. 1982. "Multiple Equilibria and Structural Transition of Nonmonocentric Urban Configurations." *Regional Science and Urban Economics* 12:161–196.

Fujita, Masahisa, and Tony E. Smith. 1990. "Additive-Interaction Models of Spatial Agglomeration." *Journal of Regional Science* 30(1):51–74.

Fujita, Masahisa, and Jacques-François Thisse. 2002. *Economics of Agglomeration*. Cambridge and New York: Cambridge University Press.

Fujita, Masahisa, and Jacques-François Thisse. 2009. "New Economic Geography: An Appraisal on the Occasion of Paul Krugman's 2008 Nobel Prize in Economic Sciences." *Regional Science and Urban Economics* 39:109–119.

Gabaix, Xavier. 1999a. "Zipf's Law and the Growth of Cities." *American Economic Review Papers and Proceedings* 89(2):129–132.

Gabaix, Xavier. 1999b. "Zipf's Law for Cities: An Explanation." *Quarterly Journal of Economics* 114:739-767.

Gabaix, Xavier. 2009. "Power Laws in Economics and Finance." *Annual Reviews of Economics* 1:255–294.

Gabaix, Xavier, and Rustam Ibragimov. 2011. "Rank $-1/2$: A Simple Way to Improve the OLS Estimation of Tail Exponents." *Journal of Business Economics and Statistics* 29(1):24–39.

Gabaix, Xavier, and Yannis M. Ioannides. 2004. "The Evolution of City Size Distributions." In J. Vernon Henderson and Jacques François Thisse, eds., *Handbook of Urban and Regional Economics*. Vol. 4: *Cities and Geography*, 2341–2378. Amsterdam: Elsevier North-Holland.

Gabriel, Stuart A., and Stuart S. Rosenthal. 2004. "Quality of the Business Environment versus Quality of Life: Do Firms and Households Like the Same Cities?" *Review of Economics and Statistics* 86(1):438–444.

Galambos, Janos. 1987. *The Asymptotic Theory of Extreme Order Statistics*. New York: John Wiley and Sons.

Galeotti, Andrea, Sanjeev Goyal, Matthew O. Jackson, Fernando Vega-Redondo, and Leeat Yariv. 2010. "Network Games." *Review of Economic Studies* 77:218–244.

Galster, George 2001. "On the Nature of Neighbourhood." *Urban Studies* 38(12): 2111–2124.

Gan, Li, and Qi Li. 2004. "Efficiency of Thin and Thick Markets." Working paper no. 10815, NBER.

Gan, Li, and Quinghua Zhang. 2006. "The Thick Market Effect on Local Employment Rate Fluctuations." *Journal of Econometrics* 133(1):127–152.

Gans, Herbert J. 1968. *People and Plans*. New York: Basic Books.

Garreau, Joel. 1991. *Edge City*. New York: Doubleday.

Gaspar, Jess, and Edward L. Glaeser. 1998. "Information Technology and the Future of Cities." *Journal of Urban Economics* 43(1):136–156.

Ghiglino, Christian, and Sanjeev Goyal. 2010. "Keeping up with the Neighbours: Social Interaction in a Market Economy." *Journal of the European Economic Association* 8(1):90–119.

Giesen, Kristian, Arndt Zimmermann, and Jens Suedekum. 2010. "The Size Distribution across All Cities—Double Pareto Lognormal Strikes." *Journal of Urban Economics* 68(2):129–137.

Gladwell, Malcolm. 1999. "Six Degrees of Lois Weisberg." *The New Yorker*, January 11.

Glaeser, Edward L. 2000. "The Future of Urban Research: Non-market Interactions." *Brookings–Wharton Papers on Urban Affairs* 1:101–150.

Glaeser, Edward L. 2008. *Cities, Agglomeration and Spatial Equilibrium*. Oxford: Oxford University Press.

Glaeser, Edward L., and Joshua D. Gottlieb. 2009. "The Wealth of Cities: Agglomeration Economies and Spatial Equilibrium in the United States." *Journal of Economic Literature* 47(4):983–1028.

Glaeser Edward L., and Joseph Gyourko. 2005. "Urban Decline and Durable Housing." *Journal of Political Economy* 113(2):345–375.

Glaeser, Edward L., and Matthew E. Kahn. 2001. "Decentralized Employment and the Transformation of the American City." *Brookings–Wharton Papers on Urban Affairs* 2:1–63.

Glaeser, Edward L., and Matthew E. Kahn. 2004. "Sprawl and Urban Growth." In J. Vernon, Henderson and Jacques-François Thisse, eds., *Handbook of Regional and Urban Economics*, Vol. 4, *Cities and Geography*, 2481–2527. Amsterdam: North-Holland.

Glaeser, Edward L., and Matthew E. Kahn. 2008. "Why Do the Poor Live in Cities? The Role of Public Transportation." *Journal of Urban Economics* 63:1–24.

Glaeser, Edward L., and Janet E. Kohlhase. 2004. "Cities, Regions and the Decline of Transport Costs." *Papers in Regional Science* 83(1):197–228.

Glaeser, Edward L., and David C. Maré. 2001. "Cities and Skills." *Journal of Labor Economics* 19:316–342.

Glaeser, Edward L., Bruce I. Sacerdote, and José A. Scheinkman. 2003. "The Social Multiplier." *Journal of the European Economic Association* 1:345–353.

Glaeser, Edward L., and José A. Scheinkman. 2001. "Measuring Social Interactions." In Steven N. Durlauf and H. Peyton Young, eds., *Social Dynamics.*, chap. 4, 82–131. Cambridge, MA: MIT Press.

Glaeser Edward L., José A. Scheinkman, and Andrei Shleifer. 1995. "Economic Growth in a Cross-section of Cities." *Journal of Monetary Economics* 36:117–143.

Gnedenko, Boris V. 1943. "Sur la Distribution Limite du Terme Maximum d'une Serie Aleatoire." *Annals of Mathematics* 44:423–453.

González, Marta, César A. Hidalgo, and Albert-László Barabási. 2008. "Understanding Individual Human Mobility Patterns." *Nature* 453(5):778–782.

González-Val, Rafael, Luis Lanaspa, and Fernando Sanz. 2008. "New Evidence on Gibrat's Law for Cities." Working paper no. 10411, MPRA, September.

González-Val, Rafael, and Marcos Sanso-Navarro. 2008. "Gibrat's Law for Countries." Working paper no. 9733, MPRA, July.

Gould, Eric D. 2007. "Cities, Workers, and Wages: a Structural Analysis of the Urban Wage Premium." *Review of Economic Studies* 74:477–506.

Goux, Dominique, and Eric Maurin. 2007. "Close Neighbors Matter: Neighborhood Effects on Early Performance at School." *Economic Journal* 117:1193-1215.

Goyal, Sanjeev. 2005. "Strong and Weak Ties." *Journal of the European Economic Association* 3:608–616.

Goyal, Sanjeev. 2009. *Connections: An Introduction to the Economics of Networks*. Princeton, NJ: Princeton University Press.

Goyal, Sanjeev, and Fernando Vega-Redondo. 2007. "Structural Holes in Social Networks." *Journal of Economic Theory* 137(1):460–492.

Graham, Bryan S. 2008a. "Identifying Social Interactions through Conditional Variance Restrictions." *Econometrica* 76(3):643–660.

Graham, Bryan S. 2008b. "On the Identification of Neighborhood Externalities in the Presence of Endogenous Neighborhood Selection." Working paper, Department of Economics, University of California Berkeley, June 26.

Greenstone, Michael, Richard Hornbeck, and Enrico Moretti. 2010. "Identifying Agglomeration Spillovers: Evidence from Winners and Losers of Large Plant Openings." *Journal of Political Economy* 118(3):536–598.

Griffith, Rachel. 1999. "Using the ARD Establishment Level Data: An Application to Estimating Production Functions." *Economic Journal* 109(456): F416–F442.

Grinblatt, Mark, Matti Keloharju, and Seppo Ikaheimo. 2004. "Interpersonal Effects in Consumption: Evidence from the Automobile Purchases of Neighbors." Working paper no. 10226, NBER, January.

Grossman, Gene M., and Elhanan Helpman. 1991. "Quality Ladders in the Theory of Growth." *Review of Economic Studies* 58(1):43–61.

Grossman, Gene M., and Esteban Rossi-Hansberg. 2010. "External Economies and International Trade Redux." *Quarterly Journal of Economics* 125(2):829–858.

Guimarães, Paulo, Octávio Figuerdio, and Douglas Woodward. 2003. "A Tractable Approach to the Firm Location Decision Problem." *Review of Economics and Statistics* 85(1):201–204.

Guimarães, Paulo, and Richard Lindrooth. 2005. "Dirichlet-Multinomial Regression." Working paper, Department of Biostatistics, Medical University of South Carolina, August.

Gyourko, Joseph, Christopher Mayer, and Todd Sinai. 2006. "Superstar Cities." Working paper no. 12355, NBER, July.

Hadar, Yossi, and David Pines. 2004. "Population Growth and Its Distribution between Cities: Positive and Normative Aspects." *Regional Science and Urban Economics* 34:125–154.

Hall, Robert E., and Charles I. Jones. 1999. "Why Do Some Countries Produce So Much More Output per Worker Than Others?" *Quarterly Journal of Economics* 114(1):83–116.

Hanson, Gordon H. 2005. "Market Potential, Increasing Returns and Geographic Concentration." *Journal of International Economics* 67:1–24.

Hardman, Anna M., and Yannis M. Ioannides. 2004. "Neighbors' Income Distribution: Economic Segregation and Mixing in U.S. Urban Neighborhoods." *Journal of Housing Economics* 13:368–382.

Harris, Chauncy D. 1954. "The Market as a Factor in the Localization of Industry in the United States." *Annals of the Association of American Geographers* 44:315–348.

Harrison, J. Michael. 1990. *Brownian Motion and Stochastic Flow Systems*. Malabar, FL: Kreiger Publishing.

Head, Keith, and Thierry Mayer. 2004a. "The Empirics of Agglomeration and Trade." In J. Vernon Henderson, and Jacques-François Thisse, eds., *Handbook of Regional and Urban Economics*. Vol. 4, *Cities and Geography*, 2609–2669. Amsterdam: Elsevier North-Holland.

Head, Keith, and Thierry Mayer. 2004b. "Market Potential and the Location of Japanese Investment in the European Union." *Review of Economics and Statistics* 86:959–972.

Head, Keith, and Thierry Mayer. 2008. "Detection of Social Interactions from the Spatial Patterns of Names in France." *Journal of Regional Science* 48(1):67–95.

Head, Keith, and Thierry Mayer. 2011. "Gravity, Market Potential and Economic Development." *Journal of Economic Geography* 11(2):281–294.

Heckman, James J. 1979. "Sample Selection Bias as a Specification Error." *Econometrica* 47:153–161.

Heckman, James J. 2007. "The Technology and Neuroscience of Capacity Formation." *Proceedings of the National Academy of Sciences* 104(33):13250–13255.

Heckman, James J., Rosa L. Matzkin, and Lars Nesheim. 2009. "Nonparametric Identification and Estimation of Nonadditive Hedonic Models." Discussion paper no. 4329, IZA.

Helpman, Elhanan. 1998. "The Size of Regions." In David Pines, Efraim Sadka, and Itzak Zilcha, eds., *Topics in Public Economics*, 33–54. Cambridge: Cambridge University Press.

Helpman, Elhanan, and Oleg Itskhoki. 2010. "Labor Market Rigidities, Trade and Unemployment." *Review of Economic Studies* 77(3):1100–1137.

Helpman, Elhanan, and Paul Krugman 1985. *Market Structure and Foreign Trade*. Cambridge, MA: MIT Press.

Helsley, Robert W., and William C. Strange. 1990. "Matching and Agglomeration Economies in a System of Cities." *Regional Science and Urban Economics* 20(2):189–212.

Helsley, Robert W., and William C. Strange. 2004. "Knowledge Barter in Cities." *Journal of Urban Economics* 56:327–345.

Helsley, Robert W., and William C. Strange. 2007. "Urban Interactions and Spatial Structure." *Journal of Economic Geography* 7:119–138.

Henderson, J. Vernon. 1974. "The Size and Types of Cities." *American Economic Review* 64(4): 640–656.

Henderson, J. Vernon. 1977a. "Externalities in a Spatial Context." *Journal of Public Economics* 7:89–110.

Henderson, J. Vernon. 1977b. *Economic Theory and the Cities*. New York: Academic Press. 2nd edition, 1985.

Henderson, J. Vernon. 1983. "Industrial Bases and City Sizes." *American Economic Review* 73(2): 164–168.

Henderson, J. Vernon. 1987. "Systems of Cities and Inter-City Trade." In Pierre Hansen, Martin Labbé, Dominique Peeters, Jacques-François Thisse, and J. Vernon Henderson, eds., *Systems of Cities and Facility Location*, 71–119. Chur, Switzerland: Harwood Academic Publishers.

Henderson, J. Vernon. 1988. *Urban Development: Theory, Fact, Illusion*. Oxford: Oxford University Press.

Henderson, J. Vernon. 1994. "Where Does an Industry Locate?" *Journal of Urban Economics* 35:83–104.

Henderson, J. Vernon. 2000. "Comment on Glaeser (2000). 'The Future of Urban Research: Non-market Interactions.'" *Brookings–Wharton Papers on Urban Affairs* 2000:139–146.

Henderson, J. Vernon. 2003. "Marshall's Scale Economies." *Journal of Urban Economics* 53:1–28.

Henderson J. Vernon 2005. "Urbanization and Growth." In Philippe Aghion and Steven N. Durlauf, eds., *Handbook of Economic Growth*, Chap. 24, 1543–1591. Amsterdam: Elsevier North-Holland.

Henderson, J. Vernon, and Yannis M. Ioannides. 1981. "Aspects of Growth in a System of Cities." *Journal of Urban Economics* 10:117–139.

Henderson, J. Vernon, Ari Kuncoro, and Matt Turner. 1995. "Industrial Development in Cities." *Journal of Political Economy* 103(5):1067–1090.

Henderson, J. Vernon, Peter Mieszkowski, and Yvon Sauvageau. 1978. "Peer Group Effects and Educational Production Functions." *Journal of Public Economics* 10:97–106.

Henderson, J. Vernon, Adam Storeygard, and David N. Weil. 2011. "Measuring Economic Growth from Outer Space." *American Economic Review*, forthcoming.

Henderson, J. Vernon, and Jacques-François Thisse, eds. 2004. *Handbook of Regional and Urban Economics* Vol. 4, *Cities and Geography*. Amsterdam: Elsevier North-Holland.

Henderson, J. Vernon, and Anthony J. Venables. 2009. "The Dynamics of City Formation." *Review of Economic Dynamics* 12:233–254.

Henderson, J. Vernon, and Hyoung G. Wang. 2007. "Urbanization and City Growth: The Role of Institutions." *Regional Science and Urban Economics* 37(3):283–313.

Hicks, John R. 1970. *A Theory of Economic History*. Oxford: Clarendon Press.

Hohenberg, Paul M. 2004. "The Historical Geography of European Cities: An Interpretive Essay." In J. Vernon Henderson and Jacques François Thisse, eds., *Handbook of Urban and Regional Economics*. Vol. 4, *Cities and Geography*. Amsterdam: Elsevier North-Holland.

Holmes, Thomas J. 1998. "The Effect of State Policies on the Location of Manufacturing: Evidence from State Borders." *Journal of Political Economy* 106(4):667–705.

Holmes, Thomas J. 1999. "Scale of Local Production and City Size." *American Economic Review Papers and Proceedings* 89(2):317–320.

Holmes, Thomas J. 2002. "Geographic Concentration and Establishment Scale." *Review of Economics and Statistics* 84:682–690.

Holmes, Thomas J. 2004. "Step-by-Step Migrations." *Review of Economic Dynamics* 7:52–68.

Holmes, Thomas J., and Wen-Tai Hsu. 2008. "Optimal City Hierarchy: A Dynamic Programming Approach to Central Place Theory." Working paper, Department of Economics, Chinese University of Hong Kong, December.

Holmes, Thomas J., and Sanghoon Lee. 2010. "Cities as Six-by-Six-Mile Squares: Zipf's Law?" In Edward L. Glaeser, ed., *Economics of Agglomeration*, 105–131. Chicago: University of Chicago Press.

Holmes, Thomas J., and John J. Stevens. 2004a. "Geographic Concentration and Establishment Size: Analysis in an Alternative Economic Geography Model." *Journal of Economic Geography* 4: 227–250.

Holmes, Thomas J., and John J. Stevens. 2004b. "Spatial Distribution of Economic Activities in North America." In J. Vernon Henderson, and Jacques-François Thisse, eds., *Handbook of Regional and Urban Economics*. Vol. 4, *Cities and Geography*, 2797–2843. Amsterdam: Elsevier North Holland.

Hong, Sung Hyo. 2008. "Some Evidence on External Benefits from Labor Market Pooling." Working paper, Department of Economics, Syracuse University.

Horowitz, Joel L. 1986. "Bidding Models of Housing Markets." *Journal of Urban Economics* 20(2):168–190.

Horst, Ulrich, and José A. Scheinkman. 2006. "Equilibria in Systems of Social Interactions." *Journal of Economic Theory* 130:44–77.

Hsu, Wen-Tai. 2009. "Central Place Theory and City Size Distribution." Working paper, Department of Economics, Chinese University of Hong Kong, September.

Hsu, Wen-Tai, and Thomas J. Holmes. 2009. "Optimal City Hierarchy: A Dynamic Programming Approach to Central Place Theory." Working paper, Chinese University of Hong Kong.

Huang, Rocco R. 2008. "Industry Choice and Social Interaction of Entrepreneurs: Identification by the Separation of Residential and Business Addresses." Working paper, Research Department Federal Reserve Bank of Philadelphia.

HUDUSER. 2004. "MTO Research Solicitation." May 21. http://www.huduser.org/Publications/pdf/MTO_RsrchSolicitation_FINAL_REVISED06042004.pdf

Ichino, Andrea and Armin Falk. 2006. "Clean Evidence on Peer Effects." *Journal of Labor Economics* 24:39–57.

Imaizumi, Asuka, Kaori Ito, and Tetsuji Okazaki. 2008. "Impact of Natural Disasters on Industrial Agglomeration: A Case of the Great Kanto Earthquake." Working paper CIRJE-F-602, University of Tokyo, November.

Ioannides, Kimon L. H. 2007. "Exploring the Spectral Index of Segregation in a Social Network." Senior honors thesis, Department of Mathematics, Stanford University, June.

Ioannides, Yannis M., 1994. "Product Differentiation and Economic Growth in a System of Cities." *Regional Science and Urban Economics* 24:461-484.

Ioannides, Yannis M., 1997. "The Evolution of Trading Structures." In W. Brian Arthur, Steven M. Durlauf, and David Lane, eds., *The Economy as an Evolving Complex System II*, 129–167. SFI Studies in the Sciences of Complexity. Reading, MA: Addison-Wesley.

Ioannides, Yannis M. 2002. "Nonlinear Neighborhood Interactions and Intergenerational Transmission of Human Capital." In George Bitros, and Yannis Katsoulacos, eds., *Essays in Economic Theory, Growth and Labour Markets: A Festschrift in Honour of Emmanuel Drandakis*, 75–112. Cheltenham, U.K.: Edward Elgar.

Ioannides, Yannis M. 2003. "Empirical Nonlinearities and Neighborhood Effects in the Intergenerational Transmission of Human Capital." *Applied Economics Letters* 10:535–539.

Ioannides, Yannis M. 2004a. "Neighborhood Income Distributions." *Journal of Urban Economics* 56:435–457.

Ioannides, Yannis M. 2004b. "Random Graphs and Social Networks: An Economics Perspective." Presented at Conference on Networks: Theory and Applications. Industris Utrekning Institut, Vaxholm, Sweden, Working paper, Tufts University, June.

Ioannides, Yannis M. 2006. "Topologies of Social Interactions." *Economic Theory* 28:559–584.

Ioannides, Yannis M. 2008. "Emergence." In Steven N. Durlauf, and Laurence E. Blume, eds., *The New Palgrave Dictionary of Economics Online*. New York: Palgrave Macmillan.

Ioannides, Yannis M. 2009. "Discussion of Mori and Smith (2009a)." *Brookings–Wharton Papers on Urban Affairs*, 206–211.

Ioannides, Yannis M. 2011. "Urban Business Cycles through a Mortensen–Pissarides Lens." Presented at the Search and Matching Meeting, Bristol, U.K., July.

Ioannides, Yannis M., and Linda D. Loury. 2004. "Job Information Networks, Neighborhood Effects, and Inequality." *Journal of Economic Literature* XLII:1056–1093.

Ioannides, Yannis M., and Henry G. Overman. 2004. "Spatial Evolution of the U.S. Urban System." *Journal of Economic Geography* 4(2):1–26.

Ioannides, Yannis M., Henry G. Overman, Esteban Rossi-Hansberg, and Kurt Schmidheiny. 2008. "ICT and Cities." *Economic Policy* 23:203–242.

Ioannides, Yannis M., and Esteban Rossi-Hansberg. 2008. "Urban Growth." In Steven N. Durlauf and Laurence E. Blume, eds., *The New Palgrave Dictionary of Economics Online*. New York: Palgrave Macmillan.

Ioannides, Yannis M., and Kurt Schmidheiny. 2006. "Estimating Equilibrium Models of Local Jurisdictions: A Discrete Choice Approach with Individual and Community-Level Data." Presented at the Regional Science Association International, Toronto, November.

Ioannides, Yannis M., and Tracey N. Seslen. 2002. "Neighborhood Wealth Distributions." *Economics Letters* 76(3):357–367.

Ioannides, Yannis M., and Spyros Skouras. 2009. "Gibrat's Law for (All) Cities: A Rejoinder." Working paper, Tufts University, September. Revised 2011: "U.S. City Size Distribution: Robustly Pareto but only in the Tail." August.

Ioannides, Yannis M., and Adriaan R. Soetevent. 2007. "Social Networking and Individual Outcomes beyond the Mean Field Case." *Journal of Economic Behavior and Organization* 64:369–390.

Ioannides, Yannis M., and Win (Wirathip) Thanapisitikul. 2008. "Spatial Effects and House Price Dynamics in the Continental U.S." Working paper, Department of Economics, Tufts University.

Ioannides, Yannis M., and Giorgio Topa. 2010. "Neighborhood Effects: Accomplishments and Looking beyond Them." *Journal of Regional Science* 50(1):343–362.

Ioannides, Yannis M., and Jeffrey E. Zabel. 2008. "Interactions, Neighborhood Selection, and Housing Demand." *Journal of Urban Economics* 63:229–252.

Ioannides Yannis M., and Gulio Zanella. 2008. "Searching for the Best Neighborhood: Mobility and Social Interactions." Working paper, Tufts University, April.

Irwin, Elena G., and Nancy E. Bockstael. 2002. "Interacting Agents, Spatial Externalities and the Evolution of Residential Land Use Patterns." *Journal of Economic Geography* 2:31–54.

Jackson, Matthew O. 2008. *Social and Economic Networks*. Princeton, NJ: Princeton University Press.

Jackson, Matthew O., and Asher Wolinsky. 1996. "A Strategic Model of Social and Economic Networks." *Journal of Economic Theory* 71(1):44–74.

Jacobs, Jane. 1969. *The Economy of Cities*. New York: Random House.

Jaïbi, M. Rauf, and Thijs ten Raa. 1998. "An Asymptotic Foundation for Logit Models." *Regional Science and Urban Economics* 28(1):75–90.

Jones, Charles I. 1999. "Growth: With and Without Scale Effects." *American Economic Review Papers and Proceedings* 89(2):139–144.

Kaldor, Nicholas. 1970. "In Defence of Regional Policies." *Scottish Journal of Political Economy* 17:337–348.

Kanemoto, Yoshitsugu. 1987. "Externalities in Space." In Takahiro Miyao and Yoshitsugu Kanemoto, eds., *Urban Dynamics and Urban Externalities*, 43–103. Chur, Switzerland: Harwood Academic Publishers.

Kelejian, Harry H., and Ingmar R. Prucha. 2008. "Specification and Estimation of Spatial Autoregressive Models with Autoregressive and Heteroskedastic Disturbances." Working paper series no. 2448, CESifo. November.

Kendricks, Lutz. 2006. "Educational Attainment in U.S. Cities." Working paper, Iowa State University, Ames, IA.

Kiel, Katherine A., and Jeffrey E. Zabel. 2008. "Location, Location, Location: The 3L Approach to House Price Determination." *Journal of Housing Economics* 17:175–190.

Kim, Sukkoo. 2000. "Urban Development in the United States, 1690–1990." *Southern Economic Journal* 66(4):855–880.

Kim, Sukkoo. 2007. "Changes in the Nature of Urban Spatial Structures in the United States, 1890–2000." *Journal of Regional Science* 47(2):273–287.

Kim, Sukkoo. 2008. "Urbanization." In Steven N. Durlauf and Laurence E. Blume, eds., *The New Palgrave Dictionary of Economics Online*. New York: Palgrave MacMillan.

Kim, Han E., Adair Morse, and Luigi Zingales. 2006. "Are Elite Universities Losing Their Competitive Edge?" Working paper no. 12245, NBER, November.

Kirman, Alan P. 1983. "Communication in Markets: A Suggested Approach." *Economics Letters* 12(1): 101–108.

Kleinberg, Jon M. 2000a. "Navigation in a Small World." *Nature* 406:845.

Kleinberg, Jon M. 2000b. "The Small-world Phenomenon: An Algorithmic Perspective." *Proceedings of the 32nd Association for Computing Machinery, Symposium on Theory of Computing* 163–170.

Kleinberg, Jon M. 2008. "The Convergence of Social and Economic Networks." *Communications of the Association for Computing Machinery* 51(11):66–72.

Klier, Thomas, and Daniel P. McMillen. 2006. "Clustering of Auto Supplier Plants in the U.S.: GMM Spatial Logit for Large Samples." Working paper, Department of Economics, University of Illinois at Chicago, June.

Kling, Jeffrey R., Jeffrey B. Liebman, and Laurence F. Katz. 2007. "Experimental Analysis of Neighborhood Effects." *Econometrica* 75(1):83–119.

Knies, Gundi, Simon Burgess, and Carol Propper. 2007. "Keeping up with the Schmidts: An Empirical Test of Relative Deprivation Theory in the Neighborhood Context." Working paper no. 2007-19, Institute for Social and Economic Research, University of Essex, August.

Koopmans, Tjalling C., and Martin Beckmann. 1957. "Assignment Problems and the Location of Economic Activities." *Econometrica* 25(1):53–76.

Kotz, Samuel, N. Balakrishnan, and Norman L. Johnson. 2000. *Continuous Multivariate Distributions*. Vol. 1, *Models and Applications*. New York: John Wiley and Sons.

Krauth, Brian. 2005. "Peer Effects and Selection Effects on Smoking among Canadian Youth." *Canadian Journal of Economics* 38(3):735–757.

Krauth, Brian. 2006. "Social Interactions in Small Groups." *Canadian Journal of Economics* 39:414–433.

Kremer, Michael. 1997. "How Much Does Sorting Increase Inequality?" *Quarterly Journal of Economics* 112(1):115–139.

Krugman, Paul. 1991a. "Increasing Returns and Economic Geography." *Journal of Political Economy* 99(3):483–499.

Krugman, Paul. 1991b. *Geography and Trade*. Cambridge, MA: MIT Press.

Krugman, Paul. 1992. "A Dynamic Spatial Model." Working paper no. 4219, NBER, November.

Krugman, Paul. 1995. "Innovation and Agglomeration: Two Parables Suggested by City-size Distributions." *Japan and the World Economy* 7:371–390.

Krugman, Paul. 1996. "Confronting the Mystery of Urban Hierarchy." *Journal of the Japanese and International Economies* 10:399–418.

Krugman, Paul. 1998. "Space: The Final Frontier." *Journal of Economic Perspectives* 12(2):161–174.

Kuhn, Peter, Peter Kooreman, Adriaan R. Soetevent, and Arie Kapteyn. 2010. "The Effects of Lottery Prizes on Winners and Their Neighbors: Evidence from the Dutch Postcode Lottery." *American Economic Review* 101(5):2226–2247.

LaFountain, Courtney. 2005. "Where Do Firms Locate? Testing Competiting Models of Agglomeration." *Journal of Urban Economics* 58:338–366.

Lagos, Ricardo. 2000. "An Alternative Approach to Search Frictions." *Journal of Political Economy* 108:851–873.

Laschever, Ron A. 2009. "The Doughboys Network: Social Interactions and Labor Market Outcomes of World War I Veterans." Working paper, Department of Economics, University of Illinois Urbana–Champaign.

Lee, David S., and Thomas Lemieux. 2010. "Regression Discontinuity Designs in Economics." *Journal of Economic Literature* 48(2):281–355.

Lee, Lung-fei. 2007. "Identification and Estimation of Econometric Models with Group Interactions, Contextual Factors and Fixed Effects." *Journal of Econometrics* 140(2):333–374.

Lee, Lung-fei, Xiaodong Liu, and Xu Lin. 2009. "Specification and Estimation of Social Interaction Models with Network Structure, Contextual Factors, Correlation and Fixed Effects." *Econometrics Journal*, forthcoming.

Lee, Sanghoon, and Qiang Li. 2011. "Uneven Landscapes and the City Size Distribution." Working paper, Sauder School of Business, UBC, March.

Lehrer, Jonah. 2009. "How the City Hurts your Brain . . . and What You Can Do about It." *The Boston Globe*, Ideas. January 2.

Leibenstein, Harvey. 1950. "Bandwagon, Snob, and Veblen Effects in the Theory of Consumers' Demand." *Quarterly Journal of Economics* 64:183–207.

Lerman, Steven A., and Clifford Kern. 1983. "Hedonic Theory, Bid Rents, and Willingness to Pay: Some Extensions of Ellickson's Results." *Journal of Urban Economics* 13:358–363.

Levy, Moshe. 2009. "Gibrat's Law for (All) Cities: Comment." *American Economic Review* 99(4):1672–1675.

Lewis, W. Arthur. 1954. "Economic Development with Unlimited Supplies of Labor." *Manchester School of Economic and Social Studies* 22:139-191.

Li, Ji, and Lung-fei Lee. 2009. "Binary Choice under Social Interactions: An Empirical Study with and Without Subjective Data on Expectations." *Journal of Applied Econometrics* 24:257–281.

Liben-Nowell, David, and Jon M. Kleinberg. 2008. "Tracing Information Flow on a Global Scale Using Internet Chain-Letter Data." *Proceedings of the National Academy of Sciences* 105(12):4633–4638.

Lin, Xu. 2010. "Identifying Peer Effects in Student Academic Achievement by Spatial Autoregressive Models with Group Unobservables." *Journal of Labor Economics* 28(4):825–860.

Lösch, Augustus. 1944. *Die Raumliche Ordnung der Wirtschaft*. Jena: Fischer. English translation by William H. Woglom, *The Economics of Location, 1954*. New Haven, CT: Yale University Press.

Loury, Linda Datcher. 1982. "Effects of Community and Family Background on Achievement." *Review of Economics and Statistics* 64:32–41.

Loury, Linda Datcher. 2006. "All in the Extended Family: Effects of Grandparents, Aunts, and Uncles on Educational Attainment." *American Economic Review Papers and Proceedings* 96(2):275–278.

Lucas, Robert E. Jr. 1988. "On the Mechanics of Economic Development." *Journal of Monetary Economics* 22(1):3–42.

Lucas, Robert E. Jr. 2001. "Externalities and Cities." *Review of Economic Dynamics* 4:245–274.

Lucas, Robert E. Jr., and Edward C. Prescott. 1971. "Investment under Uncertainty." *Econometrica* 39(5):659–681.

Lucas, Robert E. Jr., and Esteban Rossi-Hansberg. 2002. "On the Internal Structure of Cities." *Econometrica* 70:1445–1476.

Ludwig, Jens, Jeffrey R. Kling, Laurence F. Katz, Jeffrey B. Liebman, Greg J. Duncan, and Ronald C. Kessler. 2008. "What Can We Learn about Neighborhood Effects from the Moving to Opportunity Program?" *American Journal of Sociology* 114(1):144–188.

Luttmer, Erzo F.P. 2005. "Neighbors as Negatives: Relative Earnings and Well-Being." *Quarterly Journal of Economics* 120(3):963–1002.

Lyons, Russell. 2011. "The Spread of Evidence-Poor Medicine via Flawed Social-Network Analysis." *Statistics, Politics and Policy. Berkeley Electronic Press* 2:art. 1.

Malevergne, Yannick, Vlaviden Pisarenko, and Didier Sornette. 2009. "Gibrat's Law for Cities: Uniformly Most Powerful Unbiased Test of the Pareto against the Lognormal." arXiv:0909.1281v1 [physics.data-an].

Malthus, Thomas R. 1798. *An Essay on the Principle of Population as It Affects the Future Improvement of Society with Remarks on the Speculations of Mr. Godwin, M. Condorcet, and Other Writers*. London: J. Johnson.

Mankiw, N. Gregory, David Romer, and David N. Weil. 1992. "A Contribution to the Empirics of Economic Growth." *Quarterly Journal of Economics* 107:407–437.

Manski, Charles F. 1993. "Identification of Endogenous Social Effects: The Reflection Problem." *Review of Economic Studies* 60:531–542.

Manski, Charles F. 2000. "Economic Analysis of Social Interactions." *Journal of Economic Perspectives* 14(3):115–136.

Mansury, Yuri, and László Gulyás. 2007. "The Emergence of Zipf's Law in a System of Cities: An Agent-based Simulation Approach." *Journal of Economic Dynamics and Control* 31:2438–2460.

Marris, Peter. 1974. *Loss and Change*. London: Routledge and Kegan Paul.

Marshall, Alfred. 1920. *Principles of Economics*, 8th ed. London: Macmillan.

Mas, Alexandre, and Enrico Moretti. 2009. "Peers at Work." *American Economic Review* 99(1):112–145.

Matsuyama, Kiminori. 1995. " Comment on Paul R. Krugman, 'Complexity and Emergent Structure in the International Economy.'" In Alan V. Deardorff, James A. Levinsohn, and Robert M. Stern, eds., *New Directions in Trade Theory*. Ann Arbor, MI: University of Michigan Press.

Matsuyama, Kiminori. 1996. "Why Are There Rich and Poor Countries? Symmetry Breaking in the World Economy." *Journal of the Japanese and International Economies* 10:419–439.

Matsuyama, Kiminori. 1999. "Geography of the World Economy." Working paper, Department of Economics, Northwestern University, January.

Matsuyama, Kiminori. 2007. "Beyond Iceberg Costs: Towards a Theory of Biased Globalization." *Review of Economic Studies* 74:237–253.

Matsuyama, Kiminori. 2008. "Symmetry Breaking." In Steven N. Durlauf and Laurence E. Blume, eds., *The New Palgrave Dictionary of Economics Online*. New York: Palgrave Macmillan.

Mayer, Adalbert, and Steven L. Puller. 2008. "The Old Boy (and Girl) Network: Social Network Formation on University Campuses." *Journal of Public Economics* 92(1-2):329–347.

Mayer, Thierry. 2008. "Market Potential and Development." Background paper, World Development Report 2009, International Bank for Reconstruction and Development, January.

McFadden, Daniel F. 1978. "Modelling the Choice of Residential Location." In A. Karlqvist, L. Lundqvist, F. Snickars, and J. Weibull, eds., *Spatial Interaction Theory and Planning Models*, 75–96. Amsterdam: Elsevier North-Holland.

McFadden, Daniel, and Kenneth Train. 2000. "Mixed Multinomial Logit Models for Discrete Response." *Journal of Applied Econometrics* 15:447–470.

McGrattan, Ellen R. 1998. "A Defense of AK Growth Models." *Federal Reserve Bank of Minneapolis Quarterly Review* 22(4):13–27.

McKelvey, Richard D., and Thomas R. Palfrey. 1995. "Quantal Response Equilibria for Normal Form Games." *Games and Economic Behavior* 10(1):6–38.

McMillen, Daniel P. 1996. "One Hundred Fifty Years of Land Values in Chicago: a Non-Parametric Approach." *Journal of Urban Economics* 40:100–124.

McMillen, Daniel P., and Stefani C. Smith. 2003. "The Number of Subcenters in Large Urban Areas." *Journal of Urban Economics* 53:321–338.

Melitz, Marc J. 2003. "The Impact of Trade on Intra-Industry Reallocations and Aggregate Industry Productivity." *Econometrica* 71(6):1695–1725.

Michaels, Guy, Ferdinand Rauch, and Stephen J. Redding. 2012. "Urbanization and Structural Transformation." *Quarterly Journal of Economics* 127(2):535–586.

Milgram, Stanley. 1967. "The Small World Problem." *Psychology Today* 1(1):60–67.

Miller, Harvey J. 2010. "The Data Avalanche Is Here. Shouldn't We Be Digging?" *Journal of Regional Science* 50(1):181–201.

Mills, Edwin S. 1967. "An Aggregative Model of Resource Allocation in a Metropolitan Area." *American Economic Review* 57(2):197–210.

Miranda, Javier, and Ron S. Jarmin. 2002. "The Longitudinal Business Database." Working paper no. CES-WP-02-17, Center for Economic Studies, U.S. Bureau of the Census, July.

Mirrlees, James A. 1972. "The Optimum Town." *The Swedish Journal of Economics* 74(1):114–135.

Mitzenmacher, Michael. 2003. "A Brief History of Generative Models for Power Law and Lognormal Distributions." *Internet Mathematics* 1(2): 226–251.

Miyao, Takahiro. 1977. "A Long-Run Analysis of Urban Growth over Space." *Canadian Journal of Economics* 10(4):678–686.

Miyao, Takahiro. 1978a. "Dynamic Instability of a Mixed City in the Presence of Neighborhood Externalities." *American Economic Review* 68(3):454–463.

Miyao, Takahiro 1978b. "A Probabilistic Model of Location Choice with Neighborhood Effects." *Journal of Economic Theory* 19:347–358.

Miyao, Takahiro. 1979. "Dynamic Stability of an Open City with Many Household Classes." *Journal of Urban Economics* 6:292–298.

Miyao, Takahiro. 1981. *Dynamic Analysis of the Urban Economy*. New York: Academic Press.

Miyao, Takahiro. 1987. "Urban Growth and Dynamics." in Takahiro Miyao and Yoshitsugu Kanemoto, eds., *Urban Dynamics and Urban Externalities*, 1–42. Chur, Switzerland: Harwood Academic Publishers.

Miyao, Takahiro and Yoshitsugu Kanemoto. 1987. *Urban Dynamics and Urban Externalities*. Chur, Switzerland: Harwood Academic Publishers.

Møen, J., Kjell G. Salvanes, and Erik Ø. Sørensen. 2003. "Documentation of the Linked Employer-Employee Data Set at the Norwegian School of Economics." Norwegian School of Economics.

Moffitt, Robert A. 2001. "Policy Interventions, Low-Level Equilibria and Social Interactions." In Steven N. Durlauf and H. Peyton Young, eds., *Social Dynamics*. Cambridge, MA: MIT Press.

Molloy, Michael, and Bruce Reed. 1995. "A Critical Point of Random Graphs with a Given Degree Sequence." *Random Structures and Algorithms* 6:161–179.

Moody, James. 2000. "Using the Social Network Data from Add Health." Add Health Users Workshop, Bethesda, MD.

Moretti, Enrico. 2004a. "Workers' Education, Spillovers, and Productivity: Evidence from Plant-Level Production Functions." *American Economic Review* 94: 656–690.

Moretti, Enrico. 2004b. "Estimating the Social Return to Higher Education: Evidence from Longitudinal and Repeated Cross-sectional Data." *Journal of Econometrics* 121:175–212.

Moretti, Enrico. 2004c. "Human Capital Externalities in Cities." In J. Vernon Henderson and Jacques-François Thisse, eds., *Handbook of Urban and Regional Economics*. Vol. 4, *Geography and Cities*, 2243–2291. Amsterdam: Elsevier North-Holland.

Mori, Tomoya. 2008. "Monocentric versus Polycentric Models in Urban Economics." In Steven N. Durlauf and Laurence E. Blume, eds., *The New Palgrave Dictionary of Economics Online*. New York: Palgrave MacMillan.

Mori, Tomoya, and Koji Nishikimi. 2001. "Self-Organization in the Spatial Economy: Size, Location, and Specialization of Cities." Working paper, Institute of Economic Research, Kyoto University, November.

Mori, Tomoya, Koji Nishikimi, and Tony E. Smith. 2005. "A Divergence Statistic for Industrial Localization." *Review of Economics and Statistics* 87(4):635–651.

Mori, Tomoya, Koji Nishikimi, and Tony E. Smith. 2008. "The Number–Average Size Rule: A New Empirical Relationship between Industrial Location and City Size." *Journal of Regional Science* 48:165–211.

Mori, Tomoya, and Tony E. Smith. 2009a. "A Reconsideration of the NAS Rule from an Industrial Agglomeration Perspective." In Gary Burtless and Janet R. Rothenberg, eds., *Brookings–Wharton Papers on Urban Affairs* 10:175–205, 215–216.

Mori, Tomoya, and Tony E. Smith. 2009b. "A Probabilistic Modelling Approach to the Detection of Industrial Agglomerations." Working paper no. 682, Institute of Economic Research, Kyoto University, September.

Mori, Tomoya, and Tony E. Smith. 2009c. "An Industrial Agglomeration Approach to Central Place and City Size Regularities." Working paper no. 687, Institute of Economic Research, Kyoto University, December.

Mortensen, Dale T., and Christopher A. Pissarides. 1999. "New Developments in Models of Search in the Labor Market." In Orley Ashenfelter and David Card, eds., *Handbook of Labor Economics*, Vol. 3, chap. 39, 2567–2627. Amsterdam: Elsevier North-Holland.

Muth, Richard. 1969. *Cities and Housing*. Chicago: University of Chicago Press.

Nakajima, Ryo. 2007. "Measuring Peer Effects on Youth Smoking Behaviour." *Review of Economic Studies* 74:897–935.

Neisheim, Lars. 2002. "Equilibrium Sorting of Heterogeneous Consumers across Locations: Theory and Empirical Implications." Working paper CWP08/02, CeMMAP, University College London, March.

Neumann, George R., and Robert H. Topel. 1991. "Employment Risk, Diversification, and Unemployment." *Quarterly Journal of Economics* 106(4):1341–1365.

Newman, Mark E. J. 2002. "Assortative Mixing in Networks." *Physical Review Letters* 89:208701.

Newman, Mark E. J. 2010. *Networks: An Introduction*. Oxford and New York: Oxford University Press.

Newman, Mark E. J., and Juyong Park. 2003. "Why Social Networks Are Different from Other Types of Networks." arXiv:Condmat/0305612v1.

Newman, Mark E. J., Steven H. Strogatz, and Duncan J. Watts. 2001. "Random Graphs with Arbitrary Degree Distributions and Their Applications." *Physical Review E* 64:026118-1–17.

Nitsch, Volker. 2005. "Zipf Zipped." *Journal of Urban Economics* 57(1):86–100.

Nordhaus, William D. 2006. "Geography and Macroeconomics: New Data and New Findings." *Proceedings of the National Academy of Sciences* 103(10):3510–3517.

Ober, Josiah. 2008. *Democracy and Knowledge: Innovation and Learning in Classical Athens*. Princeton, NJ: Princeton University Press.

Ogawa, Hideaki, and Masahisa Fujita. 1980. "Equilibrium Land Use Patterns in a Nonmonocentric City." *Journal of Regional Science* 20:455–475.

Ogawa, Hideaki, and Masahisa Fujita. 1989. "Nonmonocentric Urban Configurations in a Two Dimensional Space." *Environment and Planning A* 21:363–374.

O'Hara, Donald J. 1977. "Location of Firms within a Square Central Business District." *Journal of Political Economy* 85(6):1189–1207.

Oreopoulos, Philip. 2003. "The Long-Run Consequences of Living in a Poor Neighborhood." *Quarterly Journal of Economics* 118(4):1533–1575.

Ottaviano, Gianmarco, Takatoshi Tabuchi, and Jacques-François Thisse. 2002. "Agglomeration and Trade Revisited." *International Economic Review* 43:409–436.

Overman, Henry G. 2010. "'GIS A Job:' What Use Are Geographical Information Systems in Spatial Economics?" *Journal of Regional Science* 50(1):165–180.

Overman, Henry G., and Diego Puga. 2010. "Labor Pooling as a Source of Agglomeration: An Empirical Investigation." In Edward L. Glaeser, ed., *Economics of Agglomeration*, 133–150. Chicago: University of Chicago Press.

Overman, Henry G., and Yannis M. Ioannides. 2001. "Cross-Sectional Evolution of the U.S. City Size Distribution." *Journal of Urban Economics* 49:543–566.

Owyang, Michael T., Jeremy M. Piger, Howard J. Wall, and Christopher H. Wheeler. 2008. "The Economic Performance of Cities: A Markov-Switching Approach." *Journal of Urban Economics*. 64:538–550.

Page, Marianne E., and Gary Solon. 2003. "Correlations between Brothers and Neighboring Boys in Their Adult Earnings: The Importance of Being Urban." *Journal of Labor Economics* 21:831–855.

Page, Scott E. 2007. *The Difference: How the Power of Diversity Creates Better Groups, Firms, Schools, and Societies*. Princeton, NJ: Princeton University Press.

Pancs, Romans, and Nicolaas J. Vriend. 2007. "Schelling's Spatial Proximity Model of Segregation Revisited." *Journal of Public Economics* 91:1–24.

Papadimitriou, Christos H. 2003. "Networks and Games." Lecture, Departments of Economics and of Computer Science, Tufts University, September.

Papageorgiou, Yorgos Y., and David Pines. 2000. "Externalities, Indivisibility, Nonreplicability, and Agglomeration." *Journal of Urban Economics* 48:509–535.

Papageorgiou, Yorgos Y., and Terence R. Smith. 1983. "Agglomeration as a Local Instability of Spatially Uniform Steady-States." *Econometrica* 51(4):1109–1119.

Patacchini, Eleonora, and Yves Zenou. 2011. "Neighborhood Effects and Parental Involvement in the Intergenerational Transmission of Education." *Journal of Regional Science*, forthcoming.

Perälä, Maiju Johanna. 2008. "Increasing Returns in the Aggregate: Fact or Fiction?" *Journal of Economic Studies* 35(2):112–153.

Peri, Giovanni. 2002. "Young Workers, Learning, and Agglomerations." *Journal of Urban Economics* 52:582–607.

Petrongolo, Barbara, and Christopher A. Pissarides. 2001. "Looking into the Black Box: A Survey of the Matching Function." *Journal of Economic Literature* 39: 390–431.

Pissarides, Christopher A. 1985. "Short-run Equilibrium Dynamics of Unemployment, Vacancies, and Real Wages." *American Economic Review* 75(4):676–690.

Pissarides, Christopher A. 2000. *Equilibrium Unemployment Theory*. 2nd edition. Cambridge, MA:MIT Press.

Plato. ca. 350 BC. *The Laws*. http://classics.mit.edu/Plato/laws.html

Pollak, Robert A. 1976. "Interdependent Preferences." *American Economic Review* 66(3):309–320.

Porta, Sergio, Paolo Crucitti, and Vito Latora. 2006a. "The Network Analysis of Urban Streets: A Dual Approach." *Physica A* 369:853–866.

Porta, Sergio, Paolo Crucitti, and Vito Latora. 2006b. "The Network Analysis of Urban Streets: A Primal Approach." *Environment and Planning B: Planning and Design* 33:705–725.

Pritchett, Lant. 2006. "Boom Towns and Ghost Countries: Geography, Agglomeration, and Population Mobility." In Susan M. Collins, and Carol Graham, eds., *Brookings Trade Forum; Global Labor Markets?* 1–56. Washington, DC: Brookings Institution.

Quah, Danny. 1993. "Empirical Cross-Section Dynamics in Economic Growth." *European Economic Review* 37(2/3):426–434.

Quah, Danny. 1997. "Empirics for Growth and Distribution: Polarization, Stratification and Convergence Clubs." *Journal of Economic Growth* 2(1):27–59.

Quigley, John M. 1985. "Consumer Choice of Dwelling, Neighborhood and Public Services." *Regional Science and Urban Economics* 15:41–63.

Raaum, Oddbjørn, Kjell G. Salvanes, and Erik Ø. Sørensen. 2006. "The Neighborhood Is Not What It Used to Be." *Economic Journal* 116:200–222.

Rapaport, Carol. "Housing Demand and Community Choice: An Empirical Analysis." *Journal of Urban Economics* 42:243–260.

Rauch, James E. 1993a. "Productivity Gains from Geographic Concentration in Cities." *Journal of Urban Economics* 34:380–400.

Rauch, James E. 1993b. "Does History Matter Only When It Matters Little? The Case of City Industry Location." *Quarterly Journal of Economics* 108:843–867.

Redding, Stephen J., and Daniel M. Sturm. 2008. "The Costs of Remoteness: Evidence from German Division and Reunification." *American Economic Review* 98(5):1766–1797.

Redding, Stephen J., Daniel M. Sturm, and Nikolaus Wolf. 2011. "History and Industry Location: Evidence from German Airports." *Review of Economics and Statistics* 93(3):814–831.

Reed, William J. 2002. "On the Rank-Size Distribution for Human Settlements." *Journal of Regional Science* 42(1):1–17.

Ricciardi, L. M., and L. Sacerdote. 1987. "On the Probability Densities of an Ornstein–Uhlenbeck Process with a Reflective Boundary." *Journal of Applied Probability* 24:355–369.

Rice, Patricia, Anthony J. Venables, and Eleonora Patacchini. 2006. "Spatial Determinants of Productivity: Analysis for the Regions of Great Britain." *Regional Science and Urban Economics* 36:727–752.

Rivera-Batiz, Francisco L. 1988. "Increasing Returns, Monopolistic Competition, and Agglomeration Economies in Consumption and Production." *Regional Science and Urban Economics* 18(1):125–153.

Roback, Jennifer. 1982. "Wages, Rents, and the Quality of Life." *Journal of Political Economy* 90(6):1257–1278.

Rockafellar, R. Tyrrell. 1990. *Convex Analysis*. Princeton, NJ: Princeton University Press.

Romer, Paul M. 1990. "Endogenous Technological Change." *Journal of Political Economy* 98(5):S71–S102.

Roos, Michael W.M. 2005. "How Important Is Geography for Agglomeration?" *Journal of Economic Geography* 5:605–620.

Rose, Andrew K. 2006a. "Cities and Countries." *Journal of Money, Credit, and Banking* 38(8):2225–2245.

Rose, Andrew K. 2006b. "Size Really Doesn't Matter: In Search of a National Scale Effect." *Journal of the Japanese and International Economies* 20(4):482–507.

Rosen, Kenneth T., and Mitchell Resnick. 1980. "The Size Distribution of Cities: An Examination of the Pareto Law and Primacy." *Journal of Urban Economics* 8: 165–186.

Rosen, Sherwin H. 1974. "Hedonic Prices and Implicit Markets: Product Differentiation in Pure Competition." *Journal of Political Economy* 82:34–55.

Rosen, Sherwin H. 2002. "Markets and Diversity." *American Economic Review* 92(1): 1–15.

Rosenthal, Stuart A., and William C. Strange. 2001. "The Determinants of Agglomeration." *Journal of Urban Economics* 50:191–229.

Rosenthal, Stuart A., and William C. Strange. 2003. "Geography, Industrial Organization and Agglomeration." *Review of Economics and Statistics* 85(2):377–393.

Rosenthal, Stuart A., and William C. Strange. 2004. "Evidence on the Nature and Sources of Agglomeration Economies." In J. Vernon Henderson, and Jacques-François Thisse, eds., *Handbook of Regional and Urban Economics.* Vol. 4, *Cities and Geography*, 2119–2171. Amsterdam:Elsevier North-Holland.

Rosenthal, Stuart S., and William Strange. 2008a. "Agglomeration and Hours Worked." *Review of Economics and Statistics* 90:105–118.

Rosenthal, Stuart S., and William C. Strange. 2008b. "The Attenuation of Human Capital Spillovers." *Journal of Urban Economics* 64:373–389.

Rossi-Hansberg, Esteban. 2004a. "Optimal Land Use and Zoning." *Review of Economic Dynamics* 7:69–106.

Rossi-Hansberg, Esteban. 2004b. "Cities under Stress." *Journal of Monetary Economics* 51:903–927.

Rossi-Hansberg, Esteban. 2005. "A Spatial Theory of Trade." *American Economic Review* 95(5):1464–1491.

Rossi-Hansberg, Esteban, Pierre-Daniel Sarte, and Raymond Owens III. 2010. "Housing Externalities." *Journal of Political Economy* 118(3):409–432.

Rossi-Hansberg, Esteban, and Mark L.J. Wright. 2007. "Urban Structure and Growth." *Review of Economic Studies* 74:597–624.

Rosvall, Martin, Ala Trusina, Petter Minnhagen, and Kim Sneppen. 2005. "Networks and Cities: An Information Perspective." *Physical Review Letters* 94:028701–028704.

Rothenberg, Jerome. 1967. *Economic Evaluation of Urban Renewal.* Washington, DC: Brookings Institution.

Roy, Andrew D. 1951. "Some Thoughts on the Distribution of Earnings." *Oxford Economic Papers* 3(2):135–146.

Royal Swedish Academy of Sciences. 2008. "Trade and Geography—Economies of Scale, Differentiated Products and Transport Costs." Stockholm, October 13. http://nobelprize.org/nobel_prizes/economics/laureates/2008/ecoadv08.pdf

Rozenfeld, Hernán D., Diego Rybski, Xavier Gabaix, and Hernán A. Makse. 2011. "The Area and Population of Cities: New Insights from a Different Perspective on Cities." *American Economic Review* 101(5):2205–2225.

Sacerdote, Bruce. 2001. "Peer Effects with Random Assignment: Results for Dartmouth Roommates." *Quarterly Journal of Economics* 116:681–704.

Samuelson, Paul A. 1983. " Thünen at Two Hundred." *Journal of Economic Literature* 21(4):1468–1488.

Samuelson, Paul A., and S. Swamy. 1974. "Invariant Economic Index Numbers and Canonical Duality: Survey and Synthesis." *American Economic Review* 64: 566–593.

Sanbonmatsu, Lisa, et al. 2011. *Moving to Opportunity for Fair Housing Demonstration Program; Final Impacts Evaluation*. NBER, November. http://www.huduser.org/publications/pdf/MTOFHD_fullreport_v2.pdf

Saxenian, Anna Lee. 1994. *Regional Advantage*. Cambridge, MA: Harvard University Press.

Schelling, Thomas C. 1969. "Models of Segregation." *American Economic Review Papers and Proceedings* 59:488–493.

Schelling, Thomas C. 1971. "Dynamic Models of Segregation." *Journal of Mathematical Sociology* 1:143–186.

Schelling, Thomas C. 1972. "A Process of Residential Segregation: Neighborhood Tipping." In A. Pascal, ed., *Racial Discrimination in Economic Life*, 157–184. Lexington, MA: D.C. Heath.

Schelling, Thomas C. 1978. *Micromotives and Macrobehavior*. New York: W.W. Norton.

Schlicht, Ekkehart. 1981a. "Reference Group Behavior and Economic Incentives: A Remark." *Zeitschrift für die gesamte Staatwissenschaft* 137:125–127.

Schlicht, Ekkehart. 1981b. "Reference Group Behavior and Economic Incentives: A Further Remark." *Zeitschrift für die gesamte Staatwissenschaft* 137:733–736.

Schweizer, Urs. 1988. "General Equilibrium in Space and Urban Agglomeration." In Jean Jaskold Gabszewicz and Jacques-François Thisse, et al., eds. *Location Theory*, 151–185. Chur, Switzerland: Harwood Academic Publishers.

Seabright, Paul. 2004. *The Company of Strangers: A Natural History of Economic Life*. Princeton, NJ: Princeton University Press.

Sieg, Holger, V. Kerry Smith, H. Spencer Banzhaf, and Randy Walsh. 2002. "Interjurisdictional Housing Prices in Locational Equilibrium." *Journal of Urban Economics* 52:131–153.

Silverman, B. W. 1986. *Density Estimation for Statistics and Data Analysis*. New York: Chapman and Hall.

Simon, Herbert. 1955. "On a Class of Skew Distribution Functions." *Biometrika* 44:425–440.

Simon, Curtis J. 1988. "Frictional Unemployment and the Role of Industrial Diversity." *Quarterly Journal of Economics* 103(4):715–728.

Simon, Curtis J. 1998. "Human Capital and Metropolitan Employment Growth." *Journal of Urban Economics* 43:223–243.

Simon, Curtis J., and Clark Nardinelli. 2002. "Human Capital and the Rise of American Cities, 1900–1990." *Regional Science and Urban Economics* 32:59–96.

Sirakaya, Sibel. 2006. "Recidivism and Social Interactions." *Journal of the American Statistical Association* 101(475):863–875.

Skouras, Spyros. 2009. "Explaining Zipf's Law for U.S. Cities." Working paper, Department of International and European Economic Studies, Athens University of Economics and Business. http://ssrn.com/abstract=1527497.

Smith, Adam. 1776. *An Inquiry into the Nature and Causes of the Wealth of Nations*. London: W. Strahan and T. Cadell.

Sobel, Michael. 2006. "Spatial Concentration and Social Stratification: Does the Clustering of Disadvantage 'Beget' Bad Outcomes?" In Samuel Bowles, Steven N. Durlauf, and Karla Hoff, eds., *Poverty Traps*, chap. 8, 204–229. Princeton, NJ: Princeton University Press.

Soetevent, Adrian R. 2006. "Empirics of the Identification of Social Interactions: An Evaluation of the Approaches and Their Results." *Journal of Economic Surveys* 20(2):193–228.

Soetevent, Adrian R., and Peter Kooreman. 2007. "A Discrete Choice Model with Social Interactions: with an Application to High School Teen Behavior." *Journal of Applied Econometrics* 22:599–624.

Solon, Gary, Marianne E. Page, and Greg J. Duncan. 2000. "Correlation between Neighboring Children in Their Subsequent Educational Attainment." *Review of Economics and Statistics* 82(3):383–392.

Solow, Robert M. 1956. "A Contribution to the Theory of Economic Growth." *Quarterly Journal of Economics* 70(1): 65–94.

Solow, Robert M., and William Vickrey. 1971. "Land Use in a Long Narrow City." *Journal of Economic Theory* 3(4):430–447.

Soo, Kwok Tong. 2005. "Zipf's Law for Cities: a Cross Country Investigation." *Regional Science and Urban Economics* 35(3):239–263.

Starrett, David. 1978. "Market Allocations of Location Choice in a Model with Free Mobility." *Journal of Economic Theory* 17:21–37.

Stevens, Margaret. 2007. "New Microfoundations for the Aggregate Matching Function." *International Economic Review* 48(3):847–868.

Storper, Michael. 2008. "Why Does a City Grow? Specialization, Human Capital, or Institutions?" Working paper, Institut d' Etudes Politiques de Paris and London School of Economics, July.

Storper, Michael, and Anthony J. Venables. 2004. "Buzz: Face-to-Face Contact and the Urban Economy." *Journal of Economic Geography* 4:351–370.

Strange, William, Walid Hejazi, and Jianmin Tang. 2006. "The Uncertain City: Competitive Instability, Skills, Innovation and the Strategy of Agglomeration." *Journal of Urban Economics* 59(3):331–351.

Tabuchi, Takatoshi. 1998. "Urban Agglomeration and Dispersion: A Synthesis of Alonso and Krugman." *Journal of Urban Economics* 44:333–351.

Tabuchi, Takatoshi. 2009. "Self-Organizing Marketplaces." *Journal of Urban Economics* 66:179–185.

Tamer, Elie. 2003. "Incomplete Simultaneous Discrete Response Model with Multiple Equilibria." *Review of Economic Studies* 70:147–167.

Tang, Heiwai. 2009. "Labor Market Institutions, Firm-Specific Skills, and Trade Patterns." Working paper, Tufts University, revised, August.

Tauber, Karl, and Alma Tauber. 1965. *Negroes in Cities: Residential Segregation and Neighborhood Change*. Chicago: Aldine.

The New Yorker. 1978. "The Talk of the Town: New President." *The New Yorker*, November 13, 40–42.

Thisse, Jacques-François. 2000. "Agglomeration and Regional Imbalance: Why and Is It Bad?" *European Investment Bank Cahiers/Papers* 5(2):47–67.

Thompson, Clive. 2009. "Are your Friends Making you Fat?" *New York Times Magazine*, September 13.

Thünen, Johann H. von. 1826. In Heinrich Waetig, ed., *Der Isolierte Staat in Beziehung auf Landwirtschaft und Nationalökonomie*, 3rd ed., 1930. Jena: Gustav Fischer. English translation by Carla M. Wartenberg. Oxford: Pergamon Press.

Topa, Giorgio. 2001. "Social Interactions, Local Spillovers and Unemployment." *Review of Economic Studies* 68:261–295.

Topel, Robert H. 1986. "Local Labor Markets." *Journal of Political Economy* 94 (3): S111–S143.

Uchida, Hirotsugu, and Andrew Nelson. 2008. "Agglomeration Index: Towards a New Measure of Urban Concentration." Background Paper, World Development Report

2009 http://siteresources.worldbank.org/INTWDR2009/Resources/ 4231006-1204741572978/Hiro1.pdf

Veblen, Thorstein. 1899. *The Theory of the Leisure Class: An Economic Study in the Evolution of Institutions*. New York, London: Macmillan.

Vega-Redondo, Fernando. 2007. *Complex Social Networks*. Cambridge: Cambridge University Press.

Venables, Anthony J. 1996. "Equilibrium Locations of Vertically Linked Industries." *International Economic Review* 37:341–359.

Ventura, Jaume. 2005. "A Global View of Economic Growth." In Philippe Aghion and Steven N. Durlauf, eds., *Handbook of Economic Growth*, chap.22, 1419–1497. Amsterdam: Elsevier North-Holland.

Vinković, Dejan, and Alan Kirman. 2006. "A Physical Analogue of the Schelling Model." *Proceedings of the National Academy of Sciences* 103(51):19261–19265.

Wasmer, Étienne, and Yves Zenou. 2002. "Does City Structure Affect Job Search and Welfare?" *Journal of Urban Economics* 51:515–541.

Wasmer, Étienne, and Yves Zenou. 2006. "Equilibrium Search Unemployment with Explicit Spatial Frictions." *Labour Economics* 13:143–165.

Wasserman, Stanley, and Katherine Faust. 1994. *Social Network Analysis: Methods and Applications*. Cambridge and New York: Cambridge University Press.

Watts, Duncan J., and Steven H. Strogatz. 1998. "Collective Dynamics of 'Small-world' Networks." *Nature* 393(6684):440–442.

Watts, Duncan J. 2007. "A Twenty-first Century Science." *Nature* 445: 489.

Weinberg, Bruce A. 2007. "Social Interactions with Endogenous Associations." Working paper no. 13038, NBER April. Revised December 2008.

Weinberg, Bruce A., Patricia B. Reagan, and Jeffrey J. Yankow. 2004. "Do Neighborhoods Affect Hours Worked? Evidence from Longitudinal Data." *Journal of Labor Economics* 22(4):891–924.

Wheaton, William C. 1977. "Income and Urban Residence: An Analysis of Consumer Demand for Location." *American Economic Review* 67(4):620–631.

Wheeler, Christopher J., and Elizabeth A. La Jeunesse. 2008. "Trends in Neighborhood Income Inequality." *Journal of Regional Science* 48(5):879–891.

Wilson, William Julius. 2009. *More Than Just Race: Being Black and Poor in the Inner City*. New York: W.W. Norton.

World Bank. 2009. *World Development Report: Reshaping Economic Geography*. Washington, DC: International Bank for Reconstruction and Development.

Xiong, Kai. 1998. "Intercity and Intracity Externalities in a System of Cities: Equilibrium, Transient Dynamics and Welfare Analysis." Unpublished Ph.D. dissertation, Department of Economics, State University of New York, Buffalo.

Young, H. Peyton. 1998. *Individual Strategy and Social Structure: An Evolutionary Theory*. Princeton, NJ: Princeton University Press.

Zabel, Jeffrey E. 2004. "The Demand for Housing Services." *Journal of Housing Economics* 13(1):16–35.

Zenou, Yves. 2009a. *Urban Labor Economics*. Cambridge: Cambridge University Press.

Zenou, Yves. 2009b. "Urban Search Models under High-relocation Costs: Theory and Application to Spatial Mismatch." *Labour Economics* 16:534–546.

Zhang, Junfu. 2004. "A Dynamic Model of Residential Segregation." *Journal of Mathematical Sociology* 28:147–170.

Zhang, Junfu. 2011. "Tipping and Residential Segregation: A Unified Schelling Model." *Journal of Regional Science* 51(1):167–193.

Zhang, Qinghua. 2007. "Microfoundations of Local Business Cycles." Working paper, Department of Economics, University of Texas at Austin, December.
Zheng, Siqi, and Matthew E. Kahn. 2008. "Land and Residential Property Markets in a Booming Economy: New Evidence from Beijing." *Journal of Urban Economics* 63(2): 743–757.
Zipf, George K. 1949. *Human Behavior and the Principle of Least Effort*. Cambridge, MA: Addison-Wesley.

INDEX

Add Health data, 29, 56, 57, 59, 60, 61, 62, 74, 75, 460, 477, 507; and education outcomes, 59; and health outcomes, 60; and network empirics, 54
agglomeration, 8; and employment concentration, 258; of firms, 148; GIS-based index of, 376; identification of, 183, 233; index of, 77, 161; information-theoretic measures of, 175; and spatial concentration, 258; testing for, 158, 182
agglomeration economies, 8, 169, 258, 468
agglomeration effects, 168, 256, 439
agglomeration spillovers, 182
Alonso–Mills–Muth model, 201; and firms, 212; and job matching, 234; and uncertainty, 226; canonical urban, 201, 212; monocentric vs. polycentric, 217 amenities, 3, 5, 6, 80, 88, 94, 101, 187, 201, 231, 248, 262, 323, 378; dispersed: 188, 202, 205, 407, 442; endogenous, 231–34; exogenous, 205; and the canonical urban model, 231, 290
American Housing Survey (AHS) data, 74, 97, 101, 103, 114, 123, 124, 125, 133, 204, 460, 461, 462
autarkic cities: and divergence vs. convergence, 428; and growth, 412, 418, 424, 426, 445, 454, 478
autarky: fully autarkic cities, 310; and law of motion, 414; partially autarkic cities, 314; in social structure, 22, 50; and total factor productivity, 414; and urban structure, 306, 310, 316, 318, 323, 337, 340, 347

Brock-Durlauf model, 6, 14, 18, 30, 81, 463, 488; estimation with, 34, 63, 67; and multinomial discrete choice, 156
buzz, 2, 66, 210, 212, 492; identification of social interactions as, 66, 210

capital, 198; accumulation of, 405, 409, 423, 429; and estimations, 275; inputs of, 183, 220, 249, 251, 253, 259; physical, 224, 248, 253, 256, 378; social, 14; and urban transportation, 404, 416
capital, human, 65, 236; accumulation of, 268, 290, 405, 429; parental involvement and, 278; synthetic neighborhoods and, 284; spillovers of, 220, 224, 248; firms and spillovers of, 264
central business district (CBD), 81, 200, 217, 226, 300; and job matching, 234; predetermined, 202; not predetermined, 206
centrality, 65; Bonacich on, 25; and empirics, 57; in social structures, 24; of the Web graph, 454
central place theory, 368; and Christaller-Loesch hexagons, 371; and city size distribution, 370
choice: discrete, 20, 83; of firms' location, 189; of neighborhood by individuals, 20, 58, 88, 95, 102, 135, 140; of social group, 50
city: autarkic, 306, 310, 318; Brazilian, 187, 199, 408, 480; diversified, 306, 316; European, 395, 407, 453; French, 210, 265, 266, 268, 286, 346, 350, 365, 400; German, 191, 192, 250, 329, 368, 393, 394; and growth, 412, 415, 447; heterogeneous, 236, 247; homogeneous, 236, 247; isolated, 388, 401
—definition: clusters, 176; metropolitan area (MSA), 19, 71, 74, 81, 123, 158, 171, 175, 187, 194, 211, 218, 224, 249, 252, 258, 294, 331, 371; micropolitan area, 469; places (U.S.), 372
—system of cities: 6, 293, 299, 305, 321, 330, 384, 398, 425, 429, 440, 448. *See also* Duranton model; Henderson model; Krugman model; Rossi-Hansberg and Wright model
—U.S. cities: 118, 204, 260, 294, 350
city size: classical views on, 6, 7, 302; equilibrium, 293, 301, 302, 303, 312, 320, 321, 324, 339, 342, 343, 442; optimum, 293, 302, 304, 305, 320, 321, 324, 347, 425, 428, 442, 449; socially optimal, 424, 429, 441, 442, 449, 480
city size distribution, 350; and city definition, 371; empirical models of, 350; estimates of, 350; evolution of, 379; global aspects of,

city size distribution (*continued*)
395; and intradistribution dependence, 379; and urban accounting, 378
clustering: and cultural buzz, 211; geography and spatial clustering, 375, 379, 390; industrial, 158, 175, 177; in networks, 27, 29, 455; spatial, 115; and urban specialization, 294
clustering algorithms, 284
community, formation of, 21, 126
concentration: industrial, 77, 158, 170, 179; spatial, 248, 258, 259, 292, 374; urban, 6, 292, 385, 397, 444, 446. *See also* Ellison–Glaeser index; agglomeration, testing for
contextual effects. *See* effects
correlated effects. *See* effects

data: city GDP, 221, 249, 407, 411, 446, 469, 478; community-level, 126; confidential, 71, 72, 173, 243, 268, 271, 282, 462; contextual information, 4, 14, 16, 34, 44, 49, 58, 60, 71, 72, 95, 99; experimental, 21, 38, 39, 41, 43, 182, 393, 452; French, 65, 78, 181, 265, 266, 268, 300, 346, 365, 400, 466; geocoded, 71, 73, 77, 206, 211, 270, 275, 282, 462; Geographic Information Systems (GIS), 66, 74, 76, 376, 397, 446, 509; National Longitudinal Survey of Youth (NLSY), 73, 243, 263, 264; panel, 49, 55, 71, 122, 182, 193, 243, 263, 265, 269, 379; on population densities, 349, 371, 374, 375, 376, 444; on social network, 28, 54, 56, 60, 61, 74, 76, 507; with unusual features, 39, 58, 182, 346, 444, 457; Panel Study of Income Dynamics, 71, 263, 269, 270, 275, 278, 282, 460
data, merged, 71, 77, 287; combining aggregate and micro, 133; microgeographic, 76
decisions: housing, 97–112; location of firms, 148; location of individuals, 79, 97; joint neighborhood and housing demand, 99; joint location and factor demand by firms, 185
density, 3, 55; of amenities, 203; and increasing returns, 157, 171, 256, 439, 445; population, 77, 207, 218, 223, 375, 376, 392
distance, 65, 69, 76, 81, 158, 171, 172; between firms and externalities, 219; and intercity interactions, 382; localization and distance-based measures, 173
distribution: city size, 350, 353, 357, 370, 371, 377, 378; income, 48, 268; intra-distribution dependence, 379; neighborhood income, 50, 123, 127, 228
distribution, extreme value, 31, 83, 103, 121, 135, 154, 227, 287, 458, 461, 486; as an asymptotic model, 139. *See also* generalized extreme value distributions (GEV)
Duranton model, 364

economic geography, 65, 67, 149, 208, 307, 364, 382, 383, 384, 399, 448, 466, 480, 497, 504, 514; and firms' location decisions, 188; and urban evolution, 382, 383, 384, 399, 448, 466
economies of scale, 7, 9, 184, 187, 188, 194, 212, 219, 235, 254, 257, 285, 302, 309, 313, 347, 368, 385, 399, 400, 405, 411, 414, 418, 420, 425, 426, 429, 434, 445, 480; external, 289, 297, 300, 450
effects: contextual, 4, 14, 16, 56, 59, 79, 82, 88, 95, 97, 112, 270, 282; endogenous social, 4, 13, 14, 17, 19, 30, 33, 37, 43, 53, 57, 58, 62, 79, 82, 95, 97, 98, 101, 109, 131, 157, 226, 233, 256, 272; neighborhood, 4, 14, 39, 40, 42, 71, 80, 95, 99, 103, 104, 105, 109, 112, 115, 130, 131, 146, 226, 232, 243, 268, 269, 270, 569; peer, 14, 34, 39, 41, 44, 59, 62, 126, 132, 457; social, 4, 5, 13, 14, 15, 16, 19, 22, 23, 30, 33, 37, 38, 46, 54, 56, 59, 60, 62, 67, 79, 82, 88, 95, 97, 101, 109, 112, 131, 134, 157, 161, 226, 243, 256, 268, 272, 299. *See also* interactions
Ellison-Glaeser index: definition,161; empirics with, 165, 170, 174, 198. *See also* agglomeration endogenous effects. *See* effects
entry, by firms, 145, 169, 170, 175, 181, 186, 188, 215, 220, 298, 299, 302, 428; by cities, 360, 381, 382, 420
Epple and Sieg models, 127, 284, 288
equilibrium: multiplicity, 22, 29, 32, 33, 35, 96, 97, 149, 188, 217, 274, 283, 337, 380, 298; and social interactions, 15, 18, 31, 80; spatial, 115, 143, 198, 201, 204, 206, 220, 226, 232, 233, 234, 237, 246, 251, 258, 259, 329, 331, 357, 378, 392, 418, 420, 421,450; urban, 202, 206, 213, 233, 234, 237; urban spatial: 200, 206, 226, 228, 232, 234, 290
externalities, 3, 11, 12, 29, 170, 173, 180, 209, 231, 233, 248, 255, 289, 305, 309, 397, 404, 430, 442, 444, 448; consumption, 25, 26, 131, 464; human capital, 220, 223, 225, 250, 264, 269; intercity, 324; Jacobs, 180, 199; localization, 157, 185, 188, 193; pecuniary, 310, 312, 400, 420, 428; production, 131, 169, 198, 219, 220, 224, 256, 289, 321, 400, 435, 438; search, 195, 234; urban, 2, 443; urbanization, 157, 169, 180, 185, 187, 188, 193, 293, 378, 441; and urban wage premium, 225, 252

exit, by firms, 169, 170, 175, 181
experiments, 38; field, 454, 455, 481; laboratory, 41, 43; natural, 38, 39; quasi-experimental, 67, 182, 393; "quasi-natural," 393; randomized, 41
extreme value distribution. *See* distribution; generalized extreme value distributions (GEV); logit model.

firms' location decisions. *See* decisions
frictions: labor market, 234, 240, 295, 297, 308, 330, 333, 397; and urban structure, 330

generalized extreme value distributions (GEV): 103, 136. See also distribution; logit model.
geography, 65; economic/new economic, 5, 6, 7, 8, 149, 161, 169, 191, 208, 218, 289, 309, 328, 347, 349, 358, 361, 364, 391, 393, 396, 399, 401, 448; and the Krugman model, 188, 191; and market potential, 382, 384
geometry of the urban model, 206, 226, 290, 300, 329
Gibrat's law, 352, 356, 367, 372, 394, 387, 433; geometric Brownian motion and, 353, 355, 363; spatial, 356
Geographical Information Systems (GIS), 66, 76, 376, 397, 446
graph: dual urban, 65–66; Erdös and Renyi random, 26; primal urban, 65–66; random,13, 26, 27, 28, 68, 70, 458; and small world, 53, 66, 451, 455
graph theory: basics, 68–71; and the city, 65, 451, 452, 454; and social network modeling, 22, 25, 65, 68–71
growth: endogenous economic growth, 7, 391, 401, 409, 416, 429, 434, 435, 440, 449, 480. *See also* urban growth

hedonic price: and housing demand, 103–8; properties of, 91, 93, 112–15
hedonics, 84, 87; and housing decisions, 143; and neighborhood information, 93, 95, 112; regressions, 105, 112; and sorting, 91, 93; theory, 143
Henderson model, 6, 7, 148, 289, 293, 294, 297, 298, 300, 302, 323, 325, 381, 388, 416, 429, 430,441, 442, 448
hierarchy principle, 176, 179, 199, 345, 346, 361, 363, 368, 369, 371, 396, 476; hexagons, 368, 371; versus number–average size rule, 369, 370
housing: demand for and neighborhood effects, 97–112; Ioannides and Zabel model, 99

identification of social interactions, 4, 16, 34, 37, 38, 40, 42, 54, 56, 60, 67, 96, 132, 145, 173, 183, 249, 257, 264, 287, 288, 347; and Manski's reflection problem, 4, 14, 16, 67, 101, 127, 287; partial, 16, 33, 96; and self selection, 20, 21, 30, 48; and social multiplier, 17
information: contextual, 49, 71, 72, 99, 194; as contextual effect, 37, 43, 44, 56, 59, 60, 62, 79, 88, 90, 95, 97, 101, 104, 109, 112, 131, 170, 243, 260, 270, 282, 288, 465. *See also* hedonic: regressions; neighborhood
infrastructure: 7, 206, 378, 398, 401, 404, 440, 442, 447, 452, 454, 470, 477, 479; transportation, 404; urban infrastructure and social interactions, 452.
interactions: face-to-face contacts, 2, 65, 222, 226, 438, 451; among governments, 63, 64; interfirm, 169, 181, 198, 220, 224, 289; interfirm vs. self-selection, 181; and linear models of human capital accumulation, 270; and nonlinear models of human capital accumulation, 272; social (*see* social interactions); strategic, 63, 64; urban, 2, 9, 65, 210, 216, 397, 455
intercity trade and growth: Rossi-Hansberg and Wright model, 429; Ventura-based model, 409
interdependence, 14, 40, 64, 123, 140, 149, 152, 153, 154, 156, 157, 166, 198, 253, 287, 310, 345, 365, 380, 391, 456
isolated cities. *See* autarkic cities

Jane Jacobs, 7, 293, 330, 453, 457

Koopmans-Beckmann model, 150, 153
Krugman model, 5, 7, 148, 188, 192, 195, 294, 299, 307, 323, 326, 328, 377, 382, 383, 384, 390, 444, 448

labor market frictions. *See* frictions
labor turnover. *See* frictions
land use, 204, 205, 213, 217, 223, 289, 290; and social interactions, 34, 65, 148, 200; and socialist cities, 213
learning: classroom, 132, 457; social, 1, 58, 64, 181, 247, 274, 300, 451; in urban settings, 64, 330, 451
localization, and the marketing industry, 171. *See also* externalities
logit model, 140; and firms' location decisions, 154, 156, 159, 160, 172, 190, 191, 198; and individuals' location decisions, 83, 103, 106, 137, 139, 140. *See also* extreme value distribution

Lucas and Rossi-Hansberg model of urban spatial structure, 219

Manski's reflection problem. *See* identification of social interactions
market potential, 175, 189, 290, 361, 382, 383, 389, 391, 395, 408, 466
matching: firms to locations, 150; job, 192, 194, 234, 240
moving: Moving to Opportunity (MTO) program, 41; in the Schelling model, 121; and social interactions, 28; and urban interactions, 263
multiplier, social: 14, 17

neighborhood: choice of, 102, 140; and ethnicity, 271; and human capital accumulation, 44, 270, 272, 275, 280, 283; and income distribution, 50, 120, 125, 126, 130, 230, 231, 285; micro-, 74, 97, 112, 123; synthetic, 284; neighborhood sorting, 20, 21, 80, 88, 124, 126, 261, 265, 271, 278, 288, 290, 346, 448
neighborhood tipping. *See* Schelling's models
neighborhood choice models, 88, 140
neighborhood effects; and the canonical urban model, 226; identification of (*see* identification of social interactions); and moving (*see* moving); in networks, 23, 69
network: endogenous, 43, 44, 50, 51; neighborhood, 23, 70; social (*see* social networks); urban, 65, 451
networking, 9,13, 22, 51, 75, 171, 453
network modeling, 43; basics, 68–71
norms, social, 32
number–average size (NAS) rule. *See* rule

peer effects, 14, 34, 39, 44, 59, 62, 126, 131, 132, 457; and school integration, 21
place(s): central place theory, 368, 370, 371; data on U.S., 371, 372
politics: and peer effects, 126, 131; and social interactions, 9, 131, 452, 453; urban, 9, 126
price, hedonic. *See* hedonic price
price index of tradable goods, numeraire, 412
productivity differences: across regions, 250; across space, 253, 254, 258, 265, 266; across states, 249

rank. See rule, rank-size; Zipf's law
rank clocks, 395
rat race, urban, 266
returns to scale, 185, 187, 188, 219, 254, 305, 399, 400, 405, 414, 419; increasing, 7, 9, 194, 257, 302, 394, 395, 411, 414, 418, 434
returns to scale, constant, 9, 184, 235, 285, 286, 302, 305, 309, 368, 399, 400, 406, 411, 415, 429, 435; at the national economy, 425, 435
risk, of job loss, 236, 336
risk pooling, 149, 166, 168, 192, 193, 196, 199, 333, 337, 345, 426
—and firm location, 192, 345; dynamic Krugman-Overman-Puga model, 195
Rossi-Hansberg and Wright model, 471
rule: hierarchy principle versus NAS and rank-size, 369; number-average size (NAS), 179, 199, 368, 369, 370; rank-size, 176, 179, 199, 349, 350, 351, 369, 370

Schelling's models, 29, 82, 115; empirics with, 118, 122; Schelling's location model, 115, 118; Schelling's neighborhood tipping model, 119, 122
self-selection, 20, 21, 29, 38, 84, 130; and identification, 20, 288; and interfirm interaction, 181; and sorting, 229, 251, 448
serendipity, 9, 211
small world. *See* graph
social context. *See* effects
social effects. *See* effects
social interactions: as cultural buzz, 210, 212; and education, 9, 14, 15, 19, 21, 59, 62, 79, 88, 94, 109, 132, 249, 260, 262, 264, 268, 272, 279, 281, 284, 456; empirics of, 11, 56; identification of, 20, 55; and job referrals, 244; and sigmoid maps, 226, 272; and social networks, 53, 56; and synthetic neighborhoods, 284; and urban redevelopment, 3, 209, 232; and urban spatial equilibrium, 200
social networks, 22, 23, 44, 86; empirics of social interactions in, 56, 57; and education outcomes, 59; and health outcomes, 60; and prices, 24; social interactions in, 53; and urban politics, 9, 452, 453
spatial econometrics: empirics, 62; strategic interactions as, 61
spatial equilibrium, 200, 220, 222, 226, 228, 230, 232, 234, 237, 246, 252, 258, 262, 264, 290, 299, 308, 319, 322, 329, 342, 346, 392, 402, 418, 421, 427; and hedonic theory, 143; and Schelling's models, 115; social interactions and, 200, 206, 251; urban wage premium and, 259
spatial interactions, 63, 254; in TFP, 254, 256, 389
specialization, 294, 297, 306, 344; and intercity trade, 306; sectoral versus functional, 324; urban, 344

spillovers: human capital, 221, 248, 249, 265, 290; spatial attenuation of, 225
stratification, 129, 132, 229, 464; and Epple and Sieg models, 127
social structure, 12, 23, 29, 31, 68, 274; centrality of, 24; endogenous, 22, 27, 44; probabilistic, 26; and income distribution, 48
symmetry breaking, 322, 347, 398, 506; and unstable spatial equilibrium, 198; urban specialization as, 322
system of cities, 6, 7, 223, 259, 262, 293, 299, 301, 302, 305, 307, 321, 330, 350, 383, 384, 398, 425, 429, 440, 448. *See also* Duranton model; Henderson model; Rossi-Hansberg and Wright model

topology: of graph, network, 9, 18, 23, 27, 30, 32, 48, 51, 55, 57, 59, 67, 68,117, 274; of social interactions, 9, 57, 274; of urban interactions, 65, 453, 455
total factor productivity (TFP), 411, 413, 414; externalities as, 253, 256, 430, 434; of firms, 181, 182, 262; functional equivalence of for autarkic versus specialized cities, 423; increasing returns to density via, 256; location-specific, 254, 256, 266; and spatial Gibrat's law, 356; spatial interactions in, 253
total factor productivity (TFP), augmented: and autarkic cities, 415; in specialized cities, 423, 424
town: factory, 302, 303, 305, 306, 330, 368, 371, 372, 407; ghost, 442, 480
trade, 292; and economic growth, 409; intercity, 292, 306; Rossi-Hansberg and Wright model of intercity trade and economic growth, 429; Ventura-type model of intercity trade and economic growth, 409
transportation, 8, 65, 66, 152, 169, 201–4; intercity, 292, 323, 346, 383, 393, 399, 401; intracity, 81, 201–4, 224, 289; investment in urban, 224, 242, 403, 416, 427; and urban growth, 416, 427
urban evolution: linear models, 380, 388; nonlinear models, 379, 382–88
urban growth, 5, 8, 9, 64, 221, 262, 292, 332, 347, 353, 355, 356, 360, 363, 379, 380, 387, 390, 392, 394; and autarkic cities, 401, 412; and Brazilian cities, 408; controls on, 64; and decay, 440; and European cities, 407; divergent versus parallel versus convergent, 418, 380, 399, 400, 419; growth-accounting viewpoint on, 222, 223; and information and communication technologies, 436; and intercity trade, 409; and investment in transportation, 415–16, 423, 427; questions about, 447; and specialized cities, 420; sequential, 440; and U.S. cities, 407
urban interactions. *See* interactions
urban model, 200, 201, 212, 246; monocentric vs. polycentric, 217. See also Alonso–Mills–Muth model; Duranton model; Henderson model; Krugman model; Rossi-Hansberg and Wright model; system of cities
urban renewal, 3, 43, 209–10, 233, 467
urban structure: evolving, 379; and Germany's division, 191, 329, 394; and information and communication technologies, 436; Ross-Hansberg and Wright model, 471
urban wage premium, and spatial equilibrium, 259. *See also* wage premium

wage premium: urban, 225, 252, 259; and selection into cities, 262, 290
wage setting, 335

Zipf's coefficient, 350, 356
Zipf's law, 350, 351; and central place theory, 368, 370; for cities, 350; and Duranton's model, 364; and Gibrat's law, 361; estimates for, 357; and geometric Brownian motion, 353, 355, 363; and heterogeneity in growth rates, 361; and hierarchy principle, 368; and ICT, 436; and power (Pareto) laws, 351; and rank clocks, 395; and rank-size rule, 350; and Rossi-Hansberg and Wright model, 433; spatial, 356